FOUNDERS AT WORK

STORIES OF STARTUPS' EARLY DAYS

———————

Jessica Livingston

apress®

Founders at Work: Stories of Startups' Early Days

Copyright © 2007 by Jessica Livingston

Lead Editor: Jim Sumser
Editorial Board: Steve Anglin, Ewan Buckingham, Gary Cornell, Jason Gilmore,
    Jonathan Gennick, Jonathan Hassell, James Huddleston, Chris Mills,
    Matthew Moodie, Dominic Shakeshaft, Jim Sumser, Matt Wade
Project Manager: Elizabeth Seymour
Copy Edit Manager: Nicole Flores
Copy Editor: Damon Larson
Assistant Production Director: Kari Brooks-Copony
Compositor: Dina Quan
Proofreader: Linda Seifert
Cover Designer: Kurt Krames
Manufacturing Director: Tom Debolski

Library of Congress Cataloging-in-Publication Data

Livingston, Jessica.
  Founders at work : stories of startups' early days / Jessica
Livingston.
    p. cm.
  ISBN 1-59059-714-1
  1. New business enterprises--United States--Case studies. 2.
Electronic industries--United States--Case studies. I. Title.

  HD62.5.L59 2007
  658.1'1--dc22
                        2006101542

Printed and bound in the United States of America 9 8 7 6 5 4

Distributed to the book trade worldwide by Springer-Verlag New York, Inc., 233 Spring Street,
6th Floor, New York, NY 10013. Phone 1-800-SPRINGER, fax 201-348-4505, e-mail
orders-ny@springer-sbm.com, or visit http://www.springeronline.com.

For information on translations, please contact Apress directly at 2855 Telegraph Avenue, Suite
600, Berkeley, CA 94705. Phone 510-549-5930, fax 510-549-5939, e-mail info@apress.com, or visit
http://www.apress.com.

For Da and PG

Contents

Foreword

Apparently sprinters reach their highest speed right out of the blocks, and spend the rest of the race slowing down. The winners slow down the least. It's that way with most startups too. The earliest phase is usually the most productive. That's when they have the really big ideas. Imagine what Apple was like when 100% of its employees were either Steve Jobs or Steve Wozniak.

The striking thing about this phase is that it's completely different from most people's idea of what business is like. If you looked in people's heads (or stock photo collections) for images representing "business," you'd get images of people dressed up in suits, groups sitting around conference tables looking serious, Powerpoint presentations, people producing thick reports for one another to read. Early stage startups are the exact opposite of this. And yet they're probably the most productive part of the whole economy.

Why the disconnect? I think there's a general principle at work here: the less energy people expend on performance, the more they expend on appearances to compensate. More often than not the energy they expend on seeming impressive makes their actual performance worse. A few years ago I read an article in which a car magazine modified the "sports" model of some production car to get the fastest possible standing quarter mile. You know how they did it? They cut off all the crap the manufacturer had bolted onto the car to make it *look* fast.

Business is broken the same way that car was. The effort that goes into looking productive is not merely wasted, but actually makes organizations less productive. Suits, for example. Suits do not help people to think better. I bet most executives at big companies do their best thinking when they wake up on Sunday morning and go downstairs in their bathrobe to make a cup of coffee. That's when you have ideas. Just imagine what a company would be like if people could think that well at work. People do in startups, at least some of the time. (Half the time you're in a panic because your servers are on fire, but the other half you're thinking as deeply as most people only get to sitting alone on a Sunday morning.)

Ditto for most of the other differences between startups and what passes for productivity in big companies. And yet conventional ideas of "professionalism" have such an iron grip on our minds that even startup founders are affected by them. In our startup, when outsiders came to visit we tried hard to seem "professional." We'd clean up our offices, wear better clothes, try to arrange that a lot of people were there during conventional office hours. In fact, programming didn't get done by well-dressed people at clean desks during office hours. It got done by badly dressed people (I was notorious for programming wearing just a towel) in offices strewn with junk at 2 in the morning. But no visitor would understand that. Not even investors, who are supposed to be able to recognize real productivity when they see it. Even we were affected by the conventional wisdom. We thought of ourselves as impostors, succeeding despite being totally unprofessional. It was as if we'd created a Formula 1 car but felt sheepish because it didn't look like a car was supposed to look.

In the car world, there are at least some people who know that a high performance car looks like a Formula 1 racecar, not a sedan with giant rims and a fake spoiler bolted to the trunk. Why not in business? Probably because startups are so small. The really dramatic growth happens when a startup only has three or four people, so only three or four people see that, whereas tens of thousands see business as it's practiced by Boeing or Philip Morris.

This book can help fix that problem, by showing everyone what, till now, only a handful people got to see: what happens in the first year of a startup. This is what real productivity looks like. This is the Formula 1 racecar. It looks weird, but it goes fast.

Of course, big companies won't be able to do everything these startups do. In big companies there's always going to be more politics, and less scope for individual decisions. But seeing what startups are really like will at least show other organizations what to aim for. The time may soon be coming when instead of startups trying to seem more corporate, corporations will try to seem more like startups. That would be a good thing.

Paul Graham

Acknowledgments

I'd first like to thank my aunt, Ann Gregg, for her unfailing support and encouragement. She's an extraordinarily perceptive reader and she provided a lot of advice that helped make this a better book.

Thanks to the people I interviewed for sharing their stories and their time. One thing I noticed in the interviews that I didn't mention in the introduction is how much I *liked* the founders. They were genuine and smart, and it was an honor to talk with them. I know the candid nature of their stories and advice will inspire would-be founders for years to come.

Thanks to Gary Cornell for being willing to do a different kind of book, and to the Apress team for working on a different kind of book.

I'd like to thank many people for their willingness to make introductions: Jim Baum, Patrick Chung, Mark Coker, Jay Corscadden, Rael Dornfest, Jed Dorsheimer, Randy Farmer, Steve Frankel, Anand Gohel, Laurie Glass, James Hong, Mitch Kapor, Morgan Ley, Mike Palmer, Tom Palmer, Bryan Pearce, Andrew Pojani, Will Price, Ryan Singel, Langley Steinert, Chris Sacca, and Zak Stone.

Thanks to Kate Courteau for creating cozy offices for me to work in; Lesley Hathaway for all her advice and support; Alaina and David Sloo for their many introductions; and Sam Altman, Paul Buchheit, Lynn Harris, Marc Hedlund, and Aaron Swartz, who read early chapters of the book. I owe thanks to Lisa Abdalla, Michele Baer, Jen Barron, Ingrid Bassett, Jamie Cahill, Jessica Catino, Alicia Collins, Caitlin Crowe, Julie Ellenbogen, John Gregg, Chrissy Hathaway, Katie Helmer, Susan Livingston, Nadine Miller, Sara Morrison, Bridget O'Brien, Becky Osborne, Allison Pellegrino, Jennifer Stevens, and Suzanne Woodard for their encouragement.

Thanks to others who shared their insights on startups at Y Combinator dinners or with me personally: Rich Bacon, Greg Benning, Tom Churchill, Michael Ellenbogen, Jonathan Gertler, Hutch Fishman, Sara Harrington, Bill Herp, Bradley Horowitz, Joel Lehrer, Carolynn Levy, Simon London, Page Mailliard, Udi Manber, Fredrick Marckini, Greg McAdoo, Mark Macenka, Mike Mandel, Jerry Michael, Rich Miner, Mark Nitzberg, Peter Norvig,

Steve Papa, Tom Pinckney, Stan Reiss, Olin Shivers, Hugues Steinier, Jeff Taylor, Rob Tosti, and Stephen Wolfram.

Thanks to the founders of all the startups we've funded at Y Combinator. They are inspirations and I know they will have valuable stories of their own to share.

Special thanks to Trevor Blackwell and Robert Morris for all of their support. I'm lucky to work with them.

To my grandparents, Baba and Bob, who I admire and whose advice from their own experiences as authors helped me a lot. Extra special thanks to Dad and Michele, who supported me even when I had crazy ideas like quitting my job to start a company and work on a book. Over the years, my father never seemed to doubt that I could do something I'd be really proud of, and I'm very appreciative.

Most of all, thanks to Paul Graham. He inspired this book and was a source of encouragement and advice throughout the entire process. I'm grateful to have benefited from his extraordinary understanding of technology, startups, and writing. But mostly, I'm glad to know him.

Introduction

Some kind of magic happens in startups, especially at the very beginning, but the only people there to see it are the founders. The best way to understand what happens is to ask them, so that's what I did.

In this book, you'll hear the founders' stories in their own words. Here, I want to share some of the patterns I noticed. When you're interviewing a series of famous startup founders, you can't help trying to see if there is some special quality they all have in common that made them succeed.

What surprised me most was how unsure the founders seemed to be that they were actually onto something big. Some of these companies got started almost by accident. The world thinks of startup founders as having some kind of superhuman confidence, but a lot of them were uncertain at first about starting a company. What they weren't uncertain about was making something good—or trying to fix something broken.

They all were determined to build things that worked. In fact, I'd say determination is the single most important quality in a startup founder. If the founders I spoke with were superhuman in any way, it was in their perseverance. That came up over and over in the interviews.

Perseverance is important because, in a startup, nothing goes according to plan. Founders live day to day with a sense of uncertainty, isolation, and sometimes lack of progress. Plus, startups, by their nature, are doing new things—and when you do new things, people often reject you.

That was the second most surprising thing I learned from these interviews: how often the founders were rejected early on. By investors, journalists, established companies—they got the Heisman from everyone. People like the idea of innovation in the abstract, but when you present them with any specific innovation, they tend to reject it because it doesn't fit with what they already know.

Innovations seem inevitable in retrospect, but at the time it's an uphill battle. It's curious to think that the technology we take for granted now, like web-based email, was once dismissed as unpromising. As Howard Aiken said, "Don't worry about people stealing your ideas. If your ideas are any good, you'll have to ram them down people's throats."

In addition to perseverance, founders need to be adaptable. Not only because it takes a certain level of mental flexibility to understand what users want, but because the plan will probably change. People think startups grow out of some brilliant initial idea like a plant from a seed. But almost all the founders I interviewed changed their ideas as they developed them. PayPal started out writing encryption software, Excite started as a database search company, and Flickr grew out of an online game.

Starting a startup is a process of trial and error. What guided the founders through this process was their empathy for the users. They never lost sight of making things that people would want.

Successful startup founders typically get rich from the process, but the ones I interviewed weren't in it just for the money. They had a lot of pride in craftsmanship. And they wanted to change the world. That's why most have gone on to new projects that are just as ambitious. Sure, they're pleased to have more financial freedom, but the way they choose to use it is to keep building more things.

Startups are different from established companies—almost astonishingly so when they are first getting started. It would be good if people paid more attention to this important but often misunderstood niche of the business world, because it's here that you see the essence of productivity. In its plain form, productivity looks so weird that it seems to a lot of people to be "unbusinesslike." But if early-stage startups are unbusinesslike, then the corporate world might be more productive if it were less businesslike.

My goal with these interviews was to establish a fund of experience that everyone can learn from. You'll notice certain classes of problems that constantly bit people. All the founders had things they wished they'd known when they were getting started. Now these are captured for future founders.

I'm especially hoping this book inspires people who want to start startups. The fame that comes with success makes startup founders seem like they're a breed apart. Perhaps if people can see how these companies actually started, it will be less daunting for them to envision starting something of their own. I hope a lot of the people who read these stories will think, "Hey, these guys were once just like me. Maybe I could do it too."

Max Levchin
Cofounder, PayPal

PayPal was founded in December 1998 by recent college grad Max Levchin and hedge fund manager Peter Thiel. The company went through several ideas, including cryptography software and a service for transmitting money via PDAs, before finding its niche as a web-based payment system. That service became wildly popular for online vendors, especially eBay sellers, who preferred it to traditional payment methods. PayPal went public in early 2002 and was acquired later that year by eBay for $1.5 billion.

PayPal was started during the Internet Bubble, but it was in no sense a Bubble startup. Its success was a direct reflection of the intelligence of the people who built it. PayPal won because they built a better mousetrap.

With any new method of moving money comes new forms of fraud. In large part, PayPal succeeded because it could deal with fraud—and its competitors couldn't. The software that Levchin and his team developed to combat fraud runs quietly and invisibly. To this day, PayPal doesn't talk much about it. But Levchin's software was just as much the reason for PayPal's success as a more visible product like the Apple II was for Apple.

Livingston: Tell me a little about how PayPal got started.

Levchin: The company was really not founded to do payments at all. My focus in college was security. I wanted to do crypto and stuff like that. I had already founded three different companies during college and the year after, which I spent in Champaign-Urbana, where I went to school. Then, in favor of not doing graduate school, I decided to move out to Silicon Valley and try to start another company.

So I was hanging around Silicon Valley in the summer of '98 and was not really sure what I was going to do with my life. I was living in Palo Alto, squatting on the floor of a friend. I went to see this random lecture at Stanford—given by a guy named Peter, who I had heard about, but never met before.

The lecture turned out to have only six people in it. It was in the heat of the summer, so nobody showed up. This guy was like, "There are only six of you, OK." Afterwards I walked up to talk to him. He was this really intense guy, and he said, "We should get breakfast sometime." So we met up the next week.

I had two different ideas that I was considering starting companies around, and I pitched him on both evenly. Peter was running a hedge fund at the time. For a few weeks we kept talking, and eventually he said, "Take this idea, because this one is better, and you go start a company around it, and then I can have my hedge fund invest a little bit of money in it"—like a couple hundred thousand dollars. That was a good thing, since I was starting to run out of money.

I had just moved from Champaign; most of my contacts and friends were in Chicago. One of them I was trying to convince to be the CEO. He wasn't really available, so I wound up being without a CEO. I called Peter and said, "This investment is a great thing, but I have no one to run the company. I'm just going to write the code and recruit the coders." And he said, "Maybe I could be your CEO." So I said, "That's a really good idea." The next 2 weeks we were sort of playing with the idea, and by 1/1/99 we agreed that he would be the CEO and I would be the CTO.

Livingston: How did you have the idea?

Levchin: The initial idea was actually very different. At the time, I was really into developing software for handheld devices, which is sort of an art and a science unto its own. And I was really into security. This idea that I had in college, which I was vaguely successful with—if you've ever seen these authentication devices, like a little card that spits out numbers at you that you can log in with. It's like a one-time password generator, like S/Key, Digital Pathways, and CRYPTOCard. Most of the algorithms are variations on the standard called X9.9, which is a public standard. The algorithms don't really use it correctly. In college one day I had bought all the different kinds of cards. Each costs like $50 or $100, so it's not that expensive. They weren't that difficult to reverse-engineer because you already know the standard, so you know it can't be too far outside the standard. I reverse-engineered most of them except for one which was very proprietary. I decided not to touch that one since I was too poor to handle a lawsuit.

Once I got them all reverse-engineered, I wrote an emulator for every single type of them for a Palm Pilot. I had a lot of friends on campus who were really into security as well—most of them were sys admins—and they carried a whole bunch of these things in their pockets, because most of the time you can only use one per computer, per system. If you adminned a lab with ten servers, you'd have a stack of these things in your pocket, and that adds up. They are heavy, and they need batteries. I basically emulated the whole thing on a Palm Pilot so my friends were able to throw out their stupid devices and use my thing.

I posted it on the Web, which was young and silly then, and I got hundreds and then thousands of downloads, and people were offering me money to get more features in. So I thought, "This seems to be a business." At the time, I was just keen on getting any sort of business off the ground. So, when I moved to the Valley, I basically pitched Peter on the following concept. There's clearly demand for moving these cryptographic operations that are poorly understood. Even though it's not rocket science to reverse-engineer this stuff, no one else had done it before me, so there's some complexity involved.

The real difficult thing actually was getting an implementation of a cryptographic algorithm on a Palm Pilot, because Palm Pilots are very low power, and, back then, they were *really* low power—like a 16 MHz processor. So, to do an encryption of a public key operation on a Palm Pilot was really expensive. There is some art involved in how you speed it up—both from the user interface perspective and the math perspective. In math, you have to see how much you can squeeze out of it, and in the user interface, you have to make it feel like it's not taking that long, even though it really is taking like 2 seconds, which is a really long time.

On these handheld devices, the cards that you get, you type in the password and it's done. I was able to get it to the point where it was instantaneous on a Palm Pilot. These things are all sort of child's play at this point, but at the time they were very important. Anyway, I wanted to start a company that would take this scarce skill of implementing crypto on handheld devices and then packaging it into libraries and products. The assumption was that the enterprises are going to all go to handheld devices really soon as the primary means of communication. Every corporate dog in America will hang around with a Palm Pilot or some kind of a device. What I wanted to do was capitalize on that emergence of technology. And then, of course, enterprise requires security; security requires these scarce skills; I have the skills; start a company.

So that's what Peter funded. By the time he joined, we had realized that, even though the theory was pretty much logical, the move of the enterprise to handheld devices was actually not forthcoming. Kind of like the early Christians in the first century were all really hard at work waiting for the second coming. Still waiting. So it felt like the early Christians. "Any minute now, there'll be millions of people begging for security on their handheld devices." It just wasn't happening. We were correct to change our strategy, since it still hasn't happened.

Livingston: Tell me about how you adapted the strategy.

Levchin: Initially, I wanted to do crypto libraries, since I was a freshly minted academic. "I won't even need to figure out how to do this commercialization part. I'm just going to build libraries, sell it to somebody who is going to build software, and I can just sit there and make a penny per copy and get marvelously rich very quickly." But no one was making the software because there was no demand. So we said, "We'll make the software." We went to enterprises and told them we were going to do this and got some positive reception, but then the thing happened again where no one really wants the stuff. It's really cool, it's mathematically complex, it's very secure, but no one really needed it.

By then we had built all this tech that was complicated and difficult to understand and replicate, so we thought, "We have all these libraries that allow you to secure anything on handheld devices. What can we secure? Maybe we can secure some consumer stuff. So enterprises will go away, and we'll go to consumers. We'll build the wallet application—something that can store all of your private data on your handheld device. So your credit card information, this and that." And we did, and it was very simple because we already had all the crypto stuff figured out. But, of course, there was no incentive to have a wallet with all these digital items that you couldn't apply anywhere. "What's my credit card number?" Pull out your wallet and look, or pull out your handheld wallet and look? So that was really not going to happen either.

Then we started experimenting with the question: "What can we store inside the Palm Pilot that *is* actually meaningful?" So the next iteration was that we'd store things that were of value and you wouldn't store in other ways. For example, storing passwords in your wallet is a really bad idea. If you store them in your Palm Pilot, you can secure it further with a secondary passphrase that protects it. So we did that, and it was getting a little bit of attention, but it was still very amateur.

Then finally we hit on this idea of, "Why don't we just store *money* in the handheld devices?" The next iteration was this thing that would do cryptographically secure IOU notes. I would say, "I owe you $10," and put in my passphrase. It wasn't really packaged at the user interface level as an IOU, but that's what it effectively was. Then I could beam it to you, using the infrared on a Palm Pilot, which at this point is very quaint and silly since, clearly, what would you rather do, take out $5 and give someone their lunch share, or pull out two Palm Pilots and geek out at the table? But that actually is what moved the needle, because it was so weird and so innovative. The geek crowd was like, "Wow. This is the future. We want to go to the future. Take us there." So we got all this attention and were able to raise funding on that story.

Then we had the famous Buck's beaming—at Buck's restaurant in Woodside, which is sort of the home away from home for many VCs. Our first round of financing was actually transferred to us via Palm Pilot. Our VCs showed up with a $4.5 million preloaded Palm Pilot, and they beamed it to us.

The product wasn't really finished, and about a week before the beaming at Buck's I realized that we weren't going to be able to do it, because the code wasn't done. Obviously it was really simple to mock it up—to sort of go, "Beep! Money is received." But I was so disgusted with the idea. We have this security company; how could I possibly use a mock-up for something worth $4.5 million? What if it crashes? What if it shows something? I'll have to go and commit ritual suicide to avoid any sort of embarrassment. So instead of just getting the mock-up done and getting reasonable rest, my two coders and I coded nonstop for 5 days. I think some people slept; I know I didn't sleep at all. It was just this insane marathon where we were like, "We have to get this thing working." It actually wound up working perfectly. The beaming was at 10:00 a.m.; we were done at 9:00 a.m.

It was one of these things where you can't just be done. With crypto, if you are one bit off, nothing's going to work. We started testing at midnight the night before and fixed all the bugs and tested more. There were definitely some memory leaks, but it was secure. It was one of these things where the software wasn't perfect, but the security path where the money changed hands was definitely provably secure. The danger was that the Palm Pilots might crash, but the transaction was perfectly safe. I could have bet my own life on the transaction. The thing that was not safe was just the software was not really perfect. It was clunky; I was worried that it might crash.

So we had stacks and stacks of Palm Pilots preloaded with the same software. Obviously, money could only reside in one of them, but the plan was that, if I see that any one of them is crashing, I'm going to make a fresh pair, because we needed two Palm Pilots, one for the receiving and one for the sending. I was fully prepared. They were marked, "Sender A, Sender B, Sender C, Receiver A, Receiver B, Receiver C." So I had this stack of Palm Pilots, I hopped in a car, drove to Buck's, and it was like 9:50 a.m. Peter was getting very anxious about the whole thing. That's where everything becomes very blurry, because I was so tired by then.

There were about a dozen TV cameras and journalists—there was really big coverage. We did the beaming, and some group showed up late and said, "Well, can you do it again?" I said, "No, I just slaved away for 5 days straight—for 5 months straight. The whole point of the security is that you can't replicate the transaction. Once it's done, the money has changed hands." So these guys actually made Peter pretend like it was going to happen and turned away the screen—because the screen was actually saying, "Security breach! Don't try to resend the same money again." Which was a triumph for me, but a pain in the ass for the camera.

As I was getting interviewed by the *Wall Street Journal*, or some big pub guy, all I remember was that he went off to the bathroom for a second, and they brought out my omelet. The next thing I remember, I woke up, and I was on the side of my own omelet, and there was no one at Buck's. Everyone was gone. They just let me sleep.

Livingston: What did you do first after you got this new funding?

Levchin: As soon as we got funding, we started hiring aggressively, and we built this app for the Palm Pilot, which was getting pretty good growth. We were getting 300 users a day. Then we built a demo for the website, which was functional, so you could do everything on the website that you could do on a Palm Pilot, except the website was unsexy and we didn't really care. It was like, "Go to the website and download the Palm Pilot version. It's really cool."

Livingston: Three hundred people were downloading it per day? For fun?

Levchin: Well, there are lots of geeks. It slowed down pretty quickly too, but initially we got a lot of publicity about it.

Sometime by early 2000, we realized that all these people were trying to use the website for transactions, and the growth of that was actually more impressive than the growth of the handheld device one, which was inexplicable, because the handheld device one was cool and the website was just a demo. Then all these people from a site called eBay were contacting us and saying, "Can I put your logo in my auction?" And we were like, "Why?" So we told them, "No. Don't do it." So for a while we were fighting, tooth and nail, crazy eBay people: "Go away, we don't want you."

Eventually we realized that these guys were begging to be our users. We had the moment of epiphany, and for the next 12 months just iterated like crazy on the website version of the product, which is today's PayPal. Sometime by late 2000, we killed the handheld one because we peaked out at 12,000 users. They were still using it a little bit, and they were really upset when we killed it. They said, "You were about the handheld transactions, not about this web stuff." We're like, "No, we're pretty much about the web stuff."

Livingston: How many users did you have for the website when you killed the handheld product?

Levchin: I think we must have been 1.2 . . . 1.5 million users. It was an emotional but completely obvious business decision.

Livingston: When did you first notice fraudulent behavior?

Levchin: From day one. It was pretty funny because we met with all these people in the banking and credit card processing industry, and they said, "Fraud is going to eat you for lunch." We said, "What fraud?" They said, "You'll see, you'll see."

I actually had an advisor or two from the financial industry, and they said, "Get ready for chargebacks. You need to have some processing in place." We said, "Uh huh." They said, "You don't know what a chargeback is, do you?"

Livingston: So you didn't foresee this fraud?

Levchin: I had no idea what was going to happen.

Livingston: But you weren't too surprised?

Levchin: We tried to attack the system for ourselves, like a good security person would. How can you cheat and steal money and do whatever? We made some provisions from day one to prevent fraud. We prevented all the obvious fraud, and then, I think 6 months into it, we saw the first chargeback and were like, "Ah, one per week. OK." Then it was like an avalanche of losses; 2000 was basically the year of fraud, where we were just losing more and more and more money every month. At one point we were losing over $10 million per month in fraud. It was crazy.

That was when I decided that that was going to be my next challenge. I started researching it, figuring out what could be done and attacking the problem.

Livingston: So you made a conscious decision to attack this problem?

Levchin: It was actually sort of a side effect. We had this merger with a company called X.com. It was a bit of a tough merger because the companies were really competitive—we were two large competitors in the same market. For a while, Peter took some time off. The guy who ran X.com became the CEO, and I remained the CTO. He was really into Windows, and I was really into Unix. So there was this bad blood for a while between the engineering teams. He was convinced that Windows was where it's at and that we have to switch to Windows, but the platform that we used was, I thought, built really well and I wanted to keep it. I wanted to stay on Unix.

By summer 2000, it seemed like the Windows thing was going to happen because Peter was gone. He took a sabbatical to make sure there were no clashes between the CEOs. So, this other guy was pushing me toward accepting that Windows was going to be the platform. I said, "Well, if this is really going to happen, I'm not going to be able to provide much value, because I don't really know anything about Windows. I went to a school that was all Unix all the time, and I spent all my life coding for Unix."

I had this intern that I hired before the merger, and we thought, "We built all these cool Unix projects, but it's kind of pointless now because they are going to scrap the platform. We might as well do something else." So he and I decided we were going to find ourselves fun projects. We did one kind of mean project where we built a load tester package that would beat up on the Windows proto-type (the next version was going to be in Windows). We built a load tester that would test against the Unix platform and the new Windows one and show in beautiful graphs that the Windows version had 1 percent of the scalability of the Unix one. "Do you really want to do that?"

It was me acting out, but it was kind of a low time for me because I was not happy with the way we were going. Part of having a CEO is that you can respectfully disagree, but you can resign if you don't like it that much.

But then eventually I became interested in the economics of PayPal and trying to see what's going on in the back end, because I was getting distracted from code and technology. I realized that we were losing a lot more money in fraud than I thought we were. It was still early 2001. If you looked at the actual loss rates, they were fairly low. You could see that we were losing money, but, given the growth of the system and the growth of the fraud, fraud was not that big of a problem. It was less than 1 percent—it was really low. But then, if you looked at the rate of growth of fraud, you could see that, if you don't stop it, it would become 5 percent, 10 percent of the system, which would have been prohibitive.

So I started freaking out over it, and this intern and I wrote all sorts of pack-ages—very statistical stuff—to analyze "How did it happen; how do we lose money?" By the end of the summer, we thought, "The world is going to end any minute now." It was obvious that we were really losing tons of money. By mid-summer, it was already on a $10 million range per month and just very scary.

Livingston: Did the rest of the company know you were right?

Levchin: Through the summer, I think various people were slowly coming to understand that this thing was really serious. It was pretty obvious at a certain point. I didn't have to really convince anyone. In the beginning some people said, "Yes, it's a lot of money, but we're really growing, too. As an absolute amount, $5 million is a lot of losses, but, if you are processing $300 million, whatever."

There was actually a bit of an altercation at the very top management level, which caused the CEO to leave. Peter came back as the CEO. The first decision that he and I took was that my new job—in addition to technology—was going to be this fraud thing, because I already spent so much time looking at it. This guy Bob, the intern, and I—I convinced him to drop out of Stanford for a year and work with me more on it—for the next year, we just worked nonstop on trying to understand and fix these problems.

Livingston: So the CEO left and Peter came back?

Levchin: The three of us are pretty good friends now. At the time, already I had hated the guy's guts for forcing me to do Windows, and then, in the end, I was like, "You gotta go, man." My whole argument to him was, "We can't switch to Windows now. This fraud thing is most important to the company. You can't allow any additional changes. It's one of these things where you want to change one big thing at a time, and the fraud is a pretty big thing. So introducing a new platform or doing anything major—you just don't want to do it right now." That was sort of the trigger for a fairly substantial conflict that resulted in him leaving and Peter coming back and me taking over fraud.

Livingston: When was the first time that you said, "This is working"?

Levchin: Bob and I built this package called IGOR. We had all these different things that were all named after various Russian names—and they had to be four characters long and start with an *I*. It was sort of a random requirement that I came up with. We had IGOR, INGA, IVAN—at least two more. So we built this tool—actually we have a patent on it now—and it was very impressive. It's based on the assumption of all sorts of convoluted guesses on our part, but the guesses turn out to be mostly right.

We actually had these human investigators, like 20 to 30 human investigators, that would try to unravel particularly large fraud cases and see if we could recover some money or send the Feds after somebody. We didn't really have much success sending people after criminals. All they'd try to do is see where the money went and see if we could recover some of it before it left the system. That was pretty difficult to do because the tools we had available to us at the time allowed you to look at only a couple of accounts at the same time. If you had a well-coordinated fraud, with thousands of accounts or hundreds of thousands of accounts involved, you basically didn't know how to follow it.

I remember walking into the cubicle of one of the investigators, and he had volumes and volumes of printouts. I asked what it all was, and he said, "I'm tracing some money." I said, "How many cases is this?" And he said, "This is just one case." I said, "How much money are we talking about?" He said, "It's like $80,000 worth of losses." "Well, that's a lot of money, but it's taken you clearly at least a week to print this stuff out."

We realized that the way we were attacking these things was just fundamentally flawed. So Bob and I built this system that was part visualization package, part graph balancing tool, that would try to represent large-scale travels of money in the system in a visual form. Taking that as a base, we built all these different tools that would allow computers to predict where particularly expensive losses would be and then represent the networks of losses to the investigators in such a way that they could very quickly make a decision whether or not to pursue a particular case.

Once we had that, I sort of had this tearful moment with one of the investigators where she was just crying in happiness—"You don't even understand what you did, Max"—when we showed it to them. They were really overworked.

Once that happened, there was this huge reduction. It wasn't like 80 percent or anything. But, all this time, we had all these different ideas and we'd bring the fraud down one-tenth of a percent or one-fifth of a percent, but it was really not noticeable. Then, one day, we brought the fraud down with that tool, a lot. So we're clearly getting better at this.

Then a woman named Sarah Imbach went into a sort of self-initiated exile. She moved to Omaha and first became the manager of the fraud group and then eventually became the manager of the whole center. When the fraud group operations moved to Omaha, that made it a lot cheaper for us to run. She was working on the human management part—all the investigators—and I would be supplying her with software. Between those things, we got fraud pretty well under control in about a year.

Livingston: So the fraud solution was a combination of humans and software?

Levchin: Depending on who you ask. I think Sarah feels that it's probably more humans and the coders think it's more technology. It's one of those things where, in the end, fraud is so nondeterministic that you need a human or a quantum computer to look at it and sort of make a final decision, because, in the end, it's people's money. You don't really want some computer saying, "$2.00 for you, nothing for you." You need a human with a brain to say, "Hmm. This looks like fraud, but I really don't think it is."

Then there are various processes and exception handling where you say, "Even though it's fraud, you don't handle it because . . ." We got really good at it later on. Initially, we sorted things by loss, but then we started sorting things by expected loss. We'd estimate the probability of losses programmatically, and then we'd get the amount of money in question calculated, figure out the expected loss, and then sort the cases for the investigators by expected loss.

The investigators would only have to deal with the top 5 percent. You'd never go through the entire queue of things for them to judge, but, because they judge things pretty quickly, they would go through half the queue, and they would inevitably start with the ones we thought were the highest possible loss. So, the highest probable, the highest possible. That was one of the techniques that we used to guide development.

Livingston: Were any of your competitors doing anything similar?

Levchin: We kept the stuff under wraps for a very long time. We never really showed IGOR to anyone. We never talked about it in the press. I was definitely very paranoid. Initially, when we built it, we had a conference room where there was the IGOR terminal, and people would go in there, use it, and leave. There were no other copies available.

Eventually, various federal and state authorities wanted to use it too, because they started to see that we were getting pretty good at this stuff. We would invite them in, and they would have to go into the room and use it and leave. They couldn't take it with them, couldn't print.

Livingston: Did you patent this technique?

Levchin: I didn't really want to patent it because, for one, I don't like software patents, and, two, if you patent it, you make it public. Even if you don't know someone's infringing, they will still be getting the benefit. Instead, we just chose to keep it a trade secret and not show it to anyone.

After a while, IGOR became well known to the company, like all the other tools that we had built early on. We had patented some of it, and some of it we said, "OK, it's open for wide use now." There's still a whole bunch of tools that they are using today that are not public. They don't talk about it much at all, and I think that's a good thing.

Livingston: So is PayPal in a sense a security company?

Levchin: I think a good way to describe PayPal is: a security company pretending to be a financial services company. What PayPal does is judge the risk of a transaction and then occasionally actually take the risk on. You don't really know the money's good; you just sort of assess the riskiness of both parties, and you say, "I'll be the intermediary with the understanding that, on occasion, PayPal will be on the hook for at least part of the loss if the loss occurs." Which is very tricky; it's a hard position to be in.

So the company's core expertise, by definition, has to be in this ability to judge risk—to be able to say, "Is this the kind of transaction I really want to take on or is this something I should steer away from because you people look like thieves?" I think that's the security part. I mean, security not in any sort of a sense of anti-hacking defensive, but just security in a broader sense: risk assessment, figuring out what's the sane thing to do, what's unsafe, what's safe. Everything else that PayPal has built is sort of a commodity. The reason we had so many competitors in 2000 was because it looks really simple on the outside: you sign up, give us some credit card numbers, let's trade some money, done.

Livingston: What did you do that your competitors couldn't?

Levchin: The really complicated part is figuring out the risk. The financial industry people understood the risk, but they weren't willing to do the sort of stuff we did, where they would basically say, "Bad guys over here. Let's get all the bad guys out."

There are tools to just say, "Give me your social security number, give me your address and your mother's maiden name, and we send you a physical piece of paper and you sign it and send it back to us." By the time that's all accomplished, you are a very safe user. But by then you are also not a user, because for every step you have to take, the dropoff rate is probably 30 percent. If you take ten steps, and each time you lose one-third of the users, you'll have no users by the time you're done with the fourth step.

The point is, the startups didn't realize there was this risk. We didn't really realize there was this risk component either when we started. But we were just lucky enough . . . Maybe I should be thankful for that happy year of boredom when I was expecting Windows and digging into stuff, figuring out what fraud was all about. But one way or the other—whatever caused that—we were smart enough to realize that fraud was a huge issue very quickly, and then were successful enough combating it while the startup competitors of ours did not and got buried very quickly. I remember all these companies announcing that they were going out of business and they expected PayPal to go out of business soon too, because the fraud numbers were so staggering that they could not see anyone handling this sort of thing.

There was one company—I think it was eMoneyMail—that shut down the company at a conference basically saying that the Internet is not a safe place to conduct transactions. They had 25 percent fraud. So for every $4.00 changing hands in the system, $1.00 was stolen. And it was all coming out of their pocket. They said, "We lost a ton of money," and they just quit.

Then, people like Citibank and other large financial institutions that also competed with us that understood the fraud thing very well—they knew from many years of practice that this was going to become a big problem—didn't really approach it with the same happy abandon that we did. We started with this, "Fraud is going to kill us. What can we do to save ourselves?" They started from, "We have no fraud. How can we build this and not let any more fraud in?" Which is the wrong position to start because you are limiting your users, and new users learning about a new system really don't want to be restricted.

Livingston: Why do you think they thought that way?

Levchin: I think there's a very strong power of default where, to them, certain behavior to solve a particular problem is well understood. There are people that make careers out of risk management in big banks. They know that what you do is this and you don't do that.

The other part, I think, is that a lot of them are public companies. We didn't go public until we had the fraud thing figured out. Somebody like Citibank or anyone with a substantial public visibility announcing that they are suddenly bleeding out $10 million a month in fraud would send serious shocks through the investor base. But I think, even if they did that, it's likely they wouldn't have been successful because—we had talked to a lot of them both as a potential acquirer and as partnership potential—none of them had actually ever gone to the sort of stuff that we did for our anti-fraud work.

The default of how you do these things is very powerful, if you've been in the industry for a long time. So we were sort of beneficiaries of our naïveté. We thought, "We don't know how to do this; let's just invent it."

Livingston: What else worried you?

Levchin: There was always something, every day. I could not sleep well for 4 years. If you are in charge of technology at a really fast-growing company that gets lots of publicity, there's always something that worries you. In early 2000, it was scalability. We had a few days when the site was down. Even though we were adding servers and rewriting code to be more scalable, at a certain point the original design was starting to crack. It was kind of painful.

Peter was pretty good at insulating me. He'd be talking to the reporters saying, "We're growing so fast." eBay lost, I think, 20 percent of their market cap one time—they had this downtime, when the system went down because of scalability concerns a few years before and so the reporters were asking, "Is this like eBay? Are you guys going to be down for a week?" So it was really tense.

Livingston: What were some of the more intense moments?

Levchin: One of the more intense moments was when Peter and our PR guy were flabbergasted with this reporter who demanded to talk to someone technical, because he wanted to hear from the horse's mouth what's going to happen. I was on the phone with the guy, and he asked, "Is this just like eBay? Are you guys going to crash? Are you not going to be able to scale?" I said, "Dude, I haven't slept for 3 days trying to fix the problem." Of course he said, "I'm going to quote you on that." Peter was worried.

It's one of those things where you have to fly by the seat of your pants all the time. It would be nice to test some hardware and set up a big lab: "We have x systems now; let's 2x the systems and get twice the amount of hardware and see if it can scale." But, it doesn't work that way because, by the time you are done testing 2x, the real system is 3x because the growth is so fast. We were getting 20,000 new active users every day. The transactional growth is exponential because people are sticking around. It's not like people came in, did one thing, and left. They came in, did one thing, and stayed. And they kept doing more.

Livingston: Was the growth viral?

Levchin: We built the system to be viral from day one. The idea was: I can send you the money, even if you aren't a member. If I send you $10, you get an email saying, "You have $10 waiting for you. Sign up, and you can take it." That's the most powerful viral driver there is. Free money available to you.

For eBay buyers and sellers, it became this crazy loop where buyers would be like, "I want to pay you with PayPal," and sellers would be like, "I don't accept PayPal." And buyers would say, "That's OK. I'll just send you $10, and you can sign up." So the seller would get infected, and the seller would say, "Oh, this is really simple, so I only accept PayPal."

Livingston: Any other turning points?

Levchin: Peter and I like to reflect on the fact that we got lucky so many times. Pick any one episode in the company history, and we got lucky and lucky and lucky again.

I think it's luck in the sense that we could have collapsed under this particular one, and we didn't. Mostly we didn't because we did something about it, and we corrected the problem or caught onto it early enough. But I think the fact that we caught the signs early enough in part is a luck thing because we could have just missed it, or we could have been too tired or too bored.

Livingston: Was there ever a time when you wanted to quit?

Levchin: The Windows thing was the closest I ever came to contemplating being out, but I probably wouldn't have done it anyway. I was still really attached to the company.

Livingston: What was one of the most surprising things to you?

Levchin: It was all surprising. Nonstop learning of things that I didn't really know before.

The most surprising thing was how big it became. I never thought it was going to be that big. I think I told Peter, "If we ever get to be 25 people, I'll probably quit because I like small companies. Is that OK?" The next time we talked about it, we already had 75 people, so I sort of missed my window. He said, "Why don't you stick around till 100, and we'll see what happens?" Next time we talked, we had 1,000 people.

Livingston: What advice would you give to a young programmer who's thinking of starting a startup?

Levchin: Try to have a good cofounder. I think it's all about people, and, if you are doing it completely alone, it's really hard. It's not impossible, in particular if you are a loner and introverted type, but it's still really hard.

One of the ways PayPal changed me is that I used to be really introverted, and I sort of still am, but not anywhere near to the extent that I used to be. A big part of it was that I had run a company before PayPal, alone, and I thought it was fine. I could deal with it. But, you only can count on energy sources and support sources from yourself. There's really no one else who you can go to and say, "Hey, this thing is going to fall apart any minute now. What the hell are we going to do?"

The thing that kept us going in the early days was the fact that Peter and I always knew that both of us would not be in a funk together. When I was like, "This fraud thing is going to kill us," Peter said, "No, I've seen the numbers. You are doing fine. Just keep at it. You'll get it." On the flip side, when Peter would be annoyed by some investors or board dynamics or whatever, I was usually there trying to support him. That sort of sounds touchy-feely, but I think you have to really have good people. If you have a good team, you are halfway there. Even more importantly, perhaps, you have to have a really strong cofounder. Someone you can rely on in a very fundamental way.

Livingston: Did you feel that way about Peter when you started?

Levchin: We hit it off really quickly. I have this IQ bias—anybody really smart, I will figure out a way to deal with.

It was very positive. Both of us are really competitive and really—not mistrusting, but not willing to assume that the other guy knows what he's talking about. When we met, we sort of hung out socially, and then one night we had this showdown where we sat around in this café for like 8 hours and traded puzzles to see who could solve puzzles faster—just this nonstop mental beating on each other. I think after that we realized that we each couldn't be total idiots since we could solve puzzles pretty quickly.

We would constantly try to come up with ones that the other person wouldn't be able to solve. I'm really into puzzles. I'm not a very quick solver, so I tend to take a long time. Not always, but on occasion, I will take a lot longer than an average time to solve it, but I almost always will succeed.

I think in a big way, the reason for PayPal's success is that I got very lucky with Peter as a cofounder, and I'd like to think he got pretty lucky with me.

Livingston: Who did you learn things from?

Levchin: There are different segments to running a startup. Different people taught me different things. A lot of the top management people at PayPal were really good. It was very fun and meaningful to work with them and pick up their various interests and skills.

I never really paid much attention in college in econ, and I never really took any accounting classes. One night I came over to our CFO's office, and I said, "I really don't understand a lot of the balance sheet math and all this stuff. I'm pretty good at math, so I should be able to get it, but I just don't understand the language, so teach me accounting." We had this crazy multihour session where he was explaining accounting to me. I learned debits and credits and why certain things are called what they are; liabilities versus assets and capital. Until then, I had no idea. It was maybe a year into the company, and I thought, "I really should understand this balance sheet stuff. It's kind of an art."

I had never really raised money before, so when Peter was raising money, I was tagging along as much as I could, trying to pick that up.

Livingston: Did you have a good relationship with your investors?

Levchin: It's one of these things where, if you look back now, when everyone walked away with a ton of money, everyone loves everyone. We had this great time, etc. It's generally more complicated than that where, when the company is doing well, they're happy and they think they're great. The company's not doing well; they've overpaid and they've been too nice. It's half and half. I think I was blissfully spared a lot of it because Peter managed the board much more than I did.

I was on the board all through my tenure there, but a lot of the more unpleasant conversations were handled by Peter. I got involved more as the fraud thing grew. For a long time, it was one of these things where—I was really much younger than now—my whole "brand" both to the investors and to our board members was this crazy Russian boy-genius who comes out and sprinkles magic dust on technology and things just work.

So for a long time I got away with, "Don't ask how it works. Max will solve it." It worked OK until the scalability problems hit us, and then I had to be much more vocal and explain to the board, "Here's what's going on. Here's what I'm doing about it. It will be OK. Just chill out." Then, when the fraud thing became my primary concern, obviously I had to get involved much more because it had to do with things they dealt with on a daily basis: money. So I had to prepare much more thoroughly. The whole boy-genius thing had to be discarded for the much more serious attitude and language.

Livingston: Looking back, is there anything you would have done differently?

Levchin: No.

Livingston: You didn't make any mistakes?

Levchin: There are all sorts of tactical decisions that we made here and there that played out to be wrong, but it's not like I could have predicted it. It's not one of these things that I'm now smarter and therefore I could have done it even better. I think, given the information available at the time, I would have likely chosen the same outcome. There are some business decisions that I think we made incorrectly, where we partnered with some companies, but generally in financial industries, partnerships are not . . . we got screwed and had to back out, but, in retrospect, these are not major.

I think we hired the absolute best people, we were able to do things pretty well on average, and we had lots of fun.

Livingston: Did things change a lot after PayPal was acquired?

Levchin: I think the acquirers tend to be more—it pays to be different from the founders; otherwise, you still have this clinging-on of the original culture. It's very sad that, when you buy a company, you have to sort of squash a lot of the original stuff, but if you don't, you foster this festering of distrust and dislike. So you just have to get through the unpleasant bits as fast as you can and go on doing business. Which doesn't make it any easier for the early people or the founders, but I don't know any other format in which you can acquire companies. You could let them be on their own, but then you aren't really getting any of the benefits.

Usually, when you acquire companies, you sort of calculate these synergies, which is this nebulous number: if we take you and we take me and we combine it, we can get rid of this much stuff and this many people. It's really painful to hear about it, but that's why people buy companies. eBay bought us because, for a while, they had their own floundering payment service. They had 65 people that were doing this thing called Billpoint that was an also-ran in the payment space. They did particularly poorly. Even though they were bought by eBay and they were the eBay solution, they still got completely smashed by us.

The ultimate justice was carried out when they bought us and they announced to those people that they were going to be let go. It's really painful. I wouldn't want to be on their side at all. Finding out that you're being told to pack up and being replaced by these people that you'd fought all this time with. The mothership has capitulated, and they're replacing us with the people we've been fighting against.

Livingston: What can big companies do to preserve a startup culture?

Levchin: I don't know. Less PowerPoints. I think PayPal—even by the time we were acquired—still felt really startup in a variety of ways. But not as much as originally. People were definitely grumbling about how the startup culture was being lost, even internally. But then, when we got to eBay, which was three times the size, it was even less so. But, as you grow larger, you need more structure and coordination and meetings.

My theory is that you sort of subdivide, and you make smaller units and you give them a lot of power and responsibility. You let them make it or break it. But I have no practical knowledge as to whether this works or not.

Livingston: Was there anything that was misunderstood about what you were trying to do?

Levchin: No, because I think we didn't know what we were doing. I think the hallmark of a really good entrepreneur is that you're not really going to build one specific company. The goal—at least the way I think about entrepreneurship—is you realize one day that you can't really work for anyone else. You have to start your own thing. It almost doesn't matter what that thing is. We had six different business plan changes, and then the last one was PayPal.

If that one didn't work out, if we still had the money and the people, obviously we would not have given up. We would have iterated on the business model and done something else. I don't think there was ever any clarity as to who we were until we knew it was working. By then, we'd figured out our PR pitch and told everyone what we do and who we are. But between the founding and the actual PayPal, it was just this tug-of-war where it was like, "We're trying this, this week." Every week you go to investors and say, "We're doing this, exactly this. We're really focused. We're going to be huge." The next week you're like, "That was a lie."

One of the interesting moments was after we got funding from Nokia Ventures, the first VC firm that funded us. The beaming at Buck's was still done under this, "We're doing this handheld device thing and there's some payment component, but it's really handheld device, share your lunch bill with your Palm Pilot." By the time we had our first board meeting a month later, we had already realized that that wasn't going to work and that we had to do the web stuff much more prominently—and we had all these other ideas that we wanted to do, which we later on threw out. But we started the board meeting basically saying, "Hi, John. Hi, Pete"—the new VC guys—"We changed our business plan." And these guys were like, "What?" They just put down $4 million to see something happen, and we said, "Sorry, we're not going to do that; we're going to do this."

To their credit, they were like, "All right, you guys are smart. Let's do it." Usually VCs get freaked out by that, but these guys were like, "OK. You're so crazy. Let's go."

Sabeer Bhatia
Cofounder, Hotmail

When coworkers Sabeer Bhatia and Jack Smith began working on their first startup idea—a web-based personal database they called JavaSoft—they were frustrated because their employer's firewall prevented them from accessing their personal email accounts.

To solve their problem, they came up with the idea of email accounts that could be accessed anonymously through a web browser. This idea became the startup. In 1996, the first web-based email was born, offering people free email accounts that could be accessed from any computer with an Internet connection.

Less than 2 years later, they had grown Hotmail's user base faster than any media company in history. On New Year's Eve, 1997, Microsoft acquired Hotmail for $400 million.

Livingston: Take me back to how the idea got started and evolved into Hotmail. How did you know Jack?

Bhatia: I met Jack Smith when I joined Apple Computer. We were working on the same project building PowerBook portables. Our manager left the company to join a startup in the Valley called FirePower Systems. Jack and I knew Apple would have given us steady, stable employment, but it wasn't with grand stock options. So we decided to leave Apple and join this startup.

We worked very hard, cranking out products: chips that were used to design PCs that ran on the PowerPC processor. These would run multiple operating systems, and at that time the idea was that if the insides of the computer were better and faster, then people would switch because it ran multiple operating systems, including either the UNIX or Windows architecture. If the processor was better, obviously that would eliminate the need to get Intel-based processors, because the architecture of RISC-based systems was better. But what happened over time is that Intel itself caught up on the price/performance curve.

After 2 years the company really wasn't doing very much. Our manager who hired the two of us left and went on his own. So I was kind of looking around to see what I should do with my life—whether I should go to business school or look at other things. The Internet was just unfolding, so I started spending more and more time on it, and it was interesting. It was exciting to see these little companies get started. Two of my colleagues from Stanford had gone on to start Yahoo, and I thought, "Wow. This is just a list, a directory which tells you what is where. And somebody put $1 million in them." I mean, that was huge. So I thought, "This Internet thing is here to stay," and I started playing around with it and came up with the idea to do a simple-to-install database at the back end. Then you'd use the browser as the front end. It could store any piece of information at the back, but the browser would be used to display it. So people could just look for it and be able to create a personal database of anything: contact information, phone numbers, special files, or whatever it is that you would do on a local PC.

So I wrote a business plan and didn't know what to do with it. I was the only guy, so how do you build a company? I knew Jack and knew that he was a great software and hardware engineer. So I shared this idea with him. He read the business plan and said the next day, "This is great, where do I sign?"

So we started and I said, "The next thing we need to do is go raise some money and try to figure out how to hire more people and take this to the next level."

Livingston: Had you quit your jobs?

Bhatia: No, we were actually both working, so we decided to spend all of the time on the weekends and evenings building this product. Then it came to a point that one of us had to quit our job to focus full-time on it, so I told Jack, "I'm single and don't have a family. Why don't you quit and start working on this and I'll give you half of my salary?" So at least he could support his family. I didn't need that much money.

We started building the product and then started looking around for funding. We went to a number of VCs and many of them turned us down because they were like, "How are you going to make money if you are going to give it away for free? What's the revenue mechanism?" We said we would capture detailed demographic information about people and that detailed quality of information on individuals would help us advertise to them. But of course advertising was not a proven revenue model at that time.

Livingston: How did the JavaSoft idea morph into Hotmail?

Bhatia: While we were putting the business plan for JavaSoft together and were working at FirePower Systems, they installed a firewall around our corporate intranet that prevented us from dialing out to our personal email accounts. I had an account at Stanford and Jack had one at AOL, so we would dial out and email each other. But we couldn't do that anymore because the firewall prevented us from accessing our personal accounts. So we ended up exchanging information on floppy disks and on physical pieces of paper. That's when it occurred to us, "Wait a minute, we can access any website in the world through a web browser. If we made email available through the web browser, that would solve our problem."

And then it occurred to us, "If that would solve our problem, it would solve the problems of many others." We didn't know how many others, but email was something that everyone used. To provide ubiquitous access to that email from any web browser from anywhere in the world was the killer idea.

Livingston: This killer idea emerged because you guys were trying to solve the personal email exchange problem for yourselves?

Bhatia: Absolutely. That we could access our email from only two places: our homes and our work. And while we were at work, we could not access our personal email accounts.

Livingston: Once you were onto the concept of web-based email, did you immediately discard the JavaSoft database idea and go full throttle with Hotmail?

Bhatia: We were kind of torn. Our plan was to use the JavaSoft idea to get money from venture capitalists. But actually the killer arrow in our quiver was always email because we thought that it was even bigger than the original idea.

Livingston: But you didn't want to tell people about the killer idea because you were afraid they'd copy you?

Bhatia: That they would copy us, or what if they just shared this idea with Netscape? Or shared it with anyone else. You have to realize that in those days we had nothing—just the idea. When we were approaching venture capitalists, they would shoot us down for one reason or another—for reasons we thought were frivolous like, "You guys, what is your background?" So we would tell them that our background was in hardware engineering. "Why are you building software?"

Many of them also said, "But you're too young. Do you have any management experience?" "No," we said, "we're two young kids; we have a great idea."

The whole VC community has so many links with each other—you never know. Netscape was building email servers. What if the VCs were just to say to them, "Hey, why don't you do web-based email?" And that's it, that's the idea, right? There was not that much to protect in terms of IP. Whoever built it first would win the market.

So we were afraid and that's why we kept that as the secret. But we were going to do web-based email no matter what, even if we got funding for the other idea.

Livingston: I read that you judged the VCs by their reaction to the JavaSoft idea. Did you plan this clever approach?

Bhatia: We actually planned to do this. You can't get an audience with any venture capitalist without sharing a business plan, but we didn't want our business plan floating around somewhere with the email idea. So we would go in with the JavaSoft business plan.

If they passed the litmus test of not rejecting us for the wrong reasons and said, "OK, we don't mind that you're young, we don't mind that you don't have management experience," only when they would start poking holes in the actual idea would we share the Hotmail idea with them. That was actually just because we didn't trust them.

Livingston: You finally pitched Draper Fisher Jurvetson (DFJ) and they passed the test. Tell me about getting funding.

Bhatia: They liked the idea right off the bat. They said, "We're going to get one of our partners to come in and take a look at this because it could be big." So Tim Draper came in the following week and he liked the idea. After another meeting he said, "OK, we're ready to fund you. We like this very much. How much do you want?"

I did some calculations on the back of an envelope and asked for $3 million, which was our plan based on hiring a few engineers.

They said, "No, that's too much. How much money do you need just to prove to us that you can do this—that it's even possible to make email available on the web?" So I asked for half a million and he said, "I'll give you $300,000." I said, "Alright, I'll take it."

They wanted 30 percent of the company, which would value us at $1 million. It was an intense negotiation; I threatened to go to the other VCs if they didn't pony up the money. We finally settled on a 15 percent split with them and they valued the company at $2 million post money. But they'd put in a right of first refusal. Since I was a young entrepreneur at the time, I didn't understand that this basically meant that you couldn't go to any other VC. So even though they didn't get their chunk in the first piece, in any subsequent round they would have the ability to take up the entire round.

Livingston: Your lawyer didn't point out that clause?

Bhatia: We didn't have a very good lawyer back then. Of course it was touted to us as "We love you so much that we want to have the right to buy the next round. You can go to other people too."

But that's the one that got us. It impeded our ability to go to another VC. What ended up happening was that we could not get a higher valuation because DFJ wanted to put more money in the company themselves. So any time we would talk to another VC, they would talk him out of it: "This is not a good company, don't worry about it." So we were really stuck with DFJ for the next round.

Livingston: They put you down to other VCs?

Bhatia: They did. Of course, that was very early on and now everything is all fine and dandy, but at that point in time . . . we had a term sheet for a much higher valuation. But when we would talk to any other VC, the other VC would call the guys at DFJ and they'd say, "No, don't invest in them."

Livingston: Were they helpful at all?

Bhatia: Yes. Steve Jurvetson was very helpful; he introduced us to a lot of people and, on the whole, they're a good VC firm in the sense that they try to put deals together. But sometimes they don't play by the rules.

Nobody knows this, but the round before the deal with Microsoft, they literally put $5 million in the company just because they knew it was going to get sold and that we needed some bridge money. This came at a very expensive valuation with certain rights that should not have come with it—like participating preferred, which is they first get their money out and then they participate in the rest, which was OK for the earlier rounds, but not for the later ones. That was just bridge money that we needed while we were negotiating with Microsoft. They knew full well that we were going to get acquired; we were negotiating about the final price.

Livingston: I'll come back to the Microsoft negotiation in a moment. Did your background in hardware help you in terms of building servers that could handle massive loads?

Bhatia: It helped us because we knew what kind of hardware we would need to be able to handle the kind of traffic to our site. Also, when you are hardware designers, you have tremendously more discipline in writing and describing software because in hardware you cannot get it wrong. Every turn of every chip costs you millions of dollars, so when hardware designers design any piece of software, they normally get it right. They use something called state machines to describe the functioning of the software. When you do that, you are very deterministic: if this is the input, then this will be the output.

So you write it in a very deterministic fashion and therefore you tend not to make too many mistakes. Whereas the pure software writers—the way they think and architect software is very creative. They put in lots of bells and whistles, but they think, "No big deal. If there is a bug, we'll fix it. Put in a patch." You can't do that in hardware. There's no patch. Once you ship a chip, it has to work all the time. So in terms of being able to test it out, there is somewhat of a difference, but I just think that hardware designers would be pretty good software designers as well.

Livingston: Were you at all worried about intellectual property issues when you left the company to start Hotmail?

Bhatia: No, they were totally different. We were designing chips, which had nothing to do with the Internet.

Livingston: So you now have $300,000 and you're working full-time on Hotmail. What happened in the 6 months before you launched?

Bhatia: We got funded on February 14, 1996, and the site launched on the Fourth of July. We had 100,000 subscribers in the first 3 months and we were growing very rapidly from then on. We were literally getting 1,000, 2,000, 5,000 sign-ups every day.

Livingston: How?

Bhatia: It all spread by word of mouth. We launched a massive PR campaign with a PR firm and started talking to different journalists. We did a West Coast and East Coast press tour, and it just took off from there.

Livingston: You had a tagline in the body of the email encouraging email recipients to set up their own free Hotmail accounts. How did you come up with this?

Bhatia: It was actually Jack's idea to do that. We ran it by our VCs just to make sure it was OK. When you alter somebody's email, you've got to be very careful. You're sending an email to a friend of yours, and we are kind of violating the sanctity of that email by putting in a tagline at the end of it that says "This message has been sent from Hotmail. Get your free email at hotmail.com."

So we asked Tim if it was OK that we did this. We said, "We don't want to be perceived as the evil company by altering their email." And he said, "Absolutely, you should do it."

And the next thing we know, he claims that this idea was his. He's given a number of interviews literally claiming that he was the father of web-based email—without him it would not have happened. I can't believe he's just taken credit for everything—including the tagline (which later became known as the classic example of viral marketing). He blatantly claims this at conferences, which I don't think is right.

Livingston: He claimed that web-based email was his idea?

Bhatia: That it was our idea, but without them, it would not have happened and that we would have done JavaSoft. Their version is that "we told them to do web-based email at that [first] meeting." Why would they tell us to do web-based email?

Livingston: You grew Hotmail's user base faster than any other company in history at that time. Do you believe it was more because you had a great product or you had a good PR campaign?

Bhatia: That's one thing about the Internet: if you have something that's good, it spreads by word of mouth and like wildfire. You just have to hire a small PR firm and do it.

Livingston: Had you always planned for Hotmail to be free for users?

Bhatia: Yes.

Livingston: How did you convince people you could make money from targeted advertising? That was so novel at the time.

Bhatia: It was novel, but at the same time it wasn't novel, because Yahoo had gotten funding (and later went public) on that basis. Their whole concept was to grow by advertising, even though it was a directory, because people would pay for advertising.

Our whole idea was that, if page impressions are a commodity that can be sold, can be monetized, then we would generate far greater page impression than they were able to because you interact a lot more when you do email. You click on something and a page comes up and you click on something and another page comes up. So we were thinking of the number of pages and the number of page impressions as the monetizable quantity. In our estimate, we believed we would overtake Yahoo in the number of page impressions that we would deliver, which was what Yahoo was touting.

What has happened in the last 10 years is that advertising has grown even more. It's not just page impressions, but the number of click-throughs. The most monetizable part of advertising (at least online advertising today) is the click-through to another advertiser, which is search. When people search, they're most likely to click through because that's when they're looking for something.

Google has proven remarkably well that click-through is a monetizable quantity more than page impressions. You can have 100 page impressions and that has some value, but the click-through has far greater value because that's how advertisers measure, "Is this advertising working for us or not?"

Livingston: Did you have a hard time signing up advertisers at first?

Bhatia: It takes a long time before you can break through to an advertiser and get them to start paying you. In fact, the first 3 or 4 months we were doing advertising for our advertisers for free. We had them give us their banners, just to show that this was a mechanism for people to get their product in front of millions and millions of consumers.

People would ask, "So, how are you going to make money?" And the whole thing about making money was all those pesky ads. Ads were perceived to be kind of a negative. And that's the reason why, when there used to be 25 search engines, only 2 or 3 have survived. The others have died because they made their front pages look like Las Vegas casinos as opposed to preserving that simple, clean interface that Google has. I think the strategy that Google took was far better. They earned the trust of the end consumer.

Livingston: Did Hotmail ever become profitable from advertising?

Bhatia: No, we didn't become profitable. But we weren't losing that much money. We found that we were not the best at selling ads, so we outsourced the whole thing to another company and said, "You guys go sell the ads for us. We'll just focus on delivering these ads to you no matter how much you sell them for. Just give us a percentage of revenue with a minimum commitment and we won't go to anybody else."

That minimum commitment they gave us, which was about $1 million per month, was alone sufficient for us to break even. Our costs were so low; we were spending about $1 million a month. So though we were not wildly profitable, we were not losing that much money.

Livingston: Getting back to the first 6 months before you launched, tell me about the major turning points.

Bhatia: Before we launched, I think the first major turning point was getting the $300,000 in funding. That was huge for us—two young kids to get that much money. The second turning point really was when I started using it and I told my friends and family about it and everybody who used the product (50 or 100 or so people) loved it.

And then of course, the interesting thing was that when we finally did launch, each of us had pagers that would send us a page every hour, so we would know how quickly our user base was growing. It was just phenomenal— 100 people signed up last hour, 200 people this hour. Everyone knew how many users were signing on and that was very motivating to the whole company.

Livingston: Was there ever a time when you thought you were in trouble?

Bhatia: The only time was when we had to go in for the second round of financing. We didn't have any money and Tim was at the Olympics in Atlanta and he refused to fund us because we wanted a slightly higher valuation. This was what all the other VCs were telling us, but he wanted to invest at a lower valuation. We had only a couple of weeks worth of money left and I would not have been able to meet the next payroll. So as soon as he came back, we literally had to accept his terms and move on.

Livingston: Couldn't you have argued legally that by not agreeing to a higher valuation that they had "refused" you?

Bhatia: At that point you are stuck; you've got to make a decision one way or the other and move on.

Livingston: So really the biggest challenge in the early years of Hotmail was the funding?

Bhatia: Yeah, it was the funding. And of course then the tough part was in scaling up to that growth. Our servers would break down and we had to worry about scalability problems and how to add servers and make it more reliable. It was not all smooth sailing.

Livingston: Did you ever go out of service?

Bhatia: We went out of service for a few hours sometimes and we didn't have proper backups, or the ability to restore things. Reliability was an issue and it took us some time to cross the reliability curve.

Livingston: Was there ever a time when you felt you couldn't keep up?

Bhatia: We just handled the problems as they came around: we put in a new system, rearchitected some of the things. The engineers worked really hard, and we kind of made it work. But even now there are times when you log into Hotmail and it says, "Sorry, the server is down." These are just issues when you have a very large user base.

Livingston: Web-based email was so new to the world. What did consumers misunderstand?

Bhatia: We had a sales guy who signed up his mom, and his mom said, "Yes, I can see that there's an email from you, but how do I read it?" And he said, "Mom, go and click on it." She didn't know you had to click on it!

I heard another story from a man who said his sister would get into the Hotmail account not directly by going to http://hotmail.com, but by going to Yahoo, typing in the word "hotmail," and then it would bring up the Hotmail page and then she'd log in. And he'd say, "Why do you do it that way?" and the sister would say, "My friend taught me this is how you get to Hotmail, so that's what I've been doing." The usage patterns of how people used the Internet were baffling to us.

Livingston: Who were you most nervous about from a competitive standpoint?

Bhatia: Anybody in the Internet space. We were most nervous about companies like Netscape, because Netscape was building email servers and they would provide web-based access to the servers. Their whole point was that they provided web-based management to servers that you could set up. So, as system administrators, you could check to see how many had people signed up or whatever, but they were not offering web-based mail to people.

The good news was that a lot of people said, "I'm not sure email is a browser-based product. Email is best done on an email client like Outlook Express. It doesn't belong in the browser." That's what Jerry Yang said at Yahoo. We were like, "Great!" So we had no competition from them for the first 8 months or so, till we reached a certain point and then they had no choice but to buy a company.

I heard that Yahoo gave up the opportunity to buy Google for $1,000,000—that at one point, Google would have been happy to be sold to them for a million bucks.

Livingston: Yahoo ultimately wound up buying Rocketmail. They were your first real competitor, right? Tell me about them.

Bhatia: They were our partners. We needed to have a directory of users that people could search and send email to. Instead of building our own directory, we partnered with Rocketmail. We said, "OK, we'll use your directory on our website and we'll send you our registration data so you could register these people's email accounts." We didn't want to build a directory just for people to search for email. All they had was a directory, that's what they specialized in, that was their business.

They found out how many registrations we were sending them daily—they saw our growth from hundreds to thousands to tens of thousands, and that's when they said, "Even we ourselves cannot get these kinds of registrations on our website. We should do email." So they decided to do email and that's how they came up with Rocketmail.

Livingston: Were you pissed?

Bhatia: They are also funded by Draper Fisher Jurvetson. So Draper was seeing two of its own companies create two different email systems.

We felt bad that they had done it, but we couldn't go to Draper and say anything. It was a decision that the company took, that's what DFJ told us, and we were pissed at them, but at that time we knew we had to not share too much information with DFJ as well.

Livingston: So you didn't have a showdown with Rocketmail?

Bhatia: We just scrapped our partnership and decided, "OK, competition is competition."

Livingston: Then you started to get into talks with Microsoft?

Bhatia: Talks with Microsoft started after our first anniversary, which was July 1997. In August or so, Microsoft contacted us and said, "Wow, this is really big. Do you really have 7 million subscribers?" They knew that we were growing and they wanted to find out how we provided email to 7 million subscribers because they were having a hard time providing email to just 2.5 million MSN customers. So we began talking of a partnership deal and that's how we started talking to each other.

We worked out a detailed business plan about how we would provide email to their subscribers, and then they said they wanted a tighter relationship between us and their company—that they wanted to invest in our company. So they looked at our business plan and saw very quickly that we wanted to be more than just an email company. We wanted to incorporate all of the other functions as well, such as personalized news and those kinds of things.

We wanted to be a portal at that point in time. So that's when they came to us—they wanted to be a portal as well—and they said, "We cannot have one of our providers of email be a competitor of ours, so have you thought of an acquisition?" And I said, "I really haven't thought of an acquisition, but at the right price I can think of anything."

Livingston: Tell me about the negotiation process.

Bhatia: They called us to meet with Bill on October 13, 1997, and we were shown the Microsoft campus, headquarters, the whole works. We were taken to Bill's office, met with him, and then we were taken to a room with a gigantic table, and there were about 15 Microsoft negotiators sitting on the other side: business development people, lawyers, accountants, all of them.

They gave a presentation about how much they liked the company and this and that, and they said they wanted to buy us and placed an offer of $160 million. I knew that that was the opening shot and I said, "Thank you very much for making an offer. We really, really like your company and like the fact that you like us so much. We'll go back to our board and discuss this and get back to you."

And the CFO said, "C'mon, is that in the right ballpark?" He wanted me to open my mouth, but I was told beforehand that if I opened my mouth, there was no way I could negotiate with so many people. It was just the three of us: Jack Smith, myself, and our VP of marketing.

Livingston: The VCs gave you the liberty to negotiate, right? That surprises me.

Bhatia: Luckily it was very early on; had we been burning through a lot of cash, had we been around for a while, they probably would have put pressure on us. But we were under no pressure at that point in time.

Livingston: What drove you to keep on negotiating until you got the $400 million?

Bhatia: Once you've got a lead in terms of a subscriber base, that is unassailable. It can't be replicated easily. So I knew even if they started developing the product—I have no doubt in my mind that they could have developed it, so many engineers and smart people in Microsoft. At that time they had something like 16,000 engineers, and I had a total of 60 people in the company, only 14 engineers, so it would have been easy to pick 15 guys from 16,000 and build this product. But I knew we had that momentum behind us and that is very hard to replicate.

Livingston: You arrived in this country with only $250 in your pocket. Wasn't it tempting for you to agree to sell for, say, $300 million?

Bhatia: Once you have tasted this kind of success, once you've tasted that it works, that you've got subscribers who are telling you it's good, you know you are going to get there. In fact, that's exactly what's happened. That 6-month lead that we had already over any of our competitors today has translated into about a 50 to 100 million–user lead.

Seeing how they did a lousy job of providing email to their 2.5 million subscribers, I also knew that they didn't have the technology in house. Because if they did, they wouldn't have been asking to license this from us. If we had gone the licensing route, I think we would have been as big as Google. Because that's what Google did, right? Initially, they said, "We've got search. Why don't we license search to everyone else?" That was their original business model. They licensed it to Yahoo, Microsoft, and AOL and grew big based on their subscribers.

Livingston: Do you wish you had gone the licensing route?

Bhatia: No, it would have been a lot more difficult, because the cost of providing email was much higher than the cost of providing search—even though search is far more profitable than email in terms of the advertising monetizability of search. Because when somebody searches, they are looking to find something; they are in the mood to click. Email is more of a destination. When you are doing email, you don't want to be disturbed by what's on the right, you want to read whatever your friend has written to you. So it's the end product. It not a click-through kind of a product. So I don't know where we would have ended up had we done that.

Livingston: Looking back on your experience with Hotmail, what surprised you most?

Bhatia: I think I knew that Hotmail was going to become successful one day. I was just shocked that all of that happened in a span of 20 months from start to finish. Those kinds of things don't happen very often; from the time you start to the time you see an exit in less than 2 years. That's what shocked me. And I have not been able to replicate that kind of meteoric growth and success yet.

I was lucky also; I was at the right place at the right time. I have been thinking about new ideas and new companies in the last 5 years and have been working on some really exciting things. But I don't think that any one of these will become successful in that short a period of time.

Livingston: Web-based email was one of those big ideas that was waiting right under people's noses. Why did you and Jack come up with the idea first?

Bhatia: I don't know why. Let me tell you one other thing about the Internet: there are thousands of such ideas under our noses even as we speak. Why things happen, I just don't know. Maybe somebody has a need and, in our case, we had a need. That's what triggered the idea. Sometimes ideas are born out of necessity: you solve a problem for yourself, and you hopefully solve it for a number of other people too.

The one lesson that I've learned in my experience while I did Hotmail and since I've done Hotmail is you have got to own the customer. The customers came to us for free at Hotmail. Even though they were free customers, what the last 10 to 15 years of my experience of the Internet has taught me is that it's OK if you don't monetize them right up front. Eventually you will be able to. But having that customer base and being able to tap into that customer base and upsell them on services, or advertise—you can always make money off them.

Livingston: Is there any advice you would give to someone thinking of starting a startup?

Bhatia: The general piece of advice, which is fairly mundane and oft repeated, is: make sure you write a business plan because it will crystallize your thoughts to communicate your ideas with somebody else. Make sure that once you have written your business plan, you have somebody read and critique it and ask you questions.

It doesn't have to be a cookie-cutter business plan with glossy pages and lots of information. Essentially it's a plan that says what the company is going to do, what problem it is going to solve, how big the market is, what the sources of revenue for the company are, what your exit strategy is for your investors, what amount of money is required, how you are going to market it, what kind of people you need, what the technology risks are, marketing risks, execution risks. Those are the fundamentals of what goes into a business plan, and many people have it in their heads but don't write it down.

Second is, don't try to change user behavior dramatically. If you are expecting people to dramatically change the way they do things, it's not going to happen. Try to make it such that it's a small change, yet an important one. For example, the reason that Hotmail succeeded was because people were accustomed to going to different websites. All they had to do was put in their name and password and a little bit of information and they got an email account. So in that regard, it was the ease of use of getting online and having an identity.

The other reason why Hotmail became kind of like its own phenomenal PR was every time somebody sent an email out, it was sent from @hotmail.com. That's of huge branding value, to have that moniker in people's email IDs. So when people would give a business card to somebody that said @hotmail.com, it perpetuated the brand.

And the other lessons are you've got to own the customer and make sure there is a full loop between your product and that it has the least amount of resistance before you get to your end customer. Do partnerships; what Google did with partnerships was phenomenal—giving the search away to other companies to help them make their so-called portals. But in the end, Google got the customer because they got the branding.

Livingston: You were a programmer. How did you learn how to write a business plan? Tell me about the one you wrote for Hotmail.

Bhatia: There are some things that, even though you go to school for a certain reason and you gain skills, are just natural talents that people have. One of the natural talents that I believe I have is the ability to communicate. A business plan is nothing more than your own communication to a person not sitting in front of you—an imaginary person who will read it. Try to answer every possible question that that person could raise. That's the description of a business plan, really.

I didn't take any formal lessons. I just sat down and I wrote about the problem we were trying to solve, and in two paragraphs I described the World Wide Web and how it had grown and what its future potential could be. I said, this is the problem today that we are trying to address, this is how we hope to address it, with this idea. This is how we hope to monetize it and this is what page impressions are able to fetch you in the print world. If you translate it into the online world, this is how it will happen. And that's it, that was the core of our business plan.

I wrote it in one night, and the next day I went to work looking really sleepy and tired. My boss said, "Another one of those days of late-night partying?" I'm like, "Yeah, something like that." He said, "Alright, you'll be productive only in the afternoon. Take the morning off." Little did he know that I was actually up all night writing a business plan, not partying.

Steve Wozniak
Cofounder, Apple Computer

If any one person can be said to have set off the personal computer revolution, it might be Steve Wozniak. He designed the machine that crystallized what a desktop computer was: the Apple II.

Wozniak and Steve Jobs founded Apple Computer in 1976. Between Wozniak's technical ability and Jobs's mesmerizing energy, they were a powerful team. Woz first showed off his home-built computer, the Apple I, at Silicon Valley's Homebrew Computer Club in 1976. After Jobs landed a contract with the Byte Shop, a local computer store, for 100 preassembled machines, Apple was launched on a rapid ascent.

Woz soon followed with the machine that made the company: the Apple II. He single-handedly designed all its hardware and software—an extraordinary feat even for the time. And what's more, he did it all while working at his day job at Hewlett-Packard. The Apple II was presented to the public at the first West Coast Computer Faire in 1977.

Apple Computer went public in 1980 in the largest IPO since Ford in 1956, creating more instant millionaires than any other company up to that point.

The Apple II was the machine that brought computers onto the desks of ordinary people. The reason it did was that it was so miraculously well designed. But when you meet Woz in person, you realize another equally miraculous aspect of his character. A programmer might describe it by saying he's good in hardware.

Livingston: Take me back to before you started Apple.

Wozniak: Even back in high school I knew I could design computers with half as many chips as the companies were selling them with. I taught myself, but I had taught myself in a way that forced me to learn all sorts of trickiness. Because you try to make valuable what you're good at. I was good at making things with very few parts by using all sorts of tricks—almost the equivalent of mathematics—so I valued products that were made with very few parts.

That helped in two ways. When you are a startup or an individual on your own, you don't have very much money, so the fewer parts you have to buy, the better. When you design with very few parts, everything is so clean and orderly you can understand it more deeply in your head, and that causes you to have fewer bugs. You live and sleep with every little detail of the product.

In the few years before Apple, I was working at Hewlett-Packard designing scientific calculators. That was a real great opportunity to be working with the hot product of the day. But what I did that led to starting a company was on the side. When I came home from work, I kept doing electronics anyway. I didn't do the same calculators we were doing at work, but I got involved through other people with the earliest home pinball games, hotel movies . . . The first VCRs made for people were actually made by an American company—not Betamax, it was before Betamax even—called Cartravision. It was put in some Sears TVs. I got involved with that. I saw arcade games—the first arcade game, Pong, that really made it big—so I designed one of those on my own. Then Atari wanted to take my design and make it the first home Pong game. They said to do one chip, which was better for the volumes that they would have—to do a custom chip. Steve Mayer came up with that idea. But I was kind of in with Atari and they recognized me for my design talents, so they wanted to hire me.

Livingston: How did they know you?

Wozniak: Steve Jobs worked there part-time. He would finish up games that they designed in Grass Valley. He brought me in and showed me around, and Nolan Bushnell offered me a job on the spot. I said, "No, I'm never going to leave Hewlett-Packard. It's my job for life. It's the best company because it's so good to engineers." It really treated us like we were a community and family, and everyone cared about everyone else. Engineers—bottom-of-the-org-chart people—could come up with the ideas that would be the next hot products for the company. Everything was open to thought, discussion, and innovation. So I would never leave Hewlett-Packard. I was going to be an engineer for life there.

Then I designed a game for Atari called Breakout, and that was a really incredible product. That was just so neat, to have my name associated with a product that actually came out in the field in video games. Because this was the start of a whole industry and I wasn't really a part of it. But I wanted to be a designer and just have some little connection to it.

In doing all those projects, I got involved in another one. The ARPANET then had about a dozen computers connected with a network. You could select which computer to visit, and they had certain access that you could get into as a guest; or, if you had passwords, you could get deeper. I just saw somebody typing away on the teletype, just talking about playing chess with a computer in Boston, and I said, "I have to do this. I just have to have this for myself." For a lot of entrepreneurs, they see something and they say, "I have to have this," and that will start them building their own.

I couldn't really afford to buy the pieces I needed. I couldn't buy a teletype, so I had to design my own terminal. The only thing that was free (because I had no money) was a home TV to see characters on. I got a keyboard for $60, which was amazingly low-priced then. That was the most expensive thing to getting my terminal built. Then it was just a matter of designing logic to put dots on a TV screen that add up to the letters of the alphabet and spell out what's coming from another computer far away. The keyboard types the data to the computer far away, and I built a modem for that. So now I had a TV terminal. This is while I'm working at Hewlett-Packard. I'm just doing these things on the side for fun in my apartment in Cupertino.

Back in college, I had designed a neat deal called a blue box, for making free phone calls. Steve Jobs came along and said, "Let's sell it." So now I had this video terminal, and he said, "There's a local time-sharing outfit that buys these expensive terminals. Why don't we sell this to them?" So we actually sold some of the video terminals that I had built. It was to become a portion of the Apple I.

I had wanted a computer my whole life. Back in high school I told my dad, "I'm going to have a computer someday." And he said that it cost as much as a house—the down payment on a house. And I said, "Well, I'll live in an apartment." But I was going to have a computer someday. So it starts with a huge dedication. You start with a lot of motives and values and who you are going to be in life. You start with those very early—some of mine even go back to elementary school. I decided there that I was going to be a fifth grade teacher, and I stuck to it and was. But some of these things you want so badly in life that, when the door opens, you are going to get there.

Now, I still was in this mode where I had to build everything for free. Then I discovered that microprocessors had come out. I had sort of slipped out of the electronics world, out of the computer world, due to working in calculators at Hewlett-Packard. All of a sudden I discovered these microprocessors. What are they? I didn't quite understand it fully, so I took a datasheet home.

There was a club that got started up. It was a club of young people—every one of them could have been an entrepreneur—the sort of people that liked to put together gadgets at home and make them work. But it turned out that not very many of them were real engineering designers that actually sat down and designed new things. Maybe they had jobs as technicians at work wiring stuff up, analyzing it, spotting inputs that were the wrong voltage. They were that kind of electronics person, but most of them weren't designers.

Livingston: This is Homebrew right?

Wozniak: This is the Homebrew Computer Club. There were a lot of software people that had no hardware background, and it took hardware to build these first machines. I was embarrassed because the world had somehow jumped ahead of me—they had come out with little cheap microcomputers based around microprocessors and I hadn't heard of it and I hadn't been a part of it. I felt very weird—that was the direction in life that I was going to be a part of when it happened. Well, I analyzed what a microprocessor was in one night, and discovered it was just like the minicomputers I used to design back in high school that were so good.

Then I looked at the Altair computer that started the whole thing going. It was the first microcomputer, but it wasn't really a computer. To me, I needed one thing. In high school, I told my dad that I was going to have a 4K Data General Nova. Why 4K? 4K bytes of memory. The reason is that's the minimum computer to run a programming language. You've got to be able to program in Fortran or Basic, or some language to get your programs done. The Altair that was being sold at a ridiculously low price, all it was was a glorified microprocessor from Intel, with some chips to protect the voltages. All they did was bring it out and say, "You can now plug in all the things that a microprocessor is designed to have added to it." You can add RAM, you can add cards that know how to talk to teletypes, you can add a big cable over to a teletype, you can buy a teletype for thousands of dollars. By the time you added enough RAM and everything else to have a computer that would really run a programming language, you're talking so many thousands of dollars, it was still out of the price range of anyone. It would be like $5,000, and, I'm sorry, but we were all low-level, just barely-getting-along-type people that had this interest in having our own computers.

Secondly, 5 years before that, in 1970, I had built a computer of my own design that was exactly what an Altair was—only I didn't have a microprocessor; I had to build it out of chips. So I built a little processor and it was only on one small—almost 3-by-5—card, very tiny. It had switches, it had lights, it looked like an airplane cockpit, just like the Altair. It had just as much memory as the Altair (256 bytes was the starting amount of memory). I could toggle these switches, punch some buttons, get ones and zeros into memory and run it as a program, and I could verify it really was in there and running. So I had done this 5 years before. Now I saw the Altair and I saw the microprocessors and I knew that they weren't enough. You needed something to run a whole computer language. But it was close.

So I searched around. My thinking was always, in making something possible, you've got to get it down to a reasonable cost, but I needed 4K bytes of RAM minimum. The first dynamic RAMs got introduced that year, 1975—the first 4K dynamic RAMs. That was the first time ever that RAMs were lower in price than magnetic core memories, which every computer up to that day had used. So all of a sudden, the world was going to change to RAMs. Silicon was going to be our memory.

Everybody else in the world—the Altair, the Sphere computers, the Polymorphic computers, the Insight computers—every one was designed by basically insufficient engineers, not top-quality engineers. They were designed by technicians who knew how to look at the datasheets for some RAM, look at the datasheets for a microprocessor and see if the microprocessor had some lines called "address"—and the RAMs had lines called "address," and they would hook a wire from one to the other. It's a very simple job—if your RAMs are static RAMs.

The dynamic RAMs were going to be one-half to one-quarter the price. The dynamic RAMs meant that instead of 32 chips to have enough memory for a computer to have a language, you only needed 8 chips of RAMs. But dynamic RAM needs all this circuitry to get into every single address in the RAM every 2000th of a second, read what was there and write it back, or it forgets it. Dynamic RAM (this is what we have in our computers today) will forget every single bit in a 2000th of a second unless something reads it and writes it back the way it was to hold its state. It's like little electrons stored on a plate and they'll leak off in a 2000th of a second.

Well, that took some extra circuits and thinking on my part, but when I put my computer together, good lord, I already had these counters that were counting regular sequences for a TV screen, for my terminal, and I said, "I'll just use those counters to supply the counts to sneak in every so often and update part of the RAM." So constantly the microprocessor would get to my RAM and the video addresses would get to my RAM—not to really read video (video wasn't in the RAM back then because I was using the same terminal that I had built before and it had its own memory for the screen), but it would get in and just sample things in the right sequence to make sure the RAM stayed alive. It took a little more designing, but in the end it was a lot less chips. It was not only a lot less chips, but it was smaller in size. It was more impressive to anyone who saw it. It was cheaper and it was faster. You get all these things at once if you use the right approaches.

In the late 1960s, a ton of minicomputers were coming out, and they all used the same chips: 7400 chips that would have 4 gates on a chip—or they'd have an adder on a chip or a quad adder on a chip or a multiplexer on a chip. They'd all use the same chips in all these computers, but what they did was say, "Let's build a computer. Like all the computers before, it has an instruction that can add 1 to an accumulator, has this many registers, it can move a register to memory, it can add, it can exclusive-or them, it can exclusive-or them with memory." They make up an instruction set that will make this computer usable. It will grow into an operating system, it will grow into programming languages, if we design enough instructions into the machine.

Then Data General came up with the Nova minicomputer and, instead of having 50 instructions to do various types of mathematical type things, they had 1 instruction; 1 instruction of 16 bits—6 ones and zeros. A couple of those ones and zeros told it which of four registers to put on one side of the arithmetic unit. A couple more bits told it which other of the four registers to use. Another couple of bits told it whether to shift or rotate the result after it finished, left or right, which is equivalent to multiplying or dividing by 2. There were bits as to whether you should set a carry (just like you learned addition in elementary school, you have carries—well, computer circuits worked the same way). By the time you were done, all of these 16 bits had certain meanings. I looked at it when I went to design a Nova, and it turned out that two of the bits selected one of the four registers, so I ran them to a four-way multiplexer chip and it just flowed in. It's like those two bits fit a chip. I didn't have to make up a bunch of logic that decides "do this and this and this, and gate those over here, and put a signal down there." I didn't have to do all that stuff. It just flowed logically. Three of the bits flowed down to a logic chip to tell it whether to add, or, or exclusive-or. Another bit just got fed in as the carry into the adder. By the time I was done, the design of the Nova was half as many chips as all of the other minicomputers from Varian, Digital Equipment Corp., Hewlett-Packard—all of the minicomputers of the time (I was designing them all). And I saw that Nova was half as many chips and just as good a computer. What was different? The architecture was really an architecture that just fit right to the very fewest chips.

My whole life was basically trying to optimize things. You don't just save parts, but every time you save parts you save on complexity and reliability, the amount of time it takes to understand something. And how good you can build it without errors and bugs and flaws.

Livingston: You were designing all of these different types of computers during high school at home, for fun?

Wozniak: Yes, because I could never build one. Not only that, but I would design one and design it over and over and over—each one of the computers—because new chips would come out. I would take the new chips and redesign some computer I'd done before because I'd come up with a clever idea about how I could save two more chips. "I'll do it in 42 chips instead of 44 chips."

The reason I did that was because I had no money. I could never build one. Chips back then were . . . like I said, to buy a computer built, it was like a down payment on a good house. So, because I could never build one, all I could do was design them on paper and try to get better and better and better. I was competing with myself. But that's just the story of how my skill got so good. It's because I could never build anything, I just competed with myself to come up with ideas that nobody else would come up with.

I knew that I had a lot of approaches in computers that basically no human really would use. They couldn't even be taught in a school program. I did a lot of it in my head. Taught myself everything. We didn't have computers in our high school even. And I was designing them. So, I just came across some lucky journals and then I discovered a way to get computer manuals. The computer manuals described the computers and my dad got me chip manuals. So I just figured out, "How do you take the chips and build a computer?"

My skill was that, if I know what I want for the end result—in those days it was a computer, in later days it might be a certain floppy disk that had to read and write some data—but if I knew what my end goal was, I know how to combine chips together very efficiently to get that goal done. Even if I've never designed anything before. My skills weren't that I knew how to design a floppy disk, I knew how to design a printer interface, I knew how to design a modem interface; it was that, when the time came and I had to get one done, I would design my own, fresh, without knowing how other people do it. That was another thing that made me very good. All the best things that I did at Apple came from (a) not having money, and (b) not having done it before, ever. Every single thing that we came out with that was really great, I'd never once done that thing in my life.

Livingston: Do you think that that's a recipe for being good at something: you've never done it before and you are trying to do it on the cheap?

Wozniak: Yup. But you have to have skills. We had a guy that designed the Macintosh and he was the same way. He'd never gone to college, but, boy, he just studied circuits that had been done by others and just became that good on his own.

Livingston: You went to college and then dropped out, right?

Wozniak: Not exactly. But I didn't learn anything about designing computers in college. I never had a class, for example, in writing a computer language, and, when I got my computer done, I had to write a Basic. It needed a Basic, there was no other choice. I also knew how to combine low-level software to build a program that was immense. I didn't know anything about computer languages except—a friend of mine had gone to MIT and, while he was there, he would Xerox pages out of books that were good topics, and he had sent me a lot of pages back from compiler design books. So I had actually read some compiler design books. I hadn't taken a course, I hadn't had a teacher, but I had some ideas of some of the parts involved in parsing a computer language.

So when I got my computer built, the Apple I, I just took the terminal that I already had. It was a shortcut computer; it was not designed to be an efficient computer from the ground up—that was the Apple II. This one was: take the terminal that I already have that works on my TV set and has a keyboard. And then I said, "All these computers are coming out and they've got switches and lights and look like airplane cockpits, and they're just like the one that I built 5 years before"—Cream Soda Computer we called it. And I said, "That was just too slow and sloppy. It was neat to have a computer, but it didn't do what I wanted to do. I want to write a program in Basic; I want to type in a game and play it; I want to write a program that solves my simulations for my work at Hewlett-Packard." (I used their big computer. They had a minicomputer that was shared by 40 engineers so you'd sign up for time on it.)

I knew that I wanted a good enough computer and it meant a microprocessor (once I discovered that a microprocessor was like those minicomputers I used to design), dynamic RAM was the choice to save money and parts, and I already had the terminal. Then I sniffed the wind and I said, "I need a language. I've got a 4K computer. It can run a language, but there's no language yet for this microprocessor. So I was (a) a little bit disappointed because I wanted a computer language, but (b) I was excited and exuberant because I got to be the one to write the first language for this processor. I would get a little bit of fame out of that, and I was super shy, so the only way I could ever get noticed was if I designed great things.

So I got to write a computer language, but remember I've never written one in my life. I'd never taken a course on it. So I opened up the Hewlett-Packard manual at work and saw the Basic. I read all the different commands in the Basic, and I started creating a syntax table that showed the grammar of that language: what words, what commands are allowed in what order, how you put in variable names, how you put in numbers, what size they can be, what formats. Then I came up with an idea—and I have no idea where it came from—just a weird, weird idea that, as a user types in a statement, I will just scan his statement, character by character, from left to right, and I'll see where it fits into the syntax table. I typed my whole syntax table into memory. I said, "I'll just follow along in memory and, if what he types fits the syntax table, then whenever he hits return, I know all the elements he typed in." I just output a list of little tokens that represented what had been typed in, if it matched the table. This was just an idea I had, not knowing how other people did it. I don't know to this day how compilers are written.

I also knew that there were numbers and variables and you have operations like plus and minus, times, divide. (I was just a very low-level person here . . .) Numbers are nouns and a plus is a verb. Even in a statement like "print," print becomes a verb. So I had these lists of verbs and I had noun stacks and verb stacks and figured out ways to push them on and make their priorities such that we could turn it into reverse Polish notation.

I was very familiar with reverse Polish notation from books I read in college (or that my friend had sent me in Xerox form); and also our Hewlett-Packard calculators used reverse Polish notation, and we thought we were more advanced because we were doing what computer science people do. You take an equation like "5 + 4" and you change it into "5 ENTER 4 +" so you do the addition last. But how do you convert between one and the other? That one wasn't too bad for me. I had some knowledge of that.

I built this whole Basic up and it worked, and that was the hardest project I did. Normally you type a computer program into a computer; that's the only way it's done. You type it into a computer or you feed it in on cards. What I did was I handwrote it on the left side of the pages in my program, in what's called machine language. That's as close as you can get to the ones and zeros. And then I looked at a little card and I translated my program into ones and zeros on the other side. If it said, "Jump ahead," I'd have to count—if it's jumping ahead 19 bytes, I'd have to write 19 in zeros and ones. I would write the zeros and ones myself because I couldn't afford a computer program that did this assembly job. I went down to the absolute lowest-level jobs you could do. For the computer itself, I not only designed it on paper (I was the draftsperson, I would draft it on my drafting board), I would hook up all the parts and figure out where to plug them into some boards, and I would solder wires between each one.

In my minimalist approach, I made the wires the shortest, straightest, thinnest wires possible, instead of having these big old looped-up hairy messes of wire-wrap type stuff. So I did all that and I was also the technician. I would test things out and look for the voltages first and apply it carefully and look for signals and analyze what was wrong and fix the bugs and resolder and come up with new ideas and add some chips in. I was the technician and everything for all of the Apple projects I ever did.

Livingston: So where were you when you first realized that you could build the Apple I?

Wozniak: I got this idea that I was going to have the computer that I had wanted my whole life at the first meeting of the Homebrew Computer Club. That night, I realized it, when I found out what a microprocessor was. I went home and studied it and said, "Oh my god, I'm here. Because now I can come up with the money to buy it someday." At first it was quite a job to come up with the money because the Intel processor was $400, and I just wasn't going to come up with that soon. It's like coming up with $2,000 nowadays. That's a big deal. Then I found out there was a Motorola one I could get for $40 at Hewlett-Packard and then the company introduced the 6502 for $20, so that's what I bought. I bought it because it was just super-cheap and it was also the best one of the day.

Now I had to build the hardware. I looked at all the other computers that were around me and they were like the standard old computer—switches and lights and slots to plug boards in and connect them to teletypes. I said, "No, I want the whole thing, because it's affordable now." I've got my terminal and my terminal already has a keyboard for typing on. It's kind of like our Hewlett-Packard calculators have human buttons—a human can understand what they are doing. None of this zero-and-one stuff. So I said, "But the trouble is you have to get programs into memory." I'm starting out with a microprocessor that didn't even have a programming language, so you've got to still stick some zeros and ones into memory. I said, "Why don't I write a simple little program"—a 256-byte program that took two chips to store. And my program read what you typed on the keyboard and did the stuff the front panel would have done, but did it at 100x the speed in the end. And it could also display on the TV screen what was in memory. It could let you enter stuff into memory, and it could run a program at a certain address. And that allowed me to develop further to start typing my ones and zeros. As I developed Basic, I would type the ones and zeros in by hand, and it got up to where I would type for 40 minutes to get my whole program into memory. I would type not ones and zeros, but base 16 actually, get the program into memory and test out bits of it at a time, and see what's going on. So this was not at all a normal project where you have tools. I had no tools; my approach in life was to just use my own knowledge. I know what's going on better if I'm not going through a tool.

Livingston: You had your Sears TV and a tape cassette for data storage, right?

Wozniak: Yes. Once I got that much of the Basic done, we had to store a big program efficiently somehow on mass media. I used a tape recorder so I wouldn't have to type it in for 40 minutes. But that came pretty late in the game. I had developed the whole Basic without it really.

Livingston: And you showed it off at the Homebrew Computer Club?

Wozniak: Every 2 weeks I brought my computer, which became the Apple I, down. We hadn't decided to start a company. Because companies weren't my thing, technology was. I'd bring it down and show it to people, and I brought schematics. I'd make Xeroxes at work of all my schematics and pass them out, because—I made sure my name was on it—I was so shy and I thought, "I'll get known by doing good stuff." And I'm telling other people, "You can build your own. This is how easy it is." And I was really trying to say, "You can have a complete computer at a very low price. And not the Altair way." Trying to say that there was a whole different way of computers. Some people got it and some didn't.

Livingston: Did the people who got it try to build their own?

Wozniak: It was still too much of a job. A lot of them were software people, not hardware solderers. I went over to one young kid's—he was in high school—I went over to his house and helped him wire his own up. I started doing the soldering. A lot of people in the club didn't even know how to solder. It really was more a software group. So not many built it, and that's really where Steve Jobs came in saying, "Let's start a company." He said, "Look, there are a lot of people that want to build it and they can get the chips, but they don't want to solder it all together. So why don't we make a PC board and they can plop their chips in the PC board"—soldering a printed circuit board is easy, there are no wires—"and then they've got it done."

So the idea was that we'd start this company and build PC boards for $20 and sell them for $40. Well, I only knew the club as a place to sell it and I thought, "Are there 50 people at the club"—I had a group gathering around me—"who are going to buy this computer instead of the Intel?" I didn't think so, but Steve said, "Even if we don't get our money back, at least we'll have a company." So it was like two good friends having a company.

Livingston: Do you remember where you were when you guys talked about making a company out of this?

Wozniak: I don't. I don't remember if he phoned me at work, if I was at his house, if he was visiting me—I can't remember.

Livingston: How did you know Steve?

Wozniak: That computer that was like the Altair that I'd built 5 years before— Cream Soda Computer—I'd told a friend down the block, Bill Fernandez, about it, and we agreed to solder it up in his garage. We spent about 2 weeks soldering my design together. We'd ride our bikes down to buy cream soda and come back and drink it, so we called it the Cream Soda Computer. Bill went to our high school, and he said, "There's another guy at Homestead High School, younger than you, and he's interested in electronics and pranks and things too and you really should meet him." So he thought we were alike.

The way I remember it is that Steve came right out there in front of his house. We're out there on the cul-de-sac on the sidewalk and we're just talking. We started out by comparing pranks we'd done and talking about different types of electronics and chips. We both had a lot of similar experiences so we had a lot to talk about. Then we became best friends for so long. There weren't that many people that young that knew technology. Steve and I weren't similar personalities, which was strange, but I'm the sort of person that goes along with anyone that wants to talk technology. And then we both agreed on music too. We had very strong music influences in those days, and it was more songs about living and life and where we're going and where we're from and what's it all about and what works and what doesn't. It was a lot more Bob Dylan stuff than normal popular music that intrigued us. So we'd go to concerts. I was going off to Berkeley, but I'd be down on weekends. Every time I was down, we'd link up, have a pizza, whatever.

Livingston: What were the first things you did after Steve suggested starting a company? You were still working at HP, right?

Wozniak: The very first thought in my mind was, "I think I signed a document that everything I design belongs to Hewlett-Packard." Even just on my own time, I thought that they deserved it first. And I wanted Hewlett-Packard to build this. I loved my division. I was going to work there for life. It was the calculator division; it was the right division to move into this kind of a computer.

I went to management, and I had three levels of bosses above me in a room and a couple of other engineers, and I presented the ideas and told them what we could do at what price and how it would work. They were intrigued by it, but they couldn't justify it as a Hewlett-Packard product for some good reasons. Hewlett-Packard couldn't do a simple project, which was really what was interesting. They had to do a real finished-for-scientists type of computer that would be too expensive and really wouldn't start the mass movement. They were a little concerned about using a TV set that didn't come from Hewlett-Packard. When there's a problem, how do you decide where the solution is? But I know they were intrigued by it quite a bit. That was when we were going to sell PC boards for $40 each.

When Steve called me one day at work and he said he got an order for $50,000—100 built computer boards for $500 each—that was high money. That was twice my annual salary at Hewlett-Packard. So then I got Hewlett-Packard's legal department to search every division—I wrote down what we were doing and had them search every division—but the thing is that the calculator division was the lowest one in Hewlett-Packard. The others wouldn't want to touch anything cheap. It was too cheap for our division, and the other ones wouldn't touch it even more. So I got a written response back from them that no divisions were interested.

Now it was almost like we were big-time. We were going to sell some computers. Sure, we only sold 150 (maybe less) of the Apple Is, but it was a real computer and we had our name in all the magazines with charts and comparisons. This whole industry's springing up and there are articles about it. And no article could skip a company with a name like Apple.

Livingston: How'd you come up with "Apple"?

Wozniak: Steve came up with it. I do remember that one. I picked him up at the San Francisco airport and I was driving down the Bay on 101 and then on 85, and it was on 85 that he said, "Oh, I've got a name for the company. Apple Computer." Both of us were sitting there trying to come up with techie names that were clever, but nothing was going to be better than Apple. And I said, "But what about Apple Records?" (Which is funny because we're still having problems with them.) And he said, "They're a different company."

So we said, "OK, we'll do Apple Computer." In those days there was no money yet in this microcomputer business, and big experienced companies and investors, analysts—those kind of people, that are trained in business and much smarter than we were—they didn't think that this was going to be a real big market. They thought it was going to be a little hobby thing, like home robots or ham radios, that a few techie people would get into and really it wasn't going to go to the masses.

In the Homebrew Computer Club, we felt it was going to affect every home in the country. But we felt it for the wrong reasons. We felt that everybody was technical enough to really use it and write their own programs and solve their problems that way. Even when we started Apple, we had very mistaken ideas about where the market was going to be that big. We didn't foresee the VisiCalc spreadsheet.

Livingston: Had you quit Hewlett-Packard?

Wozniak: That was very tough. We started selling the Apple Is, and I stayed at Hewlett-Packard. I still intended to be at that company forever. Our calculator division moved up to Corvallis, Oregon, and my wife didn't want to move to Corvallis and I did, so that was lucky because otherwise I would have been up in Oregon and Apple never would have happened. So I stayed here and I moved into another division of Hewlett-Packard across the street that made the Hewlett-Packard 3000 minicomputers.

I was working there for a while getting educated on the HP 3000 . . . for the Apple II, we knew it was so good . . . that was a product that broke ground in every which way. The Apple I, oddly enough, was probably more important, because it said that a computer of the future is going to have a keyboard and a video display and it's going to look like a typewriter. It's going to be roughly that size. And it's funny, but every computer since the Apple I, including the Polymorphics technology Sol computer that came next (it was out of our club), had a keyboard and a video display. No computer had done this before that. No small computer was coming with a keyboard yet. The Apple I was the first and the Apple II was the third. Basically every computer since then had a keyboard and a video display. The world has never gone back from that day. Now the Apple II was the great design. I designed it very efficiently with very few parts—amazing design. We added color. How could you ever have color and still cut the chips in half? It was half the chips of an Apple I. It had color, and it was just a clever idea that popped in my head one late night at Atari.

When you get very, very tired—and I had been up four nights all night long; Steve and I got mononucleosis—your head gets in this real creative state and it thinks of ideas that you'd normally just throw out. I came up with this idea of taking one little cheap (less than $1) part with 4 bits in it. If I spun it around at the right rate, the data that comes out of that chip looks like color TV. And I could put 16 different patterns and they all look like different colors, sort of. Would a digital signal that goes up and down actually work on a color TV the way there are sine waves and complicated calculus to develop how color TV was established in the television world? Would it work?

Man, when I actually finally put together this little circuit and put some data into memory that should show up as color and it showed up color, it was just one of those eureka moments and you're just shaking inside. It was just unbelievable. Here we had it in just a couple of chips. I had color, and then I had graphics, and then I had hi-res, and then I had paddles and sound to put games into the machine. It had dynamic memory—it had the newest right type of dynamic memory that could expand almost forever. All sorts of slots with a little mini–operating system that actually worked incredibly well. The Apple II was just one of those designs. Anybody could build things to add on to it, anybody could write programs, they could write sophisticated programs, they could write it in machine language, they could write it in my Basic. So that machine, there was just nothing stopping it.

We knew we'd sell 1,000 a month, but we couldn't afford to build them. So we sought money, and one of the first places we went to was Commodore. To the guy who had been the product marketing manager for the 6502 microprocessor that I had chosen. I had actually bought them at a show in San Francisco over the counter for 20 bills. He and his wife would hand them to us at the table. That's how we bought our first microprocessors that became the Apple I and Apple II, from this guy Chuck Peddle. He now was moving to Commodore to do a computer. We said, "We've got to show him the Apple II."

So we brought him by the garage. I really respected the guy; he designed the microprocessor that I had chosen. He came to the garage and looked at the Apple II, and I put it through all its specs of bringing up quick patterns on the screen and scrolling text and playing games—all the things I'd done on it. He looked at it and didn't say too much. I figured he'd be more impressed. We later heard that Commodore turned it down.

We went in and spoke one day to Commodore's head of engineering, Andre Sousan, and Andre told us that his boss who ran Commodore, Jack Tramiel, had basically brought in Chuck Peddle and Chuck had talked him into "No, you don't want to put all these exotic things like color into it." The truth is, he didn't know how to. No one knew how to do color cheap. There were boards out for small computers. Cromemco had a color system. You buy two boards for your Altair; each of those had more chips than the Apple II on it. So, just to add color, that's what it was like for most people. And Chuck Peddle said, "You should do it cheap. We should just have black and white; we should have the cheapest keyboard you can imagine, the smallest screen, and just keep the costs way down." They wanted to make it cheap enough to be affordable. The funny thing is that the Apple II had so few parts, it was cheaper to build and still was much more of a computer. We didn't have to include a TV set, because we assumed everyone had their own.

Livingston: Why didn't Commodore want it?

Wozniak: Good question. Andre Sousan very soon after (within weeks) left Commodore and came to Apple saying that he felt we had the right product and he wanted to be with us. They just missed the boat. I think it was that Chuck Peddle knew what he could design, but he knew that he couldn't design what the Apple II was. They should have bought it. They would have had a real good deal cheap. After that, we were still seeking money. I wasn't really seeking the money, Steve Jobs was. I mean, I almost couldn't have cared less. If I could show it off at the club and get credit for having a great computer design in my life, that's what I wanted. We went down to visit some Atari friends. We went to Al Alcorn's house, and he had a projection TV—the first time I ever saw a projection TV in my life, really. And we put it on his projection TV and he looked at it and he liked what we were doing. He was real interested. Atari would do this, but they had a hot project coming out—the first home Pong game—and they were going to have so many millions of those that every effort in their company had to go that way. They didn't have the ability to do two things at once. So they turned us down, very friendly though.

Then we talked to some venture capitalists. Don Valentine came to the garage and he looked it over and he didn't seem too impressed. He would ask questions like, "What's the market?" And I'd say, "A million." And he'd say, "How do you know?" And I said, "Well, there's a million ham radio operators, and computers are more popular than ham radio." Nobody in the world could ever deny that. But it's not the sort of analysis that they wanted. And there were no analysts yet that were predicting that this was going to be a big marketplace anyway.

So Don wasn't that interested, but he gave us the name of Mike Markkula— Mike being a person who was interested in technology, who was looking around for things to do. So Steve went over and talked to him and Mike really thought we had a great thing, that there was going to be a huge market for small computers in the home. Home computers. We didn't even have the word "personal computer" yet; that came about a little later. Because we were trying to say, "How do we establish this new type of computer? What's special about it?" In the old days, several people would use one computer all at the same time. This was the first time you'd have one computer all your own. So it's a personal computer. It's almost maybe a negative in some ways, but we're making it a positive.

So Mike said that he would put in the money we needed to make 1,000 computers—$250,000. Boy, that sounded astounding. $250,000 back in those days was like a couple million today, maybe.

Livingston: Were you still in Jobs's parents' garage?

Wozniak: Well, actually we never did much in the garage. People think we had a garage where we sat down with soldering irons and we designed stuff. No. The only designs that ever took place in the Apple I or II for hardware or software were in my apartment in Cupertino or my cubicle at Hewlett-Packard late at night. That's the only place any building got done.

The computers were manufactured at a place in Santa Clara. They made the PC boards, they stuffed the parts in, they wave-soldered it. Steve would drive down and then drive them back to his garage. We did use the garage at his place—we had a lab bench there and we would plug in the PC boards of the Apple Is and test them on a keyboard. If they worked, we'd put them in a box. If they didn't work, we'd fix them and put them in a box. Eventually, Steve would drive the boxes down to the Byte Shop in Mountain View or wherever and get paid, in cash. We had the parts on credit and we got paid in cash. That was the only way we could do the Apple Is.

Livingston: So you'd keep self-funding?

Wozniak: Yes, we kept self-funding and we probably built up a bank account of about $10,000. Not a huge amount, but it was enough to move into an office. Steve really wanted to make a company.

Livingston: Where was the first office?

Wozniak: The first office was even before we worked a deal with Mike Markkula. We arranged to get a place at an office complex I could drive to in Cupertino. It's not too far from where Apple's places are now. Not too far from where our first building on Brandley was. We had one office and Steve had arranged that we only pay for half of it until a certain date when we'd use the rest. It was kind of cold and empty when we finally did move in.

So Mike was going to finance us, and then one day he said to me, "You have to leave Hewlett-Packard." And I said, "Why? I designed two computers and cassette tape interfaces and printer interfaces and serial ports and I wrote a Basic and all this application software, I wrote demos, and I did all this moon-lighting, all in a year."

He said, "Well, you have to leave Hewlett-Packard." It just wasn't open. I went inside of myself and thought about it. "Who are you? What do you want out of life?" And I really wanted a job as an engineer forever at a great company (which was Hewlett-Packard). I wanted to design computers and show them off and make software. And I can do that on my own time. I don't need a company to do it. So there was an ultimatum day—I had to decide by a certain day if I was willing to do this. I met Mike and Steve at Mike's cabaña at his house in Cupertino. Eventually we got around to it, and I said, "I've decided not to do it, here are my reasons." Mike just said, "OK." Steve was a little more upset.

About the next day after I said no to starting Apple, my parents called me and said, "You really ought to do this." (Because $250,000 was a big deal in any-one's life.) And then friends would start calling me. That day my friend Allen Baum called me in the afternoon, and he said, "Look, you can start Apple and go into management and get rich, or you can start Apple and stay an engineer and get rich." As soon as he said it was OK to do engineering, that really freed me up. My psychological block was really that I didn't want to start a company. Because I was just afraid. In business and politics, I wasn't going to be a real strong participant. I wasn't going to tell other people how to do things. I wasn't going to run things ever in my life. I was a non-political person and I was a very non-forceful person. It dated back to a lot of things that happened during the Vietnam War. But I just couldn't run a company.

But then one person said I could be an engineer. That was all I needed to know, that "OK, I'll start this company and I'll just be an engineer." To this day, I'm still on the org chart, on the bottom of the org chart—never once been any-thing but an engineer who works.

Livingston: So you called Steve?

Wozniak: I made my decision by that evening and I called Steve and told him I would. Then the next day I came in (to Hewlett-Packard) and I told a couple of friends, who had come over with me from the calculator division. I told them that I was going to leave Hewlett-Packard and then I went over to tell my boss, and he wasn't there. He was in a meeting or something. All day long people started coming up to me saying, "I hear you're leaving." And my boss hadn't heard. Finally he showed up at his desk, and I went over and I told him that I was going to leave and start Apple. He said, "When do you want to go?" and I said, "Right now." So I left that day and the deal with Mike Markkula was that I'd have the same salary starting Apple. It was like $24,000 a year.

Livingston: Did you go straight over to Apple?

Wozniak: I walked out that day. We didn't have an office yet so I was still at home, but I was doing the Apple stuff. I was finishing up things on the Basic, finishing up some hardware things, writing code for some special graphics, that sort of stuff. Then Steve and I met a friend of Mike Markkula's named Mike Scott, and we liked him very much as a strong, forceful guy (he was a director at National) who got things done that needed doing. We decided that we wanted him to be our President. He was our President from the day we started Apple as a real corporation—until the day we went public, he was still our President. So he had a rather important role in history, and he's very much forgotten. I just think that he was the greatest thing ever.

Livingston: How did you find him?

Wozniak: Mike Markkula knew him as a friend. Their friendship kind of came to a breaking point where Mike Markkula sort of ousted him as President for making rash decisions. There was a day that he laid a lot of people off. Apple kind of grew and grew and grew and had a bunch of engineers assigned to different projects, and we weren't getting out really good stuff really fast like we had been. Mike Scott came in and told our engineering manager, Tom Whitney (a guy that I worked for three times in my life: once at Hewlett-Packard's calculator division, later on at the Hewlett-Packard 3000 division, and now at Apple), to take a vacation for one week, and he went around and talked to all the engineers and found out who was doing stuff and who was slacking off. He pretty much fired the right ones—that weren't working. But he should have given them chances to go around and bring their abilities to play and all that.

Mike Markkula was close to Ann Bowers at the time (she was the wife of Robert Noyce, I think), and she was taking over our human resources. So to have this poor of an example of human resources was almost a blot on the face of the company. Mike Scott was starting to make some real rash, quick decisions, and not be as careful as was needed, and as he'd been in the past. The board gave him another job and he wrote a very shocking resignation letter that, basically, life was too important for this political type stuff. It was sad to see him go because he supported good people so well in the company.

Livingston: What about Ron Wayne? Wasn't he one of the founders?

Wozniak: Yes, but not when we incorporated as a real company. We had two phases. One was as a partnership with Steve Jobs for the Apple I, and then for the Apple II, we became a corporation, Apple Computer, Incorporated.

Steve knew Ron at Atari and liked him. Ron was a super-conservative guy. I didn't know anything about politics of any sort; I avoided it. But he had read all these right-wing books like *None Dare Call it Treason*, and he could rattle the stuff off. I didn't realize it until later.

He had instant answers to everything. He had experience with businesses and times he'd been gypped out of stock deals. He always had something very quick to say and, wow, it sounded like he was very knowledgeable about this stuff. He sat down at a typewriter and typed our partnership contract right out of his head using lawyer-type words. I just thought, "How do you know what to say, all rights and privileges and all the different words that are in there"—I don't even know what they are. He did an etching of Newton under the apple tree for the cover of our Apple I manual. He wrote the manual. So he helped in a number of ways. Steve had 45 percent of this partnership, I had 45 percent, and Ron had 10 percent, because both of us agreed that we could trust him to resolve any dispute, and we would trust his judgment.

Then what happened was that we were going to sell PC boards for $20 each and fund it out of our own pockets. I sold my HP calculator, Steve sold his van, so we had a few hundred bucks each. Then Steve got the $50,000 order. Over at the company that was making our PC board, as soon as the PC boards were made, they opened up a closet that had our parts and it started a 30-day clock ticking. We had 30 days to pay for the parts. The parts got stuffed into the computers, we made them work, we delivered them to the store and got paid in cash. The parts suppliers—the distributors in Mountain View—had checked with the store owner and knew that he was going to pay us. So basically, we didn't have the credit; he was good for it. But, here was the problem: What if he didn't accept them one time or didn't pay us? We would owe a ton of money on those chips.

I had no money and Steve had no money. We didn't own cars, we didn't have savings accounts, we didn't have houses. So Ron Wayne figured they'd come after him for his golden nuggets that he kept under his mattress. (He actually tells me it was in a safe—but he was afraid they'd come and get his gold.) So he sold out. It was too risky for him, so he sold out his 10 percent of Apple to us for a few hundred bucks. Maybe $600, maybe $800, maybe $300— but a few hundred bucks. And this was even when we had an Apple II designed and were heading toward future business. He was just scared that something was going to catch him.

Livingston: Way back then, how did you guys divide the work between you?

Wozniak: We actually never talked about it even once. If there was any engineering to do, hardware or software, I did it, because Steve could do stuff, but he couldn't do it as well as I. So never once did he even try. Never did he look at a circuit and suggest anything. I don't want to mess around running a company—my whole life's engineering—so he's on the phone talking to reporters, talking to stores, "Do you want us to ship you some computers, do you want to start buying them?" Talking to the dealers on the parts, ordering the parts, negotiating process, getting brochures made up or ads for magazines.

Livingston: So you two fit together nicely in terms of your skills.

Wozniak: Well, we added up to the total everything that was needed. If there was anything that neither one of us knew how to do, Steve would do it. He'd just find a way to do it. He was just gung ho and pressing for this company to be successful. And me, I was pretty much only in my technical head with the circuits.

Livingston: Do you remember any disagreements you had in the early days?

Wozniak: Extremely minor. There were a couple, maybe. One was that we're getting close to shipping it and we wanted things to be low-cost. Steve says, "Can we save any chips?" He's pressing me and pressing me. I am down to like what is just amazing in the world. People to this day that understand circuitry tell me how they looked at my design and it was the most beautiful thing they ever saw. So I said, "I could cut out two chips if I skipped high-res. I don't know if anybody's really going to use high-res." (It became very important actually.) And Steve said, "Oh no, if it's only two chips, leave it in." But it wasn't like we were really arguing. I was just telling him that that's the only place I could save any chips.

We had a real argument over slots. Mike Markkula's coming on and we were going to build the Apple II, and I had designed a clever system on the suggestion of a friend—Allen Baum again—that decoded eight slots you could plug little computer boards into. Each board had the ability to have its own programs on it running in its own addresses, and it didn't have to have all the normal chips to decide, "Well, if the addresses are such and such, I will respond to them." That was done on the main board. In the Altair world, each board you had to dial in the address that it would look at, and that took a couple of thumbwheel switches to dial the address on (they cost money), and a bunch of chips that would compare the address coming from the microprocessor to the one that they were good for, to see if they equaled, and that cost about 5 chips a board. So if you had 8 boards, that would be 40 chips. In my case, I used 2 chips, and I had double sets of address to all 8 boards already in 2 chips instead of 40. So I was very proud of that.

Now Steve said, "All people really need is a printer and a modem." And that was just false because he'd come from a different world than I. He'd never done software and he'd never really been around computer users. He'd been around Hewlett-Packard where they make them, but he hadn't been around computer users that plug in boards that do an oscilloscope out of a computer board, and another board that controls some equipment on the factory and runs some motors, and all these little boards that were just a big part of my life. Every computer I'd ever seen, some of its greatest things came because of boards plugged into it. And he wanted just one slot for a printer and one for a modem. Today, we're sort of in a much different, freer world.

We got the computer finished up enough. We don't have much to add on besides a printer and a telecommunications of some sort. So Steve was arguing for two slots. And the trouble is, two slots wouldn't save me a single chip. And I wanted to show off that I had eight slots and so few chips. If I only had two slots, I would have had parts of chips unused. I was really dead set to hold my chip count, so I said, "If you want two slots, get another computer." That was the only time we had a real argument.

Livingston: Did he keep pushing?

Wozniak: No, he had no choice. I gave him no choice. We had to have eight slots. And it turns out that it was very important; it was very beneficial. Because we came out with a floppy disk. Not only that, other people came out with cards that put 80 columns of text on the screen so you could see more. People came out with extra memory cards, people came out with other languages in cards, people came out with cards that had CPM. People came out with cards to connect all kinds of equipment in the world, to operate your house over your power lines. It was just a world of cards. Many people had their Apple IIs filled up with cards—every single slot.

Livingston: When you showed people the Apple computer, were they amazed?

Wozniak: Every single time I showed the Apple II, before we started the company and even slightly after we started the company—before there was much word around about it, every single person who ever saw it . . . The engineers at Hewlett-Packard came to me and said, "That's the best product I've ever seen." And they're around one of the greatest products of all time—the Hewlett-Packard calculator—and one of the greatest companies, and they're saying things like that. The Apple II had so much intrigue to me, but I knew it intrigued all technical people. And the Apple I just worked. I actually wound up doing some great work at Hewlett-Packard using that as my computer.

Livingston: What is the key to excellence for an engineer?

Wozniak: You have to be very diligent. You have to check every little detail. You have to be so careful that you haven't left something out. You have to think harder and deeper than you normally would. It's hard with today's large, huge programs.

I was partly hardware and partly software, but, I'll tell you, I wrote an awful lot of software by hand (I still have the copies that are handwritten), and all of that went into the Apple II. Every byte that went into the Apple II, it had so many different mathematical routines, graphics routines, computer languages, emulators of other machines, ways to slip your code in and out of an emulation mode. It had all these kinds of things and not one bug ever found. Not one bug in the hardware, not one bug in the software. And you just can't find a product like that nowadays. But, you see, I had it so intense in my head, and the reason for that was largely because it was part of me. Everything in there had to be so important to me. This computer was me. And everything had to be as perfect as could be made. And I had a lot going against me because I didn't have a computer to compile my code, my software.

Livingston: Did you have a hard time getting everyday people to say, "Yeah, I want a computer in my office, my home"?

Wozniak: Almost everyone who saw it wanted one, but usually the idea was, "What's the cost?" A couple thousand bucks. "Well, I want one of those." But they weren't jumping because it's enough money—you have to plan and maybe some months ahead downstream, you'll be able to buy one.

But we never found one person who said, "I wouldn't have any need for this at all." (We didn't talk to elderly people.) But people not only in their offices, but just at home, you play one game on it, and an awful lot of people—adults and children—want a machine to play games. The Apple II really started the whole gaming industry, because it was the first time a computer had been built with sound, paddles, color, graphics—all the things for games. And it was really so that I could implement Breakout in software.

Back a year before, when I had worked at Atari, they were starting to talk about coming out with microprocessor games. Up till then it was all hardware. In other words, you solder wire to the right sort of chips and put it through some more chips and some other chips, and it determines where the score is on the screen. It's not like you type it in software and say "put the score at this location." No, it was all done with wires and gates and chips and registers, and it was very difficult back then.

So now I had a machine that I could program a game in (or somebody could), and I got this crazy idea to try to do Breakout in Basic. Basic is like a hundred to a thousand times slower than machine language, so I don't know if it's possible. I sat down one night and finally put in all the commands in the Basic to draw color, and I started typing away in Basic and, within half an hour, I not only had my Pong game working, but I had done about 50 or so variations of colors and speeds and sizes and where the score was and all that stuff. I had changed so many things around and put in little features that would just take forever to do in hardware. Little words pop up on the screen when things happen. I called Steve over and I was just shaking, I was quivering, and I showed him the game running, and I said, "This game was so easy to write! Look at this, go ahead—change the color of the bricks." This would have taken me a lifetime to do in hardware and I did it in half an hour.

And that was true. It would have taken an entire lifetime for any engineer with a soldering iron to try all those variations. So I said to him, "Now that games are software, it's going to be a different world for games." And the Apple II, so many people just started trying to figure out how can you get rocket ships to launch, how can you get things that sound like sound when you have a real cruddy voltage to a speaker. How do you listen to somebody talk and figure out what they said? They started using the Apple II. It was just open to all these things. We made it easy for anyone to do what they wanted to do. And I think that was one of the biggest keys to its success. We didn't make it a hidden machine that we own—we sell it, it does this, you got it—like Commodore and RadioShack did.

We put out manuals that had just hundreds of pages of listings of code, descriptions of circuits, examples of boards that you would plug in—so that anyone could look at this and say, "Now I know how I would do my own." They could type in the programs on their own Apple II and then see "that's how that works" instantly, and know how to write their own programs. Running cards was the most important thing. All these companies started up making cards that you could plug into your Apple II and write a little software (mostly games at first) on cassette tapes. You'd go to the store and they'd just have all this stuff that you could buy to enhance the Apple II. So one of our big keys to success was that we were very open. There's a big world out there for other people to come and join us.

In the years 1980 to '83, when the Apple II was the largest-selling computer in the world, we didn't advertise it once. Everybody else who was making products for it was advertising for it. All of our ads were for the Apple III, which never sold in that time frame. Because we were trying to make the Apple III the big business machine instead of IBM.

Livingston: That didn't happen, right?

Wozniak: That didn't happen. I think it was a total fallacy. I think we should have advertised the Apple II. If you've got the world's best-selling computer, keep it going as much as it can. But the company kind of wanted the Apple III to win and the Apple II to lose. It was really weird because you'd walk into the company and everybody had an Apple III on their desk—nobody had an Apple II. The Apple II was the largest-selling computer in the world, and the only guy working for it in the company was the guy reprinting the price list.

Then by '83, the IBM PC took over. It was selling more computers than the Apple II.

Livingston: You had left by then, though, so you weren't part of the Apple III, right?

Wozniak: I didn't exactly leave. I didn't leave college either; I didn't drop out. Between my second and third year of college, I worked for a year programming to earn money for my third year. After my third year of college, I crashed my car and totaled it. It was a very famous night, the night I met Captain Crunch of blue box fame. Later that night, I got home, picked up my car, drove back to Berkeley at 3:00 a.m., and I fell asleep on the freeway and totaled my car. I walked to my dorm and told my roommates, "It's a good thing I didn't pay the quarterly parking fee."

So after my third year of college, I took a year off to work, to earn money for my fourth year. Then I got that job at Hewlett-Packard. What an incredible job. And then my career started going up, and I had all these side projects that I was working on and then Apple. So I never really had a chance to get back. But I was close, and I wanted to get back. And in 1981, I had a plane crash. As soon as I came out of amnesia from the plane crash—within 5 minutes I knew that this was the time I was going back to college. I'd never get another chance. So I went back and got my degree. I always liked school and was a good student, a top student. And my parents had college degrees and I thought something of that. My kids should see their dad with a college degree.

Livingston: Any other eureka moments in the early days?

Wozniak: I've told you two major eureka moments. One was getting color to work, with this weird scheme that I had no idea if it's going to work or not. The other was that I didn't know if I was going to get Basic to program an arcade game, and it worked. In both those cases, I didn't even know if it was possible and lucked out. The floppy disk was probably the third real major eureka story.

We had the computer out, and I got to work designing parallel cards to talk to early cheap printers. Then serial cards to talk to better letter-quality printers that are more like the quality work that a business could put out. Then cards that would talk to modems, other serial cards. I actually did a phone card that could control your phone line and control cassette tape recorders and make an answering machine for you and do all this stuff, but it didn't do a modem, just controlled your phone line. Apple never put it out, because they didn't like the guy that I had brought in to do it, which was Captain Crunch. He designed it. It was a great card.

Then came a point where we only had a cassette tape interface at first. To read a program in, you'd stick a cassette tape in a tape recorder and type something on the keyboard and then press a button on the tape recorder. I think on the keyboard you would just type something like "100R" and it means the program goes into address 100. You press the button on the tape recorder and there's a long lead-in period and then data (there's a twiddling sound if you're listening), and you have to wait for a minute and it goes "beep," and now your program is in memory. It worked surprisingly well, but it took a long time.

Mike Markkula wanted to get going right away on the marketing. He ran the marketing for the company. Marketing largely meant, how are you going to present the computer to be acceptable in the home? How do you move "computer" from a word that's yucky and airplane cockpittish to acceptable in my home? And that had to do with different types of photography, pictures, settings, words to the press. He also wanted us to start getting to work on software that would apply.

He basically wanted us to write a flash card program. So Randy Wigginton and I did a flash card program called Color Math and it shipped with every Apple. We also did one called Checkbook, which would let you reconcile your checks on the computer. But here's the problem: you had to first read the Checkbook program in off of a tape, then twiddle your thumbs for a minute and it goes "beep"; then you have to pull out another cassette tape of your own and read your checks in and it goes "beep"; then you have to do the stuff on the screen, enter some more checks and reconcile them; and then you have to put that data cassette back in and record onto it and it goes "beep." You have all these waiting periods, and it was just too awkward and too slow. So Mike said we needed two things: a floating point Basic (that's a Basic with decimal points, which I didn't have) and a floppy disk.

Just before I left Hewlett-Packard, a new chip had come out. The chips in those days were in 14-pin packages and 16-pin packages. This new one was like an 18- or 20-pin package, a little longer than normal, but it had this beautiful little 8-bit chip register, and 8 bits is a magic number—it's a byte. And I had thought, "That chip would be beautiful for getting 8 bits of data off of a computer and shift it out to a cassette tape recorder, or whatever, to a floppy disk. I'd thought about using that chip for a floppy disk, because Steve Jobs had talked about floppies back before I left Hewlett-Packard.

So I said, "I'll look into this floppy disk." And I started pulling up the datasheet on that chip, and I started coming up with my first ideas of "How do I have that chip get the data to a floppy disk?" And then I came up with this clever little approach. I needed a little bit of logic in here, but if you put in logic, you only get four gates on a chip. And you have four gates and four gates and four gates—you need lots of gates to do all this figuring out what to put out, and it's chips and chips. So I said, "Why don't I do a clever little scheme? Data's going to come back from the floppy disk and I'm going to sit there and, within small portions of a microsecond difference, I am going to tell when the signal went from high to low and low to high and tell what the data is."

I needed a little bit of intelligence running at a very high speed, and I came up with a device called a state machine. I'd had a state machine class at Berkeley. I built just a very simple state machine, which basically was a register that contains an address that you're at—a certain place in a program. It held an address as a number and it fed its data into a ROM that took where you are in the program, plus a couple of inputs coming from the floppy disk and from the computer, and decided what it would do next. It would send out signals to cause the right things to happen, and the next address, the next place—it's called a state. So you're in one state and you say, nothing happened, I stay in this state; nothing happened, I stay in this state. Aha, the data from the floppy changed to a 1. I pop down to state number 5 and now I'm in state number 5 and nothing happens, and then the data from the floppy disk just went to a 0, and I pop down here and I also tell a ship register up there to ship in a bit of data, so it actually worked like a small microprocessor even though it was only two chips. It was very successful, a little 256-byte ROM and a little 6-bit register, I think.

So that's three chips, and then I had a couple more interface chips, and I took Shugart's floppy disk. They had a new 5-inch disk, and Steve got me one. Smaller than before—the prior ones were 8-inch. I'd never seen a floppy in my life, by the way. I'd never used or seen one. So I didn't know the first thing about them. I'd never taken a course in floppy controllers, I'd never seen a floppy controller, I didn't know what they did. But I knew on a cassette tape, I generated signals of certain timing patterns and, when they came back from the cassette tape, I analyzed them to figure out what were the ones and what were the zeros. The microprocessor did the timing, because the timing was loose; it wasn't in fractions of a microsecond. I just wrote programs that waited a certain amount of time and saw when the signal went from high to low or low to high, and made decisions right in the microprocessor of our Apple II. But I couldn't do that on the floppy disk. So I looked at Shugart's design to figure out how it worked. And I figured out, oh, you put some data here and some signals here and you set a clock bit at a certain speed every 4 microseconds, and you shipped in some new data. I went through chip after chip after chip on theirs, and I said, "If I take all these out, it's just as easy for me to run the wires straight over to the head that's writing onto the disk. And the signal coming back from it, I just run a wire over to my controller and I just do all the timing here and I don't need all their complicated interface to work." So I took 20 chips off their board; I bypassed 20 of their chips.

Steve Jobs really liked this because, when it came negotiation time, he said, "That's a good reason to sell it to us at a lower price. We don't need your controller board. All we need is a little bit of it. So you can sell it to us cheaper than you are selling it to other people." It was a good deal for Shugart, a good deal for Apple.

I thought I could write some data onto a floppy disk and interpret what was coming back as ones and zeros. Here's the problem: you got a whole big track of data and there's thousands and thousands of ones and zeros and then the track repeats. The head goes around and around. You have to know where and when data starts and stops. And that was an issue I'd never done in my life. I came up with an approach of writing a certain kind of data, a certain pattern—AA D5 AA 55—some pattern like that. I just wrote it for a long enough sequence at the start of every section of data, and it was something that would somehow get my circuits into sync so they knew when a one and a zero started a byte, instead of was in the middle of a byte. It just automatically caused it to just sort of slip into place. By the time it got to the data, it read it correctly. So that was a lucky find. I was afraid, partway through my floppy disk design, that I would never be able to solve that problem. But I did. I lucked out.

Early on in the design, we were going to the very first CES (Consumer Electronics Show) show that was going to allow personal computers—which meant RadioShack, Commodore, and Apple. I had never been to Las Vegas and I wanted to see this beautiful city, but only marketing was going. There was no need for me to go. So I said, "If I get the floppy disk done, then could I go to show it off?" It was 2 weeks away. Something like a floppy disk design, you'd give it 6 months lead time, normally, to write down all the sheets and documents of what you're going to do and get them approved by managers. It's a horribly long cycle. This was 2 weeks away and Mike Markkula said yes. So that was my motivation. I always had these little fictitious motivations that motivated me and got me to do such great work. So I sat down and designed the floppy disk, and Randy Wigginton (he was the guy just out of high school) and I came in every single day including Christmas and New Years for 2 weeks. I came in every single day leading up to, I think it was January 3 or 5, when we went off to Las Vegas. I almost had this floppy disk done.

I got it to where it was writing data on a track, reading the data on a track. Then I got it to where it was reading the data in the right byte positions. Then I got it to work with shifting tracks, and we wanted a simple program where we would say "run Checkbook" or "run Color Math," and it would run the programs that were stored on the floppy disk. So we went off to Las Vegas, and Randy and I worked all night and we got it done to where it was working. At the very end, it was 6:00 a.m. and I said, 'We have to back up this floppy disk." We had one good disk that we prepared with the data hand-massaged to get it just right. So I stuck it in the floppy and wrote a little program, and I typed in some data and I said "read track 0;" stuck in the other floppy and said "write track 0, read track 1, write track 1." There were 36 tracks—I had to switch floppies back and forth.

When I got done, I'm looking at these two floppies that look just the same. And I decided that I might have written onto the good one from the bad, and I did. So I had lost it all. I went back to my hotel room. I slept for a while. I got up about 10:00 a.m. or so. I sat down and, out of my head and my listings, recreated everything, got it working again, and we showed it at the show. It was a huge hit. Everybody was saying, "Oh my god, Apple has a floppy!" It just looked beautiful, plugged into a slot on our computer. We were able to say "run Color Math," and it just runs instantly. It was a change in time.

But the real eureka moment for me was the very first time I ever read data back. I wrote it on the floppy, which was easy—but read it back, got it right. I just died.

Livingston: Where were you when you did this?

Wozniak: I was actually in Apple's office for the entire floppy disk creation. We were in that office building that I described earlier. There were about five of us in there, then there were about eight or ten. Then I moved out to a second little room that we got—a smaller room in the same office complex but down in another building. Randy Wigginton and I were in there, and Captain Crunch who developed the phone board for me.

Livingston: What advice would you give to hackers who are thinking about starting a company or making something on their own?

Wozniak: First of all, try to have the highest of ethics and to be open and truthful about things, not hiding. If you have to hide something for company reasons, at least explain what you're doing. Don't mislead people. Know in your heart that you are a good person with good goals because that will carry over to your own self-confidence and your belief in your engineering abilities. Always seek excellence: make your product better than the average person would.

If you can just quickly whip something out and it's done, maybe it's time, once in a while, to think and think and think, "Can I make it better than it is, a little superior?" What it does is not necessarily make the product better in the end, but it brings you closer to the product and your own head understands it better. Your neurons have gone through the code you wrote, or the circuits you designed, have gone through it more times, and it's just a little more solidly in your head, and once in a while you'll wake up and say, "Oh my god, I just realized a bug that's in there, something I hadn't thought of."

Or, if you have to modify something, or add something new, you can do it very quickly when it's all in your head. You don't have to pull out the listing and find out where and maybe make a mistake. You don't make as many mistakes. Just believe that what you have is better than whatever has existed before. We should only move forward in technology and not backwards.

Lack of tools: find a way to do it. If you say, "I have to have a tool," and you are a prima donna—"I have to have a certain development system"—if you can't figure out a way to test something and get it working, I don't think you're the right type of person to be an entrepreneur. Entrepreneurs have to keep adjusting to . . . everything's changing, everything's dynamic, and you get this idea and you get another idea and this doesn't work out and you have to replace it with something else. Time is always critical because somebody might beat you to the punch.

It's better to be young because you can spend a lot more nights, very, very late. Because you have to get things done, and there's almost no other way to get around that. When the times come, they are critical.

Livingston: You got mono once because of this?

Wozniak: That was the Atari Breakout, because I didn't sleep for 4 days and nights. How could you design a game—this would be months of design—build it, breadboard it, get it working, debug it in 4 days? Steve needed the money quick. He didn't tell me. He also didn't tell me the full amount of the money. He got paid a lot more than he told me, and he only gave me half of a smaller amount. Which he didn't have to; I would have done it for 25 cents. So that wasn't the point. I was glad to just be in there doing it. To get to design a game for Atari, who was bringing arcade games to the world—what a thing to remember for the rest of my life. So I would have done it for 25 cents.

But we both got mononucleosis. There was one Coke can I think we'd shared.

Livingston: So he took more money than you did, but you both worked on the project?

Wozniak: Yeah, I found out 12 years later.

Livingston: That's awful.

Wozniak: I know, but he didn't have to. He probably needed the money. And I didn't; I had an engineering job at Hewlett-Packard. It was very little to me. It would have been better if he'd been open about it and honest. And what if I remembered something wrong, too? It's so long ago.

Livingston: Did you ever get any investment from Mike Markkula?

Wozniak: $250,000. What he did was $80,000 of it was investment for an equal share to Steve and I, and the rest was a loan, paid back to him.

Livingston: And that's all Apple ever took?

Wozniak: Yeah. But we did right away meet with some people he'd met through Intel that were investment people. Hank Smith of . . . I can't remember the name of the company out of the East, but a venture group. They came in and met us all early on, and they did put in . . . Mike figured out that we were going to need some cash, we were going to be so fast growing. And when you are fast growing, you need more cash right away. So we did have a venture deal in place from well before we shipped an Apple II. And sometime after we were shipping the Apple IIs, we got, I think, $800,000 or $300,000—some large amount—from one venture capital place.

Livingston: On the East Coast?

Wozniak: I believe that's where we arranged it. Mike Markkula had worked with this guy Hank Smith at Intel, so that's how they knew each other. And I think Don Valentine actually put some money in, but then it came to a point where he wanted to make some good money and buy some stock off Steve Jobs for like $5.50 before we went public. $5.50 a share, and Steve thought it was too low. Oh, those two. Don Valentine doesn't like it when people don't agree with him.

Livingston: Is there anything that people have wrong about the early days of Apple?

Wozniak: Steve and I never really had an argument. Nobody ever saw us have an argument. The disputes were very rare and minor, of any sort between us, and they were usually just misunderstandings. He'd read something in the paper like I had said it. A lot of times papers got things wrong. They made it sound like I was leaving Apple because I was upset once about things inside of Apple and quoted me on a lot of things. The *Wall Street Journal* did. I told the reporter, "The reason I'm leaving is to start a new startup company to build a remote control. It's something I want to do." I had gone on a whiteboard and shown all the Apple executives what it was so nobody would accuse me of trying to go out and start a company that was competitive. As a matter of fact, they kept me on the payroll. They kept me as an Apple employee. They wished me well and told me that it was non-competitive in writing. But the *Wall Street Journal* got this story down that I was leaving Apple because I didn't like things going on there.

I had complained about the way some Apple II engineers were being treated like they didn't exist in the days of the Macintosh. I mean, we weren't even allowed to buy the floppy disk from Sony that we wanted in the Apple II division, because it would be better than the one that was going to go in the Macintosh. But it was the right one. So that sort of thing. Salaries, bonuses, etc. So I spoke up for some of those engineers in that article, but they made it sound like I was leaving, and I wasn't, not for that reason. Misconceptions . . . there are so many. It's like every book I read that I just think, "God, this is not how this person was at all." So I don't really care, I don't try to correct anything. But the world doesn't really have that much of it wrong in the end. I'm surprised when I go on the Web and I read all sorts of discussions about the Apple II and my role. It's actually very flattering and accurate.

The hardest thing was, though, after having a big success . . . see, I didn't seek the success—I wasn't like the entrepreneur who wants it. So the money to me didn't really mean much. Pretty much I gave it all away to charities, to museums, to children's groups, to everything I could. It almost was like an evil to me. That was because it wasn't the motivation that I was after, and I wanted to remain the person that I would have been without Apple. So that's why I went back and did the teaching. I would have done teaching were there no Apple.

Livingston: Didn't you give away your Apple stock early on to other employees?

Wozniak: As a matter of fact, when we went public, I was a little disturbed that five people who had been with us in our little office from the start and had been so important—Randy Wigginton, Chris Espinosa, a couple of young kids, and a couple of older ones, just hadn't gotten any stock. I felt that they were a part of this whole energy and excitement and passion for what computers were going to be and what we were doing and how right it was. If somebody is sitting there working till 2:00 a.m. with you, helping to write a little code, and says, "Wow, that is a cool one," those words mean a lot to you and they deserve something. So I gave each of those five a large amount of stock, probably a million dollars in that day. And that was an early day for a million dollars.

I also did a program where I sold stock to about 40 Apple employees . . . I had a chance to sell some stock and get a house. There was an outside bigwig investor type that was willing to buy it all at a certain price. And I said, "Rather than sell it to somebody who's already got a lot of money, why don't I give the Apple employees the opportunity?" We were going to go public soon and it was going to be worth a lot more (and was eventually), so basically I sold it to 40 Apple employees. Our legal department was very concerned because they were supposed to be sophisticated investors. They finally gave me the OK. I did the deal and sold it to them, and they each pretty much got a house out of it.

Livingston: That was so generous.

Wozniak: But it's that whole thing I was talking about: Hewlett-Packard, we're a community. There was a recession in '73 and Hewlett-Packard had to cut back 10 percent. Instead of laying off 10 percent of the people, they cut everyone's salary by 10 percent and gave us one day off every two weeks. So basically they said "nobody goes without a job." And I like that sort of thing. So a bunch of Apple engineers and marketing people got to benefit from going public. Otherwise, they'd have no stock at all. Mike Markkula kind of felt that some of these people didn't deserve it; some people shouldn't get stock. But I disagreed with him on that. Nobody stopped me, so I did it.

Livingston: But you still kept enough stock for yourself to buy a house, right?

Wozniak: The money I got from Apple employees, I used to buy a house. It was kind of an early state to be selling out 15 percent of your stock, but hey, that was a great opportunity for me. When I designed the Apple stuff, I never thought in my life I would have enough money to fly to Hawaii or make a down payment on a house. So it was huge deal for me.

Steve Jobs (left) and Steve Wozniak (right) in 1975 with a blue box
Photo by Margret Wozniak

Joe Kraus
Cofounder, Excite

Joe Kraus started Excite (originally called Architext) in 1993 with five Stanford classmates. Though they began by developing technology for information search and retrieval, their decision to go into web search ultimately made their site the fourth most popular site on the Web in the late 1990s.

Excite got venture capital funding in 1994 and launched its web search engine into a market crowded with competitors. Excite went public in 1996 and in 1999 merged with high-speed Internet service @Home.com to become Excite@Home.

In 2004, Kraus and Graham Spencer founded JotSpot, an application wiki company.

Livingston: How did Excite get started?

Kraus: We decided to start a company together before we had any idea what we were going to work on. But we were so committed to the idea of starting something together that we knew we were going to figure it out.

For me, that idea came from a formative experience after freshman year of college. As soon as I had arrived home to Los Angeles from Stanford, my parents said, "Good news"—and that usually meant something bad—"We went to your high school fundraiser last night and we bought you a summer job."

And I thought, "Oh, that's terrible news." I had thought I would pump yogurt or bag groceries and then I could surf and hang out with friends, which was really what I wanted to do.

I said, "Well, where is this job and what is it?" They said it was at an architectural engineering firm. I thought, "Well, that sounds kind of interesting. I don't know what that is, but OK." So I show up for work on my first day and the job is to duplicate microfiche with three 70-year-old women. For a 19-year-old guy, this is hell.

You had to expose the microfiche to ultraviolet light and then run it through this developer, which had this ammonia smell. It was really bad. I did that for 3 weeks and I quit and bagged groceries. I kind of determined from that point forward that my life wasn't going to be about being in an office, working with people I didn't want to work with and doing jobs I didn't want to do.

The next summer, to avoid the risk of my parents buying me another job, I contacted a high school friend who was an artist and said, "Let's start a T-shirt company together over the summer." How do you start a T-shirt company that runs only 3 months and then evaporates? The answer is that we found a group of clients that actually buy summer wear in the summer—which is very unusual because in retail, you buy your summer goods in the winter and winter goods in the summer. Nobody's buying T-shirts in the summer in traditional retail. But it turns out that private school bookstores have a lot of gear: T-shirts, sweatshirts, hats, etc.

We went to some of the larger printing houses in Los Angeles, who laughed at our orders because they were so small. They wouldn't do them. But in touring the facility, we inevitably met the foreman of the line, who usually had a backyard operation—some silk screening units in the backyard.

That summer we made $25,000. For college students that was huge. Also, our days were great: we'd get up a little late, do sales calls in the morning and show our portfolio and designs. In the afternoon, we'd go surfing or some outdoor activity and at night we would get together and do designs. It was a blast.

So I definitely had the bug. I also worked for Domino's Pizza in college, at a prepress house—all sorts of ways to try to earn some money. But the stuff I loved was doing something on my own. By the time senior year rolled around and my parents were saying that I should get a job, my whole thing was, "No, I don't want to get a job. I want to figure out how to do something in tech."

Even though I'm not technical—I was a political science major—your role models at Stanford if you're at all entrepreneurial are tech entrepreneurs. You don't have to look very far and you see buildings with names like Hewlett Packard, etc. There were even classes on this stuff that I started taking.

The smartest person I knew, by far, was my friend Graham Spencer, who was my next door neighbor freshman year. I thought, "If I can convince him to do something, then I bet we can make something interesting happen." He was being courted by Apple, Microsoft, and all the big players of the day, and my pitch was "Look, those guys are always going to want you and it's rare that you are going to be in the position in life where you have so little responsibility, except to yourself. So now's the time to do it. Yeah, we don't know anything. We're dumb and we're just coming out of college. But now's the opportunity."

Once Graham agreed, we gathered four of our other friends and went to a taqueria down in Redwood City and the dinner was focused around figuring out what this company was going to work on. "We are a company. Now what on earth do we do?"

Livingston: How did you choose to involve your four other friends? Because they were friends and you trusted them, or they were technically good?

Kraus: They were willing, capable, and friends—all of those things at once. They were all technical, they were all enthusiastic about starting something like this—it sounded like a good idea to them, as opposed to something they were scared of. Actually, every one of us was in the same freshman dorm. This was a company started out of essentially freshman dorm relationships.

So we get together at our favorite taqueria. We each had brought ideas to the table and they all sucked. There were things like applications for the Apple Newton—that was my brilliant idea. My other brilliant idea was automatic translation software, which to this day doesn't work. Everybody had ideas and they were all terrible, and by the end we were all very depressed.

And then Graham started talking. It's hard to remember exactly what he said, but it was something like this: "Look, between CD-ROMs and command line stuff, more and more information's being made available electronically." (We'd all been using command line email systems at Stanford since '89, and there were tools like Veronica, Archie, and Gopher. And WAIS had just come out, which was kind of a big thing at the time.) "But, as far as I know, the tools for searching through all that stuff were built in the '50s. There's got to be an opportunity to do something there."

So we thought, "Well, that's the best idea we've heard, so that's what we're doing." We came up with our slogan, which was "We are unencumbered by reality." We were so naïve we didn't know we could fail, and therefore we almost had to succeed.

We set off trying to research what was happening in R&D in search technology. We had no idea how we were going to make any money. But we started spending a lot of time in the math and science library, trying to figure out what had happened over the last 30 years in search.

Livingston: Was it search for the Web?

Kraus: No, it was just search. We didn't know what the application was going to be. Was it going to be a search engine that you'd include on CD-ROM when they distributed online encyclopedias? Was it going to be for law firms who had a lot of text documents to be searched through? In 1993 we weren't thinking Internet search because the Internet was very nerdy. There wasn't anything there. Those weren't people who would pay for stuff.

We all tried to get $3,000 from each of our parents, and five of the six parents put up, so we had $15,000. After graduating, three of us lived in one house in Palo Alto and three of us lived in another. We set up shop in the garage of the house that I was living in. It was the classic setup. My parents came up and they saw the garage and wound up buying us some nasty carpet. The tables were all Formica. I won a fax machine at Office Depot. We stole our chairs from Oracle Corp.

One of the founders was working a part-time job at Oracle, and back in those days, you could take home VT100 terminals to work from home. The way you got them to your car was by going to the supply closet: you took a VT100 and you put it on this $1,000 Herman Miller chair, and you rolled the chair out to your car, put the terminal in your car, and brought the chair back into work. So we thought, "That's a good idea. We could get some VT100s and some chairs all at once." We rolled up a U-Haul and brought down six chairs and six terminals and rolled away.

We bought two Sun machines. I bought one from an earthquake researcher in Berkeley for $600. Honestly, the biggest fight we had in those early days was over a used copier that I bought for $300. I'd used a substantial fraction of our capital on a copy machine while Graham was out of town, and we had this major fight about having spent all that money on a copy machine. Graham thought it was foolhardy to spend that much on a copier, and my view was that I was spending all my time having to go to the bank and get dimes for the copy machine at the math and science library, so I'd rather just buy this thing. It was used, and it never worked, so he was right and I was wrong—it was a stupid purchase.

We basically sat in the garage coding for around 18 months. In retrospect, it was really fun. But I remember a lot of worry. "Are we doing anything of value?" We were building the core engine, the indexing engine that would actually index the text, and the search libraries that would query that index.

It got cold in the garage and we didn't have a heater, so we would use the dryer for heat. We'd tape the little button down that made it run with the door open.

In about mid-'94, we now needed to put an interface on the software to start showing demos.

Livingston: Were you still living off the original $15,000?

Kraus: Yeah. Some of us had part-time jobs. I got my nickname during that time: "Phone Boy" (which it still is). My job every morning would be that—I was doing some coding, but not very well—I would read the *Wall Street Journal* to find out if there were people that I might call that could be interested in search stuff. So I invariably just did cold calls most of the time, "I saw your name in the *Journal* and we're this little startup . . ." I didn't know any better. Why wouldn't somebody take us seriously?

Livingston: Was there a cold call that you made that turned out to be pivotal?

Kraus: No, the pivotal things were all unintentional. Like the way we got turned on to the Web: it was about '94 and we were deciding between two technologies for the interface. How do you present search technology to the user if it's not a command line?

One was HyperCard and the other was this Web thing. And Graham, wisely, chose the Web. I believe it was because of that particular chance moment that we ended up being web-oriented and got known as a web search thing.

The intentional things were rarely pivotal in those early days, but the being persistent, following-your-nose thing made a big difference. The chain of events that led to our funding had no connection. You write them all down in a line and you wonder how these all led to each other, but the chain was very direct from step to step.

When I graduated, my college girlfriend gave me a book called *Accidental Empires*. It was a gossip history of Silicon Valley by a guy whose pen name is Bob Cringely. In it he writes, "Here's a tip for entrepreneurs. Call me, I'm a cheap date." So I call him and we get together for lunch and I tell him what we're working on. He gets very excited about it and we get the whole group together and he says that he wants to join the company. We think, "If he joins, we are golden, because he's huge, he's an author." It's funny to say now, but we felt that way.

He didn't end up joining, but he did introduce us to his bosses at InfoWorld (where he wrote a column), Amanda Hixson and Stuart Alsop. InfoWorld was interested in the search stuff we were doing so they said, "We'll give you a $100,000 contract if you can index our archives and make them available on the Web." They said that, if we did a good job, they'd introduce us to their parent company, IDG.

So we did a good job and they introduced us to IDG and we attended a board meeting where we presented what we had done. They were talking about investing and one of the people on the IDG board was a guy named Steve Coit, who was a partner at Charles River Ventures. Charles River started getting interested in investing, but they wanted a West Coast partner and they introduced us to Geoff Yang.

Geoff didn't know what to do with us. In fact, many of the VCs we met with didn't know what to do with us at all. They were very excited through the course of the demo until they got to the first question, which was "How do you make money?" Especially given that search had never made money for VCs before. Verity, PLS, Open Text—these had never been big and profitable businesses. We were saying, "We think advertising is interesting, and if not, we kind of hoped you would help us figure that out." And the conversations usually went very poorly from there.

But it was Geoff's introduction to Vinod Khosla, who ultimately funded the company along with Geoff, that really made the difference. Vinod interrupted the demo and said, "Can your technology scale? Can it search a big database?" And we said, "That's an interesting question. Nobody's asked us before." We liked the fact that he didn't ask us the "how do you make money?" question. We answered honestly, "We don't know because we can't afford a hard drive that's big enough to test." In a kind of Jerry Maguire "you had me at 'hello'" moment, he takes out his cell phone, calls his assistant and says, "I'm meeting with Joe Kraus and Graham Spencer of Architext and I want you to buy them a 10-gig hard drive." Which at the time cost like $9,000. And we were forever indebted to him.

As it turned out, yes, it did scale. We figured out how to make it scale, and we worked and worked and worked and ultimately put together a $3 million financing with Kleiner Perkins and Geoff Yang's firm, which was called IVP at the time.

Livingston: So you went from your families' $15,000 to a $100,000 contract to a $3 million VC financing?

Kraus: That's right. Because there wasn't a lot of angel money around at that time—at least that I knew of or had access to.

Livingston: Did the VCs let you keep your original stock?

Kraus: They adjusted the vesting schedule a little bit. I think by the time we did the financing we had been working on it 2 years, but they only vested us a year. So, they got a year of free vesting from us.

Livingston: Had you incorporated when you were in the garage phase?

Kraus: Yeah, we must have. How did we do that? We had to in order to accept the $100,000 from InfoWorld, so we incorporated pretty early. I think we got a lawyer to do it for us really, really cheaply. I had a friend whose father was a lawyer, so I called that friend and talked to his father and asked, "How do I do this?" and I think they actually just did it for us.

Livingston: Did you wind up doing something for IDG?

Kraus: No, we didn't. I think they might have put in a small amount of money—I actually can't recall. But we never ended up doing anything big with them.

Livingston: When you got the VC money, I read that you had to think hard about how you were going to redistribute the stock. You described it as a "couch moment," right—where you would pull the couches face-to-face to discuss difficult situations?

Kraus: Yeah, it sucked. People ask me all the time, "Would you start a company with your friends again?" This presumes that starting a company with your friends is bad. And there are some things that are bad about it. It makes it hard to be objective about personnel decisions. I love the show *Entourage* on HBO. In it, the lead character is a rising movie star and his best friend really wants to be his manager and is quite competent at it. The lead character says to his friend, "Remember, I can't fire my friend, but I can fire my manager." And that's the hard one, right—if you have to make personnel decisions, you can't fire your friend, but you can fire your business partner.

That's a very difficult line. But we would have never, ever survived as a company without having something bonding us other than the pursuit of a business idea. Because we came together to start a company before even knowing what that company was doing. We were more committed to the idea of starting something together and figuring it out than a bunch of people who were only personally interested in how much money they could make or what could be built around a particular idea.

That morphs over time as the business actually starts to take off, but that commitment carried us through a lot of very dark moments and no money and difficult nights and toiling away in a garage. It is the thing that got us through the couch moment of redistributing the equity.

We originally had the company divided evenly: everybody had a sixth. When Kleiner came in, Vinod said, "You know, you can leave it that way if you want, but I think you guys are going to want to look at this." And so Graham and I went and had a meeting with the whole team and said, "We think we need to redistribute equity in a way that isn't even." And that's no fun to hear. I think, quite honestly, nobody had a problem giving Graham more, because Graham was clearly the man among boys in terms of his technical ability. The other guys were smart, but they did what Graham asked them to do and Graham was the guy who really architected the whole thing. The hard part was, "How do we value Joe, who's not technical. He does stuff, but I don't know whether I could do his stuff better." Basically it was, "I don't know how to measure myself against Joe, and therefore how do I feel comfortable that he has more?"

But we ended up working through it. I don't remember the specifics of the conversation. I remember it being very awkward and I remember it being quiet. People were unhappy. No screaming or anything like that, but awkward.

I think the fact that Vinod was talking about it helped, as an outside instigator. But we never would have made it through if we had not been friends. I think you needed something stronger than greed pulling people together at that moment when greed alone would have caused huge fractures in redistributing. In the end, I think it made a lot of sense to do because those conversations only get harder and harder to have.

Livingston: What about your first version? Did it seem like you were onto something huge?

Kraus: No, it was never clear that we were on to something huge. You never know anything. The hardest part in a startup is that you wake up one morning, and you feel great about the day, and you think, "We're kicking ass." And then you wake up the next morning, and you think "We're dead." And literally nothing's changed. You haven't made some big deal, you haven't sold something new. Maybe you wrote a few lines of code over the course of that last day. Maybe you had some conversations with people, but nothing's really moved.

It's completely irrational, but it's exactly what you go through. The thing is, you never know. I am certainly sort of a paranoid competitor. I was always worried about who was going to kill us and what they were going to do. I'd feel like "We're going out of business any day and anything could upset the applecart." I really wanted it to get to a point where I'd say, "OK, I know we're on to something huge."

Even up to the time when Excite was several hundred people and we were the fourth largest website in the world, it didn't feel real. It doesn't feel like you're really doing something huge. On some level it feels like you're fooling people—like, are we really doing this?

It's the whole sausage and sausage factory problem: when you're outside and you only see the sausage coming out you think, "That's pretty tasty." When you're on the inside and you know how it's made, it's terrifying. That's the feeling. You just don't ever feel like the progress is smooth. It's never, "We set out this well-orchestrated plan, we're executing it, it's going exactly according to plan. We're getting bigger by the day and it's just as I thought."

It's never been that, ever, for me. It's always been, "I know this can be huge, I believe it in my heart. How on Earth do we make this happen? Why don't other people think it's huge yet?" It's just this complete, everyday banging your head against the wall trying to figure out how to convince other people that this thing is the biggest thing in the world.

Livingston: What did people misunderstand most?

Kraus: First, back in those days, it was legitimate to ask, "Why would I use a search engine more than a couple of times to find the sites that I like? Then I'll bookmark those sites and never go back to a search engine again."

Microsoft made a buyout offer for Excite in late '95, and even then I had Microsoft's CTO, Nathan Myhrvold, yelling at me, "Search is not a business. People are just going to search a few times and then bookmark what they want to go to."

The second was that nobody knew what the business model was going to be. In fact, Excite really never got the business model right at all. We fell into the classic problem of how, when a new medium comes out, it adopts the practices, the content, the business models of the old medium—which fails, and then the more appropriate models get figured out. For example, all the television programming in its early days looked like radio. It was literally the same guys reading the radio program on television, and it was extraordinarily boring. And advertising was radio advertising—the announcer reading the ad.

We too adopted the business model of the prior medium, which was print. Cost per thousand impression (cpm)-based advertising was how we made money in search, and that was wrong. We never figured out the cost-per-click piece of it. We got too buried in our legacy of cpm-based advertising and that's how we died. Or at least that's how the Excite piece of the business wasn't as much as it could have been.

By 1997 everybody was diversifying into portal strategies, because nobody knew how to make money from search. Search was viewed as the traffic director to other more profitable businesses, when in reality, search was the business. That wasn't obvious at the time.

Livingston: What competitors did you worry about?

Kraus: Early on you worry about the ones that don't matter, because you don't know any better. Early on, as a search technology company, we worried about Verity, PLS, Open Text. We were too young to realize that existing companies' biggest problem is legacy. Period. They can't focus on new businesses because they've got to manage their old ones. And so when we moved to web search, it was never clear to us that Verity, PLS, and Open Text wouldn't actually go and do this. But they couldn't because they were servicing all their existing businesses and could never invest enough in this new kind of business.

We worried about Yahoo, Lycos, and Infoseek the most when we started getting into the web search business, for sure. There were some rumors of entries from big companies, like MCI. Was AT&T going to play in this space? What was AOL going to do?

Livingston: You felt there was the threat of the larger companies with deep pockets getting into the space?

Kraus: Right, and they never did. When Microsoft made its buyout offer for Excite in late 1995, they offered about $70 million. We'd just launched in October '95 and they're offering $70 million. We said no, and we told them the number needed to be more like $100 million. And apparently what happened is—and I only learned this story recently—the negotiator we were working with went back to Gates and said, "I think the number's going to be $100 million if we want to do this." And Gates said, "How much would it cost us to do it ourselves?" So the guy went away and built a plan and said it would be about a year and $25 million and 25 people or something like this. And the interesting thing is that they didn't buy Excite for the $100 million, and they didn't invest and build it themselves. Instead they did nothing.

Which is really interesting to me in terms of the longer-term history of Microsoft and the search wars. It's interesting that MCI and AT&T and these guys never got into the business.

Livingston: How did you get the Netscape search button deal?

Kraus: That was a gut-wrenching moment. We needed distribution—we needed eyeballs and more people to be trying Excite. The natural point of distribution was the browser. The only real point of distribution. No websites had any traffic of any size to do a deal with. It was the browser getting bundled in that made the big difference. So we went to Netscape. They had two buttons on the browser: NetSearch and NetDirectory. NetSearch was pointing to Infoseek and NetDirectory was pointing to Yahoo. And those deals were free; it was just free traffic to those services. Unbelievable.

But nobody knew how to make any money off traffic or that traffic itself was valuable. Netscape wasn't a media company; it didn't view that as valuable. What Netscape wanted was more downloads of its client, which would help them sell more servers and more client licenses. So they finally decided to put these two buttons up for bid and there were three bidders: us, Infoseek, and MCI (with a rumored new service).

We had $1 million in the bank and we didn't know what we were going to bid. We sat down in my office, all on the floor. Vinod said we should bid $3 million. I was like, "How do we bid $3 million? We only have $1 million in the bank." And he said, "Well, if we win, I'm pretty sure we can raise it, but if we don't win, I don't know how we're going to raise it." And so I thought, "OK, this is really scary."

(If you are 22 and trying to make these big decisions, it's great to have a very active guy like Vinod helping you out. And I mean active. I was talking to Vinod twice a day easily. He's one of the senior partners at Kleiner Perkins and he's spending multiple hours a day on my business, which you just don't get. But that's Vinod's style.)

We decided to bid $3 million. We had no way to pay for it, but we weren't going to reveal that. We bid the $3 million and we lost. It was horrible to lose; it felt like somebody had died. It was just this feeling of, "Oh my God, what are we going to do?" Because you spend so much time wanting to get the deal that when you don't get it, you're like, "Oh, are we really screwed?" (And I think we would have been screwed.)

Vinod told us this whole story about how he'd gone through a similar situation at Sun in losing a deal, and he just never gave up and won the deal back. He said, "We haven't lost. Let's meet with them. Let's show up in their lobby unannounced." We did all this stuff; we called them constantly; we just basically acted like the bidding wasn't over. And made a total pain in the ass of ourselves. It would have been embarrassing if it weren't so serious.

Then luck struck: MCI couldn't deliver its service to Netscape on time. Netscape wanted its money and they wanted to have a vendor in that slot, so they came back to us and said, "OK, we'll take your $3 million and you can be in the NetDirectory play and good luck." I can tell you that, had we given up, we never would have gotten the deal back. And without that deal I don't think Excite would have had its run at all.

That was what helped launch the company. It's so ironic. If you look at the way that a lot of huge companies get built . . . Microsoft built itself off IBM, unwittingly. Excite built itself unwittingly off Netscape. Google built itself unwittingly off Yahoo. I don't think we would have gotten where we got without the Netscape deal and we certainly wouldn't have gotten the Netscape deal without a really valuable lesson in persistence.

I see way too many people give up in the startup world. They just give up too easily. Recruiting is a classic example. I don't even hear the first "no" that somebody says. When they say, "No, I'm not interested," I think, "Now it's a real challenge. Now's when the tough part begins." It's hard to identify talent, but great people don't look for jobs, great people are sold on jobs. And if they're sold they're going to say no at first. You have to win them over.

For example, we had this VP of marketing that I worked to get for about 3 months. He was the former VP of marketing at QVC. He called me literally the day before he was supposed to move out to California and said, "I can't do it." I said, "Well, we're going to have dinner tonight, so I'm coming out to New York." I got on a plane and went to New York and sat down with him. And I got really lucky: we're at the restaurant and we were quiet for a second and you could hear people talking about the Net. They were talking about Hotmail and AOL and the Internet boom going on. So I said, "Look, these people aren't talking about home shopping, they're talking about the Internet. So your choice is, 'Do you want to be part of the past or do you want to be part of the future?'"

I love this stuff; the persistence part is the part that I like. It's actually not fun when it's happening, but you know it makes a difference because 99.9 percent of the people give up. And Vinod gave me that lesson in spades. I think I would have given up with Netscape. I wouldn't have known what to do. I wouldn't have had the chutzpah to just say, "No, we haven't lost, we're still negotiating, aren't we?" And treating it as if I didn't hear their "no." It was very unfamiliar to me originally.

Livingston: What was most surprising to you?

Kraus: That opportunity creates opportunity. One of our first acquisitions was a company called Magellan, an editorially oriented search engine. The primary reason for doing the deal was to show that in a space that was ripe for consolidation, we were going to be doing the consolidating, not being consolidated. Because otherwise the deal didn't make a whole lot of sense to me. It was a momentum play.

People asked a lot of questions about why we did that deal. We couldn't predict it at the time, but it led to the acquisition of WebCrawler. The acquisition of WebCrawler happened because we had acquired Magellan and because AOL saw it and said, "Hey, this company is doing something." When we were at a very bleak stage—we were public and running out of money—we were saved by Intuit, who we did a $20 or $30 million deal with. The original impetus was something related to some other deal we had done, which in turn was built because of the WebCrawler deal.

Reading the Cringely book, which led to a lunch, which led to an introduction, which led to a $100,000 contract, which led to a board meeting, which led to a VC, which led to another VC, which led to a financing. It's the same as Magellan leading to WebCrawler leading to AOL leading to Intuit, and you can't predict these things going forward.

Some famous person said, "Success is 50 percent luck and 50 percent preparedness for that luck." I think that's a lot of it. It's being ready to take advantage of opportunities when they arise.

The other thing that surprised me was how well companies can do if you challenge them with these big, crazy goals. When we launched in October '95, we were number 17 in a 17-horse race. We said to the company in January '96, "We're number 1 or number 2 by the end of the year or we don't matter." We did a lot of crazy things—from acquiring companies to building new products to distribution deals. How is it realistic to say that you'll go from 17 to 1 or 2 in a year? It's crazy, but the company rallied around it. I'm surprised really pleasantly by the ability of people when challenged to rise to the occasion.

So I guess the last lesson is that people make all the difference in the world. Everybody says that people matter most, but boy, I've never worked with a finer group of people. They just were inspired.

Venture capitalists, with the exception of people like Don Valentine, would tell you that they'd rather fund a great team than a great idea. The reason is that if they have a bad idea, great teams can figure out a better one. Mediocre people even with a great idea can screw it up in its execution. Or if they have a bad idea, then they aren't going to be in a position to think about how to change it. They're just going to pursue it blindly.

Livingston: What important lessons did you learn at Excite that you are carrying over to JotSpot?

Kraus: One is hiring slowly and more carefully. Another is be cheap, cheap, cheap. Also, get the legs of the business underneath it before you run terribly fast. We were always playing catch-up at Excite and I never liked that feeling. You always felt like the traffic, the momentum, the deals were all ahead of where the business naturally was. You want to be ahead of where it naturally is, but you don't want to be two times ahead of it. So, I think really taking the time to understand the dynamics of the business, so we can scale it, is important, along with being cheap and hiring well.

Dan Bricklin
Cofounder, Software Arts

Photo by Louis Fabian Bachrach

Dan Bricklin and his friend Bob Frankston founded Software Arts in 1979 to produce VisiCalc, the first electronic spreadsheet. Spreadsheets used to be made on paper. As a student at Harvard Business School, Bricklin thought how convenient it would be if they could be made on desktop computers instead. He wrote a prototype in Basic over a weekend, and then he and Frankston set about turning it into a product.

When their first release shipped in October 1979, it ignited the personal computer software revolution. VisiCalc was the "killer app" for personal computers: businesses bought Apple IIs just to use it.

Unfortunately, VisiCalc was not produced by a company organized like a modern startup. VisiCalc was developed by Software Arts, but distributed by Daniel Fylstra's Personal Software (later renamed VisiCorp), which paid royalties to Software Arts. Friction between the two culminated in a lawsuit in September 1983—just as Lotus 1-2-3 hit the market. The distraction proved fatal.

As a business, Software Arts's fall was as fast as its rise, but it had more influence than many longer-lived companies. Bricklin and Frankston's ideas live on in all the software we use today.

Livingston: How did you know Bob?

Bricklin: I met Bob when I was a freshman at MIT. I was working in the labs as my student job—because a really good way to learn an area in college is to work on a real project in one of the labs. I worked at the Multics project, which was a major project in the history of operating systems. Out of it came the Unix system and the 386-style chipset and a whole lot of things about how we do software and operating systems today. The first job I was given was to make some modifications and finish the work of this other guy, who had just graduated, in his bachelor's thesis. And that was Bob Frankston.

Bob's thesis was a project called Limited Service System. We used time sharing then; we all shared the same computer over a terminal. The Limited Service System was a way to throttle your usage so that nobody would use more than a certain amount, so they could just give it away for free and know that nobody would hog more than a certain percentage—because this one system was being shared that could handle maybe 50 users or 100 users, and this is for the whole campus.

Many of us working at that project were undergraduates or graduate students. Those of us who were young and single would get together socially, too. Bob had a car and lived off campus. He would drive us places, so we all got to know Bob really well.

Bob and I always wanted to found a business together. We both had parents who were entrepreneurs, so the idea of running your own business was a normal thing. There are people who come from backgrounds where they're used to working for a company, and they couldn't dream of doing it themselves and not having that safety net. When your parents and family are entrepreneurs, you know it's nothing special. I worked at big businesses and I worked at small businesses beforehand, so the idea of starting your own business was just a normal thing.

Bob and I were sort of looking for years for something to go into business with together, and clearly it would be in computers. It's not uncommon to get together with friends that you meet in college. You see that in a lot of startups. The other advantage of the two of us being friends, and not just business associates, was that a lot of the structure of our deals together was based on friendship and not on other things. The friendship was stronger than a lot of the business stuff. So even though we came to odds about things, even though there might be a "Well, did you do more, or did I do more?" because we liked each other and had a relationship, we were able to keep that from messing up the business.

We'd be arguing all the time about stuff, but, on the other hand, we have a strong friendship that still continues. Twenty-five years later, we're still close friends. So that was a help, because we didn't have to think, "Do you get 35 percent and I get 65 percent? How are we going to do this?" So many things were just, "We'll just do it 50/50. I'll do this one, you'll do that one." That did make a difference. Also, because we knew each other, there was a lot of trust, which you need, especially in families, because family money was involved when we started the business.

Livingston: Is that how you first got money to start a company?

Bricklin: We first started on our own. I was in business school, living as a student on loans and savings. Bob was actually working as a consultant, so he was getting money. We went through very little money to begin with, because we used time sharing to do the programming. It was done on a separate computer that you would log into, and then the resulting product was downloaded into an Apple II we borrowed from our publisher, and then it was tested.

Bob already had equipment. He had an acoustic coupler modem and a terminal to edit on, from his other consulting work. So we just had to pay for the time-sharing time, and he used it late at night, when it was cheap. I mean really late. Basically, he slept during the day.

Livingston: That was at MIT, right?

Bricklin: We used MIT's Multics system, the one we worked on.

Livingston: Did they mind?

Bricklin: No. We paid for it. Luckily it took a few months to be billed. So money went into that, and Bob had some money and was able to pay for it. Eventually we borrowed some money from relatives, because we wanted to buy our own computer. We borrowed money from a bank and from relatives, and we bought a Prime minicomputer, which had an operating system based on the ideas of Multics, done by people who used to work at Multics. We bought one of those of our own, and we sublet space through some other friends who had a business, and that's how we started our business—in a basement. The original business was started in Bob's attic in Arlington, Mass.

Livingston: At this point, you had graduated from MIT and were at Harvard Business School?

Bricklin: Right. I graduated and worked for a few years, which was important.

I had worked for DEC—Digital Equipment Corporation, a big company. Then I worked for FasFax Corporation, a small company. I got to see the differences and see that small companies were just as exciting and just as cutting-edge. You didn't have to be in a big business, which was an eye-opening thing for me.

Then I went to Harvard Business School, which was where I came up with the idea. I saw the need for it. But that was coming off of my experience with word processing and typesetting at DEC. I worked in computerized typesetting at DEC because I like practical stuff. My father and grandfather were printers. Out of typesetting, I got into video editing for typesetting, and out of that, I ended up in the word processing group. I was project leader of the first word processing system that DEC did. So that got me into this whole interactive, screen-based, what-you-see-is-what-you-get type system.

When I was at business school, taking the experience of what I had done at MIT with interpreters . . . I worked on the APL system, I worked with Bob on his Basic system; I had done interpreters (in high school I was building interpreters). So the idea of an interpreted language, together with the word processor—and you're sitting there in business school running numbers—the idea of word processing with numbers to me was a natural thing. The traditional way a lot of people think of spreadsheets is as rows and columns, and it really isn't. It's really a two-dimensional layout of words and numbers. If you look at what we had in all our cases at Harvard Business School, at documents you have in business, you have tables of things, but they're organized in a way that is appropriate to the data, and there's a lot of other text, and the text is just as important as the numbers.

I took this general layout idea of the word processing and computerized typesetting world, together with the calculating world of APL and Basic and stuff, to the needs of business, where you need to be able to ad hoc throw anything together and make changes. That's where the idea for the spreadsheet came from. Then through business school, I met this publisher, Dan Fylstra, of Personal Software, and his partner, Peter Jennings. Dan was a second-year Harvard MBA student when I first met him.

When I started programming, he had graduated and was running this business selling software on cassettes out of his apartment in Allston, Mass. He was looking for new stuff, like a checkbook program. I actually prototyped VisiCalc on one of his machines over one of the vacation weekends. I went to his place and wrote a prototype in Basic. Then we started discussing that they would publish it. As MBAs (both he and his partner were MBAs), they understood the value of this thing. They already had a need listed in their list of things they wanted of financial stuff. And they were looking at other financial forecasting tools, but this also would do checkbooks and other stuff. So they knew they could sell it as that; they knew that they would use it. And we made a deal to produce it.

I had already prototyped it and said what it would do, but I didn't have time to program it since I was in school. So, since Bob was out of school, he would program it.

Livingston: You did it over one weekend? When was that?

Bricklin: The fall of '78.

Livingston: You just wanted to see if it would work?

Bricklin: No, I had been thinking of the idea; I had daydreamed about it. I had actually done a prototype on Harvard's computer system that was available to us as students. As part of the prototyping, I came up with what we have today: the A-B-C 1-2-3 type of thing, the columns and rows ways of indicating things; the idea of having a formula on what we call the contents line that tells you what you're pointing to; moving around where you could move the highlight around from cell to cell—that whole thing. The idea and some of the prototyping had been done. The actual trying it on a personal computer was written in Basic to see what it would feel like. And then we actually programmed it in assembly language starting the winter of '78/'79.

Livingston: When you first wrote the prototype that you did in Basic, what surprised you most?

Bricklin: I had originally wanted the thing to use a mouse. There was no mouse on the Apple II at the time, so I was using the game paddle and turning it. But the way I was doing it with the game paddles, the cursor was just too unstable. So I switched to the arrow keys, which were much more discrete.

I learned some computer things. I had it make a sound every time it recalculated a cell, but it turned out that the making of the sound on the Apple used up three-quarters of the CPU time, because it did it with a timing loop. I learned little things like that. But I saw that it was a useful thing and that it actually felt good and that I could start describing it to some classmates. One of them was also an MIT grad and computer person, John Reese. I would tell him how it was, and he'd say, "Well, Dan, it would be easier if you did this," and I said, "You're right." There was a lot of feedback that way.

Livingston: Were you nervous to tell anyone about your idea?

Bricklin: No, not those people. Once we started working on it and were in business, yeah, since we thought it was obviously such a great idea. Though we realized it takes forever for it to become big in the world. We didn't think it would be as big as it is now, because nothing had done that in the past, though we thought it was real important. But you always do, as an entrepreneur. Everybody feels that way about what they're doing. You need that drive. And, yeah, we were afraid that Texas Instruments would find out about it and they'd steal the idea. So we were careful; we would have people sign nondisclosure agreements.

Livingston: The idea of a startup was pretty new. How did you know what to do first?

Bricklin: There were always startups. A huge portion of the economy in Massachusetts came from people who got their start at DEC, which started as an entrepreneurial thing. Then the same thing happened on the West Coast with Hewlett-Packard and places like that.

But there was this other business, Personal Software, the publishing company, which was the model that they used of how to do software. This was a different model of author-publisher. We now know that author-publisher is not a very good model. We were the poster child of it not being good. But we set up that way, so when Bob and I made a deal with the Personal Software people in the fall of '78 to produce this product and they would sell it, we needed a business.

We incorporated the business on January 2, 1979, and then we negotiated the deal with Personal Software. We were developing the product, but before it was announced we had already agreed on the general terms. The actual specific contract wasn't signed until the night before we announced it at Ben Rosen's conference. We had our lawyer (a general lawyer) negotiating on our side, and we had a publishing lawyer on the other side, I think, negotiating, which wasn't exactly right for software. Our contract ended up having problems long-term. But, it actually ended up being the model contract for many, many software things afterwards, because it did have a lot of interesting stuff in it.

Livingston: So VisiCalc was the first to use the author-publisher model?

Bricklin: We weren't the first, I'm sure, but in the personal computer software business, we were one of the first.

Personal Software later renamed themselves VisiCorp. Dan Fylstra, who was the head of the company, was one of the founding editors or something of *Byte* magazine. So he was involved in many ways in the publishing business. I assume that his lawyers were from that business too.

Livingston: You incorporated over your winter break, right?

Bricklin: Yes. When I graduated business school, I graduated as chairman of the board with no salary. We announced the product on Monday, and I graduated Wednesday or Thursday, something like that. The first time it was shown to the public was at the National Computer Conference in June of 1979. It had actually been announced privately at Ben Rosen's conference and then shown at the West Coast Computer Faire in May of '79, but only shown to dealers behind closed doors.

Livingston: When you were giving these private demos, was there any part of the demo where you just saw the audience say, "Oh my God"?

Bricklin: It depends on the audience. We announced it at the National Computer Conference; it was written up by a Morgan Stanley analyst in the summer . . . you think it would be mentioned in any publication? A business publication? No. Eventually, in a publicity thing about the software publishing that Personal Software was doing, *BusinessWeek* mentioned it a little bit. And eventually *Fortune* magazine and *Inc.* ran stories that we were featured in on the business of publishing software. But, the concept that the spreadsheet as a type of software was available (other than in the personal computing software magazines like *Byte* or *Creative Computing*) just wasn't mentioned. I think *Forbes* finally mentioned it in a comparison of new computers—did it have VisiCalc or not? So it sort of was missed.

People who saw it, who needed it, got it. Sorry, no—*some* of the people who needed it got it. You have to be a person who is able to look at a general-purpose tool and be able to think, "How would I use that to solve my problem?" Most people are not that way. They look for a tool that is being used already for something close to their problem and then understand what it is. Many people who saw the spreadsheet with an example, if the example wasn't in their field, they couldn't make the leap. Because they're not programmers in their mind.

But, if you showed it to somebody where it clicked, either because they understood the general-purpose nature and could apply it to their own needs, or you showed them an example, like financial forecasting or something that they did, and they knew the other tools in the world, they got very excited. If you showed it to a computer person who didn't have those needs, they'd say, "That's kind of cool, but what's so special about that? I could just do it in Basic." Now, there were those that hadn't seen as interactive a computer before, weren't as aware of word processing and some of the other things, and, when they saw it, it really opened up their minds to what you could do interactively with computers. Jean-Louis Gassée, who went to Apple, is one of the people who says that.

There were those people—not that many, but enough that it got a lot of people going in computer software. And then there were people—the general public—who thought computers could do everything, and they weren't at all surprised. They'd say, "Well, of course, computers can do so much more than that. What's special?" Luckily for us, the people who funded things—the MBA types got it, the investment banker types got it, because this was something they would need. And that made them get the personal computer.

Livingston: Did it drive sales for the Apple II along with VisiCalc?

Bricklin: Well, for Apple, yeah. Eventually we could track Apple sales by how many we sold. But the first year we were only selling a thousand units a month.

Livingston: Who were the very first users?

Bricklin: There was Al Sneider, locally, who was at Laventhol & Horwath, which is an accounting firm, and he started pushing them to use personal computers. They did a lot of accounting for the gaming business. They actually used VisiCalc to figure out how to lay out a casino and where to put which slot machines, I'm told. There were doctors who had bought personal computers because they thought it would be kind of cool, who used it for, I think, anesthesiology calculations in open-heart surgery.

We got cards back where people said what they used it with; we asked them in their registration card. They were people who liked technology and were enamored with the personal computer, who knew business. But, as I say, only a thousand units a month. It took a while for people to get what it was, and these people evangelized it.

Hewlett-Packard got it. One of my classmates from Harvard Business School worked in the group that was developing a personal computer there, and they read Ben Rosen's write-up, and Hewlett-Packard licensed it and did their own implementation based on our software.

Livingston: What were the biggest conceptual hurdles for you as you were building the product?

Bricklin: The original vision was of an electronic blackboard or work area. In fact, initially I also thought of it as a head-up display (like in a fighter plane) where—using a mouse together with a key pad, like a calculator with a mouse ball on the bottom or something—you could lay things out and you could use it real time while looking at people or something. So this electronic blackboard type of thing, like the typesetting layout software that was being worked on at the time. The Harris 2200 was one that I was very interested in, which nobody knows about, but I have the Seybold write-up of it.

I had seen what we now call desktop publishing, because in computerized typesetting, that's what they were doing for display ads. Classified ads are automatically laid out, more or less, but in the display ads, where you're putting "Sale!" and all this stuff, that general-purpose layout—that was the hot thing, developing that two-dimensional, general-purpose layout stuff like PageMaker. The PageMaker people came out of computerized typesetting—out of Atex, which is a local company that did computerized typesetting and one of my competitors when I worked at DEC.

So I had this idea, this general two-dimensional layout, and I had the idea of calculating and then recalculating, because it's like word wrap; it does that. So those ideas came up right away for me. But then how do I really express that? What exactly are the keystrokes that you do? What exactly is the metaphor? How do I make it easy to learn? I had struggled with this in the word processing world, when we invented things for word processing, because when we did word processing at DEC in the mid-'70s, there weren't many screen-based word processors. A lot of them were page-based, which meant that you edited one page at a time, and if something was more than a page, you had to cut it and paste it onto the beginning of another page, because they were thinking like paper. In fact, some of them had things like platens to turn to make the paper go up and down, and you set the margins with something you slid back and forth. That was the Lexitron. But some of them, like NBI's (Nothing But Initials) system, were document-oriented.

This was before Wang did their first screen-based word processor. I came out of the Multics project, which used the Runoff system, which Jerry Saltzer had developed for the CTSS (the Compatible Time Sharing System), which was one of the first time-sharing systems. To write his thesis, Professor Saltzer invented this thing called Runoff, which was used basically to do the word processing for it. It was a document-oriented word processor, as opposed to the page-oriented ones. The big word processors were the Mag Tape and then the Mag Card Selectric, from IBM. Those were relatively early in word processing. There were a few things before that, none of them screen-based.

The idea of a long document that's automatically broken up and that embeds commands was like typesetting. So put those two together and we had to invent the ruler—the embedded ruler. Now, others invented it simultaneously, but we had to invent our idea of the embedded ruler that, when you put the cursor above it, it does one thing, and below it, another. In the word processors of the day, the ruler was active as you were typing and applied to what you were typing, but it wasn't really remembered in it. So we had to figure this out.

We were selling it to places where secretaries would use it. People were paid by the keystroke in typesetting, in some cases. And in word processing, they were paid by the hour, which is basically by the keystroke. So we were very much into keystroke minimization. How many keystrokes does it take to do things? Hours of arguments and design about that in the typesetting world and the word processing world. I applied that to the spreadsheet. My whole mindset was, "How do I make it easy to learn to use? How do I make it minimum keystrokes for everything? How do I make it natural, so, if you're doing this repeatedly, it's the natural thing to do?"

Day one I wasn't thinking computer-like. The whole idea was not to think computer-like. We used decimal arithmetic so it would act just like a calculator. We didn't use binary arithmetic, which might end up with some anomalies that you might not understand.

I had Professor Jackson at the business school, and I had her look at the prototypes as we were doing it (she consulted to CEOs of big companies). She said, "You're competing against the back of the envelope. It's got to be really easy to use." I was constantly worrying about those things, and that affected the design quite a bit, because I had a lot of experience in that user interface world. I had also trained people on my product, so I had a lot of experience training people. So I knew what it was like, what people learn to use, etc.

The challenge was, how do you express the value you're typing in, the formula you want to calculate, its location, and the precision of the decimal points, and how wide are the columns and all this stuff? Is it an integer, is it a floating point number? How do you specify all that? In computerdom in those days, that was the most yicky stuff of any computer language—the format statement in Fortran, and COBOL's pictures and all that. It was just such a mess. How do you get the output specification of how it looks?

I ended up with WYSIWYG, like people had done in typesetting. How do you marry that with calculating? There I came up with use of the grid as a way to be able to name things. The big problem for me was, how do you name things? How do you name the value? In the old days, it's like, variable name equals expression, right? That's how computers work. Well, this was, "What's the variable name going to be?"

Today it seems so natural: you use A1. Well, first of all, it was A1, not 1 comma 1. It is too many keystrokes, it's not normal for people, and there's a whole lot of problems with it. By going to the map coordinate type of thing—A1, G7, or something like that—that was something I knew regular people would understand. But it also parsed well: anything that starts with a letter was obviously a variable name, because numbers always start with a number, or a plus and a minus or something. So it made it really easy to make it obvious what you were typing in. So, if you said 1 + A1, I knew exactly what it was. But, if I said 1 + 1,1?

So coming up with that idea, coming up with the fact that you'd be editing the output as the input—you'd basically be inputting into the output; what you see is what you get—with a separate location that showed the contents and all the attributes of it at the top, with the menu tree being shown at the top. We had very little memory space to give you in the way of help, but if you hit /, it listed all the letters you could type. If you typed a letter, it would give you the name of the command that you were doing and any options. So basically, it was always prompting you with what you could do next, once you learned to do the / key. And, of course, we could use /, because / is an infix operator, not a prefix operator, so you always knew that if something started with a /, it had to be a command. But, if it started with a +, it's going to be a number. So it was one of the few characters around that was good for that. And it was not shifted (I hate holding control keys down), and computers had used / as commands before, so it was a natural thing to use, for me.

So working out those problems was the thing. But then, after that, everything else was just, "What are the required features?" Adding replication, the ability to copy a cell with absolute and relative, that was sort of a natural thing for me to come up with, and it was not uncommon in other financial forecasting systems that existed—the time-sharing systems that were not as interactive. So that just all flowed. And it was just, "What can we throw out to make this thing useful and to fit in memory?"

Livingston: What kind of interesting features did it launch with? Any that you wish you had included?

Bricklin: Well, it would have been nice to have a better help system, but there was no space to store that.

Livingston: Space was an issue?

Bricklin: Oh God, the whole system, the operating system, the screen buffer, the program, and the data that you're running on, fit in 32K. A screenshot of VisiCalc doesn't fit in 32K nowadays. The Apple II only had 48K max. So this program launched in 48K, and you're going to put in a help? When Lotus launched with their help system, it was a separate disk that you put in that had the whole system in it.

Livingston: Didn't Lotus design 1-2-3 with the IBM in mind?

Bricklin: It ran in 256K or maybe 128—I don't remember—but you had to have an extra disk in the drive if you wanted help, as I recall. Just think about it: if a help screen has a thousand characters and you're going to have 10 help screens, there goes 10K! Where are you going to fit it when you only have 20K of memory for the whole sheet? How much are you willing to give? So I printed a reference card up, which my father actually helped me do—my father's printing business typeset and printed that whole thing for us. An awful lot of people learned the product from the reference card.

It had the ability to lock—because, remember, you had a very small screen, 40 characters by 24/25 lines on the Apple II—it allowed you to lock columns or rows on the screen. They call them panes now, I think, in Excel; you could lock the panes. We called them titles. You could lock the title area, and, as you scrolled, they'd synchronize, so that if you scrolled sideways, the stuff stayed in place.

It had two windows—you could actually split the window and watch two parts of the screen at once—so you could type numbers in one place and look at the sum somewhere else. And you could scroll them in unison. You could lock them in synchronous, so as you scrolled one, the other scrolled, and in one of them you might have the titles locked. And in fact, you got different column widths in different ones. Bob put in all sorts of cool stuff. They don't do that stuff today.

But it didn't have commas in numbers, because we had some bugs in that. We never shipped that, which was a real problem. And all the columns were the same width. You could change it, but they were all the same width, and that was bad. If you had a label that was longer than a column and there was a blank cell next to it, it didn't automatically go into it. You had to cut it into two pieces. Those were real killers. Those were things that 1-2-3 had, among others.

When 1-2-3 came out, those were the things people asked. "Does it have commas in numbers? And dollar signs before the numbers?" I think we had dollar format, which meant .00. But did it do commas, did it have variable column widths, and did it have the long labels? I remember Vern Raburn telling me those were three of the main questions that he was asked, and then people said, "Fine, I'll buy it." So those were features we didn't have that would have been nice if we did. We knew we needed those, but there was just a limit to what we could get done and would actually fit and work in the original product.

Livingston: You publicly announced VisiCalc in June. When did you first ship?

Bricklin: We worked out of Bob's attic until around when we got delivery of this computer that we bought, a time-sharing computer. Bob wrote an assembler and linker for it, and I wrote an editor for it so that we could do our work. We hired an employee or two, and they helped us finish the actual product and then convert it to other machines.

Bob wrote most of the code, and then this person we hired, Steve Lawrence, and myself wrote the rest of the code. I got the transcendental functions to work, the sine and cosine, stuff like that. There were bugs in divide, and Steve got those things working. We had the beta version of it ready, I think, in the late summer, together with a self-running demo version of it that was actually macro-driven—that basically had a long macro that would just run that was just keystrokes driving the thing.

You could just put that disk in—the computer store could do that—and people would just leave it in the window, and it would run through an entire demo, explaining what the thing was. Personal Software sent those to every known computer store. Some of them had no idea what to do with them and just sold the demo. Some lost it. And some figured out what it was, and became rich, hopefully.

In the fall of 1979, the manual was finished, production was finished, and it shipped. I think I got my first copy Saturday, October 20.

Livingston: Were there any panic moments before October 20?.Any times when you thought, "We can't pull this off?"

Bricklin: There were panic moments in the business, but they had nothing to do with programming. We were working in a basement in Central Square. We were next to the T (the subway) right near the Kendall Square Station. The T went right by us, and every time it went by, everything would shake, because, literally, it was a few feet in front of us.

We were below street level, so, when it rained, the toilets would back up. When it rained, whenever you left the building, you had to remember to turn off the toilet, or else they would back up. We missed one, and it started flooding, and the water started pouring toward our computer. I have some pictures of me there with one of those wet vacs as the water just missed our computer! Our life savings are in this one computer—life savings plus some money from relatives, plus personal guarantees on the loan.

There was getting the contract finished. Dan Fylstra came over with the latest version of the contract. We didn't have word processing. We had a correcting Selectric that I was writing stuff on. Dan didn't have a real word processor or a good printer for it, but he was doing advertising, so he went to Typotech, which was a place in Harvard Square where you could do your own typesetting by the hour. So he used it as a word processor, and he would typeset the contract. Then we would be sitting there negotiating some of the stuff, and he would run off to Typotech and make changes, and he'd literally cut and paste the results.

The final contract we signed—because it was up until late at night, making some changes about advances and royalties and future versions, I don't know, whatever we were doing—we needed a copy of it, and it was late at night; there were no all-night things. Bob had a copier. In the old days, Xerox's patents hadn't run out, and people didn't have Xerox machines at home. We had a thing which had a lightbulb in the bottom and used this heat-sensitive paper or something, and you put one page over another, and you end up with this brown-on-brown output. And that was the actual contract that we signed. Dan had the contract in hand, and he jumped on an airplane and flew off to New Orleans, where Ben Rosen was having his conference (later it became Esther Dyson's conference), and that's where he first showed it off to people.

Ben had seen a prototype, and it was being announced, semi-publicly, at the conference. So that last-minute getting that done, that was the type of thing we were doing.

I wrote an accounting system. Not only did I write the editor, I wrote an accounting system for us, and I did all the bookkeeping. I mean, here I am, a business school student taught to do accounting by a wonderful professor of accounting and then taught cost accounting by Jim Cash, who's now on the Board of Microsoft, but I'm now trying to figure out doing debits and credits by hand. I didn't know what the real world had on that. And I was doing my own bookkeeping. I wrote a system to do it.

Livingston: Did you have any competitors?

Bricklin: We were nervous that competitors would come out. But there was just so much optimism in those days. And we were doing this as a stepping stone to do other things. We didn't know this was going to be such a big thing. We figured we'd just keep on figuring out all sorts of cool stuff.

Livingston: Do you remember when you finally thought, "OK, this is a big deal?"

Bricklin: It felt like a really big deal when I started having people I didn't know in the regular part of the world knowing about spreadsheets and taking them for granted. When the *Wall Street Journal* ran an editorial about the budget in Washington and said, "Yellow ledger pads and VisiCalc spreadsheets all over Washington are trying to figure this out," that really hit me.

IBM came to us wanting VisiCalc on the IBM PC, and when they ran the advertisements on TV, they showed VisiCalc (or they showed what they said was VisiCalc; it was a mockup that they did) with Charlie Chaplin pushing a button. When Apple ran an ad, they had Dick Cavett—who had never done ads on TV before—and he would push a button and up would come VisiCalc on the screen. He didn't know what the hell he was doing, I'm sure, but I thought, "Wow! That was really cool! Dick Cavett!"

One thing that really hit home was when I was going back to the airport from a conference where Ross Perot had spoken—he was the head of EDS. A few of us from Software Arts shared a limousine with senior EDS people, and they knew about VisiCalc. This is EDS, which is the big mainframe company. They said, "Oh yeah, we did some deal, and we used VisiCalc to do all the calculations for the deal." Now, here's EDS, that has infinite computing power available, with any software of the big financial forecasting systems, and all that, and they're using VisiCalc to price multi-million-dollar deals! I found out that investment bankers who were doing real deals were using it. When the people you looked up to as the pros have switched to your stuff, that meant something.

And the other was when I heard from Don Estridge, who was the head of the IBM PC project. Don had told me that, when he was about to demonstrate VisiCalc to one of the real senior people, the executive said, "No, I know how to do it. Hold on. Let me do it." And I think he was demoing on an Apple II. "Whoa!" Then you realize that you did make a mark, and people did get it.

Livingston: VisiCorp and Software Arts had some legal disputes. Is there anything important that you learned from that?

Bricklin: Stay out of lawsuits if you can help it. It's bad for both sides, especially small businesses. That's lawyers' business, to them, solving things through lawsuits. But it's very, very expensive. It's a sport of kings, and it uses up a lot of time. Unless you're a very big business that can make it a very small part of what you do, it's much better to find other ways to solve things. Frequently, individuals can do it better face to face. People who are the heads of companies understand that.

The boards involved there let it happen, and they shouldn't have, since it ended up being bad for both companies.

Livingston: And it distracted you.

Bricklin: Distracted? It killed us.

We had just finished negotiating a deal to sell our company, for cash—a lot of cash—to a major company. It would have changed the whole industry. We had been approached by H&R Block to buy our company for, I think, $50 million in cash, plus stock. It was based on the numbers we had. It was kind of bogus, but whatever. They had a division called CompuServe, and we were going to be bought by CompuServe. We had board approval from both sides. We got sued a day or two before the deal was consummated. This was not very good. I was used to bad things happening at the last moment.

If that had happened, we would have ended up with all the stuff we were doing over at CompuServe. The world would have been quite different. One of the pioneers of the Internet, David Reed, worked for us. He would have worked at CompuServe instead of at Lotus, because it ended up, when things went down, Lotus bought us out. Thank you very much, Lotus! It was the right thing for them to do, business-wise. But also it was the right thing for them to do, and Mitch [Kapor] was very good about that, to save us from bankruptcy. It was just a few million bucks to take us out of our misery, to pay off our loans.

But we weren't able to run the business. It killed the deal; we weren't able to sell the business while we were in a lawsuit. VisiCorp was in bad shape. Their legal fees were running about the losses they had every month. It killed VisiCalc—well, VisiCalc was being killed by 1-2-3 anyway. They thought the new product, VisiOn, would have saved the day, but new products don't do very well right away, often. It was a precursor to Windows in the days when the PCs weren't powerful enough to do it. So for all of its advancing the art of things and cool stuff they did, it wasn't its time, and they ended up selling it off to make some money, and they ended up going belly up. It was bad all around.

What I do realize is there are advantages to selling at a peak. You don't know when the peak is. I know people who sold their businesses when everybody thought you were crazy. "The business is going through the roof; why are you selling now?" And in hindsight, of course, it turned around. Six months, a year later, the business started crashing. They didn't get the peak, but they came pretty close.

There are some people to whom it's worth taking the risk, because you risk going for the big one, and, in a portfolio, that's good. But as they say on Wall Street, the bulls make money, the bears make money, but the pigs get slaughtered. In other words, don't be greedy. Whether you think things are going up or things are going down, you can make money going both ways. But, if you are piggish, are greedy, that's when you have problems; you'll be irrational about that.

It is worth it sometimes, if you can do it, to reach for the stars. Microsoft didn't reach for the stars. Microsoft was step by step by step to where they got, and it was profitable all the way to it. So that's the traditional way of doing it. The Google, Netscape way, those things, sometimes it works, and sometimes— usually—it doesn't. But sometimes it does, and the payoffs are incredible. But, if you're a business person who wants your business to succeed, as a business, because you like that business, you take a different view. So the risk profiles are different.

A lot of people make money because they're very good at timing. We were close. If we hadn't been sued, I would have done pretty well financially, because Bob and I owned most of the company at the time. And we would have had an interesting next step, going into what was probably the leading online business at the time. Maybe it would have ended up into the Internet or something, or it would have made the jump better. Who knows? But it didn't happen.

Livingston: Do you have any regrets? That one was out of your hands.

Bricklin: Yeah, it was out of our hands. If we had been able to settle in advance, the thing would have closed, and we would have made a lot of money, and we'd have a bigger house, and whatever. But, you know, as I always tell people, here it is, 25 years later, and you're still interviewing me. There's fame and fortune. I didn't get much fortune out of it, but, on the other hand, the fame has basically given me a meal ticket ever since, and I learned a lot from it, and the rest of my life has been pretty good. All in all, I can't complain. I did a lot better than I ever expected to, in all sorts of ways. So there are no regrets about that. I mean, each thing, you think, "Well, if I had put this feature in, it would have been better."

Livingston: Do you remember any disagreements that you and Bob had?

Bricklin: Oh, we had lots of disagreements, all the time. People always thought the company was going to die, because we'd yell at each other on all sorts of issues. It was usually over technical stuff. Bob's much more aggressive in many ways than I am, and I'm much more conservative. So we're very complementary. While I'm disorganized, he's more disorganized, in certain things, so he depends on me for the drive to get things to completion. On the other hand, I depend on him for some of the reaching for the stars.

So we were very complementary, but that's tough. It's like having old married couples who spat all the time, always yelling at each other. It wasn't as bad as some businesses, where it actually is a married couple. But our friendship has continued to this day. As people know, in the business—like Bill Gates is known for this, about being really tough in meetings, and arguing and stuff like that—that's just a way of testing your own understanding of things. By arguing with others about it, that's how you learn. And, if somebody can't take the arguing with it, then maybe they don't really believe in what they're talking about and they don't understand it well enough.

We'd argue and then we'd go out to lunch together, because it wasn't based on animosity. We had enough problems with people outside.

Livingston: Do you remember a time someone tried to take advantage of you or cheat you?

Bricklin: We needed to move, so we bought a building and rehabbed it, because it was not in the best of shape. It was an old factory, and we turned it into programmer heaven. It turned out that we spent too much time on that, and we should have spent more time on the product. So stick to the knitting, and focus. But, we did really well by that, and, basically, the only money I got—other than my salary—out of Software Arts was the money I made on selling the building.

When we got the building, we got a loan to pay for it. We had a bank we'd been working with for years at the time, and we told them we wanted to do a loan, but we wanted no personal guarantees. When you have personal guarantees, they'll take your house. So, we wanted no personal guarantees. And the bank said, "Sure." We came down to the last closing papers, and we looked at the papers, and what does it say? Personal guarantees! They said, "Oh well, that's standard. We always do that." We got another bank, and sure enough as they were about to close, in came the personal guarantees. It wasn't until the third bank—we finally got one—that we did it with no personal guarantees.

Livingston: How did Lotus end up buying you?

Bricklin: At the last minute, when the company was about to go under, we found some people who were willing to buy the company, but they wanted me to spend a year working for them, and I was not happy about this at all. I ran into Mitch Kapor on an airplane, and we talked. That's Monday. Friday night, Lotus bought our company—they bought the assets of the company. So finally we sold the company, and I'm out, with no strings attached. That was great. And then we have to finally sell off all our stuff, because they did an asset deal. So people had to stay on to close down the company and all the liabilities for a year or two; it was a mess.

All those things happen, all the time—the wonderful ups and horrible downs, but that's what business is all about. And it's very personal. There are a lot of personal things. It's running into people. And how did I know that I should talk to Mitch? Well, our insurance agent was also his business insurance agent, and he talked to Mitch. So I knew that Mitch knew what was happening with our business. He knew our business was in rotten shape, because we had to work out all this stuff about insurance and getting the right things done and what we were going to do in case we were going to declare bankruptcy, because we came within days, within minutes, of declaring bankruptcy at one point. And so we had to work closely with him. But, he also worked closely with Lotus. So he was able to tell me, "Look, why don't you talk to Mitch? He's a good guy. He'll help."

I had known Mitch from the Apple II days and all those other things. And we were like sister companies until they competed with us, and even then. And a lot of our people were at Lotus, so I liked a lot of the people there. So when I ran into Mitch, I was willing to actually tell him how bad things were.

Even though it seems like it's big business and impersonal, and "they" take care of it, it really isn't. There is no "they." It always comes down to an "I" of somebody, and in many cases, it's a principal.

Bob Frankston (standing) and Dan Bricklin, circa 1982

Mitchell Kapor
Cofounder, Lotus Development

Mitch Kapor founded Lotus Development with Jonathan Sachs in 1982. Their spreadsheet software, Lotus 1-2-3, quickly surpassed VisiCalc to become the new industry standard.

VisiCalc had been the original "killer app" for personal computers. Kapor was a VisiCalc product manager at Personal Software when he wrote VisiPlot and VisiTrend, companion products to VisiCalc. He left to found Lotus just as legal conflicts were distracting VisiCalc's developers, and the arrival of the IBM PC opened a window of opportunity for a better spreadsheet. Lotus 1-2-3 could handle larger spreadsheets and added integrated charting, plotting, and database capabilities. It became the killer app killer.

Lotus went public in 1983. Kapor served as president and CEO from 1982 to 1986, and as a director until 1987. IBM acquired Lotus in 1995 for $3.5 billion.

Kapor cofounded the Electronic Frontier Foundation (EFF) in 1990 and now leads the Open Source Applications Foundation, a nonprofit that promotes the development and adoption of open source software.

Livingston: How did Lotus get started?

Kapor: I bought an Apple II in the summer of 1978 because I had become obsessed with personal computers and just had to have one. I didn't know what I wanted to do. I very quickly and fortunately started generating some consulting income, writing programs for individuals who had bought them, like an ophthalmologist who wanted to use it in his practice and an investment analyst who wanted to look at stock market data. And I met other people in those days that had Apple IIs, because it was very much a hobby phenomenon. Several of us started an Apple II user group called New England Apple Tree.

One of those people was Eric Rosenfeld, who was a graduate student in finance at MIT. As a favor to him, and because it was kind of a challenge, I helped write a statistics routine that ran on the Apple II that he could use to analyze data in his dissertation. It took me a weekend. He actually had to explain the math to me; once he explained it, I understood the math. Afterwards, we kind of realized, hey, this might actually be useful to other people if we built a statistics and graphics product on the Apple II. It was called Tiny Troll after something called TROLL, which was a time-sharing thing at MIT.

At the same time, Dan Bricklin and Bob Frankston were developing VisiCalc, also in Cambridge, and when it came out, it set the world on its ear. It was far and away the most useful piece of software ever done for a personal computer. It was incredibly innovative. It started generating sales of Apple IIs, and it was a cut above everything else.

The authors of VisiCalc were Software Arts. The publishers were Personal Software, which then changed its name to VisiCorp somewhere along the way. I knew the VisiCalc authors because they came to the meetings of the Apple II user group that I had cofounded, and that's where I first saw VisiCalc in probably 1979.

They introduced their publisher to me—this is Dan Fylstra and Peter Jennings—and they said, "We would like you to take Tiny Troll and rewrite it and clean it up so that we can bring it out as a companion product to VisiCalc." They wanted to have more offerings since they had such a hot product. And I agreed to do that. I still had a partner, but I think he was probably beginning to teach at Harvard—anyway, he was otherwise engaged. I was at business school; I decided, when this happened in November 1979, that I needed to learn about business because that's where the market was going to be.

I thought I was just going to clean up this little product over Christmas break so I could finish my education. I would make some money and that would be that. And I only thought that because I was totally ignorant about how long things took. I had no background in computer science. I was self-taught—I was still writing in Basic. I had no management experience; I was in business school at the time. In fact, I had spent my years after college as a radio disk jockey on a progressive rock station. I was a transcendental meditation teacher, and a mental health counselor at a psychiatric unit of a community hospital. That was OK, because there wasn't really a personal computer software industry. It was still kind of a hobby thing becoming a business, and nobody really took this stuff seriously, so I wasn't ludicrously unqualified by the standards of the day.

But I was wrong about how long it was going to take to do this thing. I was inspired to want to do a really great job by VisiCalc, which was so much better than anything I could ever write. But I said, "I want to try to do something that could stand up well." And I faced a difficult decision because school was starting again. I took a leave of absence from school to finish the product.

It then came to be the spring of 1980, and I thought I was done, and I wasn't done. I didn't know what *done* was with software. I had, roughly speaking, an alpha version of the product—it had some demonstrable features. I decided that I needed to totally rewrite Tiny Troll to be much better, and give it a totally new user interface, and so on. Based on that misunderstanding of what done was, I said to the publisher, "What I want to do is to come out to California"—which was where they were—"and you should hire me to be your new product manager. I can finish this thing in my spare time. It's almost done."

Now why did I want to go out there and be the product manager for the publisher? There were a couple of reasons. The main one was that I had come to understand that the big economic opportunity was to get stock in a startup, and this was a way of doing it. I had a royalty contract—like a book contract—and they said "fine." So I moved out to California without my program having been completed.

So now I had gone from writing and rewriting Tiny Troll, which eventually was called VisiPlot, to being product manager for several versions of VisiCalc—not the flagship Apple II version, but the other versions. I worked for the publisher, for Personal Software, with the Software Arts people. And a number of things transpired. I was in California for 6 months and had no time to work on getting my own products finished. But I found it incredibly fascinating to be in Silicon Valley and learned a lot.

Personal Software had brought in venture capital just before I arrived, and while I was there they brought in more management. The VCs brought in more senior management from places like Intel, and I was moved aside. I could see that my power and my access were being marginalized, which I didn't like, and I didn't feel that the business was being conducted with the degree of integrity that met my standards. And we had actually never consummated this swapping royalties for stock. So I said, "You know what, I'm going to go finish the product that I promised you. Let's unwind this." And I moved back to Boston and then I finally finished the product. It took another 6 months.

They brought it out in the early part of 1981. And it started generating a huge amount in royalties right away—a huge amount relative to what it was. It generated about $100K a month in royalties, but I had essentially no expenses, so that's a lot of money.

Now, all of a sudden, I had options about what to do next. In the course of developing VisiPlot, I had come to certain conclusions. And there was one other factor: somewhere while all this was happening, I had worked in assisting the VisiCalc guys in devising a way to exchange data between VisiCalc and VisiPlot. That was important because it provided a way to actually make graphs out of spreadsheet data, which was an obvious piece of functionality.

Bob Frankston had developed something called the data interchange format, and VisiPlot was one of the first other software applications to support it. I'd worked with Bob on that—he played the lead role, far and away. But while there was a way of moving data between these two programs, it was really cumbersome. There were no hard drives in those days. Everything was on floppy disks, which had limited capacity. And furthermore, VisiCalc had a copy-protected floppy disk to prevent piracy. So if you wanted to make a graph, you had to boot up VisiCalc, you would make your spreadsheet, and then you would save a file in this special data interchange format to the second floppy drive—you had to have a second drive because you couldn't save it on the first drive. Then you had to quit out of VisiCalc completely and then start up VisiPlot and then read in the file and then you could see the graph. If you wanted to look at another graph and you hadn't saved the data, you had to repeat the whole process.

I could think of several ways to make this process less cumbersome, one of which would be to put both programs on a single disk. I raised the issue with the guys at Software Arts who did VisiCalc and they weren't interested in it at all. In fact, at various times I raised a number of ideas with the publisher about combining the programs and they weren't interested at all.

Why weren't they interested? The people who did VisiCalc had serious technical backgrounds and a bunch of computer science training. They knew what they were doing and they had the hot product. I had no credentials or background, at best sort of minor league success. So I don't think they really saw me as an equal. And the publisher was even worse in my view, in that they were firmly convinced, between the venture capitalists and the people they brought in, that they knew how to build this thing into a big business. And they saw me, when I was there as a product manager, as an annoyance—as a marginal person without experience or credentials who was kind of a pest. And I suppose I was kind of a pest.

So they had no interest in doing more stuff with me. They were trying to figure out how to technically get rid of me. And I took advantage of that fact. I didn't like it, but I took advantage of it. The royalty rate that VisiCalc was getting and that I was getting was very high. My royalty rate was 33 percent of their gross margin. And VisiCalc's was higher—they got 35.7 percent. At the time the contracts were done, the economics of the business, which was a new business of packaged software for PCs, was not well enough understood to know that that was obviously an insupportable thing to do. But it quickly became apparent, because huge sums were flowing back to the authors, but the publisher was the one that was incurring very significant expenses for support—which was their responsibility—and all the marketing and sales expenses. Anyone who is familiar with the business understands that royalty rates adjusted downward pretty quickly.

So here's the way the world looked to me at the time: I have a hit product—not a number one product, but it's making money. And it has an insupportably high royalty rate. I no longer work for the publisher, but I know how they think and I'm uncomfortable with them. And I know they don't want to work with me. So I felt what I should do is to have them buy me out. They would get control of the code, close out the royalty stream, and I would go do whatever I was going to go do next. I saw that was in everybody's interest. And that's in fact what happened. They bought us out for $1,200,000, so I made a whole bunch of money. I had never made more than $14,000 a year—I told you what kinds of jobs I had. We had taxes to pay and I had a partner to take care of, but I wound up with $600,000, which I divided into two piles. (I'll talk about that in a minute.)

The non-compete was the hinge issue. I'd been thinking about what I wanted to do next and in fact had hired Jonathan Sachs, who was the person who architected and implemented the original version of 1-2-3. We had the basic concept in mind, which was an integrated spreadsheet and graphing program with other stuff. They bought me out 6 months after we started, which was in November '81, and Sachs had started in the summer of '81. We didn't have any code. We were considering a bunch of different ideas. It was still very, very early, but I knew I wanted the ability to go do this thing.

I also knew the publisher wasn't going to do the buyout if they didn't have a really strong non-compete. But remember, I had done a graphics and statistics program, not a spreadsheet, and I proposed that they carve out an exception in the buyout to do this integrated graphing calculator program, betting that they would be sufficiently motivated to get the deal done that they would look at this thing and go, "This is a very big ambitious thing. We don't really think he has the ability to pull this off. This gets us what we need, and for the sake of getting the deal done, we'll sign off on it." So basically, I told them what I was going to do, taking advantage of the fact that I didn't think they would take me seriously, because I know they didn't take me seriously. And that's what actually happened.

It just goes to show you shouldn't underestimate people. You shouldn't judge from appearances like that.

Livingston: So now that you were free and clear, what were the first things that you did?

Kapor: Jon had implemented spreadsheets previously; he was one of the few people. And that's how I knew him. But he had made the mistake of being in a business with technical people and no business people. He had been at Data General, and the first spreadsheet that they implemented was for the Data General minicomputer. Well, there was no market for that.

And then Sachs and his partner were sort of going, "What do we do now? This didn't work." I forget how I ran into Sachs, but I convinced him to come workor my fledgling little thing. Remember, I had the royalties. He had some ideas; I had some ideas; we succeeded in spite of ourselves.

I was so convinced that VisiCalc had a lock on the market that I had to convince myself that we were going to do something that wasn't fundamentally a spreadsheet. Of course, what we did was fundamentally a spreadsheet, but the self-deception I engaged in wasn't sufficiently damaging to be fatal. But there was a big push to call it integrated software, to add other capabilities, to wrap other things in it.

The galvanizing event was when IBM announced the IBM PC in August 1981. It was very important in the history of PCs because it legitimized the whole field—because of IBM's imprimatur. Until then, the personal computer hardware companies were Apple, Tandy, and Commodore. IBM was the first "real" computer company to come out with a PC, legitimizing it for the business marketplace. And that was not lost on me.

So we decided to bet on doing something for the IBM PC, which proved to be one of the reasons why we were successful. They had decided to outsource a lot of the key elements of what they were doing, right to the distribution. Rather than selling it just through their own sales force, they were selling it through retail stores like Computer-Land and Sears, which at the time was a very radical idea. They had gone to Intel for the microprocessor; they had gone to Microsoft for the principal operating system. And I said, "They're smart. They realize they don't understand this business, so they'll go to the best people. They're not going to have a lot of ego, and this is the way things are going to work." Also, they had put a 16-bit chip in the machine with greater memory capacity. And memory capacity was an enormous issue.

The Apple II had 64K—not megabytes, kilobytes—of memory. It was tiny. And not all of that was available. Actually, if you wrote programs on the Apple II, you started with a 48K memory space. So the programs were tiny and the user data was tiny and people were building spreadsheets that exceeded memory. It was a fundamental limit of the Apple II, because it was an 8-bit microprocessor. IBM used a 16-bit microprocessor and I said, "Ah, this will permit people to build bigger spreadsheets." The memory space of the IBM PC when it came out was 640K, 10 times the size. So I said, "16-bit, faster processor, more memory says IBM. We should target it. We should build a product that is optimized for it."

Now, the IBM PC came out day one, August '81, with a version of VisiCalc, and with a version of MultiPlan, which was Microsoft's spreadsheet, but neither of them took advantage of the full capabilities of the IBM PC. In particular, because they had been put under a lot of pressure to get a product out, they had taken the code for the 8080/Z80 Intel/Zilog processors—8-bit code—and tweaked it a little bit. The point is that VisiCalc on an IBM PC still ran in 64K of memory. You had 640K available, but you couldn't address it in a spreadsheet, so it was as if it wasn't there. And I said, "This is really an opportunity here."

Plus another factor: because I knew all of the individuals, I knew that Software Arts and Personal Software were fighting with each other over the royalty rate. And I knew that they were essentially distracted and they were not working together, and I knew that Personal Software was hiring its own developers. I felt guilt-ridden about coming out with a product that was going to be competitive with VisiCalc, so I did my best to pretend to myself that it wasn't going to be competitive. I ultimately said to myself that the fact of the matter is that I didn't create this opportunity, they did. If they had been on the job, I would have gone and done something else because the opportunity wouldn't have been there. But I saw a gap in the marketplace and I said, "We should do something that lets you do bigger spreadsheets, that's faster, that takes full advantage of the IBM PC, that integrates the graphing, so you could hit one button to get a graph"—because I knew people wanted that—"and have a better user interface for non-expert users"—which we did—"and allow user customization and user programming"—which we did in the macro language. So there was a set of ideas that gave 1-2-3 its character, that really made it a second-generation product, that had sufficient differentiation that was immediately visible when you demoed it, and that was what gave it its market entrée.

Being at the right place at the right time also helped. The business world was poised to adopt personal computers. They were reasonably priced and they did something useful, which turned out to be Lotus 1-2-3. So the market just expanded dramatically, far faster than anything any of us in the company would have imagined.

Livingston: When you demoed it, were there parts where you knew people were going to go "wow"?

Kapor: Yes, I think the one-button graphing in particular, and the speed of the calculation. VisiCalc users *loved* VisiCalc; they just wanted it to do more. And it didn't. And when we showed that this did it right out of the box, they went, "I get it." I used to get applause doing demos all the time.

This was all so new then, in a way that was recapitulated in the early days of Netscape, the first time people saw a web browser, web content; the first time people looked at Amazon. So we had our version of that in the '80s.

Livingston: I read you spent 10 months programming it. Did you program it?

Kapor: No, Sachs did. He wrote virtually all of the code of the original version. We came out with it in January '83. He started working on that code base probably in October of '81, so that would be 14 to 15 months. All written in assembly language, for speed. This was the fifth time he'd implemented a spreadsheet, so he was pretty good at it at this point.

Livingston: Wasn't VisiCalc written in assembly language too? Why was Lotus faster?

Kapor: Because they were writing for an 8-bit machine, and they didn't take advantage of the 16-bit architecture in a whole variety of different respects. We just had more optimized code. And we had a different recalculation algorithm. We were the first spreadsheet to do something called "natural order of recalculation." If your spreadsheet had forward references in it, VisiCalc would take multiple passes over the whole thing to calculate stuff, but we did one pass through the entire formula chain, and as long as there weren't circular references, it would calculate properly. So it was much faster for certain cases.

Livingston: Was the code tuned to the IBM machine?

Kapor: It was tuned to the Intel 808X 16-bit architecture. And Sachs was also very, very good. He was just an artist at high performance with limited resources. I didn't know how good he was; I got lucky. I knew he was good, but he was a genius at this sort of stuff. The two of us together was essentially 1 + 1 = 3, because I had a vision about the product and very strong ideas about the feature set and the user interface, and he was generally willing to let me drive things at that level. He had the responsibility for the technical architecture and implementation, but I'm actually quite technical, so I was able to talk with him to fully understand a number of the issues and limitations and modify the design in a way that was consistent with what we could actually do. So we had a critical mass of knowledge between the two of us that neither of us had alone.

Livingston: What went wrong?

Kapor: A number of things went wrong or almost went wrong. I almost ran out of money. Lotus 1-2-3 wasn't the only idea that we had. I had done this thing with some other people called Executive Briefing System for the Apple II that was like a precursor to PowerPoint. We did some other projects; I had hired another group of people and basically had spent down the $300,000 that I'd allocated. It was almost gone and we were nowhere near product, because of doing all these other things and not having done this before.

I had $600,000 after taxes and paying my partner, and I divided it into two piles. I took half and said I'm going to buy a house. It was $89,000, the least expensive house in Cambridge—this was in 1981. I said that I could live on $40,000 for at least 5 years. So I had the other $300,000 that was my own seed money, but I almost ran out.

I got lucky in that Ben Rosen at Sevin Rosen decided to invest. He was the only VC that I pitched (I didn't understand anything about venture capital). And that was fortunate, because without him, I don't know what we would have done.

Most of my mistakes came after we launched the product, not before—after we started shipping in January of '83. I had no significant experience in building an organization or building a management team. And I intuitively did well when I was leading the whole team, but once we got past 25 people, you can't do that. And so I made a series of classic mistakes in hiring. And not building a good middle management structure. And not recruiting a board that could help me build the company. Big mistakes in picking a successor, big mistakes in having an undisciplined product strategy—I was much more interested in having distinctive, innovative products and thinking about what would make sense for a product line for our business overall—and big mistakes in expanding too fast and not having discipline about what we were doing. So I give myself a C or C– on all that stuff.

Livingston: You guys grew to 1,000 employees before you went public. Did you know you were going to go public when you started?

Kapor: I didn't know when, but this was what I'd learned from my time in Silicon Valley. To be honest, here's what I was driven by: I wanted to do really a great product. Almost from day one I understood that I was passionate about the applications themselves, that they'd be integrated, easier to use and be powerful. They'd help make people more productive and I cared a lot about that. The other thing I wanted was financial independence. I had an enormous desire not to be dependent on other people, or to have to have a job. I wanted to dictate the terms. So I knew if you had an IPO, then you had a liquid currency and you had the ability to cash in and get that.

So I actually pushed for an early IPO, which we did successfully. But that brought all the usual problems. The main problem we had as a very young public company was that people did not understand the industry or its dynamics and therefore they consistently misvalued the stock and misunderstood what it was about. Because it was new and it was different. Eventually, people figured it out, but I was very impatient.

I did not set out to build a big company. I actually wanted to be a software designer. I saw having a company not exactly as being a necessary evil, but there wasn't a good alternative. My experience had convinced me that being a program author and having somebody else publish it wouldn't give me enough control over the process. In Hollywood, the very successful directors like Steven Spielberg quickly understood that they also needed to be producers and have their own studio in order to retain control. It was a similar thing.

There were some other funny things about it. In the '60s, when I came of age, business was not a cool thing. We were all counterculture people with long hair and sex, drugs, and rock 'n' roll. It was the '60s; I have the pictures to prove it. I don't remember any of it, but as someone said, if you can remember the '60s, then you weren't there. But it turned out I also have some entrepreneurial talent. It's not surprising—my father was a small businessman, my grandfather was a small businessman, it kind of runs in the family. But I think I had cultural biases against seeing it or valuing it that took a while to get over. So while Lotus was getting started, I just saw it as a vehicle to doing great product. I never wanted to have a big company.

Livingston: The word "creative" comes up a lot when you do a search for Lotus. Did you make a conscious effort to have a creative atmosphere at the time when programmers were considered dull and nerdy?

Kapor: Yeah. I was interested in really cool products, so I guess that's where that came in. I had a very unconventional background and really no interest in building a button-down business culture. And I'm not an engineering geek, either. These types of companies tend to reflect the personalities and interests of their founders. Microsoft is very much cast in Bill Gates's image; and Apple, Steve Jobs; Borland, Philippe Kahn. And so we tended to have more creativity and innovation.

The other thing that I cared about a lot right from the very beginning was creating a workplace that treated people well. At Software Arts, they felt I had attitude problems. I didn't respect authority. I basically thought, "The people that are running this are stupid and they don't listen to me and I don't like being here, being told what to do." It was a mixture of keen insight and adolescent emotions that I carried for a very long time. So when I unexpectedly found myself running this high-growth successful software company, the thought of making it be the kind of place that I would want to work at and different from all those other places was incredibly appealing.

There were some other key people there who shared that feeling and I think I probably hired them. And so we did all sorts of very progressive things with the corporate culture. We invested in the human resources function extensively. We surveyed all the employees annually on quality of work-life issues, and took what we heard very seriously. We had a corporate values statement that wasn't just on a piece of paper. We actually at one point tied a portion of the managers' bonuses to how well their direct reports viewed them exemplifying the corporate values. I made every single manager get on the support lines and listen to customers, no matter what function they were in.

When I was running Lotus, we never had a single employment discrimination lawsuit; we had a whole bunch of different alternative dispute resolution conflict management approaches, through the employee relations function. And then we had a diversity committee that had out gays and lesbians on it—this was in 1984. We were the first corporate sponsor of an AIDS walk. We had a corporate philanthropy committee in which the employees actually made decisions about where the money went, not the pet projects of senior management. So for many people what was memorable and important about Lotus was that it was the best place they ever worked.

The other thing to say is that because I lost control of the company—I felt overwhelmed by what I had created, did not know how to step up to it, put enough brakes on, hire the right people and be collaborative—I wound up jumping ship and leaving pretty early, in 1987. And my successor, a very poor choice on my part, did not share the same vision or values and he wound up disassembling most of what we put in place. So it was a bittersweet sort of thing. It was ultimately not sustained. Learn from that, too.

Livingston: Can you remember anything else that surprised you?

Kapor: Oh, almost everything. I didn't expect to find myself in this situation. I really didn't. Being successful surprised me enormously, shocked me, especially the magnitude of it. VisiPlot was a success and I had made some money, but I didn't understand how big the industry was going to get; how big we were going to get.

Our original business plan called for $3 to $4 million in sales. Ultimately, in 1983 it was $53 million. So it was a 1,700 percent forecasting error. And then it tripled the next year to $150 million. I was totally unprepared for the magnitude of the success and the rate of growth. It would have been psychotic to say it was going to get that big that fast. Or you'd have to be prescient, but I'm not.

So mainly what I was thinking in those days was "We'd better make sure that we don't blow it, having gotten here." And worrying that it could all fall apart as quickly as it came about. So I was terrified! Inwardly. And excited. And unprepared. I became a minor league celebrity in Boston, being recognized in restaurants, and that was weird. And people started to act differently around me, because when people are seen as having power or they're seen as having some special resources, people get weird because they project their fantasies onto the person or they start telling you what they think you want to hear. If you watch people around Sergey Brin and Larry Page from Google, it's very amusing, but, to be the recipient of that . . . I wasn't particularly prepared for, nor did I want most of that. I mean, I liked attention, but it's a lot to get used to and a lot of it made me profoundly uncomfortable.

And there was a series of values challenges that came up with running a business that I was unprepared for that were very painful.

Livingston: Can you describe one?

Kapor: Lotus as a company wound up suing some other companies that were copying our look and feel. Now, that was not done on my watch. I was transitioning out. But I was actually still on the board at the point when we voted to bring the first two suits, and I voted in favor of the suit out of company loyalty—a decision that I regretted the next day and have regretted since then, because I felt that it was an inappropriate use of copyright law to try to prevent someone from making a product that looks and works the same if they develop it independently.

I was really torn about how to handle this, and all my net worth was tied up in Lotus, so it was kind of a mess. There was too much, too soon, and not a lot of time to grow up in and not a lot of mentoring. There weren't elders or people to learn from who had been through it whose values I shared.

Livingston: Who were your mentors?

Kapor: Ben Rosen for a while in some respects, but then he made his money, cashed out, stepped off the board and went on to other things. And plus, he was not a business guy, he was an investment analyst. So there were some people that were somewhat helpful, but nothing like what I would have liked or what exists today.

I try to give back now and help other people try to sort through stuff. I'm also much clearer about my values, and have been for quite a while now. I think business at all costs is just wrong. I think there are certain things that you just don't do, and that acting with integrity and decency in business to me is just a given. I simply don't compromise on those things. When a person has those types of values, you have to be careful what type of project you undertake, because as soon as you undertake a project and you have those values, you're just going to be so conflicted you won't know what to do.

Livingston: What advice do you give to people who want to start startups?

Kapor: It depends on what type of advice they want. You can't tell people what they don't want to hear because they won't care and it's just a waste of breath. And everyone comes in with some kind of agenda.

I like working with entrepreneurs who have a compatible set of values and are inspired by a vision and are passionate about some piece of disruptive technology—who are going to create something that actually has value for people in a way that can be a game changer. That's sort of my sweet spot. But every project is different, so the specific advice needs to be customized.

The most important thing for me is, I don't want to work with someone who says, "Just help me make the business be more successful." I want to work with entrepreneurs who are personally passionate, committed, and believe in what they're doing. Not all entrepreneurs are like that. Some people may be just as happy selling canned tuna—"Just show me an opportunity where I can make money and I'm going to go do that." You think Mark Cuban really cared about what they were doing at Broadcast.com? This is not to criticize him as a businessman—I'm just observing—but I don't think he had a fundamental passion about that business. There was an opportunity, he saw it, he built something, he sold, and he cashed out at the right time.

Livingston: When you were developing Lotus 1-2-3, you always had working code. Wasn't that type of incremental development very much ahead of its time?

Kapor: Yes. I think Sachs and I saw it the same way. We figured out a number of things very early on that became conventional wisdom. I'm not sure that we were that much smarter than anyone else. But we had the requisite smarts and we were in the right place at the right time. So this developing close to the target machine and having code running, it seemed obvious once you looked at it that there were enormous benefits to it. The reason it wasn't obvious is that the machines were barely powerful enough to do development on.

Typically, the systems you develop on could usefully consume a lot more computational power than what you might actually need in the delivery platform, and so that's the argument for doing the development not on the target platform. But there were corresponding disadvantages because it tended to produce bloated—not optimized—code if you're using a cross-compiler or cross-assembler. And optimization of limited resources was the name of the game when you were talking about a 64K machine. So what worked in the minicomputer world—the techniques and best practices—just didn't work for microcomputers. I shouldn't say that, because Sachs did come from the minicomputer world, so that's not right. But a lot of the conventional wisdom was just wrong and that's what saddled a lot of people. They just didn't think things through from first principles.

And always having something running was a Sachs thing, because it was just his experience it was a good thing, and I saw it and said, "Yes indeedy, we should do this," long before extreme programming.

Livingston: Was there ever a point when you wanted to quit?

Kapor: After we shipped and the business felt like it was getting out of control, yes. The most fun parts were from time-equals-zero till 1984. I was terrified about stuff—how's this going to come out, what's going to happen?

I did almost walk out. We raised a second round of venture capital, which I think, if I had been more sophisticated about business, we wouldn't have needed to do. We could have just borrowed the money. We turned cash flow positive so quickly. If I had been a little bit less risk-averse . . . but that's another story.

We got to the closing for the second round and they had a very sharp lawyer on their side—our lawyer wasn't so good—and all these things were happening at the last minute, all these onerous terms, and I got up and said, "I'm not going to do this. I don't have to do this today. We don't have to close here and I'm just not going to agree to this. I'm gone." And they backed down completely on their onerous terms.

I was just pissed off about this for a long time. These were supposed to be our investors, they were supposed to be on the same side, but they were highly adversarial and totally willing to take advantage of us. And saw absolutely nothing wrong with that. I don't really like conflict, was a conflict avoider; it takes a lot for me to get up. And I really was going to get up and go home and we really weren't going to close.

Livingston: You weren't bluffing?

Kapor: No, I wasn't bluffing. I was prepared to take whatever—run out of money or find financing elsewhere. My attitude was: that's the wrong way to do business. I don't care that that's the way the world works, it's wrong. That is the way most of the business world works, but sometimes you just have to stand up and say, "Not on my watch, not here, not this way."

I think there were these minor problems—the Blue Sky clearances hadn't come in from some of the states—and they wanted me to personally take the liability. The investor didn't want to take any risk. It was absurd. They only do this because they can get away with it, because they have the money and you need it and "fuck you." (I hope that goes in the book.)

It's just wrong, but the fact is that when the VCs do their deals and they do the paperwork, they take advantage of entrepreneurs who haven't been through this before. They do things on terms that favor them in a way that really can't be justified—that take advantage of their ignorance. It's not a good way to do business. Some of the VCs try to rationalize it, "This is just the way things are done." Well, I'm sorry but they're wrong. Why do you think venture capital also enjoys a reputation as "vulture capital?" It's not an accident; it doesn't have to be that way.

Livingston: Did you try to change this when you joined Accel Partners?

Kapor: Yeah. And I think that a more nuanced version of what I was just saying would be that there are contradictions inherent in the venture capital business because there are significant aspects of what VCs do, including Accel, that are collaborative with entrepreneurs, and there are other aspects that are not. I thought that Accel was more different than I ultimately concluded they were. But I don't think that they were worse than everyone else. There are norms and practices that cut across individual firms that are really problematic. So I tell people, "Know what you're getting in for. Here's the way it works."

If the VCs were more transparent and disclosed stuff so that entrepreneurs could make a choice, that would be better. They wouldn't have to change the terms, just disclose them and explain what they mean, and what's likely to happen. But they don't do that. They see it as a negotiation in which having information that the other side doesn't have gives you an advantage. It gives an advantage in terms of that individual negotiation, but if you're trying to form a genuine partnership where you have repeat encounters and you withhold critical information in the first and most important one, you're undermining long-term collaboration.

Why should they trust you? What they've demonstrated is that you are going to act in your own self-interest at my expense if you know better than me about something and you don't feel under any obligation to share that. That's actually not collaborative. But it's completely standard.

You know why VCs are like this? It's not that they are bad people; it's the limited partners. And who are the limited partners? Our great institutions—Harvard University, Stanford University, UC Berkeley. So if you want to point up the chain of accountability, when those people stop measuring performance just based on the return numbers, things could change, because they'll change the incentives.

Livingston: What would you tell an entrepreneur to understand before he/she meets with a VC?

Kapor: I try to explain how it works. There are more choices nowadays for people—angel money, for example. And many things are much less expensive to do now. You can go further on your credit card than you could before. I want entrepreneurs to make informed choices when it comes to financing. Understand what the impacts and implications are for different financing options.

Livingston: Plus, many people don't need to have as much money to get something started.

Kapor: You can also do some interesting things in a seed round of $100,000 to $200,000 and it's available on very different kinds of terms.

Livingston: Did you ever do anything to seem more impressive to investors?

Kapor: I'm pretty terrible at artifice; I don't play poker for that reason. But there's one thing I did. When we were raising money, I hadn't heard from the VCs (Ben Rosen and L.J. Sevin) for a long time, and I was worried. So I got a call from L.J. (he's from Texas)—"Mitch, I'm in town. Would y'all like to get together for dinner tonight?"

So I made a reservation at the fanciest French restaurant in Boston and raced home to change from my jeans to a suit, and we came to dinner. I ordered a very expensive bottle of wine, and I knew he was paying for it, so I was kind of stepping up here like, "This is serious, so I hope you're serious." I wasn't feeling like French restaurant, three-piece suit, expensive wine. And he's making small talk through the appetizer course. I was thinking to myself, "If he doesn't get to the point when they have the main course, I'm going to ask him, 'Are you doing this thing or not?'" Because I knew that we were out of money. And finally at the end of the appetizers—about 45 minutes, but it seemed like all night—he said, "Mitch, Ben and I would like to invest in your company. How much do y'all think it's worth?" And I dropped my fork, like a cartoon.

Livingston: How much did you tell him?

Kapor: I think I said probably $2 to $3 million. We had *nothing*. We had an early-stage under-development spreadsheet, and me and Jon Sachs. So that was the biggest number I felt I could ask for without being totally absurd.

Ray Ozzie

Founder, Iris Associates, Groove Networks

At the University of Illinois, Ray Ozzie worked on PLATO Notes, one of the earliest collaboration applications. Later he wanted to develop collaboration software of his own, but couldn't find funding. After he led the development of Lotus Symphony, Mitch Kapor and Jonathan Sachs decided to invest in Ozzie's idea, which would become Lotus Notes. Instead of working as an employee, Ozzie founded Iris Associates in 1984 to develop the product for Lotus. It was an unusual form of startup, but it worked.

Lotus Notes was the first widely used collaboration software. The first release shipped in 1989, and Iris was acquired by Lotus in 1994.

In 1997, Ozzie founded Groove Networks, which built Internet-based workgroup collaboration software. Microsoft acquired Groove in 2005 and named Ozzie chief technical officer. In June 2006, he took over as chief software architect from Bill Gates.

Livingston: When you started Groove, where were you and who was there? What was the first piece of code anyone wrote for Groove? What did it do?

Ozzie: When we first started Groove in the fall of '97, we worked out of my house. Initially, it was my brother Jack, Eric Patey, and Brian Lambert. A few weeks later, we moved to an office space at the Cummings Center in Beverly, Massachusetts. A couple months into the project, another former Iris engineer, Ken Moore, joined our team. The first thing we coded was a primitive version of our synchronization algorithm.

Livingston: How did you come up with your ideas?

Ozzie: The common theme to both Iris and Groove was the fact that the ideas were not based on technology, but on a need I saw for users or potential customers for the product. I'm an engineer by training and I tend to be one of these people who believes he can accomplish basically anything in software—it's just a big toolbox. So if you know that you can accomplish anything you set your mind to, what's worth accomplishing?

I've never taken the perspective of "build a cool piece of technology and see where it goes." It's more or less been based on an intuition about a hole in the market—or, more accurately, a future hole in the market. At any given time, you've got to have a technology roadmap in your mind and a market roadmap as to where things are headed—broadband is getting increasingly pervasive or wireless is getting increasingly pervasive, or something is going on—and trying to project out several years, because it will take you several years to build anything that's worth building. So you don't want to fill today's needs, but try to capture some window that will happen in the future.

In Notes, it was (and this is hard to imagine because it was a different time) the concept that we'd all be using computers on our desktops and therefore we might want to use them as communication tools. This was a time when PCs were just emerging as spreadsheet tools and word processing replacements, still available only on a subset of desks, and definitely no networks. It was '82 when I wrote the specs for it. It had been based on a system called PLATO that I'd been exposed to at college, which was a large-scale interactive system that people did learning and interactive gaming on, and things like that. It gave us a little bit of a peek at the future—what it would be like if we all had access to interactive systems and technology.

With Groove, it was an observation that the nature of work was changing. Technology at that point had largely been applied to helping people work together within corporate boundaries. People were increasingly going to be challenged trying to apply that same technology across boundaries, because you can't control the technology chosen by your business partners. I might choose Notes, you might choose Exchange, the other person might choose someone else.

We saw a lot of frustration when our customers tried to deploy systems across enterprises. So we came to the conclusion that what we really needed was to build a system that just worked instantly, right after download, for the end users.

Livingston: Were you trying to basically build a "better Lotus Notes" for the Web?

Ozzie: Lotus Notes ended up being a multifaceted piece of software; it had email, it was used for collaborative workspaces for people to do dynamic work together. It was used as a content management system, as an application server.

Groove was really meant to fulfill just the collaborative workspaces piece. We were laser-focused on the notion of people needing to dynamically assemble in a virtual environment, share documents and their thoughts in order to get work done very quickly, and then disassemble. In the work environment now, increasingly you have to work with partners or customers directly, and this concept of rapidly forming virtual workgroups would be an increasing challenge and opportunity moving forward. The Web itself on the open Internet is an alternative way of doing this, but we were really targeting people who needed to work in a highly mobile fashion, behind the firewall, outside the firewall, and in a secure manner. So we went for a desktop architecture.

Livingston: So this is a big problem that you were approaching. How did you start?

Ozzie: Before I start a company, I typically write a couple of founding documents. One of them is very outside-in: it's a scenario-based document, describing the high-level challenge that I'm trying to address and the end user scenarios that we are trying to solve. This attempts to explain what we're trying to accomplish to anyone who joins the company or we might need to get financing from.

Then I create a second, bottom-up document describing the different technologies that will have to be assembled to accomplish that vision.

The first thing we did in both Iris and Groove was get a big open office and recruit a core team of people. Generally these were people I'd worked with before, so I wouldn't have to get past the trust issue involved in understanding what they are good at and what they're not.

And we'd just sit down with the whiteboards and just try to work through some of the more difficult algorithms, make key tooling decisions. Early on in Groove, we had a very big decision to make: do we do it in C++ or do we do it in Java? These types of decisions are important because you can never go back on them once you've started down that path.

In Groove's case, there was a very risky piece of technology—a certain algorithm for synchronization that we didn't even know if we could do. And we didn't want to hire more people and really get going until we knew we could accomplish it. It took about 3 to 4 months before we were confident that we'd be able to actually build what we wanted to.

Architecturally, Groove was a real contrarian play at the time. This was in '97, an era where most people were saying, "Things will move from other architectures to the Web." We were basically saying, "The Web will hit its limits at some point for certain applications, and we want to go to a peer-to-peer architecture that would complement the Web, not replace it." For a certain class of applications it would be very effective. It's a masterless synchronization where people could do things like work independently on all these different peer nodes and the algorithms would get everyone in sync.

It can get very complex when you have a dozen people and they're in different subnets. Eventually these people come together and it's complicated to make sure all the changes get applied in a uniform fashion for everyone. So we worked through that on the whiteboard and then in a prototype. Once we were sure we could build it, we decided to hire the first 15 to 20 people and just embarked on the project.

Livingston: Masterless synchronization was a novel technology that you guys really had to work through?

Ozzie: It had been done for years in a variety of settings—especially in an academic setting. But the commercial PC environment is a very harsh one. People reboot PCs, they restore them from backups, they lose them. It has to be very resilient. We wanted to make sure the algorithms we were using would scale to what we needed.

All those early technology choices were like that. Initially we thought we'd be using Java, but we ended up not using it because we concluded that there would never be a stable runtime environment that we could count on on all desktop PCs. It didn't seem like Sun, with all due respect, really was on a path to having a stable client-side environment. And we needed the thing to work within several clicks on random PCs worldwide without anybody supporting them. So we ended up having to do a lot of extra work using C++.

Livingston: Was there an initial customer who was so happy with the product that you just knew Groove was going to fly?

Ozzie: We launched Groove in beta in October 2000, 3 years to the month when we first formed the company. We didn't ship the first commercially available version of Groove until April 2001. When we did, we announced a 10,000 seat deal with GlaxoSmithKline, the major pharmaceutical company. They are a big Notes customer, but saw the opportunity for Groove to address some of the cross-boundary collaboration needs they have in bringing new products to market. In hindsight, that initial sale may have hurt us more than it helped. We deluded ourselves into thinking we could sell Groove into enterprises like GlaxoSmithKline far more quickly and systematically than turned out to be the case. We really hadn't paid our dues yet in terms of making Groove "enterprise ready." We did that in subsequent releases of the product, but still struggled to develop a successful, repeatable sales model for the enterprise. It was extremely difficult to sell new technology like Groove into enterprises at a time when their sole focus was on reducing costs and increasing security.

Livingston: What else was hard in those 3 "stealth" years?

Ozzie: The thing that's not really characteristic, that doesn't really translate from both of my startups to what other entrepreneurs do, is that I think of the challenges I take on as 10-year challenges, not filling a quick market niche. There tends to be some time where I'm building up a level of technological advantage for when we get to market. With technology, there's no such thing as a sustainable advantage, but you can get a good running start if you concentrate on doing something hard really well.

In Notes, it was the database and replication environment and the security aspects. In Groove, it was the security aspects again and this transaction synchronization and the peer-to-peer XML-based communications. Most people find risk and uncertainty very daunting. In both Notes and Groove, there was both technological uncertainty and market uncertainty. We knew we were embarking on something that was technologically very difficult and would take several years. But you know that the market is going to change during those years, so virtually everything you do, you have to late-bind the decisions. You can't completely predetermine all the user interface or integration decisions.

You cannot early-bind marketing and positioning decisions because the market and competitive environment will be different.

Some people cope with uncertainty by being really comfortable in their own little box. Some developers, for example, will divide the problem and divide the problem until they only have to work on this little piece of the database or this little piece of the communications, and they just don't worry about the stuff above that. They leave that to people like me to deal with, in terms of the risk and continuing to be on the right path. To be on that long of a time frame, you have to be able to change as the market changes.

So there were a number of things over the course of the years at Groove that changed dramatically. At one point early on, we were giving an equal focus to the media/entertainment and productivity applications of our technology. When we started Groove in '97, it was the Bubble, and because you can apply technology in many ways, we thought that we'd bring it to market to serve a number of different things. By the time we brought it to market in late 2000, things were starting to get a little serious, and we decided to concentrate on the productivity realm instead of consumer applications.

Then once we really doubled down that path, it meant that we had to take a lot more enterprise manageability things seriously than we had early on, which brought with it a lot of burden and a lot of changes within the company.

Livingston: If you do have this long time frame, are you extra nervous about competitors? And do you have to manage people's expectations differently?

Ozzie: In a startup, you're on this mission together. Everyone has to feel that, and you have to hire people who are willing to believe in something they are trying to accomplish. And in that era, it was very challenging in two dimensions. Hiring in the dot-com era, when a lot of these people's friends were getting rich, was hard. But the other thing was that the type of software we were building had many systems software elements to it. A lot of it was lower-level communications, storage, application framework–type code, and hiring was more difficult for that type of talent at that time. In an earlier era when DEC was big, it was easier to hire systems software talent.

But what held people together was the belief that you're really going to change the world. I think that's the nature of many startups. You believe that what you are doing is going to have a dramatic impact. You might not exactly know how, but you really have a belief. That keeps you going and going through many changes and a lot of uncertainty.

Livingston: What about managing your investors' expectations?

Ozzie: That's a difficult subject. There are pros and cons to taking money. The best kind of company is one where you don't have to take any money.

Livingston: Did you use your own money for Groove?

Ozzie: Yes, I funded the first few years myself. But eventually I took some money from Mitch Kapor and then others. Not so much because I needed it at that point, but because I knew that, ultimately, you cannot accomplish something completely on your own. You really need to develop a network of people who win when you win. Being on the East Coast, I believed that it was very important to establish a good network in Silicon Valley, where I didn't have a presence.

I'd worked with Mitch for many years, and I felt that he could make the right introductions. So I first took money from Mitch, then he made some introductions to VCs. One of them was Accel, and I took money from them. I ended up spending quite a bit of time in the Bay Area, meeting a lot of people, and ultimately that network helped a lot.

Iris was a corporate partnership with Lotus. I was 27 years old and didn't have the money to fund it then. Getting the product built was an amazingly positive experience. We had structured a great contract that funded the product—it was a unique partnership, a corporate startup kind of R&D partnership. But that brings its own challenges. When you have an alliance with a major corporation from an early stage, what you build really has to relate to the other, larger goals of that corporation. You may not be completely tied up, you still can accomplish your vision, but it would make no sense to be funded by a company and be completely aligning yourself with their competitors' offerings.

In a startup environment, it's much rougher in terms of making your numbers. There's much less patience. Once you start down the treadmill of taking venture capital, it's "how many rounds before people give up on you or you have a positive exit event?" So you're really setting yourself up. The best by far is to structure it such that you don't have to take money.

Livingston: You also took money from Microsoft. I know they thought very highly of you, but do you think they also invested to keep an eye on what you were doing?

Ozzie: That's exactly why they did. They were a straight investor, meaning there was no technology sharing or anything like that as part of the investment. I think Notes probably got a little bit out of control from Microsoft's perspective. They didn't really track its market very closely while it was emerging, and, had they watched what was going on, perhaps they might have been able to respond a bit more quickly.

So I think with Groove, it was essentially buying a look at what kinds of customers found this technology attractive. More than anything else it was market tracking. They knew enough about the technology, because once we came out of our stealth phase we were very open with everyone about the kind of technology that it was built on. And we were very confident about that because we knew how hard it was to build.

At both Iris and Groove, we believed Microsoft was our prime competitor.

Livingston: Even at Groove? But Microsoft seems so ambivalent about the Internet . . .

Ozzie: If there's going to be a trend that's largely horizontal, Microsoft cares. Because Microsoft's bread and butter is serving the masses—whether it's consumers or enterprises—with low-cost technology that solves many problems. And other people layer upon it more vertical solutions.

We were pitching Groove as a fairly horizontal technology. We were applying it to productivity challenges, but to the extent that it had the potential to catch on broadly, they would certainly have been the biggest competitor.

Livingston: Looking back, was the Microsoft threat real?

Ozzie: Oh yeah, they are brilliant technologically and from a business strategy perspective. If you believe that Microsoft is your competitor, it's better to keep stealth and then embrace them at the right time, when you believe it can be to your advantage to embrace them. In the case of Groove, we were having distribution challenges, we needed money, we were raising a round. One of the biggest questions we were encountering with our enterprise customers was "Why isn't Microsoft just going to crush you tomorrow?"

And although I brought some credibility to the table because of my background at IBM, having Microsoft as a backer only helped us within those enterprise accounts.

Livingston: Back to Lotus Notes—were you already working on an application when Lotus discovered and then funded you? What was the history there?

Ozzie: As I mentioned earlier, I first wrote the spec for Groove in 1982. But I couldn't find funding for the idea. So in 1983 I was hired by Mitch Kapor and Jonathan Sachs at Lotus Development, just after Lotus 1-2-3 release 1 had shipped. I did a small amount of work on 1-2-3 1A, then led a small team to create Lotus Symphony, one of the first "suite" products. I agreed to do Symphony, if Mitch would help make introductions to VCs and help get Notes off the ground. The day Symphony shipped, Mitch made good on his word. But because Lotus was in a good cash position, rather than introduce me to VCs, Mitch suggested Lotus supply the capital. I then formed Iris Associates in Westford, Mass., with three other programmers in December 1984.

Livingston: What surprised you the most?

Ozzie: How difficult the go-to-market challenges are. I suppose it shouldn't have surprised me, but in both the cases of Notes and Groove, building a market in something that's new can be as, if not more, challenging than building the technology. We were building some very complex technology, and I thought, since we were developing to what seemed to be a fairly straightforward customer value proposition, going to market would be a lot easier.

Changing people's habits is extremely difficult. Notes came out at a time when things were kind of booming from a tech perspective. But Groove came out at a very difficult time. It was just post-Bubble and IT spending was really down. If you are serving the consumer, everyone expects not to have to pay for anything. In business, if you're talking with IT, it's just very difficult to justify any incremental spend.

I guess as a tech entrepreneur I would nurture relationships with people who are outside your skill set on the marketing and sales side or business development side. Relationships you know you can trust. As a technologist, it's very difficult to hire someone on the marketing and sales side because they're so different than technologists and you don't know who to trust. It takes about a year to really understand whether the people who you are partnering with trust you and know they will rely upon you just as much as you know you will rely upon them.

That's where I think working for another company and building those relationships is extremely valuable. Frequently, people think just running from school out into doing a startup is the best thing to do. But I think that getting some experience within a number of companies is really positive because you meet people and you start to develop patterns in your mind of the types of people that you need, and the types of people that you can trust, and the types of people you never want to work with.

Livingston: What advice would give someone who was thinking of starting or joining a startup?

Ozzie: For someone who's joining a startup, just learn about leadership from the people at the top of the company. Watch how they talk to people, watch how they present to people. Companies take their shape based on the personality characteristics and human interaction characteristics of the founders. This is true in every company. Learn about the kind of culture that you want to create in your own company based on the positive and negative aspects that you witness in the people that are your leaders.

Learn to respect and appreciate other people's skill sets, because you are going to need other people if you do start a company and you are a technologist. Understand that it's a rare, rare case when a tech entrepreneur is the right one to lead a startup for a long period of time. You have to feel comfortable in your own skin in terms of what you're good at and what other people are good at. Know when the shift to chief technologist is the right thing for the company.

You have to be comfortable with the fact that you are separate from the thing that you're building, and that the team and the people financing you will have joint custody over the asset that you create. You have to respect that and not associate your own success and failure with the success and failure of your "child."

Livingston: Is there anything that you learned from Iris that you applied to Groove?

Ozzie: In terms of the culture, there were some really strong positive things. People doing things for the right reason. Never say to people that you are doing it for the money. Don't do it for the money.

Everyone knows that one reason you go to work and do what you do is the hope that ultimately you'll be compensated. But you don't have to say it, and it doesn't have to come through. It should be about the mission. It should be about changing the world. It should be about how you can impact the lives of users, partners, and the employees themselves. It's not just about this big payday. The more you focus on the things that matter when you are talking to people who want to believe in you, the more they will believe in you and the more it will be a sustainable entity.

Evan Williams
Cofounder, Pyra Labs (Blogger.com)

Evan Williams cofounded Pyra Labs in 1999. Originally, Pyra intended to build a web-based project management tool. Williams developed Blogger to manage his personal weblog, and it quickly became an important mechanism for sharing ideas internally at Pyra.

Once launched publicly, Blogger grew rapidly, and Pyra Labs decided to focus on it full-time. But Blogger.com did not generate a lot of revenue at first, and as the Bubble deflated in 2001, Pyra seemed near death. Williams remained as the only employee and managed to bring the company back from the brink. By 2003, Blogger had one million registered users. That attracted the attention of Google, who made Pyra their first acquisition. Williams left Google in 2004 to cofound a podcasting company called Odeo.

Livingston: Tell me about how you started Pyra Labs.

Williams: I have always been pretty entrepreneurial, and I had started a couple of other companies. In late '98 when I decided to start Pyra, I had been doing Internet stuff for about 5 years. I actually started a company in Nebraska.

I had never even really worked anywhere. I was just totally self-taught technically, but I started a company and kind of ran it into the ground over 3 years or so, and it was a very educational, painful experience. But I knew I was going to do that again. I just always knew I was going to start my own thing.

I went to college, and I dropped out because I didn't need to have a degree—because I wasn't going to try to get a job with anyone. I came to California after playing with the Internet for a few years because Nebraska wasn't the place to be, very clearly.

I moved to California to take a job with O'Reilly, which ended up being very fortunate as you'll find out later. I worked there for a few months, though I knew I didn't want to work for anyone. I taught myself web development—this was in the middle of the boom and there was lots of work to be had as a contractor. I knew I was going to start another company. I just wasn't ready yet. So I was a web developer on contract for about a year and a half, and worked in various companies like Intel and HP. Finally I got to the point where I said, "OK, I am going to start another company." This was very much in the middle of the boom.

I had visions of raising money and building something cool, but originally the idea for Pyra was around web-based project management, or collaboration, which was an area I had been interested in for a long time. The idea for Pyra was the personal and project information management system: to build projects for clients around their intranets and help them organize their work and personal information. It is a web application where you would put your stuff, things you are thinking about, things you had to do, things you wanted to share with other people. There is not exactly a corollary to it today, but it is along the same lines as Basecamp or Ta-da List (but more complicated). There are a lot of products that are about organizing your work and stuff. That was what I saw as the big idea, and I had specific ideas about how that could be done better than it had ever been done before.

Around the time I was thinking about starting the company, I was talking to a friend of mine, Meg Hourihan. She got excited about the idea and said, "Hey, let me start it with you." She had been a management consultant and was really smart, so I said OK. I had been contracting, so I had a little bit of money, so I could coast for a little while, but we didn't know anybody. We weren't hooked into the startup scene.

Everyone was getting funded, but it is still completely just a network. You have to know the right people. Whether it's good times or bad, you have to know people and you have to talk their language, and we were just from a different place and not hooked into that at all. So we just said, "OK, here is the product we are going to build," and we started building it. We actually kept contracting on the side—I had a contract with HP. That's how we paid the bills—we turned my personal contract into the company's contract and we did a little work on that and we did a little work on our project, and that is how we started.

Livingston: What was the point where you really said, "I know this is going to work and I am going to do this full-time"?

Williams: Well, for me it was always the point of no return. Meg actually kept her other job, but only for a couple of months. We were pretty hardcore. So we formed the company and said, "OK, we are building this thing." We hoped to raise money. We just didn't know how yet. We focused on building the product first.

Livingston: So, you built the product and then did you have to raise money or did you keep relying on consulting fees?

Williams: Well, we kind of tried. We started talking to the few people we knew, but we just didn't have any inroads for that. We wrote a business plan, I think.

The first year was entirely self-funded. It was just doing this work mostly for HP. HP basically funded Pyra for the first year, unbeknownst to them, because at the time you could charge a decent amount of money for doing pretty simple web application development. If one of us was working on that full-time, it would pay for three of us (not that we were paying ourselves much). We started working on things in November '98. We technically started the company in January. Meg started full-time in February, and we hired our first employee, Paul Bausch, in May. Then we got an office down here in SOMA.

Livingston: So is that when you focused on developing Blogger.com?

Williams: No. We had personal websites and we were web geeks, but those things were separate. At the time, blogs (or weblogs as everyone called them back then) were just beginning to be talked about as a distinct thing. There are those who argue that the first website was a weblog. It didn't really matter, because early '99 is when people started saying, "OK, I have a weblog." And the form and community were just sort of developing. Paul and I already had personal websites for a few years. They weren't blogs; they were just kind of typical homepages—experiments with web technologies. But we were reading folks like Dave Winer.

Paul turned his site, onfocus.com, into a blog before I did. Being web app developers, I think we both wrote our own scripts to do it—basically the same functionality as Blogger. It seemed like not a big deal at the time, but it did change my relationship with my website—even with the Web.

Livingston: It was easy?

Williams: It was easy, and that was a key thing for me because I wasn't lacking the knowledge about how to publish to the Web . . . For a long time, people understood Blogger as "It makes it easy to have a website." But a lot of things before that made it easy to have a website. GeoCities made it easy to have a website, but they didn't make it easy to publish anything on an ongoing basis. So, for me, the idea that I could have a thought and I could type in a form and it would be on my website in a matter of seconds completely transformed the experience. It was one of those things that, by automating the process, completely morphed what it was I was doing. If I could have a thought and then put it on my site, then obviously I am going to potentially do that much more and it is a stream for communication of a whole different type.

So that was a little bit of an insight. To me it was, "Heck, that's handy." But it was not dissimilar to what other people were doing with weblogs. They were either doing it by hand or maybe they wrote their own little script to do it. But it's the little thing that clicked in my mind: "This is that little tweak that makes it kind of maybe a big deal." Not that the future lit up in my head and I said, "We are doing that." It was just sort of a hint, more in retrospect than at the time.

We took the script I wrote to publish my site, and we made an internal site where we could do the same thing. So, even when it was only Meg and I, we had this little internal blog we called "Stuff," and we just put stuff in there.

It was a blog, but it was just, "Here's a thing from a competitor or a potentially useful page or just information for each other." It was a place where we collected everything and, as we grew, it was the center of Pyra. It was where things happened.

So this whole time we are building our real collaboration tool, with all kinds of structure and big ideas trying to be implemented into it, but we were really using Stuff a lot. And then Paul wrote a little addition to Stuff so that certain things we posted to our internal blog we could put on our external company blog.

We were one of the first companies to have a blog on their site—not that many people were reading. But it was neat. We were publishing news, random things we liked, whatever.

This must have been around March of '99, so all of this happened fairly quickly. That's when I got the idea for Blogger—I know because I registered the domain then. I totally pictured what it was because it was based on what I was already doing and then the way we were publishing our own blog to an external site. I said, "Let's turn that into a product." I have always been a product guy and am just always thinking about products and thought this would be a cool little idea.

While it did seem fairly easy to build, it was a dilemma, because one of the big lessons from my first company was to focus. After my first company died, I did an inventory of the projects I had worked on in the last year. There were something like 30 projects that I had started on and not finished. My total weakness was not focusing on things. So I had this idea and I loved it, but very clearly we were only three people and we had to contract to pay the bills and we couldn't start another product. We had this big thing we were trying to do. So it just kind of sat in the back of my head, but it wouldn't go away. It kept bugging me. Of course, what made me still think about it was that we were using it for our own purposes and we were building this collaboration tool, but we were doing this kind of collaboration with Stuff. We actually said several times, "Maybe Stuff should just be our product?" And we agreed, "That's too simple, that is too trivial." And also we didn't have the resources for two products. So that went on for a long time, and it was in July, I guess, when we finally launched Pyra, the app, and that actually got a pretty good, if limited, reception.

People started using Pyra and it was in evolving it that I came up with the justification for why to do Blogger. That was based on the idea that we were trying to solve a really, really big problem, which is organizing people's information of all types. We said, "That is too big a problem to start with, so we should focus it." We decided to focus it on people who were building websites, as a place for them to collaborate. Then we thought up this architecture where there would be little mini-apps, and Blogger would be one of those. So, with that justification (Meg was actually on vacation for a week), Paul and I built Blogger and launched it while she was gone. Which was a terrible thing to do, but ultimately a good thing to do—but not a cool thing to do.

Its functionality was really dead simple at first, but it did what we needed it to do and we already had the script. We thought it would take a couple days—it turned out to take a week, but we just launched it, while Meg was gone. She was pissed, of course, rightfully. We launched a whole product, and she's the cofounder of the company. But we talked her into thinking that it made sense. "It will be this little thing that won't take any effort. We just push it out the door and it will attract people to our real thing and we can go back to our real thing."

Livingston: Did it catch on quickly?

Williams: It caught on a lot more than we expected. It was really designed to appeal to web geeks. It wasn't a mass consumer product. It was, "If you're a web geek like us, you might find this interesting." It's good to appeal to the alpha geeks sometimes. I thought it would be pretty cool if 1,000 people used Blogger. It didn't explode at first because it was fairly technical. You had to have a website and you had to know what FTP was. You had to know a bunch of stuff, but things that you would know if you were a web geek. We put it out there and people started using it and the existing weblogs started pointing to it. Like Peter Merholz (he is credited with coining the term *blog*), who pointed to it. It started getting traction and a lot of people who were like the "cool kids" were using our product, and we were really excited.

We launched it in August and we had a dilemma on our hands right away, of course, because we now had a product that people were using, but it wasn't the "real" product.

The problem was, we didn't see a business in Blogger. This was during the boom, but we weren't one of these companies that was just, "Let's get eyeballs." We talked a lot about the stupidity of a lot of the dot-coms and raising too much money. We were very product driven. We wanted to create cool stuff, and we wanted it to have a sustainable business. We wanted to probably sell the company to somebody eventually, but we didn't see any business model with Blogger. Also, we hadn't raised money, so making money was pretty important.

The other product served a business need and was something we thought people would pay for. We thought Blogger was this free little thing that would get people to pay for the real thing. So we very clearly had a dilemma on our hands: we could focus on the stupid little Blogger app that people were using, or we could work on our real product. We tried to split our time amongst those two things and contracted to pay the bills. We were three people, so that was a little bit difficult. We had endless debates about what to do about that. I think we ended up doing another rev on Blogger in November that made it much better, and then people really started using it.

Livingston: Did you start to make money?

Williams: No, not until much later. But we did get wired in, so to speak. Blogger was how people found out who we were, within a community that was at first San Francisco–based web design geeks but bled into a lot of different communities, like Silicon Valley and a lot of leading Internet thinkers. They were attracted to publishing blogs, and this was a thing you used to do that. So it got us known a little bit, which was very helpful. For example, we met Jerry Michalski, who emailed out of the blue and then became an advisor. Jerry knows everybody and was tremendously helpful.

People were using our other app, too, a little bit, but it wasn't very mature because it was much more complicated.

In early 2000, we started actually raising money, and O'Reilly invested in us. They were some of the only people I knew. I guess I left an OK impression on O'Reilly. I only worked there for seven months as an employee and then another couple as a contractor doing a completely different job, but left a good enough impression that I was able to go back there and say, "Hey, look at this thing." They were aware of Blogger, but we were still doing Pyra, too, and they agreed to invest.

Livingston: So, you had Blogger out there but you weren't totally focused on it. Were you worried that competitors, since it was a simple thing, would try to copy it?

Williams: There were a couple other products out there, but they weren't very substantial. No one was really paying attention to it. It's hard to fathom now, but blogs took a really long time to be taken seriously. But, yeah, we felt we needed to make it a lot better and spend a lot more time on it, and we didn't have the resources to do that. But at the same time, we didn't think there was a business there, so we weren't that concerned about it. All the time, of course, we are debating whether or not there was something there and debating why it was appealing to people. I thought about it a lot and I came to the conclusion why it was appealing and the impact it had, and I started to get some insight about its potential.

I started leaning more and more toward Blogger by late '99. I think Meg and Paul were pretty much pro-Blogger and I was the one who was still on the fence. Pyra was my baby and I had all these ideas I wanted to see realized. I felt the need to focus, but it was also like, "This is the cool thing that's taking off." I couldn't decide.

The money was actually raised around both. There wasn't a very specific plan. We had this thing that had buzz and then we had this thing that had all of this potential. So it was like, "Here's some money, go do whatever." We ended up not really getting the money until April or May of 2000, which was around the crash, but (around here anyway) it wasn't like everything was over all of a sudden. People had faith.

We were still able to get money without a lot to go on. We raised a half of a million dollars from O'Reilly, Advance.net (Condé Nast's parent company), Jerry, Meg's parents, John Borthwick from AOL, and Jerry's father-in-law. A half a million dollars was a ton of money to us at the time. We ramped up to seven people and shortly thereafter decided we were going to focus on Blogger and developed it.

Livingston: Do you remember why you finally decided, "OK, we will do this"?

Williams: I had come to the conclusion that blogging was going to dramatically impact the Web. After I thought about it a lot and saw what people were doing, I decided that this made tons of sense. The conclusion I came to then was kind of the one I stuck to, which was that this is going to impact the Web because it is a native form for this medium, just like all new mediums start out imitating what came before them and then they kind of find out what they are good for.

We even looked at Blogger and, technically, it was trivial (at least until it came to scaling it). It wasn't based on any new technology. But that made sense to me because it was not that the technology was new, it was that we had figured out this medium, at least one of the native forms of what the Web was good for. It was about freshness and about frequency, and it was about the democratization of media and giving power to everybody and the universal desire for personal expression and the attraction to a real, compelling personal voice. And hyperlinks. And all of those things were just inevitable forces that were going to terrifically impact the Web and media in general.

It was kind of the first time that I had started really seriously thinking about media, and then at the same time Pyra had all these big ideas that were going to take a really long time to build, and this was much more fun. So I said, "Well, we can figure out a business. We can charge for pro accounts and we can license it to companies and we can just make up the obvious businesses around it (even though they weren't necessarily that strong)."

Livingston: Was it easy to make up businesses around it to make money off of it?

Williams: It's easy to make up things to write down about how we are going to make money off of it.

Livingston: Well, how did you make money off of it?

Williams: Well, that didn't come for quite a while later. So, we had raised money at this point and we decided to focus on Blogger. I wrote the business plan for Blogger after we raised the money and said, "Here is what we are going to do." We hired some people. We were seven people in the middle of 2000, just focusing on all types of things. We redesigned Blogger, with the help of Derek Powazek, who created the famous orange "B," which was great. It just kept growing; there were probably hundreds of new users a day.

Livingston: But you weren't charging them?

Williams: No, we weren't charging any money anywhere. And we had all of these features planned. We had most of the features planned that later became standard in the blogging world—and some that haven't yet. We were totally focused on building the product and community around it once we had raised the money, because this was still, "you get enough eyeballs, you have buzz, you'll be fine." And the extent of the crash didn't dawn on us that quickly. I don't think it dawned on a lot of people. We just wanted to build momentum with this $500,000 and then raise more money later in the year.

At the time it was pretty much the belief that, if you have buzz and you have users and you have good seed investors, you can raise more money. We said, "We'll make money, but this is down the road so we don't need to focus on that. We are going to focus on building more features and getting more users."

We just went on that path, and in the fall we knew that we were running out of money and started trying to have some conversations with folks. I also wasn't sophisticated at all about how you do that. We felt connected at that time, but it wasn't necessarily to the money crowd, and we probably wouldn't have been able to talk the talk of VCs anyway. So the money wasn't coming. We scrambled around. We decided we could launch some for-pay stuff.

Other companies at the time were going into enterprises, since companies had money. At the time it was like, "Consumers aren't spending money. Go to companies—they're the ones with money." So many companies at the time took their consumer Internet thing and made it an enterprise Internet thing and then died anyway. We debated that a lot. We had a good story about why this was really useful inside companies, and we had a friend at Cisco who wanted to use it and we got it installed inside of Cisco. It was just a pilot and we started saying on our site, "We have enterprise Blogger." But there was a lot of pressure internally, a lot of debate about just doing enterprise, which I was pretty adamant that we didn't want to do because, whether or not it would make money, I thought it was pointless. At this time I was very much excited about the idea of democratizing media and that's what mattered. It mattered more than the company, really. When you are in that mode, it's hard to say that the company doesn't matter, since everyone's heart and soul is in it, not to mention their livelihood.

Livingston: But you're changing the world?

Williams: Yeah. I didn't think we could do enterprise and still do the consumer site well, even though we had talked about it from the beginning. I sort of realized later on that, if we do enterprise, we are going to have to focus on enterprise and the consumer stuff is going to suck and that doesn't sound fun. Also, we probably won't be good at enterprise, because we don't know how to sell and service companies. So, we had lots of arguments about that. Then I said, "What we need to do is charge money from the consumers, just to have a Blogger Pro," which was always in the plan, and everyone said, "We can't make money doing that. No one pays for stuff on the Web."

In late 2000, we built a version with many more features but never felt that we had it to the point where we could feel comfortable charging money for it. So, we talked to a couple of companies about merging—private companies who had funding. We had a couple of serious conversations and came close to doing a deal. Actually one deal was with Moreover, which did headline aggregation before there was much RSS out there. It was started by Nick Denton, who is the guy who runs Gawker Media. Nick and his cofounder, David Galbraith, were fans of Blogger and wanted to buy us. It wasn't a particularly attractive offer, but we were on the brink and thought, "Maybe we can get in there and everyone would have jobs."

Everyone in the company wanted to do the deal but me. But I had conceded, because I wasn't going to be the asshole who denied the chance everyone had to still be employed. We were out of money. Fortunately Moreover's board wouldn't approve the deal. It was some ridiculously lowball offer—it was something like a million dollars worth of their stock. But they're a private company. So it was basically like, "We'd give everyone jobs."

Livingston: And your financial future is contingent on them getting acquired or going public.

Williams: Right. After two years of pouring our hearts and souls into this, it seemed like a crappy option. Fortunately it didn't work out, though. There was another company in New York that was a startup but that had some funding we talked about merging with. And the group that was funding them actually gave us a bridge investment. They gave us $50,000 while we tried to figure it out. But that didn't seem like a good deal either. They wanted to do it, but we decided not to. (That company went away fairly quickly.)

Livingston: Then you ran into Dan Bricklin.

Williams: Yes. So this is December or January of 2001 and the second potential acquisition hadn't worked out, so basically we got to the point where we sat everyone down, and I said, "OK, everyone is laid off as of today, including me." We had warned them a few weeks earlier that we didn't have money in the bank to meet payroll. Obviously when you are in that state, tensions rise a lot and morale wasn't good and relationships with my cofounder weren't good. I said, "I am going to stick around because I took a half of a million dollars of other people's money. And we have all of these users." (The service was still running.)

This whole time, this service is growing. In terms of users, we were getting more and more successful. Which also caused other problems in that we needed more hardware and we had all of these scaling problems. In January, right around the time that the rest of the company was being laid off, we did what we called the Server Fund Drive. We posted it on our website and it said, "Hey, we know Blogger is really slow. It's because we need more hardware. We don't have the money to buy it. So give us money and we will buy more hardware and we'll make Blogger faster." Surprisingly, it worked really well. We had a lot of goodwill and people liked us and we had a good brand within our users because we were very personable and used the blog and we were just honest. We just said, "We can't buy hardware, but we have plans and we are not going to go away if we can get past this hump, so send us some money." So people sent us money.

Livingston: What was the biggest check you got?

Williams: We used PayPal, and I think we got bigger amounts from fewer people than we expected. We had several thousand users. 100 people or so gave larger amounts, and I am not sure what the absolute biggest was. We suggested $10, $20. Several people gave us $100, and then a company, CMP, which published *Web Techniques* magazine, offered to buy us a server outright, up to $4,000 worth. So between the users and them, we had around $17,000 to spend on servers, which is more than we had ever spent on servers, so it was a bonanza. It worked better than we had ever expected.

We told people we were only going to buy hardware, so I wasn't going to use that to pay people. I just spent that money on hardware, but it got the site back up and running well and meanwhile we laid everybody off. Meg and I weren't getting along well at all and she decided to leave and everybody else decided to leave too.

Livingston: So you had a major difference of opinion?

Williams: Yeah. I think a lot of that came back to the enterprise thing, which she and some other people felt strongly was our best chance of making money. If I was the guy in charge and we were dying, it's reasonable to conclude it's my fault. And certainly there were other things I could have done. So everybody left but me. (A lot of them needed to leave since we couldn't pay them anymore.) Everybody left, and the next day, I was the only one who came in the office.

Livingston: How did you feel that morning?

Williams: That was a really bad time. Actually the day that everyone told me they were leaving . . . I told everyone they were laid off and said, "Work with me if you can." And at the time, everyone had already missed one paycheck, and they'd had it. These are, of course, my friends, and we were hanging out all the time and we socialized together, so it's much more than just the employees. I think that same night I broke up with my girlfriend of 6 months.

Livingston: Sounds pretty grim.

Williams: Yeah, it was just the craziest bad time. The good news about all that was Blogger was still running and, with no employees, we didn't have expenses. So we went from having $50,000 a month worth of payroll, to a couple of thousand for our server infrastructure and our rent. It is probably closer to ten, between five and ten, but a manageable number, not paying me anything. I took some money every once in a while to pay rent, and I had long since put all my money in and credit cards and everything else, but that was actually a much more reasonable place to be because we didn't have to make $50,000 a month to pay people. We had to make a few thousand dollars a month.

So then other ideas started being much more feasible, and I was in some other conversations. Now that we were known, opportunities came up. One of the first opportunities was a little company called KnowNow, who wanted us to build something, and later actually two of the people who worked at Pyra, including Meg, worked for this company, and I did a little deal with them to build something that was never launched. They killed the project, but it got me $35,000, which was like months of burn rate at that point.

Shortly after that, in February, I ran into Dan Bricklin. Dan wrote me after reading my blog. We were pretty public in terms of our communication, so I posted when everybody left, and I wrote this whole story on my blog that was pretty widely read, "Here's what happened: everyone's gone. It's just me." I got a huge outpouring of support from that, and one of the messages was from Dan Bricklin, who said that he thought what we did was great and he wanted to help. We ended up meeting at an O'Reilly conference, which was in February 2001. We met and he basically agreed really quickly. He assessed the situation—what I needed to keep going. (We had a lot of back bills at this point; we needed to pay our hosting bill to keep the lights on.)

There were some confusing stories about what that deal was. Dan had a company called Trellix that he later sold, which was a web publishing platform.

Trellix licensed Blogger in order to add blogging to their feature set. They did it in such a way—Dan drove it in such a way—that if it was a traditional license (months of due diligence and really figuring out if we wanted this), it wouldn't have helped and he knew that. So, he was like, "a) there's a legitimate business reason to do this, but b) we are going to push this through so it is really good for you." It wasn't a lot of money—it was around $40,000—but with a contract later on that ended up helping as well. But it was what we needed at the time.

Livingston: So you were back in business?

Williams: Sort of back in business, but both of those deals didn't get me ahead. They bought me a few months, but between just keeping the service running and fulfilling on those deals, I didn't have any other time. I wasn't really making progress, because it was just me. First of all, I had to keep the service running, which was a really big deal in itself—we had several thousand users and I had to teach myself Linux system administration and Java, so I could just keep the servers up and fix bugs here and there. Things would break, and I'd go in and fix them on the live site and figure it out as I went. That was very time consuming. The technology wasn't rock solid by any means, and it kept growing and growing and I didn't want to shut it off. Between that and fulfilling on these deals, which were mostly giving stuff to other people, I wasn't building in the real things that were going to make a business. That was a lot of just day-to-day, by-the-skin-of-my-teeth stuff for several months. Still I had the idea to build a paid version of Blogger, but that was going to take a lot more development and work to launch that.

Then there is another part going on around this time that I can't talk too much about. Suffice it to say my former teammates didn't all go away happy, and I spent almost as much money on my lawyer in 2001 as I paid myself.

The other thing was that all those people left, and then I was being bad-mouthed within this community of people we knew. The story apparently was that I fired all my friends and I didn't pay them and took over the company. It was really ugly, and of course we had all these mutual friends and there were parties we were at. I basically went underground and did nothing but try to keep Blogger going.

Livingston: There was a whole social component to cofounding a startup with a friend.

Williams: Which I think is a theme for startups in general because people live and breathe them and become friends, date and merge their lives together. And then, if things go bad, it's bad in ways that are much more devastating than your work going badly.

So that was pretty much 2001. The funny thing about Pyra is that every calendar year was pretty distinct—'99 was the first year, we were self-funded; 2000 was the year we got money and ramped up; 2001 was the year that it was just me and it sucked. But somehow by the end of 2001 I started rebuilding. We cleared up the legal thing, and things were looking up.

Then eventually I started launching some for-pay features of Blogger. Things that people would actually pay for. So 2 years into it, Blogger itself was starting to make money—not directly but through some little ways. Like the blogs we hosted, we had advertising, which never made any money because it was during the time when web advertising didn't make money. (After it made money the first time and before it made money again.) I created a mechanism to charge people to take their ads off and that actually made money. I said, "Pay me $12 a year, and I'll take the ads off your blog." I started with this "product" because it was probably the easiest thing I could build that I thought people would pay for. And they did.

I did a couple other small things like that and got to a point where it was paying the hosting bill. I had gotten rid of my office by then, and I had no place to work at home. So I posted on my blog that I needed to rent a desk somewhere. This company, Bigstep, offered me a free desk, which was nice.

Then I just started building more things. Working from the Bigstep office, I designed and launched the Blogger API, which didn't make any money, but became important later. I actually hired a contractor programmer and had started working with Jason Shellen on business development stuff. So things were looking up. And then 2002 was a completely different year altogether.

We finally launched Blogger Pro, the paid-for version of Blogger. The paid-for version of Blogger did very well for us and we brought in some other people. With Jason's help, we did a big deal in Brazil with this company that wanted to license Blogger. So 2002 was a ramping-up year again. Everything was on the uptick, and we had a completely different team. We were getting by and the money was increasing and we were building new stuff and it was looking good.

October 2002 was when Google came knocking. We had a small office downtown—more of a conference room than an office. It was Adaptive Path's first office, which we moved into after them. And we had brought on a tech support guy and a sys admin. Then Google called us up. I forget how that happened . . . I think that was O'Reilly again.

At this point I think it looked like Pyra came back from the dead. Blogging in general had exploded all this time. We got a lot more competitors, but the phenomenon just exploded. We were a less substantial part of blogging, but blogging was a much bigger deal. So it drove our growth and it legitimized us as being a major player in an increasingly big space.

So O'Reilly was talking and they said, "I guess Pyra's still alive." We had a meeting up at O'Reilly around this time, and Tim [O'Reilly] and Mark [Jacobsen] were trying to figure out how they could help us. One of the suggestions was to introduce us to folks like Amazon and Google.

Soon after, according to the story I heard, Larry or Sergey were on a call with Tim and Tim mentioned us, and Sergey had recently been at this conference where everyone was talking about blogs, and was interested in blogs and he said, "Yeah, we want to talk to them."

We're like, "Alright. Why?" It didn't even occur to us that they might want to buy us because Google hadn't bought anybody at this point. And they were a search company. So we brainstormed all these ideas maybe we could do with Google and we went down there, and it turned out that we were meeting with their corporate development people—meaning the people who buy companies. We started talking about ideas and within the first 5 minutes they said, "Yeah, there're lots of ideas, but it's hard for someone like us to really partner with someone so small as you; why don't you just come here and do all that stuff?" So we were like, "Oh, that's interesting." (We tried to play it cool.)

I had had one or two other conversations with possible acquirers. One was Lycos back in 2001, which would have been terrible—though it would have made a lot of sense for us because they had Tripod and Angelfire (two of the biggest publishing sites that there were). But they didn't have any money for that area, so that didn't go anywhere.

What Google said was, "Would you consider being acquired?" And we said, "Well, we've talked to people, but Google's never asked before." Like everyone else, we thought very highly of Google, and we said, "Let's talk about it." Four months later, we were sitting in Google.

Mind you, it wasn't an easy decision. I struggled hard deciding if going to Google was the right thing to do. We weren't desperate. We actually had a term sheet on the table for $1 million in investment from Joi Ito's Neoteny (who ended up investing in Six Apart). And after 4 years of pouring my heart into Blogger, I saw a lot of risk in giving up control.

Eventually I decided Google was right. I really thought we could do huge things at this point, and Google had done bigger things than most, so I wanted to get in there and learn and get those resources.

Livingston: At what point did you most want to quit?

Williams: There were a lot of points in 2001 that I seriously considered quitting. Everybody I knew just thought I was crazy. And I was getting negative feedback on the Web; people who used to be my friends were posting negative things about me. We'd gotten enough press at that point . . . the *Industry Standard*, which was the bible of the dot-com era, had this annual list, the Net 21, titled something like, "The 21 people who had made lemonade out of lemons," and I was one of them. It was pretty cool, but the title for me was "The Idealist" because I hadn't sold out. Like I had a chance to have riches and I didn't. Someone took that and wrote a parody: "The Egoist." Because there was a story—not really on the surface, but very clearly underneath the community that I was previously a part of—that was a very negative story about what happened in the last days of Pyra, because all those people left and they weren't very happy (completely understandably).

For the most part, the old Pyra employees were cool with it later. But, during 2001, these stories got out that I took over this company and kicked everyone out and was just this terrible guy. That was the worst part.

And I was writing this service that was free and thousands of people used it, and all I heard were the complaints when it wasn't working. So for many reasons it was bad. I don't know how close I came to quitting. I don't think I was terribly close, even though I should have been. I was always hallucinogenically optimistic. That's the only reason I kept going. Not because I thought I could take this suckiness for a long time, but that it's going to be better tomorrow. I had all these big ideas, and I could never stop thinking about the product and the thing I was going to build next.

That always being around the corner in my mind is basically what allowed me to go through all the bad stuff. As well as the fact that, at that point, it was just pride. It was so public. If I would have stopped, that would have been very public also.

Livingston: Were there any other really stressful moments?

Williams: That's an understatement. I can think of many. For example, when the site got hacked on Christmas day. I was in Iowa, visiting my mom, and I didn't find out until the next morning. Someone was able to run an update on the database that changed thousands of users' passwords to the number 1 (which people started to realize when they couldn't log in and used the forgotten password feature to get theirs via email).

Having your site hacked is stressful enough, but here I was in Iowa trying to assess the damage over a dial-up connection and a tiny laptop. And I didn't have a sys admin or anyone else working for me at the time. I ended up spending most of the day in a Kinko's doing damage control. So much for enjoying the holidays.

Livingston: What advice would you give someone?

Williams: I think one of the things that kills great things so often is compromise—letting people talk you out of what your gut is telling you. Not that I don't value people's input, but you have to have the strength to ignore it sometimes, too. If you feel really strongly, there might be something to that, and if you see something that other people don't see, it could be because it's that powerful and different. If everyone agrees, it's probably because you're not doing anything original.

I had the personality that never liked school and rejected the normal way of doing things. Even when I was in school, I'd try to make up alternative solutions to math problems. When I was at Google, they had this huge focus on academia. Grades were super-important. Getting good grades at a good school is one filter of brains, but it might also suggest you like following rules.

Another thing is that luck comes in many forms—and often looks bad at first. I always look back on the deals that we didn't do and the things that didn't work out, and realize what seemed like a bummer at the time was really lucky. Like the early acquisition opportunities. These obviously would have been really bad, as opposed to what happened later. Through that whole experience that's one of the biggest things that I've taken away: if you have some plan and it doesn't go that way, roll with it. There's no way to know if it's good or bad until later, if ever.

Livingston: What was the most surprising thing?

Williams: One thing that I used to be bad at was paying attention to how other people are feeling. So when problems came up with some of my coworkers, it totally surprised me. That stuff shouldn't surprise you, and it did.

I think I was also surprised by the success of something so simple. That's a mantra for many people in the technology world—simplicity. But what we built wasn't that amazing. It was the idea of putting a couple of things together and being able to establish a lead by doing something really, really simple. How far you can get on a simple idea is amazing. I have a tendency to add more and more—the ideas always get too big to implement before they even get off the ground. Simplicity is powerful.

Tim Brady
First Non-Founding Employee,
Yahoo

Yahoo began in 1994 as a collection of links to research papers maintained by two Stanford grad students, Jerry Yang and David Filo. They gradually added links to new types of information, and the site grew rapidly in popularity. By the end of 1994, Yang and Filo were considering turning the site into a startup, and they asked Tim Brady to write a business plan for it.

Brady had been Yang's college roommate and was by this time getting his MBA at Harvard Business School. Brady initially expected to be able to finish the semester, but as Yahoo's potential grew, it became clear that he couldn't wait. He turned in the company's business plan as his final assignment in the courses he still needed to pass, and jumped on a plane west to become Yahoo's first actual employee.

Brady's title during his 8 years at Yahoo was VP of Production. His responsibility, as he puts it, was "product." He was effectively the editor of Yahoo's site. Yahoo went public in April 1996, and for nearly all the period since has been the most popular network of websites in the world. Ultimately, Yahoo won the portal wars because it was a better site, and it was the site it was largely because of Tim Brady.

Livingston: You were the first employee the Yahoo founders brought on. How did you get involved?

Brady: I met Jerry when we were undergraduates at Stanford and we studied electrical engineering together. We were in the same freshman dorm and were good friends throughout college and after. He continued on—he's much more adept at EE than me—and I went to Japan and worked for Motorola doing marketing and engineering.

Stanford has a program in Kyoto, and Jerry studied there for a quarter and took a summer job just outside of Tokyo. I had been there for a couple years so we hooked back up. Then I went back to business school, he went back to finish up his PhD, and we kept in touch. We always talked about dream jobs even when we were undergraduates and what we hoped to accomplish. "Wouldn't it be great one day if . . ."

So Jerry gives me a call in the beginning of my second year of B-school and says, "My trailer mate and I started this thing, and it's really starting to ramp up. I'll have you take a look at it." He wasn't looking for advice; he was just telling me what he was up to. I looked at it and was blown away—the whole Web thing. I had been on AOL, I knew a bit about the Internet, but nothing about the Web. It was still pretty early then.

I just looked at it and said, "Wow, that's really cool." And he said, "Well, things are going great with us." I said, "What does that mean, great?" He said something like, "This thing's growing and, if it keeps growing, maybe you'd be interested in doing some moonlighting after school or something like that." I thought, "Yeah, it seems interesting and I love small companies; I'd love to work with Jerry, sounds great." That was at the end of '94. They had been doing it for about 8 months before I had any idea it existed.

Livingston: They had just been doing it for themselves, to index cool things on the Web, right?

Brady: The story I've heard from Jerry and Dave is that they were both doing their PhD theses and all the technical papers that they would have to reference were online, so they were trying to keep track of them all. They had this big list, and then the EE graduate community—not just at Stanford but all the major EE graduate programs—found out about it and sent them emails saying, "Can you add this?"

In their spare time, Jerry and Dave would add categories they were interested in. Jerry, having just come back from Japan, was very interested in sumo wrestling, so he had this great sumo category. Everything on the Web related to EE they had in their list and then these other interesting areas. It was early enough that it was really the only thing out there—big lists, anyway. There were small lists, but nothing big, and so people just kept sending emails asking them, "Add this to the list. My friend told me about this list; I'd love to add this."

So Jerry and Dave did, and they kept adding categories and all of a sudden both of them went from doing their graduate work to adding websites to their list for 8 hours a day. As chance would have it, their thesis advisor was on sabbatical, so there was really no one looking after them, so it all worked. Had their advisor been there, it might not have happened. So they did it for 8 hours a day, maybe even longer, every day for 8 months. They created this huge list, at the right time, in the right place. So it just started taking off.

It had a ton of momentum when I first started talking to them. The tenor of the conversation when I first got involved was, "Hey, maybe next summer when you graduate, you can come and get a 9-to-5 in the Valley and moonlight with us afterward. Then 3 months later, the conversation was more like, "This thing is going crazy, get out here now." They had no idea how much momentum they had behind them and between October '94 and January '95—I don't know the stats off the top of my head, but traffic increased 10 times in just a handful of months.

All of a sudden, the VC community recognized what they were doing. A bunch of others—everyone who was thinking about new media at the time—

recognized it as well. So they got a lot of calls—the *LA Times*, AOL, Microsoft—wanting them to join their companies. Those conversations were, "Why don't you come and bring your project. We'll host it and you can blow it out." It started getting them to think about their project as a business, not just a hobby. Then an article in *Newsweek* happened—I think it was November of '94 or something like that. Those 3 to 4 months were the critical period from going hobby to full-fledged business.

They were entertaining taking money and had decided, "We don't want to sell ourselves. Let's go for it, why not?" Even though people were more than happy to give them money, they thought, "We need a business plan to take around on our VC visits. Even though we can talk to them about it and they would probably give us money without it, it would be better if we had a business plan." I said, "Well that's good, because I'm taking a couple classes where I need to produce a business plan. Why don't you send me your thoughts, and I'll put something together." They sent me their stuff, I wrote a business plan, they took it around to a couple VCs, and I ended up turning it in for final grades for a couple classes.

This was fortunate because, as it turns out, by February of '95, they were saying, "We need you now; we don't need you in June when you graduate." My reply was, "I'm in school, and my dad paid for it. Are you suggesting I tell my dad that I'm not going to come away with a degree?" And Jerry was like, "I'm not telling you to do anything. You don't have to do anything, but we need you now." So I talked to some of my professors, and you can fail a certain number of classes at HBS throughout your tenure—it's a pass/fail grading system. I hadn't failed any yet, so I could fail three classes and technically graduate. I was taking five classes, so I turned in my business plan as a final paper for two out of five, and passed with those.

That was at the end of March '95, and there were four of us: Jerry; Dave; Dave's friend, Donald Lobo; and me. There was a whole lot of enthusiasm, but not a whole lot of knowledge about what to go do.

Livingston: When you wrote the business plan, the Internet was so new. Do you remember what your strategy was when you wrote it?

Brady: No one had any idea how big the Internet was, but the model was advertising. Advertising was well known, so it wasn't like we were making up advertising. HotWired, which was the online version of *Wired* magazine, was online by that time, and they were selling advertising. So there was a model out there, but certainly there were no search engines or directories selling advertising. I just used your basic business plan format, incorporated Jerry's and Dave's ideas, and added a few of my own.

Livingston: So you leave business school early and move out to California. Did you have an office? What did you first start doing?

Brady: There was a consumer electronics show down in San Jose in March '95, so Yahoo's coming-out party was a booth at this show. The show was mostly hardware and software companies. There were no other Internet companies there; it was just us. That was kind of everyone's first day of work. We were still doing it mostly out of Jerry and Dave's trailer—their graduate desks were in this temporary trailer at Stanford. And some out of Jerry's apartment. A couple weeks after the show, we found space in Mountain View and moved in. We got funding and that allowed us to go find office space.

Livingston: Sequoia was your VC?

Brady: Yes.

Livingston: How much money did you get?

Brady: $1 million.

Livingston: That was a lot of money back then, especially for a company doing something so new.

Brady: Absolutely. Two graduate students who had never held a job, another programmer, me, with no experience in the US in an industry that didn't exist yet. Yeah, it was a lot of money.

Livingston: What were your main goals when you first started? Did you want to get more people on the Internet?

Brady: We had enough traffic to go sell advertising. We knew if we sold ads on all our pages as of then, at a $20 CPM, that would cover our costs. It's hard to remember back what your mindset was, but I know it wasn't, "Let's get everyone on the Internet." That was way beyond us. The mindset was more like, "Let's not let this sink the company; let's keep it going." And part of that was just making money, so we did a bunch of crazy things in addition to advertising to try to bring in money. We made book deals and a bunch of little things that really didn't add up to anything. But we did anything in the name of getting money while we looked for proper management. Because we all knew it wasn't us.

"If this thing is going to be as big as we want it to be, we're not the people to run it,"—although we'd have loved to. So we had a CEO search for 6 months. It was really 6 months of struggling between then and when we got Tim Koogle to come.

Livingston: What were some of the important turning points during those 6 months?

Brady: Netscape was the only browser back then, well before Internet Explorer. They had a directory button that was part of the browser, and they linked to us from that button for free. Netscape's job actually was to grow the Internet—the way they were going to make money was to get everyone on the Internet and then sell servers. So anything with the purpose of getting people on would help them. They thought Yahoo was the best thing out there, so they gave us the link. It made sense for them at the time. That was big. It sent our traffic through the roof.

We hired an outside sales firm to help us start advertising. We sold five packages to five big companies; MasterCard was one. We got our first round of advertising before Koogle came.

We put up graphics, which was a big thing. That sounds really ridiculous now, but at the time Yahoo was all text. The connection speeds were so poor that any website that used a lot of graphics made the site unusably slow . . . Most of the traditional media folks didn't get it because they didn't realize that people were dialing in on slow modems. But we knew that if we were going to have any sort of brand, it would have to be a graphic. So we made the graphic switch at the same time we put up advertising.

We started to hire and build an organization without the CEO. We had temporary management that Sequoia helped us find—a CEO and CFO. Because we weren't having success finding a CEO, Sequoia insisted that we hire these managers. That didn't go great. They weren't as vested in helping Yahoo long-term as we were. There was a clear divide between someone who was interim and someone, like myself, who was fully invested in making it work. I had moved my whole life from the East Coast for it; my fortunes were tied to this thing, whereas theirs weren't necessarily.

In my estimation, they neither hurt nor helped us. They helped steady the ship for 6 months until we brought in Tim Koogle.

Livingston: Was it hard to convince people to join Yahoo, since it was so new?

Brady: Yeah, it was tough. We hired a lot of friends and friends of friends. You always hear "Never go into business with friends." But with the first 20 hires, everyone knew each other. Consequently there was a high level of trust. Everyone was young. It was pretty much everyone's first job, with the exception of the interim management. So people weren't worried where the Internet was going; they were just looking for something interesting to do, and joining Yahoo qualified.

The Internet really started to take off in July '95. Netscape went public, and that set off a chain reaction of PR. Not only was the Internet cool, but, all of a sudden, people could make money. The press was all over Jerry and Dave, so we spent a lot of time handling the press. We hired a temp PR firm that didn't work all that well. We didn't even need it because people were just calling in, and Jerry was so naturally good with the press, so things just kind of happened.

Then when Tim came in, he hired Jeff Mallett within a month, and then Jeff hired out his staff within 2 to 3 months.

Livingston: What were you personally focused on?

Brady: Product. I worked for Jeff Mallett, who was essentially COO under Tim Koogle. I became part of Jeff's staff, running product. There was also business development, and sales and marketing under Jeff.

Livingston: Did you ever worry about competitors?

Brady: There were a couple of seminal events where we thought we were going to get crushed by competitors. The first one was the directory button on the Netscape browser became a search button, and Netscape started selling the right to be linked from that button. Architext (later called Excite), which was funded by Kleiner Perkins, was a bunch of undergraduates from Stanford. They bought the Netscape search button with their venture capital money. Netscape was also funded by Kleiner Perkins.

Livingston: Did you make a bid for the button?

Brady: We bid up to a certain point in which we felt comfortable that we could make a return on money. After which point, we knew it became "investing in the brand," and I don't think we felt comfortable investing in the brand at that point. Because we didn't know how big the Internet was going to be at that point. Even though the press was going crazy, the numbers were still pretty small compared to any other media. I think it was $5 million that Excite paid for that button.

We definitely worried about Excite, and we were worried about Microsoft. In the summer of '95, Bill Gates sent out one of his famous memos on the Internet. I think this was one of the first ones. It talked about Microsoft needing to get in the game, and he ended the memo with: "My favorite site: Yahoo. Cool. Cool. Cool."

At first our reaction was, "Yeah, cool, cool, cool," and then our next thought was, "Oh no. Does that mean we're in Bill's crosshairs or does that mean we're just cool?" Any time you talk to Microsoft, just the way they do business, they have the potential to do whatever the hell they want, so when you go to them their mindset is always, "We could partner with you, or we could do it ourselves."

We were always very nervous about them doing anything. At the time, I think IE had just come out, and it was a poor effort, their first crack at a browser, but still, you knew that they were going to grow. There was always that threat looming over us.

There was also a handful of other competitors: Lycos, WebCrawler. Also, AOL was growing faster than the Internet for a period of time. Everyone heard "Internet," but then they went and signed up for AOL because it was the easiest way to get online. Although we thought it was crazy, AOL's walled garden was bigger than the Internet for a handful of months there, which made our strategy impossible. That was definitely a threat.

Livingston: Did you ever see anything on a competitor's site where you said, "They just launched this feature; we have to do it now."

Brady: In the early days, not too much. Jerry and Dave were way ahead of the curve. The ideas that they had really early on were right strategically and creatively. So everything we did through the middle of '97, invariably we were first and we did it very well.

The one thing we didn't do that all our competitors were spending a lot of time doing was search. They were crawling the Web and doing full text search, and our strategy was, "Look, that's a technology game. We're not a technology company, we're a media company. Since there are so many of them out there, we're always going to be able to rent it." That was the thought back then, and until Google came along that strategy was perfect. Because, as things played out, that's exactly what happened.

We had this searchable directory. It was big, and it had all the popular sites, so you could search for anything on it. But it didn't have everything. If you really wanted to search for that needle in the haystack, that wasn't us. But we had a lot of those people. They would read an article, then go to the Web and think, "I can find anything on Yahoo." The expectation when they came to Yahoo was that they could find anything, but we didn't necessarily deliver on that needle in the haystack expectation.

So what we did was that we searched our directory first, we gave you those results, and then, if we didn't find anything, we kicked you over to a full-text search. So, when I say we "rented" that technology, we essentially partnered with full-text search companies to be the falloff searches that we had.

Livingston: That's what you did with Google?

Brady: Yes. Strategically, it was spot-on until Google showed up. Because we always thought it was going to be a leapfrogging game. No one is ever going to be able to get so far ahead that we'd ever be in strategic risk of kingmaking a full-text search engine, because you just can't do that. Google ended up doing exactly that. At the time, until 2000/2001, we had Open Text first, then I think we had AltaVista, then Inktomi. So we just switched off as better technologies became available. We just switched out the old partners with the new ones and always had the best-of-breed search as our falloff.

Livingston: Was this invisible to the users?

Brady: Yes, it was largely invisible to our users. Even though their brands were there, you came to the front page of Yahoo; you searched; the search result had a Yahoo brand on the upper-left and the technology provider had a smaller brand. We tried to make it as seamless as possible.

Livingston: When you were writing the original business plan, did you have any idea that you'd go public about a year after getting funding?

Brady: None. Neither did Jerry and Dave. They may have hoped, but I don't know what their hopes were. At that time you had no idea how big the Internet was going to be. It had less to do with us, and a lot more to do with just how quickly the Internet grew and the fact that we were able to survive as the Internet got as big as it did.

Livingston: Do you remember the rationale behind going public, or was it your VCs who wanted you to?

Brady: No, it really wasn't driven by the VCs. There were a bunch of different reasons—and I wasn't privy to all those conversations. However, there were a couple of considerations. One, IPO windows don't last forever. Markets get hot and then they don't. If you go out, you can only go IPO while the market's hot. Netscape lit that market afire for us. The other consideration was that we saw that one of the ways we were going to have to compete was to acquire companies. The best way to do that was to have a currency other than the cash in the bank—to have a stock to pay people for their companies. So, in order to get big fast, which we thought we needed to do, we had to have a public stock. That was probably the biggest reason. Then raising money was obviously a third very important thing we needed to do.

Livingston: Were you nervous that Stanford would claim to own Yahoo? Wasn't it running on their servers?

Brady: It was. I was never part of those conversations. I was obviously nervous, and I asked, and Jerry and Dave said, "No, it's taken care of. Don't worry about it." And it was.

Stanford is very progressive in that. Yahoo is far from the first startup that originated there and will be far from the last one. It was new enough, and it wasn't a specific technology; it was a brand. It wasn't really an invention; it wasn't a piece of technology. They were smart enough to know that anything they would do to stifle it would kill it, so their best hope was to just let it go and hope that Jerry and Dave gave money back later, which they did. They optimized their outcome, trust me.

Livingston: Was Stanford concerned that Yahoo was going to crash their servers?

Brady: Yes. That's why they told them to get off. That's what forced the issue. It became so big that it was starting to bog down Stanford's pipes, so they said, "You guys need to leave."

Livingston: I heard that you guys used Netscape's offices at one point.

Brady: We did. Mark Andreessen loved what Jerry and Dave were doing and heard that Stanford was kicking us off at a certain point and offered to host it for 30 or 60 days.

Livingston: Do you think your mixed background of business and engineering helped you?

Brady: It's hard to know, since you don't know the alternative. Probably more than anything, the business education gave me the confidence to know what I knew and what I didn't know. I knew my zone of operation and things that I was good at and things where I knew I should go ask because I didn't know what I was doing.

Livingston: Were you better at some things than you thought?

Brady: I knew that I liked doing certain things, and, with most people, things you like you tend to be better at anyways. I'm good at building things, products specifically. Creative marketing, product marketing, which I had done earlier in my first job in Tokyo, was what I ended up gravitating toward.

Livingston: Think back to the first year. What do you remember that surprised you about life at a startup?

Brady: There wasn't a whole lot of time for reflection. It was moving so fast, so I don't ever remember stopping and thinking, "This is different than the way I thought it would be." It certainly was a surprise, because no one had any idea what the Internet was going to do.

Looking back, I don't think I understood the time commitment or the emotional commitment it takes to get something off the ground. Despite how everything grew, it was a task just staying on the wave that was the Internet.

Very, very long hours. The group of people that we had assembled was just great, so the hours were never dreaded. You enjoyed being at work, even though sometimes it was 16, 18 hours a day. That's the only thing really specifically that I think back on a lot.

Livingston: I wonder if it was because it was on the early side of the Bubble and there weren't as many people going through that?

Brady: It was definitely exciting for the right reasons. As the Internet got bigger and bigger, we were saying to ourselves, "We're in the vortex of a pretty big storm." And most people don't get the privilege to know that they are at the center of something while it's happening. We were in the middle of everything. But we knew we were going through it while it was happening, which added a sense of enjoyment to it. And responsibility.

Livingston: Do you remember anything in the first year that you guys might have done wrong?

Brady: Nothing major. Because any screw-up we recognized and were pretty good at correcting it to the extent it could be corrected. There weren't a whole lot of egos, so people wouldn't defend a dumb idea just because it was theirs.

But there were certainly companies that we missed. We missed Hotmail. Jerry and I had dinner with Sabeer Bhatia and Jack Smith, and they were explaining it to us and—I hate to admit it—we were saying, "I see it, but I don't see how it can get big." We were on this rocket ship, and they were talking about something that really hadn't caught on.

All we knew was that you got your email through work. They were like, "No. There's a bunch of people that hate their work email because it gets screened." The whole notion of the ubiquitous, dialing in from home, access everywhere was still so far away that we just didn't think it was going to catch on as fast as it did. We didn't pursue it as hard as we should have, clearly.

We screwed up. But, we went and found the #2, Rocketmail, made it work, and now Yahoo's bigger than Hotmail. Mea culpa, but we fixed it.

Livingston: Was there anything you remember about Yahoo that mainstream people just didn't get that was a big idea?

Brady: What was really central to our understanding of the Internet was that it was this open system where you couldn't really put up walls. One of the things that I think Filo did a great job of making happen was that, when someone did a search and you didn't find what you were looking for on Yahoo, rather than just saying, "It's not here," or "Go check out this other thing," he put links to our competitors, then prefilled the query, so you'd just click on Excite and they would do a search on Excite for the same thing.

Certainly they don't teach you in business school to go point to your competitors, but it sent the right message to the users, which was, "It's all about you. We're going to get you the data you want. If it exists on the Web, we're going to find it for you, even if we don't make money off of it directly." But it keeps people coming back because they know we have their best interest in mind. I think that was a big idea. It was an acknowledgment that you, as a single company, can't be everything to everyone. We're not a walled garden like AOL. We're this connection point, and it's our job to get you to where you want to go.

Livingston: What were the most popular link categories at first?

Brady: The sex category was probably a quarter of everything on the Web. Not just Yahoo, but everything on the Web. Just like the VHS industry when it first got going. The Internet was no different in that respect.

There was also a lot of product information. People quickly began to do research before major purchases—about cars and reviews and things like that.

One of the big things we did in the first 6 months was that we brought Reuters online. CNN was online at the time, I think, but done poorly—slow, a ton of graphics, just didn't get it. And Reuters had this rich set of news that back then they didn't get to display anywhere. They would just sell it to people in bits and pieces, and no one would ever see it in its entirety, and that turned out to be really huge.

Livingston: How did you handle pornography?

Brady: It's a tough issue. It was always talked about. It was never taken lightly. But we were also in support of free speech. It was one of these things where we were always struggling with "whose responsibility is it?" People come to us to find information; we're not displaying the pictures, per se. Is it our responsibility to find out what age users are before we pass it off, or should that wall be at the site, etc., etc.

Ultimately we ended up removing all of our links to those sites, after probably about a year and a half of just struggling with ways to do it appropriately and responsibly and not really being able to find a good way. At the time the child protection laws were coming out, but I believe we had pulled everything down even before that.

Livingston: Do you remember the biggest debate that you got into?

Brady: There was always speed versus look-and-feel. In trying to grow a brand, look-and-feel has a lot to do with it, as does speed, so there's always that balancing act. Arguing the necessity of graphics with Filo was always a big argument. I'll never forget our 8-year debate.

How to handle pornography was another one. There were just so many. There's no one that just stands out as a watershed per se. There was a lot of Internet-related legislation in the first couple of years, and Congress, in my opinion, didn't have a clear idea what was going on. They were obviously influenced by lobbyists from traditional media who had very specific agendas that weren't necessarily in the best interest of the Internet's development. "Should we say anything? How should we react?" There were certainly those. We turned our site black a couple of times—the background black and the text in white—in protest. I forget what the proposed legislation was.

Livingston: Was new legislation a big concern?

Brady: Absolutely. Just a few things here and there—copyrights, digital rights written in a slightly different way—and we could have a different Internet.

Livingston: Do you remember any other interesting new turning points?

Brady: I remember one day when Rabin, the Prime Minister of Israel, got shot. It was the first time that we put new news on the front page. For us to think of our site as a public service to some degree—to find things on the web and use it to communicate news—was a big deal. "Rabin Assassinated" was our first foray into news, and the reaction we got from everyone about using Yahoo for that purpose was overwhelmingly good.

Livingston: Any proud moments?

Brady: The Gates memo was a pretty cool moment—scary and proud at the same time. Going public was a proud moment. Being added to the NASDAQ 100 was an even prouder moment.

Livingston: Was it hard for Yahoo to turn down acquisition offers in the early days?

Brady: I obviously never had equal weight in that decision. It was always Jerry and Dave, and I don't know the full list of suitors. I know AOL was a suitor, I know the *LA Times* was a suitor, and I know they had gotten informal offers from Microsoft—never anything concrete. A lot of them were very early on, before they even took venture money. For Jerry and Dave—neither grew up with a lot of money—to turn down a lot of money at that stage with no guarantee of the company doing anything afterwards, was, in my estimation, a big deal. They had a lot of confidence in what they were doing.

Livingston: What was one of the funniest moments early on?

Brady: The funniest thing I can remember was when there was a huge storm in May of '95, and the power grid went down for a few days. We had to go rent a power generator and take turns filling it with diesel fuel for 4 days. 24/7. We were laughing, "How many pages to the gallon today?" It was a crazy storm and it also started leaking in our building. We had all these meetings scheduled and couldn't just shut it down. We had meetings by candlelight with a bunch of prominent companies. They walk in; there are no lights; there are cords running everywhere leading to the generator out back; water dripping from the ceiling. We were trying to convince them, "Oh, yeah, we're a real business," when you say, "Hold on, I gotta go fill up the tank." So I remember that set of days pretty vividly.

Livingston: Did you ever have to pull off any tricks to make yourselves seem bigger than you actually were?

Brady: I don't have a good story for this, but I remember clearly Jeff Mallett's coming on board. I'm working like a dog and he had just started. In addition to everything else I'm doing, I'm also trying to do all the PR stuff. Even though I had our PR kits professionally bound, they were a startup's PR kits. He had just come from Novell. He looks at me, and he's just like, "This is C+ work."

I hadn't slept for a couple of days, and I felt like taking a swing at him. But he was absolutely right. "If we're going to appear big, we'd better act big, and this is what we hand out? You can't hand that out." I remember that very clearly, and that was a really good lesson for me—"I know you're tired, I know you're working hard, but it's not an excuse for putting out something that looks like a startup."

When Jeff came in, I'd been working hard for 8 months, and I was already a little bit tired, and I didn't think he would keep up. I didn't know him all that well, but he had twice as much energy as anyone. We started doing two red-eyes a week to New York for business. "OK, we have to go meet MTV tomorrow. Red-eye out. Meeting. Come back that same day." We did that for 3 to 4 months, and I just remember thinking when he walked in the door, that I couldn't work any harder. But we worked harder, faster, smarter. That was definitely a step up in both effort and professionalism.

Being everywhere all the time made us look bigger than we were; "Oh yeah, we'll be in New York, we'll be there." I'd say, "Jeff, I have all these things on my plate," and he always responded, "No, we're going." It was someone who had come from a big company who knew how to act like a big company, even though behind the scenes it was startup.

Livingston: Was there ever a time when you wanted to quit?

Brady: No. There were a few days where I was really upset, but never close to the point where I wanted to quit. It was too much fun. After the first 4 to 5 months, you could see what was coming; you knew you were on the wave; things were only going to grow.

In the first couple of months there were a few days where I felt, "I left school for this?" Because when I left school, I didn't know that I was going to graduate—I just left. I was 70 percent sure that I was going to get a degree, but that 30 percent was still sitting out there. And my dad had paid for it, so the thought of telling him I didn't get it and having this company go belly-up was like, "That's a bad scenario."

Livingston: Was your dad supportive?

Brady: Very. He knew Jerry from undergraduate days.

Livingston: Any advice you'd give to someone who was starting a startup?

Brady: Part of it is "know yourself." Try to do as much thinking up front as to what your breaking points are. One of the things I think I did well was that I never spent any time thinking about quitting or any of these doomsday scenarios, "Oh, God, what if this doesn't happen."

Before I joined, I knew where the line was, when I would quit, at what point, and so when I was in the game, it never crossed my mind. I also knew why I was involved, what motivated me, and I didn't spend a lot of time perseverating on that stuff. At the end of the day, it wasn't going to get you anywhere. It mattered, but only in an abstract way, compared to the day-to-day of getting stuff done. Doing all that thinking all up front: why am I getting in, when do I leave, if I leave then why am I doing it, what gets me up in the morning, what could happen that could make me stop getting up in the morning? I've seen a lot of people get so emotional because they start something on a whim; they are doing this thinking while they are doing business, and, when things don't go well, you don't act rationally, to say the least. There's a lot to it; it can get really emotional because you get tired and there's a lot of work and you're invested in it. All those personally motivating things—think them through before you get things started.

Jerry was one of my best friends before we started the company, and it's his company, so doing business with friends—you always hear, "Don't do business with friends, bad idea." So one of the things that really helped me was that he and I had a conversation before I joined, "OK, here are the ground rules." And this is really what made me think about it. "OK, if this happens, I walk away." We had the conversation in order to preserve our friendship, having no idea what was going to happen, but that conversation got me thinking about it and why was I involved.

Livingston: Is there anything about Yahoo's early days that the world should know?

Brady: I know it's a bit of a cliché, but the people that started it were awesome. In every aspect of the word, not just in effort or handling the responsibility they were given, but just good people, doing it for the right reasons. You could see it in the product and the way we acted.

The early Yahoo team (1995): Donald Lobo (left), Tim Brady (second from left), Jerry Yang (seated in front), and David Filo (in his Ford Pinto)

Mike Lazaridis
Cofounder, Research In Motion

Mike Lazaridis founded Research In Motion (RIM) with his friend Doug Fregin in 1984 while still an undergraduate at the University of Waterloo. One of their first projects was a local area network that ran industrial displays. Near the end of Lazaridis's senior year, they landed a $600,000 contract to build a similar network for General Motors. A few weeks shy of his graduation, Lazaridis left school to focus full-time on the company.

RIM was one of the first companies to appreciate the importance of wireless networks. In the early 1990s, when email was still largely unknown in corporate America, Lazaridis foresaw the potential of mobile email. A series of projects in this area culminated in 1999 in the BlackBerry, now the dominant product in this market.

The BlackBerry was one of those innovations that not only became popular, but changed the way organizations operate. Some of the most powerful people in business and politics run their lives with this device.

RIM went public in 1997, and is one of Canada's most admired technology companies.

Livingston: How did you get started with Research In Motion? How did you know Doug?

Lazaridis: I knew Doug from grade school, but we started working together in high school. Our high school had a state-of-the-art electronics and shop program that was the result of a donation from a local industrialist. When all this equipment had arrived, it was still in crates. I had asked to open some of the boxes and pull out the equipment, and I remember the teacher saying, "Well, you can open any box you like, but there's one condition: you have to read the manual first."

This doesn't sound like a big deal, but, to a student that just came to high school—to read a manual on how to use an oscilloscope, how to use a signal generator, a computer trainer, how to use all this advanced equipment—these were tricky textbooks to get through and understand. Of course, once I was able to prove that I knew how to use the equipment and what it did, I was able to open the box. And we opened every single box.

Livingston: This was at a high school?

Lazaridis: Yeah. It was a tricky time back then because a divide between the honor roll students and the shop students was beginning. The shop teachers tried to correct it before it got out of control and became the culture there. Many of us down in that shop program were also honor roll students. It was sort of "Upstairs, Downstairs"—the upstairs math and computer science classrooms, and then there was the downstairs shop program.

We tried to bridge the gap and explain to the teachers and students upstairs what we were learning down there and how we were applying the mathematics and science we were learning upstairs. Literally we were. I was able to give lectures to the math program, showing them how trigonometry could be applied to power generation, power control, power transformation that we were learning downstairs.

Livingston: I read that your high school electronics teachers said that connecting computers to wireless would be the next big thing. Did you realize how big it would be?

Lazaridis: Of course not. The thing back then is that you are juggling all these courses and work, and at the same time you've got these passionate interests that you just can't find enough time for. You're just trying to juggle it all, knowing that you want to get to university, so you have to get good marks. It was a bit of a challenge because you really had an extra course load. These shop programs were almost like a course to themselves, there was so much work to do. You just spent every waking hour—you come to school early, you go to the shop, work a little bit further on it, then after school you go down there and hope that you can finish your homework in time to keep working on what you were doing.

It was a grueling time, but it was rewarding in the sense that we had all these resources, and we basically had a brand new curriculum, so it could go as far as we were prepared to take it. Doug and I started learning about computers on our own. This was back in the late '70s. Computers were still punch card systems that were in some other building that you never got to see. But Doug and I started playing with these computer trainers—they were Digital Equipment Corporation computer trainers—and what we learned there was the actual fundamentals of computers: how to build gates, how to build recent memory circuits, how to build registers, and how to wire them all together and sequence them with a clock. It was very fundamental knowledge, and it really made a difference as time went on.

At the same time, my electronics teacher was also the president of the local amateur television and ham radio club. So he had us taking apart televisions and converting their tuners for use at the amateur band. Back then, we knew how to tune them, but we didn't really understand what we were doing. It wasn't until university that we started to get that understanding, but we saw how the stuff worked; we saw the potential. When my teacher started to see us really get seduced by the computer and what we could do there, I remember him saying, "Don't get too caught up with computers, because it's going to be the person that puts wireless technology and computers together that's going to make a big difference." I don't think he was seeing what we eventually did, but he understood the fact that computers gave us two fundamental things. One was the ability to send information unambiguously, and the second was that it allowed us to control the RF process and make it more efficient. It wasn't until years later that I understood what that meant.

So we went to university and, again, this is the early '80s, so you're talking about stuff that was going on at university that most people had no clue as to what it was, what it meant, and its relevance. The University of Waterloo had this massive computer system. It was a big IBM mainframe system that was the centerpiece of the campus. But more importantly, it was the centerpiece of the vision of the founders and the faculty there. It was in a massive room we called the Red Room, which was literally right out of a science fiction movie—it had a raised floor with a windowed mezzanine going right around it, and inside you had all these computers.

In all the classrooms around the mezzanine area were these terminals. We were just converting from punch cards to video terminals, so again, it was that transition period. I arrived just in time not to have to use punch cards. I went straight to terminals. And we started using something called "email" to get and submit our assignments—as well as using it to collaborate between ourselves. We started working with the Internet. It was called the ARPANET back then, and it was a collaboration between universities, researchers, businesses, and the military. We didn't think much of it, but we were being trained to use something that really wouldn't become mainstream for at least another decade.

At the same time, we were working with computer networks. This was when computer networks were research projects at universities. In fact, we had our own research program called Watlan (Waterloo Local Area Network Project). We had compilers, real-time operating systems—you don't really see the relevance these things are going to have in your life because you're so caught up in the workload and the social environment. You don't realize that you're being trained with state-of-the-art technology, applications, and techniques. As time went on, we started realizing that this stuff was pretty cool—it was pretty advanced technology—and we started getting more and more involved with the various aspects of these different programs and research projects.

In my later years, I took on projects where I was helping some of the faculty projects, just basically trying to pay my way. When the last year came, I had already been doing some computer programming contract work. It was then the 1984 recession, and it really impacted the high-tech industry. A lot of the engineers weren't getting jobs. University of Waterloo prided itself with its very high placement record for both co-op and graduate programs, and that was one of the worst years we ever had.

I remember a lot of the students were very upset. They said, "We worked really hard, and now we can't even get jobs." I just couldn't believe that, because you're talking about students that had to work very hard and had to be very talented to get to this university. We were being trained with stuff that was right out of a science fiction novel, so I couldn't imagine how we couldn't be in a better position. I remember us having these arguments, and they knocked me off my soapbox one day when they said, "If you believe this so much, why don't you start a company?" Literally, I went out and started it within a few weeks after that.

Livingston: Weren't you a month away from graduating?

Lazaridis: Yeah. I started a company before then. We got a contract that just got us so busy, we started hiring people, and I couldn't actually keep working at school. I had to take a leave of absence.

Livingston: When did you start this?

Lazaridis: Contract work would have been in my third year. Then, in my fourth year, I started what became RIM.

Livingston: In the third year, you were just doing this work to earn some extra money to pay for college?

Lazaridis: It was that, and there was also some very interesting work going on at the university. In university I was working on some new languages that were sort of the beginnings of what became Java. The whole virtual machine. I'm drawing a difficult parallel, but I was working on something called STOIC. It was an interpretive language that we were getting working on various microcomputers at the time.

In fact, we ended up buying one of those computers when the university put it up for surplus. Apparently, it had broken, and I remembered that computer system because we were using it in our engineering class. We were doing all our assignments on that one computer. I put a bid in and I got it for—I can't remember now, but it would have been $400 or $600, because it didn't work. I took it back to our office—it was massive—and took it apart, and, as I powered it up part by part, I realized that the power supply had broken. Once we fixed the power supply, the computer just came right up. So we did our big contract on that computer.

Livingston: How did you land these contracts as a young undergrad?

Lazaridis: When you have access to state-of-the-art education, and you know how to use these machines—and you are comfortable with them—you just have to make that one leap to realize that you can actually help people. There is a need for that kind of experience, but the problem was that a lot of these companies didn't know they had that need. It was just a matter of breaking out of your shell and going out and talking to them—looking in the newspapers, looking in local message boards, talking to different companies, asking if they needed any work done. Basically, you had to do a little bit of sales.

But what was interesting was that, in every case, you were able to bring this experience to bear on a tricky problem that had been there for a while and that you found that you could solve it very elegantly and quickly using what you'd learned. That's how we got these projects with General Motors and the National Film Board and Kodak, which eventually led to the Emmy Award and the Technical Oscar.

When you go back, you realize that the exposure you had in high school and in university was actually preparing you for a decade and two decades out.

We need to make sure that we are allowing students to be exposed to future technology and not reducing it to current—what a lot of people would like to say, "relevant" teaching. What's relevant teaching? What's relevant research? When I was at university, if you went in and started looking at what we were doing, you would say, "Why don't you guys get a life and do something relevant? What is this stuff? Nobody's going to use this."

When we were there, that's what people were thinking. "How many people are going to have a computer in their house? What is this networking stuff? You are talking about science fiction; you're not talking about important things. Why don't you do something important?" "Important" back then became "obsolete" very quickly after we left university.

Livingston: Was Doug part of the consulting business?

Lazaridis: Doug was at University of Windsor, and we collaborated. It wasn't until I decided to start RIM that I called Doug up and told him what I wanted to do and I needed his help. He was up within 2 weeks of that call.

Livingston: Did you have to tell your parents you weren't finishing school?

Lazaridis: Oh yeah. But what was actually harder was having to go to the president of the university and ask for a leave of absence. I had never met him before. It was quite interesting because he apologized for having to try to dissuade me from it. After he finished his speech, he wished me the best of luck and shook my hand with a big smile. I remembered that and, ironically, 20 years later he's one of RIM's board members.

Livingston: So you start RIM, and you have a $600,000 contract with General Motors. What were you doing?

Lazaridis: One of the things we did was that we listened to what General Motors was trying to accomplish. The RFP had been out for over 2 years. We got a copy of it and looked at it, and we recognized a couple things in there that you couldn't do without some of the state-of-the-art techniques that we'd learned at university. One was that it was begging for a local area network. So we had to create one, based on what we remembered.

I went back and talked to some of the teachers there and looked at some of the research that was being done. We had to develop that LAN from scratch, but we had to also make sure that it was very rugged, because it had to be used in a very hostile environment in these manufacturing plants. There were things like arc welders and 4800-volt systems. It was a tricky thing to do. Then we made sure that the display systems could boot from a central computer. If you think about it, even today, we're just starting to realize the "diskless PC"—PCs that boot up remotely, sort of the Internet appliances today. We had to come up with a system that could do that.

Then, of course, what was interesting was that we got to play with one of the first IBM PCs. I remember it was just about the time when we ordered it that the big hard drives were coming out. We changed our order from the tape system to a hard drive system. We thought that was just a luxury. That was a whopping 10-megabyte hard drive.

Livingston: I read that you got a grant from the Canadian government. Why did you apply? Were you seeking money to grow?

Lazaridis: You have to realize that the early days aren't pretty. You are worrying about paying rent. Doug and I were sharing a leased Honda Civic. The big luxury in that car was the option we took out for a five-speed transmission instead of a four-speed. We lived in the same apartment, but the whole thing was just trying to conserve expenses because we had no idea how long it would take before we'd be established.

We heard about these government programs, and we started applying for them. It was a lot of work to actually apply for these things, and then it was a lot of paperwork to maintain them. In the early days, they weren't really big grants. They were rather small, and sometimes you wondered if it was worth all the trouble. But it was very helpful when we needed it. As you became experienced, and as the government agencies that we were working with became comfortable with what we were doing and recognized that we were onto something, the grants became more interesting.

But the real boost for us was when we started recognizing this wireless data technology. That's when it hit me. I was at a conference in 1987 where someone was talking about what was happening in Japan, where they had put in a wireless data system just for Coca-Cola. It was expensive to have to keep driving these trucks out every 2 days covering all of Tokyo to make sure all of the vending machines were full. They'd find that, most of the time, the vending machines didn't need to be refilled. The system went in and was able to pay for itself just because of the reduced number of truck trips and fuel expenses, because the machines were able to signal that they needed refilling. Then a computer system was able to schedule deliveries to make sure that none of the machines ever emptied out.

When I saw that, I remembered what my teacher had said in high school. I looked at it and said, "This is interesting. I want to do this." Back then, I also remembered some of the things we did at university with a lot of signal processing work. I had received a contract at that point because of my interest—and this is just weird how this happens, but you happen to be in the right place at the right time. I received interest from Cantel, which is now Rogers. The president of Cantel asked to meet, and we started talking about this system that they had just bought called Mobitex. It was a wireless data system, and they needed someone to write some software and help them make it work.

It was a strange request, but I went and saw what they had bought and realized that this was brand new stuff. It was very primitive, and the documentation hadn't even been fully translated from Swedish yet. I remember meeting with someone and he said, "If you can make this stuff work, you've got the contract." Michael Barnstijn, one of my early partners, looked at it and said, "Mike, I think I can read this well enough"—because he was from the Netherlands—"that we could probably get this stuff to work." We spent the next few hours hooking everything up, and we surprised them because we got it working.

We got the contract and started writing software to make it all work, and the rest was history. We wrote most of the very first wireless protocol software, application programming interface (API), the development tools—all the early stuff for the first wireless data networks.

That was our first break. That was our first chance to break out of a consulting role and really start producing products.

Livingston: Would you say this was one of the biggest turning points for RIM?

Lazaridis: I would say it was the beginning of a turning point. No one knew what wireless data was. You couldn't go in and apply for loans to do wireless data. It was bizarre. Cell phones were just happening—you started seeing lawyers and real estate agents with cell phones. When you started talking about wireless data, no one knew what you were talking about. Think about it; there were no computers in people's homes at the time. It was a very rare occurrence to see a computer in somebody's home. They weren't dialing in to the Internet. Everything back then was very specific. It was proprietary; you were dialing in to servers. So it was a different world than it is today.

Livingston: If you were doing things that were so ahead of their time, how were you so successful?

Lazaridis: The tricky part was, how do you intercept a market trend? How do you intercept an industrial trend? How do you package what you've learned and what's happening in the technology space so that it has new value to customers? How do you find those customers?

What we learned with Mobitex and later Datatech was that there were some really interesting applications that were being developed, and we were right there while it was happening. But it took a lot of faith. You call it vision, but it's a combination of vision and faith that 1) it's going to happen someday, and 2) it has value, and 3) you can actually accomplish it in an economic way and promote it so that you can fund the development and growth of the business. That's pretty tricky stuff.

Livingston: Can you tell me about any of the other major turning points?

Lazaridis: One of the dreams that I had all through high school was to build some kind of space-based technology. You have these visions when you are young of working for NASA and building a space probe or part of a spaceship.

At about the time when I was getting deeper into wireless data, I had an opportunity to work for SPAR Aerospace, a Canadian company. They had contacted us and asked if we wanted to bid on something that was very similar to something that we had done before. They needed this product for what was going to be the Canadarm2 on the International Space Station.

You have to remember that people were just starting to understand what Canadarm1 was. And the space station was still a document before Congress, and Canadarm2 was something that was going to be built later. You look at that, and you go, "Holy smoke, this is what I always wanted to do! In a strange way, I had been preparing myself to do something like this, and here it is in front of me and I could have this contract."

That's when the business sense kicked in, and I had to ask the question, so I asked SPAR, "How many of these are you going to need?" They said, "Six." "Six for what—initially, over time?" Although these circuit boards were going to be very, very expensive, the opportunity for mass production was six. Then I asked, "When are you going to need them?" "We'll need a couple prototypes first; then, of course, we won't need them until the space station is built." I said, "When is the space station going to be built?" They said, "It hasn't quite passed through Congress yet." So I had to make a decision—and I believe I chose wisely. I gave up my childhood ambition, to continue building wireless data products.

Ironically, years later I was meeting with Sean O'Keefe, the former director of NASA, at his office. He was a big proponent of BlackBerry. NASA is a user of BlackBerry. They found them extremely useful when the hurricane season went through there—just being able to coordinate and having a backup system—but now they use them daily. I remember Sean telling me this story that one day he was going home (he got driven home and he does his work on his BlackBerry on his way home), and he gets an email from someone that he recognizes and it's asking all these questions about the space shuttle. He's answering them, and he gets more questions and he's answering them. And he says, "This name is really familiar." And he looks it up, and he realizes that name is on the active duty roster. It turns out to be an astronaut on the space station, and he was basically asking, in a nice way, when's he coming home. Years later, ironically, the BlackBerry allowed me to enjoy part of that childhood aspiration, because the BlackBerries were used by NASA, and they were using them to communicate with the International Space Station.

Livingston: Fast-forward a little bit to when you came up with the idea for the BlackBerry. You were in your basement—it seems like you have a thing for basements!

Lazaridis: When you try to get away from it, the basement is a nice place to hide.

All through this, I was always looking for value. I was trying to find, "Where's the value of wireless data?" Early on, we had realized that wireless push email had some serious value. But it was really tricky to do. There was a lot of work, a lot of trial and error, a lot of R&D that had to be accomplished and invested in to actually get the system to work properly. To this day, the BlackBerry is the only system that works well and is reliably secure under those conditions.

Fifteen years ago, this was still a bit of a research project, and we were spending a lot of time on that. But the product itself, its final form, was still too unwieldy to be able to put in your pocket. That was our goal. We realized early on that the function was there, but the value was limited by the packaging and limitations of the technology of the day.

So we started working on this, and it was just about the time when my son was born. I remember coming home, and my son had had a more difficult day, and I had to take over. I remember just getting him to bed, and then I went downstairs and got on the computer, and I put on some music and just started writing. Three hours later, I had just put the finishing touches on what became the plan for what eventually became the BlackBerry. Back then, it was called an interactive pager—I coined the phrase "interactive pager." Then what I did was come up with five improvements to the wireless data networks that would allow us to provide a reliable experience that was also power efficient. I came up with the basic premise as to where the value was and what became the foundational underpinnings of our technology for almost a decade after that point. As soon as I sent it to the office, that's when my son woke up.

That was a turning point, because we've used that document for years. It's still used by people here because it defines the essence of the BlackBerry experience, and it has allowed us to remain true to that and really bring value to our customers. It helped us stay away from the fads that really didn't bring any value and just made the product more complicated and more expensive and impacted things like battery life.

Livingston: Back in 1997, was it hard to convince people that they should want to travel with email access?

Lazaridis: The key thing to remember was that email was not a new idea for anyone that went to school in the early '80s. But industry was rather slow to adopt it. Not because of anything with industry, but because the technology just hadn't reached the kind of ubiquity that it needed. It had to reach a certain critical mass so that there was somebody to send it to.

What we realized was that, in 1997 and before, there was a paging culture in North America. (These networks were fundamentally North American.) We decided to build a very advanced pager. It looked like a pager; it was the size of a pager; it even seemed to operate like a pager. Except that it was a full-blown two-way email terminal. It took a lot of back-end processing to make that work. Something that a lot of people don't realize is that the BlackBerry product is a system, and the email posting and reception is actually done by a server. We spent a lot of time getting it right, knowing that the market was not ready for it. We disguised what later became the BlackBerry as a pager.

Livingston: Because people knew what a pager was, they could say, "Hey, I need one of those"?

Lazaridis: That's right. We gave them the opportunity to go two-way, so that they could send a message as well as receive it. That people found very valuable. But the system was expensive—the monthly fee was expensive, because it was brand new; it was embryonic. But we knew that email was catching on.

We had email at RIM as soon as we started the company. We had email on our business cards back when other business cards had telex numbers on them. Every time I gave out my card, people would ask me, "What's an email address?" It wasn't until about 5 years later that we started to converge on something called a fax number. It wasn't until 15 years after university that you really started to see people adopting email in the Fortune 1000 in a big way. So in 1999, we knew the time was right, and we had done a lot of research to make sure we were launching at the right time.

We decided to launch it in New York, in the financial markets, because they were big users of systems and email. They were also affluent, so they could afford the service early on. They were big users of data and information, and they needed it in real time. To them, time was money in a big way. The BlackBerry system gave them that in spades.

What was interesting was how we named it, because it goes back to our research roots. We decided to do it very scientifically. We went out and found one of the leading naming companies at the time, called Lexicon, and we worked with them for 6 months to come up with the name. It was probably the most expensive word I ever bought.

BlackBerry ended up being one of the all-time most famous brands worldwide. It works everywhere. We tested it around the world. It was one of 40 names that were on the list that we narrowed it down to. We did a lot of testing to see what it meant to people. Could we build a brand, an experience, around it? There was a lot of thought around that name.

Livingston: As a Canadian founder, do you think there's anything that readers should know about advantages to being in Canada? Were you ever tempted to move to Silicon Valley?

Lazaridis: I have to tell you, we were so busy that we never really thought it made a difference. One of the great things about being in Canada is that there's this education that is available to everyone at the highest level, and that's really what helped us. There was never a thought in my mind as to "should I put it somewhere else?" Regardless of whether we should put RIM in the United States or not, even the idea of where I should put it in Canada. There was never any hesitation. I had to have this company next to University of Waterloo and Wilfrid Laurier, a university down the street, because I knew that we needed to draw this talent to grow. There's something about having the proximity to the students and university in terms of brand awareness.

In fact, when we first leased our building here right next to the university, we could put a sign up, and I remember they were asking, "Do you like this sign? Do you like that sign?" I said, "Actually, I don't care about that. What's important to me are the signs on the back of the building." Of course, everyone recoiled from that. I explained to them, "I don't really care if anyone else knows where the building is. All I want is the students to know where the building is." From then on, all our buildings have had signs in the back, toward the university.

One of the things I realized was that to get strong co-op students, you had to start early because, by the second year, you've lost them already to some other company. So we started hiring first- and second-year students, knowing that they were not really going to be full-time employees for 3 to 4 years after that. It was a 3- to 4-year investment we started making with students early on because I knew their value. We treated them like full-time employees. We're the largest co-op employer in Canada.

Arthur van Hoff
Cofounder, Marimba

Arthur van Hoff was part of the Java development team at Sun Microsystems when he left in 1996 to found Marimba, a software distribution company. Joining him as cofounders were two fellow developers from the Java team, Sami Shaio and Jonathan Payne, and Kim Polese, Java's product manager.

Marimba received lots of attention from the press and venture capitalists early on. The company grew from a 4-person startup to a company with more than 300 employees at the time of its IPO in 1999. van Hoff left the company in 2002 to start another startup, Strangeberry. Marimba was acquired by BMC Software in 2004.

Livingston: At what point did the four of you start talking about leaving Sun and starting your own company?

van Hoff: Jonathan had left Sun, and, when I tried to convince him to come back, he said, "Well I don't know if I'll ever come back to Sun, but I'll do a startup with you."

So we decided to do a startup, though we literally had no idea what we were going to make. The first thing that we did was drive around and find office space, which was getting pretty hard at the time. We found a little office above a flower shop on California Avenue in Palo Alto, and we went to a second-hand office furniture store and bought these heavy metal desks—$25 apiece. They weighed a million pounds, but we somehow carried them up the stairs.

Livingston: How did you fund your company at first?

van Hoff: Initially we all put in a little bit of money, I think $25,000 each. If you don't take a salary, that can last you a long time. Because starting a company is free, right, if you have a friend who is a lawyer. The law firm that we used, Gunderson Dettmer, will basically not take payment until you get funding. Silicon Valley is that way; everything is geared toward getting you started, and then you pay.

We spent about $1,400 to furnish the entire office, including equipment like a fax machine and printer. We all used cell phones at first, and we had no Internet access for the first couple of weeks, just the whiteboard.

Livingston: You took a pretty big risk to decide to start a company without an idea. You must have known that the four of you were pretty compatible?

van Hoff: You know, in a hot market like that, you saw a lot of people with crazy business ideas that were never going to work but they were getting funded. We were coming out of the Java project and felt that it was a pretty safe bet that if you are part of a core team and you leave together, getting an idea is not that hard. Anybody can have good ideas.

Over the years, I've learned that the first idea you have is irrelevant. It's just a catalyst for you to get started. Then you figure out what's wrong with it and you go through phases of denial, panic, regret. And then you finally have a better idea and the second idea is always the important one.

After Marimba, when I started Strangeberry with Jonathan, we had no plan whatsoever. We just put in some money and decided to spend a year brainstorming. We built all sorts of things, and everything we did turned out to be very relevant, because you're in the right area and you are giving yourself time to investigate. Eventually, you run into an interesting idea and you execute on that. People are really the key.

Livingston: When you left Sun, did they try to stop you?

van Hoff: Kim and I did a very dramatic thing. We arranged to have a meeting with Scott McNealy. He asked what we were there to talk about. When we told him that we were leaving to do a startup, he said, "Well, I can't wish you good luck, because everybody would go and do this. But I'll tell you one thing: don't fuck with me."

One of the things that we wanted to build was a user interface builder. Java was an interesting model, but there weren't any tools for it. So we spent the first few months working on a user interface, and then these guys from a small startup visited us and showed us their product, and it was pretty much what we were doing. They were acquired by Netscape like the next week, and they turned into the IFC (Internet Foundation Class). It was ironic because that eventually turned into the JFC, or Swing, the Java toolkit.

Livingston: Were you devastated that another company was doing the exact same thing?

van Hoff: Not really. Once they were acquired, we sort of threw in the towel because Netscape was so popular and there was really no way we could compete with that. We hadn't spent a lot of time on it yet. We had some prototypes and it was working quite well, but we moved on really quickly.

It was very surrealistic at the time because we had a lot attention from the press. There was a full-page photograph in *Wired* with no information at all. We weren't telling anyone what we were doing—mostly because we had absolutely no clue and we didn't want to let on.

But we then focused on software distribution, because the system that we helped build at Sun was not really scaling very well for real applications. We came up with the idea for subscription-based software where, rather than buying software, you subscribe to it and you get updates automatically.

That was an interesting idea, but it's only now that it's really popular. These days, a Windows computer updates automatically and so everybody expects that—but at the time this was a very new concept.

By the time we announced that we were doing software distribution, PointCast had come out. PointCast did push technology, which had some similarities to what we were doing, but we were immediately filed under "push." And that became a real problem, because for years we had to explain to people why we weren't a push company.

Livingston: Did all the publicity help or hurt your cause?

van Hoff: Well, all press is good press. It definitely helps. Whenever we wanted a meeting with an executive at a big company, we'd get it because we were very well known. Nobody had a clue what we were doing. So the mystique around Marimba gave us a lot of inroads to companies, which is incredibly helpful to get deals done.

In the end, it can work to your disadvantage because you always have to reeducate the market—you have to keep explaining what you really do. And you never have anyone coming to you saying, "I want what you have," because they don't know what you have. So it can work both ways.

There were always reporters talking to Kim because she was a female CEO of a technology company. I don't know if that was a good thing. There was so much focus on her and so little focus on the company. I'd go to parties and people would ask where I worked and when I'd tell them they'd say, "Marimba? Oh yeah, Kim Polese works there, right?" And I'd say, "Do you know what we do?" And they'd say, "No, I have no idea."

So if we were selling Kim Polese, we did really well. But that's not what you're there for. You're there for the product. So I think all the media hype did not work to our advantage. I think that Kim fell into that trap early on, and it was hard to get out of.

I remember one particularly bad article by *Fortune* magazine. This reporter came and visited the company for two days while we were on a company outing. We really opened up the kimono and spent hours with her, telling and showing her everything. Then the article that came out was an exposé on Kim and it was made even worse because they'd taken these photographs of her that were real extreme close-ups. It was terrible; it just made us look very bad since it was all about her. And all this time we spent with the reporter on our technology had been a complete waste of time, which was incredibly unfair.

But that's the problem: it's so much easier to write an article about Kim than it is to write an article about the company. It's not very interesting to write about mediocrity. You have to write about the extreme, because that is what people want to hear about. So when companies are all about selling product, traveling and working hard, it's all really boring stuff.

Livingston: Did you ever suggest to Kim that she stop talking to the press?

van Hoff: Yes, we did, but she ignored it. Kim was a good CEO in the startup phase, but as startups grow it can get more difficult. Marimba went from 0 to 40 people in the first year and grew to 300 people during the IPO. Anybody can run a company up to 100 people. You just have to be intelligent and have good intuition. There's a lot of tedious work you need to do, but it's not that hard. But there's a point when the company gets bigger that it just becomes a management problem; it becomes something that you have to have experience in.

Managing people and motivating teams requires a very different skill; it's not something that you can do by the seat of the pants. So the lack of experience eventually begins to show if you don't have somebody who can make decisions, for example.

We had this really funky power balance in our company where we had a really strong VP of sales and a really strong CFO and a really inexperienced CEO. And whenever there was a decision to be made, she couldn't break the tie. And what do you do? Once Kim got replaced by John Olsen, he was completely different. John had run big companies and it was really easy for him to make decisions that were very hard for us to make. And that tells you that as a founder, you have the skills to start companies from scratch, but it doesn't necessarily mean that you have the skill to grow it till they're larger.

Livingston: Did you have a plan in the beginning to get that big and take it public?

van Hoff: Well, every business plan has an exit strategy and ours was IPO. That was the right choice at that time. Right now, you'd aim for an acquisition. Everybody that joins a startup hopes to get rich. They also do it because it's fun, but you're taking a bet on winning a lot of money. But the odds are skewed against you because not a lot of startups actually succeed in fulfilling that bet.

We exceeded our own expectations in the end. But a business plan is a tool that you use to sell the idea to VCs. The VCs look at it and say, "There're no spelling mistakes and the math seems right. But I like the people so let's invest." A lot of the decision-making is very emotional. There's no formula that identifies good business plans versus bad business plans. So I think it's not really a fair question to ask "Did you execute on your business plan?" because every business plan is just a wild guess, right? You could easily add a couple of zeros everywhere and sell the same thing to people. Instead of 10 percent market growth you make 20 percent market growth, and suddenly you make $200 million more in the fifth year, but so what? They're marketing tools.

Livingston: What big turning points occurred in the first year?

van Hoff: We did a first release of the software, which was a really important thing. We hired some executives and lots of great people. We hired some really bad people too—we had to fire somebody in the first year. We had our first lawsuit filed.

Livingston: Was there any time when you wanted to quit?

van Hoff: Marimba is an unfair case because we were willed on like crazy by the investors. We really had an unfair opportunity because when we got funding, the VCs were calling us. They all wanted to invest because they had heard about us and wanted to find out what we were doing.

So we got a really good first round of funding—$4 million from Kleiner Perkins. Though I thought they wired the money in these situations, they actually gave us a check. So we had two checks—from the Kleiner fund and the Java fund—and Sami goes, "Let's go to Kinko's and make copies!" So he takes the checks to Kinko's and comes back with the photocopies, and he forgot to take the checks out of the copy machine! Luckily they were still there.

Another story I remember from our first round of funding was when they gave us the checks—the lawyers were there, Kleiner was there, and I said, "Oh great, now I can buy that espresso machine!" and they all jumped me and said, "No, you're not going to buy an espresso machine with this money. This is to start the company."

And it became a sticking point. We were very frugal and we didn't spend money on frills, but after the IPO there was a really bad time for Marimba when it was very difficult to hire people, and all the early people that had been there 3 to 4 years were starting to leave. Morale was very low, and so I went to the CFO and said, "Look, I want to buy an espresso machine." And he said, "No, we can't do that, it's too expensive."

A few weeks later, when another senior engineer quit, I said, "Screw it, let's go buy an espresso machine." So Jonathan and I went online and bought this super-duper Italian, fully automatic, $15,000 espresso machine on his credit card and submitted the expense form. The CFO almost had a baby. It was unbelievable.

This was a beautiful piece of work, and they came and installed the espresso machine and it was the best money we ever spent. Every morning, people would meet and crowd around it. This thing was just it, the bee's knees, people loved it, they couldn't stop talking about it. A month later, the CFO came and said, "I'm sorry, we should have done this years ago." And it tells you something about where you spend your money and what you spend your money on. It's not just business-related expenses. You also have to create an environment that you like so that people are happy and feel they are valued.

Livingston: Did you get along with your VCs?

van Hoff: VCs are an interesting bunch; you can't live with them, you can't live without them. They are instrumental in your success because they give you money and a really strong endorsement. They have this mafia-like network of connections and they help you with deals and find the right executives. They are really working your case.

In my experience, it rarely happens that they turn against you, because you're a team and if the team isn't working, the company will likely fail. Occasionally, when you're a screw-up, they'll have to make a tough decision and fire someone, but that's rare in my opinion. Because they wouldn't invest in your company if they didn't believe in you and your team. So I've always had a good experience working with VCs.

Livingston: Was there anything about your technology that people misunderstood?

van Hoff: We spent a lot of time talking about subscription-based software distribution and that took a long time for people to get. In hindsight, we were probably a little early with that. Now it's a very well-understood thing. The Microsoft operating system updates automatically. Updates to virus programs come over automatically. In the beginning, a lot of people we talked to said, "It's too early. Do I really want to do this?"

But we had a couple of really big successes—Morgan Stanley and Bear Stearns. These companies that had thousands of traders all over the world really needed to use the same software or it wouldn't work. They needed to roll this out at 100,000 endpoints and needed to get a report and warn people that didn't get updates. And we did that very, very well. Over time, Marimba went from a consumer software distribution/push technology company to an enterprise software distribution company—which is a lot more boring than in the early days, but there was a lot more money to be made in that market.

Livingston: What would you tell someone who wanted to start their own company?

van Hoff: If you have the energy to do it, then you should try it yourself. But you do need to have the ability to form a team around you with good people. Talent attracts talent.

A lot of people get stuck on the idea. They all want to invent something and go execute on it. I think that's a fallacy. You have to have an unfair advantage in that you have to be good at something, or you have to have a direction that you're interested in or a market that you see an opportunity in—but you shouldn't get stuck too much on the details, because you can't foresee your future anyway. Because you'll go through so many changes, I don't think it pays off to overanalyze the first business plan, for example. The first business plan is there to make sure you can use Microsoft Word.

Eventually, you need to go to VCs and attract money, and at that point you need to be able to put your plan in writing and sell it. That's something you need to practice a lot. Start with your friends and your parents and eventually go to VCs. If you get good reactions, then keep doing it. If you get bad reactions, then stop immediately, because it's a really bad idea to sell a bad plan. You can screw up once, but it's hard to screw up multiple times, because the VCs won't give you the time if you come up with a few bad plans.

Another good idea is to join a startup that already has funding. That way you can experience the startup atmosphere and all the pros and cons without really taking all the risk yourself. Because doing a startup does mean that you have to give up your job and your income and take the plunge. That's what holds a lot of people back.

I'm lucky I really don't need to work anymore. If I do a startup, whether it succeeds or fails is somewhat irrelevant—I do it because it's fun. I'd like to succeed. When it comes to taking a salary, at Strangeberry we worked for several years without taking a salary because we had fun doing what we were doing.

Livingston: What do you remember as being the most frustrating things early on?

van Hoff: The thing that was most frustrating for us very early on was that we got a lawsuit that just kept dragging on and on, and it took so much time and attention, and that became a real pain in the ass.

Livingston: What was it about?

van Hoff: It was a patent infringement case, without merit. Patents are pretty frivolous overall anyway. But if you're at the receiving end of a lawsuit, it can make things difficult.

One of the problems for the founders, after the IPO, is that you can't sell for a certain period of time and, after that, every time you sell and the stock goes down, you'll get personally sued—shareholder lawsuits. So every time there was an opportunity for us to sell, our lawyers would say, "You better not because if you lose the lawsuit then you'll get sued. You'll replace one lawsuit with the other."

So we had to see the stock go down from $75 to almost nothing and we weren't able to sell. We were legally able to sell, but you kind of talk yourself out of it because you think the risk is too high. If you do a startup and the company goes bankrupt, the shareholders lose their money, but you don't personally lose your house. But a shareholder lawsuit is a personal lawsuit—if you lose, they take your house, so it's a totally different ball game.

There're all sorts of crazy schemes that people use to get around this stuff. But at the time, we were pretty naïve about these things. You don't want the employees to focus on that, so you take the burden and deal with it.

There's a lot to be learned from doing a startup. It's much broader than you think. Although I was the CTO, I wrote a lot of code, I did a lot of depositions, interviewing, selling, traveling, moving furniture. That's the great thing about it; it's not a regular job. I like that, and that's why I've done a couple more since then.

Livingston: Was there anything you found you were better at?

van Hoff: You grow into it a little bit. We had just received the President's Award at Sun, which is a really prestigious award that they gave out every year, and it's a whole bunch of stock options. And we were going to walk away from that. It's sort of ironic, because the Sun stock split three times since we left, and if we had sold at the peak, we would have made about as much money as we did with Marimba, personally. But would I do it differently? No, I had a great time at Marimba.

Livingston: Did you have regrets?

van Hoff: When it's your first startup, there are a lot of people involved. You take advice from a lot of people, and that advice is not always the best advice. Very often, your intuition tells you to do something different, but then you go with the advice from the experienced guys anyway. And there were a few occasions where I look back and think, "If only I had gone with my intuition, things might have been different." So I might rely more on my intuition if I were to do it again.

Livingston: Were you the ringleader to start the company?

van Hoff: Well, in a way. Jonathan and I came up with the initial idea to do a startup, but you're talking about a difference in weeks. Very quickly it became the four of us. Then you need to make some decisions about when do you want to leave and how much money are you going to put in. Then once you've left, it gets quite interesting. Because then you've got to go for it whether you like it or not.

Livingston: Were the founding shares divided equally?

van Hoff: Yes, we split it four ways. We were very lucky because at the time of the IPO, the founders still had a fair amount of stock. Financially, the company was structured really well. That's mostly because early on, we had some really good VC deals. Especially with four founders, if you're not careful, you end up with such a small portion of the company.

Livingston: What advice would you give to a group of people who worked together and wanted to go out on their own?

van Hoff: Don't take anything with you. Especially if you go and do something that is somewhat competitive with your previous employer. Although you might not have actually taken anything—ideas, physical things, or time—if you're successful, they'll come and sue you just for fun. They'll have a really good starting point because you are a previous employee. You must have taken something because you're successful now, right?

So unless you go into a completely different area, you have to be very careful about the intellectual property. So really what you've got to do is: don't plan anything, don't write anything down. Talk about it over a beer and then leave. And then you start. Don't use any office equipment or email.

It's irrelevant if the company fails, but if the company succeeds, that can be a big problem. The funny thing is that they won't sue you until you're successful, because why sue someone who is a failure? And this is particularly important if you start out at a big company like Google or Amazon, because they have a lot of time and money to spend on these kinds of things.

Paul Buchheit
Creator, Gmail

Paul Buchheit was Google's 23rd employee. He was the creator and lead developer of Gmail, Google's web-based email system, which anticipated most aspects of what is now called Web 2.0. As part of his work on Gmail, Buchheit developed the first proto-type of AdSense, Google's program for running ads on other websites. He also suggested the company's now-famous motto, "Don't be evil," at a 2000 meeting on company values.

Although not a founder, Buchheit probably con-tributed more to Google than many founders do their startups. Gmail was in effect a startup within Google—a dramatically novel project on the margins of the company, initiated by a small group and brought to fruition against a good deal of resistance.

Livingston: Take me back to how things got started. Was Gmail a side project or commissioned by Google?

Buchheit: A little bit of both, actually. I started working on email software a long time ago. I think it was maybe 1996, but it was just a little project. I had all these ideas that never really went anywhere. Oddly enough, I think I was call-ing it Gmail at the time, for some other reason. It was just a random project—not necessarily the predecessor to Gmail—but it was something that I'd been thinking about because I'd been sort of unhappy with email for a long time.

It was before Hotmail and I was in college at the time. If you wanted to check your email, you'd have to go back to your dorm room. I thought, "That's so stupid. I should be able to just check it anywhere." So I wanted to make some kind of web-based email. But I really didn't know what I was doing, so it didn't go anywhere. I wrote something, but it was never useful and never got off the ground.

So fast-forward to much later: I was here at Google and I had worked on Google Groups, which is not exactly the same, but it's related. After the first generation of Google Groups had mostly wrapped up, they asked me if I wanted to build some type of email or personalization product. It was a pretty non-specific project charter. They just said, "We think this is an interesting area." Of course, I was excited to work on that.

Livingston: So they didn't ask for an email product?

Buchheit: They were very general—just kind of saying, "Yeah, we think there's something interesting to do here," but it wasn't like they gave me a list of features. People really weren't sure what it was. And this was when Google was still pretty much thought of as exclusively search, so even the idea of doing something like email was strange. A lot of people were kind of unsure. At this point, it wouldn't seem like a big deal, but at the time it was a little bit controversial.

For quite a while I was just working on it by myself. I actually started out with some of the Groups code, just because I was familiar with it. I built the first version of Gmail in 1 day, just using the Groups code, but it only searched my email. I released that to some Googlers and people said it was useful, so it progressed from there.

Livingston: When you built this first version, was your vision to create a better email program or was it to build something that would allow you to search through your emails?

Buchheit: Both. Search is obviously very important. It was central to what we were doing at the time and it's really useful for managing your email. I had ambitions of doing more than that, but search seemed like the natural first step—it was one of the things that was most obviously a problem.

Everyone here had lots of email. This company is a little bit email crazy. I get 500 emails a day. So there was a very big need for search. That was the most obvious thing that I could do, and it was also one of the easiest. So I built this first version and it only searched my email, but even that was useful for other people, because we had a lot of the same email. So then they said, "It would be even better if I could search my own email."

Livingston: You could search for keywords, senders, etc.?

Buchheit: Yes, it was free text, just like Google is, but for email.

Livingston: Was it supposed to be your full-time gig or was it part of your 20-percent-of-your-time projects?

Buchheit: Nothing's totally full-time, but it was mostly full-time. I still had some other projects that I would have to spend some time on, and inevitably I end up with side projects just because something catches my eye and I go off and work on it for a little bit. I think I may have something to do with 20 percent projects as well because I've created a few things on the side. AdSense, the content-targeted ads, was actually something that, if I recall, I did on a Friday.

It was an idea that we had talked about for a long time, but there was this belief that somehow it wouldn't work. But it seemed like an interesting problem, so one evening I implemented this content-targeting system, just as sort of a side project, not because I was supposed to. And it turned out to work.

Livingston: This is Google's AdSense now?

Buchheit: It's the same concept. What I wrote was just a throwaway prototype, but it got people thinking because it proved that it was possible, and that it wasn't too hard because I was able to do it in less than a day. After that, other people took over and did all the hard work of making it into a real product.

Livingston: You have done two groundbreaking things at Google.

Buchheit: Probably. I've done a lot of random things. Mostly what I do doesn't turn into anything, because I like to just try out ideas and a lot of them don't go anywhere.

Livingston: So you work on Gmail for a day, you can see you're on to something—then what happened?

Buchheit: For quite a while, it was just myself; and then another person, Sanjeev Singh, started working on it. But switching projects here, especially back then, wasn't easy. It wasn't like one day, you're suddenly on a new project. So he still ended up spending a lot of his time on enterprise search, which he was working on at the time. It was quite a while before Sanjeev could really spend most of his time on Gmail. So it was pretty slow for a long time.

It was mostly just me; then me and Sanjeev; then later on another person, Jing Lim, started. It was a very slow kind of progression. And people were still a little bit uncertain about the whole idea of doing something as different as email.

Livingston: When was the moment when you said, "This is big and we're going to launch this"?

Buchheit: Several days after launch! It was a big project. Sometimes it seemed as though we weren't ever going to make it out.

Livingston: Tell me about some of the most challenging parts.

Buchheit: There's a lot that was challenging about it, just because it's very big, for one thing. We gave everyone a gigabyte of storage to start with. At the time, the standard was around 2 or 4 megabytes.

A lot of people actually didn't think that was real. They thought it was a joke—partially because we launched on April 1.

They also thought it wasn't possible. It can be a little bit tricky, because it's a lot of data if you actually do the math: you have millions of users and they all have a lot of data, and then, to make the system really reliable, you need to keep several copies of the data, backups and everything like that. It requires a lot of research. It's a lot of machines and a lot of systems to make that all work without requiring an army of people to maintain the system and keep it running. There's a very complicated system problem there.

We were also doing a lot of things that were new to Google. And I guess this is one difference between a regular startup and starting within Google—I think it's a little bit different now, but at that time there was still this vision that, "We only do web search." Now we do lots of neat products that go beyond that, but at the time, a lot of people inside the company were sort of unsure. The idea of doing this product that was receiving all the email—and we had to store the email, which is a different systems problem, really, from web search, because in web search you go out and you crawl the web and index that data and the latencies are different. We go fetch a page and it gets searchable a little bit later. But in email, everything has to be instant, and of course you can't lose any of the data either.

It turns out to make a big difference in how you build things. A lot of the strategies that you might use for web search can be problematic when you apply them to email at a systems level, simply because you need to make everything so fast. It has to happen right away. You can't say, "Well, we receive email and then in half an hour it will appear." Which is actually how it worked in one of my early versions—the email would come in and I had this little script that would incorporate it into the index, but it generated this long lag, and so that wasn't really great.

All of those little details add up to creating a lot of challenges, just to get it all right. The JavaScript was a big deal as well, because at the time that we first started doing the interface in JavaScript, most people thought of JavaScript as a tool for pop-up advertising and other obnoxious things like that. This was before the whole Ajax thing, so a lot of people were pretty skeptical that JavaScript could work reliably. Not without justification—it is a little bit tricky because if you do things wrong, you'll crash the browser.

So making all of that work and work really well took some learning and figuring out the right techniques and where to draw the line about which features are a good idea and which aren't.

Livingston: Which was your favorite feature?

Buchheit: That's hard to pin down. Actually one of the things that we added very early on, which at this point seems pretty obvious, but it turned out to be really nice, is the autocomplete when you type in the email addresses. Once you have it, it just seems so obvious. "Why wouldn't you have autocomplete?"

Livingston: This was a first?

Buchheit: None of the other web mail providers had autocomplete. Now you don't really even think about it, but it makes a big difference. You can send email so fast and you don't have to remember the addresses. To my knowledge, we were the first web mail provider to do it. Desktop products would have things like that sometimes, but no web mail was doing that at the time.

Livingston: Was it always your plan to archive everything and not delete emails and have the massive storage needs?

Buchheit: You can delete email. The idea was that there's valuable information in email and we thought, "Why would you perform these actions?" For deleting, we found three or four reasons why you might delete things. One is that you're running out of space—which was the most common reason for deleting things, because you only had a 2-megabyte quota. We said, "If we give people enough storage, then they won't run into that problem."

The second reason was that people would delete things just because email quickly became unmanageable if they didn't. So we said, "We've got search, we'll try to make that efficient." I can handle—I don't know how many millions of messages are in my email now—but it's not a problem. They don't get in the way. They're just there, and if ever I want to find that message from four years ago where someone made some funny comment about Gmail that is ironic at this point, then I can go back and find it. I guess the third reason was that there's something in the email that the person's really nervous about and they just want to get rid of it. But that's pretty uncommon. So we said, "You want to provide the ability to delete things, but ordinarily it isn't really necessary, because most of the reasons are actually just consequences of limitations elsewhere."

Livingston: What else were brand new features that the world hadn't seen?

Buchheit: Conversation view was new—when you click on a conversation and you get all of the messages as cards instead of separate emails.

Livingston: Was that your idea?

Buchheit: This was a consequence of a few things. One is that I'd worked on Groups, where we had done some of the same threading. Second was the fact that we have so much email internally.

We'd have these conversations where someone sends out an email and then four different people reply to the same thing, and some of them would be like five hours later and you'd think, "This has been covered five times already and you keep responding."

It turned out part of the reason people were organizing their mail so aggressively is because they were trying to put the conversations back together. They'd put them all in the same folder—or they would forget and put them in the wrong folder and then the conversation would get split and they could never find the reply to this message.

There were all these little tools and tricks that people had for reassembling the conversations. Why not just put them all together to start with? At some point, we said, "Let's hide the quoted text too." Because that way you can just read it much faster without having to read the same content over and over. We were also looking forward to integrating chat/IM. We didn't have time to include chat in the original launch, but it was in the early prototypes because we very much wanted to integrate chat and email—they belong together. So one thing we did was to think about email from a chat perspective, as though we were adding email to chat instead of the other way around. Of course chat is very much conversation-oriented—nobody thinks about individual chat messages. So the conversation view also came out of that—for a while we even formatted the email to look more like a chat conversation.

Livingston: It sounds like you really took the user's perspective when you designed Gmail.

Buchheit: Absolutely, that's very much how it developed. Every time we would get irritated by some little problem, or one of the users would say, "I have this problem, it isn't working for me," we'd just spend time thinking about it, looking at what the underlying problems are and how we can come up with solutions to make it better for them.

Livingston: How big was your group by the time it launched? Only three of you?

Buchheit: There were a lot more people at that point. It depends which people you count, but it was about a dozen.

Livingston: Was there a time then when you said, "We need more programmers to get this going"?

Buchheit: I was always asking for more people. We still ask for more people. There's so much more we could do. The product is nice, but every day there are things that I find that I want to change. But when you're operating a big service, it also takes a lot of work just to deal with growth and improvements. A lot of the improvements are invisible. For example, I think we added 43 new languages. You don't necessarily notice that as an English user, but for most of the world, it's a big deal. There's just so much work as the product becomes big and needs to support millions of users.

Livingston: When you launched, had you already had users?

Buchheit: Literally from day one, we had users internally. One nice thing about Google is that we can just release things internally and have this great population of testers, essentially. So people inside have been using Gmail for a long time. The code name was Caribou. Initially, I called it Gmail, and then we realized that was not really very subtle, so we changed it to Caribou.

Livingston: Did you choose Caribou?

Buchheit: Yeah. There's a Dilbert cartoon where he's talking about "Project Caribou," and I thought it was a funny name, so I used it.

Livingston: Tell me about one of the darkest days of the project, when you felt that you couldn't do this. And tell me about one of the most euphoric days.

Buchheit: There are a variety of dimensions to the darkest days. Like I said, a lot of times it was sort of controversial, especially in the very early days, because people weren't sure if we should even be doing this. So the general attitude would swing, and when it would swing against us, that was very hard to deal with. Later on, not as much.

We would have some system problems internally. In a previous generation, it wasn't as redundant as what we finally released, and the hard disk in one of our machines that had everyone's email stopped working. I came in and everyone I walked past would ask me, "When is Caribou going to be back up?" I was walking into the machine room with screwdrivers, and people saw me and were like, "Oh no!"

I managed to take apart the hard drive and transplant the electronics from another drive, so nothing was lost. Through the whole thing, we've never lost any data, which is kind of unbelievable considering everything that happened. A lot of the machines that Google is built on—commodity is the polite word for them—they're regular PCs and so they're not always the most reliable.

The most fun was, of course, launching. Nothing is more exciting than finally getting it out there for the world and seeing that people like it.

Livingston: Were there any disasters on launch day?

Buchheit: Nothing major. It went surprisingly smoothly. There are always little problems but nothing so bad that I remember it. But then again, I'd been awake for 70 hours at that point. I was awake for about 3 days, because I was furiously assembling the last bits—sort of stitching together some systems to actually make it public, like the login system. And just testing everything.

Livingston: Did you sleep well that night?

Buchheit: Strangely enough, when I went home, I had a hard time going to sleep.

Livingston: Since Google was totally focused on search at the time, was there ever a point where you worried that your project would get canned?

Buchheit: All the time. Again, it was sort of a much earlier time than now where it fits in nicely. It was really kind of the first thing that diverged from the simple idea of web search. Even Groups is still basically search—it's just search over public usenet posts.

So it took a while for people to get used to the idea of something different. You have to remember that the situation between Google and Yahoo was different at that time. It was sort of a different company with different concerns.

Livingston: Is Gmail still invitation-only?

Buchheit: No, you can sign up with a cell phone.

Livingston: And on Blogger, right?

Buchheit: We've extended it in a bunch of different directions. All university students can sign up, because we wanted to make it available to students.

Livingston: What was the idea behind the invitation-only signup?

Buchheit: There were a few different factors. Again, I mention that this is a really big thing in terms of the amount of data and everything else. A big concern has always been that I don't want to lose any of that data, because of course nobody wants to lose their email. If something goes wrong with web search, you can go back and crawl the Web again, but with email, if it's gone, it's gone.

I was very concerned about keeping the systems operational. So part of it was just controlling the rate of adoption so that you don't exceed any of those limits. You always want to make sure that the current users are getting a good service. Also, it controls some of the abuse, by making it harder for, let's say, a spammer to get 10 million accounts, which also would be bad.

Livingston: Who did you learn things from at Google? Did you have mentors?

Buchheit: I didn't know anything about building these large systems before working at Google. So I'd look at how different parts of Google work and sort of say, "Does that apply to us? Can we reuse that technique?"—since there was already a successful model of how to do these things. That was part of the challenge, just figuring out when to copy other parts of Google and when to say, "Our problem is too different from theirs. We have to do something new."

That took us a while to figure out. You don't want to ignore all of those lessons, because that would be a big mistake, but at the same time, sometimes you really are just solving a different problem. For example, the update issue: we needed to be able to update instantly. Something like search, you can have a little latency. If a document doesn't get added for a few minutes, it's not a big deal. So at a system design level, that actually makes a huge difference, even though it's a seemingly small difference when you describe it.

Livingston: It seems like one advantage of having a startup-like project within a big company is that you have access to all its resources. Tell me about some other valuable things.

Buchheit: I think the people are the biggest resource. There are really smart people around, so you could just go talk to them and say, "How are we going to do this?" and brainstorm solutions. You can just go talk to people, whether it's the engineers . . . and Larry and Sergey are actually really smart.

Yesterday, I heard someone making a comment like, "These guys get lucky and now they think they're smart." But in fact, they really are smart and have good ideas. Sometimes people think that these guys just got lucky, and luck is always a factor in everything, but it isn't sufficient. It takes more than luck to build something that successful.

So there are lots of good resources, in the people and also systems. We get machines—we don't have to build the machines ourselves—so it's nice to have that infrastructure.

Storage turns out to be a surprisingly difficult problem. It's not solved. There are network attached storage (NAS) appliances, but they tend to be expensive and they have some other problems. Then you have what we do with PCs, and that's technically pretty challenging—to take this big network of machines that are unreliable and build a big, reliable storage system out of it. We're getting a lot closer, but it probably isn't something that some startup could pull off the shelf, at least not without paying for it.

Livingston: Was there anyone else at Google commissioned to work on an email program at the same time?

Buchheit: No. It's possible someone else was doing something on the side, but I don't know of any.

Livingston: Did you get a Google's Founders Award?

Buchheit: No, most of what we did predated the Founders Awards. But things mostly worked out for us anyway.

Livingston: What surprised you most looking back on the whole process? Was it about 2 years?

Buchheit: It depends where you draw the line, but it was a couple of years. I think some of the systems problems were a little bit harder than we realized to start with. I keep mentioning this idea of updating data quickly. It really soaks in at a lot of levels when you have to make your latencies be very low. If you have a machine that's down, what do you do? You have to be able to respond to everything that goes wrong very quickly, so that's challenging.

I was actually surprised to some extent at how positively some of the things we did were received. We were pretty nervous about some of our features. The idea of doing the whole thing in JavaScript—internally a lot of people were very unsure about that, but I think that our users loved it. It actually worked better than we expected it to. We were pretty nervous about it, because there are so many browsers out there and they all have plug-ins and some of these plug-ins will cause problems for you. It's really worked out better than we thought it would.

Livingston: Earlier, you said "it worked out" for you. Most founders take the risk of starting a startup for the potential reward of a liquidity event. Did you get a bonus or something similar?

Buchheit: There are lots of bonuses inside of Google and I don't know what the average is, but the bonuses in general can be very significant—much more so than at other companies. For me personally, I've been here long enough that there's only one bonus that matters, right? Which is part of why, for newer employees, things like the Founders Grants are much more important, because they're not going to get stock at a nickel a share or whatever. So something like a Founders Award isn't necessarily that important to me, but would be for newer employees.

Livingston: What number employee were you?

Buchheit: 23.

Livingston: How did you join Google?

Buchheit: I was working at Intel in the area and was kind of bored. I was looking around for something more interesting and I emailed Google my résumé. Interestingly enough, the first time I emailed my résumé, it bounced because their mail server was down. But I emailed it again the next day and it got through and they called me up. I came in and took a job.

It worked out well, but it wasn't like I saw this company and said, "Oh wow, this is going to succeed!" I just thought it would be fun. It looked like there were some smart people and it was kind of interesting work—that it would be more fun than my old job.

Livingston: Did you get any compensation for doing this project that was such a big success within the company?

Buchheit: It's hard for me to know even, because, even after the initial stock grants, throughout the history of the company they've given follow-on grants. So I don't know what mine would have been if I wasn't working on Gmail.

Livingston: I heard you came up with the famous "Don't be evil" principle. Can you give me the background?

Buchheit: I believe that it was sometime in early 2000, and there was a meeting to decide on the company's values. They invited a collection of people who had been there for a while. I had just come from Intel, so the whole thing with corporate values seemed a little bit funny to me. I was sitting there trying to think of something that would be really different and not one of these usual "strive for excellence" type of statements. I also wanted something that, once you put it in there, would be hard to take out.

It just sort of occurred to me that "Don't be evil" is kind of funny. It's also a bit of a jab at a lot of the other companies, especially our competitors, who at the time, in our opinion, were kind of exploiting the users to some extent. They were tricking them selling search results—which we considered a questionable thing to do because people didn't realize that they were ads.

Livingston: The users didn't know?

Buchheit: Companies would just mix the ads in with the regular search results so people would think it was a search result. It's kind of like fake news or something. In a newspaper, they're usually pretty good about separating out which things are advertisements and which aren't. But the search engines at the time were all selling search results and mixing them in with the real ones, so it was a little bit of a differentiator that we always said that we would never do that— and haven't.

So it was all those inspirations, and I just thought it was a catchy little phrase. But the real fun of it was that people get a little uncomfortable with anything different, so throughout the meeting, the person running it kept trying to push "Don't be evil" to the bottom of the list. But this other guy, Amit Patel, and I kept kind of forcing them to put it up there. And because we wouldn't let it fall off the list, it made it onto the final set and took on a life of its own from there. Amit started writing it down all over the building, on whiteboards everywhere. It's the only value that anyone is aware of, right? It's not the typical meaningless corporate statement or platitude.

Livingston: You mentioned that Gmail was "controversial" internally. Can you expand?

Buchheit: I think, in general, people are uncomfortable with things that are different. Even now when I talk about adding new features to Gmail, if it isn't just a small variation or rearranging what's already there, people don't like it. People have a narrow concept of what's possible, and we're limited more by our own ideas about what's possible than what really is possible. So they just get uncomfortable, and they kind of tend to attack it for whatever reason.

But for me, I am more interested in things that are new, and so I'm always excited just to see what will happen. That was actually one of the biggest reasons I joined Google in the first place. It wasn't so much that I was convinced that it was a good business; I just thought it was interesting and I was excited to see what would happen.

Likewise, with Gmail, part of the excitement was just seeing how the world would respond. I kind of like uncertainty to some extent, because it's a little bit of suspense and excitement and adventure, almost, right? And you can learn a lot even if things don't work out. But not everyone likes adventure. A lot of people seem to be against uncertainty, actually. In all areas of life.

I'm suddenly reminded that, for a while, I asked people, if they were playing Russian roulette with a gun with a billion barrels (or some huge number, so in other words, some low probability that they would actually be killed), how much would they have to be paid to play one round? A lot of people were almost offended by the question and they'd say, "I wouldn't do it at any price." But, of course, we do that every day. They drive to work in cars to earn money and they are taking risks all the time, but they don't like to acknowledge that they are taking risks. They want to pretend that everything is risk-free.

Livingston: Wasn't it controversial when you tried to test out the AdSense idea?

Buchheit: Yes, absolutely. Everyone hated it. Many people were kind of mad at me because they didn't really go for the whole concept. It was something that had been talked about, and people agreed that it was not workable, it was not a good idea. So, to some extent, they were agitated that I wasted my time.

Livingston: But you did it in one day?

Buchheit: Yeah, pretty much.

Livingston: And they were still annoyed?

Buchheit: Different people to different degrees. There were only a few people who were sort of upset about my distracting from the main task. Other people just didn't like the concept, because it's obviously something that's very controversial and it isn't immediately obvious when you just hear about the idea and you haven't really used it.

At first, it kind of seems a little bit wrong, right? Just because it's very unfamiliar. So it takes some getting used to. But people got used to it and then they were OK with it.

Livingston: Most startup founders have investors, but you had Larry and Sergey to answer to. What's it like having them as your investors, in a way?

Buchheit: I think it's probably reasonable. I've never had other investors so I don't have a lot of perspective, but they are very open to crazy ideas—more so than almost anyone I've ever met. I used to tell people my ideas, and then they'd explain to me that I just didn't understand how the world worked and why I was wrong about whatever. One of the exceptional things for me, coming to Google, was that it was the first time that I would tell people my crazy ideas and they'd say, "Oh, yeah, that's a good idea. I was thinking the same thing." So it was an environment with many people who are open to these kind of unusual ideas, and this is especially true with Larry and Sergey.

Livingston: So they aren't "risk-averse" like so many investors.

Buchheit: Obviously they consider risk and so forth, but they are definitely more open to the idea of something unexpected or different. Which I believe is very much their own thinking.

Livingston: What advice would you give someone who was working at a big technology company (that wasn't like Google in terms of encouraging new ideas) if they had a great idea that they thought could help the company?

Buchheit: It depends on your situation. It depends how risk-averse you are. You should consider going to work at Google, start a startup, or go to another place where you are going to have that opportunity. For someone who's pretty far down in a company, if they are going to try to change the whole culture of the company, I'm skeptical. When I was leaving Intel, one of my managers there was trying to convince me, "You don't have to leave to do the startup thing. There are startup opportunities inside of Intel."

Livingston: When you were working on it, were you working startup hours? Did it feel like a startup?

Buchheit: Oh yeah. We had a pretty tight little team. We have really smart people and they are fun to work with. I'm not a morning person, so I'm always here at night. My normal hours were something like noon until 3:00 a.m. It's hard to go home at night, because you get working and you say, "I'm just going to make this one last improvement." Then, the next thing you know, it's 3:00 a.m.

Livingston: Did it affect your relationship with your wife?

Buchheit: No, it was nothing new. I've always been like this, so she was used to it. It's actually a much bigger change now, because I see her every day. But, as I say, for these people, it depends on their situation if they can take that risk of joining a startup or moving to a new city if they don't live in the right place. For me, I was actually single at the time, I didn't have a mortgage, so the idea of joining a little startup that may well be destroyed was just like, "That will be fun." Because I kind of thought, "Even if Google doesn't make it, it will be educational and I'll learn something." Honestly, I was pretty sure AltaVista was going to destroy Google.

Repairing the disk electronics on an early Gmail prototype.

Steve Perlman
Cofounder, WebTV

One weekend in 1995, Steve Perlman tested his theory that the Web could look as good on a TV screen as it did on a computer monitor. In 3 days of round-the-clock effort, he built a thin client for surfing the Web, using a television as a display. He invited his friend Bruce Leak over to see what he'd built, and they knew right away it was a big enough idea for a startup.

It was a natural project for Perlman, by then one of the leading experts on display technology. At Apple, he helped bring color to the Mac. Later, at his first startup, Catapult Entertainment, he built one of the first systems for network games. Now he wanted to bring the Web into people's living rooms.

A little over a year after that first prototype, Sony and Philips sold the first WebTV set-top boxes to the public. In 1997, WebTV (now called MSNTV) was acquired by Microsoft for over $500 million.

Livingston: Take me back to the weekend in '95 when you built the WebTV prototype. How did you get the idea? Why did you decide to do this?

Perlman: For many years, I've been interested in making television interactive. What I mean by "interactive" is something beyond just changing channels up and down, to get it where people can have access to content that's more interesting—to be able to find what they want and then to be able to view it on demand. For example, what we now consider to be DVR, or what you do with your TiVo. At the time, it was considered something you'd only do in an editing suite. If you were a network professional, you might have a disk-based digital editing system.

I wanted to do all those things, and I even did a lot of the work at Apple. In fact, just a month ago on the History Channel they showed some of the early stuff I did at Apple. It was 1989. I was showing a system where we had video on the screen, images moving around, and animation, and several video sources. You could pause, rewind, and manipulate the things. That was a big prototype system, but we could never get it out the door because there wasn't enough content to drive a system like that. You could theoretically bring in live video, but in 1990 there wasn't a hard disk big enough to hold live video. Theoretically, you could try to create all sorts of content for it, but who would ever create all the content if there are no devices to receive it? So we had a chicken-and-egg problem. Nobody would buy the devices because there was no content, and there was no content because the devices weren't out there.

But there were lots of offshoots from that work; QuickTime came out of that work. We took the video decompression technology, developed it, reduced it to just a software algorithm, and that was turned into a product by Bruce Leak and his team. A whole bunch of other things grew out of it—some of the video products from Apple and so forth.

Then, at General Magic, I went to work on a PDA—but I worked half-time at General Magic and half-time I was still working on how to make inexpensive delivery systems on a television for interactive TV, and work with video and games and things like that.

Livingston: You worked on your own projects on your own time?

Perlman: On my own time. I relinquished half of my stock options. I worked out a deal with them where 2 and 1/2 days a week I worked on my own stuff, 2 and 1/2 days a week I worked on General Magic stuff. And then what happened is General Magic, in my last year there, said, "Hey, we want to do video stuff too." MagicTV is what they called it. So I worked full-time then to try to create an interactive system for them. But they ran into financial difficulties and other problems getting the product out, and shut down the MagicTV effort.

I said, "OK, it's time for me to move on." That's when I first started—and cofounded with three other people—Catapult Entertainment, which made a modem for Sega and Nintendo video games that would modify the execution of the games, so people could play existing titles with each other over the phone line. That involved building out the network infrastructure to connect people together—remember, people didn't have the Web in their homes back then—designing the hardware, and also reverse-engineering the games. So I learned a lot about the consumer market and about getting stuff out into stores. From the founding of the company to the point where the product was on store shelves at Toys"R"Us and the network was up and running, was 6 months—including custom silicon that we did, as well as shooting the plastic molds for it, boxing it, and getting it through distribution.

Livingston: And you did it in 6 months?

Perlman: Six months. We reverse-engineered four video games: NBA Jam, Mortal Kombat, a hockey game, and some other one. We were just working around the clock, literally. What I would typically do is not sleep for 2 nights; then I would get 4 hours of sleep and go back to work for another 2 days in a row, and then get 4 hours, and so on.

It was the hardest I've ever worked in my life. Sometimes I'd take 10-minute cat naps by just laying my head down on my shoulders—just so I'd get some REMs. As soon as the dreams come, it resets your brain a little bit and you're able to work again. We were sleeping at our desks. People would bring in pizza. My wife would sometimes cook some turkey meatballs and spaghetti in a big pot and then bring it over, and everyone would just chow down.

Livingston: Surely your wife was nervous about you sleeping only 4 hours every 2 days?

Perlman: She was. She got one of those fold-out futons that would fold under my desk. She didn't like me sleeping on the floor.

My admin, who came with me from General Magic, tells stories about coming in in the morning and trying to clean up. She'd pick up a folded pizza box and get scared because she'd find a guy sleeping underneath it—it was covering his face. It was really bad. My dog, when my wife would bring him over, he would find burritos, because the place was just a pigsty.

But we had the product out in 6 months because we knew we had to meet that Christmas. It was out by September.

Livingston: So you had a deadline?

Perlman: We had a hard deadline. But, it was a great learning experience for me. The guys that we hired to get our network software working, they just did not deliver. They couldn't work on that kind of schedule. So we pulled it in and did it all ourselves. It was a matter of just cranking it out.

We used a programmable gate array that we could then freeze into a permanent gate array to make it cost-effective. That was the only way we could get the hardware working that quickly. Then it was just a matter of hard work on the games and everything. We partnered with THQ, which is a video game company who had a distribution channel to all the video game retail outlets, so we could get the product out quickly.

I also learned about working with people, because one of the guys I cofounded it with, it just didn't work out between us. He had his perspective of where he wanted to take the company; I had mine. I realized that these things are like a marriage. When you cofound something, you've got to have people that have a similar kind of perspective on where you're going to take the thing. Otherwise you're just locking horns all the time.

Livingston: Had you worked with him before?

Perlman: I knew him before. General Magic was developing products for Sony, and Sony was particularly interested in MagicTV. I'd known him at Apple because he'd done some industrial design there. He went and got his MBA and then went to work at Sony. And so I was seeing him at Sony. We weren't friends, and I didn't know him very well outside of work, but, when I left, he said, "They're shutting down MagicTV. So what are you going to do?" I said, "I don't know. I had an idea for this thing I wanted to do with video games."

I had figured out a way to make existing video games work online—you know, a two-player game like NBA Jam—we hacked it so the software, instead of looking to the second controller, actually would set up a link through the dialup connection to another box, and the two kids were able to play each other. And of course they didn't have to buy new software because we were working with game software that's already written. Great way to bootstrap an online game thing.

Of course, we were way early for the online game market, and we were at the tail end of the cartridge market. There were a million things I learned from that, because it ultimately did not succeed as a business. Financially it was OK, but as a business, it was not successful.

But the biggest lesson I learned was: I wasn't getting along with this guy and it was time to move on. So I stayed there for about a year. We started that in the spring of 1994; I left in the spring of 1995. And then I was very tired. I was physically, bodily tired, as you can imagine after such a hard effort.

I was determined to just go and tinker for a while and explore things. I saw Netscape 1.0 and thought, "The World Wide Web is kind of cool." I'd been on the Internet since college—then it was the ARPANET. Back then, the ARPANET only connected up a few institutions, but through the years I continued to use it as a software engineer might use it.

Livingston: Were you an engineering major?

Perlman: No, I have a liberal arts background. My engineering background is as a hobbyist. I built a computer when I was 16 and then designed a graphics display to go with it and things like that. I'd read *Kilobaud* magazine and *Byte* magazine, and I'd go and print up some company letterhead, which I'd send to the chip companies—that are now people I work with officially—and I'd say, "Hey, we have great plans for new products. You should send me some samples." So I'd get all these chips for free. The ones I could get for free, I'd design circuits around their capabilities. They weren't the ideal chips, you know. But what are you going to do—you're a kid in high school; you had no money.

I was in Connecticut and everyone else was in California, so I was 3 hours off. I ended up shifting my schedule and actually was getting up around noon because that's when stores would open: Jameco Electronics would open at 9:00 a.m. in California, which is noon in Connecticut. So what's the point of getting up before noon, right?

I've always been a hobbyist, and it's one of the reasons I kind of seamlessly go between software, hardware, networking, and material science. I don't care—it's whatever it takes to make the damn thing work. I don't have much formal education in these things, but you learn. You build enough stuff; after a while, you see it. And if you reverse-engineer enough things, you learn what other people have done.

I designed a software-based modem when I was in college and I got an F for it because the professor said it would never work. But I got it working at my first company. The professor was quite nice about it. I sent him an email later on and said, "This email is being sent to you on the modem that I designed at

Columbia." And he said, "We try to make the right judgments and we don't always. I'm glad that I did not dissuade you from continuing on with its development." I thought that was a very nice thing to say.

Livingston: So you leave Catapult and say, "I'm just going to tinker around and see what happens?"

Perlman: Netscape 1.0 comes out. I get it working, and I said, "Wow, this is really great," because people are putting up websites that anybody can go to. I went to campbellsoup.com, and there was a Campbell's soup can and recipes. It was the early days of the Web, so there wasn't too much, but I thought, "The kind of people that would be interested in these recipes probably aren't using computers and connecting to the Web."

Remember, this is before a lot of people got computers in order to get email and be on the Web. And then I thought, "This could be the thing I need to break that chicken-and-egg problem." Because if I can get these pages that were really designed for PC screens to work on a television screen, then . . . It's not ideal content; a lot of it is stuff really suited for someone on a PC. But some of it, like this Campbell's soup site—and there were many other sites, music sites and all that—is suited for the casual television entertainment experience. That might be enough to bootstrap us so we could do what I really want to do, which is these richer—what we now call broadband—interactive experiences. Things like DVR and so forth.

Before Apple, I was at Atari and Coleco. I designed video game systems there, and I knew an awful lot about how to create a very high-resolution image on a television screen by doing special image processing. If you try to put a high-resolution image on a TV screen, it's interlaced. Interlaced means it draws all the odd lines in 1/60th of an second, and then it draws all the even lines. If you have a continuous-tone image—the kind of image you see in the real world—and you capture it with a video camera, your eye, even though the whole screen is only refreshed 30 times a second, will look at each of these individual fields, all the odd lines and all the even lines refreshed at 1/60th of a second, and think it's flashing 60 times a second. At 60 times a second, if you stand back in the room, it's your foveal vision; it seems like a non-flickering image. So you look at a TV, and it doesn't seem to flicker.

But, if you now put content in one of those fields and then very different content in the other fields—for example, take black-and-white horizontal lines as you might see at the top of an old Macintosh window, and you put that on a TV screen, it flashes like crazy. In fact, it can put an epileptic into a seizure; it's that bad. So what they would do before is only have the TV draw half the lines vertically. All the video games back then, instead of having 480 lines, they would only draw 240 lines. I had figured out techniques where I could do image processing on images that would be intended for a computer where they would be smoothed out in such a way that you would not see them flicker. They would look extremely sharp on the TV, but they would not flash, so you could now do a high-resolution image on a TV. The technology was in some of the Macintoshes, but not many people were hooking up Macs to TVs.

The other thing—and this is an interesting point—back in the 1980s, when I developed this technology for Apple, software patents were not things that people filed. It was mainly hardware patents. Later on, people started filing software patents. The reason is software was considered an algorithm, and an algorithm is not patentable. A Fourier transform is not patentable. It's considered a mathematical function. This technique for stabilizing the image—the basic underlying principles of it—were things that patent attorneys said we couldn't file patents on, so it was open for anyone to use.

But still, the way I did it at Apple wasn't enough for what we needed to do with the Web. We had other things to accomplish, and so what I did was take those basic ideas and added on a whole bunch of other stuff and filed some basic patents around it. I knew that it was possible to take an image intended for a computer screen and get it to work on a television. So I went to Fry's and got about $3,000 worth of parts and built something over 3 days and 2 nights. (Much like I was working at Catapult. Back then, that's the way we worked.) I then got this image up of these web pages on a TV, and it looked perfect. It looked just like the image looked on the computer screen. I grant you, back then, computer screens were largely 640×480 and web pages were a little bit smaller and so on, so it did happen to work for the time and place we were in.

I called my friend Bruce Leak, who I mentioned before is the guy I worked with at Apple. He had taken a lot of the technology that we had developed in the Advanced Technology Group, like QuickTime and also the color QuickDraw stuff, and then developed these technologies into products. We had a good partnership working together. He was at another startup at the time, Rocket Science Games. It was the middle of the night—it was midnight or something—I called him up on his cell and said, "Bruce, get your ass over here." He said, "Why?" And I said, "I've got something to show you. I'm about to pass out."

So he comes over and looks at it and says, "Well, so what? What did you do to the TV set?" And I said, "I didn't do anything to the TV set. It's what I did to the signal going into the TV." And he's like, "No way!" And I said, "Yeah!"

I remember he said, "Man, we've got to form a company." And I said, "Ah, yeah." I think that was the first moment I even thought about it. Then I was thinking we should get a good name for the company, and immediately we knew it was going to be called WebTV.

After that, one thing kind of led to another. We were able to attract Phil Goldman to come, another top-notch developer. He created MultiFinder for Mac, and he wrote a lot of the OS for the General Magic device.

Then we went to Marvin Davis, a wealthy financier in Hollywood. He had made a lot of money because he invested early in Catapult. As I said, Catapult was financially successful although it was not successful as a product. He told me that, whatever I did next, he wanted to put money into it—because he had turned around his Catapult shares and sold them to Viacom and made some outrageous profit in about half a year. So I went down to Hollywood with Bruce to meet with Marvin Davis, and we demonstrated WebTV to him—the prototype I had—on a TV set in his office. I'm not sure he immediately saw what the value of it was, but he nonetheless committed to put some seed funding in. We ended up raising $1.5 million from Marvin, and that's what we started the company with.

That was in July of 1995. I think I got the thing working first in April 1995, so from April to July, I kind of pulled together the business plan and at least the first couple of guys that were going to help me, spent a lot of time calling different people who we might be able to work with, went looking for office space, and so on. We were working out of my dining room in my house.

After we got the money from Marvin, we went and found an old BMW dealership that was vacant. It was mostly garage, but they had a little bit of office space. There was no connectivity there; I think there were three phone lines going into it. But, it was about 90 cents a square foot per month, so I thought, "OK, perfect." It was right near downtown Palo Alto, and so we moved in there. Literally, we had three phone lines. There was always one of them with a dialup connection, because we were doing experiments and everything. I was trying to do business calls on the other one, and there were modems always interrupting.

We finally were able to convince Pac Bell, the phone company at the time, to bring a T1 line in there. I remember talking to the guy and saying, "We want a T1 line here. We've got this big business we're growing. We're eventually going to need very high bandwidth connections and optical fiber, and all this kind of stuff." I hear some paper flipping in the background, and he says, "Is this some kind of a joke? It says here on the manifest that this is a car dealership." And I said, "No, no. We're running a big online service business. It's going to affect people all over the United States. It's going to be really huge." The guy says, "OK. Who put you up to this?" It was like a joke trying to get connectivity there. We literally had to go to several levels up in Pac Bell until they finally believed that we were a startup using an old car dealership to set up an online service.

Livingston: How many cofounders did you have when you started?

Perlman: There were three total: Bruce Leak, Phil Goldman, and me. Phil passed away 2 years ago of a sudden heart attack, sadly. That was a real tragedy.

So then we started hiring people and getting things going. I'm doing something that I wasn't that familiar doing, which was business development. That was all new for me. As I said, I may not have an engineering degree, but that's what I've always done for my vocation.

I called Sony and said, "Hey, we should go and do this cool thing." Sony was interested—I networked through some of the contacts I had made at General Magic, but they were slow getting through the company. We also began to speak with Philips. Sony finally said they wanted to go forward with WebTV, but they'd have to be exclusive for a year. They'd brand WebTV with a Sony logo, and they'd distribute it through their stores, and so on. But we could begin to have other licensees for the technology after a year. So we told Philips that they would have to wait a year, even though they were all hot to trot. At the time—and probably still today—Sony was the stronger brand in the United States.

Then we went to raise more money. The Davises had committed to $3 million that was going to be in tranches. We had $1.5 million, but the last $1.5 million was contingent on us closing a deal for a consumer electronics partner . . .

Livingston: . . . who would manufacture it?

Perlman: If we could get the deal through Sony, they would manufacture WebTV. Sony's a big company. It takes a lot to get through the system there, and we just could not get the deal through the system. As hard as we tried—they were almost ready to go—we couldn't get a commitment. So we went back to the Davises, and they got very nervous. They don't know about technology, and they said, "Well, we're only going to put in a million and a half."

Well, now we had hired all these people—I think we had over 30 people then. Though we were quite frugal, it still was a high cash burn. We were just about out of money. So I mortgaged my house, liquidated all my assets, and brought in all the cash I could to help it. (Although I did make some good money from General Magic and Catapult, it wasn't until after that point. Both companies did their IPOs after that. There was a holding period for General Magic, and so on.)

We didn't tell the employees that we were running low, because we didn't want people to be in a panic. We were going to tell them if we were really hitting a wall, but I could keep the company going a little bit longer.

Then we started going and talking to other investors and VCs, much sooner than we thought we were going to have to.

Livingston: Because you were expecting the second tranche?

Perlman: Yes. These days I look at it, and I think, "Jeez, even $3 million is a fairly modest amount for the scope of thing that we were trying to do."

I remember we spoke to one semiconductor company that we got very far along the road with that made a processor. When it came down to literally days before we signed the investment document, they added in a section that said we would be obliged to use only them as the provider for all of our silicon. In other words, they set it up so that our backs were against the wall, and they were getting us locked in. We knew that, if we were locked into one provider for silicon, we would have no way to negotiate prices. That would drive up the cost of the unit, so we couldn't do that. We even tried to explain to them that, "You guys are investing in a company. You don't want that to happen." But they felt very clever about this strategy and taking these wet-behind-the-ears entrepreneurs.

So there was another 2 months wasted. We were watching the bank account dwindle. Then we started speaking to VCs, and we talked to a whole bunch of different ones. We spoke to Paul Allen at Vulcan and a couple of other companies. We talked to Sony and Philips about possibly investing, but they weren't in a position to invest. We found that nobody was willing to make that first step. In fact, I think a lot of them were sort of like vultures waiting for us to fail, and then pick up the pieces—because they saw the value of what we were doing—for a bargain.

Livingston: Can you describe the investors' initial responses? Did they say, "What the heck is this?"

Perlman: The biggest issue they had was the concern that people did not want to interact with their TV. I mean, we showed working prototypes, but that wasn't enough. By then we had a browser working that we had written from scratch. In less than a year, we had a browser working. To give an example, when Microsoft did Internet Explorer, they started with Mosaic. We couldn't fit Mosaic into our system. We only had 2 MB of RAM, and we had a 112 MHz MIPS CPU, and we had 2 MB of ROM and 1 MB of flash memory.

None of these existing browsers could fit into a memory footprint so small. So we had to go write the thing up from scratch. Of course, we had to deal with the reality that a TV screen was very narrow. We had a different user interface for the remote control. We had a custom chip, and we had a programmable gate array doing the video. We were doing the image processing that I mentioned to eliminate the interlace flicker and to sharpen the image. We were building the whole network side, which was all the servers and the network that would handle and proxy the information. For example, if a large JPEG came in that we knew that a TV could not display, we would resize it in servers and send that down to the box to make a faster experience.

Then we had to go set up a whole dial-up network. We had to make relationships with dial-up providers all around the country, so that they would automatically find a local phone number to dial. So there was huge range of things we were doing to make this thing work. I don't know, but, if I were advising a VC, I'd see a bunch of guys with all these pieces of the puzzle and they were executing and working with so little capital—I'd say, "Wow. I don't care what they're going to do; something's going to come out of it." But that's not the way that most investors look at it.

Now, looking back, I think some of the investors saw us as potentially carrion ready for the taking, if we ran out of money. None of them said that, and at the time I wasn't thinking that, but now I've seen it happen. I think other investors were just nervous. Because all the other Internet plays are happening—this was 1996, and huge deals are being done with the Internet. But, they are all purely web-based: software running on servers somewhere. There were no actual capital costs. We were talking about building a box that was going to be deployed to people's homes. It has to be manufactured; there are inventory risks, all those kinds of things. It was just not something they were used to doing.

But the biggest thing people would say is they didn't think people would want to interact with their TV. They could imagine them changing channels with their remote control or playing a video game, but, as far as doing something more advanced with the TV—like surfing the Web or doing email, or the future things we were doing, where you had video content on the TV along with the program guide (believe it or not, back then there weren't program guides on TV) or having video eventually recorded on a disk with pause/rewind—people thought that was crazy. I know it sounds so obvious now, but back then they thought it was crazy.

Then we found one venture capital firm, Brentwood Venture Capital. Jeff Brody, a VC there, saw it and he thought it was great. He said, "We want to invest." And they were prepared to put in $4.5 million.

We were just about to sign all the paperwork. It was great, since we were plumb out of money. I would have lost everything: my house; I would have been deep in debt; the company would have folded; it would have been a bad scene. Then we get a certified letter from Sony, and it said, "After due consideration, we've decided not to proceed with you in deploying this product." Remember, they had told us they had to have a 1-year exclusive. So we weren't very far along with anybody else. We'd begun discussions with Philips, and we told them it was a year out.

You have to disclose this to an investor, so we went and told Jeff Brody. It was a real seminal moment for the company. He could have said, "OK, then, I'm not going to invest if you don't have anyone to deploy your product." But he said, "I believe in you guys, and I think this is going to make it. We'll still go forward on the same terms." As soon as he moved forward, Paul Allen wanted to get in. So he put in the other $4.5 million, and we ended up raising $9 million that round.

After that, everything began to change. First of all, Philips came back, and they immediately said, "We want to do a deal with you." Because they had been sitting on the sidelines. We said, "We think we might be able to do a deal sooner than 1 year." They said "Great."

Meanwhile, we had hired a consultant, Spencer Tall of Asia Pacific Ventures, who had done a lot of deals with Japanese companies. He spoke Japanese fluently and, in particular, he had a personal relationship with Idei-san, who was the CEO of Sony at the time. We told him, "Look, we got this letter from Sony. They said they're not going to do the deal with us." He says, "Well, let me find out why this thing got bottlenecked, how it actually got shut down."

He went and called Idei-san while he was in the United States—this must be April of 1996, maybe May. It turns out that he was at a business meeting in New York and he had his chief technology officer with him. We're busily working, and, when you're building stuff, you're always doing different builds. They always have bugs in them. None of them were really working, because we were in the development stage. And I got a call from Spencer, who said, "I just got off the phone with Idei-san. He said that his guys didn't think the thing really worked and they're skeptical this would ever be successful as a product. I told him he really should reconsider. So he dispatched his chief technology officer on a private jet to your offices to get a demo. This is your big chance to show it to them."

I said, "Great. When's he sending him?" He said, "No. He *dispatched* him. He's in the air now. He's going to be there in 2 and 1/2 hours."

I said, "Spencer, we're in the middle of development here! We need more warning than 2 and 1/2 hours!" We had been adding a bunch of code, so it was really crashing all the time at that stage. So I went back and talked to Bruce and Phil and said, "Look, we have one last chance with Sony. Their CTO is coming here in 2 and 1/2 hours."

Phil said, "Well, we do have a build that's compiling now"—it took a long time to compile all the source and then we had to release and test it—"and it's going to be done in about 2 and 1/2 hours." I said, "How do we know it's going to work?" He said, "Well, it probably won't." So I said, "What do you mean?" He said, "All the recent builds we've done had major bugs and serious crashes. We did do a lot of fixes here, though." And so I'm thinking, "Holy cow. This is our big chance, and we're in a really bad stage of development." But we had no choice, so I said, "OK, let's roll the new build out when the CTO comes and see what happens."

The guy arrived about 15 minutes before the compile was done, and so we kind of wined and dined him. We brought in a vegetable tray and had some drinks there and were talking with him and tried to be polite. He said, "I really don't have a lot of time. I need to see your WebTV prototype now." So then I look over to the prototype area, and Phil had just walked in with a WebTV prototype, "Here it is. The new build is loaded into this box."

So for better or worse, it was ready to go, and we sit Sony's CTO down on the couch. I remember saying to Phil and Bruce, "What happened when you tested it?" And they said, "What do you mean? This *is* the test." So I thought, "Great. We're doomed."

We turned the thing on, and I don't know how, but it was perfect. It ran perfectly. It just happened to be a good build. It was pure chance, but it went through all the paces. We could go to websites and we typed in URLs and went to all the different things, and there it was: WebTV did what it was supposed to do. You could see the Web on TV.

We talked about the image processing and flicker elimination and showed him the hardware and everything, and he looked very impressed. In fact, shortly thereafter, we got a call to come to Tokyo to present to Idei-san himself and his staff. In the end, he brought in engineering teams from all over the company simply to see the image processing we were doing to make such a sharp image on a TV, because they had never seen that before at Sony, even that one element of technology.

The one website that the CTO went to that didn't work when he was in Palo Alto was a Japanese website, because we didn't support the Japanese characters. We had one engineer, Mark Krueger, who we had worked with at Apple, working from Japan. He married a Japanese woman, so he lived there, and he had an ISDN line to a house in the middle of a rice paddy, literally. He was picking up a little bit of Japanese. When we went to Japan, we got to the Tokyo Hyatt, and I remember Bruce had a development system there—we had hauled these big computers with us. Mark had a development system at his place in the rice paddy. And the night before our demo with Sony, they went and did another build. They didn't tell me about this, but Bruce stayed up all night working with Mark, and he integrated Japanese language support into the code. So, literally, we arrived in Japan with an English-only browser, but by the next morning we had it running English and Japanese.

Livingston: You didn't know they did this?

Perlman: I didn't know. Bruce told me on the cab ride over. I said, "What about the stability? Bruce, Japanese is nice but . . ." And he said, "Don't worry. It won't crash. It will be fine, it will be fine."

We gave a great demo in Palo Alto, and now we're going to give this demo to the president of Sony Corporation, and we're going to fall flat on our face! Well, it didn't crash. It worked beautifully. The CTO was there, and we said, "By the way, there was one web page that you went to in Palo Alto that didn't work. Well, it does work now." We typed it in, and, sure enough, it showed beautiful Kanji, and we won him over.

Then they said, "We want to go back to the original contract we negotiated with a 1-year exclusive." And we said, "We would love to do that, but now we have a deal with Philips, and so we can no longer offer you an exclusive." They were very unhappy about that, but, in the end, they felt it was worth doing. So there it was. We had a deal with both Sony and Philips—at the time, the two powerhouses in consumer electronics.

Now that we had these deals in place, we raised Series C. I think we raised about $35 million.

Livingston: Did you get funding from the same people?

Perlman: Well, Brentwood re-upped, and I think Vulcan re-upped, and the Davises did what they did at Catapult—they flipped. They sold their shares to other investors. They're not technology people, so they saw it purely as an investment. And they were happy as clams. I think they got seven times their money in less than a year.

And then Microsoft came in, interestingly enough, and Citicorp and St. Paul Venture Capital. Some individual investors came in, and also Seagate, I think, put some money in. And Washington Post Group. A lot of people were interested in the subject area. We expanded the board then, so the board was now the three cofounders; we had Randy Komisar as an outside director, and we had representatives from Brentwood, Vulcan, and I think that was it. Maybe we had one other guy.

Then we cranked. We introduced the product in July of 1996—one year almost to the day after I got that first check from Marvin Davis to fund the company. It had custom hardware, a browser from the ground up, proxy servers, and so forth. The whole network was supported, and I was true to my word when I called the guy at Pacific Bell and told him that we were going to be running a nationwide online service.

Livingston: How did the idea for WebTV evolve? Was it to make the Web available to people who might not have computers?

Perlman: Yes. I should go back even further. My mission, even before then, was to connect average people together doing non-engineering things, the things that interest them—to foster better communication, sharing of ideas, and for pure entertainment. I love storytelling; my favorite college class remains "The Novel."

I wanted to figure out how to do communication. I wanted to figure out consumer electronics. I wanted to figure out ease of use, you know, interfaces.

I wanted to work with televisions, audio systems. That's what I've been interested in, and it has driven all the things I've done.

When I joined Apple and interviewed with them, they weren't even interested in doing color, and we brought them over to doing color. We created the whole color model as well as the rest of multimedia for the Mac—music and sound and everything. We made the Macintosh from a little black and white computer into a multimedia powerhouse. And it was driven really by what my ultimate desire was: as a delivery vehicle for multimedia and a means by which you can interact. Video games are one kind of interaction. That's great, but there is more than just that.

I think that, in the end, if you have enough people communicating with one another, it's going to be really hard to go and blow each other up. They may send nasty messages on blogs, and they may argue and maybe somebody will write something unpleasant in Wikipedia about you, but that's a lot better than blowing someone else up.

Livingston: Was it hard designing something for non-technical users?

Perlman: It's extremely hard, because you have to design for someone who's not you. After a while, as you develop interfaces and have experience with them, you begin to think with the intuition of a person who does not understand the inner workings of the system. And you also have to do a lot of testing. You have to be good at testing. You have to know what questions to ask people and what problems to present to them.

The following is not something from my personal experience—it's a story told to me by the Mac team—but they said that, when they first did the dialog boxes for the Lisa, instead of saying "OK," it said, "Do It." They found that people were reluctant to click on that, and they couldn't figure out why. Then, once they had a test subject there who just wouldn't click on it, they said, "Why didn't you click on that little button there?" He said, "I'm not a dolt. Why would I click on that?" People were reading it as "dolt," not "do it," because it was an unusual combination of words. So they changed dialog boxes to say "OK." That little change greased the skids for people to click on dialog boxes.

It's very small stuff like that, very often—that somebody sees something and has the wrong impression. The only way to learn that is by doing a lot of testing. In fact, that's one of the reasons why the iPod was such a phenomenal success where the MP3 players before were not. The iPod had the design sensibility of an average person just trying to listen to music, whereas the previous MP3 players were kind of technical exercises in understanding how music files are stored, and perhaps required very delicate balancing of your fingers to hit the buttons the right way, and so on.

Livingston: Were you inspired by the Apple II's use of TV as a monitor?

Perlman: Well, Apple IIs did work on TV screens, and I was inspired by the fact that it was a friendly-looking computer and that it had color. But it was not an easy-to-use computer. That's one of the reasons I didn't join Apple earlier. I didn't see where that was going to go.

I was very impressed with the engineering. When I looked at the floppy disk drive for the Apple II and I saw that it was a Shugart SA-400, but it was missing most of the chips that every other computer had in it, and realized that Woz had hacked the thing and was doing a lot of it with a combination of software and hardware, I was deeply impressed with the engineering. But it was not something that I could see an average person using. I could see, probably, more likely someone using that than a CP/M machine. Remember, this is before even the IBM PC.

But I was ready to leave the world of computers. I was working at Coleco in 1983. At the beginning of 1984, I was calling up Lucasfilm and other people in the film industry because I thought, "Well, the IBM PC"—which was introduced in 1982—"is taking over the world. Its graphics display is so poorly architected. It doesn't even have square pixels. It has a palette of just eight primary colors—actually two grays and six colors. Clearly, it's being driven by business applications and so on. My dream of where computers would go turns out to be the wrong one. It's not going more toward the average person; it's going more toward businesses. And that's OK." So I figured, "If I can't do it in people's homes, at least I want to be involved in creating exciting experiences on the silver screen and on television."

Then I saw an ad in 1984 for a Macintosh, and it changed everything. I saw that it had all this cool graphics capability. They clearly were interested in the user experience: it was designed for an average person in simplicity; it was very graphically oriented, albeit in black and white. I decided that there was hope.

I kept calling Apple again and again, trying to find somebody who would talk to me, to get an interview there. Finally, Alan Kay, who I had worked under at Atari and now was running a research group at Apple, came to visit Connecticut to give a talk. I told him what I thought about the Macintosh and said, "I want to make a color Mac and make it low cost." He said, "OK, OK. I'll see if I can talk to somebody and get you an interview with the Mac team." That led to three interviews, and I ended up not working on the Mac team, but for the team secretly making the color Macintosh.

Livingston: Then you moved out to California?

Perlman: Yes. Actually, it was the second time. I moved out here before to work for Atari. Then that went bust, so I came back to Connecticut and worked for Coleco.

Livingston: Do you think there are major differences for a new startup in Silicon Valley versus the East Coast?

Perlman: Oh yeah, phenomenal differences. I can't speak for every kind of startup, but for something involving technology—and even a lot of things involving content—it's just so much easier to do it here. You have resources here and people who understand technology. There's a high concentration of talent that you can draw on. You don't have to relocate people to get them there.

Then there's Sand Hill Road with all the VCs and other potential investors, who are all clustered together. You literally might do two or three presentations to different VCs all in the cluster of buildings on Sand Hill Road.

The other thing is that there's kind of an attitude here that people should try things, and, if they fail, if they understand why they failed, they may actually be a better investment in the next round than somebody who quickly succeeded just by sheer luck.

Livingston: Were there any powerful interests who did not like what you were doing and tried to stop WebTV? Like maybe Microsoft saw it as a threat to Windows?

Perlman: With WebTV . . . Microsoft, I found out over time that they probably . . . I mean, they're a very cautious company, and they proactively worry about any potential threats. I don't know if they saw WebTV immediately as a threat, but they saw it as a potential threat.

We didn't sell that many units the first Christmas. We were too high-priced. We were $329 when it came out, and the lesson learned there is that you don't charge both a high price and a subscription fee. Just one or the other, right? When we repriced WebTV at $99, then we sold a lot of them.

So when Microsoft came to acquire us, we only had 56,000 subscribers, which was a fairly modest number. But they still were very interested in us and that convinced me—perhaps wrongly, but nonetheless convinced me—that their real objective was to capitalize on this market, to grow from what we were doing. Also their desire to create the campus here in Silicon Valley was the other thing. So I kind of thought—and maybe even this was their objective at the time—that they really were going to develop this area of advanced television systems. But, as time went on, it became apparent that they simply wanted to make sure that nobody else successfully deployed a product in this area. I think they saw WebTV as the only viable player out there.

Who knows? Maybe it was a compound decision for them. Maybe they thought, "Well, maybe there's a market here, and maybe we can protect our flank to make sure nobody else does it." I don't know.

But there were some things that I was not allowed to do, which made it impossible for me to stay. They reneged on their commitment to support RealNetworks and Java, and I didn't know how we were going to build a good web-surfing experience without Real and Java compatibility. Then, as we went through the budgeting process and everything else there, and I began to get to know the other top executives at Microsoft, they were talking about negotiating this and that funding, and cutting back products to the point where they no longer made sense. I said, "Look, can't we all agree on what is the right objective for the whole company and then fund that? I don't care if it's in your group or my group or whatever, but we should do the right thing." It didn't work that way and, of course, any big company is like this. People have certain things they control. That's why there's politics in large companies.

I can't operate in that environment. I'm just far too focused on the end result. And so for all those reasons—the fact that they were very resistant to adopt other technologies that they felt might be competitive, and the fact it was just a large organization, no worse than any other large organization, I'm sure, but, nonetheless, it was a large organization with a lot of politics—it became unbearable.

But I think in the end they recognized that WebTV was a profitable thing for them, because they ended up investing in it more, and now it's become MSNTV. And it actually is a significant profit sector. WebTV was marginally profitable in its 18th month of operation and has been profitable every month since then, to this day. In 2005, 10 years after founding, WebTV (now called MSNTV) grossed about $150 million for Microsoft with 65 percent gross margins. Over its 8 years in the market, WebTV has grossed over $1.3 billion. We never expected people would still be using a dial-up connection and browsing on their TV in 2005, but there's still a significant market there for a device like WebTV, primarily for older people who want to be connected to the Web and email, but just will never buy a computer.

The other things we did with it that I was very excited about—that I was hoping to really capitalize on, which was moving to satellite with DVR and adding more interactivity and eventually moving to broadband cable—they have not been successful at pursuing. I think with the satellite stuff they actually introduced a couple of reasonably good products, but they got tripped up in the business negotiations with that, and the cable operators are very resistant to working with Microsoft.

Now their new thrust, which I think there's some significant opportunity with, is with IPTV. And that sort of is what the legacy of WebTV moved into. Peter Barrett is heading up that effort. He was the person who created the first browser on WebTV. And here he is still at Microsoft—over 10 years later, if you can believe it—and he's now trying to get television to work through the Internet, while what we started doing was trying to get the Internet to work through a television.

Livingston: What has the potential to go most wrong in the first year when a startup is such a fragile organization?

Perlman: The worst thing that can happen to a startup is if the founding team—or the people who are leading the thing—do not get along. And it's deadly when they don't get along in front of the troops. I've come to realize over the years that companies are just the people that make them up. We like to think of them as business enterprises and having this value and that value. Well, if you are going to distill it down to just patents and you are just going to go after people for infringing your patents, I agree. Those companies are simply made up of intellectual property assets. But any organization that actually has a product they are trying to ship and/or service they are trying to provide, it mainly comes down to the people. And the attitude of the company distills from the top.

In an organization that is very large and has existing businesses that have been running for a long time, you could have some not-so-great things happen in the top of the company, and it doesn't have as much impact. Maybe the employees aren't so happy, maybe they don't think so highly about their jobs, maybe they don't work as efficiently, but the company can keep plowing along. But, in the early days, you've got nothing. All you've got are problems— problems that need to be solved, obstacles that need to be overcome. You need to have an incredibly strong bond and an incredibly synchronized view of the world amongst the key players if you are going to succeed.

A synchronized view of the world doesn't mean you don't argue about things, that you don't have disagreements. You must agree on the philosophy, though, and on the vision. There are many ways to get there, but if you can't agree on the vision, then obviously you're never going to agree on how to execute. And you've got to respect each other. You've got to have cordial relationships. You've got to be decent people. I can't tell you how many times I've seen companies where people are fighting or arguing or nasty things are happening—fists punched through walls.

There's one example where a pair of pliers was tossed by the CEO at the controller. They sailed over her shoulder and lodged into the wall behind her. She dropped her papers and said, "I quit," and stormed out the door. I've seen this stuff happen at different places, and these companies—no surprise—have not prospered.

But, then again, I've seen companies that really have a lot of execution problems. General Magic is a good example of that. They really did not execute well in what they were doing. The product was very expensive; it was over $1,000. It was heavy. The battery didn't last long. The screen was not very bright. And it was loaded with all sorts of features that were not really needed by a mobile professional, which is what a PDA—this was 1990—was targeted for. Palm, on the other hand, made something small, light, the battery lasted a long time. It was inexpensive and focused on things like a calendar and address book. I saw General Magic working on getting bunny rabbit animations working to make it cute. It had infrared output, and they were making it so it could tune channels on a TV. They were doing things that were just taking sideways turns from the core product, which were interesting things to work on in a playground kind of environment as engineers, but were not focused on the product execution.

But the thing about it is, the three founders were very, very closely bound together. They worked together well, for better or for worse. They projected a common vision. They exuded stability, which made everyone else feel stable in the company. And it made the company strong. They were able to survive. The company ended up lasting over a decade. It did an IPO, though it finally fizzled out. And the product was never successful in the market. It only sold a few thousand units. But it shows an example of where you have so many things working against you—the product was not one that was marketable, and you are facing all these problems—but because they had a very strong core, they were able to survive as an organization. To me, that was the most important thing.

The key thing about Phil and Bruce is that they had hearts of gold. They were nice people. They were not in it to get rich. I mean, money certainly is freedom. But they both had a vision of creating something great that people would love. That attitude from the three of us permeated the rest of the organization. And the organization functioned well. On top of it, we had a strong business model and good execution on the technology. We were actually profitable 18 months after we launched.

We could have had all the technical talent and engineering know-how and business knowledge, but, if we were acting like Chinese fighting fish in a tank together, the whole company would have failed. And through those really difficult things that I told you about, where we were running out of money, when we got the certified letter of rejection from Sony—all those different things I think would have easily knocked over a weaker triad. We persevered through all of it, and we never stopped. None of us ever doubted that we were going to succeed. And none of us ever stopped to question whether or not we trusted the other. We never had to look at our back. And that is what allowed WebTV to persevere.

Mike Ramsay
Cofounder, TiVo

Mike Ramsay and Jim Barton founded TiVo in 1997. Their original plan was to create a network server for homes. Realizing it would be hard to explain to consumers why they needed one, they narrowed the idea down to one component of the original plan: the digital video recorder (DVR). The first version was launched in 1999.

TiVo was ground-breaking in that it took all the information that existed on television and gave the viewers the power to manipulate it. With TiVo, you could skip commercials, pause live TV, schedule the recording of every episode of a series—all the things one might expect to be able to do with data. But these new features sparked controversy in Hollywood. Networks worried about losing control over how people watched TV.

By skillfully navigating the border between what's possible with technology and what television executives would tolerate, TiVo brought about a revolution in the way people watch TV. Like Google, its name became a verb.

TiVo went public in 1999. Ramsay stepped down as CEO in 2003, but remained as chairman.

Livingston: You came to the United States when you were in your mid-20s. What brought you here? Had you planned to stay for as long as you have?

Ramsay: The reason I came was because I worked for HP. I joined HP right out of school. I was educated in Scotland, and they had a factory over there. Through good fortune, I got a chance to come over here with HP and check the place out, and loved it so much that my wife and I decided to come here.

It was the mid-'70s and Britain was in bad shape. That was when there was 25 to 30 percent inflation; there were strikes everywhere. By today's standards, it was a complete mess. A lot of people, not just myself, were disillusioned. This was like Disneyland for technologists, so off we came. I had a great career with

HP and kind of moved on from there. It was definitely the American "looking for opportunity."

Livingston: Wasn't the time around the start of the microcomputer revolution?

Ramsay: It was very early on. There were no PCs. The microprocessor idea had just gotten going, and they were 4-bit microprocessors—that was state of the art. Designs were all basically custom hardware designs, so it was very different. I was involved in chip design at that point. That felt like rocket science. That was the leading edge, and therefore it was the most exciting thing to work on.

When I left HP in the early '80s, I went to a startup company called Convergent Technologies. They had been founded before the PC revolution—that happened during the formative stage of the company. The idea of Convergent was to build a workstation. That notion of a CRT and a CPU and a keyboard was brand new. Computers were things that sat in rooms and had terminals, and this was completely self-contained. I thought that was really exciting.

It was during that period that the IBM PC came out. I remember the entire company was run on an Apple II—this thing that looks like a little wedge. Because it had to do all this stuff for the company, it got too hot and it had fans bristling out of it. By today's standards, it was pretty archaic, but it was also very exciting.

People like Bill Gates were young kids then. A lot of the people who are now very famous were just young engineers that were trying to come up with a good idea. And they did. So the rest is history.

We were definitely at the center of the universe, and that was fun. You felt like whatever you did, you had the best opportunity and you could go to the best places and work with the brightest people. They had energy and enthusiasm and they couldn't fail. There was nothing that was impossible. Culturally, in the UK, it was much more subdued; people were much more cautious.

I was just back there, and I was looking at a bunch of venture firms and their portfolio companies. I was curious to see what's the attitude of a typical startup in Scotland compared to here. I found that they are just culturally a whole lot more conservative and cautious. And somewhat lacking in self-confidence. You come over here and . . . I had a meeting recently with a couple of early 20-year-olds who have decided to drop out of Stanford because they got bored, and they are trying to raise money to fund their startup. They believe they can do it, and nothing's going to hold them back. They have confidence, they have that spirit, which I think is great and is probably unique to this part of the world. Being part of that for so long, for me, has been very invigorating.

Livingston: Take me back to when you decided to partner with Jim and start TiVo.

Ramsay: I had a couple of stints at HP, and it was during that second stint that I met up with Jim. We were building a team inside the company, and we hired some very talented people, including Jim, and Tom Jermoluk, who went on to run @Home. We all kind of became pals.

After a year or so, I realized that I couldn't go back to a big company thing; it just wasn't going to work. I got recruited to this opportunity at SGI, which then was a couple of hundred people. Mark Perry just joined (he's one of the partners at NEA), Dick Kramlich was on the board, and so I went over there and thought this was the greatest thing I'd ever seen. The technology was phenomenal. I thought Jim Clark was great. The people there were super bright. Sometimes you just walk into an environment and you know. There are no questions to be asked; you just kind of know and that's it. And that's how I felt about SGI.

When I decided to join, I told T.J., Jim, and some others, and they said, "Great, when do we start?" So there was a whole exodus out of HP.

We actually ended up in different departments at SGI. We never worked very closely together, but we always kept in touch socially. Jim went off and became a world-class technologist in his own field. He invented things at SGI that nobody else had done. He made UNIX work in parallel processing systems. He made UNIX work in real time. You had to have real-time systems to do graphics, because the flight simulator couldn't hiccup once in a while. So he went off and did that stuff, and I was very impressed with what he had done. I was off doing all the low-end workstation things for SGI. I was hanging out with the movie studios and special effects people and got to know that whole crew.

I started to get really interested in what you could do with computers in the entertainment space, things that I considered not-boring, because most computer applications are pretty boring. I got interested in how you can use computing technology to do things that are really entertaining and very different from what you might expect it to be used for.

Jim, on the other hand, coming from his technical background, started to work on a video-on-demand system that SGI was doing with Time Warner. It was in Orlando, Florida. They did the very first video-on-demand system, called the Full Service Network. Technically it was brilliant, but the experience turned him against all things institutional in the TV world, like cable companies and satellite companies. He felt they were like monopolies and we were going backwards. But nevertheless, he kind of liked that space.

So Jim was doing that and left SGI and went off and tried to start a company. About a year later I left, and just by happenstance I got hold of him. I can't even remember who called who, but we ended up going out to lunch and we kicked around a few ideas. We said, "It would be kind of fun to work together on some ideas, because we come at it from different angles. Maybe we'll come up with something. Maybe we could do a company."

We thought that was a fine idea, so we kept going out to lunch and talking about it. We had some great lunches. We started to home in on this idea of using computing technology in home entertainment. At the time, it was like home servers and home networks. You wired everything in the home network, and it was a little bit ahead of its time, which got us interested.

After a while, we put this together in a presentation. It wasn't a business plan, but we had some ideas of what we'd like to do. We came here [to NEA] and other places and peddled it around. Most people just kicked us out because the model for venture capital was—and it is still to some extent this way today, but certainly was 10 years ago—their ideal companies are ones where people come in and say, "We have this idea. Here's the market. Here's the size. I want $5 million, and I'll be profitable from day one. And I'll give you half my company."

We came in and said, "It's not like that in our case." First of all, it was a consumer play, and that was new. Second, it was a service company—because early on we had really wanted to do that. At that time, VCs generally didn't invest in service companies. Number three, we said, "It's going to be capital intensive. It's going to require a lot of money. You can give us a little bit of money right now, but it's going to require a lot more." So we had three things going against us, and they all kind of freaked out. The only two people that didn't freak out were Stewart Alsop of NEA and Geoff Yang of Redpoint.

Livingston: Why do you think they thought differently?

Ramsay: Geoff told me that he was fascinated by this space and wanted to do something, but he hadn't seen too many companies with any ideas. We kind of wafted in, and he thought, "Great. Suddenly we've got a couple people who could probably run a company and who've got a creative idea and can make it happen." So he was all fired up about that.

Stewart is a visionary. He's way out there. So this was a natural for him. He looks for companies that are trying to push the envelope and do something radically different. It kind of fit him emotionally. Neither of these guys were thinking about, "How much money do we make? Is the market ready?" They certainly weren't thinking about, "Are they going to violate copyrights or get sued?" or all that stuff that we got threatened with. They just thought, "Here's a couple of people that have got a fascinating idea. Who knows if it's going to work or not, but we'll give them some money and see what happens."

Livingston: Your original idea was not just a DVR, right?

Ramsay: It wasn't. It was this flamboyant, home server network thing. And we actually got funded based on that. When we got into the technology, we realized, "Hey, network technology isn't quite there yet. The idea of a server is fine, but how do you explain it to the average consumer?" We learned very quickly that this was going to be a hard sell and a hard thing technologically.

At the time, this server had a ton of apps that we thought up, one of which was DVR. We said, "Look, you can't do everything, so let's design a simple server based on very low-cost technology. Let's decide on one app that we think is the killer app to run on it, and let's do that. If that's successful, then we'll branch out. Forget the network thing and forget the massive amounts of storage and high cost and hardware models and all that."

We thought the DVR idea—we called it PVR at the time, personalized television or something like that—we thought this was a cool idea. It fascinated us because, once you looked under the covers, you realized it was a very difficult technical problem. The fact that it was a consumer product and it had to be television meant that it had to be completely reliable and bulletproof. Jim immediately flipped into this mode of "How do you make that work?" He started thinking about this, and all his real-time UNIX and video-on-demand experience started to come together, and we thought, "This could be very cool." So we clicked on it.

We went back to the VCs and said, "Thank you very much for the money. We've changed our minds. Here's what we're going to do and here's why we think it's a good idea." They said, "Oh, that just sounds like a VCR." (Anytime anyone says that to me, I go completely nuts.) So we had this challenge of explaining, "It's actually not a VCR. It's a lot more sophisticated and uses a hard disk, and therefore you can record and playback simultaneously and do clever things like pause live TV, and so on."

We then hired people who came in and were very creative and thought a lot about the user interface and how you actually make this work internally. In a very short space of time—like 6 months from when we got started—we had a good-sized team of people who were all working on this from different aspects.

One of the things I worried about in starting a company was . . . you come from a high-tech background and, depending on the technology, if it's cool, it attracts the brightest. If you go back in history and you look at all the different phases of technology evolution, you find there are certain things that are in vogue that attract very bright people. Certainly through my tenure at SGI, the big thing was UNIX. All the best people wanted to work on UNIX. UNIX was the sandbox that they could be creative in and solve difficult problems. That's where they wanted to be. So companies that did that, like Sun and SGI and others, attracted very bright people, and therefore you got great work done.

I thought, "I'm going to start a consumer company. It's going to be a little box that can't cost more than $200 or $300. It's going to do a very simple function. It's got to work with a remote control. Is that going to be challenging enough for us to attract the brightest people? Because I don't want to run a company that has a second-rate engineering organization. I want to run a company that has a top-rate engineering organization." So I was worried about that.

Then Jim hired a guy that he had known from SGI who was really bright. That was kind of the first key hire. We'd begun to realize that inside this thing it was very difficult, and, as we identified these great engineers and they came in, we sort of explained a little bit about it to them, and they said, "It sounds like a very difficult problem. Sign me up."

I think TiVo became the first company, certainly in this area, that created a new playground for those really great people. It was nothing to do with UNIX, although it was a Linux-based system. It was to do with creating an integrated system that really worked well and was inexpensive. Hide the technology from people—that was the challenge. When you used it, you never thought of it as anything. You thought of it as a remote control.

That, I think, really got people's imaginations going. They said, "Yeah, I'd love to work on that. That sounds interesting."

Livingston: Can you tell me about some of the biggest technical challenges?

Ramsay: While people had talked about storing video data on a disk before, actually creating a consumer product that used a disk to store video was pretty radical because, at the time, it was really expensive. We had to make a bet on whether the price was going to come down fast enough to make this any kind of consumer product. Originally, this thing had 14 hours of recording time and we were going to have to charge $1,000 for it. We better be on a pretty steep curve, right?

But once we had decided that, the big deal was, "How do you use the disk?" A disk has got fast seek. It's not like a VCR, where you have to record something on the VCR and that's all you can do with it—once it's recorded, you can play it back; it's a linear thing; you can only do one thing at a time. What we saw on the disk was—because it's a random access device and that little head moved really fast—you can essentially create the illusion of doing things simultaneously, so you can record and play back at the same time.

How to do simultaneous record and playback, pause and fast-forward and rewind and stuff like that cheaply and efficiently was the key attribute. In fact, that idea of how you implemented that through a device called a media switch and sort of managed all that flow of data—that became part of the Time Warp patent, which was one of our most important patents.

That was one of the first patents that we filed. Figuring that one out was critical, and had not really been done before—simultaneously recording and playing back video in a very low-cost way that "just worked." Maybe somebody had built a massive professional video editing system that cost a million dollars that could do that, but certainly nobody had done it to cost a few hundred dollars, and that was a big breakthrough.

The second was the harnessing of the program guide data to actually drive the function of the machine. Prior to that, and still to some extent today, that program guide data was generated by companies who had armies of people that were literally going through newspapers and calling up the TV stations. An entirely manual process of writing down what was on when, and a description of it. It's scary, but I think most of that still happens today. Very labor intensive. They would create a database of stuff and then they would sell that to the newspapers and magazines, so that when you opened the newspaper, it would tell you what was going to be on.

We looked at that and thought, "I wonder how accurate it is?" If it's off a little bit, it's not life and death, but, if it's a database that you want to drive a DVR, and when you say, "Get me *The Sopranos*" or "Get me *24*," you are very intolerant of not getting it. So that data has to be accurate. We went to this company, Tribune Media Services, and we said, "We'd like to use your data for this purpose."

So we start to use their program guide data, and we had to massage it and figure out what was wrong with it and change it and modify it and bend it into shape for what we wanted to do with it. Then we had to try it out. It was pretty wild and crazy. There were things wrong, and it was not clear how it was all going to work. But we plugged away at it and we finally got it to a place where it was pretty reliable, and you could download and it worked. It could drive the

DVR. That had never been done before. Nobody had ever thought of it before. It was a brand new idea.

I remember complaining to the team once that we were like 6 months from release of the product and we hadn't recorded anything yet. I said, "Don't you think it would be a good idea to test that out?" And everyone would go, "No. That's easy. That's not the hard bit. The hard bit is pausing and all this kind of stuff." And I'm going, "I know, but if you try and record something, the chances are that it's not going to work and you are going to learn a lot." So finally I persuaded them to record something, and, sure enough, it all fell apart and we had to scramble at the end to make all that work.

That idea of driving the thing from this program guide data was brand new. Then we had to decide, "How do you get it?" Today, you can switch on your TV and you get a program guide. It comes down through the TV signal. We thought, "Well, why don't we just do that?" We realized that not all TV signals have it, and you could only get a certain amount of coverage.

So we finally decided, "All right, let's get it over the telephone line." We had to put a modem in this thing and it had to call up, and when it called up, we had to have a server at the other end that had all this stuff. It would tell the server, "I'm in ZIP code 94022 and I'm getting Comcast cable and I have the basic service; therefore, send me the program guide for just that." And everybody was different. There were like 65,000 different combinations of program guide that we had to sift through so that you got exactly what you wanted and it matched exactly what your TV service was.

And we had to design this thing so nobody could hack into it. We wanted to make sure that nobody went in and stole your TV programs, or, perhaps more importantly, nobody could go in and find out what you were watching, because people don't like other people to know what they are watching on television. It's their business. So we had to make it very secure and very robust. We created a reliable and secure back-end server farm—that we created from nothing—and nobody had ever done that before in this kind of an environment. Stuff like that was really radical at the time, and even when we released it, most people kind of took it for granted. They hit the TiVo button and they got what they wanted, and there's all this stuff going on in the background they had no idea was going on.

We had our fingers crossed. I remember once the thing broke, and we had to literally go in there and change people's DVRs. It happened very early in the company. We responded instantaneously, and our customers hardly knew what had happened and we got them back on air. We looked at each other after that, and we said, "Thank goodness that happened right now, and not 5 years from now." We put in place some things after that that made sure that you could never send data to a TiVo that would break it. Because you have 4.5 million TiVos out there, and if you get something wrong in a software release and you issue the software to all these TiVos and it breaks them, you are in a lot of trouble. So we had to ensure that that was impossible.

One of the things we did was this thing called TiVo phone home. It's like controlling satellites that are orbiting Mars. You can only get a certain amount of information to them, and if they lose their way, they have to go into a safe mode. So we had this safe mode for TiVo, where it would ignore everything and it would phone back to TiVo and say, "I'm lost." When we contacted it, we would then redownload the software so it could come alive again. Right now it's 4.5, but it has to scale for 10, 20 million. You got them all out there, and it's a massively distributed, incredibly complicated system. So when somebody says, "It's just like a VCR," you want to attack them.

Livingston: When did you first start getting users? You raised the first round of money in '97 and then homed in on your plan. Then, you raised a lot more money, right?

Ramsay: We raised a lot more money. We were able to get the first round done because we had Jeff and Stewart and they were into it and it wasn't a lot of money. The second round was a lot harder, because we wanted an uptick in valuation and we needed to bring in some more investors. That was a very difficult round. I can't remember all the numbers of what we raised, but the combination of the first and second round was probably $10 or $15 million. Not a huge amount of money.

For the third round, I believe we got Paul Allen—I think it was either the third or fourth round. Paul Allen came in with Vulcan and invested a significant amount of money. After Vulcan came in was another interesting time. That was when the media companies started to get interested in us. We raised a lot of money from major movie studios and content holders prior to our IPO. Then we had an IPO; then we got an investment from AOL—$200 million. We did a bunch of other rounds and if you add it all up from then till now, it was about half a billion dollars that we raised. So we were in money-raising mode from day one.

Somewhere in that process we hired Dave Courtney as CFO, which I think was one of the most successful hires for us. Dave had not been a CFO; he was an investment banker. I thought, "Though the accounting part of a CFO's job is very important, the capital-raising part is so difficult and specialized. Why don't I find somebody who is really good at that?" So we found Dave, and he joined us. He had a ball raising all that money, and he got us through our IPO.

I would say that one of the reasons that TiVo is thriving today is that we were well-capitalized. We were able to power our way through the downturn—that early 2000 period when Replay went away. We were capitalized enough that we knew we could ride through it. While we had to make a few adjustments to the company, there was never a question that we were going to survive. We knew we were going to survive.

Livingston: Tell me about the launch and the first users.

Ramsay: We launched at the end of March of 1999. It was the last day of March, and we called it the Blue Moon event. It turns out that month was a blue moon. Because it was such a momentous thing—our first product shipped—we declared it a company holiday. It's still a holiday today.

We were manufacturing it through a third-party manufacturer in Milpitas, and we took the whole company over there and we all put on little blue jackets and caps and we watched them making TiVos. That celebration was fun.

Prior to that, we had been shipping certain selective units. The previous January, 3 months before, we had launched at CES (Consumer Electronics Show), so people knew about us. We were in this hot debate with Replay, who were trying to claim that they were first, and we were first. We actually released the product and shipped first.

There were a bunch of beta users prior to that, including Geoff and Stewart, and of course these things broke and didn't record the programs properly and did all sorts of crazy things. They kept rebooting. We were a bit nervous about giving board members TiVos, but we got through that.

We had an arrangement with Philips, and they started shipping through their retail distribution system. We were fortunate because the press loved this idea of a young startup company that was screwing up the media industry, and the press loved this idea that we were locked in battle with Replay. We got a huge amount of publicity. People knew what TiVo was long before we ever put the product out. So we started to sell it and it went well.

We had to learn a lot. I remember one weekend, we took the entire company, which was about 60 people at the time, and we divvied them up and went to all the Fry's stores in the Bay Area, because they were selling at Fry's. We set up demo stations and the employees were giving demos. It was great because almost everybody had no experience of what it's really like to sell in a retail store. So we started to do all that stuff, and it began to take off. That was the end of March. By August/September, we had sold about 18,000 units and we were going to IPO.

It was not a lot of units, and we were just riding the wave of this bubble that was about to burst. We got in in September of '99 and we got our IPO done and we were oversubscribed and the company's valuation went up to billions of dollars and we thought we had died and gone to heaven.

During that period, we did a deal with Sony and we did an important deal with DIRECTV. We started to supply DIRECTV with TiVos. That became a big deal for the company and still is today for that matter. So we started to branch out to some different partnerships there, and one thing led to another, and we grew.

Everyone complained that we weren't growing fast enough, and, if the thing was so hot, why did it not just take off? But we were charging $500 or $600 for this thing, and I was pretty happy with how things were going considering that, starting off, we wanted to do this big server and we had scaled it down to a DVR. I thought we'd sell a few thousand, and then we'd go on to the real thing. Now this thing has got a life of its own. People love it and we started to get great feedback.

It was interesting because the press who reviewed it . . . there were two kinds: the technology press, like Walt Mossberg, who hated it because it wasn't techie enough for them; then there was the consumer press, who loved it because it was nice and simple.

I can't tell you how hard it was to get a bad review. It just tore the company apart if somebody wrote a bad review about TiVo and we read it. "Oh God. How can we deal with this?" It was a gut-wrenching time for the company. As everyone started to review it, some people liked it, some people didn't. But at the end of the day, it worked out just fine.

Livingston: Back to your first customers—were there any features you were surprised they wanted as they started using it?

Ramsay: The thing that really got them was pausing live TV. That was the hook. You go, "Blah blah blah and it can pause live TV." They'd look at you and go, "Wait a minute. Pause live TV? How do you do that?" "Well, technically, you do it this way and that way." "That doesn't work. You can't pause live TV. It's live!"

We couldn't get people to understand it. We'd say things like, "It's not like the actors take a break or anything. You pause live TV." Then you'd show it to them, and we got pretty good at this after a while, where we'd surprise them with this and we'd pause live TV and you could see them going, "Wow. I never thought that would ever be possible."

So that was a big catalyst. Once people got that idea, they realized it was something really different.

The other things that people wanted to do—and I don't know if it was because we did it and then they liked it or if it was because they asked for it and then we did it—but this idea of a season pass or a wish list where you just put in something—a very small amount of information saying, "I want this"—and, for the rest of your life, you get it. So if you want to see *The Sopranos* and you want it every week, you do a Season Pass, and that Season Pass will look out for *The Sopranos* every time it's broadcast. It's clever enough not to get any repeats, so you only get the real one. And it's clever enough to deal with times changing and durations changing. So if you have a season finale that lasts two hours, TiVo will automatically figure that one out. People loved this idea of "Get me a Season Pass," and then they can forget about it. We expanded that to WishList, which says, "Get me all the Martin Scorsese movies," or stuff like that. "Clint Eastwood westerns." Those were very attractive to people, and over time it became pretty clear that this was something very new and different.

Livingston: Tell me a little bit about times that you were most worried about competitors.

Ramsay: The Replay thing was definitely an interesting case in point. We were on parallel paths, and it was a bit of a mystery to us how we managed to get on parallel paths.

We kept hearing rumors about them, and I'm sure they heard rumors about us. They went out with a very different proposition. Theirs was much more techie. They had no monthly fees; you bought a box. They were really scrappy. We were kind of taking the high ground, and they were down there doing all the dirty tricks to try to compete with us.

During that time, both their CEO and myself were getting interviewed by the press, and they had us doing photo shoots together with dueling remote controls. We knew these guys, and there was no hatred, but there was a definite, very intense competitive attitude. Our aim was to get them out of our hair, out of our business. This wasn't, "There's enough room for everybody." This was, "They have to go. They are the enemy and we're not going to let anything stand in the way of us beating them."

While that was very angst-ridden and a lot of our employees were very concerned and sometimes upset about what Replay said about us, I think it was a great time for the company because the company learned how to compete. I know, from my standpoint, I had never worked in a company that really competed before. SGI, if it found competition, it went elsewhere. HP was not as competitive back then as it is today. They relied on doing things very new and different, so they differentiated themselves. In those days, they weren't going to say, "You have one of them, I have one of them, I'm going to compete with you, and this is not going to be clean." So we were doing that; we were competing.

I look back on that and it was a lot of fun, especially since we beat them. We saw things that they were doing wrong. If you are playing a competitive game, you worry about winning the game, but you are so much in the game that, while you are doing it, you are not thinking, "Oh, gee, I'm going to lose." You are thinking about "How do I win?" And that was very much that spirit.

The next big competitive threat was with DIRECTV. DIRECTV decided that, in addition to us, they wanted to do a deal with Microsoft. Microsoft had just bought WebTV, and they were building a DVR. DIRECTV decided they wanted to have that DVR, too. So then all of a sudden DIRECTV was selling both of them. They were under probably pretty similar financial agreements, so for them it didn't make a whole lot of difference who bought which one. Except Microsoft was pouring hundreds of millions of dollars into trying to develop this market, and here's little TiVo with—although we'd raised a lot of money, we didn't have that kind of resource at our disposal.

Lo and behold, we found out that we were outselling them by a significant amount. People loved TiVo. The brand was getting known by then, and we were better. We discovered that people preferred what we were doing to Microsoft on a fair and level playing field. It was not our doing; this was DIRECTV marketing it on an equal basis. It got so bad for Microsoft—they were putting so much money into it—that they finally gave up. We thought, "This is great, they gave up. Let's celebrate."

We then thought that the consumer electronics companies would come in, and we were worried about that, because we thought it was a natural for Sony. So what we did there was license our technology to them. We got some good license deals and that sort of took that one off the table.

Most recently, a big competitive threat is from cable companies and satellite companies, who are entering this market and essentially giving away DVR for free. That's been a big issue for TiVo over the last several years. While TiVo has been able to do deals with several cable and satellite companies, there are competitors like EchoStar against whom we have had to enforce our patents in court.

More recently, TiVo has done deals with Comcast. It's renewed its deal with DIRECTV, so it's moving in this direction of taking its technology and embedding into those third-party platforms. I think that is going to be a trend for the future.

Livingston: Do you think if the networks had realized what you were doing early on that they would have tried to do something about you guys?

Ramsay: Oh, they did. That's a whole other story in its own right. Very early on, this notion of digital recording got the attention of the networks, and it was clear that they were concerned about what we were doing.

About the same time, we had built a prototype—it was a little thing based on a PC, a little box with a handle—and we'd take it around to show it to people. We had hired a guy called Stacey Jolna, who was from the media industry. He would take me around all these places to meet his contacts and sort of try to convince them that we weren't really a threat—that we were an advantage and there were some advertising opportunities and audience measurements things and all that kind of stuff. After the statutory hugging and talking about their kids and their families and what they've been doing, it was not unusual for them to let us know how they felt about what we were doing and show us the door. "You're evil. Don't come back. You're going to destroy us."

We'd see quotes in the newspaper about how we were going to destroy the US economy. People were becoming very irrational. We got threats of lawsuits—all the time, every week. And we had people on our board from NBC and Discovery and all sorts of other media companies.

Replay probably did us a fabulous favor when they stepped across the line. There's a line in the sand that those media companies think about. You don't know where it is, but if you step over it, they're going to get you. Replay stepped over it by doing automatic commercial skipping. You didn't even have to fast-forward through the commercials. They just found out where they were and they eliminated them. And they let you share programs over the Internet. That crossed the line. They got sued. They were the bad guy; therefore, we were the good guy.

At the end of the day, actually, I think we got a lot of respect from those companies, but it was a difficult time and these are powerful companies that were hell-bent on getting rid of us. To this day, it amazes me that those companies eventually decided to invest in TiVo, actually put money into the company, and probably made the difference between TiVo surviving and not surviving when the Bubble burst. That difference was attributed to Disney, Viacom, Discovery Communications, NBC, Showtime, HBO, and Time Warner. They all put money into the company. They put one representative on the board—NBC has always had a representative, John Hendricks from Discovery was the representative for a lot of the others. There was something like $50 million that we raised from that group of people, and that got us by.

Livingston: Do you think they thought, "If we can't beat 'em, join 'em"?

Ramsay: I don't know what it was. I still don't quite understand it to this day, but it was fascinating to go through that. Though it was not without its trials and tribulations.

I'm not sure if people still get today that the combination of the technology development and the getting to market of a product, the development of a channel and the marketing and the brand building of that product, the management of the media companies and their desire to destroy you, and the management of this highly competitive situation every step of the way, where you had to win every day in the marketplace and worry about intellectual property—if you think about all these massive things that we had to deal with every single day of TiVo's existence, you realize that it was a big deal and not for the faint of heart. You had to kind of learn to have fun with it and not to take it too seriously.

Livingston: Thinking back on the early days of TiVo, what surprised you the most?

Ramsay: Probably the thing we just talked about. The fact that these media companies got involved and embraced it and invested in it and are involved in it today. I would not have anticipated them doing that. Given their earlier reaction, I would have thought it would be impossible, but it happened.

So TiVo's now a media company. It sort of transformed the company into a media company. I think we have an appreciation for what media companies are going through; that helped us develop in a way that didn't cross the line. And I think the media companies have an appreciation for what a young, scrappy, highly competitive technology company in Silicon Valley is trying to do.

They know that is a dynamic that is driven by the human spirit; that they ought to embrace it rather than fight it. All the resources they have in the world, all the billions of dollars, can't stop people being creative. There are a lot of companies who, in one way or another, have changed the rules of the game for the better. It's just going to happen. I think we helped a very conservative industry get their minds around that.

Paul Graham
Cofounder, Viaweb

Paul Graham and his friend Robert Morris started Viaweb in 1995 to make software for building online stores. A few days into writing the first prototype, they had a crazy idea: why not have the software run on the server and let the user control it through their browser?

Within weeks, they had a web-based online store builder they could demo to investors. They launched at the beginning of 1996.

Viaweb was one of the first companies to deliver on the Web's promise of creating a level playing field. Using Viaweb's software, small businesses could make online stores as good as those built by big catalog companies. And many did: by 1998, Viaweb Store was the most popular e-commerce software.

Viaweb was acquired by Yahoo in June 1998 and renamed Yahoo Store. In 2005, Graham cofounded Y Combinator, a seed-stage investment firm.

Livingston: You had a different startup before Viaweb, didn't you? Can you tell me a little about that?

Graham: Before Viaweb we had a startup called Artix. We were going to put art galleries online. The problem was, art galleries didn't *want* to be online. They still don't want to be online. We spent a long time trying to convince these people to use something they didn't want before we had the idea that maybe we should make something people actually did want.

Livingston: You scrapped Artix and switched to making software for websites for online stores?

Graham: Yeah. Actually, it's pretty similar software. We realized that if we could write software that could generate sites for galleries, we were only a shopping cart away from generating online stores. Everyone seemed to want online stores, so why not just do that instead?

At least, we thought everyone wanted online stores. There was a lot of talk in the press about e-commerce then, because Netscape was doing a big PR campaign for their IPO. They had to convince everyone that the Internet would be economically important, and they picked the most literal example they could think of. Actually most merchants didn't want to sell online, not yet. But when they started to want to, we were there.

Livingston: Take me back to when you were first working on Viaweb. What were some of the first things you did? Did you have any funding?

Graham: In the very, very beginning, no, we didn't have any funding. It was just me and Rtm [Robert Morris] in his apartment. It was in the middle of summer. Rtm was in grad school, but because it was the summer he had some free time. We just said, "OK, we'll try and write a prototype." We wrote the first version in a couple days.

One of the unusual things about Viaweb was that it worked over the Web. That's where the name came from. It was a web-based application—as far as I know, the first one. But in the very beginning, it wasn't web-based. At first it was going to be software that you would use on your desktop computer to build a website that you would then upload to a server. Then in the first couple days of working on it, we had this idea, "Hey, maybe we could make this run on the server and have the user control it by clicking on links on a web page." So we sat down and tried to write it and, sure enough, you could write a program that worked this way.

Livingston: This was a new idea, right? Do you remember when it came to you?

Graham: At the time most of the hackers we knew used this program called X Windows, where you could be using a program that was running on some remote machine, but it would be drawing stuff on your screen. There was also this idea of an X terminal, or xterm for short, which was a computer that did nothing but run X Windows—all the brains were on the server. So the way we thought of web-based applications at first was using the browser as an xterm. Could we just treat the browser like an xterm, and have the application running on the server?

So it wasn't that huge a conceptual leap if you came from our world, but it was a bit of a conceptual leap. I remember very well when I had the idea. I was staying in this spare room in Robert's apartment during the summer, because at the time I was living in New York, and I woke up one morning with the idea. As I was lying there half asleep this idea of making the software run on the server popped into my head and it was so dramatic that it woke me up. I sat up in bed, like the letter L, thinking, "We have to go try this."

Livingston: Do you remember how you felt when it worked?

Graham: I was pretty excited, because it meant we could start a company without having to learn Windows. The prospect of having to write desktop software was horrifying to us, because at the time, writing desktop software meant writing Windows software. Neither of us knew how to write Windows software and we didn't want to learn. It seemed like this huge steaming turd that was best just avoided. So the main thing we thought when we first had the idea of doing web-based applications was, "Thank God, we don't have to write software on Windows."

Livingston: So you have this major breakthrough. What were some of the next things you did?

Graham: Pretty early, we got some funding from our friend Julian, who also worked with us on Artix. He gave us $10,000. After about 6 weeks or so, it seemed like it was going to be more work than we thought, so we got Trevor Blackwell to work on it too.

Livingston: How did you know Trevor?

Graham: Trevor was in grad school with Robert. I asked Robert, "Who's the smartest grad student in the computer science program?" and he said "Trevor." I couldn't believe it actually, because at the time I thought Trevor was a total goofball.

Livingston: But you were soon convinced he was talented?

Graham: Trevor is a prodigy, in the original sense of the word. When we first recruited him, we asked him to write this little piece of image-manipulating software, to kind of test him out. For 2 weeks we heard nothing from him, and I had pretty much written him off. Finally he sent me an email asking me to come to his office to see what he'd done. I went there expecting to see this new image software, and instead he's rewritten our entire system in Smalltalk—everything I wrote, plus everything Rtm wrote.

I basically said, "OK, you're hired. Now go and write the damn image software, because we're not rewriting everything in Smalltalk."

Livingston: You and Robert were already good friends, right?

Graham: Oh yeah. We had been friends then for about 10 years—since way back. In fact, I think in the beginning it was only because he was friends with me that Robert even did this. In the beginning he was just humoring me. It was a year before he thought Viaweb had any chance of ever making any money.

Livingston: So you convinced him to spend the summer working on this project. What happened in the fall?

Graham: Things kind of came to a head with Rtm. We had this angry phone conversation where he said something like, "We've been working on this thing for a whole month, and it's still not finished." It's funny in retrospect, because we were still working on it 3 years later. At the time, I was just thinking about how to get him to keep working on it for another month. But that was the main reason we got Trevor. Robert basically rebelled, so I thought, "All right, we need more programmers."

Livingston: If Robert was so reluctant, why did you start the company with him?

Graham: Well, first of all he was my best friend, so I really trusted him, but he's also one of the best programmers in the world. I'd rather have a quarter of his brain working on some problem than 100 percent of most other people's.

Livingston: Where did you work?

Graham: In Robert's apartment. His housemate was away that summer, and I moved into his room.

Robert used to get up early, whereas I stayed up till four and got up at noon. So we would kind of work a 24-hour schedule. I would write some new code during the night and send Rtm an email saying, "OK, we've got all these new features in my part of the code." Then he would write the corresponding stuff in his part. So we got code written very fast.

Livingston: On one computer?

Graham: Uh, well, there was a large university nearby whose computers we sort of unofficially used.

Livingston: Nearby in Cambridge, Massachusetts?

Graham: Yes.

Livingston: What was the next big turning point after you realized you could make this web-based?

Graham: The next turning point was when we had a working demo—when we actually built an online store using our software and you could order from it, and edit it through Netscape. We started Viaweb in the middle of July '95 and I think we had this first demo in early August.

Livingston: Who were the first people that you showed the demo to?

Graham: The first people we showed it to were some potential investors. We ultimately decided not to take money from them, because they wanted a majority share of the company for a comparatively small amount of money. But the existence of these potential investors did spur us to write our first version, to get that demo working.

Livingston: Once you had this demo, did you start thinking about signing up customers or were you focused on raising money?

Graham: What we really thought we needed to do was write more software. We were software guys. Maybe someone who knew more about business would be thinking about going and getting customers, but frankly the idea of customers frightened us. We thought, "Before we go get any customers, why don't we just write a few more thousand lines of code?"

Livingston: Why were you frightened of customers?

Graham: Being a sales guy and being a hacker are two very different kinds of work. We were very comfortable dealing with hacking, but dealing with customers seemed like this terrifying unknown. If it seems strange to you that we were afraid of customers, imagine how the average sales guy would feel about modifying the software running on his laptop. The idea would seem terrifying. Whereas to a hacker, big deal.

Livingston: So what did happen?

Graham: We wrote a lot of software. We thought, "That's what we're good at. That's what we'll do." We just tried to put as much distance between any potential competitor and us as we could.

By that fall, we probably had a better online store builder than any of our competitors ever had, even 3 years later. In October or November I went down to New York and did demos for some angel investors and we got $100,000 more, which seemed to us more money than we could ever possibly spend. (We were wrong.)

Livingston: So what happened next?

Graham: We were very encouraged that the angel investors wanted to invest. We gave demos to two investors. We only wanted to raise $50,000, but both of the investors who saw the demos said yes. So we thought, "All right, we'll raise $100,000 then, since they both said yes."

Then we wrote more software. It didn't look then like we had an awful lot of competitors, so we took a risk and rewrote most of the code. Even though it was pretty good, we thought, "If we're ever going to rewrite this thing, now's the time to do it." Finally in December we started trying to get users.

Livingston: Who were your first customers and what did they think when you first showed them Viaweb?

Graham: Our first customers were a pair of technical bookstores. Robert actually went with me on the sales call to the first one. He just sat there absolutely silent through the whole thing. I think both of these bookstores were frightened of Amazon. Most people back then, you had to kind of twist their arm to get them to sell online, but not people in the technical book business.

Livingston: Tell me a little about your relationships with your first customers.

Graham: We felt like we had to have five or six customers to launch. And for these first customers, we basically would do whatever they said in order to get them as customers. We gave them the software for free for as long as they wanted. We built their sites ourselves. If they needed to have images in them, we would scan the images. We were basically web consultants, because we needed users; you can't launch a thing like this without having any users.

That's one of the problems with web-based software. If you're making desktop software and you launch the thing, no one can tell how many other users there are, right? But if you're making web-based software and you're hosting the websites that these guys build, then if you don't have any users, the entire world can see that.

Livingston: Were most people that you tried to pitch your software to online retailers? Were there things that they misunderstood?

Graham: One of the big things we got wrong was that we thought our users were going to be catalog companies. Now all the catalog companies are online, but back then, they just didn't want to hear about the Web. This was late '95, early '96. A lot of people didn't even have web access yet. So these middle managers at the catalog companies we called up, at that point they just wished the Web would go away. It was just making their lives more complicated. We would call them up and tell them how we could solve all their problems and make an online store for them, and it was kind of like the dentist calling up and saying, "Why don't you come in for that root canal?"

The people, it turned out, that really wanted our software were individual merchants—guys who had some kind of specialty store selling antique chess pieces or something like that, and up till now had relied on people coming to their shop to buy stuff, or maybe occasionally they would mail out a xeroxed price sheet. For these guys, the Web was huge, because it allowed them to have what the catalog companies had. Those users loved us.

Livingston: Why did users like Viaweb?

Graham: I think the main thing was that it was easy. Practically all the software in the world is either broken or very difficult to use. So users dread software. They've been trained that whenever they try to install something, or even fill out a form online, it's not going to work. *I* dread installing stuff, and I have a PhD in computer science.

So if you're writing applications for end users, you have to remember that you're writing for an audience that has been traumatized by bad experiences. We worked hard to make Viaweb as easy as it could possibly be, and we had this confidence-building online demo where we walked people through using the software. That was what got us all the users.

The other thing was, we had good graphic design. Our secret weapon was that we knew that e-commerce was really about graphic design, not transaction processing. Unless you had a site that could convince people to buy, you didn't have a transaction to process, and what convinced people to buy was how good the site looked. So we made sure that our software made great-looking sites—not just better than our competitors, but better than most of the sites that big companies paid web consultants half a million dollars to make for them.

We didn't even process credit card transactions till about 2 years in. We would just forward the order to the merchant, and they'd process it like a phone order.

Livingston: Who were your competitors? Were there any that you worried about?

Graham: We worried about different ones for different reasons. Our biggest competitor was a company called iCat. Fortunately for us, they were not very good at writing software. They were, however, very good at raising money and seeming corporate. At one point they did one round of funding that was more than our entire valuation, in fact probably twice our valuation. But fortunately they were never a threat technically.

At first they weren't web-based; they had desktop software. Finally they came out with a web-based version. Trevor and I were at a trade show when it launched, and we noticed that the URLs for static pages were something like "display-file" with a file name for an argument. So we tried replacing the argument with "/etc/passwd" and sure enough, the server displayed the password file right in the browser. *And* there were accounts with no passwords. I mean, this is programming 101.

There was another competitor called Shopsite that was better technically, but still not too dangerous. Plus they were out in Utah; they weren't really connected to the startup world. Whereas iCat was in Seattle, which was much more startuppy. For some reason there were no serious competitors in Silicon Valley.

Livingston: Tell me about some of the other major turning points in the first year or two of Viaweb.

Graham: There were a lot of turning points. Basically Viaweb's history was one turning point after another, alternately up and terrifyingly down. A couple days after we launched came the next turning point, when a giant company called us up and wanted to buy us, right on schedule. It was just like we thought it was going to be. We're these great hackers, we write this clever piece of software, we launch the thing, and rrring, there goes the phone and it's some big company wanting to buy us.

Livingston: What happened?

Graham: There was kind of a clash of cultures. First they came to check us out. They showed up wearing these Bill Cosby sweaters, like someone in corporate affairs has told them that when they go and visit startups, they're supposed to not wear suits and they're like, "Uh, what do we wear?" "Wear a sweater that looks like some macrame class knitted it collectively." So they show up in their Bill Cosby sweaters and march up the stairs past all the landlady's kids' shoes in the corridor, and walk in, and this company they're supposed to be buying is just a grad student apartment with some computers in it.

But they still wanted to buy us after that, so we arranged to have a meeting at Julian's loft in New York. One of our investors was a metals trader, so we figured that he must be a great negotiator and we'd let him handle it. The guys from the big company said, "We want to buy you for $3 million." And he said, "Well, I won't sell you the company for $3 million, but for $1 million, I'll sell you an option to buy the company in 6 months for $20 million." At that point the guys from the big company just got up and walked out.

Livingston: How did you feel?

Graham: For the first day or so, it didn't register with me what had happened. Then I felt really bad. I realized that if they'd bought us for $3 million, it would have been more than a million for me personally, so I felt like I'd lost a million dollars. I'd had a million dollars, and then lost it. I was aghast.

I called up the guy we'd been talking to at the big company and I said, "Do you still want to buy us?" and he said, "No!" He had lost face, I guess, with his colleagues for wasting their time on us.

Livingston: So that was a harsh dose of reality about the acquisition process.

Graham: That was my first introduction to something that turns out to be a very important lesson for startups: it's never a deal till the money's in the bank.

So many things can go wrong with deals, and they all do. Before we ultimately got bought by Yahoo, we probably had nine or ten different acquirers that we were talking to, and things always went wrong for one reason or another.

Livingston: So then what did you do? Go back to business?

Graham: Yeah. There were always two stories going on simultaneously with Viaweb. There was the software and the customer story, which just went smoothly and wonderfully the whole way along. We kept writing great software, we kept getting more and more customers, the customers loved us, the growth was this beautiful, smooth upward curve. Simultaneously, there was this story about the business, which was one disaster after another. So most of the actual turning points are not software or customer turning points, because everything went great there. All the turning points are business turning points.

The next one was probably when Robert went off that summer and took a summer job working for another company. He went to work at DEC SRC out in California. The problem was, he didn't tell me he was going to do this until . . . Well, actually he never told me. A few days before he left, we were having dinner with some friends and one of them said, "So Robert, are you looking forward to California?" I looked at Robert and said "California?" And it turned out he was going to leave in a week for the whole summer.

So now I had to explain to our investors why one of the founders of the company they had just invested in had gone and taken a summer job working for another company. That required all my spin abilities.

Livingston: What did you tell them?

Graham: I said that this was part of his graduate student career and that it was a common thing for people in graduate school to take jobs working in research labs during the summer and, yes, this was another company, but it was really more of a research lab than a company. That part was certainly true. When they tried to turn AltaVista into a company, it was disaster.

Livingston: What was the next turning point after Robert left for his summer job?

Graham: Our main angel investor, the metals trader, was encouraged that the big company had wanted to buy us, so that spring he'd put more money in—still angel-scale money. We weren't desperately running out of money, but we were going to run out sometime in the fall. The angel investor decided that we needed to have a business guy as CEO and that he wasn't going to give us any more money unless we got someone. So that summer, as well as trying to deal with Rtm being in California, we spent our time talking to various business guys.

The problem with all of them was that they had delusions of grandeur. This was the beginning of the Internet Bubble, remember, and I think all of these guys saw themselves as some kind of grand CEO, while we programmers labored in the kitchen cooking the food and washing the dishes. If the deal were simply that the business guy would be the public face of the company, but we would be allowed to do what we wanted and make sure everything worked right, that would have been OK. But we were worried about what might happen if one of these guys wanted to actually be the chief executive officer and tell us what our strategy should be. We'd be hosed, because they didn't know anything about computer stuff.

Livingston: So what did you do?

Graham: We lucked out. At practically the last moment, we found Fred Egan—or rather, he found us. Fred Egan saved us. That was a great turning point, when we got Fred. The lowest point, well, maybe tied for the lowest point in the company's history, was that summer when Robert was away and the investors were pressuring us to take some business guy as our boss. When we finally got Fred, that ended that summer of horror.

Livingston: What was so special about Fred?

Graham: He didn't need to be our boss. He was willing to be the COO and do the business stuff and let us handle the technical stuff. He had worked for a company that I had worked for, actually, Interleaf, and so he came with a lot of credibility. In fact, he had been a big executive at Interleaf while I was just a peon, so I was very impressed with him.

Livingston: Did he reassure your investors?

Graham: Oh God, that was so great. I remember Fred's first day. The metals trader was an extremely fearsome guy. He seemed like the kind of guy who would wake up in the morning and eat rocks for breakfast. On Fred's first day, the metals trader called up, and Fred answered the phone and said, "Hi Alan, are you buying or selling?" And I was so relieved. Finally I had someone to take over that stuff.

It was such a relief to have someone who would deal with the investors, so that we could just write software and make users happy. That's all we wanted to do.

Livingston: Tell me a little bit about your relationship with your investors.

Graham: I think, because we didn't seem very businesslike, most of the investors didn't really have any confidence in us as a company until we got bought. I think it was only then that they were really convinced we were doing a good job.

We didn't seem very businesslike for the same reason we didn't seem very well dressed. We just didn't bother with that stuff. But we did concentrate on the stuff that really mattered, which was making users happy.

Livingston: If the company that they've invested in was doing well, then why was the relationship bad?

Graham: Well, I suppose they thought it could be doing better. We were getting users at a certain rate and maybe they thought we could have been getting users at twice that rate. I don't think we could have. We already had more users than anybody else. There just weren't that many users out there to increase the rate that much.

There was one investor who I think really wanted to run the company. He had just sold his own startup, and he was pretty young. It was hard for him to just be a passive investor. For a while he actually came to work for us, as a VP.

You know, in retrospect I think the big problem with our investors was that we weren't forceful enough with them. I think investors like to be bossed around, like horses. It reassures them when you're in control. But these guys were much older than us and had given us huge sums of their money, so it was hard for us to boss them around.

Livingston: So now you have Fred on board and you are becoming more legitimate. What did you do next?

Graham: Soon after we got Fred, we raised more money. I don't remember exactly how much—maybe $800,000. A lot more money than we ever had before. We really shifted gears at that point. Up till then, we had been operating out of an apartment. In the very beginning, we operated out of Robert's apartment. Then after we got the $100,000 in that first round from the angel investors, we rented the apartment upstairs from Robert's. We had that for about a year and then after we got Fred and we got this new round, we actually rented an office and started hiring people. We really started to look like a company.

Livingston: Were you worried that you didn't look enough like a company before that?

Graham: We were big beneficiaries of that rule that on the Internet, nobody knows you're a dog. We were just a bunch of guys in an apartment with computers. Nowadays more people accept that startups look like that, but not back in the mid-'90s. People still expected a company to have a real office. I think if some of these companies whose online stores were on our server could have actually seen the room that the server was sitting in, they would have freaked. Thankfully they never did.

If anybody ever did want to come and visit us, we pulled all kinds of tricks to make ourselves seem more legit. When that first giant company wanted to buy us and sent people over to check us out, all we had in our so-called office was one computer. Robert and Trevor mostly worked at home or at school. So we borrowed a few more computers and stuck them on desks, so it would look like there was more going on.

One of these Potemkin computers was Robert's, from the apartment downstairs. And in the middle of this big visit from the company, Rtm comes upstairs boiling mad because he's come home and discovered his computer's missing. He's like "What have you done?" We said, "Shhh, shhh, we had to borrow it. We're trying to look real. Don't worry, we're not using it. It's not even plugged in." He was really mad, but he let us keep using his computer as a prop for another hour until they left.

Livingston: So you are growing as a company, you get a lot more funding, what happened then?

Graham: We started to seem more real then. By that point, we were starting to get mentioned in the press a lot. Early on, people found out about us through word of mouth. We were the underdogs—the guys who have better technology but nobody's ever heard of. This was the point where we stopped seeming like total underdogs and people started to know about us.

Part of the reason was that we hired a fabulous PR firm with this money, Schwartz Communications. We told them, "When people talk about e-commerce and they have to mention a few examples of companies, we want to be one of the companies they mention." The most valuable sort of press is not articles about you, it's when people mention you in passing as a matter of course. That's what you really want—whenever anybody talks about e-commerce, for them to say, "companies including . . . and Viaweb." Schwartz got us that within a couple months.

Incidentally, it was one of the guys at Schwartz who came up with the term "web-based software." Up till that point we'd called it "server-based."

Livingston: Were you still getting acquisition offers at this time?

Graham: There were always people trying to buy us. There was another one just at the point where we found Fred Egan—a Japanese company that later made an imitation of our software and went on to become a big success in Japan. Rakuten, they were called.

Livingston: They copied you?

Graham: Not very well. It's sort of like if you copied a dog by taking a photograph of a dog and sticking it onto a cardboard cutout. From certain angles it would look like a dog, but if you threw a stick and yelled "fetch" it wouldn't do anything. The Japanese market wasn't as far along then, so in their market, this was pretty advanced. But the entire time, there were always people trying to buy us, of various levels of seriousness.

Livingston: Did you have to take any more funding?

Graham: We did have at least one more funding round, under the most disastrous circumstances. One of these companies that tried to buy us—actually the second to last one; we were almost done—was a big Internet portal. We had a handshake deal with them and in the process of the due diligence for the deal, it was discovered that one of our programmers had signed a piece of paper with the company who had paid for him to go to graduate school, saying that everything he thought of belonged to them.

Livingston: So they owned the intellectual property?

Graham: They might have. What it said on the piece of paper was that they owned ideas relating to their business. But this was a huge company and arguably just about anything you could do with software related to their business. So we had to go and get a release from them and that took a long time, during which the acquirer welched on the deal.

It turned out to be good in the end, but we had to raise our last round of funding while this was happening. You want to raise a round of funding with an

IP cloud over your head? It's just impossible, because potential investors have no way of judging how serious it is. It could be no big deal, or it could be that this other company owns half your software.

That was the second low point—tied for lowest. Ultimately we managed to get some bureaucrat within the big company to give us a release, so we could say to acquirers we actually owned our software. But we had to do a round of funding before that, because we were out of money.

It was pretty miserable. Basically, the angel investors played chicken with us. They knew we couldn't get money from anyone else, since we didn't even know for sure if we owned our software. So they proposed to do a cramdown round where they would refinance the company, I believe, at a pre-money valuation of zero—meaning all the common stockholders were completely wiped out. To keep us around, since they kind of needed us to write the software, they were going to give us options. So we called their bluff. We said, "If you do that, we're leaving."

Livingston: You and your cofounders said you were leaving?

Graham: Yeah, all the technical guys. So when it came down to that, they compromised and we ended up doing a funding round at a low, but reasonable, valuation—$12 million, I think. We got bought only a couple months after that round closed. But we had to do the round because we were in debt at that point.

Livingston: You must have been displeased with your investors for doing that to you.

Graham: Well, everybody ended up rich, so it's hard to be too displeased. I'd rather have an investor who invested in us and made our lives hell than one who didn't invest in us at all, which is what most investors do to most startups. I mean, we needed their money to grow the company, and some amount of stress always comes with the money.

In retrospect, I think it was more about control than money. They weren't trying to rob us so much as take over the company. They were offering us quite a lot of options. The point was, we'd have to do what they said from then on, or lose them.

Livingston: Was there ever a point when you wanted to quit?

Graham: There was one point when I almost *did* quit, when the investors were telling us they were going to refinance the company. I had an appointment with a lawyer to figure out how to quit without getting sued. I was on my way out the front door when Fred Egan grabbed me and said, "Wait, let's see if we can fix this." It was pouring with rain and I was not too psyched about having to go find a cab in that, so I went back to work while he made some phone calls. I don't know what he said, but I guess he convinced the investors I wasn't bluffing. I wasn't, either.

We had some leverage, because the investors already had over a million dollars in the company. I don't know if they realized how hard it would have been to just hire a bunch of programmers and throw them in there and have them figure out the code, but it would have been really hard.

Livingston: So a few months later after this horrible low period, you have a great high period because you get bought by Yahoo. How did that happen?

Graham: We especially wanted to get bought by Yahoo. If you had asked us, "Who do you want to get bought by?" we would have said, "Yahoo." In fact, we did say that; we kind of spread the word that we saw Yahoo as the ideal acquirer.

We'd tried to do an online demo for Yahoo about 6 months before. We could do demos by phone where we'd talk people through editing a site and we could see from the log files where they were clicking. I tried to do a phone demo for Tim Koogle in the fall of '97, but he couldn't even get to our server. It turned out some router was hosed halfway between us and them.

The way we really got onto their radar screen was through Ali Partovi. He'd had Robert and Trevor as teaching assistants in CS classes at Harvard a few years before. He had a startup called LinkExchange that was talking to Yahoo at the time, and their VC was Mike Moritz, who was also Yahoo's VC. In the end they got bought by Microsoft instead, but not before they'd told Yahoo about us.

Livingston: How did it go with Yahoo?

Graham: We liked them. They were like us. They had hacker values, basically. They were from graduate programs in computer science too. They were our tribe of people, not these weird business people we kept having to deal with.

Plus they weren't jerks about the acquisition. So many companies play hardball in acquisitions. It's so stupid. Don't they realize that the people they're trying to squeeze are going to have to work for them afterward? Yahoo was very upstanding about the deal. They didn't require any vesting, for example. We could have quit the day after the deal closed. But because they'd been good guys, we worked hard to make the acquisition work out well for them.

It did, too. Yahoo made a lot of money from this software. When you tell people you sold a startup to Yahoo in 1998, they get this knowing look, like you sold someone a bag full of air for a hundred million dollars, but Viaweb was a real money-making acquisition for them.

Livingston: What was the most surprising thing about being acquired?

Graham: For me the most surprising thing was the day the deal was going to be announced. There was a point where I had to change our front page to read Yahoo instead of Viaweb and then it really hit me. Viaweb is gone. Viaweb doesn't exist anymore. That was so weird. And I told myself, "Look Paul, don't get sentimental. You built this thing to sell it. That was the whole point, and now you've sold it, so stop whining." But boy, it was strange to think that when I clicked on "publish" and replaced the Viaweb front page with the Yahoo front page, Viaweb would never be seen again.

It was also kind of weird that when the deal closed, we all became Yahoo employees. It was like one of those dreams where you have to go back to high school. Up till that point we'd been independent, and then suddenly we were employees, with bosses. And the weirdest thing was, we, or I at least, actually started to think of them as bosses. Now whatever I did was either submitting or rebelling, whereas before it had been just doing.

I think Yahoo is smarter now about dealing with startups than they were then. We were one of the first companies they bought, and I think the idea was, back then, that what you should do with an acquisition is "integrate" it, in the same way that a sugar cube becomes integrated with your tea. We basically got dissolved within Yahoo, and all the people working on Viaweb—or Yahoo Store as it then became—got dispersed to all the corresponding bits of Yahoo. The engineers got put with the engineers and the people working on customer support got put with the support people and the sales guys got put with the Yahoo sales guys.

It seemed to Yahoo that this was the most efficient, organized way of doing things, but actually it was terrible for us. We had been this little tight-knit group that worked really well together and suddenly we were spread out all over Yahoo.

Livingston: Any general thought you have on the acquisition process, since you had several offers?

Graham: Never believe it's a deal till the money's in the bank. Even at the point where you walk in that room to sign the final papers, there's still a 10 percent chance the deal's going to fall through. At the point where people say, "We want to buy you," the chances of it falling through are like 80 or 90 percent. So you can't let yourself believe. If someone wants to make you an offer, fine, but don't change your plans based on that. Just keep going.

Livingston: Looking back, what surprised you most in your experience with a startup?

Graham: One thing that was surprising was that it actually worked. There we were, in the summer of 1995, thinking, "We don't know anything about business, but we're good programmers. Maybe if we write a really good program, we'll make something all these users will want and we'll get lots of users and then some big company will buy us." And 3 years and enormous numbers of ups and downs later, that's exactly what happened. We had this theory about how business might work, and we sort of forced it to conform to our theory.

I know Robert was surprised that we made any money, because I have a real index of how he was feeling about Viaweb early on. A couple months in, he and I were having dinner, and I made a bet with him that if he ever made a million dollars out of Viaweb, he would get his ear pierced. So the day after the Yahoo deal closed, Trevor and I grabbed him by one arm each and took him down to the Garage in Harvard Square, where all the teenagers get their nose rings, and we got his ear pierced. He spent a long time trying to pick out the smallest one.

Livingston: Some aspects of business turned out to be less of a mystery than you had thought. What did you find you were better at than you thought?

Graham: I found I could actually sell moderately well. I could convince people of stuff. I learned a trick for doing this: to tell the truth. A lot of people think that the way to convince people of things is to be eloquent—to have some bag of tricks for sliding conclusions into their brains. But there's also a sort of hack that you can use if you are not a very good salesman, which is simply tell people the truth. Our strategy for selling our software to people was: make the best software and then tell them, truthfully, "this is the best software." And they could tell we were telling the truth.

Another advantage of telling the truth is that you don't have to remember what you've said. You don't have to keep any state in your head. It's a purely functional business strategy. (Hackers will get what I mean.)

Livingston: Were there things that nontechnical people misunderstood about what Viaweb was doing?

Graham: Constantly. No one ever seemed to get that the software ran on the server. Nowadays there are so many web-based applications that you take this for granted, but this was a year before Hotmail. We would explain to people how the thing worked and give them a demo and they would say, "Great. Where do I go to download it?"

After we got bought by Yahoo, a reporter who had been covering us for the past 2 years wrote an article about the Yahoo acquisition and at the end said "It only takes 10 minutes to download." After covering us for years, the guy still thought this was client software.

Livingston: Is there anything that you would have done differently?

Graham: I wouldn't worry so much about seeming like a real company. Now I would just say, keep it a bunch of guys operating out of an apartment for as long as you want, because there's nothing to be ashamed of in that, especially if you're writing great software.

Another thing I would do is open an online store ourselves. We did use our software for building our website. We were the only one of all our competitors who actually used our software for building our own corporate website. But we didn't have anything people could buy online. If we had been selling stuff, we would have understood what life was like from the merchant's point of view.

Livingston: What was one of the funniest moments?

Graham: Probably the time we tried starting a gas generator inside our office. There was this huge blackout in Cambridge that lasted for about five hours. We always had our servers in our offices with us. We didn't trust this collocation stuff. Nowadays, collocating is the standard thing to do and even big companies do it, but we felt like we had to have those servers in the room with us. So when the power went out, our servers were really dead.

We had some battery-powered UPSs, but they would only last for half an hour. They were really designed for power spikes, not for the power going out for 5 hours. So I dispatched Trevor to Home Depot to buy a gasoline-powered generator as fast as possible, while I sat there watching the UPSs' power go down, turning off servers one by one—thinking about which customers were on each server and which ones would be the maddest, and turning off whichever server would have the least mad customers on it. Eventually I had to turn off all the servers, because it took Trevor a while to get to Home Depot and back.

Finally he showed up with this gas generator, and we weren't really sure where to put it because we were in this small office building in Harvard Square.

We were on the top floor; we didn't really have a place to put a gas generator. The first thing we tried was putting it in the office next to the server room. We started the thing up and it sounded like the end of the world. It was the loudest thing I have ever heard in my life. You might think the problem with starting a gas generator inside your office would be the exhaust, but it never got to that point. It was so terrifyingly loud. We thought, "Even to avoid our customers calling us up angrily because their stores are offline, we cannot endure this." After about 5 seconds, we just looked at one another and shook our heads and turned it off.

Then we tried putting it out on the street in front of our building. The problem was, we were up on the third floor. We got every extension cord we could find in the place and stuck them together end to end, and they were just long enough to get out the window and down to the street. But only just—it was so close that the extension cord was actually tight. It was running through our office at chest height and you could kind of twang it and it would go "boinnnnnggg." Then we started the gas generator up in the street and that was just about bearable, so we ran the servers on that for a couple hours until the power came back.

Livingston: Can you remember any other hair-raising moments?

Graham: At one point, in the Spring of '96, when we only had about 20 users, we all went off to this trade show down in New York—the first trade show we ever went to. We came back and it turned out the server had crashed soon after we'd left and had been down for 11 hours. And nobody noticed! We kept waiting for the angry phone calls, and they never came. It was so early in the history of the Web that nobody was ordering from these stores anyway, and they weren't even checking themselves to see if their sites were up. Half of these people who had online stores with us probably didn't even have Internet access.

Livingston: Do you have any regrets from the experience?

Graham: One thing I regret is how pathetic we were during much of this whole process. We all had practically zero assets when we started, and this was during the Internet Bubble, remember—very early in the Internet Bubble, but still, there were people starting companies and getting them bought for like $5 million. *Millions* of dollars, when the most money I'd ever had in my bank account was about $10,000. There was a point where we started to seem like a real company—that is, real enough that someone might actually buy us—and this made us just pathetically eager to sell the company. We must have seemed like such losers.

So I can understand now when founders want to sell out for a couple million. Investors say, "No, you should wait," but it's easy for them to say. A million dollars seems just overwhelmingly attractive when you have nothing. You don't care if it's a good deal or not.

I also kind of regret being a zombie for several years straight. I really had no life during Viaweb. If people are talking about some famous movie and I've never seen it and have no idea what it's about, it's usually a movie that came out between 1995 and 1998, because at that point, I was on Mars. I was not part of the ordinary world of humans. I was sitting glued to a computer all day long, or asleep.

Livingston: What did you worry about the most?

Graham: Running out of money. That was the big worry. Running out of money and having to go and get more funding. Getting funding is very painful. It's so much harder than actually making a successful company.

Livingston: What advice can you give about raising money?

Graham: The advice I would give is to avoid it. I would say spend as little as you can, because every dollar of the investors' money you get will be taken out of your ass—literally in the sense that it will take stock away from you, but also the process of raising money is so horrible compared to the other aspects of business. You can't work your way out of it like you can with other problems. You're at other people's mercy.

The way not to have to raise money is not to spend money. Do everything as cheaply as you possibly can. What you want in a startup is this feeling of cheap and hip. Not miserly cheap, but cool, bohemian cheap. That's what we strove for.

Livingston: So investors were your biggest worry?

Graham: Probably, but I worried about all the different things that could kill us and all the different ways they could kill us. People start startups to get rich, but what keeps them going day to day is the fear of failure. You've said, "OK, I'm starting this startup and I'm going to get all the users and be successful," and once you've told everybody that's what you're doing, if you fail you'll look like a fool.

So when we did sell the thing finally to Yahoo, in the eyes of the world, because we got bought, we were a success. Arguably we were already a success, since we had more online stores than anybody else. But getting bought kind of locked that in. At that point you would think someone would be thinking, "Wow, this is great. I'm rich. I can go buy everything I want." But all I was thinking was, "Thank God we didn't fail."

Livingston: You write a lot of essays with advice for startup founders. What is the most important piece of advice?

Graham: What Y Combinator prints on our T-shirts: make something people want. If you make something users want, they will be happy, and you can translate that happiness into money. That is the basis of a startup. A startup is a company that builds some kind of technology that people want. The mistake that a lot of founders make is to build something they think users want, but that users don't actually want.

Livingston: Do you think having done a startup yourself makes you a better judge of startup founders now that you are an investor?

Graham: Oh yeah. In fact, I don't know how people who haven't done it can pick founders. How can they tell? I often see people who seem kind of clueless, and I can remember, "Yeah, we seemed clueless in exactly the same way." So those are the guys we invest in.

Trevor Blackwell, Paul Graham (standing), and Robert Morris in 1996

Joshua Schachter
Founder, del.icio.us

Joshua Schachter started the collaborative bookmarking site del.icio.us in 2003. As often happens with startups, del.icio.us began as something Schachter built for himself. He needed a way of organizing his collection of 20,000 bookmarks, and he hit on the idea of "tagging" them with brief text phrases to help him find links later. He put del.icio.us on a server and opened it up to other people, and it began to spread by word of mouth.

For the first several years, Schachter worked on del.icio.us and other projects, like Memepool and GeoURL, while working as a quantitative analyst at Morgan Stanley. But all the while, del.icio.us was growing. By November 2004, a year after its release, it had 30,000 users.

In early 2005, Schachter decided to turn del.icio.us from a hobby into a company. In March of 2005, he left his job to "found" del.icio.us and focus on it full-time, raising $1 million in funding.

In December of that year, Yahoo acquired del.icio.us for an amount rumored to be about $30 million.

Livingston: Take me back to how you got started with del.icio.us.

Schachter: It goes back quite a while. In 1998 or so I created a website called Memepool. There was an editor, with reader submission. We had a contribution pool, and we'd edit and post stuff. It was chronologically sorted, updated every couple of days—so it was basically a blog before that word came out. We put a link at the bottom, "Send us an email. Give us good links." And people would email us stuff they found on the Web. I would dutifully look at it and write it down. It took me a long time to post anything, because I'm not a great writer.

Over time, I had these links that just piled up—links that I'd found, or surfed for, or had been sent in, or whatever. By 2001 or so, I had a text file filled with 20,000 links. I couldn't find anything in that file anymore, so I started putting in notes. I'd put the URL, a space, a hash mark, and then a word or two describing it. I think the first one was "math," so I could grep out all the things that were #math and get all my items marked as math. In some sense, these were the first tags.

After a while, I couldn't really do this, so I built a sort of next generation of that text file, which was called Muxway, in 2001. It was a lot like del.icio.us. There was a bookmarklet; you saved things; you could describe and tag them. It was single-player—no one else could use it—but the actual website was visible to other people. I discovered over time that people were subscribing to my bookmarks. There were some 10,000 daily readers looking at my stuff. That was interesting.

I did several other projects along the way. I did GeoURL. Something called Reversible, that is long gone. Reversible was also like del.icio.us in many ways, but different in a few key ways that made it fail.

In late 2003, I started working on del.icio.us, which is a multiplayer version. I was actually trying to come up with a better Memepool—something between Muxway and Memepool which was more vital somehow, and we ended up with del.icio.us. I had it partially done for the first Foo Camp. I'd been invited to Foo Camp for GeoURL, and I had stuff to show for del.icio.us, but I didn't show anyone. I chickened out because I was embarrassed at the state of the thing. So people were using it then, but it was more generally released later—I think toward December of 2003.

Through 2004, I kept working on it and started to get press and lots of users. By the end of 2004, I had 30,000 users.

Livingston: How were the users finding out about it?

Schachter: People were telling each other about it.

Livingston: You were at Morgan Stanley this whole time, right? What were you doing there?

Schachter: I was doing data mining and proprietary trading algorithms.

Livingston: Why did you choose not to focus full-time on del.icio.us and what finally tipped the scale?

Schachter: The economics didn't make sense. It still made sense to keep the day job. But in late 2004/early 2005, my group at Morgan Stanley began to come apart. There were a bunch of people leaving, so it was a natural time to leave. It was a "Should I find a new job elsewhere?" kind of thing.

Livingston: When you were doing this in your spare time, did you ever say, "Ugh. This is too much work"?

Schachter: Not really. I was always very careful (not anymore, because the guys that I work with are better programmers) to structure the code—each chunk of code wasn't larger than the screen—such that I could come in and look at it, figure out what I'm doing, do it, and be done for the day in 15 minutes. So if I could get one thing done a day, I was happy. A lot of stuff, if I could spend more time, I did, but as long as I could get one or two things done a week total, if I didn't have time, I didn't have time.

So it moved pretty slowly. I worked on it for years.

Livingston: Looking back, do you wish you had left Morgan Stanley earlier to work on del.icio.us full-time?

Schachter: I think it would have been very challenging to sell this as a venture to VCs if I didn't have a great deal of user base and press to show. I think that would have been a challenge. If I said, "Hey, I'm going to build a bookmarking service," I would have never been able to get off the ground.

Livingston: Because the idea was so new?

Schachter: No. There had been plenty of other startups that failed doing this. Backflip and God knows what else. So it had been tried and failed in the past.

Livingston: Why did del.icio.us succeed?

Schachter: First of all, because it was not a venture to start. I was building a product and that's it.

Livingston: Did the others fail because they had too much money?

Schachter: I think in general being overcapitalized is a path to failure. The VCs want you to spend. There are general ills with being overfunded.

I don't think they ever really quite thought out the problem. We live in a different world now where people value the data differently.

Livingston: Was there anything about del.icio.us that was much better than your competitors?

Schachter: I think the competitors had already disappeared by then. The tagging thing was probably essential.

Livingston: Can you tell me more about how you came up with tagging?

Schachter: There was no point at which I said, "I'm inventing this wonderful new thing." I just sort of realized that I had evolved my own filing system, and it worked for me. I'd used it for a long time before del.icio.us even showed up. This was the codification of that practice.

Livingston: But you were one of the first companies to do tagging?

Schachter: Yeah. For example, in Muxway, the internal table that tracked that stuff was called Tags. The name had come along at some point, but I don't remember exactly how it showed up.

Livingston: When you decided to leave Morgan Stanley and focus full-time on del.icio.us, did you know you had to raise money?

Schachter: I was getting a lot of interest in acquisitions—there were a bunch of offers/buyouts, and they were increasing in value over time. At the same time, I wanted to be able to pay the rent, but I didn't want to chew into life savings. At the end of the day, my Morgan coworkers were pretty supportive, "You should go do this. Try it out and let us know how it goes."

Livingston: Union Square Ventures was your VC, right?

Schachter: They were Union Square and Amazon.

Livingston: Did they come to you?

Schachter: I had met Jeff Bezos at Foo Camp, and he was very interested.

Livingston: How much did they put in?

Schachter: We never announced the amount, but it was not a huge amount of capital.

Livingston: And that's because you didn't want to take a huge amount of capital?

Schachter: Well, there was a lot of risk. It was sort of hard to justify a large valuation and so on, so we sold a small chunk for enough money to work for a while and see if it turned into something. That was the plan: see where this goes.

Livingston: Did you hire anyone?

Schachter: We did. There were eight employees total at the end.

Livingston: Were most of them shareholders?

Schachter: We gave shares to everybody.

Livingston: Did you have vesting?

Schachter: Yes. Even I vested.

Livingston: What were some of the first things that you did once you were officially a startup?

Schachter: One of the most challenging things was getting payroll going. PEOs typically don't want to do less than five employees.

Union Square introduced me to this guy, Albert Wenger, who had some operations experience. He helped a lot. I lucked out in that he's a smart guy who knew how to do not just the corporate operations stuff, but he had a good product sense and ended up doing a great deal of product work as well. The first version of the Firefox toolbar, he dealt with, for example.

Livingston: What were some of the biggest technical problems that you encountered?

Schachter: Scaling, inevitably. Scaling, dealing with bandwidth, dealing with routing, networks. This is for consumer Internet kind of stuff, but there's a great deal of stuff that you have to flawlessly execute on. It has to be done well, but everybody does it well, so it doesn't differentiate at all. Like your connection has to be up. Your office needs to have DSL. There's a great deal of crap that has to be executed better than competently that is no value for you to actually do yourself. So outsource that.

For example, the payroll. I was capable of going 2 to 3 months without salary, but other employees certainly were not. So that kind of stuff.

But you need to pay attention to the important stuff. Scaling was important and core to the product, but dealing with the network, getting the hardware racked, building machines, ordering stuff, getting pricing out of Dell, you name it. That was a lot of work that was not useful.

Livingston: Outside of the scaling requirements, can you remember any technical problems that you guys solved?

Schachter: Tagging basically was the thing. And then there's a gagillion little improvements in marketing things. We actually thought about the product always with an eye toward innovation. Everything we did we questioned—and I think we didn't even go far enough. Whatever it is, question every single aspect of conventional wisdom. "Is that the right way to do it or can we break that and make it better?"

That's also dangerous, because, if you are doing a lot of paradigm innovation, call it—which is not a good word—but if you are breaking boundaries elsewhere, maybe you need to be very within boundaries on other fronts.

Livingston: Do you remember a time when you were worried about something?

Schachter: Site's down. Site's slow. Table crash—MySQL corrupted a table. That happened all the time. A great deal of what we did was putting out fires. We didn't have a lot of process management in place, which probably hurt us a great deal.

A week after the acquisition, the power of the data center dropped and corrupted every single machine. We were down for like 48 hours. That was horrific. The power bounced in the network; the machines didn't come back up because they weren't configured quite properly. We weren't careful about that.

In general, assume that whatever you are doing is going to go wrong. How can you make it so that it will go faster when it does go wrong? Because it will. For example, the rebuild script takes 24 hours, but that's not a big deal because this part of the system isn't live yet. But when it is live and it takes 24 hours to redo, that's a big deal. So fix it. Make it work in 2 or whatever. There's a lot of stuff that you can't get around due to SQL, like you can't change the database without bringing the site down.

Livingston: What kind of technology inspired you?

Schachter: Inspired? We built in Perl, MySQL, Apache. Very standard LAMP stack kind of stuff. That was the standard mechanism for everything.

Livingston: Would you do anything differently if you could?

Schachter: Knowing what I know now, I would have designed the back-end architecture differently, and that would have saved a lot of work now. Scaling past one machine, one database, is very challenging, even with replication. The tools that are there are not quite right.

For example, when you add things to a table and it numbers them, that means you can't have a second machine also adding to them because the numbers will collide. So what do you do? You have to come up with some completely different way to do it. Do you have a central server that hands out number sets, or do you come up with something that's not numbers? Do you use random numbers and hope they never collide? Whatever it is, auto-assigned IDs just don't fly. There's a stack of about 15 things that I have, a big list of pitfalls.

Livingston: Can you remember any features from del.icio.us that the users wanted or really loved that surprised you?

Schachter: There's always stuff. I tend to be careful about that. I think people ask for features—they want to do something, but they don't say, "I want to do that something." They translate it into some feature that typically they've seen somewhere else and ask for that instead. I want a feature that does this. "Why do you want to do that?" Then it turns out there's some better way to do that. So, stuff that people ask for, I tend to try and dig to the root cause, before reducing to practice.

People frequently aren't quite sure what they want. Then there's a whole bunch of stuff that's like, "Feature 1 and feature 2 suggest feature 3; ask for feature 3." And I just know that people are never going to use feature 3 and the implementation thereof would be quite expensive. So leave it out.

Livingston: How did your user base evolve over the years?

Schachter: I think it's still a very technical, early adopter audience. It's broadening over time, but we're sticking with that for now.

Livingston: Can you tell me about some of the major turning points in del.icio.us?

Schachter: Nothing really comes to mind. It was like a roller coaster always going up, so it's always increasingly bigger, faster, more and more people.

I had a bunch of conceptual revelations on how to build stuff. For a long time, it would go slow and I'd figure out some clever thing to do—"I know we're doing extra work here." Figuring out caching. My own education was kind of interesting. But that was ongoing; there was always something new that I learned every couple weeks. So I never really broke it up into large milestones. Getting the funding, working on it full-time, selling it—these were all big parts of it.

Livingston: How was working on it full-time different than when you were at Morgan Stanley?

Schachter: Constraints breed creativity. So now, instead of only having 15 minutes two or three times a week, it would be more like, "I have the entire day to work on it, every day." I don't work in bursts like that. I do a little bit of work and then go wander around the city and come back. Then work all night. Once everyone has gone to sleep and it's quiet, I can get a lot of work done. I didn't really get to stay up late when I was at Morgan; I don't really do it now. But during that I did, and I think it was incredibly productive. Probably very alienating to my wife though.

Livingston: Did you find you were better at some things than you thought?

Schachter: I could focus on it more and do slightly larger stuff. I've always had a short attention span, so that's probably the actual limiting factor. The amount of coffee I can consume to mitigate that and that's about it.

Livingston: Were there things about del.icio.us that users misunderstood?

Schachter: We named things differently. I wouldn't say that we had awesome execution. It was very techy. It bred a strong priesthood, which was helpful in getting the message out initially, but it was harder for people to adopt. We continue to work on that, and struggle with that now.

It is a challenging product to do conceptually. It's not something like, "Let you file your taxes better." There's no clear value proposition here. It is valuable, but hard to understand. You will be able to remember more things this way, and with that, people don't even realize there's a problem. So that's a challenging value proposition to explain or get across.

Ultimately, I think people who understand it are better for it, but it's a challenge.

Livingston: Was there anything that you learned from your earlier projects that you were determined not to do with del.icio.us?

Schachter: There were a bunch of things. I released a bunch of projects—I've done a bunch more that are halfway done. I keep an idea journal of stuff. I make ideas and I work on them a bit to see what they feel like, and then I move along. One was called Bookbook—because I never came up with a name for it—in which you could say, "I'm at this location and I don't want these books and I do want these other books." You would put that in an XML file on your website, like a feed—you would provide a feed and other people would do this and create a central crossing engine that would say, "You have this book and he wants that book, and you are not that far from each other." This was basically a distributed geomarket for books.

The problem was, the way I wrote it was fully decentralized. You didn't log in and create your data; it was just, "Here's a URL to my data" and the system would do the best it could. The problem is that it was so hard to use. You had to make an XML file. If that's your beginning user interface proposition, you fail. I think 12 people signed up for it, maybe. The UI was too hard. The elegance of a distributed system trumps the usefulness of centralized UI and control.

Similarly, there was a system called Loaf that I did with Maciej Ceglowski that was a fully distributed social network—no central server whatsoever. It used email as a carrier and could tell people you talked to about other people you corresponded with in an encrypted and compressed way. If I emailed you, it would attach a Loaf file. You couldn't open the Loaf file and read the contents of it; it just didn't work that way. It used Bloom filter, so it was sort of a statistical object. But you could take another email address and see if it was in there. With 99 percent accuracy, you could tell if someone was inside that file. So if you got email, you could say, "I think Joshua Schachter corresponds with this person." Without me exposing my address book to you, you could tell who in your address book you talked to. It was a pretty neat idea, but it was complicated to install.

The other problem was that it didn't work without Loaf. So that didn't do very well, but we got press for it. It was sufficiently innovative. Maybe I'll return to that idea someday.

Livingston: So press helped you get the word out about your projects?

Schachter: I was in *USA Today* in the late '90s for Memepool, so it was always from there I got a great deal of press and sort of had early training. My father was the consumer advocate for the Long Island Railroad and was in the newspaper all the time, so I got training sort of that way. When this stuff started happening, I knew that you have x messages and when you talk to the press, any question they ask is answered with one of the messages.

I understand talking to the press as an essential part of marketing. At the same time, I understand that the consumers are the best marketers. If they love your product and you give them the tools to market it, they will.

Livingston: What do you think about technical founders versus businesspeople founders?

Schachter: I have never had a great deal of trust for people who don't execute on core ideas. I understand the value of needing someone to deal with that kind of stuff—someone's got to do the VC pitch and there's got to be a CFO, etc. But the guy who says, "I have a great idea and I'm looking for other people to implement it," I'm wary of—frequently because I think the process of idea-making relies on executing and failing or succeeding at the ideas, so that you can actually become better at coming up with ideas. It's something you can learn. It's a skill, like weightlifting. That failed; that worked; continue. You begin to learn how to make ideas. So if you are someone who can't execute and all you can do is come up with ideas, how do you know if they are any good? You don't really know if it's a good idea until you've executed it. You need to understand the cost of execution and so on.

Also, where I worked at Morgan, they were not hyper-trustful of MBAs. All my coworkers were PhDs in computer science, mathematics, or physics.

Livingston: New York City doesn't seem to be a place where too many startups flourish.

Schachter: There's a great deal of technology going on in New York City. In financial places, there is lots of high-end, high-speed transactional technology. There are a lot of good problems in finance. The technical problems faced there are hard. One issue is that there is a lot of money to be made there and the companies that are doing that pay. Some of the big brokerages pay a lot of money annually for their technology.

Livingston: Why aren't there more good hackers living in New York City then?

Schachter: There are. They work at banks and stuff and have side projects.

Livingston: So the smart hackers . . .

Schachter: They're around. They just know when to be quiet and when not to be.

Livingston: Who did you learn things from?

Schachter: Albert, the guy I mentioned. I learned a lot from Fred Wilson of Union Square, certainly. I learned a great deal from my Morgan folks. I learned a hell of a lot about how to understand problems. It was rough sometimes, but they pushed me far. My coworkers at Morgan were smart people. One of the people we worked with won the Nobel Prize for economics while I was there. It was a fast, smart environment.

I remember when I interviewed at Google the first time around and they were making derogatory comments about where I worked: "Well, here you'll get to work with PhDs and computer scientists." And I'm like, "I already do."

Livingston: So it didn't work out when you interviewed for a job at Google?

Schachter: I went out there once and was rejected because I didn't know C++.

Livingston: Was there ever a time when anyone tried to trick you or take advantage of you?

Schachter: Yes, but it would not be polite to talk about it. There were several cases of people wanting to get equity in advance of other people, or weird deals.

Livingston: As a new startup founder who has never done a deal or negotiated, do you think you need to be careful of getting taken advantage of?

Schachter: In general, I found VCs to be significantly politer than the folks I worked with. The worst they did was not call me back. I'd never hear from them again. Brad Feld does a nice blog talking about how the VC process works. He says they never call you back to say no—they don't want to close the door in case they want to open it again, but they don't want to actually give you a response. Very few VCs actually said, "Sorry, we're not interested."

Livingston: How did the process of starting your own company and then selling it change you?

Schachter: It pushes you far. You learn a lot. I did a round of funding, I was writing code, I was hiring people, chief architect designer, negotiator, you name it. I did all of it, for the most part.

When Albert got up to speed and was working full-time, he did a great deal of work there as well.

Livingston: What surprised you most about having your own startup?

Schachter: It's a combination of sudden freedom to run things as you please and crushing responsibility in which you know you have to do certain things in a certain way at a certain time. That eradicates all of that freedom. You become a robot on rails. You know what you have to do and you are working in a certain direction.

Maybe other people are different, but I think that every step was sort of the inevitable, inexorable progress due to the previous steps in the path. It's not like I had no choice, but everything I did was the only choice because it was the only thing that made sense at the time. It's not that long ago, but no regrets, that was the path to take. Everything that had to be done was done.

Livingston: What is your favorite bit of advice you'd give to a technical person who wanted to start a startup?

Schachter: Reduce. Do as little as possible to get what you have to get done. Do less of it; get it done. If you've got two things that you want to put together, take away until they go together. Don't add another thing. Because you can understand it better, you can analyze it more cleanly. The UI will be easier. Doing less is so important.

People often wind up adding features, adding stuff. Making it bigger is the typical way you engineer out of a problem, right? It's the traditional, "I apologize for the long letter. I didn't have time to make it shorter."

Mark Fletcher
Founder, ONElist, Bloglines

Mark Fletcher was a senior software engineer for Sun Microsystems when he started ONElist, a free Internet email list service, in 1997. He ran ONElist as a side project until he received venture funding a year later. Yahoo acquired ONElist (later renamed eGroups) in June 2000.

In 2003, Fletcher created Bloglines, a web-based news aggregation service. He originally wrote the program to manage his own bookmark list, but once he launched it publicly, Bloglines was fast on its way to becoming the most popular news aggregator on the Internet. It was acquired by Ask Jeeves in February, 2005.

Fletcher's startups typify many of the Web 2.0 aspects that we value today: building inexpensive web-based companies that grow fast. ONElist got to one million users before it took outside investment, and Bloglines took only $200,000 of investment before its acquisition.

Livingston: Take me back to how you got started with Bloglines.

Fletcher: I had started ONElist, it became eGroups, we sold it to Yahoo, and then I left at the acquisition in September of 2000. I decided I needed to take time off—I hadn't had a vacation since eighth grade, between work and school. So I traveled around a lot, got really bored, and realized—I had been around computers all my life, that is really what I like doing, so why am I depriving myself of the fun of working on startups?

It really came down to solving a need of mine. I had started another company—an anti-spam company—called Trustic, and that wasn't going very far. But as I was starting that, I was doing this other thing on the side, which became Bloglines. I had a bookmark list of about 100 sites that I went to every day just to see if there was new stuff. Things like Slashdot, CNN, my friends' blogs. It was taking a long time; I figured there had to be a better solution to this, and that's how I found out about RSS. At that time, there were a couple of desktop-based aggregators—programs that you could download. But those weren't really applicable to me because I'm on several different computers every day and the quality of the programs weren't very good. With my background of building server applications, it wasn't a great leap to figure out that I should just build something for myself.

So I did that while I was running this spam thing. Then it became very apparent that the anti-spam business is not a fun one to be in, because everybody hates you. You're never perfect. You either don't block enough spam or you block somebody's favorite emails. I quickly got out of that. This other thing, Bloglines—which was working at the time, but I was just using it for myself—I wasn't even sure was going to be very popular. Nobody really knew about blogs; aggregators were the next level up, kind of difficult to explain to people. So I decided, I'd already written it, might as well just throw it out there and see how it goes. So that was it. I put it out there in June of 2003, and it started getting coverage pretty quickly after that. I realized that I should probably put some effort into it, so I brought some friends in and started doing some marketing and went from there.

Livingston: So Bloglines was something that you created for yourself to use and then backed into doing a startup around it?

Fletcher: I had an inkling that it could be interesting, but I guess I thought it was a little ahead of the curve. I started ONElist because I wanted to start a mailing list for my parents, and at that time you had to download software and you had to have a computer connected to the Internet. It was just really difficult for an average person to put together a mailing list. So it was the same thing. I guess my advice is: solve a problem that you have, first and foremost, and chances are, other people may have the same problem.

Livingston: You brought on some people that you had worked with before?

Fletcher: Right. A core group of people that I had worked with at ONElist: a great marketing person, a great PR person, a UI guy, and eventually a programmer. But I was the only full-time person until around September of '04.

Livingston: Were you doing this out of your home?

Fletcher: Yeah, the den over there.

Livingston: Was it self-funded?

Fletcher: Yeah.

Livingston: So you didn't have to deal with any of the investor headaches?

Fletcher: Didn't have to deal with any of that. That's the other thing. Doing startups like this is so cheap that it just doesn't require a lot of money. I think I put in a total of $200,000. And I didn't do it nearly as smartly as I could have. I ended up buying all the computers. My recommendation would be: don't buy any computers. Just use the virtual dedicated hosting services.

Livingston: Tell me about some of the biggest turning points for Bloglines once you decided, "We're a real company." I assume you incorporated and did all the legal stuff.

Fletcher: I just used the same company that I had set up for the anti-spam company. That's why the official company name was Trustic. I thought, "I've already done the work to set up this company, so it's just another product from it." I was using the same lawyer that I had used with ONElist, who was a family friend.

Livingston: So you just did a quick shift into a different product.

Fletcher: Yeah.

Livingston: Does that mean that you were the only shareholder?

Fletcher: No, the people that I brought in who weren't working full-time were working for stock. I'm very fortunate that I can bring in people who don't need money right away to do this; they can just work for essentially deferred compensation. So you give them some chunk of stock as a contractor. You say, "You have a 6-month contract, you get this amount of stock over that time."

Livingston: Tell me about some of the big turning points.

Fletcher: We went online in late June of 2003. I guess the first thing is that we started getting press coverage almost immediately—and this is even before I brought in my marketing friends. There's a newsletter called NTK, or Need to Know, and we got a big old blurb in that within 2 weeks or so. Then it kind of went from there.

The amazing thing about this company is that . . . I can show you the press binder and it's literally this thick, for something that really a tiny percentage of people actually use.

Livingston: Why?

Fletcher: I think we got really lucky because blogs in general started to become really big and the downturn was ending, so you had all of these people looking for the next big thing. Also a lot of reporters used Bloglines. They like to talk about things they use, so we got really fortunate in that regard. But there was no planning with that; it was just serendipity.

Livingston: I'm surprised, because I feel like reporters are often the last people to write about what's new.

Fletcher: In general, yeah, but it became comical. I'd talk to these reporters, and they'd all tell me they were Bloglines users. Maybe I was talking only to people who were using Bloglines, but I don't know. If you compare the press that we got with Bloglines versus the press that we got with ONElist and eGroups, it doesn't even compare. Whereas with the first company, we had 20 million users at the acquisition, with Bloglines, we only had a tiny fraction of that. It was this huge, disproportionate amount of press for this little company. We were all amazed.

Livingston: Were blogs as mainstream in 2003 as they are today?

Fletcher: Not at all. Nobody knew about blogs. I was kind of embarrassed about this little thing that I wanted to put out, because nobody knows what the hell a blog is.

Livingston: Did you think that blogs would someday surpass the mainstream media as the source of information? Did you know how popular they'd become?

Fletcher: No, not with the speed that it happened. I mean, we were incredibly lucky in that we latched onto this trend which kind of developed at about the same time. But there was no planning. It was just me trying to solve my own problem.

Livingston: Did you have a blog back then?

Fletcher: Yeah, wingedpig.com. I've had that for a few years. It's more of a marketing thing for myself than anything.

Livingston: You weren't trying to say, "Blogs are going to take over—let's get into that"?

Fletcher: I wish I could say I was that smart, but no. I was just some idiot who had a bookmark list 100 sites long and it was taking too much time to go through. I was addicted to reading these things. That's all.

Livingston: What were some of the other big moments in Bloglines's life?

Fletcher: We were around for a year and a half before we were acquired, so it wasn't very long. Because I was funding it myself, there was no big funding event that would be a milestone. It was kind of a gradual buildup throughout the entire time in terms of interest from the press, interest from venture capitalists, interest from companies. So it got to the point where all the big companies were talking to us. But that's fairly typical of a lot of startups.

Livingston: Did you ever contemplate taking VC money?

Fletcher: I'd done that with ONElist, and I wanted to do it differently this time. It was kind of, "Let's see what I can do." Because I fully believed in the thesis of "these companies can be really cheap to run if you do it with even just a little bit of intelligence."

I took money with ONElist because at that point we were growing so quickly that we were running out of money, and I couldn't fund it myself any longer. ONElist got to be the 150-person company. But you don't have to do that these days.

Livingston: When you were developing Bloglines, were you following a purposeful plan or were you just like, "Let's build this product and see what happens."

Fletcher: My philosophy on these types of companies—consumer-based Internet companies—is that you don't need to worry about the business model initially. If you get users, then everything else follows. Basically any technology can be copied, any concept can be copied. In my opinion, what makes one of these companies valuable is the users. That can't be copied.

Livingston: Did you think about the idea of "democratization" of the media when you were doing this? Was there a social ambition?

Fletcher: No, I'm not nearly that smart. Just friends and news sites that I wanted to follow on a regular basis. But I was latching onto trends, of course, which are [that] the number of websites on the Internet is just growing exponentially over time. So if I had this problem now and I knew that I was a very early adopter, other people would probably have the problem eventually. It was just a question of when. I thought I was just way too early. But I wasn't. Who knew?

Livingston: Why did you think you were way too early?

Fletcher: Because I talked to all my friends and nobody knew what a blog was. Nobody knows what a blog is and certainly nobody knows what aggregation is. Even these days, you say, "Do you know what syndication is?" and they think, "*Seinfeld* reruns." Which is one of the struggles we had with Bloglines—trying to explain these concepts to normal people. Syndication, RSS, aggregation? What are these goofy things? But we didn't have to do the education as to what a blog is because the press was doing that for us.

Livingston: Did you worry about competitors at all?

Fletcher: Always and never, I guess. I get very competitive, very paranoid. I freak out about everybody. But, I also knew that nobody was doing a decent job when we started, so we had a head start. As long as we didn't screw that up, then it would be difficult for somebody else to come along, unless they were to grab a whole lot of money and go on an advertising blitz, for example. Yeah, I was worried, but what are you going to do?

Livingston: Who was your biggest competitor?

Fletcher: When we started, there was only one service that was at even a close corollary and that was News is Free. When I was talking to reporters initially, they'd ask the same question, "What's your competition?" It was basically the desktop aggregators, the programs you could download. We had a fairly good story around why we were better than that. Most people don't want to install software on their computers. A lot of people can't install software on their computers at work. A lot of people use multiple machines. We had several clear-cut advantages that were fairly easy to describe. About 6 months after we launched, I think NewsGator came out with their web-based aggregator, and were the closest competitor.

Livingston: Were there any lessons that you learned through your experience with ONElist that you said, "I'm not going to repeat that this time" or "I am going to repeat this time"?

Fletcher: Well, I didn't take VC this time; I didn't have to.

Some of the software design we carried over from ONElist to Bloglines, the way the website was put together and how we scaled certain things. And certainly some of the people. Everybody I worked with on Bloglines, I'd worked with at ONElist before. It felt like ONElist, version two.

Livingston: Can you remember any near disasters from ONElist?

Fletcher: Tons. We were growing so fast with ONElist—a percent-and-a-half a day for the first year or two. We had a million users at 11 months, which in '98 was an amazing thing. We had horrible scaling problems the first year. We had lots of downtime because I didn't know how to set up monitoring systems. I guess that's one thing I did a lot better with Bloglines.

I didn't even have a cell phone when I started ONElist. Now, it's easy to use your cell phone as a pager and you can set up systems. With ONElist, I was always scared to leave the computer. Just because I knew things would crash. With Bloglines, at least I had a greater degree of freedom. Especially when you get something like a Treo, where you can basically log in from your phone. I remember fixing stuff while sitting in front of a slot machine in a casino.

Livingston: Did you have good relationships with your VCs? Did it suddenly impose new requirements on your company?

Fletcher: I guess the answers would be "no" and "yes." As an entrepreneur, I'd never talked with VCs, I didn't really know how VCs thought, so it was an education the whole time. I didn't even have a mentor. No VCs were blogging. I didn't know anybody who had started a company. I was just flying blind.

We raised $4 million from CMGI and Bertelsmann Ventures in December of 1999 as our series A. We had been self-funded to that point—we'd survived the first year on $55,000. That got us to a million users, and then we took $4 million. I had never seen a term sheet before, I didn't know what I should be negotiating for, I didn't know what I shouldn't be negotiating for. So, mistakes were made, but I can't fault myself for that. I didn't know what things I should throw out from the term sheet and the lawyer couldn't tell me.

The great thing for entrepreneurs these days is that there is so much more information out there than there was in the '90s. Any number of people that have gone through this are blogging. All sorts of VCs are blogging now. There are a lot more books out now. You can just do a search and find sample term sheets, for example. All things considered, I certainly can't fault the outcome, but I made mistakes along the way.

The VCs did come in 2 weeks after we took the money and said they wanted to replace me as CEO, which was interesting. I was pretty wrapped up ego-wise with the company. When you start a company, it's your life. So you think you are the only one that can run it. You think, if you're not around, it will fall apart—or at least I did—for all of these things. It was very difficult for me to separate myself from the company in that way. So there was a fight over that for quite a while before I acquiesced, and we brought in a new CEO. It turned out that that was very good for the company and, had I been more mature, it would have been a less painful process.

Livingston: You worked at Sun before the startup, right?

Fletcher: I got to Sun via the acquisition of a startup I was working at, called Diba.

Livingston: So you had some startup experience.

Fletcher: I had worked at a couple of startups as an engineer before.

Livingston: But you didn't have any mentors?

Fletcher: No. My parents are a fantastic resource; they were both managers at IBM. But, we were all flying blind. You look at a term sheet and it talks about vesting schedules for founders stock, and you have no idea what you should expect and what you should negotiate for.

Livingston: How did you feel when the VCs said they wanted to replace you as CEO?

Fletcher: It was jarring. I think there was bad behavior on all sides. During the whole funding process they said, "We're interested in you guys because of your management team; we think you're fantastic." I'm on the phone with David Wetherell, head of CMGI, and he's saying, "We're making the investment because we believe in the management team." Two weeks later they pull me into the office—before even the first board meeting—and say, "We want to replace you as CEO."

Looking back, I can absolutely see why they would want to do that, because I was not a good negotiator with the term sheet and I'm sure they could see that. But I was so wrapped up in it at the time, it was very difficult. The good news is that we did bring in a new CEO, he did get us acquired by Yahoo, and things turned out wonderfully. So there are no complaints.

Livingston: But maybe there should be more open discussions between management teams and VCs?

Fletcher: Well, always. I've been dinged as having poor communication skills, which I'm certainly guilty of. But what nerd isn't?

The whole VC process in general has been very closed and oftentimes by design by the VCs. Because they don't want to be negotiating against other VCs, they don't want terms of the deal to get out, so it's in their best interest to keep things secret. But it is very nice that things are starting to open up now, whether they like it or not.

With VCs, it's all about power. It's great that that's changing. It's changing because more people are talking about it because it's so much cheaper to start companies these days. At least these kinds of companies. There will always be the need to raise $10 to $50 million for some companies, but for most user-focused Internet startups, you just don't need a lot of money.

Livingston: Do you remember some surprising features that your users wanted?

Fletcher: Not features, but the stickiness of the site. I thought I was a freak because I would go back to Bloglines all the time—10, 20 times a day. But then, when we started looking at user behavior, the average user came back to the site 4 times a day for 12 page views each time, which is a huge number. Usually, the average user doesn't come back to a given website more than one-half a time a day or something like that, so it was this incredibly high number of sessions and incredibly high number of page views. Whenever I quoted that to Bloglines users, they would say, "These numbers sound low to me. I go back ten times a day." People were saying that this was one thing that had changed their use of the Internet, which is incredibly gratifying.

Livingston: Can you remember one of the most surprising things about the startup experience?

Fletcher: I don't think there was any one thing. Startups are just so amazingly fun; they are so amazingly stressful. Whether you are an engineer or whether you are a founder, at least for me, it takes every emotion you've got and multiplies it 100-fold. Higher highs, lower lows than any other work experience. A startup is all-encompassing, so do it when you are young and when you don't have a family because you'll lose it all.

Livingston: Back to the money thing—you said startups can be cheap. I read that you said that a lot of the Web 2.0 principles started even back in the '90s.

Fletcher: With ONElist, we didn't own machines until years into the company. We did the virtual dedicated hosting thing. So we had 40 or 50 machines at Digital Nation in Virginia, that we had never seen. Which is smarter. That was the biggest mistake I made at Bloglines—not doing exactly what I had done in the '90s. Because when you do that, you don't have to worry about buying switches, racking the damn machines or moving them when you run out of rack space. Or going down to the colo at 2 a.m. to reboot something because it crashed—all that gets taken care of. And these types of startups are never valued on the cap x, so you don't get any more money in any sort of acquisition based on the number of machines you own. Unless you're Google. So we had 40 or 50 machines at Bloglines when we were acquired, and that didn't play a factor at all.

So just get something out there. If you find really early versions of ONElist or Bloglines on archive.org, the websites are horrible. They are crap, they don't have any features, they just try to do one thing. And you just iterate because users are going to tell you what they want, and they're your best feedback. It's critical just to get something out quickly. Just to start shipping and then you can iterate. Because shipping is just this huge hurdle. I've been a part of companies that have had big problems shipping—they just can't ship. It's a psychological thing.

Livingston: It's hard to do though, no?

Fletcher: Well, you want things to be perfect, and the great thing about user-based Internet services is that they don't have to be perfect. You got a bug, you can fix it in 5 minutes. You don't have to worry about upgrading everybody's software installation.

Livingston: What would you tell a founder who just could not release new features and was overanalyzing everything?

Fletcher: That it's very easy to do, very understandable; but, in my opinion, the best thing for your company is just release early, release often. Because then you start a dialog with your users, because they're going to send you emails saying, "This is what I want." We were getting 50 to 100 emails a day at Bloglines, and most of them were feature suggestions. Once you start acting on those feature suggestions, the users see that you are actually listening to them and they become more loyal to your site. Because they see they are able to participate in this and it's just kind of like a virtual cycle. So it is not a disadvantage—it may even be an advantage—to ship without all your features initially, for that reason, because you get all of this going and you get out there sooner.

Livingston: You called yourself a nerd. Do you have any thoughts on founders who are technical people versus founders who are MBAs?

Fletcher: I guess it takes all types. When you say a technical guy, they can range from a hardcore nerd to somebody who has some product knowledge as well. I like to think I have a little bit of product knowledge, which helps me develop these websites. A lot of engineers don't necessarily have that skill set, but they are better engineers than I am, so for those people, if they were to partner up with somebody who was a product designer, I think that probably helps out a lot.

But in terms of MBAs, these user-focused Internet companies aren't very complicated business-wise, so until you actually build something that's got users and has momentum, it's not like you're going to be doing biz dev deals or anything like that. Actually, I don't have the greatest opinion of biz dev people for these companies because they're just not needed, I don't think. You either stand on your own or fail on your own, initially. If you build momentum, if you get users, then deals may come your way, but a lot of times most deals don't make sense, so you don't need hardcore MBAs. It's more focusing on the product and engineering side.

Livingston: Do you think that the technical founders can tell if the deal doesn't make sense? A lot of technical founders might think, "Oh my god, get bought for $5 million dollars? This is amazing!"

Fletcher: Yeah, and there's nothing wrong with that. If you are two guys in a garage and if you've been doing something for 6 months or a year and somebody offers you $5 million, it doesn't sound very dumb to me. You can hire help for acquisitions, so with the Yahoo acquisition of eGroups, we had a board member, Mike Moritz, who was also on the board of Yahoo, so he was involved in that. With Bloglines, Ask was interested in us. We had talked with Google and Yahoo and some of the others, and things were getting interesting with Ask. I knew that I needed help negotiating any sort of deal. So at that point I brought in an investment banker.

What an investment banker does—and especially boutique investment bankers ([who] are guys that deal with smaller deals, up to $100 million)—what they'll do is serve as the middleman, essentially creating an auction and [trying] to drive up any price. They'll help you negotiate the deal; they'll do all of that for you and then just take 2 or 3 percent of the purchase price. I had a pretty good experience with that with Bloglines.

Livingston: How did you know that the time was right that you should be seriously considering selling Bloglines?

Fletcher: Because there was a lot of interest and Google was making rumblings that they were going to come out with something, Yahoo was making rumblings that they were coming out with something. I tend to be a lot more paranoid than I probably need to be. We weren't growing as fast as I wanted us to, and it came back again to users are really the only thing that you have with these types of companies that protects you, that makes you valuable. When somebody buys you, they buy you for the users and to a lesser degree the buzz. It depends on the acquisition. So it was a combination of factors that just felt like the right time.

I knew no investment bankers and had never dealt with any of them before, so I asked my lawyer, who's a senior partner at Wilson Sonsini, for some names. He gave me three names. I interviewed all three, and I went with one because I liked them and they had just done another deal with Ask Jeeves, who I knew was the leader in this process right now. I knew that these guys had experience and they knew all the contacts there, so that's who I went with. That was probably in late October/early November of '04, and the acquisition was announced February 7 of '05.

Livingston: Any other lessons or things that would be helpful for a founder to know about the acquisition process?

Fletcher: The biggest question is when to sell. Even with ONElist, I had acquisition offers 4 months into the company. Offers by websites that no longer exist. So I dodged a bullet. With ONElist, we were growing so quickly that it was like a no-brainer that we just shouldn't sell. And we didn't really have much in the way of competition back then, so it was basically hang on for your life and see how long you can go. With Bloglines, we weren't running nearly as fast as that. I was feeling there was competition coming. I do think we're kind of in a bubble again to some degree. Not in terms of money flowing into all these companies, but certainly . . . somebody put out the canonical list of Web 2.0 companies, and I think every company has like 30 competitors now or something like that. So I was just starting to see some of that.

And actually, thinking back to this, all the press that we were receiving was wonderful, but it was also a double-edged sword. I remember thinking back then, "Just leave us alone and let us grow for a while more before you hype us." You can't complain about it, but . . . there was a stretch where we were in the *Wall Street Journal* four times in 6 months. With ONElist, we were never in the *Wall Street Journal*, ever. I was joking with my PR person saying, "So it's been 2 weeks since we've been in the *Wall Street Journal*. When are we going to be in again?" And she said, "Don't you dare expect this kind of stuff forever."

So you have to figure out when is the right time to sell, what you want out of an acquisition—both in terms of money and whether you want to stay on. Would you be happy with somebody else running the company? It's a very personal decision. And there are better times to sell than others. If nobody is talking to you, it's going to be hard to set up an auction and you're not going to get much money and you're not going to be happy about it.

I think those are the main things. Then, in terms of selecting a banker, it's "Who are you comfortable with; who understands your company?" One of the investment bankers I talked to had no clue what we did, didn't do any research to figure out what we did and was just unresponsive. Well, how is somebody, who is essentially going to be your representative, going to make a good sale of your company if they don't know what you do?

Livingston: You were acquired by Yahoo and Ask. How does life change once you become part of these big companies?

Fletcher: There were differences. With Yahoo, I left at the acquisition, so I was never a part of Yahoo. With Ask, I stuck around for 14 months. Not that it was contingent on the acquisition in any way, it was just the right thing to do. If you compare the two companies . . . when eGroups was acquired by Yahoo, we were 150 people. I essentially hadn't played in the code base in a year, I wasn't running day-to-day operations, so it was very easy for me to go away. At the acquisition by Ask, there were two of us going over. It wouldn't be right, regardless of anything else, for me to leave. I wanted to make sure that the acquisition was viewed as a success for Ask 1 year later—5 years later, even. I've learned that your reputation is very important, as an entrepreneur, as a tech guy in the Valley, and it's a good thing to worry about your reputation. I was very concerned about that, and so, when only two people are coming over—and most of the knowledge was still in my head—it wouldn't have been right for me to leave. So that's why I stuck around for a while, helped build up a team, made sure that the knowledge in my head was transferred to all of these other people, and that, when I did leave, the place wouldn't fall apart.

Livingston: You said you started to get acquisitions offers very early on with ONElist. Is it hard to turn these down?

Fletcher: Sure. It's very flattering to have some company come up and start schmoozing you. It comes down to you have to figure out what you want to do with your startup and your life. With ONElist, it was very easy—I didn't even have to make the decision just to keep going as long as I could, because I knew I was creating all this value from the users. Otherwise it just comes down to the intangibles I guess. If you like the people you're talking to, if you think you're getting a decent deal. But what is a decent deal? It's the most money you can get, right? But what is that? Nobody knows.

Livingston: It's a confusing situation for a lot of founders.

Fletcher: Sure. Why do you start a company? Do you start a company to get rich? Do you start a company for the fun of it? That's going to play into it also. And then, what's your definition of rich, I suppose is another thing. It doesn't take a lot of money to let you live without working ever again, if you do the numbers. So what are your goals in life? You have to think that through.

Livingston: What other practical advice would you give to would-be founders?

Fletcher: I guess, get a lawyer. With ONElist, I incorporated not using a lawyer. There's a company in Delaware called the Company Corporation, so I created an LLC by myself before I had a lawyer. Then we went online and fixed things after the fact . . . it was a big hassle because VCs want a C-corp—any sort of investor generally wants a C-corp because that's what they understand.

With Bloglines, I had an accountant, at least for a good part of it, who was fairly cheap. One of the hassles of ONElist was that I was the one managing the books the first year, as well as answering the 200 support emails every night, as well as doing all of this other stuff. I guess I'm torn with how cheap do you want to go with a startup. Having an accountant is kind of a nice frill.

I also think a lot of people don't know about all these outsourcing sites, which are absolutely wonderful. One of the things that I did do differently with Bloglines was rely upon an outsourcing site, in this case eLance, for a lot of things. Not a lot of coding, but other things. So, if I wanted to put together a presentation and I needed a couple of graphics, I put up a proposal on eLance and ended up working with some lady in Australia, who turned things around in 6 hours, for $50. So sites like that are so amazingly powerful, which is just one more reason why it's really easy to do very small companies, because you don't need a graphic designer necessarily.

Livingston: Can you remember any moments in ONElist that were harrowing?

Fletcher: Sure. Many times. The first year especially when I was still working the full-time job at Sun and doing this on the side.

Livingston: You were still working?

Fletcher: Oh yeah, did I forget to mention that? In most aspects of at least my fiscal life, I'm very conservative. I had a mortgage and didn't want to take the leap of faith to do this without a salary, and so I started ONElist while I was still working full-time at Sun and did that for the first year.

Livingston: Weren't you worried they would claim they owned the IP?

Fletcher: Yeah, and I talked to a lawyer about that. Because ONElist was not at all competitive with anything that Sun was doing—and I certainly wasn't working on it while I was at Sun—it was thought to be OK. But that is absolutely a valid concern. But I was, at least in that regard, very much risk-averse, because I had a mortgage and didn't have much savings back then. So the first year was incredibly stressful. The whole thing was stressful, but the first year especially. For example, it got to be the summertime and we'd take off for the weekend. I'd come back and have 500 emails to answer for customer support on Sunday evening. And I'd just curl up into a fetal position . . . and I had to go to work the next morning, too, and how dare I not answer every single email? That was crazy.

I remember my birthday that year. I got a phone call because the phone number registered in the ONElist domain was the second line in my town-house, and there was an answering machine on it. I remember getting woken up on my birthday that year by some guy saying, "I don't know if you know this, but your site is down." So I logged in, and our whole database machine had died, in Virginia. We were Digital Nation's biggest customer and they didn't really have much experience with these database machines we were using, so they were trying to figure out what was wrong. I had to call in sick from work. It was very stressful. We had scaling issues all summer; we had to turn off new user registrations for 3 months because we couldn't handle the influx of people coming in—which is crazy, you're not supposed to do that.

Livingston: Would you recommend starting a startup on the side while you are still employed?

Fletcher: It worked out for me. Sometimes that's the only way you can do it. It certainly is one way of mitigating the risk significantly, because if you do it on the side and it doesn't work out, you still have a job. Of course, you absolutely have to pay attention to the employment issues. You can't work on your startup at work. Depending on your employment contract, they may own stuff that you do on the side, too. You have to be very cognizant of that.

Livingston: I hadn't realized that you did it on the side.

Fletcher: By the end of the first year, there were five of us, and we were all working, just nights and weekends.

Livingston: What was the tipping point to make you resign to work full-time on ONElist?

Fletcher: We got funding. We had signed the term sheet for the $4 million in our series A, and at that point we were like, "Time to quit."

Livingston: Was there any time with your startups when you felt like giving up?

Fletcher: Not with Bloglines, but certainly the first year with ONElist. A lot. Especially with all the emails every night, with working a full-time job, with the incredible amount of stress. My family was great. I just remember them encouraging me to stick with it. I probably never would have forgiven myself had I quit, too. There are always dark times with startups, always. I was in a startup in San Diego where we didn't get paid for 3 months. There are different types of dark times, but for some there is just no more fun than doing a startup.

Livingston: Did you ever experience some sort of malaise like, "This isn't going anywhere, I just can't work on it anymore"?

Fletcher: Yeah. Somebody asked me what was my greatest strength and my greatest weakness, and I think it's the same thing. I get easily bored. I think I'm able to focus on one thing, but I burn out easily. I'm still not good at the whole work/life balance thing, and with a startup it's very easy to skew that in only one direction. Sometimes you have to do that, but you absolutely get burned out. So I was burned out after eGroups; I was burned out definitely to a degree with Bloglines.

So now I'm taking a little time off. I'll do some skiing, and then I'll start something else.

Mark Fletcher and Scott Shambarger at the celebration of Yahoo's acquisition of ONElist. The two had a bet that if they ever sold the company for more than $5 million, they'd shave their heads.

Craig Newmark
Founder, craigslist

Photo by Gene X. Hwang

In 1995, Craig Newmark started an email list to pub-licize events in San Francisco. As "Craig's List" grew in popularity, he switched from a mailing list to a website and added categories. Without consciously realizing it, he was about to take a big bite out of the classified ad business.

In 1999, Newmark decided it was time to morph craigslist.org from a hobby into a real business. Jim Buckmaster joined on as lead programmer and CTO in early 2000, and was promoted to CEO later that year.

Dedicated to his mission of building a community on the Internet, Newmark has held fast to his plan to keep craigslist as free as possible. All listings are free, except help wanted ads in select cities and broker apartment listings in New York City. There are no banner ads.

Despite many opportunities to increase revenues, craigslist never compro-mised the experience of its users. And because it is able to operate cheaply and let users do much of the work, craigslist has only about 20 employees—several orders of magnitude less than other top-ten sites.

Though eBay purchased a 25 percent stake in the company from a former craigslist employee in 2004, craigslist remains a privately held company. It con-tinues to expand, and now has sites for over 300 cities worldwide.

Livingston: How did craigslist get started?

Newmark: It's now been over 11 years. I don't know exactly when I started craigslist. I do know that in '94 I was at Charles Schwab and I was working with computer security and some other stuff. But my real contribution there was evangelizing the Internet—telling people that's how the equity brokerage busi-ness would work someday.

I saw a lot of people helping other people out, and I figured, "Well, I should do something." In early '95—I don't know when—I started sending out notices about cool events—what I thought were cool events—to friends. It may have been 10 to 12 people, CC list, using Pine, and that worked out pretty well. These were usually arts and technology events, like the Anon Salon or Joe's Digital Diner. More people wanted to be added to the list. They were calling it "Craig's List." Over time, they suggested other kinds of things, like jobs or stuff for sale.

In the middle of '95, the CC listing broke and I had to give the thing a formal name and use a listserv. Somebody offered Majordomo and I was going to call it "SFEvents," but the people who were calling it craigslist said, "Keep calling it that. It will signify that it will be personal and quirky." They were right.

That's a microcosm of our whole history: people would suggest things to me, and then I would figure out what seemed to make sense—what a lot of people were asking for—and then I'd do it. Even now, with a whole company behind it, we listen. We do stuff, we follow through, and then we listen more. What we do is almost 100 percent based on what people ask us to do.

The biggest entrepreneurial lesson I've learned has been that you really do need to follow your instincts. I trusted some people who my instincts were telling me were untrustworthy, and in some cases they proved to be very untrustworthy. But that's fixed now.

I got lucky in that I realized relatively early that I'm not a good manager. Jim Buckmaster is CEO and he does a great job and that's why my title is currently "Customer Service Rep and Founder." Sometimes I exploit that George Costanza magic I have and I act in a glamorous figurehead role, where I'll do public speaking or whatever. But I spend 40 hours a week or more doing customer service. I was doing that minutes ago. I'll be doing so again in minutes. The biggest single project I have now is dealing with misbehaving apartment brokers—rental brokers in New York City.

The biggest problems are different forms of bait and switch, where they post an ad for an apartment in the no-fee section, but they actually charge a sizable fee for renting it. The standard is 15 percent of a year's rent, which can easily be $3,000 or $4,000. That's a lot of money. So we can handle some forms of that. The bigger forms will require better forms of reporting, which I'm starting to think about, but which might not happen until later.

Livingston: Take me back to 1995. Craigslist began as an email list, but at some point you decided to put it online. How did you program it?

Newmark: Sometime in late '95 I realized that, "Hey, I have a lot of this email sitting in folders." At this point, I think I'm operating on a Solaris system and I'm using Pine. I have email in several categories and I can write Perl code, which turns the email logs into web pages. So I had instant publishing. Everything has grown since that. I was, in fact, using Pine as my database tool until late '99, at which point we switched to MySQL.

Through the first years, probably through '98, it was mostly Solaris, although there was a period of maybe a year with Linux. But we used something in the UNIX/Linux family all the time. We used Apache relatively early. Perl, now more mod_perl. And MySQL since '99. Now we're running it on over 120 Linux servers—small, cheap machines. We're primarily Linux on the desktop, with some Mac and some Windows.

We do worry about liability issues relating to the use of Windows, since it's pretty insecure. We don't have much sensitive data, but we have to regard Windows as a source of compromise.

Livingston: When you put craigslist on a website, did you get a positive response pretty quickly?

Newmark: Our traffic has always been slow but sure. We're the tortoise, not the hare. Now and then we'll get a surge of growth, but it's been slow but steady.

Livingston: Were you just running craigslist at night out of your home?

Newmark: It depends on what part of my life it was. But even when I was contracting, I would work an arrangement with the people I was working for. Now and then, I would look at my email and get stuff done. I would put in a half hour. For example, I would be doing my contracting work, I'd get stuff done, then I would take a half hour off to do craigslist, and then I would get back to work.

Livingston: This was run out of your apartment?

Newmark: Mostly.

Livingston: Did you need other people's help?

Newmark: At the end of '97, we were getting about one million page views a month. At that point, Microsoft Sidewalk—or their PR people—approached me about running banner ads. I had decided to not do them, because they'd slow the site down and they were kind of dumb. Banner ads are, more often than not, kind of dumb. More importantly, I thought about my own values and I was thinking, "Hey, how much money do I need?" I was already doing well as a contractor. So I figured I would just not do that.

At that point, I got the first inkling of what I now call my "moral compass." I better understood it later—particularly since the presidential elections, because then I realized that people were claiming a moral high ground who actually didn't practice what they preached, and it's about time for people of goodwill to reassert their idea of what's right and what's wrong.

Livingston: Once you decided that the site was good the way it was and you didn't need any more money, you stuck to that?

Newmark: Yes, and expanded on it. In the '98/'99 timeframe, we took a good look at the morality of charging for something. We asked people, "Hey, what do you think we should charge for, if anything?" And they said, "The principle is: charge people who would otherwise be paying more money for less effective ads." They specifically said, "It's cool to charge for job ads and to charge landlords or apartment brokers." Beyond that, there was some mix of opinion, but we stuck with that.

Livingston: Did you come up with the policy on your own?

Newmark: Primarily the community dictated the policy. And they weren't shy about sending the feedback in. I'm mixing together a couple years worth of feedback—'98/'99 and beyond, but primarily those years.

In the end of '97, I was approached by some volunteers, and they said, "Hey, let's run craigslist and see if we can run a nonprofit." To make a long, painful story short, that effort failed. I kind of knew it was failing, probably midway through 1998, but I was in denial. A couple of our biggest job posters took me out for lunch and said, "Hey, this isn't working. Get real and make this more serious."

It took me a couple months, but I got out of denial, made craigslist into a real company—got off to an OK start. But again, it wasn't until Jim became management that we got good.

Livingston: When you say you made it into a real company, do you mean incorporating it?

Newmark: That was part of it, but the real thing was me going full-time and getting full-time people in all the areas we needed, including billing, customer service, technology.

Livingston: So you were still doing contract work while running craigslist?

Newmark: For a few months at the end of '98 through like a month or so of '99, I actually joined a startup, but left it because I had to get serious about craigslist.

Livingston: You joined another startup?

Newmark: Remember, in the conventional sense, we were never a startup. In the conventional sense, a startup is a company, maybe with great ideas, that becomes a serious corporation. It usually takes serious investment, has a strategy, and they want to make a lot of money.

We've done something very different. I've stepped away from a huge amount of money, and I'm following through. In '99, we made this real. I did make some more mistakes, but by 2000, with Jim handling a lot of stuff, we've made only the occasional mistake since.

Livingston: Will you tell me about some of those mistakes?

Newmark: Actually, there are legal settlements which prevent me from talking about a lot of them. I can answer specific questions, sometimes.

Livingston: Did a mistake have to do with personnel?

Newmark: Yes. And I didn't listen to lawyers well enough. And those two issues are swirled together.

Livingston: So you had some personnel issues that involved lawsuits, but then you were able to get some closure? Then you hired Jim?

Newmark: No, Jim helped lead us out of the difficulties. I'm being vague, but I have to.

Livingston: Going back to the time when you were still in your apartment, was there anything that worried you?

Newmark: I can't think of anything. I may be forgetting a lot, but I think the only worry I can recall was that, when you run your server on someone else's machine, if there's a problem in the middle of the night, you have an issue. Or, if you are running it at a service, and they are flaky and have weak customer service, that's another problem.

Livingston: Did your site ever go down?

Newmark: I think it did, but in a way that's reasonable and understandable. Once in a while, our site has problems this way, but the thing is that we still manage to keep it up pretty well and keep it fast, which is hard because we're in another surge of growth. We're now getting at least five billion page views a month. We're in 170 cities.

Livingston: Back to how you got people to help you with this. Did people come to you?

Newmark: Well, how can they help me run the site? We spoke about making it a nonprofit and that made some sense, given my ignorance then. Now I realize there's a lot of legal constraints in nonprofits. They're meant to prevent various forms of corruption. The thing is, like a lot of laws like that, people who are crooked always find ways around the laws, and so the constraints just make it more difficult for the honest people. We are very, very lucky we're not a non-profit. We have our own nonprofit, which is doing some really good things. I'm on the board there, but my gig is customer service.

Livingston: When you first started, did you worry about spammers and other people trying to take advantage of your site?

Newmark: We have a really good culture of trust on the site—of goodwill. You know, we're finding that pretty much everyone out there shares, more or less, the same moral compass as we do and as my personal one. People are good. There are some bad guys out there, but they are a very tiny minority and our community is self-policing. People want other people to play fair, and that works. That does mean a certain amount of our time, including mine, but that's OK.

Livingston: You set up a way for the community to regulate the site, right?

Newmark: Yes: flagging. Flagging works. By virtue of flagging, we've turned over control of our site, for the most part, on a day-to-day basis to the people who use the site. We need to figure out better ways of doing that; that's still in process.

Livingston: How did you first come up with the idea of flagging?

Newmark: I forget. I think it was my customer service team, not me. I don't recall, it was so long ago.

Livingston: But it worked pretty well?

Newmark: Yes. It works great in all sorts of ways, and it's also an expression of our values. Mutual trust. This is kind of democracy in real life. Everyone wins, except for the bad guys.

Livingston: Do you remember a time when you wanted to quit?

Newmark: Nothing like that. Sometimes I'll have some anxiety. For example, when the site is having a problem, or when there's some issue that I'm having trouble handling, but that's not usual.

Livingston: It started out as a side project. Was there ever a point when you said, "I don't have the time for this"? Or were you always very committed?

Newmark: Always very committed. I'm stubborn. As I sometimes say, "I'm one very persistent nerd."

Livingston: I'm surprised that you never had any problems that you thought were totally overwhelming.

Newmark: The problems I've had which got to me were the after-effects of some of the bad trust decisions I made.

Livingston: Who did you learn things from?

Newmark: From friends, from business people I know. I should give particular credit to our principal corporate lawyer, a guy named Ed Wes from Perkins Coie. He's been very good at a lot of issues. He's really helped us out a great deal.

Livingston: The turning point for you was when you decided to do craigslist full-time, when your advertisers took you to lunch?

Newmark: Basically in mid-December of '97, they took me out to lunch and said, "This isn't working. You've got to take more responsibility for the way things are going." And I did.

Livingston: And you thought, "This is the right thing for me to do"?

Newmark: Yeah. That meant that I coasted on savings for several months or so, but that's not a problem. And it worked.

Livingston: Did you fund craigslist initially or did you take outside investment?

Newmark: I funded it with my own time. In no form did we ever take investment money. While we were trying to run nonprofit, the nonprofit entity took a few tiny loans, but we're talking about low thousands.

Livingston: I'm interested in the concept of how little money it takes to start certain types of web-based startups.

Newmark: Good point. The deal is, I did have some help, some favors; but, for the most part, for the first few years, it was just putting my own time and energy into it. If I was billing for my own hours, it would have been a great deal of money. But that doesn't matter now.

Livingston: Who were the first craigslist employees?

Newmark: Just a handful of people that I found in '99.

Livingston: Did you work with them? How did you find them?

Newmark: I think through the site.

Livingston: How did you grow the features on the site? Did you always add new features based on user feedback?

Newmark: When it comes to features visible from the outside, yes. Internally, we figure out on a continuous basis . . . we figure out what tools we need, and then we do them. That's working to this day, because it's the job, for example, of customer service to figure out how they can do their jobs better and then to tell tech what they need. This is business process reengineering, which companies used to talk about a lot in the late '80s, but usually didn't follow through.

Livingston: Did you have investors knocking at your door, offering you money?

Newmark: They started in '99, and we had a flurry of that last year. That's how I have some idea of how much I stepped away from.

Livingston: When they first offered you money, were you tempted at all?

Newmark: Yes. But I decided to hold fast. I'm not implicitly judging anyone else. We're not anti-traditional by any means. We just made a specific decision based on our specific values and followed through.

Livingston: And you make enough money to cover costs?

Newmark: We are doing well. Again, we are currently charging for less than 1 percent of the site. We started to charge for apartment rental listings in New York City, but we're still basically free.

Livingston: Did you ever think, "Boy, we can squeeze those brokers for a little more"?

Newmark: They asked us to charge them, because they feel that it will help improve the quality of that stuff. Especially the more legitimate brokers—they want that because they feel that will help control the sleazier brokers. And we think that will work OK.

Livingston: Are you having an impact on these sleazy brokers?

Newmark: It is working. It's a long slog, but these brokers increasingly behave. The deal is that a guy without, let's say, a firm moral compass, if he thinks that other brokers are being sleazy, he feels an implicit moral sanction to be sleazy. Now I'm telling guys like that, "Hey, it's over." And that's working. So we have brokers who used to be problematic, who are no longer problematic.

Livingston: Will you tell me about one of the most frustrating situations with a broker?

Newmark: I'm thinking of one, who's now very well-behaved. They used to do all sorts of things, all the bad things we've talked about, and they would also do things to try to evade our tools—which worked, by the way, except I have a volunteer who looks at things. They would post using multiple email addresses, that kind of thing. I just kept blocking them and blocking them, and they got tired of being blocked and they finally approached me and said, "Sorry about this." And it's working now.

Livingston: So they didn't just go away; they changed.

Newmark: Yes. That is mighty good. It worked very nicely.

Livingston: Can you remember anything that surprised you about the early days?

Newmark: What surprises me, in a way, is how almost universally people are trustworthy and good. There are problems, and sometimes people bicker, which is a pain in the ass, but people are good. No matter what your religious background, we share pretty much the same values. There are some minor differences that we disagree on, but the differences are at the 5 percent level. That's pretty good.

Livingston: What about companies wanting to buy you?

Newmark: We politely say, "No." The deal is, you know, eBay got that equity. And we're happy it's eBay since they have a similar moral compass. The person who sold was a former employee selling his equity. Unfortunately, years ago I decided I'd give away equity. I would grant it, because that would help me avoid temptation. Normally I can avoid anything but temptation. But he left the company, and he decided to sell in 2004.

We are very different from any other startup you've heard about. That's just the way things happened. It's working out well. Again, a big reason for our success is Jim.

Livingston: At what point did you think you'd actually be a "real" company?

Newmark: In early '99. It's been 7 years. Jim's been running things for about 6.

Livingston: I read craigslist used to work out of an old Victorian.

Newmark: It's not really a Victorian, I think. It's a very simple home. Oddly enough, we move into an old Victorian mansion in a not-great location, but that's all we can find. We did not want to move into the financial district. We had to move some place convenient for pretty much everyone to commute to.

Livingston: How do you find your employees?

Newmark: We advertise on our site. Sometimes someone will know someone.

Livingston: What's the most important part of your culture?

Newmark: The culture of trust. The moral compass.

Livingston: And you make sure, when you hire someone, that they have one?

Newmark: The other people on my team do, yes. Since I've had such bad luck in interviewing—that's because I'm not suited to it—I have no role in the hiring whatsoever.

Livingston: Is there anything about craigslist that people misunderstand?

Newmark: People sometimes still think we're a nonprofit, even though we tell people that we're not. Sometimes people think that we sold part to eBay, and that's a misconception I have to fix now and then.

Livingston: eBay is letting you do your thing, right?

Newmark: Yes.

Livingston: What advice would you give to someone thinking about starting a startup?

Newmark: Trust your instincts and your moral compass. I've used that phrase too much in this conversation. The deal is: we're not pious about this. We try hard not to be sanctimonious. This is the way people really live; we just don't talk about it. I'd prefer to be cynical and not talk about it, and yet, that's real life.

Craig Newmark and Jim Buckmaster, circa 2005
Photo: Gene X. Hwang

Caterina Fake
Cofounder, Flickr

Caterina Fake started Ludicorp in the summer of 2002 with Stewart Butterfield and Jason Classon. The company's first product, Game Neverending, was a massively multiplayer online game with real-time interaction through instant messaging (IM). In 2004, they added a new feature—a chat environment with photo sharing—which quickly surpassed Game Neverending itself in popularity.

The team knew they were onto something big and put Game Neverending on hold to develop a new photo-sharing community site called Flickr. Flickr became extremely popular and was acquired by Yahoo in March 2005.

With its emphasis on user-generated content and its devoted online community, Flickr is one of the most commonly cited examples of Web 2.0 companies.

Livingston: How did you get started? How did you know your cofounders?

Fake: Stewart and I are married. When we met, I was living in San Francisco and he lived in Canada. One of his wooing strategies was to suggest that we start a company together. Both of us were doing web development at the time and his idea was that we do some type of transnational web development company—which is kind of a harebrained scheme. We didn't end up doing that, but we did fall in love and have a long-distance relationship. I eventually moved up to Vancouver and we got married. We went on our honeymoon and came back and two days later started Ludicorp.

The name is from *ludus*, the Latin word for "play." We were building a massively multiplayer online game called Game Neverending. It was a lightweight web-based game, and atypical for massively multiplayer games. Most of those have Sword and Sorcery or science fiction themes, and are usually CD-ROM based. Game Neverending was very much based around social interactions; you could form groups, instant message each other, and there was a social network associated with it.

When we came up with the idea for the game, Stewart had been working at the CBC, on the kids' site, and in doing research he started playing all these online games. Neopets was one of the inspirations for Game Neverending. It's really fun. I was totally addicted. They have these pets, which are Tamagotchi-like, and you can buy them presents and give them toys. But what's interesting is that it has a market and you can trade things with other people in the game. The little area that I cornered the market on was trading JubJub hats. My sister became completely absorbed in it, and we thought, "Wow, there's something interesting here."

Both of us have backgrounds in web design and development, and I have a focus on social software. Before Ludicorp, I worked on or participated in a bunch of online communities including the WELL, Electric Minds, the Netscape online communities, and various sites I'd started on my own. At Interval Research, I worked on a collaborative animation game, which was a cousin to the Game Neverending idea.

Livingston: It was just the two of you?

Fake: At the beginning it was me, Stewart, and Jason Classon. Jason and Stewart had started a company together in 1999 that was acquired by a venture-backed startup out of Boston after about 6 to 9 months. Jason went and worked in Boston for a year and came back and then the three of us started working on the game together. I did the game design, Stewart did the interaction design, and Jason did the PHP for the prototype.

Livingston: Did they fund the game with money that they made from the acquisition?

Fake: Partially, yes. It was really a friends-and-family investment.

It was the three of us and we added Eric Costello very soon thereafter. Eric is a phenomenal web developer. He's recognized as one of the great DHTML gurus. He lives in New York, so we were working with him remotely. If you have somebody who's really fantastic and they live in New York, that's OK. He likely wasn't going to move (he has a family and is very settled there), but Eric was a phenomenal addition to the team.

He's a front-end developer. Soon thereafter, we were hiring for a back-end developer. It was actually very difficult to find that person in Vancouver. We felt that person needed to be local. We didn't want to be too dispersed.

There are a lot of companies that are virtual companies—a bunch of people that are living in different places, but I think that's tough. You can do it with one or two people, but I think for the most part, everybody being in the same place is important.

Stewart, Eric, and I had worked together on a project before, so we knew how to work with him remotely. The project was the 5K contest, which was a web development competition. It emerged out of a conversation that Stewart had with somebody at his web development agency who had said, "Oh, you can't make anything worthwhile under 5K."

Livingston: Where did you start working?

Fake: We had a friend who was subletting a space, and he had a contract job that kept him out of the office all the time, so we sublet his subletted space. This was in 2002 and it was still in the great technology bust period. There were failed dot-coms all over the place, so office space was cheap. And some really awesome developers (like Eric) were available, who wouldn't otherwise have been out on the open market two years earlier. So it was actually really well timed.

I think that the timing was really important because you could operate in a much more independent mode. The money was scarce, but I'm a big believer that constraints inspire creativity. The less money you have, the fewer people and resources you have, the more creative you have to become. I think that had a lot to do with why we were able to iterate and innovate so fast.

Flickr was kind of a lark. It was a side project that we built while we were in the process of building Game Neverending. The back-end development of the game fell really far behind the front-end development, and so while we were waiting for the back end to catch up—being restless hacker types—we built this sort of instant messenger application in which you could form little communities and share objects. And we just added the ability to share photographs.

So Flickr started off as a feature. It wasn't really a product. It was a kind of IM in which you could drag and drop photos onto people's desktops and show them what you were looking at. We built it really fast; we had a lot of the technology already from the game, but we built the first instance of Flickr in eight weeks. We had the idea in December and built it out by February and then presented it at the O'Reilly Emerging Tech Conference.

Livingston: What type of response did you get when you unveiled it?

Fake: It was hard to say. The response was positive, but it didn't end up being a compelling product mainly because it was a feature. It had a critical mass problem. Unless all of your friends were already on it, the sharing feature wasn't valuable to you.

It still grew, slowly. But it really started getting traction when we added the ability to put your photographs on a web page.

Livingston: Why did you decide to make it available on a web page?

Fake: When we started it, we were under this deluded idea that we wanted to create something new, but not a photo-sharing site. This is weird, but one of the things that enabled us to innovate within this space was that we hadn't done our research. We hadn't sat down and said, "We're going to build a photo-sharing site. We're going to do the research, figure out what the business model is, and raise some venture capital." We were naïve and optimistic.

What we did was just start building stuff. And I think if we had sat down and done the research, we would have looked at --the companies that had actually made businesses in this area, like Ofoto, Shutterfly, and Snapfish. Basically their model was that photo sharing was a loss leader for photo finishing services. It was all about the funnel to get you into buying prints. Photo sharing wasn't seen as a valuable enough activity that people would pay for that itself. So I think that our naïveté was what made the whole thing possible.

Other things were happening too. Stewart and I were longtime bloggers. I'd started blogging back in 1999, and had had a personal site on the Web since 1994. At the time when we were developing Flickr, social networking services had been bursting onto the scene. The Friendsters, MySpaces, and the Tribes were all happening around that time. So it was a convergence of all of this personal publishing stuff, as well as social networking and the rise of camera phones.

One of the things that I think was new about Flickr was the idea of publicness that hadn't been there when Ofoto and Shutterfly were being built, which emerged from blog culture. There's no such thing as a public photo on those sites, whereas on Flickr and a blog, the default is for it to be public.

Social networking got people used to this idea that they could make an online digital identity. They could put up photographs online and talk about who their friends were and what their interests were. And social networking as social networking pretty briskly showed itself to be a fairly pointless activity. People would go in and collect up all their friends and then there was nothing to do; there wasn't any sort of core interest. But when you tied it to a very specific, very connective activity like photo sharing, it really flourished.

Livingston: So Flickr was taking off. How did you, as a company, respond?

Fake: We tried to do both Flickr and Game Neverending in parallel. It was really tough because we were only six people, and that just wasn't enough resources to do both. Eventually, I think in July of 2004, we had to put the game on hold and stop development on it because Flickr was really taking off.

We were sad to do that because we all really loved the game. It had a lot of avid fans and we already had 20,000 people signed up to test the prototype. It was hard to let it go; it was the thing that we had started the company to do. But you couldn't argue with the momentum and growth that we were seeing with Flickr.

Livingston: What were some of the next turning points? Did anything go wrong down this new path?

Fake: We were extraordinarily fortunate in that the road was pretty smooth. The tide completely turned for us with Flickr. We'd been trying to get the game off the ground. Raising money for the game from outside investors had been really grueling. Raising money is very hard, especially in that market. We were building something that was not really known to people. If it wasn't a shrink-wrapped game sold at Best Buy, they didn't know what it was.

Livingston: Were you talking with VCs or angel investors?

Fake: At that time we were talking to venture capitalists and they didn't get it. But with Flickr, it completely turned around because the momentum behind it was so strong that at one point, we were getting calls from three to four VCs a week. They were getting in touch with us—completely different from when we were going door to door and beating the bushes trying to raise money.

Livingston: Did you wind up taking any investments?

Fake: We did a small angel round, but we didn't take any venture capital. And we lucked out and got an interest-free loan from the Canadian government. We'd applied for it, and gotten rejected, and then just sent the same application in again when it was open again, and much to our surprise, we got it. And here's the other thing that was interesting about Flickr: almost immediately after we launched—even when we were just the IM client—we were being approached by potential acquirers. So it was clear that we were onto something. People really weren't sure what yet, but there was definitely a lot of excitement and interest.

Livingston: Why did you decide not to take venture capital?

Fake: A couple reasons. We didn't think that we were ready, and we were kind of in a holding pattern. We weren't sure we wanted to take venture capital at all. We were being approached by all the acquirers and VCs and still many angels who were willing to invest. We had enough money to carry us through six months into the future and we already had some great angel investors, including Esther Dyson and Reid Hoffman. So we didn't feel we had to go for it. That was the ironic thing, because when you need money, nobody will return your calls. When you don't need money and you say, "Sorry, guys, don't need any money," they can't stop calling you. They just can't help themselves.

At that point, we were almost at break-even in terms of our operating expenses. If we were to take venture capital, it would have been making a big bet, expanding rapidly, rather than growing organically. And we were already growing at such a fast rate, we were barely keeping up on the back end. You know, all those scaling issues that come with rapid growth.

Livingston: What else happened?

Fake: Tagging really revolutionized the way that the product behaved. Tagging is an incredibly simple concept: you just add a keyword to the photograph, and once it's networked with all of these other people, you can see not only all the things that you've tagged (so it acts like this organizational system for yourself) but you can also see what everyone else in the system has tagged themselves in the public stuff.

So if you go to Tokyo and you take photographs, you can then visit the global Tokyo tag and see what everyone else has taken. You can find photographs of anything—mountain goats, McDonald's, anything that you can think of you can find in Flickr.

The other thing that tagging enables is the ability to see newsworthy events. Suddenly there'll be photos that are uploaded all at once from Live 8 concerts or the bombings in London. You have the ability to immediately surface all of these events from people distributed all over the globe.

When the Australian embassy in Jakarta was bombed, within 24 hours three people had uploaded photographs from the site of the bombing. And this was when Flickr only had 60,000 users. Three of them were in Jakarta with cameras, near the embassy, took photos, uploaded them and tagged them Jakarta. So it was emergent behavior.

The other thing that was happening was that people were creating groups for collaborative creativity and this was a completely different behavior for people. Photographs were being used in a completely different way. The best-known group of this kind is the Squared Circle group, in which people take a photograph of something circular, and then crop it to a square. It's incredibly beautiful to watch in a slide show, as suns and manhole covers and dandelion globes melt into each other. People have made all kinds of creative groups, and giving people a forum and an audience for their creativity is a big part of Flickr.

Back when photographs were really expensive, they were like these iconic photographs. For example, my grandparents—there's a picture of them that was taken in a studio. It's very posed and it is this special photographic event. As cameras became more and more distributed, you would take photographs at weddings, birthdays, or events. But then digital photography really changed that because photos are totally inexpensive. You can take hundreds of photos and only save five. So people started taking more photographs, but sharing them became an increasing problem. Then, the next step in the evolution in the photograph was when it was attached to a delivery mechanism. A camera is now in a phone and you can send the photo immediately.

There are cameras everywhere now. Nokia is apparently the biggest distributor of cameras in the world. And people are taking photographs of things that you would not normally take photographs of—maybe a funny thing that they see on their way to work. One completely new behavior that we saw was that people were taking photographs specifically to participate in a group on Flickr.

Content gets more and more defined. For example, if there's a car accident on this corner right now, that would be really interesting to you and me and the people that live within a five-block radius: there's an accident at 18th and Sanchez. Not interesting to people who live in Istanbul, or even people who are ten blocks away. People can find things that are relevant to them more easily, and I think that tagging has a lot to do with why that's possible.

Here's an example: there's a guy who was on vacation in Maine and got an alarming phone call from one of his neighbors saying that his apartment building (in Atlanta, Georgia) was on fire. So he immediately went on line to Flickr and typed the name of his apartment complex, "Atlantic Landing Georgia," and found all of these pictures of his apartment complex on fire. He was able to see that the fire was on the opposite side of the building and that his apartment wasn't affected, so he didn't have to panic and call his insurance company; he could continue on his vacation.

Livingston: What surprised you most?

Fake: The whole thing has been a surprise. We started out expecting to do the game and we ended up doing a photo-sharing site. We never expected that, could not have planned that.

The success that Flickr has seen has been a huge surprise. Obviously when you start a business you hope and pray that it will be successful, but I think it's also something of a surprise when it actually happens.

Also, we could not have timed it better. All of these things were in the air: blogging, social networking, camera phones, the ubiquity of network, suddenly more people were on broadband. All these things converged at the same time and we were really well-positioned to ride that wave.

Livingston: Were you nervous about any competitors?

Fake: There were people that did pieces of what we did, like Ofoto, but the competition wasn't apparent.

Livingston: You weren't worried that Ofoto would try to copy you?

Fake: Well, we knew they wouldn't because they wanted to acquire us.

Livingston: Is there anything that you would have done differently?

Fake: We may be the most boring startup that you interview for your book because our path was fairly smooth. There were times when we were really broke before we had our angel investment, when only one guy who had children was getting paid. One of the big risks of startups is that they're inherently unstable. They don't have an established business; they're often trying to invent something new. They are relying entirely on investment and not on revenue.

Livingston: What was it like starting a startup with your husband?

Fake: In the beginning it was kind of tough because a lot of our skills overlapped. Both of our backgrounds are in design. So in the beginning there was a lot of jockeying for position—who did what and who made which decisions. But once we were able to figure that out, it worked out really well.

We have very complementary personalities: Stewart's very improvisational and he likes to do things in a fairly loose manner, whereas I tend to be very directed and driven toward a goal. So in combination, he sort of loosens me up and I get him on a path and those two things work really well together.

Livingston: What kinds of challenges have you faced as a female technology startup founder?

Fake: There is a lot of institutionalized sexism working against women in business and I think that people aren't even aware that it's there. One example happened when we went down to Silicon Valley to meet with a venture capital firm. After the meeting, the VC spoke to someone associated with our company and said to him, "Tell Stewart not to bring his wife to VC meetings." Which was shocking to me, and Stewart was furious about this as well. He let everybody know, "Caterina is not 'my wife.' She is instrumental to the success of this company. Her contributions have been equal to mine."

It takes a lot of nerve for women to face up to this assumption—and the assumption is everywhere, even in some of the most surprising places—that they don't measure up, that they're not good or tough enough. Twice as much will be expected of them. I hear this from women again and again in business: they have to be twice as prepared as men.

This happens to me all the time: I go to meetings and I've stayed up late preparing my presentation and I've got all my papers in order and know exactly what I'll be talking about and I come to the meeting and a bunch of guys show up and say, "Hey, so what's this meeting about?" They haven't done any of the preparation or work.

Livingston: Do women bring any advantages to a startup?

Fake: I was talking to another entrepreneur, Judy MacDonald Johnston, and she said that women are much more passionate about their businesses. They're doing it less for the money and more because they love it. There's something about that that really rings true to me. Women are able to put their hearts and souls into it in a way that many men cannot—or rather, are not known for doing.

I've been very conscious of this too, and it's important to give something back, so I've been a big participant in a lot of women-in-technology organizations, like the Forum for Women Entrepreneurs. I think it's really important for us to continue supporting each other and make sure that women have an equal shot. I do a group blog, www.misbehaving.net, with a bunch of other women in technology, and we've been working on getting women more speaking engagements at industry conferences. Being invited to conferences and elevating your profile in the industry is an important part of growing businesses, making contacts, and building partnerships, and we want to make sure that women get a fair shake.

Brewster Kahle
Founder, WAIS, Internet Archive,
Alexa Internet

Brewster Kahle started WAIS (Wide Area Information Servers) in the late '80s while an employee of Thinking Machines. He left in 1993 to found WAIS, Inc. WAIS was one of the earliest forms of Internet search software. Developed before the Web, it was in some ways a predecessor to web search engines. Kahle sold WAIS to AOL in 1995.

The next year, Kahle founded Alexa Internet with Bruce Gilliat. The Alexa toolbar tracked user browsing behavior and suggested related links using collaborative filtering. Once captured, pages visited by users would then be "donated" to the related nonprofit Internet Archive, to help build a history of the Web.

Alexa was acquired by Amazon in 1999. Kahle continues to run the Internet Archive.

Livingston: You were one of the first members of the Thinking Machines team. What number employee were you?

Kahle: I was not one of the two founders—they were Danny Hillis and Sheryl Handler. I was on the project team at MIT, so when we started the company, anybody from that team that wanted to come came. There were three or four of us. We had been working on it for a couple years before there was a company.

Livingston: Tell me about some big things back in the Thinking Machines days that helped pave the way for WAIS.

Kahle: Thinking Machines was not my doing, but I was on the project team beforehand and then helped start the company. What I learned out of that was: do your homework before you are spending your own money. We did a full couple rounds of the Connection Machine at MIT before we started a company. It was very helpful to get your lessons learned basically on somebody else's nickel, in a research phase.

Another lesson that I learned out of Thinking Machines was, if you're trying to get your company to think differently—to do something interesting—pick your setting carefully. Thinking Machines was set in an 1800s Victorian mansion on 100 acres of forest just outside of Boston. It was a park, basically. Working in an environment where, if you got stuck, you'd go for a long walk is very different than trying to do a startup and think differently if you're in Suite 201 in some major office complex. That was a lesson that I've used every startup since.

Thinking Machines had the great fortune of starting with $8 million in the bank, because some very rich individuals really believed in it. It was not venture-funded, and it was founded with the idea that it was going to take years and years and years to actually get something real done. That allowed Thinking Machines to attract a very interesting set of people. Richard Feynman worked there, Stephen Wolfram, Marvin Minsky. I found that I had better access to professors in a company than I did when I was in school. So that was an interesting way of trying to figure out, "What should the company do?"

They took a good summer to try to figure that out and, actually, through a bunch of the first year, which is a luxury that most startups don't have. Usually you have to work really hard to try to get your first release built. So being in an interesting setting with brilliant people coming by, it was quite a unique startup—very unlike the West Coast startups that I've seen.

Livingston: What were some of the big turning points early on?

Kahle: We hired a fellow from Digital Equipment Corporation—his title was VP of Reality. The idea was to try to help a bunch of folks that had great ideas out of MIT, but had never really produced a supercomputer before, figure out "How do we actually do that?" I remember being invited to give a design review of the core central processing unit of this new computer, and I really didn't know what a design review was. It was quite embarrassing. But it was very helpful to inject a VP of Reality. It stirred up the culture to try to get it so that we could actually produce working machines.

There was a lot of trust in very young people in that company. People were in their early 20s. So the basic design and building of the machines—even though we were completely underqualified, looking back on it—was entrusted to a very young set. But it made it fun. We were absolutely glued to the project. We didn't really have much of a rest of a life.

Livingston: Were there any experiences where you thought, "If I start a startup, I'm not doing this"?

Kahle: The blessing of Thinking Machines and the curse of Thinking Machines was that it had a lot of money. If you have a lot of money, then you can be detached from people that are going to pay you in the future.

My first startup upon leaving Thinking Machines was a bootstrap. We had no investment at all, and I had no savings, so it was self-funded from the beginning. That was a night and day cold bath. It was sort of like going from the Roaring 20s, when champagne is coming from everywhere, into the depression, where you are washing your baggies and reusing twist ties.

Actually I really liked the discipline that came from a bootstrapped startup. I think that everybody that goes and does a startup—even if they don't do a major startup that way—should start a business that is having to make people happy with them day one, through contracts, through small scale sales, whatever it is. How low can you go? How can you build something really inexpensively? How can you not spend money on furniture and matching carpet and those sorts of things? The biggest thing that I probably didn't do the second time around was have any money.

Livingston: Tell me about how you got the idea for WAIS.

Kahle: The idea of WAIS was to make network services—stuff that you take completely for granted now—but the idea was that you could use remote machines to answer questions. The ARPANET was just really becoming in use by universities in the 1980s, and so at Thinking Machines we were trying to figure out, "How would you make use of a machine that had 15 gigabytes of disk space and would have processors that you could run at, say, a gigahertz?" This was completely amazing. How would you possibly use that much computing power? We said, "Well, you'd put them on the Net, and they'd be smart machines that would answer your questions for you." So this was the idea. We'd prototype it around Thinking Machines.

I prototyped it in my spare time. I guess there was very much an ethos that hacking was encouraged—playing around and doing fun things, spending time doing something that wasn't your exact job responsibility, but doing it at work, and getting support from work. So I tried out the idea of remote publishing—of remotely asking machines questions. It was the first Internet publishing system. It came before Gopher and before the Web, but it was the first system that was trying to answer questions over the Net. Yes, search was a big part of it, but you could also click around and it had a URL system and it had a search system for finding servers. It had all the different pieces. It was built on an open protocol. We did it as a project of Thinking Machines, working with Apple Computer, KPMG Peat Marwick, and Dow Jones.

So my first experience with trying to start something at that scale was actually done within Thinking Machines—again, following that original lesson of "learn your lessons without spending your own money." So we tried basically building this system up within Thinking Machines. Thinking Machines wanted to make money by selling servers, so we needed to get the rest of the system going. We had Apple Computer to do the front end, the client piece; Dow Jones to do the information sources; and KPMG Peat Marwick for their corporate information and as a user base. So it was a test project. It ran about a year and a half and was successful. Everybody loved it. Each one of the organizations went forward to figure out how to make this all go. This was in 1989/90. So we were all looking into the future.

Livingston: WAIS seems to have ideas that anticipated the Web.

Kahle: All these ideas were in the air. The Web came a bit later, but, as I understand, Tim Berners-Lee was working on some of the same things, but doing them locally within CERN in Switzerland. We were doing them within a corporate environment using supercomputers and the Internet as well.

Livingston: So Dow Jones, KPMG Peat Marwick, and Apple were all involved?

Kahle: Yes, everybody was working together. It was a project that had a project team in each the companies, and I ran it. I moved out to the West Coast to try and run it, because I knew I could run Thinking Machines remotely, but I didn't think I could run Apple remotely. So I moved out to the West Coast and had a cubicle and a project team that I worked with at Apple.

Livingston: Tell me about some of the hard technical problems that WAIS addressed.

Kahle: One of the difficult things was just using the computer networks at the time. This is 1989, and the Internet hadn't quite become easy in any real sense. Trying to hook up to Dow Jones through X.25 networks and ISDN was all quite challenging. KPMG Peat Marwick started to have an intranet then that we could use, and fortunately they used Macintoshes. The Macintoshes were helpful because they had TCP/IP for them, where Windows didn't. It wasn't until Windows 95 came out 6 years later that Microsoft caught up.

What I loved about it was I got to work with four companies that were managed very differently from each other. This was my bath of "How do companies work?" Thinking Machines was a bottom-up company. In many ways, the ideas and the people with power were the young engineers. They could see where things were going better than the top level management, because everything was so new.

Dow Jones was a top-down company. If you sold the top guy, he'd say, "OK, we're going to do this." Then he'd issue a command, and the next-level guy would say, "OK, sir, I'm going to do this."

Apple Computer was explained to me to be a "beanbag chair." You had to push not only on the top, but on the bottom and the middle all at the same time to try to get it to move. This was a time when John Sculley was running Apple, and I don't know if it's any different now, but at that time you had to actually keep pushing all up and down the whole chain or it just wouldn't move. You'd push, and you'd think you were making headway, but the beanbag chair didn't move.

KPMG Peat Marwick was a democracy. It's a partnership. Each partner thought of themselves as in control of their piece of turf. And they were very much so. They controlled their own revenue; they spent it; it was a democracy. In fact, every so often they would get together and elect their upper-layer management. If they didn't like the upper-layer management—which was just another consulting office, like any other—they'd vote them out. And they did. The folks that were really supporting the WAIS project at KPMG Peat Marwick after a couple years got more or less voted out. Not because of WAIS, but the partners said, "We want a different type of management."

So this was still being done within Thinking Machines, but I found that Thinking Machines wasn't going to go and build some of the pieces needed to make this Internet publishing world work. We coined the term "Internet publishing" and tried to say, "OK, this should happen." Apple would do their piece and Peat Marwick would do their piece, but nobody would go and do the central set of tools, the software needed. So I said, "OK, well, I'll do that. And start a company to do that."

There was a decision to try and figure out where it should be. Should it be in Boston? Should it be in Silicon Valley? Should it be someplace completely else? So I went around to the smart people I knew and said, "Where should we put this company? What I'm really trying to do is build an industry." Not build a company, build an industry, so there would be all of these pieces that would make network publishing come about. Some people thought it was a little crazy to think about starting an industry, but it seemed like it made sense to me.

The best piece of advice that I got was from Bill Dunn, one of my mentors. He said, "Go someplace where people don't think you're crazy." Which sounds like a pretty simple thing to say, but it actually turned out to be a very wise piece of advice. Boston, especially back in 1990/91, was in recession and having trouble. California was also in recession, but in California there were dreamers. There were people who wanted to think about new and different things and wouldn't think we were crazy to try to build this thing.

So I decided to start the company out here and start with a contract—it was a bootstrap—doing the information system for the Perot campaign for the presidential campaign of 1992. They could really use an information system that leveraged some network. Of course, they didn't know what network, but we did. So we could build this Internet using modems and leased lines and all sorts of things to be able to build this up. The Perot campaign collapsed, but we still had enough money to make it through most of the first year to go and get our products built.

One of the interesting ideas out of WAIS was its use of freeware and shareware. This was a new idea, more or less. There had been some examples of freeware like GNU, but there were also mixed models: Kermit, where people basically would make source code available on the Net and sell something related. We gave away the client version, the equivalent of a Web browser. It was a WAIS browser and a server, so people could go and build their own system.

During that free period, hundreds and hundreds and hundreds of servers were set up. We got up to about 10,000 servers—all this is before Gopher and the Web came out—based on free software. Once people got really hooked on the free software, they wanted upgrades, or they wanted services. So we were there as a company to sell it to them. We made the free version, and there was a for-pay version. It was the same idea that we've seen now with Netscape. There's a whole set of companies that also tried to give something away and sell something else.

Livingston: You were the first company to do that?

Kahle: Well, I think we may have been the first to think of the Internet as a distribution system of software: to give something away and to sell it. I don't know of any examples before.

Livingston: That is so many companies' business model these days; it's interesting to think it was the first.

Kahle: I don't know if it was the first, but it was certainly early. We also found that people—even if we sold them the software—often didn't know what to do with it. They wanted consulting services. We started what I think became the first web studio, or web services business. We worked with big players, whether they were newspapers or magazines, that wanted to publish on the Net. This allowed us to work with the big boys very early on.

We tried very hard to work with the best of class. They were always more difficult to deal with, but they were great to work with once you got working with them: the *Wall Street Journal*, *Encyclopedia Britannica*, Government Printing Office. We worked with both the House of Representatives and the Senate. So we were working with people who had insights into what it is they really wanted. It's harder to get those customers at first, but they were terrific because they weren't just trying to catch up. They weren't trying to be number 2. They were number 1 in their fields, and we could learn from them.

As the Web came along and was a better underlying system, we became a web services company, basically. We set up, I believe, the first publisher on the Net, which was Scholastic. That was done during the Gopher era. And we put the first advertising-based service up, which was for CMP. We put the first subscription-based service up, which was the *Wall Street Journal*. So we were trying to get publishers online, and that was what the WAIS system was.

I would stand up in conferences in 1990/91 and say, "I'm the token dot-com in the room. I'm here to help people make money by publishing on the Net." The idea was to try to get the Net to go commercial enough to support publishing.

Livingston: Did these big publishers at first think this was crazy?

Kahle: Usually it would take 9 to 12 months with lots of meetings before anything would turn concrete. Eventually they wanted to do some sort of project, and they'd throw $100,000 into a project. Since we were so inexpensive—we were living based on furniture that didn't match; we had learned our lessons of how to live very inexpensively—we could do things as production that they would normally pay an Ernst & Young just to do a study.

We could deliver something that they could really learn from, and we'd learn from as well. That kind of partnership worked well for us. But, boy, was it tough running with so little money.

Livingston: When you broke off from Thinking Machines, were they OK with this?

Kahle: There was a lot of consternation. There were a lot of questions of whether Thinking Machines owned the idea or whatever. I was very careful to make sure that all the things that the (eventually) WAIS company needed were actually based on the public domain of software that had been produced. It was based on the open source software. So there weren't actually any patents or copyrights, but there was still a bond. And there was this question of, "Should Thinking Machines own it? How should it work?" But there was so little to own. It wasn't like it was a VC-started company where you could value it. It was just basically myself and one other, Harry Morris, that left to found the company.

I think there was some hand-wringing, but we couldn't figure out any way to really do a deal. The problems that slow things down the most are these things around intellectual property—especially when there's no money yet—and these are the times that you could end up talking endlessly and you can't figure it out. It's a lot easier if there's money. Then you have a mechanism of knowing how share it. But before it, it's really, really tough.

I found it was very helpful to start a company out on the West Coast. Even though I had moved out here, I made a partnership with a fellow named John During—key for me, basically the cofounder of WAIS. He was a key player because he'd been around for a long time, so he knew how to do all of this stuff. How do you get an accounting company, the law firms, what do you spend money on, how do you negotiate a lease—all the things that I had never learned by being an engineer inside another company.

Livingston: How did you meet him?

Kahle: He was a consultant for Dow Jones. Also I found that there are people that specialize in different parts of businesses. Some people just do startups over and over again. Or they are actually in the idea stage. So a lot of people that I saw in the late '80s and early '90s in this Internet world were the people that had been involved in the PC revolution 10 years before. They had seen all of that go through, and they were looking around for "what's the next thing?" and this Internet thing started to smell kind of like it. So John During had a lot of experience in that.

Livingston: So you said, "Let's do it"?

Kahle: Yes, and moved out to San Francisco, started the company in a Menlo Park mansion, sort of on the Thinking Machines model. That was as far north as I thought I could put the company and still be connected in with the Apples and the Suns and the other technology companies.

In 1992, San Francisco wasn't the place for companies. That happened in the mid '90s, with the whole South of Market rebuilding. That was another sort of "learn the lesson of going someplace where people don't call you crazy." I really needed the help of those that were in Silicon Valley, though I knew that as this industry built up, it was going to work more with the creative people. So it was going to transition more and more to San Francisco. When we moved offices in 1994, we moved it into the city, so that we could work with the publishers—basically, the people that were going to be out there on the Net, not just building the technology, but using it for something.

Livingston: So you were getting a little bit of money from clients. Did you hire anyone?

Kahle: Yes, there was Harry Morris, the key engineer that built much of the technology. It grew into a company that was about 30 people, 35 people by the time it was bought by AOL.

Livingston: Tell me about some of the most hair-raising moments.

Kahle: Going broke. When you just don't have enough money to pay the bills. We would usually live with the amount of money in the bank that would be about 2 to 4 weeks worth of the bills. We'd never have more than that. If we got up to 2 or 3 months, we would think of ourselves as being flush. Living a boot-strap in a non-market—we're trying to make a market go based on making servers in a client/server publishing environment based on the Internet, that people didn't understand. So it was very difficult, but it was a good disciplining time.

Times that were really interesting? I think working with really great customers. It sort of sounds like a cliche, but to go and learn from *Encyclopedia Britannica*, the *New York Times*, the *Wall Street Journal,* and try to learn how do they view their businesses and their lives was the most fun out of the whole experience.

Livingston: What did you learn from your customers that surprised you?

Kahle: I love working with businesspeople because they are really straightforward. Now we have lots of lawsuits around copyrights in the music industry, blah, blah, blah. But if you work with the actual businesspeople—not the lawyers that work for the businesspeople, but the businesspeople—they are very straightforward. They just want to make money. And they just want to make more money than they are making today. They understand there are going to be transitions and technology changes. So if you lay out a path of how they can make more money, potentially, at the end of this than before, then they are on board.

We got the newspapers on the Internet during that time. You take it for granted, but all the newspapers are pretty much online now. They control their own distribution. They have their own websites. It doesn't all funnel in through an iTunes. The music guys, I'm not sure why they did this, but they sold their souls. Somebody else controls not only the distribution of their product, but they control the pricing. What do you have if somebody else controls the distribution and the pricing of your product?

So the newspaper guys and publishers were great because we'd say, "You want to control the distribution of your work." And they'd nod their heads, and we'd say, "Well, there are some alternatives out there." In the early '90s there was AOL, there was Lexus Nexus from the '80s, where they would lose the control of the distribution of their work. We'd say, "Do you want that?" They'd say, "No, we don't want that. We want to control the distribution of our work." So we said, "Swing with us for a little while, while we build this Internet. Let's build this Internet together based on open systems." So these business guys were, in fact, wanting an open system.

We wanted to build this up before the monopolists got to town and said, "Oh, you don't want an open system. You want a closed system that belongs to us, and we'll do it really well." So we worked very hard to get it to go in the early '90s, to get an open system anchored. And it worked. By the time AOL announced in '94 they were going to support basically the Internet protocols and when Microsoft said in August of 1995 that they were going to support the World Wide Web, that meant that we won. We had gotten publishing on the Net, and at that point I could graduate and do the thing that I wanted to do.

Livingston: Do you remember things that your clients totally misunderstood about what you were trying to do?

Kahle: I learned to try not to make too many leaps at once. Most people have a very difficult time imagining something they can't see at least a demonstration of. If you can get a demonstration—or, worst case, a video—it communicates an idea better than hand-waving for hours. So get to a demo quickly.

This was difficult when the Internet hadn't been deployed. Often the executives didn't have computers on their desks. They had secretaries that typed for them. Remember, it wasn't that long ago that these things weren't everywhere. And they weren't hooked up to anything. Maybe they had a modem, but that was it. We had to demonstrate these things over modems. Trying to get clearance so that they could dial out from a computer to the Internet to demonstrate this system inside the CIA headquarters was actually a several-day process. So it was difficult to go and explain very many jumps forward.

Whenever I went and said, "Really what I want to do—after we get this publishing up and running, is build the library . . ." Because that's always what I wanted to do. I just thought I had to build these supercomputers first, then I had to get the publishing going, and, once we got that, then we could build a library. So it was not until '96 that I got to the place where what we had dreamed of in the late '70s as the goal—which was to build the great library—could even start.

Livingston: That was always your goal?

Kahle: Yes, that was always the goal. We just had to do a couple things first. It took a lot longer than I thought. We're now in 2006, and it's hard to believe how pathetic things are. We don't even have books online yet. I don't know why the world moves so slowly. Everybody says, "Oh, it's moving so fast." And it's like, "No, I don't think so. It's been forever."

Livingston: Besides always running out of money, how did you find having your own company different from Thinking Machines?

Kahle: Having your own company means that it's much harder to blame somebody else. If you are working inside a big company, you can always blame management, marketing, engineering, or something. But, when you are running it, you can't, because it's all your responsibility. I found that to be quite cathartic. The East Coast also has a little more of an aesthetic of complaining, and so I got a little bit over that, I guess.

Another, I thought, was expressed really well by Don Yannias of *Encyclopedia Britannica*. He said, "Now that I'm running *Encyclopedia Britannica*, I have to be Mr. Sunshine every day." Because people are looking to you, not just for the ideas, but for the general attitude toward how to make the whole thing work. Carrying a company is a lot of weight. You have to make sure that you keep on the uptick—not just financially, but also make it so that it's a fun environment and people want to work there.

Livingston: Did you have any competitors back in the WAIS days?

Kahle: There were other systems around, but one thing I tend to do is do something that is far enough out there that nobody in their right mind would possibly want to do it. In general, I usually take things from the "you gotta be crazy" period to the "of course." And once it gets to "of course," then there will be competitors, and I'm done. Because usually what I want to do is just get other people to do it. The best way to do that is to show that it's possible.

So WAIS was all about trying to get other people to copy us. And they did, and it worked great. And they did better at it, and flourished. Better web studios than we were, server manufacturers and the people that made web servers—they did much better than we did. But the idea on WAIS was to try to guide the building of it, because WAIS wasn't the goal. Building that company wasn't the goal. I wanted to get it so that publishing would happen on the Net, so then I could go and actually do something.

Livingston: Publishing was happening, you sold WAIS to AOL, then what?

Kahle: Then I tried to work within AOL, and that was very difficult. For an entrepreneur, acquisitions are very difficult to manage. That's a warning. I've been through two acquisitions. One was WAIS; that was bought by AOL. The next round I built two organizations at the same time. One was called Alexa Internet (short for the Library of Alexandria), and the other was the Internet Archive, to archive everything that was in the library. Alexa was a for-profit, and the Internet Archive was nonprofit. I didn't make enough money to go and make a nonprofit and fund it myself, and I didn't know how to ask for money in a nonprofit, but I knew how to build products.

Alexa Internet was a navigation system for the Internet. Bruce Gilliat and I started it out here in San Francisco, in a house in the middle of a park—in the Presidio. We're in a 1500-acre park in the middle of San Francisco. We're the second lease-holder here.

Livingston: You started both companies simultaneously? Did you have different people running each one?

Kahle: Everybody worked at Alexa. The idea was that everything that Alexa ever collected would be donated to the Internet Archive. Over the long term, companies come and go. They usually don't last that long. But the great thing that was going on with the Internet wasn't the technology. That gets replaced. It's the information, and it's all the people. So we started collecting the World Wide Web and making services in a commercial company, but donating all of the materials collected to a nonprofit that was designed to last the ages. It was very specifically designed to think through what happens after the commercial company is gone.

Livingston: When you first started with Alexa, did you get funding?

Kahle: I funded the first part of it with Bill Dunn. And I cofounded it with a business-oriented fellow, Bruce Gilliat, because I'm more on the visionary side. Building in a businessperson has been a good idea. Finding a good partner is extremely difficult. It's as difficult as finding somebody that you want to get married to and you'll stay married to forever. A business partner is very difficult, and if you can find a good business partner, stick with that person.

Livingston: What makes a good business partner?

Kahle: Compatibility. Mutual respect through hard times. Maybe it's clear lines of differentiation for who does what. But finding a good business partner is a fantastically valuable thing to do. So the second startup, Alexa, I started with a partner as a full cofounder and that worked out really well.

Livingston: Did you get funding?

Kahle: We got $1 million to get the first round going, and then we started talking to venture capitalists. This is 1996; some of the companies started going public, so there's some money around. But again, everything that we were talking about, we couldn't communicate it in a way that made sense to them. So we got private investment by a single individual. That was very helpful. We grew that company to around 45 or 50 people and then sold it to Amazon.com.

Livingston: The toolbar was a brand new idea. How did you entice users to download it?

Kahle: The idea of Alexa was to help guide you around the Net. We thought that search engines were going to give up steam. We just didn't think that they were going to be able to scale. I was wrong, just wrong. But the thing that we wanted to do was help people navigate around the Net. We wanted to catalog the Web: make it so that you knew where you were and where you might want to go next. The concept of the company was to show you related links to every page that you were on.

So if you're on a web page and you are looking at some car, some book, or a website about some new computer, then you'd be able to see, "Oh, if you're on this page, you might want to go to this page, this page, and this page." It may not be what the owner of that website wants you to see.

Livingston: Was that what became known as collaborative filtering?

Kahle: It came to be called collaborative filtering. The way that it worked was we collected user trails of "Where did they go?" You know, the Amazon recommendations, "people who bought this book, bought that book." This was, "people who went to this web page, went to these web pages." And we did it years before those other systems. It was based on some work by Carl Feynman, when we were talking about this at Thinking Machines. We were talking about, "Where could this whole thing go?" and he said, "Well, there might be editors, and you might be able to discover editors," based on this idea that became collaborative filtering.

He went off to MIT, and they started a company called Firefly that was based on his ideas. So anyway, this idea of doing a web-scale collaborative filtering, people who liked this web page liked these web pages, was what we did. We did the toolbar to do this and to offer information to people as they are moving around the Net. In return, all of these people would be giving us information as to where they went, what trails they took, which we'd then learn from.

Livingston: What did you learn?

Kahle: We learned what was related to other things. But in the great scale, what I loved was watching some of these users—though we didn't know who was who and we didn't care. In fact, that was very important because it's very private information. Something I think we're forgetting is that some of these other systems are collecting this information, and they do care who's who. Google's toolbar, for instance. Going and learning where people go, you learn a lot more than you want to know. So you have to go and delete some of them; otherwise, it gets scary.

Livingston: Alexa deleted them?

Kahle: Yes. Alexa deleted things. Others that sort of followed in those footsteps aren't deleting things. This is going to be a big problem. At Alexa, we started with a code of ethics in the whole approach, because we knew that we were gathering information that people often didn't know that we were gathering, or they weren't really conscious of it. Throwing away a lot of information is key in such a circumstance.

Livingston: What went wrong with Alexa?

Kahle: We couldn't get the ad model to work worth a darn. Our idea was to give very contextual ads. We knew what web page people are on, might as well give them an ad that made sense. But we couldn't find a way of selling ads in such a way that it worked. We had an unbelievable number of page turns. We had many opportunities to put ads in front of people, but we couldn't turn that into making money.

So our underlying business idea failed. We were very successful in terms of getting lots of people to use it. People liked it. Netscape bundled it into their browser. Once Netscape bundled it into their browsers, getting Microsoft to bundle it into their browsers was easily done. (We found the best way to get Microsoft to do something was to get the competitor to do something.)

So we got lots and lots of users—millions, tens of millions of users—but we couldn't figure out how to make the business work. At that point, when some folks from Amazon were looking around for data mining technology, they came and said, "Should we buy you for data mining technology?" And we said, "One, you shouldn't buy us, and the other is that we're doing something quite different from data mining. We have this toolbar we can get out there in front of people and things like that."

In talks with Jeff Bezos, the founder of Amazon.com, I said, "I tried being acquired, and it didn't work. By AOL, a great company, but my company got dispersed, and I don't know how to run a division; I know how to run a company." He said, "If we're going to buy you, why don't you run it as a company? What does that mean to you?" I said, "Well, it has a board, and I meet with the board once a month and they give general direction and I run the place." And he said, "OK, let's do it that way."

So we got acquired, and we ran as a separate company. The company is still running. It's about 200 yards away from the Internet Archive, which is where I am now. I stayed for 3 years and then moved over to build the Internet Archive—which had nobody working here—into a real organization. Because once we had enough materials, then we could build the library. So Alexa was about the cataloging of the library, and the Internet Archive is trying to build the stuff.

Livingston: This was your dream?

Kahle: Yes. One thing I learned from Marvin Minsky (one of the founders of AI) was, "Pick a big enough project, something that's really hard, something that over the years you can work on." I've found that that has been a great guiding piece of wisdom. If you just set out to go and make a lot of money, then the problem is, what happens when you make a lot of money? You're out of ideas.

So the idea of going and putting everything online is something really big and hard. How do you make a library such that everybody has access to everything? I remember talking to Richard Feynman, and we were looking at the *Encyclopedia Britannica* in one of these 1800s rooms at Thinking Machines. We had an *Encyclopedia Britannica*, and it had an index that was one volume, then a micropedia, which was about 10 volumes, and then the next level was the macropedia, which was about 30 volumes. We just imagined: how many more layers of this before we have everything ever published? It turned out there were like 5 more layers, and I said, "That couldn't be that hard. How much information is there? It's not that much." So even in the era of Thinking Machines, we knew what it was we were trying to build. It just takes longer than one thinks. That was 20 some odd years ago.

Livingston: Do you think it's a good idea for those who have a big dream like that to section it off a bit? To try to create a successful startup to get the money to give them the freedom to pursue their dream?

Kahle: Yes. I try to make sure that every year there's some accomplishment that you can actually point at and say, "OK, this year I'm going to do this." This year I'm working on digitizing books. Last year I was trying to get a storage computer to work internationally, so that we'd have copies in Europe and the Arab world, in Egypt. We made copies so that, in case we disappeared, the information lived. Every year, try to do something that you can point at. Otherwise, a couple years go by, and you say, "What really happened?"

Livingston: Who were your mentors?

Kahle: I've had two. Most people don't have mentors. They say, "Well, I've had influential teachers. I've learned a lot from this person." But they don't think of it as a mentor. A mentor is a life guide, somebody that you might work with, but somebody who is helpful toward watching bigger issues about things that guide your life.

Danny Hillis, who was 4 years older and whom I worked for at MIT and Thinking Machines, has been a guide and a help ever since. The other was Bill Dunn. I found those two men, both being very kind and smart, had the ability to know what was going to happen—even though they had way too little information. I'd always sort of note down their wild ideas and think, "Did they come about?" A few years later you find out they were right. Some people are just more right than they ever deserve to be.

Livingston: You've done startups in the East and West Coast hubs. Is one place better than the other for startups?

Kahle: Oh, I think it's much easier to do a startup on the West Coast. There are all the facilities and services available to you. You can put together a marketing department out of part-time people. You can hire an accountant to just do exactly what you need. You need a lot less infrastructure that you control to do a startup on the West Coast than on the East Coast.

If you started with $8 million, you can buy everything you need; but if you are starting, just you, you can do a startup out of your bedroom. In fact, a lot of people do. In fact, most bedrooms I think are startups! The idea that you can start on a shoestring, that you can hold a meeting in a coffeehouse and that's OK, is perfectly legitimate on the West Coast.

Livingston: Why not in Cambridge?

Kahle: Maybe you can do that now in Cambridge; maybe it's changed. But there's a more institutional idea that you have to be more proven. San Francisco is full of dreamers. It's the people with the new ideas. It may be bad, they may be inappropriate, they may fail, but I love the idea that we can do something new and different—something that hasn't been done before, something that's going to affect a lot of people. There's an idea that you can pull something off here. That sort of uplifting nature to San Francisco and the Bay Area in general really lives on. This is a city of dreamers, and that's what makes it just a wonderful place to live and to work.

Livingston: Looking back on all of your experiences, what surprised you most?

Kahle: How long things take. To start a company and to get to a point where one has a critical mass—you have an office, you've got your CFO, you've got all of the infrastructure to become a viable entity. I think about 20 to 40 people is a golden size, because you're not spending all of your time doing things that you're not that good at. There are other people in the organization with more specialization in different areas. It takes a couple years to really get that debugged.

You can grow it instantly. You can hire 40 people in an afternoon, but they won't necessarily work together well; they won't understand what's going on. It takes a while. So 6 months, 9 months goes by often just putting together all the pieces of infrastructure. With Alexa, it took a year to build the company to the extent where we could do our first real product release. WAIS was the same way. The first product release came a year after the start. It always seems like it should be much quicker than that.

Livingston: What can big corporations do to preserve the startuppyness of the companies they acquire?

Kahle: My first company was bought by AOL, and what AOL wanted to do was inject the Internet into its veins. So they went around and bought a bunch of companies. And I'd say what they'd bought the company for, if I had been more worldly, they actually achieved. It just wasn't what I was looking for. I had built a little company. It made something like $3 million a year, which I thought was pretty great. I wanted it to get to $10 million or $20 million, but that was a rounding error for AOL—it was noise. They needed us to help on the big issues. So I worked on strategy for the company for 12 months—to get the company going in the Internet direction. And that's really what they wanted. It just wasn't something that I knew how to do. I really liked running something that I knew how to run.

When I did the startup that was bought by Amazon, I said, "Leave us on our own. We're smart and independent enough to be able to do good work that will inject things from the side into your other organization." The thing that Jeff Bezos did that I thought was very smart was that he ran us through his organization and others through ours. He used us, at least for the first few years, as a think tank in some sense—a live and breathing example of how else they could do things.

Alexa's major value in the first year of its being acquired by Amazon was to take some of the lessons that we had learned of how to do things much cheaper than they had. They had gone through an explosive growth phase, and they were spending $100 million a year on hardware. We couldn't believe it. Here was this little company that had been living its whole life, and we hadn't spent $10 million.

So Jeff said, "OK, Brewster, you know how to do this stuff cheaply. What should we do?" I said, "You should stop buying hardware. You've bought plenty." He said, "OK, we're going to stop buying hardware." It caused enormous pain to their organization, but it was the right thing to do. They needed to become profitable. They learned a lot of lessons from this. They could use an outsider that was still inside. We were not as independent as a Bain Consultants or something like that, but we knew what we were talking about because we had actually built stuff. We dropped the cost of their Internet connections by 90 percent just by saying that you can go and negotiate deals in this and this way. So we paid for the acquisition of our company in the first year just by the capital costs that they saved.

AOL took our ideas and put them into their bloodstream and dispersed us—and properly, I'd say. Amazon kept it to the side and kept it moving and generating new ideas. Amazon spent the time; we had basically a full-day meeting with the top execs of Amazon every month. It was just an outrageous amount of time given to us, but that was because Jeff Bezos said "New ideas are going to come from these guys."

Charles Geschke
Cofounder, Adobe Systems

At Xerox PARC, Chuck Geschke and John Warnock developed a language called Interpress that would allow any computer to talk to any printer. When Xerox seemed slow to commercialize this technology, Geschke and Warnock started their own company, Adobe, to produce a successor of Interpress called PostScript.

PostScript made it possible to describe complex documents in a simple form. In 1983, Adobe partnered with Apple Computer to create Apple's new LaserWriter printer. When it was introduced in 1985 it created the "desktop publishing" industry. Adobe went public in 1986 and is the recognized industry leader in graphics and desktop publishing software through its typefaces and its popular Photoshop, Illustrator, and Acrobat applications.

Livingston: Take me back to the PARC days and why you started Adobe.

Geschke: I came to Xerox PARC when it was first beginning. I showed up in October of '72. When I first arrived, I had a fairly straightforward task of bringing up a machine that simulated a then-mainframe computer that, for various political reasons, the researchers couldn't buy but wanted to use. So we basically built our own mainframe. When that project was done, I got involved in programming languages and developed the tools that were used to build the Star workstation, which came out around the same time as the IBM PC—a little before it actually.

PARC was an amazing place. The recruiting for computer science was done primarily by a guy named Bob Taylor. He had been the head of ARPA's Information Processing Technology Group, which had funded many of the universities that started up in computing in the late '60s and early '70s. He knew where all of the talented people were and he did his best to hire as many of them as possible. So when you go through that list of people who were there at PARC during those early years, it's sort of a who's who of folks who eventually migrated on to other things—as did John and I—into other parts of Silicon Valley.

By the fall of 1977, in my office there, I had a personal computer with a bitmap display—oriented like a sheet of paper, not like a television set for the obvious Xerox reasons. I had a software program running on it that was as good as Microsoft Word—in fact it was developed by the fellow who left PARC and went to Microsoft and built the Office product line for them, Charles Simonyi. I had a great mail system on it that could mail to anybody in the ARPANET community, as well as within Xerox. It was on the precursor of the 3Com Ethernet technology, developed by Bob Metcalfe, who later left PARC and started 3Com. The network connected the personal computers to laser printers. We had a 60-page-a-minute black-and-white laser printer, a 10-page-a-minute color printer. We had a file server where you could store files and share them for projects. All of these computers were connected in both an internal and external network throughout Xerox Corporation and into the ARPANET, which was the precursor of the Internet. All of this was at Xerox PARC in 1977.

That fall, we put on a demonstration for the Xerox senior management. Periodically they would bring in about 250 of the leading managers around the world for a conference and a little bit of socializing. We were given one of the days to put on a vision of what the future could be for Xerox. We leased two DC-10s (personal computers weren't so small back then) and flew all this stuff out to Florida and set up the equivalent of a trade show to show Xerox management what we had.

It was a very enlightening experience. The body language of the Xerox executives was to fold their arms over their chests, sort of stand back, look at this stuff, make some pithy remarks. If you've ever been in sales, you know that this is someone who doesn't want to buy, is probably a little afraid of what he's seeing because he doesn't completely understand it, and hopes it goes away quickly.

Since this was a social event as well, everybody was invited to bring their spouses and significant others. I think all of those 250 executives were men at the time. Most of them had wives, many of whom had worked in offices. They loved this stuff. They sat down and played with the mouse, they changed a few things on the screen, they hit the print button and it looked the same on paper as it did on the screen. They said, "Wow, this is really cool. This would really change an office if it had this technology."

When that event was over and we had the postmortems and discussions with Xerox management, it became pretty obvious that we were in an uphill battle to get them to understand what they had and what its potential was. Remember that 1977 was 4 years before the introduction of the IBM PC and long before the Macintosh. In fairness to the management, I think we as researchers were a little naïve about what it would take to get these things from conceptual operating prototypes all the way to full-production, supportable products. But we sort of hoped that they would hire the people who could do that.

Shortly after that, I was given the opportunity to start up a new laboratory within PARC focused primarily in graphics and printing technologies, and one of my first jobs was to hire a chief scientist to be the head researcher. I had known John Warnock by reputation. In fact, he gave a talk when I was a graduate student at Carnegie Mellon. He was just finishing his thesis at the University of Utah in graphics. But we never really met or spent any time together. So I called him up, we had lunch. He had a beard, I had a beard; he had three kids (two boys and a girl), I had three kids (two boys and a girl); he refereed soccer, I refereed soccer. We hit it off. I made him a job offer, which he accepted, and he interviewed at PARC and became the chief scientist in this laboratory.

We began to focus on the problem of how to take a variety of different printers—different speeds, different characteristics, some black-and-white, some color (we already knew about ink jet technology even though it wasn't broadly available at the time)—how do you integrate that all so that any computer could talk to any printer? We did a project for Xerox called Interpress. It was actually the precursor of PostScript, which was the first technology developed at Adobe. The idea was that you could build a network of printers and computers and they could all talk to one another.

We showed Interpress to Xerox management and they were extremely excited about it. They said, "We're going to promote this as an internal standard that we're going to use on all our products." I said, "That's fantastic. When can we start the marketing program to go out and talk to the world about that?" They said, "Oh, wait a minute. At Xerox it takes us at least 7 years to bring a product out." I said, "7 years? In our industry, that's two to three generations. This will be very old news by the time you get a product out, and the world will have passed us by." "Sorry, that's how fast we can get a product out and so that's what we're going to do."

That made both John and me very frustrated. We were talking one day and he said, "I'm going to go and see if there's a way that we can take our ideas and start our own business." His thesis advisor at the University of Utah was a man by the name of Dave Evans, and Dave sat on the board of Hambrecht & Quist, a venture capital company up in San Francisco. He introduced us to Bill Hambrecht, and we went up and met with him. The idea that we talked about was to build laser printers and typesetting equipment that could produce not only text, but also images—imagesetters they're called today—combine that with all of the software and market it to the Fortune 500 as internal publishing systems that they could use to have more control and more rapid response in their printing needs.

Bill liked the idea—partly because he was always frustrated with the financial printers to get his prospectuses out—and so he said that he would support it. "But neither one of you guys have ever run a business before, right?" And we said, "That's correct." He said, "Well, I've checked around and you have a lot of respect in the technical community, but I'm going to hire a guy to be a consultant for you who is a marketing person. He'll help you write a business plan because I need to have a business plan to talk to the investors."

We said, "Fine." So we wrote our business plan. John and I had managed enough projects that we knew what the costs would be to bring out a first product. We put that together in a plan, gave it to Bill, and he said, "Fine, you can quit your jobs." We said, "We don't exactly have the money yet." He said, "You'll have to trust me." So John and I quit. Bill loaned us $50,000 just as a personal note so that we could go out and start leasing a Vax computer to do our work on. We eventually found the name Adobe Systems and we were in business.

Livingston: How did you choose the name Adobe?

Geschke: We originally started thinking of names that were vaguely associated with what we were going to do, and we ran into the problem that there were so many corporations founded in California that it was difficult to get a unique name. So we thought, "Well, maybe we shouldn't put too much of what we're going to do in our name, because who knows where this will lead?" At PARC, we literally threw a dart at the map when we were starting a new project and needed a code name. If it landed on a river or a town, then that was the name of the project. I was looking at a map of this area and I noticed Adobe Creek—in fact, it runs right behind my house—and I said, "How about Adobe?" John thought about it and said, "Fine." And that's how Adobe Systems came to be.

Livingston: So you and John quit your jobs at the same time?

Geschke: Yes. My father and mother thought I had lost my mind, because I had this great job at Xerox, a nice big office overlooking the whole Bay Area. They said, "What are you doing?" I said, "You know, my ego may get bruised if this doesn't work, but I'll always have a job. If you have a PhD in computer science, you're not going to be looking for work very long. This is something to give a try and branch out on our own."

Livingston: You were about 40 when you did this. You had a family; were you nervous about starting a startup?

Geschke: Both John and I were in our early 40s. Maybe my kids were nervous that I wouldn't be able to put them through college, but no, I really wasn't nervous because I knew I could get another great job, partly from the experience at PARC and from watching people in the venture world. I knew one founder who seemed to get more money every time one of his companies failed than the last time! You fail and people figure that you won't make that set of mistakes the next time.

So I never really felt scared. The only thing that would have been hard to deal with would be the stigma of failing. But I thought we had a reasonable chance of succeeding.

The first thing we did was find a place, through a friend of John's who sold commercial real estate. We got a place over in Mountain View, a few thousand square feet. We began talking to people about hiring them, and of course we talked to people we knew. Initially, most were currently at PARC or had recently been at PARC.

Before long I got a phone call from one of my professors at Carnegie Mellon, Gordon Bell, who had since left Carnegie and gone back to Digital

Equipment and was running research and development for the company. He said, "I hear you started a business and I want to come out and talk to you about what you're doing." So he came out and we showed him. We explained our business plan about building the computers and the printers and putting it all together in a package and he said, "That all sounds great, but I don't need computers. I'm Digital Equipment. I already have a deal with Ricoh for laser printers, so I don't need the printers. My problem is that I've got several development teams trying to build the software to interface between the two of them and they're getting nowhere. That's very frustrating to me. Why don't you just sell me the software?"—which we had already shown him, the precursor of what became PostScript—"That's what I need."

We said, "Well, Gordon, we raised $2.5 million and this is our business plan and that's what we're going to do." He said, "I'm disappointed, but if you change your mind, give me a call."

About 2 months later we got a call from a fellow by the name of Bob Belleville, who had been at Xerox and then had moved on to Apple and was responsible for the overall engineering management for the Macintosh. He said, "I want to bring Steve Jobs over and see what you guys are doing." So they came over, we went through the same spiel, and Steve said, "I've got this computer coming out called the Macintosh," which he showed us, and he said, "so I don't need a computer. And I have a deal with Canon on the laser printer. But the development team trying to interface between the computer and printer is just failing miserably. Why don't you sell me your company?" We said, "Steve, we're not for sale, we're really out to build a business on our own." He said, "All right, why don't you just sell me the software?" We said, "We have this business plan, we raised $2.5 million, and this is what we said we're going to do." He said, "I think you guys are crazy. Think about it a little bit and I'll call you back."

So John and I went to talk to the fellow that Bill Hambrecht had asked to chair our board, named Q.T. Wiles. He'd been in business for a long time and, when we described what had happened with both of these episodes, he said, "You guys are nuts. Throw out your business plan. Your customers—or potential customers—are telling you what your business should be. The business plan was only used to get you the money. Why don't you rewrite a business plan that is focused just on providing what your customers want?"

We called back Steve Jobs and he said, "Great! Sell me your company." We said, "Steve, we're not for sale." He said, "Well, all right." And basically he helped construct a proposal for how we would license him this software. We agreed on a royalty per printer. We also closed a deal shortly after that with Digital Equipment.

We began developing the laser printer for Apple, which eventually became the LaserWriter. We signed an agreement with Apple in December 1983, roughly a year after we went into business (we incorporated in December 1982). Unlike any startups that I'm aware of, we turned a profit within our first 12 months, as a result of that contract with Apple. So it's a very atypical story. Steve did a prepayment on royalties to make sure we had the resources to stay in business, and Apple also bought a little less than 20 percent of the company, which quintupled the value of the original investors' money. Steve wanted to make sure that we would finish this product, because it was critical for him that he have the LaserWriter.

In the meantime, we were talking to other companies—IBM and other folks. We had deliberately not gone to IBM early because we knew that, if we didn't have a couple of business deals in hand, they would be extremely difficult, if not impossible, to negotiate with.

We found that we were outgrowing our facilities in Mountain View, so after about a year, we moved into a larger building on Embarcadero across from the Palo Alto Golf Club. By about the fall of 1984, we had the LaserWriter pretty well completed and we ran into a hiccup. Steve had gone to his annual sales meeting in Hawaii with the senior sales management at Apple, and it was the first time that he really spent time talking to them about this new product, the LaserWriter. They all got very upset. They said, "We can't possibly sell a printer that costs more than the computer!" (In fact, inside of this printer was a more powerful computer than the Macintosh.)

Livingston: Because that's where all the pages were actually rendered?

Geschke: That's where the pages were rendered, and that's where all of the type was generated. It was a sophisticated computer and so it cost a lot of money. RAM prices had just gone up the preceding year. Fortunately, right before the product hit the market, RAM prices came back down. It had to have 1.5 MB of RAM, which seems tiny today, but in those days it was a lot of memory.

So he came back from that meeting and sent his marketing guy and Bob Belleville to talk to us and they said, "We think we may end up canceling this product if we can't do something about this."

John and I called up Steve and we sat down with him and said, "This will be a disaster. You really have got to get this product out because it's the only thing that's going to differentiate you from IBM." He agreed, and then he told us that RAM prices had just dipped again. So it didn't matter what his salespeople said; he said, "I'm going to put this machine out."

So he did, and it got a great deal of fanfare when it was introduced—people really loved it. There were industry analysts like Jonathan Seybold, who were very in touch with the publishing industry and were following computers' influence and the changes going on. As soon as he saw it, he completely got it and understood what was happening.

At the same time the LaserWriter was introduced, we introduced a piece of typesetting equipment, which was a full image setter, with Linotype Corporation, and announced that we had licensed the Linotype typeface library. It was extremely important for the publishing customers to know that they had the trade names of the original type vendors in the products and in the technology that we developed.

So the product launch went out and it was very well received, but as we began to track sales, while there was the initial pent-up demand, as it got toward summer, the sales began to drop off. Everybody got pretty worried about what was happening. At that time, Apple was marketing their computers and the LaserWriter around a marketing program called the Macintosh office, which was an attempt to take IBM head-on. And frankly, it was not going well. It was very hard to replace all those feet on the street in corporate America, "You've never lost your job buying IBM,"—all the stuff you've heard.

Fortunately, there was a young marketing guy at Apple named John Scull, who was aware of what was going on (as were we) at Aldus up in Seattle, because PageMaker came out at the same time as the LaserWriter did. He came up with the idea of getting the three companies—Apple, Aldus, and Adobe—together to put together a marketing campaign called "desktop publishing." That had a huge impact on Apple, Adobe, and Aldus, and on the publishing industry, and completely turned around the fortunes of the Macintosh and the LaserWriter.

Livingston: Because the desktop publishing idea was brand new?

Geschke: Yes. Up until then, people used basically analog, labor-intensive technologies.

It turns out my grandfather and father were both letterpress photo engravers, and so I knew what it was like to work with the etching baths and the copper plates and all of the emulsions and everything. It was very toxic work, very expensive and very labor intensive. What we were beginning to demonstrate pretty early on was that you could do as good, if not better, quality using a computer and PostScript than you could with the old analog technologies.

Desktop publishing became very popular. For an investment of a few thousand dollars you could, in effect, be your own printer and publisher. So it opened up a whole lot of new businesses. As graphic artists and designers began to learn how to use a computer, we brought out products like Adobe Illustrator. All of a sudden, the whole industry began to move, and within less than a decade the entire printing and publishing industry went from the old analog world completely over to the digital world. That was a tremendous thing to see, and of course it was a huge benefit to us.

Livingston: When you first started, you planned to build the computer, the printer, and the programming language that would make everything talk. Did you have a name for it before it was called PostScript?

Geschke: No, PostScript was the name that we picked shortly after we started our business.

Livingston: Did you use the same ideas that were in Interpress?

Geschke: There were several things that weren't done in Interpress. It wasn't really a programming language the way PostScript was; it was a little more static. And in the design of Interpress, we never were able to figure out how to deal with type. In the world before Adobe, the presumption was that to get high-quality type at laser printer resolutions, let alone ink jet resolutions, you would have to hand-tune bitmaps for every type style and every point size. Extremely labor intensive. Also, what would look good on a laser printer wouldn't necessarily look good on an ink jet printer and probably not look at all good on a computer screen. So in fact you not only had to design for different point sizes and different typefaces, but you had to design for different imaging devices. If you begin doing all that multiplication, you could hire all of the high-tech workers in China and not keep up. It wasn't going to work.

Livingston: So you created scalable fonts?

Geschke: We came up with the idea of using a pure mathematical description of the outline of the type and then worked on some sophisticated algorithms about how to decide which bits to turn on and which ones not to turn on to give the highest-quality rendering on the particular device. That was really the breakthrough technology that differentiated PostScript from anything that preceded it, including Interpress.

Livingston: When you were working on Interpress, what were some of the big ideas that you couldn't believe that Xerox didn't appreciate?

Geschke: At a conceptual level, it was the same idea as PostScript. From any computer running any kind of application software, you could, over the network, interface to any printer at any resolution, any characteristics, and be guaranteed that the file would transport between the two. For a company that's in the printing business, such as Xerox, that meant they only had to provide a single digital interface on the front end and they could connect to anything. The converse was also true for software writers, because they could print to this PostScript string and it would look good on any PostScript printer. And the same was true for platform vendors like Apple and Microsoft: they only had to write one print driver to be able to generate output for any PostScript device—or would have for a Xerox device running Interpress.

Livingston: Did you build the hardware for the printer too?

Geschke: We helped design it in concert with people at Apple. We did not manufacture it, but we did know some of the design characteristics that it needed to have in order to be able to handle both the rasterization of PostScript and some things about how it had to control the engine to get the best possible output. But that was a shared piece of work and the hardware belonged to Apple. Eventually we did do some hardware design, and we would offer the designs to our OEM customers so that they wouldn't have to start with a blank sheet of paper—so they could get to market faster. But we never really went into the manufacturing business.

Livingston: Why did Apple and DEC have such difficulty in creating what you guys did?

Geschke: I think it was partly a lack of understanding of the requirements of the printing and publishing industry. Even though John's background wasn't as closely tied to it as mine, he had worked for a company called Evans & Sutherland who did contract development for a lot of high-tech companies including RR Donnelley in Chicago, which was at one time the largest printer in the United States, maybe in the world. So he had a pretty good appreciation of what was involved. Plus, with his graphics background, he understood the issues about the conversion from an abstract definition in terms of the mathematics of a shape and how to get that into raster data that would drive a bitmap printer or a bitmap display.

It was a combination of all those skills and backgrounds that he and I had that put us in a unique position. And then the good fortune to get a business deal with two or three very important customers early on.

Livingston: Did your work at PARC on the programming language Mesa give you any critical insights that helped you make PostScript better?

Geschke: Not directly. Mesa was very focused on conventional programming, the kind that was done to build operating systems. It had one characteristic that conceptually is similar to PostScript, in that in both Mesa and PostScript, we had the idea that you didn't have to program at the level of the machine. In PostScript, you can program at a higher level, in a language that is more in tune with what you wanted to print as opposed to how it printed. In Mesa, we actually developed both a programming language for programmers to organize large, complex programs and a machine that would take the output of that language and operate on it very efficiently. That was built into the Star workstation that Xerox introduced in 1981.

Livingston: What were some other major turning points?

Geschke: Well, certainly if you remember back to that time in the office printing market, HP was in a very strong leadership position with the LaserJet. When we found out from HP that they wanted to come back and talk to us, that was a very important moment because we were, in fact, able to sign an agreement with HP and have them adopt PostScript on their LaserJet printers. That was a big coup for us as a company. It was at the same time that we managed to sign up IBM. So our strategy of not going to IBM early had paid off. Once they saw the market mushrooming for Apple, both IBM and HP decided they had to pay attention to it and that's how we got those business deals.

The other lesson that we had to learn, though, is that you can't be a one-product company. There's a very high risk when you're a single-product company that eventually a combination of changes in the technological landscape and changes in the competitive landscape will eventually cause you to begin losing market share. And once you lose market share, then your revenue and earnings begin to fall. Fortunately, we had decided that in order to be able to really demonstrate the capability that was inside the LaserWriter, we couldn't rely on the standard business applications—and even the graphics applications—that were out there. If you remember, Apple had a product called MacDraw, and they had another product called MacPaint. They were organized around the concept that you were going to be doing your printing on an ImageWriter; they didn't have the characteristics that could really show off the fact that the LaserWriter was in fact a full printing press. On the LaserWriter, you could combine graphics and images and text in innovative ways that none of the application packages were enabling. More importantly, designers knew they wanted to be more creative but had no tools to enable their creative expression.

But there was also another reason for developing Illustrator. John's wife was a graphic designer, and once we brought out the LaserWriter, she wanted to get some of her design concepts out on that machine. So John was programming in PostScript by hand to get this output to come out and he said, "This is stupid. I need to build a tool that behaves more like what a graphic artist would expect to have in terms of pen and ink and drawing and so forth, and then let the tool write the PostScript code." So that's where Illustrator came from.

It was introduced in the winter of 1987. We also had been working with scanning equipment and photographs. Scanners were still very expensive at that time and so there wasn't a lot of opportunity in the area of photography yet, but we instinctively knew it was going to come.

We were introduced to two brothers from Michigan: Tom and John Knoll. They had built a package that would let you work with a photographic image and change it, modify it, enhance it, do a variety of things. But of course it was doing that on a Macintosh with 512K of RAM, a little black-and-white monitor screen, no color, a disk drive that maybe held 10 or 20 megs. There were no digital cameras and scanners cost $20,000. But the software looked really good. We thought that this had to be a great idea eventually and it was the missing component. There were applications that produced text. We had Illustrator, an application that could produce line art and drawings. But we didn't have an application that could deal with photographs, even though the printer could print them. So we began investing in Photoshop, and we paid a lot of attention to the Japanese who were beginning to work on digital cameras and lower-cost scanners. We introduced Photoshop probably 2 or 3 years before the market was ready for it.

I am not a hunter, never have fired a gun, but I'm told that if you want to shoot a duck, you have to shoot where the duck is going to be, not where the duck is. It's the same with introducing technology: if you're only focused on the market today, by the time you introduce your solution to that problem, there'll probably be several others already entrenched. It will be hard to dislodge them, and hard to convince people that what you have is so much better that they should make a change. Much better to figure out where the marketplace is going to be in a few years, focus on providing a solution to that, and let the market forces catch up to you. That's what we did with Photoshop and it turned out to have been a great decision for us, and good for the Knoll brothers. It paid a lot of royalties for their work and developed a whole industry around digital cameras and digital photography.

Livingston: If you were coming out a little before the market was ready for your products, did you ever have people just not understand how great the products were?

Geschke: In those early renditions of the product, we would focus on a select community of people who understood both technology and the potential. So we would market primarily through technical analysts and product research kinds of people, and not attempt to go to a mass market, because there was no mass market.

We also had to fight the antibodies inside the company. When we introduced Illustrator, we realized that the profit margins were going to be very different because we had to actually package the software, distribute it physically, build business relationships with a different sales channel—because when we sold PostScript, we sold directly to the major OEMs, so we literally only had tens of customers for PostScript. Now we had to get thousands and eventually millions. Very different business proposition, very different market, different sales channel. So there were a lot of people inside the company who said, "This is crazy. We're going to invest all this money in this? What if it doesn't work? We're going to lose our profitability."

John and I were convinced early on not only that you couldn't restrict yourself to a single product, but you couldn't restrict yourself to a single sales channel to get your product to market either. Business relationships can eventually decay or fall apart and then you're stuck. You have no way to get your products out and no way to respond to the market.

Livingston: Did Adobe have any major relationships decay?

Geschke: Of course. The most famous one was in the fall of 1989. We had been working on technology to make high-quality text on the display, not just the printed page. Up until that time, all text on computer displays were bitmaps that were handcrafted. We wanted to be able to demonstrate that you could use the same technology on the screen that you used on the printed page.

Apple had actually been working on that for a while. Their technology was called TrueType. We were trying to market our solution to Apple, not with a lot of success. By then Steve Jobs had left. He'd been the primary Adobe champion inside Apple. Now Jean-Louis Gassée had taken over the product side of the business, and for whatever reason, Jean-Louis and Adobe never got along. So we were beginning to really have a problem with Apple. They were getting tired of paying us royalties for the LaserWriter; they thought that they shouldn't have to pay anymore.

We decided that one way to deal with that would be to convince Microsoft that they should adopt our technology for Windows. In fact, we were able to get one of their biggest customers at the time, IBM, to agree to adopt our technology on both OS/2 and on their versions of Windows. But when we tried to sell it to Microsoft, we just couldn't come to a business deal. The thing that was frustrating is that it was already proven technology. We could demo it. And we already had all typeface licenses set up with the major vendors, so you knew that you would have that requirement satisfied, and, more importantly, we weren't going to charge. We were trying to give our customers the same feeling on both Macintosh and Windows machines, so we wouldn't be forcing them to make a decision about whose products to buy in order to use our technology. It had always been our strategy to be platform-neutral.

It came to a head at the Seybold Conference in San Francisco in September of 1989. Microsoft told us they weren't going to license our technology and, in fact, that they were going to form an alliance with Apple. So our biggest customer and our biggest competitor got together on the stage, and Bill Gates announced that he was going with TrueType for Windows and that he had acquired a clone implementation of PostScript, which he would license to Apple so Apple would no longer have to pay royalties to Adobe. On the platform that morning were Gates, Steve Jobs talking about NeXT, and John Warnock (he and I used to alternate and he was the lucky guy who was on stage that year).

This quote has been repeated a lot because John spoke after Gates, and Gates had talked about how this was going to improve the world for publishing and printing—but they couldn't even demo the technology at the time. John got up and he said, "I've never heard so much garbage mumbo jumbo in all my life." And then he proceeded to talk about Adobe Type Manager (ATM) and what we were going to do. Once we learned the Apple-Microsoft alliance was going to happen, we decided that our only response would be to get to market immediately and to make ATM available on both the Apple and Microsoft platforms as an aftermarket product very inexpensively. I no longer remember the price, but it may have been $99, which at the time was considered very low-priced for software.

We sold hundreds of thousands of units in the first year, and it took Apple and Microsoft 3 years before they ever actually shipped a product. By then it was a moot point. During that time, Apple decided that they couldn't build a product using a clone implementation, so they came back and redid the PostScript deal with us.

The thing that was really most important, as a startup—though by then we weren't really a startup—by then we were public, but a young company—is the relationship that we had built with our customers. We wanted them to feel that a) they were given a decent deal and that b) they trusted us to lead them to where they needed to go. So at that same conference, the organizers decided very quickly to put an extra panel on the last day and have a live debate over whether the attendees—and this was all the major players in printing and publishing—preferred to have Apple and Microsoft take over their future or whether they wanted to stay with Adobe. Before the panel started, the moderator got up and said, "I'd like to get a feeling for what the sense of the group is before we start this. I'd like everyone who wants Apple and Microsoft to succeed in putting Adobe out of business to raise their hands." There were a few Apple and Microsoft employees in the audience, but out of about 1,500 people, only a couple dozen hands were raised.

So that reinforced a message that John and I had always preached inside the company about how to treat our customers. Listen to them very carefully. Understand what their requirements are and what their needs are. Not necessarily do what they asked us to do, but to have the vision to do more than they expected. We had worked religiously at that. We had indoctrinated in all of our employees that you treat a customer the way you'd like to be treated. That you are responsible for that customer's success and, if you fail at your job, you may cause their business to fail. I think sometimes the cynics would look at that and say, "That's sort of goody-two-shoes. Maybe this guy's reading too much of the Bible or something." But it's just good business. And that event demonstrated it; basically everybody voted for us. In fact, while there was a hiccup in the stock because of the Apple-Microsoft announcement, our business never faltered.

Livingston: Why weren't Microsoft and Apple able to make a competitive product?

Geschke: They were mostly working on speculation of what they thought they could do. When we were talking to Microsoft and Apple about licensing this technology from us, we already had working prototypes. They were an example of what a poor duck hunter does. They were shooting at where we already were, and we were long past them by the time they were able to bring that product out. It became basically irrelevant to the market.

Livingston: Was there ever a competitor out there in the early years that you worried about?

Geschke: There were some. When we got our money for that original business plan, there were about half a dozen companies who had raised money to do something similar. Not the same, but similar. Fortunately, the other five all executed that business plan, and we didn't. And they all disappeared.

It shows you the power of getting good advice and having the nerve to take that advice. Because literally, there were half a dozen companies all formed within about a 12- to 18-month period with venture capital both on the East Coast and out here in Silicon Valley, all trying to do the same thing. And sometimes, when they would get up and talk at events and conferences, that would be pretty scary.

HP continued competing with us with the LaserJet—we could see the potential that over time, some of their products, especially in the office, would become good enough. It also became clear that once ink jet technology became higher quality and lower cost and of comparable speeds, we wouldn't be able to put our software on a controller in the printer, because the printers were throwaway devices. They were just razors and the money was in the blades. So we began really pushing hard on other products and other market opportunities knowing that eventually PostScript would fade as a revenue opportunity for us.

Today we still have laser printer contracts with a number of manufacturers—probably the biggest one now is Xerox, ironically—and several image setter contracts with the companies who make high-end printing equipment, but there's very little business in the desktop market and none in the ink jet business for PostScript. So while it's still a profitable piece of our business, it's certainly no longer critical. Acrobat and our other retail products and now the acquisition of Macromedia have more than taken over for PostScript.

So the other lesson is that you have to be willing to move on, even if you've got a real success. That was, in fact, the same problem that Xerox had. Because the 914, the original copier, was so successful, they couldn't look at a business that didn't have a "b" in the dollar amount. Unfortunately, new businesses start out small and grow. You have to be willing to make some risky decisions and invest in them in the hopes that a few of them will succeed. Xerox was not very good at that. Hopefully they've gotten better over the years.

Livingston: PARC was famous for overlooking the commercial value of things. Were you surprised that they didn't see the value of what you and John were working on?

Geschke: I wasn't so surprised by our experience with Interpress, because I had seen what had happened with all the other technologies that preceded it. They never figured a way to commercialize the Ethernet. They had managed to commercialize the original laser printer (it was called the 9700), but it was for mainframe computers; it replaced line printers. Line printers were the old printers that used to be on mainframe computers, and they were big, noisy devices that could only print text. The 9700 could print pages that were more sophisticated. But it was mainframe printing, it wasn't office printing, and it wasn't focused around publishing and the graphic arts. If you look at a typical office memo coming out today, you would never have seen anything like that 20 years ago. It would have been Courier or Elite typefaces on a typewriter. It's all completely different now and people don't even think about it. They just have expectations that the text will look high-quality, that it will be proportionately spaced, and the pages will contain illustrations and photographs.

Livingston: We just take for granted what you guys created.

Geschke: That's what's really cool. That's when you know you've had an impact. I know I can speak for John on this too, but the biggest thrill is frankly not the financial success, it's the ability to have an impact. Because we're both engineers at heart and that's every engineer's dream—to build something that millions of people will use.

People with no training in the graphic arts could now develop materials that got a message across and did it more dramatically. I remember very early on, I gave a talk in Chicago somewhere—some guy in a small brokerage business somehow convinced me to give a talk. He said, "We use your stuff, but we always print it in Courier (which is the typewriter typeface) because people who see it printed in a high-quality typeface think it's old news." You see, he was on a cusp of a change. Now people don't think about it that way, but in those days, if it didn't come out in Courier, it must have gone to a printer and a typesetter and it must have taken 2 to 3 weeks to get prepared.

Livingston: What surprised you most about the early days?

Geschke: To me, the most surprising thing was how responsive people in the publishing industry were to accept and embrace change. After thinking about it later, I realized that as I had listened to my dad talk about his profession—and he of course told me never to go into the printing business—it was because he recognized intuitively that change had to happen in that industry. He wasn't sure where it was coming from but he knew it wasn't just doing what he did better or more efficiently. It was going to come from somewhere else. So I suspect it was a market that was already looking for a solution and we provided it at the right time.

The amount of printing has not decreased because of the "paperless office," it's increased. We're the people (Adobe and the others we've partnered with) who are responsible for all those catalogs you get in the mail. If you think back 25 years ago, you didn't receive many catalogs. They were too expensive to produce.

Livingston: If you had a background in printing, did you create the products to purposely encourage good design?

Geschke: I understood the difference between good and bad design. We also understood that, if you are in the hammer business, you can't require that a person who buys a hammer be a good carpenter, so we opened up our tools to a much larger community. And some of the early printouts looked like ransom notes. People would put every available typeface on one page, which is not good design. So there was a lot of bad design going on. It wasn't the fault of the technology; it was the fact that people were given a new medium from their point of view, as opposed to the professional's point of view, and they were struggling to figure out how to do it well.

I think that's gotten a lot better—not perfect, but better. More importantly, the people who are great designers have been given more creative freedom now. They can do things at a lower cost and faster than they ever could have before. A lot of design work now wouldn't have been practical to try to do some other way using hand methods, but now with the ability to manipulate layers within photographs and do all this kind of really sophisticated kind of art, people can do design that they never could do before. What we believed in very strongly was that the rules of quality for what was produced were not set by the computer industry, but by the publishing industry. It didn't matter whether or not some guy at IBM thought it looked good. What mattered was someone at Random House or Time-Life or Ogilvy & Mather or someone like that appreciated it.

I remember in the early days bringing home our first color separation work and showing it to my dad. He still had an engraver's loupe. He pulled out his loupe and he looked at the halftone patterns and he looked up at me and said, "Not very good." And I said, "I know, but it's going to get better." And then a few years later I brought home something that I knew was pretty good. I showed it to my dad and didn't say much. He looked up with a big smile on his face and said, "Now that's good." That was a wonderful moment.

Livingston: Is there anything that Adobe does now to preserve the efficiency or the "startupyness" of a young company?

Geschke: It gets harder as you get bigger. What John and I have tried to do as chairs of the board is to reinforce to the current CEO, Bruce Chizen, the importance of innovation and the importance of taking some of the investment of the company and not immediately pouring it back into the current businesses.

As I described earlier, as we were trying to develop our retail sales channel, people thought that was a waste of time and money. The product lines that are bringing in the most revenue believe that they have a right to all the resources of the company. Part of good management, and part of the attitude of a startup, is to recognize that, while those businesses are incredibly successful today and you hope they'll be successful for a long time, the law of averages and experience tells you that at some point they will peak and they will probably begin to decay. So you've got to be investing today in what your future's going to be 5 or 10 years out.

We do try to maintain that attitude; we try and have projects focused on new ideas and concepts, but it's hard. So we've done a combination of both internal investment over the years and acquisitions. We've done several acquisitions of the style of Photoshop, where we've seen a new idea and a new concept partially developed and we can bring in the resources of getting it to market and integrating it with other products to make it much more successful than the group could have done probably on their own.

Livingston: You and John are engineers and researchers, yet you were the main executives up until a few years ago. You were obviously better at running a business than originally predicted back when you raised money.

Geschke: I don't think there's any mystery in running a business. I think it helped that we were in our 40s, that we had worked for a variety of organizations. We had worked in other companies, but tried to leave their bad ideas as proprietary to them. We tried to pick the best things that we saw.

When we started, we wanted to build a company that we would like to work at and we kept applying that criterion. I remember, when we first hired people in the original days, John and I would take turns hand-delivering a dozen roses to the spouse if it was woman, a bottle of cognac if the spouse was a man, and then champagne to the employee.

We did that for the first 18 months and then it got to be too much and we started giving it to them at work. I suspect we don't do that anymore. Doing things like that to make people feel like they were part of a community helped build a rapport inside the company so that our turnover rate has been among the lowest in the Valley ever since we've been in business. Particularly with people who are the top performers, our turnover rate has been not only single digit, but typically 1 or 2 percent. And that's because we've made it an interesting and rewarding place to work. So I get frustrated sometimes by people who have never run a business who are legislating things like stock option accounting and so on. They don't have a clue of what it takes to run a business.

Livingston: Is there any other advice you would give to someone who was thinking of starting a startup?

Geschke: If you aren't passionate about what you are going to do, don't do it. Work smart and not long, because you need to preserve all of your life, not just your work life. One of the things that I felt really good about is that we—from the very first employees, including John and me—enabled telecommuting from day one. So everybody had a phone line and a modem and a terminal in their house, the day they joined the company. (Now, of course, they have their own personal computers and everything).

It's devious, because I suspect we got a lot more hours of work out of them. It's the same reason we give them a great lunch at a discount price.

Ann Winblad
Cofounder, Open Systems, Hummer Winblad

In 1976, Ann Winblad started Open Systems, an accounting software company, with the help of $500 she borrowed from her brother. The advent of the microprocessor and the first affordable PCs created a new opportunity for programmers. Winblad was one of the first generation of entrepreneurs who figured out by trial and error what a software startup was. Six years later, she and her cofounders sold the company for over $15 million.

In 1989, she cofounded Hummer Winblad Venture Partners, the first venture firm to focus exclusively on software. In the years since, 45 of its portfolio companies have been acquired or gone public. Now Winblad is probably the most powerful woman in venture capital.

Livingston: Tell me a little about your background, how you were first introduced to software, and why you first thought about starting your own company.

Winblad: I've always had to figure out ways to make a living and supplement my income, even as a young girl. I grew up the oldest of six kids. My dad was a high school basketball coach and a social studies teacher. My mom was a nurse. She didn't work while I was a young girl because I had four sisters and a brother who were even younger than me. In order to have extra money, we had to find ways to earn it. I was always trying to figure out ways to monetize anything in order to have money to go to the movies or to buy clothes or things that don't come out of a very middle class–income family.

I was given an extraordinary opportunity when I started college. They picked students with the top SAT scores and top grades as "experimental" students. As a result, I did not have to take any prerequisites, so it allowed me to take a lot more focused courseware than most students. I could do whatever I wanted. If you wanted to get in a class even though it was not your declared major, they would have to take you. In a liberal arts school at that time it was very hard to double major because, by the time you took all the prerequisites to lay the foundation for your liberal arts education, you only had time for one major. So I was able to double major in mathematics and business administration and also fill in a whole bunch of other classes, like computer science and acting, that most students wouldn't have.

In the '70s in the Minneapolis/St. Paul area, there were a number of young, but growing, colleges: College of St. Thomas, Macalester College, the College of St. Catherine, Augsburg College, and Hamline College. They had what was called a five-college cooperative. They were all within a couple miles of each other near Summit Avenue in St. Paul. You could take classes at all these colleges. So because I wasn't just cemented to my own college and I was sort of given a hall pass to anything, I said, "Well, I was planning on being a math major, but maybe I'll do this business major thing too. And by the way, maybe I'll take computer science classes." The combination of being a math and science person and then—instead of waiting linearly and taking the business classes, like an MBA, later—seeing how business is applied, that was a magical thing for me.

When I went into the accounting classes in the business major and all the guys—I was the only woman there—were sweating bullets, "How to do debits and credits?" and I was taking set theory down the hall in my math major, I thought, "Oh man, I could break into this business field pretty easily." I knew nothing about business. One of my uncles was an architect and had his own firm, but that was it in my family. So there was no sense of how businesses got started, and back then they didn't teach entrepreneurial classes. Because there was so much unknown, you felt like you were so well-equipped—sort of Superwomanish. "I have a business major, I have a math major. I must be really prepared." They didn't have a computer science major, but I took all the classes they had. At the end, I had enough credits to graduate, but I had extra time, so I thought, "OK, how do I get myself to be well-rounded? I'll take some acting classes."

I made a real attempt to be well-rounded and totally equipped—having no clue how ill-equipped you are as an undergraduate. You have no experiential knowledge whatsoever. We didn't have internships, which now even all the undergrads have at St. Thomas. We had no international travel, no semesters abroad. So you were really much more naïve as a student graduating in the '70s—even with a double major and a minor and some other good stuff thrown in. But I felt empowered.

The early '70s was a big era of affirmative action and companies were forced to go hire women. I was interviewed for some really interesting jobs, and one that I thought sounded really great was this job at the Federal Reserve Bank. It was a brand new building, built by one of I.M. Pei's designers. The president of that Federal Reserve Bank was a really young guy. They had all state-of-the-art hardware, software, and furniture for the time, so it felt like, "Wow, I get to be in this brand new hot place, the Federal Reserve Bank." That sounds like an oxymoron saying it now. The truth was that all these jobs they were recruiting for affirmative action, if you weren't really a competent young woman, you would fail. There was a gap between skills and jobs because they had to hire you and they had to hire you in stretch positions to get women populated. In fact, I got my masters degree at night and Saturdays while at the Federal Reserve Bank, and I was only the second woman in the whole Federal Reserve banking system that had a masters degree. In the whole Fed system!

When I went there, it was the first real business experience I had—although I had had part time jobs. I'd never been in a corporation, and it felt so glamorous to have a cubicle. Minneapolis is a bright city. There's the Nicollet Mall and you were right downtown in the city. It's like getting a job in San Francisco.

But it just wasn't inspiring. No one was chomping at the bit. I actually can't remember—I knew I was going to quit, but I can't remember the moment where I thought, "I'll quit and start a company." I still felt very empowered, like, "This isn't this hard a job. This is a big job and I've already gotten promoted once in the first 3 months and I know I can earn money. I can always come back to this, so why don't I break out?" So the three guys from the Federal Reserve that started the company with me—one guy did quit his job and the other two took a year sabbatical, just in case this didn't work. They held on to the safety ring.

There were not a bunch of people saying, "Start a company, start a company. Let's do this. Let's build something from scratch." It's so long ago now that I just remember the general feeling that there was very little to risk. I was somehow already fully trained for anything that might confront me. Of course, all that is false; there's a lot of risk and you are never fully equipped to . . . you just have to be very adaptable. It turned out I was adaptable. I didn't know that until I did that, but it was just a feeling of fearlessness. "What's the risk? What will I have to lose? I'm sure I can do this." It was not cockiness, just that moment you feel in your youthfulness that you are sort of empowered to achieve.

I think what does separate some entrepreneurs from other entrepreneurs is we're not handwringers. We don't worry about the unknown. We don't really worry about the risk points ahead. As you get older and you get more experience, you train yourself to think ahead about the risk points versus just to take the next hill. But non–risk-takers and non-entrepreneurs would really have big headaches about this. They would need some level of comfort and safety.

That's something that we look for in entrepreneurs—that they have the courage to do the job. That they'll have the ability to judge the business situation. They'll have the ability to lead people. They'll have the ability to interact with the marketplace and to really build confidence into strategy.

Livingston: I read that you initially started out as a consulting company and you would do the "real" startup project at night, even though you hadn't figured out exactly what you planned to do.

Winblad: Yes. We did that because no one had any money. There wasn't a Y Combinator around to even give us $6000. In fact, I exhausted all of my savings on the incorporation fees and was about $500 short, which I had to borrow from my brother, who was in high school. But he had a job. He was the only one who had $500 to borrow from that I knew. So we had to find a way to cover ourselves.

We see a lot of entrepreneurs that do this. That they actually find a way to earn some money, but they don't . . . they find a way to separate that from the business itself. Where entrepreneurs try to mush the two together like, "Well, let's compromise the real business to sort of get more money in versus let's find a way to get money to cover the real business and leave it uncompromised." But they have to perform some unnatural acts to get started, which is what we did.

We were chosen under a Request for Proposal bid to build a student accounting system for a vocational school in the state of Minnesota, which helped us focus on what we were going to do. We had to really say, "OK, how good's our accounting knowledge?"—which had nothing to do with student accounting; this was grading systems tied to student accounting. It was really a one-off. It also told us how we could underestimate a project, how we would manage a project, how we would manage engineers, how we would manage our own time. And we got paid for learning on the job. All of us owe a lot to the person who took the risk on people who looked like children, who had no work experience other than the . . . the other three guys had been at the Federal Reserve Bank longer. They were each about 4 years older than me, so they had 3 and 1/2 years of work experience and I had 13 months.

We were overly thoughtful about what we would do. When it came down to "what special skills do we have," we went back to that accounting class and in fact opened up my college accounting book and said, "Let's start programming this from scratch and build accounting systems for smaller computers."

Livingston: Was this before personal computers were even out there?

Winblad: They were coming really fast. Hobbyist computers already started appearing. Now the year is 1975—remember that's the year that Microsoft started and Microsoft was writing Basic for kit computers. We didn't have as good soldering skills as probably Bill and Paul did. And we, of course, weren't working at the systems level writing the operating systems and languages, so we first applied ours to a minicomputer. They were not on commodity processors. They basically were pretty much like a high-end PC would be today.

We skipped a whole small era of computers that all got wiped off the planet. Microsoft talks about how their first 80 customers died. Well, we had some of those customers but very, very few. We moved into the PC market as the 8080A—which was the first Intel commodity processor, came out on a computer called CADO. The company was in Torrance, California, and funded by Sequoia. This was about 1978, maybe '77 even. They were using commodity processors—the first Intel processors—but a proprietary operating system. As a result, we had to go find a language vendor because Microsoft's Basic was so weak, we couldn't program a robust accounting system in it. We worked with a language vendor that we OEMed, so we sold our product with an interpreter. A very fast interpreter, so it never had to touch Microsoft's young languages, which was good because there was not a salvageable application software business. The application vendors that started at that time all died as well.

That 13 months at the Fed and the 3 years the other guys had really was a lot of computing experience relative to most people who were the first entrepreneurs in the industry. They really were programming on kits—they were hobbyist programmers in their garage. Because it was a new generation of people starting and we just happened to catch the tip—even though we weren't any different in age than these people of the last year of computing—so we got some real computer science knowledge and that really did save our bacon and allow us not to have to restart the company. We were on a steady growth path from the beginning.

Livingston: Do you remember any major turning points?

Winblad: There were so many things that happened. Sometimes they almost feel like acts of God.

We were doing all this work for these CADO computer guys. And there were many things we didn't know—like pricing strategy or how do you collect money from people? So I remember one very unsophisticated thing, in that we had been working with CADO and they said, "We're going to get all of our resellers together. Since you're the big application vendor, come and give a presentation and pitch them."

So I get in front of these 60 or 70 guys and these guys are probably all in their 50s and I'm in my 20s, and we had a "blue light special," where we said, "If you give me a check today for $10,000, you can have unlimited rights to one of our modules"—the general ledger or something like that. "But you have to write me a check today." These guys are looking at me like I'm goofy and I'm thinking, "Well, maybe they don't believe this great offer." (This is how naïve I am.) One guy says, "Well, we don't carry our corporate checkbooks around." And I go, "Well, you must have your personal checkbooks?" And they go, "Yeah." And I'm thinking, "Oh yeah, how are they going to pay us?" So I said, "I'm sure your company will reimburse you and, if you want to, put a note not to cash the check until Monday, but I need the check today." And the CADO guys are looking at me like, "OK, what is she doing?"

That day I remember very well . . . it was in the back of a warehouse because they manufactured these computers and it was a big building in Torrance, and it was nice and sunny there. They gave me a crate to stand on because the podium was so large for me. I stood on this crate and started going through the specifications of our product, and George Ryan, the CEO, said, "We're going to take a break now." And he said, "Ann, after the break, you gotta jazz it up a little bit. If you're gonna run with the big dogs, you gotta learn how to lift your leg." That really empowered me to ask for that $10,000.

George Ryan was a great sales guy. The fact that he had this young girl there hustling software and so these guys are saying, "Well, we can't write a check." And I say, "Won't your companies reimburse you?" I went home with, I think, like 12 or 15 of these $10,000 checks in my purse. For a young company, it felt like carrying gold around. We now have $120,000—all at one time! So that was pretty seminal . . . of course today, things like that wouldn't work. It was a very unsophisticated market; we were their only choice. Probably, thinking back, half the guys wrote the check because they just wanted me to be successful.

I think this is something that people underestimate—that there are always people out there rooting for you. That is probably part of what you have to develop. They probably went back to their offices and said the following: "We got a great deal on this software and this great little company—I think those guys might be successful—called Open Systems. And this young woman got up there, and she had the balls—or stupidity—to ask us each to rip out checks for $10,000."

It was such a big victory and we didn't have cell phones at that time, so I'm on the pay phone in the airport going, "I've got $120,000 in my handbag!" We did a lot of creative things that in hindsight were very, very thoughtful. I was very fortunate that these three guys—that we all challenged each other quite a bit, that no one thought anybody's idea was better than the other's. So we had to vet our ideas against each other and sort of "win" amongst each other—the best strategy, idea, whatever. You're very lucky if you have an ensemble early on where no one just sort of accepts that you make all the calls. That you are really working in the beginning as an ensemble.

When we fund early-stage companies, even though there is a CEO named, in most cases in the ensemble, it is an ensemble. That's sort of what you look for: is there an early ensemble where everyone's rowing the oars and looking at where the boat is going and watching out for each other? That it is not sort of the "Let's get the org chart together and you'll lead us all."

We did have an office in an apartment building and the first real vacation I took, I got a phone call that there had been a fire, which, of course, was the indication that we should move out. The fire burned my old cheerleading letters, old yearbooks and memorabilia, but, miraculously, it didn't touch our computers or our software.

It was like, OK, you burn up the useless stuff. That stuff's nice to have, but you look at it once every 30 years.

Livingston: How did the fire start?

Winblad: It was in an air conditioning unit in the back of the building. It was just faulty wiring. The building was built in the '20s and it was a cheap building. It was a five-bedroom apartment I'd rented in a beautiful area of Minneapolis called Kenwood, but it was a dump of a building. It had beautiful wood floors and a bunch of rooms and a big dining room and living room. The dining room was a computer room, and the kitchen was big. So we had four offices, plus my bedroom, which I could use as my own office as long as I straightened it up every day. Then the living room we used as a cubicled area for the rest of the guys, but it was more than time to move out of there. That was another, "It's time to really either fish or cut bait here. Well, I guess we're going to have to move to a real office now."

And that does change the real demeanor of the company. Once you start committing to leases, furniture, a capital budget; it does change the cadence of a company for the better. You can only virtualize the company for a very short period of time.

Livingston: Do you remember a time when people misunderstood what you were doing because it was so new?

Winblad: My parents thought I was pretty much over the top because I had this very prestigious job at the Federal Reserve Bank and went to work every day from my apartment to this beautiful bank and got promoted and made a bunch of money for my age. Why would I quit? It was very hard to communicate to people who weren't in the very small software industry what you were doing. People didn't question you; they couldn't even converse with you.

At Thanksgiving: "What do you do again? . . . OK, thanks, that sounds really interesting." Minnesota was very different back then than out here. People didn't quit their jobs and start these companies.

Although, once you become an entrepreneur, it's sort of like becoming an alien. You notice there are other aliens! There they are, they've done that too. How did you do that? It was mostly hard to converse about . . . you couldn't get wisdom from anyone. Comments like, "What would you do with this software company?" "What's a software company?" It was such a nascent industry, and that's really a gift to join a nascent industry that becomes a real one. If you're in the group grope phase, you can make tons of mistakes. Because there is no one else competing with you or nipping at your legs. It's a completely green field.

Livingston: Did you have competitors that you worried about?

Winblad: We didn't ever worry about competitors. There were, over time, other companies that started with various different offerings in what was called "accounting software" then. But again, nobody had any market share—100 percent is available for everyone, so we wouldn't get it all anyway. It wasn't a competitive thing.

As we got into the '80s, then it was clear that we should try to find leverage points for the business versus just do it on our own, and we should also learn from other players' successes. And we weren't competing head-on for customers, because you could look this way and see different customers and they could look that way. There was the show called Comdex (Computer Dealer Exposition), which doesn't exist anymore, and everybody sold their products through computer resellers and, shortly after that, retail stores like ComputerLand or BusinessLand. Comdex was the best thing that ever occurred for us. You could see everybody there. It was pretty small in the beginning; it was all in the one Hilton Convention Center in Las Vegas. We had some really interesting experiences there because we had to decide whether we should spend a bunch of money on a really nice booth.

How do you do a booth for a trade show? Who do you ask? Nobody knows. So we started searching around for someone who has done booths for trade shows, and we find this woman. Her name was Betty. I have no idea what's happened to Betty, because she was probably in her 60s then, so she would be 90 now.

Betty was this trooper woman—she was a little woman and very skilled—and she said, "Oh yeah, I know how to build you a booth." We said, "OK, fine," and we didn't really pay any attention. She built a solid wood booth. It was not plywood, but like solid oak. It was beautiful, and it had neon signs. So then somebody says, "Well, we have to ship it." Do you know how much it costs to ship a solid wood booth from Minnesota to Las Vegas?

Of course we didn't know when you went to Comdex, you had to hire a contractor if you wanted a plant, a contractor if you wanted anything plugged in; if you had neon, you had to hire a separate contractor. So our first big Comdex, I decide to go over early to see how our big, solid wood booth had arrived and how was it looking and how we all were going to interact in the booth. You're walking in the hall and you say, "Well, there's our competitor's booth. Gee, they've got all their material lying out already (the night before); I think I'll just read it." So I went from booth to booth and read all the competitors' offers. I thought, "Well, they could be in here too; I'm not sneaking around. It's fair game."

So I thought, "I better hustle over to our booth and say, 'Don't put anything out during non-show hours,' because clearly these competitors are not that sharp in just laying this stuff around, but they might get sharper in the daytime." I get near our booth, and there was a medic there and all sorts of lights and I thought, "Oh my God, did Betty have a heart attack?" Because somebody 60 seemed like 100 then. It turns out that we had this big tower—a solid wood tower—and from the wood tower was this neon sign that said "Open Systems." It required one of those small cranes to crane it up and connect it. The guy on the crane, while connecting our neon, had fallen in the tower upside down and was stuck in there. So the medic wanted to saw our tower in half to get him out. Betty was basically hugging the tower saying, "That will ruin our booth!"

I was thinking, "Oh God. I've already invested more money than I ever thought in this thing. I shipped this heavy sucker halfway across the planet to get from Minneapolis to Las Vegas. I'm the only person who's got a solid wood booth here—it's beautiful, but, you know, it's solid. And now somebody wants to take a chainsaw to it." I said, "Is the guy dying?" And they said, "He's clearly hurt his collarbone, so he could go into shock and we don't know about his general health." I said, "Can't you just pull him up by his feet?" Of course, as a result of this, all of our neon sign had shattered. So they pulled him up by his feet and got him out of there without sawing our booth in half and now we had no signage. So we had a solid wood booth, with no signage.

So Betty says, "I'll just call up and get the neon fixed. We are in Las Vegas." It turns out that back then all the neon work was done in Los Angeles. So we had to have someone build us a new neon sign in real time for thousands of dollars overnight. It was like, "Man, this is booth hell."

I could go on and on and on about all these on-the-job training things you learn . . . We had to shrink-wrap our software to get it into retail stores. Well, how do you shrink-wrap something? I don't know. I now know. We had to buy shrink-wrap machines. Where do you get those? No one knows. So we start looking in industrial classifieds, and we find a pizza company that had gone out of business that's selling a shrink-wrap machine. So we stuck it in a back room, and whenever we had to ship 100 boxes, we'd go back there and shrink-wrap them and our office smelled like burned cheese. It would be like, "OK, let's try to do that after hours so the whole office doesn't smell like burned cheese." Later, we had forklifts and conveyor belts and the whole thing, because we had palettes of software we had to ship around the country. I never had a college class on any of this.

Livingston: There were no mentors? People who had gone through it before?

Winblad: It was so new. There were many mentors who had gone through business—we had a great lawyer. But he'd never built a software company. He didn't ship booths around the country or shrink-wrap software. Or license software. Nobody had. Rumor has it that Lotus thought it was so cool to have the shrink-wrap machines that, whenever they'd ship a new product, they would shrink-wrap the head programmer and unwrap him quick before he smothered to death. I don't know if that's fact or fiction.

So for us, it was never stressful because we didn't feel the cadence of competitors on us. It was tiring and it was hard, but it was a lot of fun. It was like, "OK, now what?"

Livingston: Was there ever a time when you wanted to quit?

Winblad: No. You also learn how to optimize your time, and you get really good at that. You do it wrong—and I see entrepreneurs do this, "Let's get up earlier and stay up later." I started putting the stuff I needed to read in my bed so, when I'd wake up, it would be there to read, so I'd maximize my time. You're young, and you are really sort of superhuman. But you are not very efficient doing that, so that's where people who become your business colleagues start saying, "That's not going to work." That's stuff that you do get help from friends and advisors. Like, "Hey, you are better off taking a month-long vacation and turning stuff over and getting fully rested and charging at it again than trying to figure out how you might personally live off 4 hours of sleep a night forever."

Livingston: Looking back, do you think you were a typical founder?

Winblad: Yes. I think that I had all the good parts of a typical founder and all the bad parts of a typical founder. You get good at figuring things out so that you don't just view every problem as if it needs a brand new lens, which, of course, it doesn't. And you learn on the job, so you do a lot of things poorly. Unless you've managed people before, you don't really know how to do that well. So you have to build skills. I think it's really interesting being a venture capitalist because, when you've got 30 years of experience, then your challenge is how to teach and not tell. Because you want people to figure it out. You want to make sure that you can grab them by the coattails if they are falling off a cliff, but you want them to discover the edges by themselves.

That's the biggest challenge of moving from being a business leader to being a business investor. Your job is not to tell, but to teach.

Livingston: Do you think you are a better judge of good management teams because you were once a startup founder yourself?

Winblad: Oh yeah. Because you see examples all the time. I do personal references myself. Whenever I'm going to join a board, I will ask people for personal references. Your friends, your business colleagues, whatever. I'll address these references as these are not going to make or break this deal, but I want to understand this person. How do they work, how do they think? How do they get themselves in corners? Or twitterpated? What do they need to be surrounded by to be successful?

You do learn that people get to be fully formed adults fairly early and it's hard to change people's behavior, although it is easy to cushion how they behave with people that buffer their weaknesses. As you go along, you get more microscopic in understanding people before you invest in them if you are going to sit on the board specifically. You can't fully trust your judgment because some people are good actors, but it's always interesting talking to people's personal references.

Livingston: What kind of mistakes do you see new entrepreneurs make?

Winblad: One of the big mistakes is that, when you form a company, there's a difference between being an inventor and being entrepreneurial to leading a company—being the CEO or, especially, the leader. You're not fending for yourself anymore. You're actually fending for shareholders.

They can't be fending for their salary; they can't be fending for their net worth. They have to really focus on building value in the company for all shareholders. That sounds very sort of lawyerish, but it's true. Some never can make that jump fully. So engagement is never on building the company while someone is watching to help them along. Just like George Ryan, at CADO, which I mentioned earlier—he needed my company to be successful in order for all the software to work for his resellers. He needed me to be successful because I was a core component of the company. So he was not just looking out for me, he was looking out for my company as well and making sure I learned how to look out for my company. And that jump to "It's not about you; it's really about a broader thing, the company, which broadly is the shareholders, which broadly is the customers, which broadly is the employees, which broadly is your mission, which broadly is the values you bring into the company." There are some entrepreneurs that never really fully get out of the "me" thing. And that changes them from being the "inventor" entrepreneur to being the business leader entrepreneur.

Livingston: Are you able to predict this better now that you have had so much experience as an investor?

Winblad: Well, if there was a perfect lens on this, it would be easier. Most companies do not fail because some competitor crushed them. There's a small amount of failures where the competition was underestimated. There's a small amount in the software category where the technical achievement needed to bring a high-value product could never be reached. But the majority of companies fail by self-inflicted wounds by the leadership team. That stuff is all under your control. We have the biggest challenge in software companies: the core value is the intellectual capital. It's everything. And when there are big flaws in the leadership team that you can't remedy quickly, the company will die of self-inflicted wounds.

Livingston: Why don't more women start software startups?

Winblad: You know, I don't know the answer to this. I was at an IBM event recently, and Sam Palmisano, in sort of the midst of his extemporaneous presentation at this event, said, "My daughter, who is 13, is a math whiz, and she was just really focused on math and now that she's 13, she's worried about appearing too nerdy." It was sort of like a segue and then he went back onto the speech, "So I don't know if she'll stick with it." I wrote him a thank you note, and I said, "It was really great to be included in this IBM event. It was a great event, and I caught that little sidebar that you said about your 13-year-old daughter, and I hope we can do a better job . . . some of the successful women in the software industry—myself, Carol Bartz, Heidi Roizen—all of us were math whizzes and we had really fun teenage lives as well as adult lives and have been very successful."

It's, first of all, a small number of women and an increasingly small number of any gender being inspired by math and science. It's a big problem. You'd think, "Hey, this week in the news, the richest guy in the world—Bill Gates—the President of China is spending more time with him than the President. Steve Jobs, with this aspirational product, the iPod. Why don't you want to be those guys?" They have inspirational products, inspirational lives, and it's not like we're under-covered in the media. Something is getting lost in the message here, where it should be really inspiring: "All I have to do is figure out this math-and-science thing, and I'm writing part of my ticket here." Why that is not pulling not only women, but pulling everybody to say, "I want to be like those people," I don't know.

You'd think that everybody would want to have our jobs. We've all been handsomely rewarded. The stories are not like, "Hey, we had patrician backgrounds and silver spoons, and we bought our way into this." We just "thought" our way into these industries. The power of thought and math and science and computing, you're given that for free—it's a choice you can make. You take that choice, and it gives you sort of a magic wand to be a captain of an industry that's still fairly young, that's driving the whole world economy. I don't know. This is just a mystery to me. Women running these companies have very rich lives. I don't know.

Livingston: What is your top advice that you give to founders starting companies?

Winblad: We try not to give too much prescriptive advice. "Think like a big dog and then figure out how you find leverage to get there." You have to have tactics to get to strategies, but you have to have a strategy, and you have to put your strategy up here and then see "Where's my gap" to get to this aspirational goal. You're always going to be short of people, you're always going to be short of money, you're going to be short of source supply value. So you have to find leverage points, versus working your way up through tiny little rungs and seeing if you get there. Think like a big dog, and find leverage to get there.

David Heinemeier Hansson
Partner, 37signals

David Heinemeier Hansson helped transform 37signals from a consulting company to a product company in early 2004. He wrote the company's first product, Basecamp, an online project management tool. He also wrote companion products Backpack, Ta-da List, and Campfire.

In July 2004, he released the layer of software that underlies these applications as an open source web development framework. Ruby on Rails has since become one of the most popular tools among web developers and won Heinemeier Hansson the Hacker of the Year award at OSCON in 2005.

In July 2006 (after this interview), 37signals president Jason Fried announced on the company's blog that Jeff Bezos had made a minority private equity investment.

Livingston: 37signals wasn't begun as a startup, correct?

Heinemeier Hansson: 37signals was founded by Jason Fried as a web design shop in 1999. It transitioned from a consulting company to a product company with the creation of Basecamp. I'm part of the 37signals 2.0 management team.

Livingston: So the launch of Basecamp was a pivotal turning point for the company?

Heinemeier Hansson: It was not an overnight transition. While we were developing Basecamp, 37signals had a lot of client work, so we couldn't dedicate more than about a third of our time to it. It wasn't a client project; it was something that we created as an internal tool to help us manage our client work.

Livingston: Take me back to the time of the Basecamp launch and the transition.

Heinemeier Hansson: I was working with 37signals as a contractor while I was finishing my bachelor's degree. They did the design and I did the programming. After a few years, it became clear that they needed a tool to manage the client project process. One person wouldn't know what the other was doing. It was pretty disorganized and starting to look unprofessional.

The idea came to us that blogging had been a pretty good way of distributing information between people. I had been blogging personally on Loud Thinking and 37signals had Signal vs. Noise. So we wondered, what would happen if you took that blogging idea and applied it to project management?

That was how we got started: the project blog was the first part of Basecamp that was made. We got it up in about a month and then we started using it to manage Basecamp itself. So it became self-contained very quickly in the sense that we were using Basecamp to build Basecamp.

As we showed it to colleagues in the industry, we quickly realized that others had the same problem; there was not a lot of software available for small companies to manage projects. Microsoft Project and the other heavyweight approaches to this relied on critical path management and things that might work fine for a 200-person project on a construction site, but not well for 3 people trying to deliver a web application.

So we started out just thinking, "This is going to help us solve our consultancy needs." And as we got more feedback, we realized it was a good time to start thinking about how we could make this 37signals's product.

Livingston: Do you remember the moment?

Heinemeier Hansson: It was more just a flow of the application coming together and the feedback we started to get from people we respected saying, "I want this too!" We thought, "This is something that it would be selfish to keep to ourselves."

Livingston: What were the features that people liked most when they saw it?

Heinemeier Hansson: The funny thing is that most people were impressed by all the stuff Basecamp didn't do. They were used to these big, honking products that tried to do everything, where they just needed something simple.

We had this dilemma that either you had MS Project or you had email, and there's a huge gap between them. Managing a project by sending emails back and forth is messy and doesn't work, but otherwise you had to adapt your process to what's mandated from these other heavyweight applications.

Basecamp was basically just trying to be one step above email. And by setting such a humble goal, we had to make a lot of decisions about how simple we could make things. We tried to make less software from the very beginning. It's one of the mantras we have. It's a win whenever we can get away with just a simple model, since we have to do less programming. I was the only programmer and I was dedicating 10 hours a week to this, while we were developing it.

37signals was paying me to do this out of its consultancy revenue, since we didn't have funds to fund it. So we had only a quarter of a programmer dedicated to the development and no funds really for doing this. The designers were giving it a third of their time at most. And we realized through this process that those constraints—which sound negative—were actually the greatest gift to the development of Basecamp.

That whole constrained development model really focused our view on what we needed, and it forced us to make tough decisions about making less software all the time. And we keep getting feedback from customers that say, "I love this, it's just so simple to use. It's got just the features I need and not all the other stuff." There wasn't time for us to say, "Wouldn't it be cool to do this and that?"

It turns out that when you build only software that you absolutely need, you don't get more software than you'll actually use. And that's why we didn't fear competition from the big guys. If Microsoft decided to go after Basecamp, they'd say, "Get a team of 20 people to do this and we'll give them 6 months to come up with something." Because when you're in a big corporate environment, you throw a lot of resources at projects. You just could never arrive at the type of product that Basecamp is when you don't work under constraints like we did. It's just too tempting to try to do it all, or at least do too much.

It wasn't necessarily that we were great programmers and designers, but because we embraced the constraints that forced that upon us. If we took the same people and put them in an environment where we had all the money and time we wanted, *we* couldn't even make Basecamp again.

Livingston: Did you worry about any competitive products?

Heinemeier Hansson: There have been a few businesses that have tried to do similar things, but most of them try to do the full management of projects: billing, time tracking, and other things that we've never tried to solve.

We picked a few simple things: a project weblog, milestones tracking, file and to-do list sharing. And we haven't really expanded beyond that; we've just tried to refine those few simple elements.

The funny thing is that another reason Basecamp is a success is because it's not more focused. We started out wanting to make a tool for creative services businesses, like us. But we never actually wound up including things that were specific to creative services, like billing, time tracking, etc. So people use Basecamp for all kinds of projects, like managing weddings, home improvement projects, and student collaboration. The only reason that we're attracting all those people who just need help with project management is because we're not trying to be more specific.

And that's why I think that if we had had more money and time to add features specific to creative services businesses, we would have shut off our entire market to all these other people who are using Basecamp for types of projects that we didn't even imagine.

Livingston: So you built this new project and didn't have a marketing budget. What happened next?

Heinemeier Hansson: We didn't spend a dollar on advertising when it launched. Though Basecamp is a monthly service, you don't need to pay anything when you first sign up. If you just need to manage a single project, the product is free for life. So a lot of people got in just testing it out for a certain project.

As soon as they realize that they'd like to use it again on another project, there's an upgrade path for them to go down. They can buy the first paid version that gives them three projects and gives them file uploading for $9 a month. So we have a shallow upgrading curve where you can go from paying nothing to paying very little. The most expensive version is only $99 a month. And because we charge on a monthly basis, customers get the advantages of low risk. People can sign up for two months, and if it's not what they want, they can cancel easily. And that's been one of the most powerful marketing tools.

Also, Signal vs. Noise had a fairly large following in the web development community. The first big market for Basecamp was these creative services firms. Since they were already reading about what 37signals was doing, we went the other way around: first we built the audience and then we figured out a product. We blogged about Basecamp even before its launch, making previews, and it was viral from there. So it helped that 37signals had a big audience and had an easy way of selling into that audience.

The majority of our new customers have heard about it from someone else or read something about it on the blog. They sign up for the free version and then, that's the best lead you could ever get. It doesn't cost us anything in the first place and doesn't cost us that much to keep the lead, because, though they get one project for life, we have a large group of people who are now friendly to the product we're selling because we just gave them something for free that they're actually using. And we're not yanking it away in 30 days. So this builds a lot of goodwill in the early phases of the relationship with the customer. It's a really powerful way of selling.

Livingston: Did anything go wrong?

Heinemeier Hansson: We made a bunch of mistakes. We got the launch pushed back by almost a month. Initially, we thought that we were going to bill people once a year, $99, $299, and $499 for the different plans. We built this entire billing system, which was a sizable amount of the development time. We didn't figure out that the bank wouldn't let us bill this way until about 3 days before we were ready to launch. The bank wouldn't let us sell a service that we were going to promise for an entire year, because they'd be on the hook for the money if we went out of business a few months into a $500 agreement. They wouldn't allow that because we didn't have a long history with them.

So now we had this extensive billing system focused on billing once a year and we couldn't use it. We had to go back and make it monthly instead. But this turned out also to be a blessing. So we pushed back the launch about a month, and now we charged monthly, *but* we charged twice as much. The plan that was before $99 a year is now $19 a month, $224 a year instead. So we actually got to raise the prices and at the same time create a less risky offer for small companies since they didn't have to buy a whole year.

One of the technical mistakes that we made early on was that we had this notion that Basecamp was for creative services firms. Set up like that, you have a firm and you have a client, so it's a one-to-one relationship. That assumption went very deep. For instance, in the database there's a client ID and firm ID, and now that people were using it, you'd have setups where people wanted two firms. So now what did we do? Basecamp simply couldn't do that. And that assumption was so deep at the roots of the system that it took us about a year and a half to fix, which was not a good thing.

Another interesting mistake was that we didn't consider time zones. Basecamp ran with the assumption for the longest time that everybody is in Central Standard Time, even though I was in Copenhagen, which is a 7-hour time difference from Chicago. So people in Australia would get their milestones one day late. We didn't really care about time, because we didn't usually have fixed deadlines. We had stuff we wanted to do, but it didn't really matter whether it was 2 hours later or 2 hours earlier. Of course, not every firm works like that.

And it was also disguised by the fact that Basecamp didn't use a lot of time. The only place where we displayed the time itself was on the comments. On the posts themselves, it just said the date and the milestone. So you wouldn't be able to discover that, unless you were in that central time zone, it was off. In Denmark, for 7 hours after midnight, the system would say it was yesterday. So it was a big deal for the firms that needed specific times. And it was always a big deal to people in Australia. Half of the time they would be off by one day. We've gone back to fix that problem too.

Livingston: Were you the only programmer?

Heinemeier Hansson: I was until February 2005 when we brought on our second programmer. Yes, for well over a year, I was the only programmer and systems administrator on Basecamp.

Livingston: In addition to all your responsibilities, you were also starting the Rails project. How did you manage it?

Heinemeier Hansson: When you have to do a project like Basecamp and you only have 10 hours a week, you can't spend your time on things that don't produce anything. So you get extremely aware of tools that aren't necessarily helping your productivity and you go seeking tools that can help.

That's how I found Ruby. It was such a nice experience for me and a nice productivity booster. I was coming from PHP. I had also looked at Java and other environments and I wasn't finding anything else that would allow me, as a single programmer, to deliver all this stuff.

And I then built Rails on top of Ruby to allow me to build Basecamp and drive this project in the way that we wanted to. Because we didn't want to bring on more programmers. We wanted to keep those constraints that we had and so we just had to make tools that allowed us to do that. And I think that's also a big explanation for why Rails is having the success that it is: it was born in an environment that was so focused on productivity and was so focused on being able to deliver within constraints. I'm building Rails while I'm building Basecamp—rather, I'm building Basecamp, and every step of the way, I'm extracting Rails.

So I'm doing what I need to do for Basecamp, then figuring, "Hey, this looks generic, I could pull this piece out and put it into the toolbox Rails." And as time goes by, this toolbox gets larger and larger and somewhere in the process I realized that this generic toolbox that I had was actually a very useful toolbox and perhaps other people could use that too to do the same thing we were doing at 37signals, use less resources and build less software.

When we launched Basecamp, it was 4,000 lines of code—so not very much. One guy who's now involved with Rails told me that they had a single configuration file in XML that was 5,000 lines!

We released Basecamp in February 2005, and by then I knew that I wanted to release Rails. We went through the hectic time after releasing Basecamp where we would keep on pushing a whole bunch of new features.

We always give a major update within 30 days after we launch a new product. Because that's really something that reinforces people's feelings about the project. If they buy in on day one and then they see a major new update after 2 weeks, they're really pleased. So for us, one of the secrets about how we market the product is to make sure that launch is not the end. We don't say, "Whew, we're done now," and then go on vacation. It's then when you keep on pushing to show this product is alive.

So that happened in February and then we had pretty much a finished framework for Rails, but I didn't want to release it yet, because I wanted to document it. I'd been using open source software for so long that I was really annoyed that a lot of it had terrible documentation. I didn't want that to happen to Rails, so I kept it back about 2 months, and then pushed it out about 3 or 4 months after Basecamp.

Livingston: Was there ever a time when you felt you couldn't do all this?

Heinemeier Hansson: Sometimes, but whenever we had those feelings we viewed them as clues that we were trying to do too much, so we'd think, "How could we make this feature require less engineering and programming?" And we got into a pretty good mode that, whenever we wanted to do something new, we would brainstorm some ideas and try to look for the idea that required the least amount of work.

And I had this same thing in the development of Rails. When you try to do 100 percent of what somebody wants, you need a perfect match, and it's pretty rare that you have a perfect match between what you thought people needed and what they actually need. If you just try instead to do 80 percent of what they need, there's a pretty good chance that you'll hit a sweet spot.

So Rails is really about trying to get that 80 percent all the time and not really caring about those last 20 percent that are really specific to the situation that you're in. When Rails launched, it was just 1,000 lines of code. So even though we've done all these things, there's no superhuman strength involved. We aren't producing more lines of software than everybody else; we're just making each line count for so much more.

Livingston: So, much of your innovation was driven by your own needs, rather than your clients' requests?

Heinemeier Hansson: Very much so. It's good to be market-driven in the sense that you should know what's going on, but you can't let your customers drive your product development. You need to be able to innovate on behalf of your customers, but they often don't know what they want. And it's the same thing for programmers. If you went around and asked them what they wanted in a framework, you wouldn't get a good product out of that. You need to be able to source input from a lot of sources, and then have your vision of what it's going to be and then drive that.

You need to drive both framework development and product development with a strong vision, where you're not afraid to turn somebody off. We're not afraid to say to a customer, "Maybe Basecamp is not for you. If you want those five things, maybe you should go look for something else."

Livingston: Now that you have received a lot of publicity, have you been wooed by investors?

Heinemeier Hansson: Yeah. We've gotten quite a lot of VC calls. But one of the things we're seeing that we really don't care too much for is that way too many companies are taking money when they don't need it. And the whole idea we had was that having too little money is a great way of getting great product, because it's a way to get focused.

So we have definitely said to ourselves, "We don't want any outside money. We actually don't even want to grow our team." We're trying to design our products in a way that they can scale with more users without us having to scale as a company. So, through Signal vs. Noise, we're trying to deliver a pushback to companies that feel like they have to hire a bunch of people as early as possible and to take money to realize their vision by saying, "If your vision of your product costs a million bucks to make, try rescoping that idea in your head so it fits in $100K and get it out there earlier. Instead of having a 1-year product cycle, what could you do in 1 month?"

And sure, that doesn't work for every company, but in the web age, it works for way more companies than are trying to.

Livingston: Might you ever get acquired?

Heinemeier Hansson: We're not that focused on that at all, but we're not ignorant to the world that we're living in. There's no urgency though, because we're a profitable company just doing what we do. If somebody comes tomorrow and offers us $100 million, I'd be pretty foolish to say, "No, never."

Livingston: What's been the most surprising thing?

Heinemeier Hansson: I think I'm fairly surprised that we've been able to stay true to our initial values. Since we launched Basecamp, we've added only one more person, even though the product has grown like crazy. I'm definitely surprised that we've been able to grow and not write a whole lot of software, and still make a difference.

Livingston: Was it challenging having several of the 37signals team in different places?

Heinemeier Hansson: We view it as advantageous actually, because the 7-hour time difference leads to "alone" time. In a company where everyone is in the same place, it's very easy to walk down the hall and interrupt somebody. If you're part of a distributed team that's 7 hours off, you're bound to have a good portion of the day where you just get work done. There are no interruptions.

Another thing is that we communicate mainly through IM, which is a fairly low-bandwidth way of communicating, so you're not going to disrupt somebody unless you're going to say something that matters. If you meet in person, it's very easy to just talk for 30 minutes, and what was the information exchange actually about?

Philip Greenspun
Cofounder, ArsDigita

Photo by Ellis Vener

Philip Greenspun founded ArsDigita in 1997. Though the company lasted only a few years, ArsDigita is famous in the startup world both as the embodiment of a new model for software consulting and as an all-too-colorful example of the dangers of venture capital.

ArsDigita grew out of the software that Greenspun wrote for managing photo.net, a popular photography site. He released the software under an open source license and was soon deluged by requests from big companies for custom features. He and some friends founded ArsDigita in 1997 to take on such consulting projects.

Greenspun and his cofounders fostered a great sense of loyalty among users and employees. Like Google later, ArsDigita created an environment in which programmers reigned supreme. The company grew fast, and by 2000 was generating about $20 million in annual revenue from its monthly service contracts.

That same year, ArsDigita took $38 million from venture capitalists. Within weeks of the deal closing, conflict arose between the new investors and the founders. They marginalized and then fired most of the founders, who responded by retaking control of the company using a loophole the VCs had overlooked. The legal battle culminated in Greenspun's being bought out, and a few months later the company crashed. ArsDigita was dissolved in 2002, but not before establishing an important new model for the consulting business.

Livingston: Take me back to how ArsDigita got started.

Greenspun: I started building Internet applications in the early 1980s. I always liked multiuser applications, and I thought connecting people over the network—if they were separated in space and time—was just going to be the best usage of computer systems.

It was pretty hard to write popular applications that way though, because whatever you built would only work on one kind of computer system. You were building a system for HP UNIX or Apple Macintosh or maybe Windows, and each particular brand of computer could talk to each other over the network and let you edit a document together or let you play a game together. But because there was no standard operating system and no real standard programming environment, if you built it for the Macintosh, it wouldn't work for Windows, or vice versa.

Then the Web came along in the early '90s and, as soon as I saw it, I said, "OK, this is how all computer applications are going to be built in the future. I don't need to write all this custom code to the operating system anymore. I'll just build something that is specified on the server side, and the user experience will be rendered by the browser. It will have a simpler user interface, but it will be guaranteed to work on any kind of computer, and it will survive changes in operating systems." It pretty much has; I have plenty of web pages that I built in 1993, and here in 2006 people can still grab them, even though there have been a lot of changes in computer operating systems and software.

I told the professors at MIT that all I wanted to work on was Internet applications and they told me I was crazy—that there was no future in it. I decided that, since they weren't going to even talk to me about what I wanted to do, I'd leave MIT for a summer.

Livingston: You were a graduate student?

Greenspun: I was a grad student at MIT and was doing a combination of research and being a teaching assistant. So I went away for the summer—a driving trip to Alaska. I wrote a book chapter every week, but really it was a letter to my friends and family so that I would get interesting email back from them. I'd email it to my friends and family to spur their thinking and let them email back to me.

When I got back, I decided that I would stick these emails into HTML and scan the photos that I had given as a face-to-face slideshow and put them on a website so that my friends in California could see them.

The book was called *Travels with Samantha*. Samantha was my old laptop computer (I was in between dogs at the time). This book was pretty popular, but most of the questions that I got about it had to do with photography. I thought, "I'll write up a couple of short tutorials on photography and then I won't have to keep emailing answers to these questions one by one. But photography is open-ended; if you answer three questions, you raise five more. So I thought I'd build a question and answer forum on my server, and when someone asked me a question and I answered, it would be a public exchange, and then the next person who came to my site would see that public exchange, and if they had a similar question, they wouldn't post it again.

Pretty quickly I found that one reader would ask a question and then a second reader would answer it. I wasn't having to do anything at all. Things took on a life of their own and voila: an online community of photographers was born. I began to write more and more software to make this community easy to manage, and I was doing it all myself. Eventually I had this big toolkit of software that I had written for my own purposes.

This was in the mid '90s, and I noticed that other web publishers were trying to build similar things where people would come register at the site and exchange information and maybe go and try to buy something. The stuff was just broken. People's sites were down. They had bugs. If you tried to buy something, you'd get halfway through the checkout process and you'd get a server error. I thought, "All these people don't even have the fundamental ideas of how to put the server together, and we could just tell them, 'Look, this is how a medium-volume online community can be run off of a computer that's medium sized. You don't need a huge server farm. You don't need ten full-time sys admins.' We'll give them a data model of table definitions in SQL (we happened to use the Oracle database, which was the best one available at the time). We'll create some web scripts that talk to Oracle's data model, and they can modify it to suit their needs. It will start from our proven working core of an application and it will save them a lot of time."

SAP was a popular toolkit for building corporate accounting systems, and I would say, "This is like SAP, but for building an Internet application or an online community." I started by giving away my software. I just tried to document it and make it as general as possible and easy to install and stuck it on my website as a free open source thing. We gave it a name: the ArsDigita Community System. A kid I worked with thought it was a good name.

Then big companies started calling, and they'd say, "We like your system, but we need ten extra features." And I'd say, "Great. You have the source code and the documentation. Good luck." They'd say, "We want you to make the changes." I'd say, "Well, I'm busy. I need to finish my PhD. And it would take me 2 weeks to do it." They'd say, "No, we really need you to do it." "How many programmers do you have in your IT department?" "Ten thousand." "Well, if you've got ten thousand programmers and I'm just one guy, why do you want me to make the changes?" They'd say, "We'll pay you $100,000." "You'll give me $100,000 for 2 weeks of work?" "Yes, we just need this system up and running now."

After a few of those calls, some of my friends and I decided that we'd band together and have a little company to do support and service. I didn't want any overhead, so I thought, "Let's just have companies hire us as individuals and pay us directly, and nobody will be taking a profit off of anybody else's labor." It didn't last long because Oracle said that they didn't want to risk getting in trouble with the IRS for hiring people as 1099 employees and having the IRS say that they should have been W2s. They said, "Look, we're not hiring anybody to be a 1099 employee, so either work for us on the payroll (and we don't want to hire you guys full-time) or form a corporation that we can hire."

So we had to trundle down to a law office and set up an LLC for the company. Right around that time, the Technology Square office complex, which housed the MIT computer science lab, decided to ban dogs from the building. So I thought to myself, "I'm making $1,300 a month as a grad student, and I can't bring my dog to work. This isn't worth it. Where can we go?"

Right around the same time a friend of mine, Elsa Dorfman, the photographer, asked if I knew anyone who would rent her house. I said, "How would you feel about renting it to a little group of programmers, and we'll use it as a company office?" She agreed.

So we moved into Elsa's house, and once you've gotten an office and you have customers, things kind of take on a life of their own. The toolkit got more and more popular, and we amazed the customers. Most computer programmers don't listen to what the customer wants. They have their own ideas of what would be cool, so they spend a lot of time building stuff that the customer doesn't want. They don't have an investment in the user experience.

A friend of mine was just telling me the other day that his company offshored a product design to India, and said, "These programmers in India, they did exactly what we told them, no matter how ridiculous!" Most programmers don't think about the user experience. They get a spec book, and they say, "Well, I'm going to meet this spec to make the customer happy." That's not really enough; you have to make something good for the user if you want to call yourself an engineer.

The third element is just meeting the deadlines. If we'd said we were going to do something by a certain date, we did it, and the customers were stunned.

Livingston: How many of you were there when you first started?

Greenspun: About five, and then we grew pretty quickly to ten. There was so much repeat business because customers would be amazed that we delivered on time and that it was more or less what they wanted and actually usable for the end user.

Livingston: When you started, it sort of grew out of your own interest in the Web?

Greenspun: Well, in response to people downloading the software. They weren't really interested in photo.net, but they had decided to adopt our software toolkit. In some cases, they'd heard from Edward Tufte in his lectures. People would ask, "What's good on the Web?" and he'd say, "Nothing's good on the Web," and they'd say, "C'mon, give us two good websites." And one of the ones he'd mention would be photo.net as an example with good design.

But most of the business was because we'd released free open source software. The 15-year-olds would just use it, and the big companies would decide that, since they had so much money and I guess not enough good programmers, it made sense for them to pay us to help them out with it.

Livingston: What was unique about ArsDigita?

Greenspun: We tried to help each programmer develop an independent, professional reputation. We had this idea that programmers could be professionals, like doctors or lawyers, and, to that end, we wanted the programmers to be real engineers—to sit down face to face with the customer, find out what was needed, come up with some suggestions or changes based on the programmer's experience with similar services, and then take a lot of responsibility for making it happen.

We pushed the profit-and-loss responsibility down to individual teams. For example, if there were two or three programmers working for Hewlett-Packard, then those guys would be solely responsible for the project and making sure that it got delivered on time and that the customer was happy. They'd get a big bonus if they did a good job and the customer was happy and the thing was profitable. Implicit in that was that, if it didn't go well, we'd know whom to blame.

Livingston: What were some of the biggest turning points?

Greenspun: One big turning point was getting Levi Strauss as a customer. They had acquired a small company that made custom-cut khaki pants, and they wanted a web front end for this new factory that they were building that could take your measurements and sew you a pair of khakis to your specs. They asked around MIT, "Who's really an expert on building this kind of thing?" They came to us and it was a happy coincidence, because they were happy to pay for lots of software and infrastructure and tools and let us keep the rights to it all.

That was one good thing about working for non-technical companies. If you worked for IBM, they make their money by owning technologies, so if you build a technology for them, they want to own it. Whereas publishers or clothing companies, they make their money by having a brand or unique content. I did a lot of work for Hearst Corporation and they don't want to give away the content of *Cosmo* magazine or their relationship with Fabio, but if you build some Perl scripts for them to do server administration, it doesn't occur to them that that's something that they have to own and prevent other publishers from getting hold of.

So Levi's was a great client and it was a big turning point because it gave us the money to build whatever we needed to build.

Another turning point was in 1998 when I published *Database Backed Web Sites*. We were working on a site and the client said, "You have to finish this site for us, because as soon as the book comes out, your phone is going to be ringing off the hook." I didn't believe him, but he was right, and that was a huge turning point. It was on my website for free, but having a hard copy in the stores gave it a bit more credibility and more readers.

That was pretty much always how we built the business—tutorial publications on our website, books in bookstores, and public lectures. Edward Tufte gave us this idea of having a one-day seminar that people would come to and learn. We would get 400 people to come to a free, one-day course, and then maybe 1 or 2 would become customers and maybe 10 of them would adopt the software.

Almost all of our marketing and sales was educational. We just thought, "We'll teach people stuff, and some tiny fraction of those people will become our customers." It seemed to work just as well as running ads, which were a hard sell and kind of empty and a waste of people's time. In this case, nobody could ever say that we wasted their time. I think the same percentage of people that read an ad in *ComputerWorld* magazine and bought something would read one of our tutorials and buy something from us.

Livingston: Did a lot of people not have resources to implement your ideas at the time, because the Web was still emerging?

Greenspun: People used to say, "Why should we pay you guys $30,000 to $50,000 a month to do this thing, when we can just hire our own programmer?" What I would tell them is, "Each company has one class of stars. In some companies maybe it's the salespeople, and in some companies maybe it's the mechanical engineers. There's going to be one class of people for whom it's really easy to hire more people like that." Hospitals are a good example. If it's a good hospital, the doctors will be good, and it's very easy for them to hire good doctors. But it's hard for them to hire any other kind of person. Hospitals don't have really good advertising people; those people want to work on Madison Avenue.

So we would say, "You're a very capable person, and you're going to have a very easy time hiring people like yourself. We don't know your business and we'd have a hard time hiring someone like you, but we have a very easy time hiring someone like me, who's an MIT-trained computer science nerd. It's cheaper for you to use us, because we have really great programmers, and great programmers are a lot cheaper than mediocre programmers. So even if you give us a profit margin, it's still cheaper than doing it internally."

That might not have been true for SAP actually. SAP was a user of our software. They had a lot of good programmers, so they weren't a customer; they just used the software without needing us.

Livingston: Tell me a little about the competitive landscape.

Greenspun: There was Broadvision. Believe it or not, people didn't agree back then on how you did websites. Today, everybody would pretty much agree that the right thing to do is to do whatever Bill Gates or Microsoft says. So you download SQL Server, Visual Studio .NET, and you have a two-tiered system where you have a data model and SQL Server and you have scripts and a scripting language talking to the database. You don't have a lot of elaborate compilation steps. If you change a script, it's written in C# or Visual Basic; the next time you load it, a new definition will be evaluated. Very lightweight programming environment. Most of the engineering is in the database.

That's how I started doing things in 1994, but there were lots of companies trying to convince people that that wasn't adequate; that you had to have something really complicated. They would say, "What you really need is lots of layers and application servers and you need our software. You don't just download Perl and Apache. You have to buy our system for a million dollars." Broadvision was almost comically difficult to use. It required people to program their web pages in the C++ language, which even a lot of professional programmers find impossible to use. Modifying a website became just as expensive and difficult as it would be to make a change to Microsoft Word, and Microsoft itself is only able to get out a new version every few years.

There was also a company called Vignette, and they had a really bad product. They had a product that let you program web pages in Tcl, which was a scripting language. But there were free open source tools that were better and let you do the same thing. Why would anybody pay for this? But they were selling it. They had hundreds of millions of dollars from their IPO, and we thought, "These companies can't just waste all their money forever."

Microsoft was another concern. But they also were very, very slow. They finally today have a product called SharePoint, which is somewhat similar to the ArsDigita Community System.

One thing that we did which enabled us to be much, much faster than our competitors was that we developed on and released our software from running real-world systems. For example, we would install our release of software on photo.net or on the ArsDigita.com site where the employees and customers were all using it. We picked one site which was a public, well-used website, and we put all our new features on there. If there was a page that was very slow because the SQL query hadn't been tuned properly, we would find out immediately. If there was a user interface that was clumsy and confused the customers, say on the photo.net classifieds, well, 100 classified ads were being posted every day and people would email us saying, "We can't figure this out." So we would get immediate feedback, and we could fix it.

Then, after a couple weeks of testing the new release on this running service, we would just tar it up in the UNIX file system and produce a distribution, and that was it. We couldn't guarantee that this toolkit would solve all the world's problems, but we could guarantee, at least for something sort of like photo.net on a medium-sized server with a few hundred thousand registered users, that the software would be adequate in performance and adequate in features. It wouldn't be too expensive to support administratively because the user interface wasn't confusing people.

By contrast, companies like Microsoft were still developing software for the Web as if the Web didn't exist.

Livingston: What does that mean?

Greenspun: Let's say you have a word processor. You send a marketing person out to interview people and find out what features they need. Then they take that back to the product manager. The product manager writes up some specs: here are the features we're going to have in the next release. Then they send that to the programmers, who are in a vacuum, who build this thing according to the product manager's specs. When they're done, it goes to QA, but it's not a real running system—they're not really trying to write documents; they're just QA people. Then eventually they burn a disk with the latest release of Microsoft Word, and they mail it out to all the world's lawyers, writers, students, and whoever else uses Microsoft Word.

That works pretty well for word processors because it's a product that was developed in the '60s by IBM, and people are pretty sure of what the minimum features should be in a word processor. It also works pretty well because people don't demand frequent upgrades. There aren't new requirements and new ideas coming out in word processors, so if you have a release every three years, that's just fine. It doesn't hurt that Microsoft has a monopoly and there's no competition, so if it takes them 4 years instead of 3, it doesn't make any difference.

They applied the same technique to SharePoint. They had to do some research. They looked at Vignette, Broadvision, the ArsDigita Community System, a few other things, and they said, "These are some features that we think we should have." The product managers spec SharePoint, they send it out after about a year or two of development, and customers don't like it. It's too hard to program; it's too hard to understand. So they interview people, find out what they don't like, refine it. It takes them years and years.

If you don't have any way of seeing how your customers are using the software except by shipping them the CD and then standing in the back of their living room while they type, maybe this is a reasonable way to develop software. But if you have the capacity to just install it on the server and essentially look over their shoulders by looking at the web server log and seeing what kind of complaints they email to the help desk or the website, then why not do that? You can shortcut the whole 2-year development cycle down to maybe 2 months. We would have releases every 2 or 3 months.

So we worried about competitors, but it was an unreasonable fear. As a friend once pointed out, most gunshot wounds are self-inflicted.

Livingston: ArsDigita was different because it was much faster?

Greenspun: Yeah. If you look at a book on how to develop software, it will always have this long cycle with all these people involved. It's very slow because it's predicated on the fact that you can't just watch people as they use your running system—which you can do on the Web.

Livingston: You had an interesting culture at ArsDigita. Was it part of your strategy to get these young, really good hackers who could develop themselves professionally? And did you know that they likely had friends who were really good hackers who you could recruit?

Greenspun: That was part of it; it was hard to hire people. No matter what you did, most of the people with really good credentials and experience were occupied. There was so much money chasing a relatively limited talent pool. The folks who were in their 30s were simply not available. They were tied up working at their own startups. So we thought, "OK, how are we going to hire and grow people?"

For programmers, I had a vision—partly because I had been teaching programmers at MIT—that I didn't like the way that programmer careers turned out. Now that I fly airplanes, I realize that the average programmer is really much less happy in his/her job than the average airplane mechanic, which is pretty sad when you consider that becoming an airplane mechanic is an 18-month trade school education. For $30,000 and a year and a half, you can become an airplane mechanic (even less if you want to work as an apprentice for 3 years and get your FAA certification). You work in a small group, you meet the customer directly. You don't have the alienation from the customer that Karl Marx talked about as being a bad thing about factory work versus craftsmanship—that you never find out if your work really connects with people because you're in a factory and the customer is at the other end of a railroad line.

Airplane mechanics have a direct interaction with the customer. A lot of the jobs require two to three people, so it's kind of social, and I noticed that they're just really happy. Programmers are isolated. They sit in their cubicle; they don't think about the larger picture. To my mind, a programmer is not an engineer, because an engineer is somebody who starts with a social problem that an organization or a society has and says, "OK, here's this problem that we have— how can we solve it?" The engineer comes up with a clever, cost-effective solution to address that problem, builds it, tests it to make sure it solves the problem. That's engineering. If you look at civil engineers, architects, they're all dealing directly with the customer and going through the whole process.

Livingston: Programmers were off in the corner programming?

Greenspun: The programmers were in the corner doing what they were told. That's one reason they were so easy to outsource. If a programmer really never talks to the customer, never thinks, just solves little puzzles, well, that's a perfect candidate for something to offshore. So I said, "I don't want my students to end up like this. I want them to be able to sit at the table with decision-makers and be real engineers—to be able to sit with the publisher of an online community or an e-commerce site and say, 'OK, I've looked at your business and your goals; here are some ideas that we can bring in from these 10 other sites that I built, these 100 other sites that I've used.' And be an equal partner in the design, not just a coder."

I wanted to grow people into being able to do that, and I thought, "Let's try to make these people true professionals in the sense that lawyers and doctors and real engineers like civil engineers are professionals."

Livingston: What would that mean?

Greenspun: They would have to develop the skill of starting from the problem. They would invest some time in writing up their results. I was very careful about trying to encourage these people to have an independent professional reputation, so there's code that had their name on it and that they took responsibility for, documentation that explained what problem they were trying to solve, what alternatives they considered, what the strengths and limitations of this particular implementation that they were releasing were, maybe a white paper on what lessons they learned from a project. I tried to get the programmers to write, which they didn't want to do.

People don't like to write. It's hard. The people who were really good software engineers were usually great writers; they had tremendous ability to organize their thoughts and communicate. The people who were sort of average-quality programmers and had trouble thinking about the larger picture were the ones who couldn't write.

Livingston: You had a different atmosphere, such as encouraging your people to be part of the process. Didn't you also have educational sessions?

Greenspun: Yeah, and we had very strict code reviews. Basically the whole idea was to grow the company by having apprentices. We would bring in some people, and then the handful of people who were already there would work with them and review their code and show them how to do things more cleanly—how to use features of the toolkit instead of writing extra software. The idea was that, once they had done two or three projects for customers, they could take on an apprentice and mentor that person.

We had younger people, and we had more women than other firms. We had Eve Anderson and Tracy Adams—two of the most senior people at the company were female, which was kind of unusual. We never wanted to have more than two or three people on a project. The consequence of that was sometimes they would have to work pretty hard. But my model of the world was MIT biology grad school.

When they're young, people need to work pretty long hours to build experience and get things done. But the benefit was that then they get a big chunk of the project, and they are able to say, "I built half of the site for the customer." They put their name on something, instead of their résumé just saying that they were part of a 20-person team.

You never really know what most programmers have accomplished. There are a handful of people that you can say that about. Linus Torvalds built the Linux kernel, but it's hard to say what the average programmer working at a big company has ever accomplished. Maybe he or she knows, but, from the outside, the projects are so big and their contributions were so small.

I wanted them to have a real professional résumé. In the end, the project was a failure because the industry trends moved away from that. People don't want programmers to be professionals; they want programmers to be cheap. They want them to be using inefficient tools like C and Java. They just want to get them in India and pay as little as possible. But I think part of the hostility of industrial managers toward programmers comes from the fact that programmers never had been professionals.

Programmers have not been professionals because they haven't really cared about quality. How many programmers have you asked, "Is this the right way to do things? Is this going to be good for the users?" They reply, "I don't know and I don't care. I get paid, I have my cubicle, and the air-conditioning is set at the right temperature. I'm happy as long as the paycheck comes in."

It's no surprise that programmers' salaries are headed down to what an illegal immigrant working at a slaughterhouse in Nebraska would get paid, because they just don't think about if they are doing high-quality work for the end users. I think because of that, managers have said, "I'm tired of these people. I don't want to see them. I haven't had a good experience. They've been late, they haven't done what they've promised, and what they've done has been bug-ridden and not very good for the end user. So if I can't have a good experience with these people, then I'll just get rid of them. I'll have them in India or China where I can't see them and they won't get on my nerves as much." So I think there's an emotional component to why programmers are being offshored: it's simply that the businesspeople hate them.

Livingston: You ran a tough ship, but you were trying to empower them?

Greenspun: Yeah, but they didn't appreciate it that much. Some of the early people did, but the later arrivals, when the venture capitalists came in and said, "Oh, you guys should just clock out at 5 p.m. and you shouldn't write, because programmers shouldn't have to do more than code," they were so happy that they didn't have to work hard anymore. "We don't have people like Philip and Jin reviewing our code and telling us to redo it to be cleaner and simpler." They were so happy to be relieved of those strictures that they very quickly lapsed. Not everyone, of course, but the majority. We built the company a little too fast, and consequently the last 50 percent of the people hired really didn't have much commitment to the corporate culture.

There were some warning signs. Consider McKinsey, which holds itself out as one of the world's leading repositories of knowledge on how to manage a business. They say they'll never grow their company by more than 25 percent per year, because otherwise it's just too hard to transmit the corporate culture. So if you're growing faster than 25 percent a year, you have to ask yourself, "What do I know about management that McKinsey doesn't know?"

I still think it's more efficient—this is just an old Lisp programmer's standard way of thinking—if you have two really good people and a very powerful tool. That's better than having 20 mediocre people and inefficient tools. ArsDigita demonstrated that pretty well. We were able to get projects done in about 1/5th the time and probably at about 1/10th or 1/20th the cost of people using other tools.

Of course, we would do it at 1/20th of the cost and we would charge 1/10th of the cost. So the customer would have a big consumer surplus. They would pay 1/10th of what they would have paid with IBM Global Services or Broadvision or something, but we would have a massive profit margin because we'd be spending less than half of what they paid us to do the job.

Livingston: So you're doing well, have great people, and are profitable, and then you decide to take VC money?

Greenspun: Here was the problem: hiring businesspeople was almost impossible. That was one of the things that drove us into the arms of the VCs.

Why is it hard to hire businesspeople for a young company? There was a guy recently hired by Microsoft to be their chief operating officer—Kevin Turner. He's 40 and was CIO of Wal-Mart. Graduated from East Central University in Ada, Oklahoma, with a bachelor's in business. That was it. (Cautionary for those of us in the higher ed biz; this guy never had much of it, but he was apparently very effective.) They could have hired anybody in the world—they have all this cash—and they hired this guy. You want somebody who's a really good manager. Managing your company might be harder than managing Microsoft because Microsoft has $40 billion in cash, so they can recover from mistakes that you won't be able to recover from. So you need a guy like that.

But entrepreneurs love their babies and never ask themselves, "Why would a guy like that want to work for me? I have no resources to manage. That same person could work at Microsoft and have tens of thousands of good employees to deploy on projects, tens of billions of dollars to invest in interesting projects.

Why would they want to come work at my company where everything is constrained?" So it's not as simple as hanging out a shingle and saying, "Here's our small company; we have $15 million a year in revenue and we're profitable; now we need a manager." The people you are likely to attract, by definition, are people who couldn't get a job at General Electric.

We were having trouble because the handful of good people who wanted to work at startups were all dazzled by the names of the venture capitalists. They'd say, "If you don't have backing from Kleiner Perkins, we don't want to work for you."

We talked to a headhunting firm, and the guy was candid with me and said, "Look, we can't recruit a COO for you because anybody who is capable of doing that job for a company at your level would demand to be the CEO." And I thought, "That's kind of crazy. How could they be the CEO? They don't know the business or the customers. How could we just plunk them down?" In retrospect, that was pretty good thinking; look at Microsoft: it took them 20 years to hand off from Bill Gates to Steve Ballmer. He needed 20 years of training to take that job. Jack Welch was at GE for 20 years before he became CEO. Sometimes it does work, but I think for these fragile little companies, just putting a generic manager at the top is oftentimes disastrous.

There was no way we could have hired first-rank businesspeople in that environment. There were too many companies that were low-risk and had more assets that were hiring the best people. All we were going to get were the second-raters. We'd get first-rate programmers because we had a company where programmers were the stars and we already had great colleagues for them, so we were going to attract great programmers, just not great businesspeople. Because we were not GE or Microsoft, we were not a place where a great businessman rationally would have wanted to work.

We did get one good guy, Cesar Brea, who had done a lot of software consulting at Bain. He came by the house to check us out because he had heard about us from a friend of a friend and was looking to work at a company instead of being a consultant. What sold him on us was that, when he came to talk, there was a check for $500,000 from HP on the coffee table that we hadn't bothered to deposit yet. He knew that if we could leave a check lying around for a few days, then we must have been doing OK.

The other thing was that the original sales pitch that I made to employees was, "Come work here. You'll make $150,000, maybe $200,000 a year if you do a great job and you make your customer really happy. We can just do that forever, making the customers happy, not spending too much. We'll pocket the profits, we'll have fun offices, a beach and ski house that everyone can go enjoy and go there for a week and do some writing. We'll collaboratively have this great lifestyle."

But they felt like they were dumb because every day they were reading the newspaper about people who had worked for 6 months at some company and now they were worth $20 million because of an IPO. They'd ask me, "Why aren't we doing an IPO?" And I'd say, "Because we have profits."

But due to a couple forces—customers and recruiting—we began to think, "Well, maybe we should hand out stock options and tell people this is going to be part of their compensation and try to go public." We did have more revenue and profits ($20 million and $3–$4 million, respectively) than almost any technology company that was then going public. Despite all of our growth, we were cash-flow positive, and we had all this profit that we had to pay taxes on. I think once we prepaid a year of rent just so we wouldn't have to pay tax. The company was growing 500 percent a year and generating so much cash that we had to find ways to spend it before the IRS got it.

So we talked to some underwriters—we were big enough that we were actually able to get meetings. They were very candid with us and said, "Look, we're not going to take you public."

We said, "Why? We've got more revenue than any company you've taken public in the last 6 months."

They said, "We get paid a percentage of the deal. The more deals we do, the more money we get paid. If we want to take you public, we'd have to waste a lot of time doing due diligence. We would have to look at your accounting and talk to your customers. We would have to convince ourselves that you were a good company."

"So what? You have to do that with any company."

"No, with all the other companies, we just look at the names of the venture capitalists who've backed them, and if it's a big name like Kleiner Perkins, we just take the company public without doing any research. We have no idea what these companies do, we have no idea who their customers are or if they're satisfied. We don't do any research. We just take them public and take our fee. So in the same time it would take to take you public, we could do five or six of these VC-backed companies. Sorry, we're not interested."

That was a wake-up call, and I think in retrospect it shows why so many of these companies that were taken public couldn't survive. They had no profit and no possibility of making it, but the underwriters never looked at them carefully.

I had brought in Cesar and another business guy who was a Harvard MBA, and we had all these VC firms knocking on our door. I was an engineer. The MIT way of doing things is that you delegate to the experts. If you are riding in a car with five guys and it breaks down and you are a math major, you don't get out and start poking around with the engine if there's a mechanical engineering major on board. So I felt like, "OK, these VC firms are all claiming they are going to provide added value and that their money is different, but it's hard for me to evaluate these things, so I'll just delegate it to these two guys who are MBAs. That's what they're supposed to know about."

Probably the VC firm that we should have picked was called Summit. They were very humble; they said, "Look, we don't know how to run your company. We know how to go to institutional investors and get their money, and then we invest it in management teams with a track record of profitability, like yours. We're not going to tell you what to do and tell you that we're going to recruit everybody for you because we don't know how to do that. We know how to get money from pension funds, give it to you, and then talk to an underwriter along the way."

There were these two VC firms—Greylock and General Atlantic Partners—that were among the group, and they would send their senior partners by to schmooze us and talk about their successful track records–building companies and management teams. I thought to myself, "I don't want to be CEO of this company where I have to repeat myself and tell people what to do and travel everywhere. It would be so nice to just be the CTO and have a brilliant management team installed in my place." So it was very attractive to me, and our MBAs said, "Yeah, these Greylock and General Atlantic guys, it's a bigger name, and it will really help us." Slightly worse terms than Summit—actually, with the deal Summit was offering, I could have sold some of my shares to them, taken some cash out, and had some money, and in retrospect that would have been a very smart idea. Especially if you are going to get into conflict with a venture capitalist later, you don't want to be a salary man with $130,000 a year while they have billions of dollars in assets.

So I let them decide, and they chose Greylock and General Atlantic. Which might have been OK, except that the senior partners in those firms were so rich that they didn't want to spend time sitting on the boards of companies they were investing in. Why should they? They had six houses each and Gulfstream jets to get among all their houses. They were going to the World Economic Forum in Davos. Why would they want to sit at my board meeting? I used to sit at my board meetings, and I would think to myself, "This is my own company and I'm bored out of my skull."

The VCs delegated very junior people to sit on our board. One guy had been a management consultant at Bain. He had never run a company; he never had profit-and-loss responsibility, which is the key. And he never started a company, and that was true with the General Atlantic board guy as well. He had been a middle manager at a big company before he went to General Atlantic. We got these guys on our board who just don't know anything about running a business.

Fundamentally, if you have a lemonade stand, you have to sell your lemonade for more than it costs you to make. That's really all you need to know to run a company. I would have been so much better off if the manager of the Central Square McDonald's had been on my board, because at least he would have understood how to do accounting.

The guys on my Board had been employees all of their lives. You can't turn an employee into a businessman. The employee only cares about making his boss happy. The customer might be unhappy and the shareholders are taking a beating, but if the boss is happy, the employee gets a raise. By contrast, the businessman cares about getting a customer, taking his money, not spending too much serving that customer, and then selling something more to the same customer. These are totally different psychologies.

The VCs found a CEO for the company, and I was like, "OK, great! Finally, I can relax." This guy was a very smooth talker. He had been the COO-type at a software consulting firm, Cambridge Technology Partners, which is a pretty bad company, actually. They never had a really good product, and I don't think their customers were very well served. If you are going to get a manager, it's probably better to get somebody from GE Jet Engines because, at the end of the day, the customer who buys a GE jet engine gets value. It's a high-quality product. They at least have that kind of culture of building something reasonable for the customer.

Livingston: Did you like and approve the hire of this new CEO?

Greenspun: I liked this guy reasonably well, but a lot of it was desperation. I really didn't like what my job had become. Until the company had about 40 people, it was a lot of fun. I felt like work was getting done that I would have done if I'd had more time. It was being done in my style and to my quality standards. It was like being pushed along by this tide of helpers.

But at the time of the VC investment, we had 80 people, and I thought, "Things are beginning to get done that I wouldn't have done." Some of my cofounders and more experienced folks were also stretched pretty thin because of the growth. I thought, "We just need the insta-manager solution." Which, in retrospect, is ridiculous. How could someone who didn't know anything about the company, the customers, and the software be the CEO?

Our customers weren't hiring us to be management experts; they wanted a really good programming team to build something of high-quality and deliver it quickly. They didn't need anyone to talk smooth to them. A lot of the traditional skills of a manager were kind of irrelevant when you only have two or three-person teams building something. So it was almost more like you were better off hiring a process control person or factory quality expert instead of a big executive type.

They brought in a new executive team very quickly, and I acceded to this because I knew that my skills weren't in management and, in theory, somebody else could have done just as good a job as CEO. But apparently nobody could do quite as good a job at making the engineering decisions on the toolkit. Jin and I and a few other experienced engineers—we knew what worked, we knew what didn't work—we should be concentrating on the product.

The CEO was a guy who had never been a CEO of any organization before, and he brought in his friend to be CFO. His buddy didn't have an accounting degree and he was really bad with numbers. He couldn't think with numbers, he couldn't do a spreadsheet model accurately. That generated a lot of acrimony at the board meetings. I would say, "Things are going badly." And he'd say, "Look at this beautiful spreadsheet. Look at these numbers; it's going great." In 5 minutes I had found ten fundamental errors in the assumptions of this spreadsheet, so I didn't think it would be wise to use it to make business decisions. But they couldn't see it. None of the other people on the board were engineers, so they thought, "Well, he's the CFO, so let's rely on his numbers." Having inaccurate numbers kept people from making good decisions.

They just thought I was a nasty and unpleasant person, criticizing this guy's numbers, because they couldn't see the errors. From an MIT School of Engineering standpoint, they were all innumerate.

Livingston: What about your board?

Greenspun: We were supposed to have two outside board members to break this kind of deadlock. They were subject to the venture capitalists' approval, and they wouldn't approve anyone. I'd say, "What about this MIT professor?" And they'd say, "No, he's not qualified." "What about this person who's started and run a $100 million company?" "Not qualified." They never proposed anyone themselves, and whoever I proposed, they shot down.

Basically, with their CEO that they brought in, they had a three-to-two board majority no matter what. And they said, "We're going to run this company. We're going to make all the decisions, and you're just going to be a figurehead."

I got very upset. It was a difficult time for me. I didn't have enough perspective to realize . . . A couple of my friends, John Gage and Bill Joy, the founders of Sun—I know John, and I don't think he'd be upset if I told this story—he would scream and yell about the direction that Sun was taking and how bad it was, and Bill Joy would say, "C'mon, John, calm down, it's only a company." Which is the right perspective to have, but I didn't have that distance. If I had been on the board of somebody else's company and the same kind of thing was going on, I could have probably contributed in a more positive manner just by having less emotional stake in the matter.

Remember, I'd financed the company and I owned most of it, so it was a big asset for me. It was my only asset, basically. It was just too personal. So after about 6 months, because they had no management experience, no P&L experience, no engineering experience, and no numbers experience, they couldn't see that what I was telling them was right and that they were headed for some serious financial and customer losses. They just thought I was injuring their self-esteem—that's what they said.

They basically fired me and all but one of my cofounders. They pushed them out of the company within a month or two. I'd been fired 2 months after they came in; I just didn't know that I'd been fired. I was still getting a paycheck, but nobody was listening to me. They were telling people, "Don't listen to him; he doesn't have any power."

I was chairman of the board. I'd been fired probably within a month and half, but it took me 6 months to realize it. They finally said, "OK, you're fired now, but you can still be on the board." I initially thought, "Maybe this is good." I was sitting in my bathtub reading the *New Yorker* magazine, and I realized that I'd been psychotic. That I'd thought, "If I don't write software, people won't have any software. If I don't write books on how to do things, nobody will learn how to do things. If I don't teach at MIT, these students will never learn anything." It hit me: I could sit here in this bathtub for the rest of my life reading the *New Yorker* magazine, and Microsoft will eventually write all the software that people need, and maybe it will be clunky and expensive, but so what? It's not my problem. They'll get the software they need, eventually. If I don't teach at MIT, they have $5 billion in assets, and they'll be able to hire somebody much better than I am to teach these kids.

That was an epiphany; I didn't have to work 7 days a week anymore, doing stuff that was repetitive in a lot of cases. I'd been building multiuser Internet applications for 20 years, with a lot of excursions into the CAD computer and engineering world as well, but basically 10 years exclusively in Internet apps. So I thought, "I can be doing something else. I'm an investor in this company. Let them build this company. Let them deal with all these issues. I'll just collect my dividends." I thought maybe this was a good thing, that I could do new stuff—new research projects that were interesting to me.

Meanwhile, because these people didn't know anything about the business, they were continuing to lose a lot of money. They hired a vice president of marketing who would come in at 10 a.m., leave at 3 p.m. to play basketball, and had no ideas. He wanted to change the company's name. This was a product that was in use in 10,000 sites worldwide—so at least 10,000 programmers knew it as the ArsDigita Community System. There were thousands and thousands of people who had come to our face-to-face seminars. There were probably 100,000 people worldwide who knew of us, because it was all free. And he said, "We should change the company name because, when we hire these salespeople and they're cold-calling customers, it will be hard for the customer to write down the name; they'll have to spell it out." And they did hire these professional salespeople to go around and harass potential customers, but they never really sold anything.

Because I wasn't a great manager—and I knew I wasn't—I said, "I'm organizing this company like McDonald's. Each restaurant is going to be managed by a few people, and they're going to have profit-and-loss responsibility. If they make a profit, they get to pocket half of it. If they make a loss, we're going to know who's responsible, and we're going to go there and fix it, and there are going to be consequences for those people." That's a very easy way to run a business. It's naturally profitable. People have all the right incentives to make their customer happy, to do the thing on time, to take the customer's money, deposit it in the bank, and then move on to the next one and get their bonus at the end of the year.

Without even realizing what a risk they were taking, the new management said, "Programmers are only good at programming. They shouldn't do anything but program. So we'll hire salespeople to sell, and not have programmers try to sit with the customer."

At the time, Anderson Consulting (now Accenture) didn't have any salespeople. They always had the people who were executing the project sell it. "You eat what you kill" was the phrase at Accenture. You don't have a salesperson go out and tell the customer, "We can do this," making promises and then handing it off to a programmer.

So they ignored the wisdom of Accenture and the history that we had of profitability, and they said, "We'll hire professional salespeople to sell. The programmers will program; they will not be responsible for anything other than coding and listening to their boss back in the head office in Cambridge. The salespeople won't have any responsibilities having to do with the project, they will only have to listen to their boss. For keeping to deadlines, the programmers won't have to do that; we'll hire project managers to keep the deadlines." And then they hired these people who, still to this day, I have never figured out what they were supposed to do. They were called "client services." They weren't the project managers. I think they were supposed to keep the customer happy.

The new management hired all these people but, if you asked, "Who's responsible for making sure that this project, overall, makes money for the company and who has an incentive to ensure that it's done on time and the customer pays?" the answer was essentially, "Nobody." You had to go way up the management chain to find somebody who had P&L responsibility. So I told them that they were taking an enormous risk, that they had no idea what the consequences were going to be.

Their response was, "Shut up, Greenspun. You're injuring our self-esteem. This is how good companies like IBM do it. You don't know anything."

They tried to make everything as much like IBM as possible. They were very conventionally minded. The problem with doing that is that those niches are occupied. If you have bland, boring marketing materials just like IBM and you have very high prices and slow delivery, there is a niche for that product and it's occupied. IBM is there. The customer doesn't need you. They just go to IBM Global Services, if that's what they want, or their own IT department, for God's sake.

In the case of open source software, it can fall apart quickly. If you become slower and more expensive and more mired in bureaucracy than the customer's own IT department, then they'll just say, "We have lazy, ineffective, slow-moving programmers right here in our back office. We don't need you."

So it was falling apart very quickly financially; I could tell that. The board meetings got more acrimonious. They actually precipitated the ultimate fight. They said, "Look, we're going to kick you off the board and sue you for injuring our self-esteem. You better talk to a lawyer."

Livingston: Didn't you also insult them by describing publicly what it was like to have VCs run your company?

Greenspun: Only after they sued me. I said it was like watching a kindergarten class get into a Boeing 747 and flip all the switches and try to figure out why it won't take off. That was before I got my pilot's license. Now I know how apt it was.

So I talked to my friend Doug, a great lawyer. He said, "You need to talk to my friend Sam Mawn-Mahlau at Edwards and Angell and figure out what to do. Sam looked at all the deal documents and said, "You own this company. You are a majority shareholder."

I said, "But these guys told me that I have no power because they control the board, three to two, and it doesn't matter what anyone else says."

He said, "Yes, but the shareholders elect the board. Just have a shareholders' meeting and elect yourself and your cofounders (or whoever else you want) to the board, and these guys will be back to their two board seats, which is what they bargained for. They have a minority investment. They bargained for two board seats and veto power over certain transactions from those board seats, but that's all they're entitled to."

I asked if there was any risk in doing this. He said, "There's some risk that they would sue you in the Delaware Chancery Court. But VCs hate to spend their own money, so I don't think they'd do it. Litigation is very expensive, and, if they can't find a way to stick it to their limited partners, then they are not going to sue you."

Basically, whenever VCs do an investment, they make the startup company pay their legal expenses. Remember, the investments come from the limited partners, the pension funds, etc. So they get their 2 percent annual management fee, but a lot of their costs, like their legal expenses, are also actually being paid by the limited partners. For example, a company is supposed to get a $700,000 investment, but right away they return $50,000 to pay the legal fees of the venture capitalists, so the limited partners actually only get $650,000 of their capital working in that business. If they can't come up with a scheme like that, they aren't going to sue you because they are not going to want to spend their own money that they could be spending on business jets and vacations and other things that are delightful to VCs.

So I said, "Great." My cofounders and I, who were shareholders, had a meeting and said, "Who wants to vote for Philip Greenspun to be CEO and on the board?" We had to change the corporate bylaws also because the default corporate bylaws in Massachusetts are that the shareholders elect officers like the CEO. The bylaws of the company, for whatever reason, said that the board elected the CEO, so we said, "Well, let's just change it back. We're the shareholders, so we'll change this bylaw so now it's back to the Massachusetts default." It was a perfectly legitimate bylaw that the shareholders in a small corporation would elect the CEO. So we changed the bylaws and elected me as CEO, which, under some other bylaws, gave me an automatic board seat, and then we elected a couple of our founders to the board. So now we had a three-to-two board majority.

Livingston: Where did you physically do this?

Greenspun: We did it by letter actually. We did it in the lawyers' office downtown at Edwards and Angell.

I knew that they wouldn't like this, and I wanted to keep things as orderly as possible, so I called up the old CEO—whom I think we had elected COO, so we had demoted him to chief operating officer and kicked him of the board— and I said, "Let's face it; you're just not qualified to run this company. You're losing money. But we don't want to have any disruption, and you are a good manager and maybe someday you can learn enough to be CEO, but that's not today." We tried to make it conciliatory—"We're not going to change anything, we're not going to go on a mass firing spree, but we have to get this company back into being cash-flow positive because, whether you know it or not, you've lost a lot of money." They still didn't know it, because their accounting was all so inaccurate; they had no idea. They hadn't been audited yet. Their accounting firm hadn't come in and shown them all their mistakes. Basically, they were flying solo.

Then Jin and I went off to California for some reason, on a guy's road trip to California and having a great time. When we got back to Boston, we discovered that we'd been sued. Me, Eve, and Tracy got sued in Delaware Chancery Court. I thought, "God damn that lawyer, Sam, he lied to me; he told me we wouldn't get sued!" And I later realized that Sam had been right and wrong. They still had control of the company checkbook. Even after he'd been voted out as CEO and the new board had been voted in, the VCs had gotten their pet CEO to write a $1 million check from the company checking account to their lawyers so that they could have this shareholder lawsuit without paying for it. This was an unauthorized looting of the company on behalf of one set of shareholders. It was probably illegal, but in Massachusetts it could take years to recover that kind of money. And they figured it's not going to be a big deal because we'll still have control of the company; we'll impoverish this guy with an onerous lawsuit. He'll never have enough money or staying power to come after us in Massachusetts for looting, and maybe he'll never find out.

So now I had to defend this lawsuit. I had to hire Delaware counsel, which was very expensive. It basically consumed all my assets over 2 1/2 months. But they had a case that really couldn't be won, since they were minority shareholders. Let's say you have one share of IBM and you go to the Delaware court and you say, "I want to control IBM; I feel like I'm entitled." There's really nothing holy left in America: religion's not holy, the family isn't holy, marriage isn't holy, but the only thing that's really left that is holy to Americans is ownership. And that's what the courts are there for. They are there to preserve the rights of owners of things. So when you go to court and say, "I don't own this thing, but I want to control it," you are almost guaranteed to have a poor reception.

Eventually, the VCs simply bought my shares, partly so that they wouldn't be prosecuted for the next 5 years in Massachusetts court for the looting, partly because they wanted control of the company, who knows. It was stupid. If they wanted to buy the company from me and run it however they wanted when I was sitting in my bathtub reading the *New Yorker* magazine 6 months earlier, they could have done it at a lower cost without all this Sturm und Drang, and everyone would have lived happily ever after. But it never occurred to them that I would want to do something else with my life. They were very worried about me competing with them and starting a new company. I had been programming sitting at a desk for 23 years, working on Internet apps for 10 years—did they really think that I would take all my newfound money and freedom and program some more? In fact, I went traveling for a while, and then I went to flight school and got my private pilot's license and bought an airplane and went to Alaska, and all through this time, they were busy losing money.

Livingston: What happened to ArsDigita?

Greenspun: They finally got a call from the bank saying that they were running out of money in their checking account, I think. That's when they woke up to the fact that the CEO and CFO hadn't been doing a very good job. Partly because they had burned through about $40 million in cash (I had left them with about $40 million in cash when I turned over the reins), and they didn't understand why. The VCs came in and fired the CEO.

There was a period where I wasn't supposed to talk about them or the company, but that's over. But I think they don't like me talking about the lawsuit, because being incompetent and running a company is embarrassing enough, but being totally incompetent in litigation also looks bad.

I had fostered an atmosphere of caring about end-user experience and education and "we're going to have fun, we're going to have the beach house and a Ferrari." We did lots of things for free—we had a foundation, we did programs for high school kids, and we did a one-year intensive computer science program for people who wanted to transition from being a poet or whatever into being a programmer. So people thought of me as a hippie. In reality, ArsDigita was my sixth company, and I knew how to make money, and I was the investor.

So while I publicly had a persona of doing all this fun stuff and money takes care of itself, I was watching the bottom line very carefully. I had set things up so that the company could not lose money while I was CEO, and if there was a problem, it would be identified very quickly and we would fix it.

If you are a for-profit corporation, your job is to make money, and if you're not making money, you're not doing a good job. End of story. It's important to have fun, but once you incorporate for profit, my attitude is that you better make a profit. When I was trying to retake control of the company, most of the programmers at ArsDigita were so relieved to be rid of me. They thought, "Now we don't have to listen to this guy, we don't have to have our code reviewed, and we can all be happy and go home at 5 p.m. and never write anything. Let the salespeople sell—we don't have to talk to customers anymore."

Some of them would email me and say, "Why are you doing this, Philip? We don't understand." I'd say, "Let me explain to you about being a shareholder in a corporation. I don't work there anymore. I'm not an employee. The only thing that you can do for me is send me a dividend check." I had to lay it out in black-and-white for them; it was a little cold. Maybe, when I was working there, there could be some brotherly love and we could all have fun together, and if the company was losing money, it would be a shared experience. But, right now it wasn't a shared experience. I was a shareholder; I wanted my return on investment. "That's the only way I'm measuring you, and if that means that you all have to have a pay cut or your jobs offshored to India, that's a shame, but for the shareholders, all we care about is the money."

The VCs also looked at the Ferrari . . . The Ferrari was something like $1,000 per month to lease. We parked it in the parking lot; it was a great symbol; we got written up in *Forbes*. I had architected the deal so we would never actually have to give out the Ferrari. You had to recruit ten friends, and then you only got to drive the Ferrari for as long as you worked at the company. I figured, "Well, programmers only stay in the job 4 years, 5 years tops. It takes them 3 or 4 years to recruit their ten friends, they'd drive the car for a year or two, and then they'd want to go back to grad school or go work somewhere else; they'll quit and then the Ferrari would go back in the pool." I had set it up so it looked extravagant, but didn't actually cost anything. But the VCs and employees thought of me as someone whose spending was out of control.

It doesn't look extravagant to hire a bunch of salespeople and client service people and a vice president of marketing. However, if you hire all these people in suits that don't do anything productive, that *is* extravagant. They went through $40 million in cash. But it doesn't appear extravagant. Nobody will fault you as a businessperson for hiring a salesperson and paying him $100,000 a year even if he is not selling. They won't fault you for hiring a $200,000-a-year VP of marketing who used to work at Oracle even if he's useless, because the guy wears a suit and shows up to work every day for 5 hours.

The Ferrari, which costs less than any of these things and sits in the parking lot, looks extravagant. But it inspired the programmers; it got us all this press; it made customers think that we were a profitable, successful business. It had all these benefits. At the end of the day, the Ferrari was the only thing that the VCs made a profit on. When they sold the Ferrari, they sold it for more than I paid for it.

Partly they killed themselves through replacing profit-and-loss responsibility pushed down to the lowest levels with a functional management structure, where you only had to report to your boss. There was a programming department, the sales department, the client services department (whatever it was), and there's the project management department, and the only person responsible for overall profit and loss is the CEO. That was really a bad problem for them.

The second thing that killed them was a common phenomenon in programming called "second-system syndrome." This is identified by Fred Brooks in *The Mythical Man-Month*, which was about the IBM OS/360 project, the operating system for their mainframe in the 1960s. We had the first system that was running photo.net, ArsDigita.com, and all of our clients. It was a set of data models in SQL and page scripts that talked to those data models to provide an online community and e-commerce site. We had all these modules do different things. We had two versions: one was in Java Server Pages, very straightforward, JSP talking to the Oracle data model, and the other one was an AOLserver Tcl, which is kind of an obscure web server used by America Online for most of their web services—very efficient. That was what we had started with in 1995. It was state of the art in '95; today you could do just as well with Microsoft Internet Information Server and Active Server Pages. Anyway, it was the first web server to have database connection pooling. We'd become a little bit identified with it, and the VCs and their pet managers were convinced that, if we just became the Java company, we'd have an increase in sales. Customers didn't seem to care.

Going back to 1998, we had plans for three versions: Java Server Pages, AOLserver, and Microsoft Active Server Pages in Visual Basic, but it turned out there was no customer demand for the Microsoft one. People said, "Look, I paid my monthly fee. I want my site up and running." We had a lot of cost efficiencies from running the AOLserver version internally for our hosted customers, and if the team was on vacation and there was a problem with the customer's site, any other programmer could go and maintain it because all the files were in the same places; everything was named conventionally. It was very easy for programmer A to debug programmer B's work.

So what was the problem? We were making money, customers were happy, people were using this. Well, with any big system, people write down a list of things that they don't like, that they could do better. It gets to be a long list. The biggest problem with our system was the same problem with SAP: you have data models, some customizations, and some scripts to talk to the data models. When you upgrade from one version to the next, you have all this SQL stuff that has to be done in Oracle to migrate the old data model to the new one—if you add columns to the tables, for example. If you are setting up a brand new system, it's easy. You just create tables. But in an existing running system, you have to alter the tables. That's kind of a pain.

If there have been customizations done to it that haven't been rolled back into the toolkit, you may have to recustomize a bit. This is a problem for SAP, and it was a problem for us. My attitude as an engineer was that SAP is a company with billions of dollars in assets and lots of smart people. They had never solved this problem, so we're not going to attack it either. Not until we have infinite money. We'll just leave it, and, if customers have to spend 2 weeks of hard programming upgrading the server, then that's the cost. So that was one of the biggest things.

The second thing we didn't like about it was that it wasn't the full Java 2, Enterprise Edition. At the time, some of these people thought that it would be cool if they had multiple layers of Java in there. They said it was a little too slow; they had all these criticisms of the system. That's true of any first system. It's new, so it's kind of got some ugliness to it. Shortcuts have been taken. So then you say, "OK, my next system, the second system, is going to fix all these problems at once. It will be upgradeable instantly, it will be super fast, it will all be J2EE, and it will be fabulous. And it will be ready real soon."

But a lot of those problems with the first system aren't there because the people who built the first system are dumb, they're there because it's kind of a difficult challenge and there are compromises involved, and that was an inevitable result of one of the compromises. And the people doing the second system are just too naïve; they haven't worked on this problem before, and they're young, maybe, and they just don't realize that it was hard.

Fred Brooks said that the second system is always late; sometimes years later than you expect. And in fact, because of the ambition, usually it won't solve any of the problems. They've got a long list of things, and it will solve almost none of them in the end. So that's exactly what happened with these guys. They told customers, "Don't use the old system, because we have a new one that should be shipping in 3 months and it will be better." It actually took them more than a year and a half.

So they suffered all these sales losses because the thing was late. They killed demand for the old product by telling them the new product was "just around the corner." Then, when the new product finally came out, some critical pages were literally a thousand times slower than the old system. So where you have had a 1-processor pizza box server, you would now need a 64-processor, $2 million server to serve the same user community. It had never been tested; it had never been released on a running system like photo.net. It was just a bunch of programmers—sitting in a vacuum and never dealing with a publisher or a user—programming whatever they thought. They were all young because they had gotten rid of some of the senior people.

The question-and-answer forum, which was one of the most heavily used parts of the site, was literally a thousand times slower than on the old system.

As far as upgrades, they said, "We're going to have this abstraction layer, and you'll never have to actually interact with the database; you'll just talk to this abstraction layer." Sure enough, the first time people tried to build a real system for a customer list, they found that the abstractions weren't the right ones, and they had to go underneath and deal directly with the database, which immediately means that, if they ever had to upgrade that to a new version, they would have all the same problems as the old system. So they didn't solve the main problem they said it would solve.

It wasn't true J2EE, either. They said it was going to be J2EE, but they didn't like some of the commercial tools or the open source tools that were available, so they built their own magic persistence layer. They built all their own stuff, so customers who looked at it said, "This isn't actually J2EE. It's a pile of Java crap, yes. It's very complicated, yes. But it is not J2EE." (To be J2EE, it has to use these other components that are standard and distributed by Sun or WebLogic.) So they failed to achieve any of their goals. The old system took the average programmer about a week to install and figure out and customize a bit. The new system was taking an experienced programmer 2 full months to understand.

There were a lot of projects where people would have gotten there sooner if they had just started with a raw Windows machine. Your competitor is always Microsoft, so you have to look back and say, "What does Microsoft have? They have Internet Information Server, Active Server Pages in Visual Basic, some example code that they distribute. So would somebody get there faster if they just got that and started from scratch?" And the answer compared to the new ArsDigita toolkit was "Yes."

Nobody wanted to use it. People would download it, but they would give up. There was no adoption in the open source world. A handful of teams at ArsDigita were installing the new system for customers, but it was taking them forever. They were all running over time and over budget. They ended up with a product that nobody wanted. At the end of the day, the programmers killed the company—the junior programmers who were put in charge. The VCs and the management team basically selected programmers according to who had an agreeable personality. They picked people who were pretty junior, who didn't have much experience with real-world customer projects, and they basically killed the company. Once you have a product that nobody wants, it doesn't matter how good your management team is.

So 4 or 5 months after our shareholder meeting, they came in and fired the CEO—demoted him to COO or something. They put in one of their own partners as the CEO. He hung out there for a while. They put in more money, I think another $10 million, and he gradually figured out that the numbers that the CFO was giving him were bogus. He began to run his own numbers, and he realized that they were losing money on every project and that, if they got one more project from a customer, because the software was so bad, it would cost them more to serve that customer than the revenue. At that point he said, "Forget this, I'm shutting it down."

So they tanked the corporate shell and welched on all of the creditors, landlords, and so forth, and they handed over the assets of the company to Red Hat, which was another investment that they had. They gave all these contracts and the software to Red Hat, essentially for free. They kind of gave people the impression that the company had been sold to Red Hat. Now, if an ArsDigita creditor came to Red Hat and said, "I want my money. You bought this corporation," Red Hat would be very careful to say, "No, we didn't buy that corporation." But it seemed to the public that Red Hat had bought this company, so the VCs could say that, "Yes, this was another successful investment." Red Hat got some advantage: they got some revenue that they could report, and since they didn't pay anything for this stuff, they didn't have to say, "Oh, by the way, this $10 million spike in revenue is due to an acquisition." So it looked like they just had growing sales. They hired a handful of the programmers and stuck them in a suburban dungeon out on Route 495.

So that was the end, but it didn't take too long. Our shareholder meeting, I think, was in April of 2001. I sold out in June of 2001. They tanked by January 2002.

Livingston: If there was one thing you could have done differently, what would it have been?

Greenspun: The one thing would probably have been slightly slower growth, I guess. Not to worry so much about the competition, concentrate on getting really good people who shared the company's vision, who could be mentored to the point where they could then recruit somebody else. Basically, just limiting growth.

Livingston: I know it was your sixth company, but was there anything that you found you were better at?

Greenspun: I think I was probably mostly worse at things than I thought. The VCs had a point when they said people remember how you made them feel more than what you said.

Managing programmers is tough. That's one reason I don't miss IT, because programmers are very unlikable people. They're not pleasant to manage. In aviation, for example, people who greatly overestimate their level of skill are all dead. You don't see them as employees. J.F.K., Jr., is not working at a Part 135 charter operation because he's dead. It's not that he was a bad pilot; it's just that his level of confidence to level of skill ratio was out of whack, and he made a bunch of bad decisions that led to him dying, which is unfortunate.

In aviation, by the time someone might be your employee, probably their perceived skill and their actual skill are reasonably in line. In IT, you have people who think, "I'm a really great driver, I'm a great lover, I'm a great programmer." But where are the metrics that are going to prove them wrong? Traffic accidents are very infrequent, so they don't get the feedback that they are a terrible driver because it's so unlikely that they'll get into an accident. A girlfriend leaves them—well, it was certainly her deep-seated psychological problems from childhood. Their code fails to ship to customers. It was marketing's fault!

If a software company dies, you can blame the marketing people. Programmers almost all walk around with a huge overestimate of their capabilities and their value in an organization. That's why a lot of them are very bitter. They sit stewing at their desks because the management isn't doing things their way. They don't understand why they get paid so little. It is tough to manage these folks. But on the other hand, there are better and worse ways to do it. If you want to ensure that the customer gets high-quality code and that the product is high-quality, you have to step on these younger folks' egos and say, "No, that's not the way to do it." The question is, how harsh can you be? I could have been kinder and gentler for sure.

I think I was good with the customers. That's one thing: I realized that businesspeople didn't have any ethics in a fundamental way. Forget how they dealt with me and other stuff, but here's one example where I realized that having basic ethics was an operational advantage. There was one customer that didn't want to pay their bill, and they were upset with us. There was a meeting about this, and I was with the new CEO and one of the MBA guys that worked for him, talking about this customer. It was out in the Los Angeles office. The managers said, "This customer's upset with us. How do we get him to pay us more money?" I said, "How much do they pay us?" They said, "$700,000." I said, "Is their site launched?" They said, "No." I said, "How much did we tell the customer that it would cost them until their site is launched?" They said, "About $700,000." I said, "Well, then why are we having this meeting? Why are we talking about getting more money out of these people? Shouldn't we be talking about getting their site launched?"

It was a perspective that was completely alien to them. What value are you delivering to the customer? Are you delivering what you said and what they paid for? I didn't think of myself as a pious, ethical expert, but at least I had that much: if you take money from a customer, you should deliver some value to them. After the meeting, I called up American Airlines and got on a plane. It was a Friday and I had some social commitments for the weekend, but I cancelled them. I flew out to LA and told the programmers that I wanted to see them on Saturday and talk about the customer.

The programmers were all pretty junior and said, "It's the customer's fault because they keep asking for these features and saying the site can't launch unless we have all these complicated features. They keep coming up with new ones because they see other people's sites."

I replied, "You guys are engineers, and you have to explain to the customer that there's a lot of learning that happens only once the site is launched. And you have to get them to accept some kind of minimum launchable feature set. You don't need 100 user question-and-answer forums on sites that are brand new. There are only 15 users. How would they find each other if they're fragmented into 15 forums?"

I said, "You can't blame the customer. You have to work with them to come up with the minimum launchable feature set, and get the site launched. You guys need it for your résumés; you want to be able to say that you worked on a project that succeeded and here's the site and anybody can look at it, not that you got a paycheck and accomplished nothing and that you worked for a stupid customer and it's all their fault."

I brought the customer in on the same day, and we talked to them and found out that, well, they didn't need the last features if it meant that their site wasn't going to launch. They hadn't understood the tradeoffs. A couple weeks later they launched.

Livingston: Was there anything that you think people misunderstood about the demise of ArsDigita?

Greenspun: I haven't written that much. I'd like to write some reusable lessons. We have some uniquely clever things that we did, like making websites that were multilingual. Just engineering stuff. I just haven't had the time or the energy for some reason.

People focus a lot on the bust-up phase. It upsets me that they remember the wrong things like, "This Greenspun guy sued the venture capitalists." This is not true, first of all, since I was a defendant, not a plaintiff.

It really upsets me that people think of ArsDigita as a venture capital–backed company. It wasn't. It was a company that I started and backed financially, basically by myself, but within a year or two brought in some other smart, good people. It upsets me that they think of ArsDigita as a company that the VCs somehow played a big role in starting; that I sued them and somehow got money trickily. That bothers me. I financed the thing. I put in money and years of labor, and right at the tail end—they were only in there for about 18 months from the time they invested to the time it went bust, and at that time the company was more than 5 years old. So it was not a VC-backed company; it was a company that took VC money just in an attempt to shortcut the underwriting process in going public.

I did not make money through litigation. I bought some shares, took a risk, sold them in the end at a much lower return than I would have if I'd never taken the VC money in the first place. I could have just taken profits out of the company on a year-to-year basis. Just take dividends, instead of giving such large bonuses to the employees—some combination of slightly lower bonuses and slightly less retained earnings in the company. So it was a simple story of investing and then selling shares. The litigation was a sideshow. In the end, they bought me out the same as if they hadn't sued. They just thought, "Well, maybe we can steal control of the company instead of having to buy it," and, when that didn't work, they bought it just like any reasonable person would have expected to.

Joel Spolsky
Cofounder, Fog Creek Software

Joel Spolsky founded Fog Creek Software with his friend Michael Pryor in 2000. They didn't have a specific product in mind, but were motivated to start the kind of software company where they would want to work—one where programmers were the stars.

Around the same time, Spolsky began writing Joel on Software—now one of the most widely read programming blogs—to share his thoughts about software development, management, business, and the Internet. Joel on Software was one of the first examples of a now common (though rarely achievable) strategy for software startups: create a popular blog to get attention.

With its popular software, including FogBugz and Fog Creek Copilot, Fog Creek Software has doubled its sales every year, even during the post-Bubble meltdown. The company never took any outside investment, and continues to operate as a profitable, privately held company.

Livingston: How you did you come up with the idea? How did Fog Creek Software get started?

Spolsky: There was no idea, in the sense that the only thing I thought was, "There's a bunch of people out there doing certain types of things and they seem to be pretty incompetent, but they're getting huge valuations. Surely if I did those same things, knowing that I am less incompetent—merely semi-incompetent as opposed to extremely incompetent—I should be able to achieve at least their level of success."

There was a period in the late '90s when starting companies was just a slam-dunk, no-brainer kind of thing. The people that were going public with $100 million valuations were punk kids [who] just graduated from college and knew nothing about anything. There were some really bad implementations of very pedestrian ideas, and we thought we could do a lot better.

Probably the key inspiration—what actually made me take the leap into starting Fog Creek—was Philip Greenspun of ArsDigita, who had a particular business plan that seemed to be working at the time. In the long run, it didn't work, because they took venture capital for a consulting business and the consulting market disappeared. But we looked at ArsDigita and said, "Wow! They're doing all this great stuff. But there are a couple of things that I would do differently." They had this weird, religious fear of everything Microsoft, which I thought came from something of a position of ignorance. I don't want to say that Microsoft is great, but they said, "We are successful because we don't use Microsoft technology." I thought they were just kind of randomly being anti-Microsoft. So that was one small thing I was going to change.

A larger thing was that they were developing this product. They had this idea; they got the consulting and they got the product—which was the ArsDigita Community System that they were developing alongside it. The theory was that the product they created would support the consulting, and the consulting would support the product.

But they thought the product needed to be open source, and we thought, "That's nice, but consulting is a business where your revenue is just a multiple of the number of people you can hire. Software is a business where your revenue can grow much faster than the people you hire." If you can make licensing fees by selling software using the same model as ArsDigita in every way, but just charging for the ACS, we thought that you would have a steady growth of the consulting side of the business.

So the idea was that the consulting would grow linearly with the number of people as you hired more good people that you could rent out as consultants, and the software business would grow like the hockey curve because, at some point when it took off, you wouldn't actually have to hire new people. You could just make more copies of the software you were selling.

That was the theory. Realistically, it didn't work, but we were able to suspend disbelief for long enough to start the company.

Livingston: Who were the founders?

Spolsky: Michael Pryor and I (we were friends from Juno Online Services) cofounded it in 2000, which was a good move. Probably starting it by myself, I never would have really had people to bounce ideas off of. I don't know if it would have gotten off the ground, really.

So it didn't work for ArsDigita, and I think they probably think that it didn't work for them because the VCs came in and mismanaged it, but actually all the other businesses that looked like their business failed at the same time. Even with good management, it's likely that their consulting business would have collapsed as ours did at the time. Luckily, we hadn't grown very much and didn't have much consulting business to lose, so we could survive that.

We had, for all intents and purposes, three consulting clients when we started in September 2000. By February or March, we had none. Other firms that were building web stuff lost something like 90 percent of their business in the course of 1 or 2 months. There was a huge dropoff; the consulting market completely disappeared.

The consulting market is the derivative of every other market. When a company is growing, they will hire a few consultants to help them grow a little bit more rapidly. When they're shrinking, they'll instantly fire all consultants. If the market is even going down by 0.002 percent instead of growing—which it did, because there was a sort of dot-com nuclear winter—then the first people to go will be the consultants. So the consulting business completely collapsed, and every company in that space more or less collapsed. The ones that remained—Razorfish, Scient, Viant, whatever—all sort of conglomerated into one company with about 120 people, and that was it.

Livingston: Were you and your cofounder working out of your apartment at this point?

Spolsky: We never wanted to do that. We had certain philosophies. Working out of our apartment was never a possibility; we got office space from the first day. It was somebody else's apartment, but we weren't living there. It was an office.

Livingston: It was someone else's apartment? Did you sublet it?

Spolsky: Yeah, it's a long story. We wound up getting ripped off. We actually sublet it from another company which, in turn, went bankrupt in a sort of disrespectful way where they just disappeared and didn't even bother to go bankrupt or give us back various deposits we'd made. But we survived that one.

Livingston: You had three initial consulting clients. Were those people that you had known while you were at Juno?

Spolsky: No, I think all of them I found. I am pretty sure those were Joel on Software readers who emailed me and said, "Hey, we've got a project for you."

Livingston: You had been writing Joel on Software back then?

Spolsky: Yeah. I'd left Juno around the beginning of the summer. I spent the summer writing a bunch of articles on Joel on Software, just because I was taking that summer off, living in a beach house. By the end of the summer, when we started, it already had enough of an audience that it was pretty easy to find people who wanted to hire us as consultants to build some stuff. But like I said, that market went south really, really quickly.

Livingston: What did you do when you didn't have any clients?

Spolsky: The market disappeared in November of 2000. I'm using specific dates because it really disappeared in that month, but nobody knew that it had disappeared until April. All the businesses' perception was that the amount of time it takes to sign up a new client was going up by about 1 day per day.

They kept saying things like, "It used to take us about 2 months to sign a client. It looks like it's going to take a little longer. The sales cycle is up to 3 months." Then the next month they would say, "Looks like the sales cycle is up to about 4 months." Nobody was ever saying, "We're never going to hire you. Go away." But that was the reality.

So for most of the firms—ArsDigita, Razorfish, Scient, iXL, MarchFirst—they didn't even understand that the market was gone and it was not coming back, and therefore they continued to pay consultants their salaries while they had nothing to do. And that caused them to hemorrhage money until most of them closed.

We didn't have enough consultants at that time. We hired a couple. But since we always knew that we wanted to be a software company on the side, around October or November we wrapped up FogBugz, which was an internal bug-tracking application we had lying around, and started selling it. And lo and behold, people started buying it.

Livingston: This was your own internal product?

Spolsky: Yeah. Basically that's where all bug-tracking applications come from. Every bug-tracking application in the world is some internal developer's idea.

Livingston: Did you think, "Hey, we'll build this for us and see if we like it?"

Spolsky: Yeah. We actually had three product ideas in mind, and FogBugz was one of them. That was the easiest one and the one closest to being able to be sold. The other two product ideas—one of them was CityDesk, which was kind of a market failure, and the third one was something called Tintin, that we never even wrote, let alone shipped.

We had this idea of a family of three applications that would work together in various ways. FogBugz would provide workflow, Tintin was going to provide a content management server, and CityDesk was going to be this content management client. That was the long-term vision, and we started launching FogBugz because we had it.

I think we started making $5,000 to $10,000 a month selling that. It was enough to pay our expenses and live off of once we laid off the two consultants we had hired. (They both immediately found jobs, so it was not really an issue. One of them is now back as a full-time employee.) I guess we were kind of lucky that we started late enough in the business cycle that we didn't waste a lot of cash discovering that there was never going to be a consulting market again.

Livingston: You were nimble enough to change your plan because you were just getting started?

Spolsky: Yeah. We just lucked out. If we started a year earlier, we would have had 37 consultants whose salaries we somehow would have had to pay for 4 months while we realized there was not going to be any money for them. That would have been a dangerous situation.

Livingston: So people were buying FogBugz. Was there another turning point for you then? Because I know you never took any outside investment.

Spolsky: We never took any investments. I put in probably $50,000 of my own money—mainly to cover people's salaries, when we didn't have clients. There was a fairly long period of time where I went without salary because I had my own savings. (Michael had less savings, and he took out a little bit of salary.) And we had some expenses, because during this entire period we had an office.

Although it was my grandmother's apartment, we were paying rent, and we were using it solely as an office. So we were paying, let's say, below-market rent for a below-market-quality office space.

Livingston: Was it in Manhattan?

Spolsky: Yeah, it was a brownstone in Manhattan. Two floors, with a garden out back. It was quite a pleasant place to go work. Nobody was living in there, but it had a kitchen.

So we shipped another product, CityDesk. There are all kinds of reasons why it was not a successful product. We misinterpreted some things, and that product was not a big hit. But FogBugz just kept growing and growing and growing. Every time we did a new release, we would double our sales. We just sort of sat there and watched this little geometric growth occur—which has been happening in the last 5 years to this day. This application is getting bigger and bigger and selling more and more copies every month.

We had to raise the price a couple of times. We didn't have to, but raising the price actually increased the number of units that we sold. I guess because it looked more legitimate with the more realistic price.

Livingston: If people have to pay more, they take the product more seriously?

Spolsky: Definitely. There was a five-user license that was like $199, and that just feels like shareware, practically. But today, when you say that a ten-user license is $999, it starts to feel like a more substantial product. In that market, it still is actually a good deal. But you really have to have a price point that conveys what you think the product positioning should be. Many people will judge where your product fits in the market based on its price.

So we increased the price a couple of times, and both times it increased the number of units we sold. We launched new versions, kept adding more and more features. It's become this gigantic monster. It's also a whole customer email management system. Your customers email bugs, it spam filters it automatically, it sorts them into areas, it assigns them to people, you can keep track of them, you can set due dates, you can automatically reply to a customer with a nice little message that gives them a link that they can click on to see the status of their message. We use it for handling all our incoming company email and make sure that it gets handled by the appropriate person.

Livingston: Would you consider when you released this product one of your major turning points?

Spolsky: Yeah, although it didn't feel like "Let's have a celebration." At the time, we thought, "Hey, we have this product. We don't know what else to do. Let's just ship it and see what happens." We had no idea. At the time, you could have told me that this thing was going to sell zero copies, and I would have believed you. You could have also told me it was going to sell $50,000 a month's worth of copies—an equally unrealistic number—and I would have believed that too.

Now I have enough experience to know that almost everything you launch is going to sell $2,000 to 3,000 in the first month, and that's the way the first month of any software product always is, if you do things perfectly. But at the time, I just had no idea what to expect.

Livingston: Was there a time during that first year when you thought, "We've lost our clients. Time to close up shop"?

Spolsky: We never thought we would close, because we had this theory that Fog Creek would continue as long as Michael and I could eat and pay whatever external obligations we had. There was no reason to completely and thoroughly give up. And that's pretty much what it got to. In the first year, I'd say revenues off of FogBugz averaged like $10,000 or $15,000, and that was enough to live on. It was growing at a reasonable rate—I remember literally every month it would grow—at least 100 percent a year. And that gave us the confidence that we could wait this out.

There was money coming in, and the amount of money coming in was going up every month. So there was no reason to give up and go home. The theory was that we would only give up when there wasn't enough income even to pay the minimum bills we had to pay. I think our monthly overhead was $5,000—mostly rent, but also office supplies and T1 and that kind of stuff.

Livingston: It seems like you have a really unique corporate culture—one that values hackers. Did you plan this from the start?

Spolsky: Absolutely. Remember, the original model was, "How can we become a big consulting company and then build a software company inside a consulting company?" The consulting company was a means to an end. It was to get cash flow, so that you could build a real software company. And when you were done, the theory was you'd still have these consultants, but software companies often need consulting arms.

The basic economic model for us and ArsDigita and those kinds of companies was that you could get a bright MIT grad or whatever and give them a salary of $75,000 to $125,000 a year, depending on experience. That comes out to, at most, $60 an hour, and the billing rate was $200 to 250 an hour for building database-backed websites.

Livingston: Wow.

Spolsky: Yeah. Obviously it was just an arbitrage condition that all these startup companies were trying to take advantage of.

The question is, how do you get the bright MIT grad to work for you and not somebody else? What was astonishing at the time was that none of these companies were making any effort whatsoever to make the work environment pleasant and to treat the people that they were hiring with enough respect that they would be able to attract people.

You would go into companies—there were a lot of them in New York: Scient, for example—and they would have millions of desks crammed into the most crowded room where they would pack people in like herrings and treat them as interchangeable cogs. It was not a fun work environment. There was not a lot of respect for the developers. There was not a lot of treating developers well and making them feel like they were the hotshots in the organization.

Things that to us are basic: Aeron chairs; private offices with doors that close for every programmer; letting programmers report to other programmers, so that your boss will understand you. We had 4 weeks of vacation and another week of holidays, which you can move I think. For the consulting business, we had a rule that you fly first class and that you never be away from home on a weekend.

We actually figured out the entire business model, and we figured that, if we spent 4 percent more or 8 percent more giving people a better work environment in these particular ways, everybody would want to come work for us and not go to the Scients and the Razorfishes of the world. And that was going to be our business model. Everybody is charging $250 an hour for these consultants and paying them $60 an hour. We would pay them the equivalent fully burdened of $64 an hour. That was our clever trick that we came up with, and that's what we thought our innovation was. It turned out not to have been what we did.

Livingston: What did you do?

Spolsky: We started a consulting business and we hired a couple really smart people. We had a few clients. We did the whole $60/$250 thing, which was great, and that business then disappeared very rapidly out from under us. So we became just a real software company.

Livingston: But you still kept a lot of your culture for the programmers.

Spolsky: Oh yeah. That was always sort of the goal, really, in creating Fog Creek. If you are in Boston, Austin, Raleigh-Durham, Silicon Valley, or Seattle, as a programmer you have a lot of choices of where to work. In New York, the choices are investment banks, some hospitals, advertising agencies—but not technology companies. There are very, very few technology companies in New York.

But New York still is the largest city in America, and there are an awful lot of programmers who are stuck in New York because their wife is going to medical school, or their family is there, or they just love the city, or they want to do improv theater and this is the best place to do it—millions of reasons why a programmer might find themselves in New York. Every programmer wants to work at a product company because it is so much better than working as a slave in an investment bank. And there were none in New York.

We would go to parties, and we'd find geeks, and they'd say, "Do you know of any software product companies in New York where I can work?" And we would say, "Gee, no. I can't really think of any." This is what programmers would talk to each other about: how can I get out of the investment bank in New York? So part of our model was, "Let's create a fun place for us to work, since we are stuck in New York City. Create a software company specifically in New York City."

With many programmers, you are sort of peripheral to the goal of the company and you are doing a peripheral path, so that you're never a part of the company and nobody cares about you.

Livingston: Why do big companies get it wrong?

Spolsky: I worked at Viacom, which is a culture of creating MTV and Comedy Central. It's not even about creating MTV and Comedy Central; it's about buying MTV and then buying Nickelodeon, and then merging MTV and Nickelodeon and creating a thing called MTV Networks and playing political games with that, and then maybe selling one of them off and buying CBS.

In order to succeed in that environment, those are the things you have to be good at. And if you need to make some interactive websites or MTV needs a web server or whatever the thing is, then you don't even hire programmers; you hire some people who know some people who might know something about the technology. Eventually, you get somebody who thinks, "Let's get some programmers in here," and they actually hire a programmer. And if they are lucky, they get a good programmer, but they will torture that programmer until that programmer wants to cry and leave.

A company that is not designed to create high-tech products is very unlikely to have the culture or the DNA that it takes to create high-tech products. So if you are a high-tech person in that company, then you're basically a glorified typist in some sense. It's very unlikely that the kind of people who would be successful in an entertainment company would even understand what programmers do that makes them more than typists.

Livingston: Looking back, is there anything you would have done differently?

Spolsky: The biggest mistake that we consistently made is that we kept getting all kinds of interesting marketing ideas. Well, the first problem we had is that we thought we didn't understand sales and marketing because, indeed, I am a programmer and Michael is a programmer. We thought that the whole business of sales and marketing, which we recognized as being utterly crucial to the success of a high-tech company, was completely mysterious to us.

When we read about it, we knew that we were bad at the particular skills that we needed to do sales and to market things. We didn't have any kind of budget for marketing. So we were just afraid of the so-called "go-to-market" strategy. I see a lot of startups in their first couple of years kind of flail around—exactly the same way we did—trying to figure out, "Oh shit, how are we going to get people to buy our stuff?"

We had this dream that we would find a company that would sell and market our products, and we would do development. There would be some kind of 50/50 split. But search as I may throughout the history of the annals of computer software, I could only find one example in which one company sold a product and the other company developed. It was Lotus Notes, which was developed by a Boston-area company called Iris Associates.

They had a deal that was a 50/50 split with Lotus, basically. Lotus Development did all the sales and marketing and bought copies of Notes from Iris for, I believe, 50 percent or something. It is probably 25 percent of the MSRP (manufacturer's suggested retail price) or something like that. That particular relationship, before Lotus completely acquired Iris, lasted long enough that I thought that maybe this model would work.

I later talked to people that were involved, and they said, "Oh my God, the tensions were unbelievable. It was a nightmare." Lotus had to acquire them.

So the next thing we looked at was selling Fog Creek to some other company that we thought could take us to market. We went through the whole song and dance and negotiations with the company that we thought would acquire us and had the cash to take us to market. It didn't work because we were prima donnas with inflated opinions of our own worth. In other words, they made an offer for about $4 million, and we thought we were worth about $12 million. We understood why they thought we were worth $4 million. That's what we would have said in their position, too. But, we really thought that we were going to go a lot further.

Lo and behold, the company that didn't acquire us did acquire another company of some friends of mine in the same scenario. They were developing software, and they were hoping that this acquiring company would be able to go to market with the software. And the acquiring company actually proved that they did not have the ability to go to market with the software products, so that was a flop. I think if we had gone that particular route, we would have disappeared, pretty much, and the products would have disappeared, and Fog Creek would have been no more.

So the mistake I made was in thinking that I had a sales and marketing problem, you know, because everybody said, "Where's your salesman? Where's your marketing department? How is anybody going to buy your software?"

In the early years, we thought, "Let's get people to link to us on their websites, and we'll pay them a little bit of money if they sell our software." When we had a consulting business; there was this little thing up on our web page saying, "Help us find some consulting clients and we'll give you $5,000"—which I thought would get people's attention. Everybody that had any kind of business experience said, "No. This looks like you're desperate and it's a bribe. Take it down from here." The only person who ever even bit at that slightly was someone who was going to hire us anyway, or thought that his firm should hire us, and was trying to get what would have amounted to an illegal kickback.

So it was just a completely goofy thing that we did. But then we took it further. We said, "Make hyperlinks to Fog Creek properties (or whatever) and if people follow the hyperlinks and buy our software, we'll give you a percentage—15 to 25 percent." It was an affiliate program, just like Amazon affiliates. That actually did get us some sales, but we put a lot of work into developing that, and the amount of sales it got us was negligible. The administration and development overhead were just not worth doing, and we eventually shut it down because I was sick of writing $19 checks every month. It was a complete waste of time; it absorbed a lot of time very early on, critically.

A third example of this was when we said, "Let's make some kind of coupon system"—because we had this idea that we would send people an automatic email when they visited our website that would tell them—and we had all these crazy ideas like, "Buy our software within the next 72 hours and get 25 percent off." (That thing was actually a bot that we wrote years ago, and it still runs. If you try CityDesk, which is our least popular product right now, you will get an automatic email with a 25 percent–off coupon that you have to use in the next 72 hours.) When we launched that, it did increase our sales a little bit. It gets people to evaluate the demo version right away—because they don't want to lose their 25 percent off coupon which is going to expire.

These were all marginally good marketing ideas. Unfortunately we spent a lot of time chasing them. The one thing we learned over 5 years is that *nothing* works better than just improving your product. Every minute, every developer hour we spent on any one of these crazy things—although they had some marginal return on the work that we put into them—was nothing compared to just making a better version of the product and releasing it. If we had taken all the effort we put into these crazy schemes and put it into moving our software development schedule ahead by the equivalent amount, it would have paid off much more.

That was probably the biggest mistake we made. And that's the advice I give everybody. All those little coupon schemes, this is what General Motors does. They figure out new rebate schemes because they forgot all about how to design cars people want to buy. But when you still remember how to make software people want, great, just improve it.

Talk to your customers. Find out what they need. Don't pay any attention to the competition. They're not relevant to you. Only talk to your customers and your potential customers and see what it is that caused them not to buy your product or would cause them to buy more copies of it. And do that, and then ship it. That was something we really, really should have focused on, but, you know, we didn't know any better.

Livingston: Do you consciously not take any investments?

Spolsky: Yeah, absolutely. We took no investments because there were so many horror stories about what VCs would do to you. ArsDigita was the most public one, obviously, of kicking out the founders and then mismanaging the company and bringing in the so-called professional management.

You can definitely see how, if you're an investor at a VC stage, when you look at your investments and you look at the kind of founders you have of companies, it's obvious that some of the founders are just hardcore geeks that are never going to develop into good managers of a large company. Some of them are founders precisely *because* they wouldn't be good managers of a large company. So in those kinds of companies, you probably do want to bring in better management, if you can find it. Although I don't necessarily believe that VCs really have the ability to do that or that it ever works trying to bring in "professional" CEOs. There is a justification for saying a lot of founders would not be good managers, but there are an awful lot of companies being run by founders that do a pretty good job of running them by themselves.

So we didn't want that to happen; we didn't want to be forced to do anything we didn't want to do. I find new reasons every day why I'm thankful that we never took any kind of outside investment. Let me give you a small example. The board of directors consists of (because we're private and we can do whatever we want) me, Michael, and my boyfriend, Jared. Jared had a friend that had an idea of some way that we could modify FogBugz to be really useful to the investment community as something—I don't remember what, but something that the investment community could really use that's 5 percent different than FogBugz. And I kept thinking, "This is a huge distraction, and there's not a big enough market. I just want to stick to our core competency, and I'm not interested in doing software for the financial markets." He kept saying, "No, no. You've got to talk to this guy. You could make a lot of money off this. It would be great."

I kept thinking, "You know what, if it was a real board of directors and the VCs were bringing you these great ideas, you wouldn't really have any choice but to say yes. And you'd keep getting distracted to do their pet projects that they dreamed up in the shower one night and they think might be a good idea, and you just don't think it's a good idea." You don't really have the ability to say no when you take those outside investments. It's hard to tell your investors, "Let me just go in my own direction."

There are things that we do, boy, that I'm so thankful that I don't have to answer to anybody. I don't think it's possible to have private offices for developers when you're VC-funded, because it looks extravagant. I think that it's worth paying for in terms of the productivity you get. We spend an outrageous amount of money on quality office space that other people don't. That makes it easier to recruit and makes us more productive, I believe. But I've heard from people that it would be considered completely unacceptable by the average VC to have private office space—because it's considered an extravagance of a successful company or something like that. And, you know, "Why aren't you all in the same room talking?"

I've had that argument whether it's better to have private offices for developers. I don't want to have that argument anymore. I don't want to have to try to convince people anymore. Certain features—flying first class, Aeron chairs, double monitors, the best computers that money can buy—these are things which might be considered extravagant, but it's nice just to be able to do things the way that we believe they should be done, without having to have a big argument educating other people as to why we know how to develop software and they don't.

Livingston: Is there any advice you would give a programmer who wanted to start a startup who wants to avoid having to take any outside investment?

Spolsky: It's totally possible. I would recommend that you create a weblog and have millions of readers every month from around the world that read it. That's not really necessarily followable. Step two is a little bit hard. I think it's Larry Wall who used to have this saying about Perl that, "Well, if you don't like it, just make your own language and make it popular." That was his way of refuting any and all complaints about the Perl syntax or whatever.

So the reason I'm saying this, even though it's tongue-in-cheek, is that we definitely got a lot of publicity—what a traditional company would call PR—through Joel on Software. And that caused us to get an enormous number of initial customers. After that, our products spread by word of mouth. Existing companies buy more, and people leave those companies and go to other companies and buy it. They've never heard of Joel on Software, but they're still buying our stuff. We've actually seen that in the curve. Whereas, in the early days, we would ask people on our website, "How'd you hear about Fog Creek?" when they purchased things, and 100 percent of the people that filled out that field would write, "Joel on Software."

Now it's down to about 30 percent. It's dramatically reduced, but it's still there, so to some extent I don't believe this is a replicable model. Because I've seen a lot of people—that maybe can't write in as exciting a way, or maybe don't have things to say that other people happen to want to read—try to replicate that model and maybe succeed and maybe not. Unfortunately, startups have to find something that works for them.

In our case, our software didn't really have a strong viral nature to it, and so using Joel on Software got the word out there that we make software products. It worked very well for us, but it's not necessarily a model that anyone else could be successful following.

I remember one of the stupidest things I ever wrote on Joel on Software. I was giving advice on writing technical specifications, and I said, "Be funny." The reason that was stupid was that I later realized that most people, when they try to be funny, aren't that funny. They just look kind of sad. That's like, "Be born to rich parents." It's not that useful advice for most people.

Livingston: Did you have any competitors that you worried about?

Spolsky: Probably, but I never really worried about them. It's sort of funny, but, because Joel on Software has such a wide readership, a lot of people say, "Hey, if Joel can do this, I can do this too." And they'll copy the model all the way down to the actual product.

I believe there have now been seven clones of FogBugz. The most extreme example was somebody that reimplemented the whole thing, but copied our user interface word for word, so the help file was actually a copyright violation, which we had to tell him to change. But it was an exact clone of FogBugz in every single way. He later used all kinds of nasty search engine optimization techniques, got banned from Google, and that was the end of his business. That was the worst extreme.

On the other hand, there are people, who we generally respect a lot more, who kind of said, "Oh yeah, bug tracking. We could do that," or "We have one of those." So all told, I think there are probably seven competitors.

The interesting thing is what they copied. They didn't really copy the code; they copied the implementation of how FogBugz works. But they missed what made us successful. They didn't really copy Joel on Software. And I think what's happening to those seven people right now is they are getting an object lesson that merely copying the product that another company makes does not make you successful. We're not afraid of those people by any stretch of the imagination. Sometimes they can be aggravating, but we don't really care.

More than that though, we've long had a philosophy of pretty much ignoring our competitors. When I first went to work at Microsoft, there was a person on my team who decided it would be useful—it would get him some notoriety internally—if he wrote a weekly email summarizing Microsoft's competitors. We were the Excel team, so it was really the spreadsheet competitors, Lotus and Borland—what they were doing and what was new and what features they had. He sent out this email internally at Microsoft to a bunch of people for 6 weeks, until he lost interest. I remember thinking that, no matter what we knew that the competitors were doing, the information was completely useless to us. It never really changed what we were doing. If it's like, "The competitors are going to do feature x," well, if that's such a good feature to do, why aren't we hearing about it from our customers?

In other words, why listen to our customers indirectly through what our competitors do when we can just talk to our customers? So my mantra has always been, "Listen to your customers, not your competitors." I don't know who our competitors are. Sometimes I'm asked to list other bug-tracking products, and by now I know about Bugzilla. I think there's something called BUGtrack. I don't know what they have, what their products are, what their price point is. I could research all that, but I can't think of a single thing I would do with that information.

I do want to talk to people who evaluated our software and then decided to go with a different product instead. I want to know why they did. "Well, one of your competitors has a wiki built in." OK, maybe we'll have some kind of wiki integration. But, again, that's something I would hear from our customers and not from paying any attention to what our competitors are doing.

Livingston: Looking back on the earlier years, what was most surprising to you?

Spolsky: Most? It was all surprising. One thing that surprised me was that, when we released a new version of our software (we're on 5.0 with FogBugz already), there would be a big jump in the number of sales. We would say, "OK, all the upgraders are upgrading right now, so that's what accounts for the boost." And the surprise is that after that initial boost, the number never went down. We expected there would be a hump after a new version was released and that would make us want to keep releasing new versions. But instead there was a step. A big step up. We kept thinking it was a hump that was going to go down, then it never went down again.

Now I understand why that is. You made a better product. When you have a better product, you will win more of the evaluations. More people who evaluate your product will decide to purchase it. So you are now on a new permanently high plateau in sales caused by the fact that you have a better product. It overcomes more of the hurdles that your software is put through when users evaluate it to see if it meets their needs.

Livingston: Who did you learn things from?

Spolsky: Oh, everyone. I can't even begin to list the number of people who taught me things.

I was in the Israeli army, and I learned some strategy there by mistake, by osmosis. In order to avoid spending too much time in uniform, I did this kibbutz army program. It was two years on a kibbutz, which is a communal farm in Israel. They usually have industry, and the kibbutz I was on had a bakery, which was this gigantic factory that made bread. I spent almost 2 years making bread every night in this factory that made hundreds of thousands of loaves of bread. It was not artisan bread by any stretch of the imagination. It was a big, noisy bakery. There are so many things that I learned from that about how people work, how to think about working, how to manage, how an assembly line might be organized, how industrial machinery works.

But my first job at Microsoft is really where I learned the software industry. I got there in 1991. At the time, there were almost—I hesitate to say this, but— no software companies that really knew the basics of how to develop software in the way that Microsoft did. They accomplished what they did because they figured out a ton of things about how to make software, repeatedly and reliably, that people want to buy, that nobody else had figured out. And they were doing things like bug tracking—like having a bug-tracking database—that seem completely obvious, and, when you looked around, 80 percent of commercial software companies did not do bug tracking. Or 80 percent of commercial software companies did not write specifications. Or 99 percent of commercial software companies did not do usability testing.

If you were an alien and you came here in 1991 and you wanted to learn how to develop software, you would learn ten times as much at Microsoft as anywhere else, I think, because I watched these companies kind of flail making mistakes. There were things—really basic things, that companies did not know. Microsoft knew that loading a segment register on the 386 was a very time-consuming operation, and therefore on the 386 architecture you can't use far pointers unless you absolutely have to because it's extremely slow. Borland did not know that. Result: Microsoft Access loaded in 2 or 3 seconds; Borland Paradox for Windows took 90 seconds to get running. Because of something that Microsoft knew that Borland did not know. And that's one of a million examples.

Now Microsoft has forgotten all these things, and they've hired a lot of morons that don't know these things anymore. I think that now Microsoft is kind of a big tar pit where you can barely move forward because there's so much bureaucracy. But I learned a lot.

Livingston: There were only 5,000 people back then, right?

Spolsky: Right, 1,000 of whom were developers. 200 were program managers. I was a program manager. I was working on Excel, which was really at the heart of the company, other than Windows and DOS, so it was really cool.

Livingston: What do you think makes a good hacker?

Spolsky: I think what makes a good hack is the observation that you can do without something that everybody else thinks you need. To me, the most elegant hack is when somebody says, "These 2,000 lines of code end up doing the same thing as those 2 lines of code would do. I know it seems complicated, but arithmetically it's really the same." When someone cuts through a lot of crap and says, "You know, it doesn't really matter."

For example, Ruby on Rails is a framework that you can use with the Ruby programming language to access databases. It is the first framework that you can use from any programming language for accessing databases to realize that it's OK to require that the names of the columns in the database have a specific format. Everybody else thought, "You need to be allowed to use whatever name you want in the database and whatever name you want in the application." Therefore you have to create all this code to map between the name in the database and the name in the application. Ruby on Rails finally said, "It's no big deal if you're just forced to use the same name in both places. You know, it doesn't really matter." And suddenly it becomes much simpler and much cleaner. To me, that is an elegant hack—saying, "This particular distinction that we used to fret over, just throw it away."

I don't know if that's what makes a good hacker. I guess that would be answering a slightly different question to what's a brilliant hack. I guess a brilliant hacker is someone who comes up with a brilliant hack.

But it's also a programmer who gets into flow—sort of what Paul Graham describes as an animal. I see it specifically as a programmer who sits down to do something and they get into a mental state where they're just cramming away. They're just generating stuff and the time is passing and they're not aware of it. They're just typing, typing, typing, typing, and great things are happening because they're in that particular mental state.

I think probably there are a lot of workaday programmers working on upgrades to Enterprise Java (now I've insulted all the Java programmers) who never achieve flow. To them, it's just kind of engineering step by step; it's never the magic of creation.

Livingston: Is that what makes a good software company?

Spolsky: To me, building a software company—and this is kind of hand-wavy—is creating the factory that was going to be equipped for, when I have an idea or when somebody has an idea, we can throw it into the factory and get the working code at the back.

The first time we ever did this was last summer with Copilot, where we took four summer interns (three programming interns and one marketing intern), and we had this idea for a particular way of doing remote desktop assistance. It was a pretty obvious idea, and we looked out in the marketplace and there were not any compelling alternatives. We realized that, lo and behold, we could do this with four summer interns in one summer, because it was not that big of a programming problem. There was a neat hack where we could reuse somebody else's code. We could accomplish this with a small amount of effort and it was a business opportunity, so for the first time ever, Fog Creek was actually able to take an idea and, within a few months, churn out the solution to that idea on a fairly small scale.

My goal is to build a company where I can take much more significant ideas—where I can say, "Golly, backup software is really, really terrible. It's awful for all kinds of reasons. Let's make good backup software." That's a big project. I want to have the organization that I don't have yet where, when we get those ideas, we can produce the products. Because the capital is sort of endless. Capital is not a problem for us. Even if it was a problem for us, there's VC. The real problem is how to deploy that capital to create software, and that's something that we want to make the machine that is able to do.

Livingston: What advice would you give to a programmer who's thinking about starting a company?

Spolsky: I've got a lot [laughs]: Don't do it. It's going to suck. You're going to hate it.

Can I steal one from Paul? Don't start a company unless you can convince one other person to go along with you. If you don't have two people (or I would even say three) that you've convinced to devote their lives to doing this, it's just going to be a different thing. There are a lot of programmers that are very tentative about starting their own companies. There are a lot of working programmers doing something they hate, with some company that they hate, but they need money to pay the mortgage. So they figure, "I'll develop something in my spare time. I'll put in 1 hour every night and 2 hours on the weekends and I'll start selling it by downloads." And you say to them, "Who's your cofounder?" And they say, "My significant other—husband or wife. My cat."

But because they never really take the leap and quit their job, they can give up their dream at any time. And 99.9 percent of them will actually give up their dream. If they take the leap, quit their job, go do it full-time—no matter how much it sucks—and convince one other person to do the same thing with them, they're going to have a much, much higher chance of actually getting somewhere. Because they either have to succeed or get a job. Sometimes "succeed" seems like the easier path than actually getting a job, which is depressing.

So quit your day job. Have one other founder, at least. I'd say that's the minimum bar to getting anywhere.

Stephen Kaufer
Cofounder, TripAdvisor

Steve Kaufer, Langley Steinert, Nick Shanny, and Thomas Palka started TripAdvisor, an online travel site, in 2000. Frustrated by the lack of unbiased, useful information for travelers, they created a site that, in addition to searching relevant content already on the Web, let users contribute personal reviews of destinations, hotels, and attractions. The online travel forum was a pioneer in the now common practice of having users pick the winners, instead of leaving the choices up to human editors.

TripAdvisor became the largest online travel community in the world, and was acquired in 2004 by Barry Diller's InterActiveCorp (IAC). As of July 2006, TripAdvisor had amassed more than five million user reviews and opinions, covering 220,000-plus hotels and attractions.

Livingston: How did TripAdvisor begin?

Kaufer: The idea came when my wife, Caroline, and I were trying to find a vacation for ourselves. We started with a travel agent, who recommended an island and some resort. This was '98 or '99, and I thought I'd use the Internet to find out more. I found a whole lot of websites that would help me book a reservation at this hotel, but nothing that would tell me whether the hotel was any good or not for what I was looking for.

Eventually I found some chat rooms that told me that the island was not particularly safe, and we really didn't want to go there. That was kind of an eye-opener. We said, "Good power of the Internet there. Let's switch travel agents." We went to a different one, who recommended a different island, different place. That time, when I did the research on the Web, after a lot of effort I found out that the hotel was really not up to my wife's standards. The picture of the hotel in the brochure was fabulous, of course, but the commentary from somebody's home page that I had found wasn't too good.

By that point, I had spent a couple of days in sort of mindless searches, trying to find the real scoop on the hotel, not the official blurb. My wife suggested, "You know something about technology. You could build a better search engine to find what you're looking for in travel—not the published opinion, but the unpublished, unbiased opinion about a place, a location, something to do."

I was employed at the time, so we put the idea on ice for about a year. In late '99, the idea resurfaced. I wanted to get out of what I was doing, and started to assemble friends that I had worked with before who might be interested in starting an Internet company to build the best travel search engine out there—where we would define "best" as not searching for prices, but really finding the unbiased information.

I was introduced by a friend to another cofounder, Langley Steinert, on the business, marketing, business development, financing side of things. So the two of us kind of took up the project as, "Hey, this is something the world clearly needs." I felt I could build it with the team of folks I had in mind from past lives. Langley had the business development experience and connections to sell and market it. Because I had started a few companies before, I knew it was important to have the right combination of skills and interests amongst the founders. We assembled four initial founders of the company and got our first round of funding in February of 2000.

Livingston: Where was your office when you started?

Kaufer: My late wife actually owned a software company that was just down the road in Needham [Massachusetts]. It was a small and declining company, which, for the first 10 months or so of our existence, gave TripAdvisor free rent, T1, computers, and other stuff that it had and wasn't using. So it wasn't technically a garage. It was closer to a second-floor attic above a pizza place. It was all one big, open floor, and the room could comfortably seat eight. By the time we busted out of there, we had 15 people. Then we just moved down the street.

Livingston: So your idea was to somehow collect the consumer feedback on different hotels, airlines—anything related to travel?

Kaufer: We were going to focus on destinations, hotels, and attractions. We've always pretty much stayed away from collecting opinions on air, for instance. But we were going to search the Web, just like Google—or AltaVista, which was king of the hill in those days—but with a focus on travel. We'd be able to come up with better results, where better was, again, not just all the booking sites that would help you book a room in a hotel, but really opinionated information.

We'd find the articles from the *New York Times*, *Boston Globe*, *LA Times*, local newspapers, etc. The back issue of *Ski Magazine* might have a great article all about Aspen, but you'd never find it, because it's tucked away in the archive section and probably wouldn't show up on Google. It was written last year— "Great Things To Do for Families in Aspen." A fantastic article, and what was good last year is probably still just as good today, but you'd never find it but for our very focused travel search engine.

Livingston: How was the technology designed to do this? Was it a crawler?

Kaufer: We tried different approaches. We tried to randomly crawl the Web and we thought, "How are we going to randomly select out of the billions of pages?" So we tried crawling from known travel hubs. We'd start from the Yahoo Travel directory and see where those sites led us. We tried to pick out good, interesting information and automatically categorize it. That didn't work so well. What we call the signal-to-noise ratio wasn't good enough—meaning that, when they got our results back, people wouldn't say, "Oh yeah, that's what I was looking for."

We ended up looking at all of the published sources of information—newspapers, magazines—and manually went through all the websites from all these places to find the ones that had free access to the back issues of their travel articles. Then we hired people to read every single travel article we could find on the Net, and classify that article into our database, and write a one-line summary. It's a fairly significant effort, and people that we talked to said, "You're nuts. You'll never finish." But if you actually do the math, you realize that you can work through the backlog (it took us a couple of years, but it was only a couple of years) and then can stay current with what's being published without too much of an effort.

We take half an hour to read an article, on average, and we'll tag that article as being relevant to everything the article talks about. If the article is about Maui and things to do in Hawaii and these two resorts, whenever you're searching for Maui or things to do in Hawaii or those two resorts, that article will come up. If that article happened to mention, "The beaches in Maui are much better than the beaches in Fort Lauderdale," and you were to search on the beaches in Fort Lauderdale, that article is not going to come up, because our search isn't keyword-based. It doesn't matter if the article happens to mention something; you only want to read the article if it's actually giving you an opinion on the topic you're researching.

What we ended up with was a much smaller database as measured by the number of documents that we'd indexed, but extremely, extremely relevant. You go to a page about Maui, and every article on that page really is about Maui, sorted to a pretty good degree based upon which article most people would rather read first. Would you rather read an article that has a paragraph about Maui in talking about fun beaches around the world, or an article all about beaches in Maui? Probably the latter, so that's why the article is sorted first. Your experience on TripAdvisor—again, this was initially, when we launched the site—was very fulfilling, because the information we found was always spot-on. We didn't always have something, but what we had was always a match.

Jumping forward in time as the site grew, all of a sudden now those hundreds of thousands of articles are dwarfed by the user reviews that our visitors have generated. It's fresher information and tends to be more detailed. To many people, it's more reliable.

There's a whole other theoretical discussion of, "Would you rather read a review about a hotel by Aunt Mary you've never heard of from Bloomingdale, Indiana, or from *Frommer's*, the trusted guidebook brand?" And the follow-up question is, "Would you rather read 20 reviews from people you don't know, or 1 review from *Frommer's*?" Near as I can tell, most people, when given the choice of only one piece of information, will take the *Frommer's*—even though they might be suspicious it's a little old or a little vague. But when you have 10 or 20 reviews, and you have a half a dozen written in the past couple of weeks, you know you're getting an unvarnished and up-to-date version of what you're looking for. And colorful.

Livingston: Were the people originally gathering all this content TripAdvisor employees, or were they contractors?

Kaufer: A combination.

Livingston: You said it took a couple years to populate the site. Did you launch the site before it was fully populated?

Kaufer: Oh yeah. We started in February 2000, and in October 2000 we launched the site, but it only covered the United States. Over the course of the next 2 years, we rolled out the rest of the world geographically. Of course, we were always adding more and more content as we found it. When we launched, if you picked the 20th hotel in our popularity index in Boston, there might have been one or two articles about that hotel, which is a heck of a lot better than none, but nothing compared to what we have now.

Livingston: How did people find TripAdvisor when you first launched?

Kaufer: When we started TripAdvisor, the notion was TripAdvisor.com was actually just going to be our demo site, because we never planned to appeal directly to end users. We were going to be selling this rich database to travel portals, online travel sites. They would be querying our database to find the best information and surfacing it to their users, and there would be a little "Powered by TripAdvisor."

Because we would have the richest database of travel information, our hope was that it would become a requirement that, if you were in the travel industry or offering a travel section of your site, you have access to our content. And we would license it out and/or get a share of the revenue generated on the page views from that. Lycos Travel, Yahoo Travel, AOL Travel, Expedia, Travelocity— all the players would have to have it. No one would try to build it themselves, because we'd always be able to stay ahead, since we were entirely focused on it. That would be our business model, and that's the model that got us some funding to begin with.

After a year and a half, we had closed one licensing deal, with Lycos, where they were featuring our content on their travel portal, and we were getting a revenue share on what they made selling advertising on the pages that we produced for them. Everyone else basically wanted to be paid to feature our content, and we wanted to *get* paid to have our content featured. So there was a pretty big disconnect. Then it turned out that with the Lycos deal (even though Lycos was a major web property at the time), the joke was the quarterly revenue check wouldn't buy the weekly free lunch that we offered to our employees. We had a rather fundamental problem in half of the business. It was a typical dot-com business problem: built the product, people liked it, and the feedback was universally positive, and we got the expansion questions that we were happy to get, like "When are you going to cover Paris?"—but we just were not making a dime.

By the middle of 2001, we were getting frustrated. Then September 11 came along, and anything we might have had in the pipeline—not that I remember it being a particularly interesting pipeline—was stalled, dead. It was a hugely traumatic time for everyone, especially for the travel industry.

We were also trying to raise a third round of funding, and we were basically looking at going out of business in 6 to 9 months. It was a little hard to go back to the existing investors and say, "Hey, pony up more money. We've got a great product. We have no revenue, and we've been trying to sell the stuff for a while. We have no takers. The one company that did license it is generating a couple hundred dollars a quarter for us. But really, toss in a couple more million, because it's a great idea." It was a tough pitch to make. We made it, and we actually did raise a small third round—more, I think, from the perspective of "Look, this is a good product. We'll figure this out."

We were 11 people before September 11, and we slimmed down to 8, so our burn rate was really pretty small. Everyone took salary cuts; we were paying $18 a square foot for office space; we had really no expenses to speak of. We were stretching the dollars, and even though it was Internet dot-com days, we had never done anything remotely lavish.

So we're approaching late 2001, and we noticed our demo site, TripAdvisor.com, had started to get some traffic. Just people finding it. We tried to be active in PR from day one, so we'd gotten some mentions in various press. I'm not entirely sure how people were finding it—search engines, whatever. And we certainly weren't doing anything monetizing the traffic. We thought, "OK, with 5,000 visitors a day, let's go run some banner ads, see if we can make some money that way."

We tried running a banner ad. We didn't try to sell it; we just copied Expedia's banner ad and put it up on our site. We wanted to see how many people would click on it. We might have had 3,000 visitors that day and we might have generated 100 clicks, so maybe it would have been a couple of dollars to us. So that was just clearly not going to work. But one of our prospects a couple of months earlier had asked us whether or not we could run ads based upon the search query. If someone was searching on "Boston," could we run an ad for Boston? We explained, "We don't run ads. That's not our model. We're trying to license you the content." But it struck us months later that we do have people that are qualifying themselves to be interested in Boston. In fact, we have people qualifying themselves to be interested in the Eliot Hotel in Boston, because they're reading a review about it. What if we created a link from TripAdvisor deep to an online travel site like Expedia and had teaser text that said, "Book a room at the Eliot Hotel in Boston," and, if the user clicked on that link, we took them all the way down to the booking page on Expedia? Our crawler technology knew how to do that, so it was leveraging something we were pretty good at.

We approached Expedia and said, "Hey, we'd like to advertise your 50,000 hotels on our comprehensive travel site, and we want to charge you only for the leads that we'll send you." I explained how our leads were highly qualified. "These are wonderful travelers, they're reading reviews, and we're going to do lots of bookings for you, so we'd like you to advertise with us." He said, "I've never heard of you guys. Prove it."

I can certainly understand why he'd never heard of us, because no one had. And he didn't really care much whether I was sending him qualified leads or not. He only cared about whether the leads I sent were going to make reservations. The way it works is, they give you a tracking code to put on the link. We said, "It's no work for you. Give me the tracking code; I'll start to advertise 50,000 properties for you." Which I did, and we ran it for a month for free for them. Then, before the month was out, I gave them a call and said, "How's it going?" And he said, "Well, I just looked at the stats the other day. You guys are doing pretty well. Can I pay you $10,000 for December to buy 20,000 (or whatever the exact numbers were) leads?" Here was a client who was on the second or third call offering to pay me money to keep the links up.

This worked. We actually got a lot of people clicking. Probably 10 percent of the time that people saw that page, they were clicking on one of those links. Click-through rates at the time were a quarter of a percent or half a percent. Here we were sitting at 10 percent because the links were so relevant to the topic at hand. Our first client was thrilled with it.

Livingston: Expedia was the first client?

Kaufer: Yes. He said, "If they stop actually doing bookings and they just click over, then I'm not renewing the order. So it's up to you guys to keep your traffic qualified." This wasn't really an issue for us, but it just drove home the point: if he got bookings, he would happily pay us for advertising.

We said, "If we do more traffic in January, are you willing to spend more?" He goes, "Yeah, we can ramp it up to $20,000 if you have more leads." Once he got a little comfortable with us that he wasn't going to lose his job over committing to a faulty buy, it quickly became, "Hey, send us as much as you can. There's no cap on this number." And the guy that I was starting with—talking at ten grand a month, we were in the hundreds of thousands not too much later— it would be another year before I actually met him, because it was just a very practical, "You're sending me leads that I'm tracking through to people that actually buy products on my site. I know how much I make when they buy my airline ticket or my hotel room, and I'm paying you a percentage of that. So the more leads you send, the more money I make."

TripAdvisor never knew whether we were earning 25 percent of their profits or 90 percent of their profits—the answer is somewhere in between—but it became a pretty easy sales cycle, if you will. And then we started growing traffic to TripAdvisor.com, and we started expanding our client set beyond Expedia, to hotels.com, Travelocity, and eventually Orbitz and others.

Livingston: Did you use the same strategy with other companies: "Try us out for a month, and, if you feel like we've driven some true leads, you'll continue with us"?

Kaufer: Yes. Once other companies saw Expedia advertising, they sometimes didn't need a free test, but we might say, "Look, our leads are normally a dollar a click, because they convert so well. But we'll let you get started at a quarter. And we'll send you 5,000 leads, and you can test with no risk. But you know, we're looking for an insertion order to show that you're committed to the test."

Invariably it would take three months to get a test going. You have to find the right person; you have to introduce yourself; you have to decide whether it's an ad agency or direct with the client and lots of other annoying aspects. But for the most part, once the client was getting the leads, the leads would convert well enough such that they would be up and stay up for years and years. So there wasn't a whole lot of maintenance involved. Our technology would automatically find the right links to advertise.

Livingston: It sounds like finally figuring out how you were going to make money was a major turning point for you.

Kaufer: Right. We went from no revenue to break-even in the course of about 4 months. That part was a testament to finding a model that worked. To break even, I had to do $75,000 in revenue for the month, something like that. We had never let our burn rate grow. We didn't do any advertising at that time. But even since, we're rarely going to do promotions that we can't tie back to actual revenue-generating activities on the site.

Livingston: Why were you so careful about spending money? Had you had a bad experience before?

Kaufer: By 2000, we'd certainly seen the dot-coms that would move into the $50-a-square-foot offices, hire loads of people to get it all done quick—to get big fast, etc. Several of them had already flamed out. That was really never in my blood, if you will. The other company I had started right out of college was self-funded, and then a tiny bit of angel investing, and then half a million dollars, and then a couple of million dollars, where the last round was purely growth capital. We had always run that profitably and had grown slowly because of it.

I guess I had toyed with the idea of doing the same here—taking my savings, building the product, not looking for any venture money—but that would have taken a long time. I had a family to support, that sort of stuff. So we certainly decided early on to go raise some money, and within the first year we had raised $3 million or so—but a comparatively small amount of money.

There wasn't anything obvious that we should spend money on, other than hiring a lot of people, and I'm just a fundamental believer in small teams do better than big teams. We were building a product, and if there were 5 people and they were all within shouting distance of each other, they were going to build a better product than if we had had 15 people. Really, even if I had the dollars, I didn't want to spend the money there. And then, did we need more sales reps without a product to sell? No. Could we have bought more PR? I'm sure we could have. We actually had a full-time PR person pretty early on. But we were never going to raise $20 million for a marketing blitz.

Livingston: When you first started trying to get customers, they said, "Pay you? You need to pay us." What were some of the other things that went wrong when you were trying to figure out your business model?

Kaufer: Building the product actually went along reasonably well. The sales and marketing and business development was the biggest challenge, because we just didn't have any takers. We finally had a major company come forward who wanted to license our database, and they were offering to pay us, I think, $50,000 a month. Maybe it was $30,000. The deal on the table would have covered half of our burn rate, right there, all at once. At the time, we looked at that deal and said, "You know, it may be this or nothing"—as in, if we don't take this, we might just go out of business. When you look at a deal in that light, a very unattractive deal, maybe that's what you have to do to survive.

As we proceeded down the negotiation path with this company, though, it became clearer and clearer that they wanted to be able to cut out of the deal after the term (I think it was 2 years) and essentially walk away with all of our intellectual property. Their point was, "Hey, our dollars are funding a lot of the creation of this thing. We're going to be building a much bigger product around it. If we can't renegotiate terms, you can't cut our product off at the knees and walk away with your database. We need to be protected, and we need a copy of your database and the tools to maintain it. You won't have to maintain it for us anymore, but we'll be able to keep going."

The notion that I take all of my time and energy, build up a business, and then hand another company who is going to be a competitor the crown jewels of the business—fundamentally the business, except for the people—after I thought about it, that ended up making it a reasonably easy decision. "No. I'd rather go out of business than take everything I'd worked for, for so long, and hand it essentially for free to somebody else."

In hindsight, we clearly made the right decision. But at the time it wasn't obvious, so we kept negotiating with them. My tip for someone in a similar situation—a company looks like it might be going out of business—this might be the only way to get enough capital to survive, on terms that really aren't very acceptable: keep pushing at it. Don't say yes too quickly, don't say no too quickly, to see whether any other options come along, or to see whether the deal gets so bad that it actually becomes an easier decision to just say no and you can go about your plans. We had a few sleepless nights back then.

Livingston: Can you think of a moment when you wanted to quit?

Kaufer: No, I never wanted to quit. I mean, it wasn't working, but I was going to find a different way to try—something different, something new.

A good chunk of our engineering team was directed to running tests for prospects who might conceivably be clients. We weren't doing a whole lot of new product innovation, because it wasn't the product that was stopping us from being successful; it was the sales and marketing strategy. I said, "Look, we will take everyone in the company and turn them into somebody that's going to help close the sale to keep this company afloat. So you're doing one of two things: you're either helping on some prospect we were chasing, or you're helping in the financing prospect we were chasing."

I was always certainly cognizant of the fact that, if we didn't do something different, we were going to run out of money in the first half of '02. But it never crossed my mind to just give it up or shut it down.

Livingston: A lot of startups that are based strongly on technology don't have the luxury of having a business guy as one of the founders. Do you think that having Langley on your founding team helped you?

Kaufer: Absolutely. We never would have succeeded without Langley on the team. If I were funding a startup, I wouldn't want to put money in unless I saw somebody identified as having an interest in the business development side of it. I'm an engineer by training myself, but at this point I have so much experience dealing with customers and what they want that I can bring that back to shape the product. Look at me 20 years ago, and at best I was a smart engineer. I didn't know much about business, knew nothing about selling, and unless you have somebody who has an interest in talking with whoever you're selling your product or service to, your product isn't going to turn out to be what the customer wants.

In almost all circumstances I can think of, if not a member of the founding team, you want to say, "With the money I hope to raise from you, this is the person—here's his/her résumé—that we're going to bring on board to take care of the business marketing aspect of it." I've always had that in the startup companies I've been associated with.

Livingston: What competitors were you most scared of as you were building TripAdvisor?

Kaufer: There weren't really direct competitors. We were fighting more of a problem of, "No one else is using your stuff. We seem to be doing OK without it. So why is your stuff critical? Why do I have to pay you for it?" The dollars that might have been spent on us were probably going to a *Frommer's* or *Fodor's*, which were branded content sites.

We would say, "No, no, no. They have one person's opinion, and it was written 6 years ago by someone that may or may not have even visited the hotel. We've got fresh stuff. We've searched for all the stuff around the Web that your visitors want."

But, there were drawbacks to our model, too. A user on Yahoo Travel looking at their description of Boston was reading it on Yahoo Travel. When they came to our Boston page and they wanted to read about fun things to do, we'd take them off to an article on the *New York Times*, or on *Frommer's*, whereupon they would be leaving TripAdvisor or leaving the Yahoo network. Yahoo, like most companies, didn't really want to send a lot of people away. Yet that was how we had such a rich database of information. So a tougher sell.

Livingston: What other things did your customers misunderstand about TripAdvisor, since it was the only one of its kind?

Kaufer: I don't know that they misunderstood too much. Today, user reviews are in many spaces a matter of course. Amazon has done a tremendous job turning that into a significant competitive advantage. In 2001 or 2000, Yahoo wanted to get more than (I'm making up the numbers) $20 million dollars for a 3-year Travelocity contract; they wanted to get $40 million dollars. They wanted to sell a sponsorship to Carnival Cruise Lines for a million dollars. They wanted to monetize their existing travel channel as opposed to improve the content by licensing with TripAdvisor.

It wasn't until around 2004 that we looked at Yahoo Travel as a competitor. It didn't change in 2000; it didn't change in 2001. I mean, the ads changed. They got better at extracting more money, I guess. But the actual content—the reason to go there—didn't change for 3 years straight. It was great to have them as a competitor, in the sense of, you know, pathetic. In 2004 they said, "Whoa!" and really made dramatic improvements, and they built a much better product.

Livingston: Did your writers edit the users' feedback submissions?

Kaufer: No.

Livingston: How did you monitor the entries? Could people say, "This place sucked! Don't go there."

Kaufer: Yes. "This place sucked. Don't go there. Found rats under the bed." Very colorful comments on all sorts of stuff. We'd frequently get threatened by hotel operators who were unhappy with the reviews that were posted.

We look at all the user reviews that come in every day and make sure they meet our posting guidelines: Is it family friendly? Are you using hate speech? Is there racist commentary? We will not edit the reviews at all. We'll either reject a review or allow it to be posted.

Sometimes we make mistakes and post stuff we shouldn't. But those are the mistakes. We'll let the horrible reviews come in and, obviously, post the great reviews as well. If a hotel complains, "Hey, this person is lying about my property. They never stayed here. We never had any record of anyone staying here, blah, blah, blah," we say, "We have a form on the site where the hotel management can post a response, so that our visitors can see both sides of the story." But we won't take down a posting if a hotel owner complains. And we make no attempt to verify the factual accuracy of a review. From our perspective, we have to be a little concerned about libel laws, and we fall under the sort of communications act that says we're a conduit for consumers talking on the Web. You can't sue AT&T for hate speech said on the phone line that they own. You can't sue TripAdvisor for libelous statements that appear on user reviews.

Livingston: Can you think of one example where someone wrote a really scathing review, and the hotel got mad at TripAdvisor?

Kaufer: There was a hotel owner in Italy who had their attorney draft a letter to us, actually all in Italian, saying essentially, "If you don't take this review down, we're going to sue your butts for $2 million." We sent it over to our legal department so they were aware of it, but our response was a polite, "We verified that the review meets our guidelines." End of story.

In 5 years, we haven't been sued by anyone—because, when you actually go look up the law, we're protected. There may be some hotel owners with a legitimate beef, but there are some hotel owners that are really just not very bright. They'll complain about how terrible this review is and their email is from abc@yahoo.com, and then the next day a review will appear on their property, written by an email address of abc@yahoo.com, saying, "I stayed at this place, and it was absolutely magnificent. The views were spectacular." I'm thinking, "You're just writing a review, posing as a guest, on your own property—24 hours ago you used the same email address to tell us that you were the owner complaining about a past review. Do you really think we're that dumb?"

Initially it really didn't matter. Our traffic is so high now that we know, for better or for worse, we have a significant impact on where visitors are choosing to stay. For every city, we kind of have a satisfaction index; we rate which hotels our travelers like the most. If you're ranked first or you're ranked 20th, the number of reservation calls or bookings you're going to get is going to change. When we changed our algorithm, it dropped some hotels and raised others. Our phones were ringing, because we had had a material effect on their businesses.

When Google changes their algorithm today or when they update things, it has a significant effect on the people who run their business based upon getting traffic from the Google search engine. For us it's a responsibility, because we want people to trust TripAdvisor. People absolutely post scathing reviews. But we don't want to be spammed. We don't want hotel owners to tell all of their employees to go write wonderful reviews of the property. So we have our techniques and our human and algorithmic ways to detect that sort of fraud, to keep the accuracy of TripAdvisor as high as we can.

Livingston: I like that your site has an impact on keeping the hotel owners honest.

Kaufer: It's not just for traveling, but for a lot of things that people are collecting user reviews on now. You may go to Cincinnati for a business or leisure trip. If you have a bad experience with a Super 8 motel, before a site like TripAdvisor, basically there was nothing you could do about it. You could file a complaint at the Better Business Bureau, but how many times have you, when making a reservation at a place you've never stayed at, called up the local Better Business Bureau to find out how many complaints were lodged? None. So here you go to TripAdvisor and you look up the place, and you see that seven out of the last eight reviews all gave it a 1 out of 5 rating and talked about smelly carpets and rude staff. You're just not going to stay there unless it's the only place in town.

That's the impact that five or six people had. Total strangers. But the hotel owner that wants to run this crappy place, preying off of the brand that they're under, and maybe their location as being near to something, that person has to kind of shape up, maybe take something out of their profits and put it back into providing a good service for the customers, because word is spreading. And TripAdvisor is the conduit in the travel space for spreading that word.

Livingston: Looking back on your experience with TripAdvisor, what was most surprising about it?

Kaufer: Certainly the most surprising to me was how much people voluntarily share their experiences. I had never written a review before starting TripAdvisor. I had never posted my comments on Amazon or anywhere else. But we're able to collect millions of opinions each year. It is 2006, and we're up to over five million now. So you have a lot of people out there that, for absolutely no reward whatsoever—we don't pay them for opinions, we never have—will take the time to write a review or answer someone else's question.

Maybe it's because we're the size we are and that people have gotten a lot of content, so now they're interested in sort of giving back to the site that helped them make a decision. But the fact that we're able to collect so much on an ongoing basis isn't something I would have predicted.

Livingston: Is there any advice that you would give to someone who is thinking about starting a startup?

Kaufer: Certainly the founding team makes the biggest difference. Usually founding teams don't stay together for very long. That happens. If the founding team splits in the first 6 months, that can be pretty devastating to the birth of a company. So getting to know someone before actually joining forces, spending some more time thinking through what the roles and responsibilities will be between the founding team members. You hear breakup stories of, "Well, I was going to do this." "No, I wanted to do that." "Oh, you're taking too much control over this." Unfortunately, odds are high that'll happen anyway. But if you can iron all that out before you actually start the company, or pick different founders, it'll improve your chances of success.

Tip number two: you can't get too attached to your vision in a startup, because things may change. It's not a sign of failure to change your vision. I remember in a previous company, we wanted to be this, but we were offered a consulting contract to do this, that, and the other thing, and, yeah, that wasn't in the plan, but we'll take that, because that's going to add $50,000 to our startup capital, and it'll only take x amount of time. Yeah, be wary of distractions, but if you're lightning-focused on just one thing and aren't willing to consider others, you probably don't have the flexibility to make it when things don't go according to plan. That's the one truism: things won't go according to plan.

At the earlier stages of the company, when you're actually out trying to get some customers, do whatever the hell the customer wants. If they're going to pay you, the customer is right. Because you need that initial money. You need that customer on the list to go get the next one. If you have to give away whatever you're doing, give it away. Get the customer. Make them into a reference account. Make that customer into the person that sings your praises the loudest, and really uses your product or service.

It's perfectly fine if you knew that customer through a past life and that's how they got to be a customer. Maybe they'll be even more honest with you. If it means adding a new feature to your product, or whatever, to close that initial sale, and it's not on strategy, screw the strategy. Do it, collect the money, get the customer, and move forward.

Then, as you're growing, sort of mid-stage, what I tried to foster here is an attitude of risk-taking, where all I want to know really is what's my downside scenario in terms of time and opportunity cost? If I can try something offbeat, weird-sounding, and it takes a few weeks, and the downside is, in my case, I rip it out of the live website, or, if you're producing software, I rip it out of the piece of software, or I don't document the feature if I'm producing a piece of hardware or whatever—if the amount of time spent making a mistake is small, don't be afraid to make a lot of mistakes without a lot of time analyzing whether you should or shouldn't do it.

On the Web, it's particularly easy to try something and get feedback. If it doesn't work, drop it. I've come up with really interesting ideas that were utter and complete failures on the site, and I make fun of myself in company meetings when I talk about those. Then I look at each group and say, "Hey, I'm hoping every one of you—in addition to all the successful ideas you'll come up with—aren't afraid to come up with some resounding failures." You just want the failure to cost you a couple of weeks, a month or two—it depends on the industry—a small, fixed cost. It's the old adage: if we're not failing at something on a regular basis, we're just not trying hard enough.

Livingston: Obviously your story ended wonderfully. You were acquired for around $200 million?

Kaufer: Yeah. I don't think of the story ending that way, but that's how the third chapter ended.

Livingston: Sorry, I didn't mean it like that. But most startups do want to have a liquidity event. Would you have done anything differently before that, to get there?

Kaufer: No. With TripAdvisor, it all really did work out well. Certainly one of the keys to our success was being fanatical on the hiring side of things. I was almost going to answer, "Well, I would have liked to have hired more top-notch folks throughout the company earlier." Because I'm still in that position now—I'm still struggling to fill positions with the types of people that we want to hire. It's not something that we do very efficiently here. It takes us a long time to fill a req.

When we do fill a req, we have a fantastic success rate. Many observers and people that have done due diligence on TripAdvisor over the years have commented on the caliber of individuals here. But if I ever start another company again, I'd love to have as a founding or very early team member someone who was a trusted recruiter. Because the difference in almost any position between someone who does a good job and someone who does a great job might be 20 percent more in salary, but it's 100 or 200 percent more in throughput. If you can have enough people in the company that work twice as efficiently as the person sitting next to them, because they just know what to do, what not to spend time on . . . I mean everyone, they're more or less all working the same number of hours. It's rarely a work ethic issue. It's just, hey, you give this engineer a task, and it's just done right in half the time as the next person. That it's done right, that's the first important part; it's done quick; and there's just less communication if the teams are smaller, because everyone's getting twice as much done. Now how the heck do you fill a company with people like that in every single department? Well, you tap out of your friends pretty quick; but absolutely, go hire your friends.

As I advise other startups from time to time, if you find someone you like, pay what it takes to get them to come to your company in options or in salary, depending on the company's stage. But getting the right people—especially in that first dozen—is so much more important than getting the req filled. Unfortunately that slows down the hiring process a lot, which slows your growth a lot, which is how I circle back to say, "In the next company, I'd hope to have a recruiter on board within the first half a dozen people to help get the right next 12 people."

Most recruiters don't work that way, don't think that way. Recruiters want to know, "What requirements do you need in the job?" My answer is, I want passion. I want people that really care about doing a great job. It's just a different mindset. That's software, that's customer acquisition, that's branding, that's PR. It's really not in any one department. It's an attitude. And it makes a company a hell of a lot more interesting to work at.

So in turn, it actually makes recruiting a little easier, because you come in, you meet the people, "Man, you've got a bunch of sharp people here." "Yeah, that's right. And Expedia did a customer survey for us, and it came back that 98 percent of the people said they really enjoyed working with the other people here."

Livingston: Does Barry Diller let you do your own thing, now that you've been acquired? How was the transition to being part of a larger organization?

Kaufer: IAC was a fantastic company to be acquired by, because they told us their history was, "We acquire companies and we let them run stand-alone." So we came on board. I have to report finances up through IAC instead of my own five to seven person board. Other than that, we were really left on our own. Even when we had ups and downs in our numbers, we were left on our own. They were true to their word. And my hat's off to them, because you so often read about small, entrepreneurial companies like ours being acquired and it being a disaster, because founders leave, teams quit, an infrastructure process is put in place that doesn't fit. IAC said, "Hey, you're running a business. Tell us what you're going to do, then do that. And let us know when you need help." That's what we've done.

Livingston: I noticed you don't have a receptionist.

Kaufer: I couldn't figure out what a receptionist would do. And executive assistants, we don't have those either. So on the subject of hiring, I don't look at a head count budget when I think of hiring people. I wait until I see the need for someone—when I can carve out a job description that's 80 percent full on the day someone starts—and that's when I'll open up a new req.

For receptionists and executive assistants, it's something of a running joke because, well, what are they going to do? Make travel plans for us? We already know how to do that. Answer the phones? Well, I can answer my own phone; it's not too much of a bother. Schedule meetings? Well, we try not to have too many meetings to schedule. So if we were to hire one, I'm sure they would be busy all the time, but perhaps not doing anything that really needed to be done at TripAdvisor. With engineering, there's usually more development that I want done, but I can look and say, "Am I willing to fund that project?" With marketing, with customer acquisition, with accounting, I first look and say, "Hey, what's taking people's time? What can we automate?" If I can't automate it, do I really need it to be done? If I do need it to be done, all right, then we'll open a req.

We're 70 people now, which is pretty small, given the revenues and profits that we're producing. Nobody in corporate would blink if I said, "Hey, I want to have 20 more people on board." Our margins would still be terrific and I could afford it, but I'm not sure it would speed things up or slow things down.

Livingston: It sounds like you're really maintaining a good atmosphere, and one where innovation can happen rather than just saying, "We've been bought. I'm leaving now. It's 5 o'clock."

Kaufer: Chapter one is starting up the company, getting anyone interested in what we do. Chapter two was hitting that profitability mark so we could break even. Chapter three is growing, and if it so happens, as it did with us, a great liquidity event. Chapter four is, "OK, are you done with the business? Do you already have a commanding number one market share and no competitors?" Well, that's pretty rare. Certainly it isn't true for us. We may be ahead of our competitors, or tied with our competitors, but how close am I to being the number one travel site in the world? Well, I'm pretty far away from that. I have some sister companies that have that spot. But I look at it and say, "Why wouldn't everyone want to start on TripAdvisor when planning a trip?" So if I have 20 million uniques a month now, why don't I have 50 million? My definition of chapter four is being the most popular travel site in the world.

James Hong
Cofounder, HOT or NOT

While looking for a job in 2000, James Hong launched a website with his friend Jim Young just for fun. HOT or NOT lets users submit photos of themselves and have others vote on their "hotness" on a scale of 1 to 10.

The site spread virally, and within hours their server was swamped. Hong and Young sensed there was a business in it, and worked frantically to scale the site to handle the load.

A few months after launching, they found the way to generate revenue from the site: they added dating for a monthly fee. Despite many acquisition offers, HOT or NOT continues to thrive as a stand-alone company. As of July 2006, HOT or NOT had counted about 13 billion votes.

Livingston: Take me back to when you had the idea.

Hong: Jim, my brother and I were hanging out drinking, and Jim mentioned that he thought a girl he met at a party was hot, and that she was a perfect 10.

My brother and I were working on a website at the time called XMethods, which was the first directory of publicly available web services, so we were talking a lot about what would be a cool consumer web service. In 1999, everyone was talking about web services in the context of B2B, and I remember thinking, "What about consumers? Aren't consumers going to do this stuff too?"

When Jim said that he thought he found a 10, an idea popped into my head: what if you had a service where people could post their pictures into the system, and then other people could rate them from 1 to 10? The original vision was that your client would call the web services, get a picture, and have it randomly float across your screen or pop up on your screen at random times during the day. The idea was that all our friends that were working in cubicles could have a window: a random girl walking by you that they could rate from 1 to 10 on if you thought she was hot.

Livingston: It was just for fun, not an idea for a startup?

Hong: Jim was burned out from working on his PhD, and I had just graduated from business school and was unemployed, so I figured what the hell, let's build it. It wasn't that hard to build in the beginning—it was hard to build later because we had to scale it—but just putting up something that looked like it worked was easy. It was not something we focused on. We had the idea one Monday, and it was coded by Wednesday or Thursday in spare time, really, and then Jim sent it to me on the weekend. There was no hurry; this was not something we were thinking about.

The weekend before it launched, I was visiting my parents and my dad walked into the room and saw me playing with the site and he asked what I was doing. I didn't want to admit that I was spending time on this thing since I was unemployed and should have been looking for a job, so I told him it was something Jim was doing. My dad was the first person that ever saw HOT or NOT besides Jim and me, and he got addicted to it! Here's my dad, a 60-year-old retired Chinese guy who, as my father, is supposed to be asexual, and he's saying, "She's hot. This one's not hot at all." We knew then that the idea had some legs, but we didn't know how much.

So we launched it on Monday with our own pictures, and at around 2 p.m. I emailed it to 40 friends and wrote, "Here's a website that Jim and I made—be nice." And I put a link to my picture on the site so they could rate me. I think we got 40,000 hits that day.

Livingston: Forty thousand hits on your first day when only a handful of people knew it existed?

Hong: I don't think I've ever told anyone this, but after I sent out that first email, I went rollerblading around a big office park where Tellme was based. I went up to a random guy and said, "Hey man, have you checked out hotornot.com yet?" He said, "No, what's that?" I said, "Dude, just go check it out!" Then I went home and watched our logs for Tellme and saw a hit come in 10 minutes later, and then more hits kept coming from different people within Tellme.

Three days later I went back to that parking lot and found someone else and asked, "Have you seen some site where you rate people from 1 to 10?" And he said, "Yeah, dude, HOT or NOT!" So that was cool; it totally spread on its own.

Livingston: You had people coming to your site from the very beginning. At what point did you decide that it could be a business? What were the next steps?

Hong: That question implies planning. We were more concerned with fear and survival at the time. I was interviewed by Salon.com the day we launched the site, and that started a string of near disasters.

Livingston: You were "not ready for prime time"?

Hong: Not at all. The site was on the XMethods server and we really needed to get it off because the traffic was shutting it down. The bandwidth was crazy; we were hosting the pictures at the time. After you voted, it took 30 seconds to get the next page—and at the end of the first day I calculated that this thing was going to cost at least $150,000 in bandwidth per year at the current run rate, and it was growing fast.

We realized quickly that the momentum would make us broke. I was already $60,000 in debt from grad school. I had turned down a consulting job paying around $170,000. I did it to roll the dice, but I was poor. I knew we couldn't afford this and thought seriously about shutting it down.

Livingston: So what did you do?

Hong: We were panicking at this point. There was no plan for a business, it was just, "How the fuck do we keep this thing going?" We weren't trying to figure out what kind of boat we needed to build, we were trying to keep from drowning. But we did know a few things: we had to reduce our costs, we had to make it make money somehow, and we needed more machines. And because the idea could be so easily copied, we had to get as much press as possible to lock out anyone else from getting publicity.

So it was panic. The whole point was just to keep going, keep going, don't stop. I got 8 hours of sleep in the first 8 days, and finally they made me sleep because I was literally shaking.

Livingston: Take me through the turning points of the first 8 days.

Hong: Basically, the feeling was: do whatever you have to do, just scrape on by. So we first addressed the biggest problem, which was getting rid of the huge bandwidth driven by the pictures. That was why we almost shut down the site. It was 12:30 a.m. after the day we launched, and I was sitting in the drive-thru at In-N-Out when I had an idea.

Three days earlier, my brother and I had launched something on XMethods, which was a web service–based file system, basically a network drive, and I showed it to Dave Winer. Though he subsequently copied it, at that time he said, "Why the hell would I need that? That's called FTP. I have a Yahoo GeoCities account that lets me FTP to it." I owe Dave a lot for his cynicism.

So sitting in line, I remembered what Dave had said, and I thought, "Holy shit, we don't need to host the pictures, we'll let Yahoo do it!

"We'll just FTP all the pictures we have now up to a Yahoo GeoCities account, and we'll change the database records so that it will point to the files on Yahoo, and then from that point on, we'll just make instructions telling people to go to Yahoo GeoCities and then submit URLs of their pictures."

We lost some users from submitting it this way, obviously, but it solved the problem. And the way I figured it, I said to Jim, "Dude, how many page views, especially at the speed of the site, will anyone have each day, maybe 25? All we need is 25 new pictures a day and we're done. We don't have to have a billion pictures, we just need 25 new pictures a day. So that's what we did. And this wasn't planning, it was survival mode. I can't tell you enough how much it was survival. Desperation is a good word to describe it.

So between 12:30 and 3 a.m. on the day we launched, we moved all the pictures to Yahoo and solved the image problem.

But the Salon.com article was coming out the next morning. I called the writer and asked her if she could push the story back, but she said it was a slow news day and she couldn't. So the article came out and the server got slammed. My brother needed the server for XMethods, so we did the quickest thing we could think of, which was that night at 3:00 a.m., we took the site down, grabbed an extra PC—a 400 megahertz Celeron, no-memory-in-it machine that I got for free when I opened an eTrade account—and drove to Berkeley where Jim had a shared office.

I remember taking the top off a case for pushpins and mounting it on top of the power switch of the machine so no one could turn it off. Then we put it in the corner under his desk and surrounded it with books, so it just looked like a bunch of stuff under his desk with a little Ethernet cable coming out.

And as soon as we turned the site back on, the access logs started flying. It was 5 in the morning!

Livingston: So what next?

Hong: We now had solved the two most immediate problems to keep the site running, so we were breathing a little easier, but the site was still slow. On day three, I started looking into managed hosts, and Rackspace came up as the clear Linux leader. Though we had no money, we were getting a lot of press, so after a failed attempt to pitch my idea to the Rackspace salesperson, I called the head of business development and said, "I know you guys want to go public and it's great to get your name out. Your whole value proposition is that you can help companies scale fast by outsourcing. If you can help us, I have all these upcoming interviews, and we can be a poster child for you."

He said, "OK, don't worry, just tell us what you need right now to scale, and we'll figure it out later." So every day that week, I would call them and say that we needed more machines. We owe Rackspace big.

At the same time, a friend suggested that we sign up for an ad network, and we were trying to get into 24/7. But we were having a lot of problems with porn and naked picture submissions to the site. And I knew that no one would advertise if this was dirty. So we came up with the motto "Fun, clean, and real" and created a system where people could click a link under an inappropriate picture and, based on an algorithm, we would kill any picture that got clicked on too much. So it was community-regulated and that worked pretty well.

I sent an email to the founder of DoubleClick telling him about us and requesting his help getting into 24/7. He responded saying that unfortunately the first picture he got when he went to our site was a naked woman. He said that right now we were innocent until proven guilty, but we needed to move to a guilty until proven innocent model in order to get advertising.

So we decided to build a moderation system. I originally had my parents moderating since they were retired, and after a few days I asked my dad how it was going. He said, "Oh, it's really interesting. Mom saw a picture of a guy and a girl and another girl and they were doing . . ." So I told Jim, "Dude, my parents can't do this any more. They're looking at porn all day." We decided to open up the community of moderators to the public. You had to apply and write an essay to get in. It was basically built on the BBSs of the old days that had different levels with different skills.

We told the moderators to reject any pictures that were inappropriate, looked like an ad, or had contact info. (Pornographers were including fake email addresses to get people to email them so they would spam them later.) And then we got a bunch of emails from people saying, "Hey, I was meeting people."

We quickly realized that we needed to make something to allow people to meet each other without letting all these porn people in. So we came up with the "Meet" system, which required a little more work than most dating sites, because it requires both people to be active. You can't just post an ad and wait for emails to come in, so it's harder for porn people to come in and take advantage of it.

As we were solving the problem of keeping the site clean so that we could get advertisers, ad rates were dropping. We had to come up with something that we had more control over, and that's when I thought, "Can we charge for anything?" We started charging $6 per month to belong to the Meet Me system. We chose the pricing based on what we thought would be an impulse buy.

In retrospect, it's easy to see that we had this dating system that was slapping us in the face, but it took us a while to think that we could charge for it, because the Meet Me system was never built to make money. It was only built in response to the porn issue. It's ironic that I have an MBA and also started a company before that had raised venture capital, but the one idea that worked was all an accident.

Another thread of what happened was that I was trying to reduce our costs. Though we weren't being charged yet by Rackspace, I now knew how much we needed to cover those hosting costs, plus enough to hire someone to manage the site. After running into a guy who worked at Ofoto at an office-warming party, I talked to Ofoto about how we were sending people to GeoCities, and since many of our users have digital cameras, maybe I should send them to Ofoto instead of Yahoo to host them, and now Ofoto would have a lead. So I did an affiliate deal with Ofoto.

It's funny to think that we took something that was originally costing a lot of money, to making them free, to actually making money on some of them. Again, all of this wasn't planned or brilliant, we were just trying to survive. At this point we thought, "OK this deal buys us more time."

On top of all this, we were constantly fixing the site to scale. We were working like madmen, only getting 3 to 4 hours of sleep a night for a long time. It became a race between Jim and me; could I bring in people faster than he could keep up with? It was a good challenge for both of us. My job was to make a bottleneck and his job was to clear the bottleneck, technically. So we didn't really get to breathe until we had the Meet Me system and it was making money. I think it made about half a million a year when we started, and we now had a scalable business model.

But we still didn't think it was going to be a business at that point; we didn't think it was going to continue growing. We thought it was just going to be there and we would hire someone to run it, and then I would go back to working on XMethods and Jim would go back to his PhD.

Livingston: At one point did you think you were really in it, you would have this startup and be the CEO?

Hong: To be honest, I never considered myself the CEO, even up until the point I quit. It was really a partnership between Jim and I. I carried the CEO title because I was the one running around talking to people. What is the CEO of a two-person company where the two people are equal shareholders? What does that mean? It just means that we had to call someone a CEO.

Livingston: So you never took any money from the outside?

Hong: It was just me, Jim, and my brother.

Livingston: What were some other hair-raising things that happened?

Hong: When we first started, we were called Am I Hot or Not? and I had been sure to check if anyone owned any similar domains. One day Howard Stern mentioned the site on his show and called it "Am I Hot?" Next thing we knew, we got a cease-and-desist letter from a site called Am I Hot that claimed they predated us. We couldn't believe it! Because we thought we might try to sell, we knew we had to keep this thing clean, so I went down to LA and tried to work it out with them. I let them keep the "Am I Hot" name, and they agreed to let us redirect our traffic to hotornot.com for at least 3 months.

So now I had to rebrand the company, too. Luckily, at that point we were getting a lot of press, so I worked hard to get the new name out there. We wound up buying Am I Hot's assets—their domain and the rights—for what I considered a paltry sum. We only really bought it to close the chapter and feel vindicated. Later I found out from someone who worked there that they thought they totally screwed us when we agreed to change our name. I guess they thought "Am I Hot" was a better name.

By the way, this was in December, in the first 4 months. We also had talked briefly to Lycos about selling. They were offering something like $3 to $5 million—this was after 2 months of work—but we didn't want to sell because we thought they would destroy it. We thought they'd stick pop-up ads everywhere and make it corporate and lame, and then it would die. Our reputation was worth more to us. I thought the company was worth more, too.

Livingston: What else kept you up at night?

Hong: The scaling issues were pretty bad. It seemed like Jim and I were nonstop everyday, trying to figure out how we could make the site better or faster. That first half-year seemed like a day. There was a lot of manic behavior going on. I was on an adrenaline rush, which felt good, but it was exhausting and sometimes I felt like I was going crazy. So much, so fast, all at once.

It was fun, too, though. We got in *People* magazine, *Time*, and *Newsweek*. By the end of the year, we got on *Entertainment Weekly*'s It List.

Livingston: Why was HOT or NOT instantly so popular?

Hong: Looking at hot chicks is fun. It's voyeurism. The concept at the time was so new and edgy. No one had ever seen it before or thought about it. It was just so funny—and painful too. Like voting for people who were so ugly that you wondered why they were voluntarily doing it.

Livingston: Did you ever catch any shit from your technology friends?

Hong: Why would I catch shit? What would they be mad at me about?

Livingston: That you were squandering your education and talent on creating a site for ranking people's attractiveness?

Hong: Most techies would dream of that, are you kidding? People in Silicon Valley are entrepreneurs, they're not the risk-averse types that would think I was wasting my education. I was the first among my MBA classmates that made it into the *Wall Street Journal*.

Livingston: Can you remember a really funny moment?

Hong: We were on the *Entertainment Weekly* It List, and we got invited to a celebrity party in New York. By chance, the *New Yorker* found out about it and got one of their writers to chronicle us for the weekend. I think the title of the article was something to the effect of "The Dorks Come to the Big City."

One of the sweetest moments happened when we went to some hip new club that had just opened and tried to get in. You know how New York is a very velvet rope culture. Well, the bouncer took one look at us and wouldn't let us in. So the writer had been passive for a while watching us trying to get in, and then he stepped up finally and said to the bouncer, "Hey, you want to let these guys in. You are a new club, I'm a writer for the *New Yorker*, I'm following these guys around, and it would probably be nice if you were mentioned."

The bouncer responded, "I've never heard of the *New Yorker*." Finally he went inside and came back out with the manager, who begged us to come inside. At that point, Jim and I were like, "This place is lame and we don't want it to be mentioned, so we really don't want to go in there." And we all walked off and had drinks at some little pub. It was definitely a nerds-strike-back moment.

Livingston: What would you tell someone who was in your shoes before you started HOT or NOT?

Hong: I'd say do it. There's kind of a backwards logic that says: when you are young, you should learn from people who are experienced, so later on, if you want to do a startup, you can take the risk. And that's a myth that was created from school. You need to learn to get to the next level.

The biggest roadblock to the entrepreneur are liabilities in your life. It's not whether or not you can be a good entrepreneur, it's whether you have to make a mortgage payment or support other people.

Experience will come when you face certain problems and live through them. And the best way to do that is to put yourself squarely in the path of those problems.

Livingston: What drives entrepreneurs?

Hong: I think entrepreneurs want to make money. It's not that they do it for the money, but they want to make money. Because money is the measuring stick; it's how they know if they've won or not. And I think a lot of what drives entrepreneurs is the kind of legacy they are going to leave. They want to make a mark in the world and feel like their life mattered. Entrepreneurs are the kind of people who love ideas and want to build things, and add value to the world.

Part of that is to quench their ego's thirst and say, "I matter." That's why people like Bill Gates and Vinod Khosla spend a lot of time doing nonprofit things. It was never about the money. Carnegie dedicated the latter part of his life to giving all his money away. He was trying to convince people to give your money away once you make it. Because that's when it can start doing real good, too.

Livingston: What else do entrepreneurs have in common?

Hong: The hardest decision you make as an entrepreneur is not one that you make while you're building the company. For me, the hardest decision was not about solving the hosting issues and all that. It was the one I made years before HOT or NOT even existed. When I said, "I'm going to be an entrepreneur," what I was really saying was, "I'm going to forgo the normal, safe route, where there's a clear path. I'm going to take a higher risk and go for a higher reward."

It's like Hewlett-Packard. Do you know what their first product was? A bowling foul line indicator. The point is, they decided that they were going to be entrepreneurs before they knew exactly what they were going to do, and that's very common.

All these things come out of new ideas. If you're not in school and you're not an entrepreneur, you're not working on new ideas. You are just a cog in someone else's wheel, and you'll never make anything new. So the hardest thing is to say, "I'm going to put myself in the position of being an entrepreneur by having ideas and trying things, and not giving up when I fail."

You never know unless you try, and we live in a world where building websites and other small things doesn't take that much time and effort to try, so why not just try different things?

Livingston: What other advice would you give to someone starting a startup?

Hong: You need the early team to be savvy in everything. And you have to have people who understand the users and the product. If you do, then you'll have users.

And nothing ever goes according to plan. You can't dwell on the fact that your plan didn't work. In our case, we didn't even have a plan, but it would have been worthless to have one anyway, since we just kept moving as fast as we could. You have to hustle; you can't just have a plan and cakewalk it. You just have to know what direction you're going in and run around like a rat in a maze trying to get out.

Livingston: Now that you're out of the maze, do you get asked out on a lot dates through HOT or NOT?

Hong: Yeah. I actually stopped using my dating service a long time ago as a way to find my own dates, because everyone on there knows who Jim and I are, and many of the ones who seek us out are crazy. I would often get random emails from women sending me naked pictures and all sorts of weird stuff. A lot of them want to date us because they have low self-esteem and they think dating us will suddenly make them hot and cool. Crazy, psycho girls can be fun to date for a while, but I'm a little older now and I'm looking for something a little more serious.

The ironic thing is that from running HOT or NOT, I care less about looks now. When I was a dork, I never really dated anyone who was hot. The models—they weren't going to date me. So you always aspire to it, they're like the untouchables. All of a sudden, HOT or NOT happened, and I was starting to date all these attractive women. I got a taste of it and I realized that looks don't make up for a good personality. Many of these girls were annoying. They were fun to hang out with, but I couldn't have a conversation with them. I'm sure there are smart and hot girls, but if you look at the hot ones first, it's harder to figure out if they are smart too. That takes time.

Livingston: Any other advice about startups?

Hong: One, do it while you're young.

Two, there's no right path. There is no one plan that fits every business; you have to figure it out yourself. There is no magic formula.

Three, even if you raise money, spend it as if it's your own and you have none. Your organization has got to remain smart and lean. Be cheap. There's no shame in being cheap. I still fly coach.

Four, there's no such thing as easy entrepreneurship. It's going to be painful, it's going to be emotionally unstable, you're going to feel insecure. If you're not already bipolar, you will feel like you are.

Livingston: How has your life had changed since HOT or NOT?

Hong: Money hasn't changed anything—well, that's not entirely true. I have a Porsche and I have a nice apartment. But I'm living within the same means as if I had gone the risk-averse route.

I don't spend that much money because once you get used to spending money, it's very hard to get unused to. Happiness is reality compared to expectations. If I have low expectations for material things in my life, then I'll be happy. If I get used to fancy meals all the time, not only will it ruin McDonald's for me, but even the fancy food would become normal, and then it's not meaningful. So I've been careful not to change my lifestyle too much.

I'm not in debt anymore, and I have financial freedom, but the first whatever million is all you really need to get that. If you had the opportunity to cash something out for x million, but you thought with some hard work you might be able to make it worth more, for some people that's the right decision to go for it; but for other people, take that money, put it in the bank, and now you can do whatever you want for the rest of your life. It depends how tied you are to that one concept as being your legacy for your entire life.

James Currier
Founder, Tickle

James Currier came up with the idea for Tickle (founded in 1999 and originally called Emode) after taking a personality test in one of his Harvard Business School classes.

A former venture capitalist with a passion for digital media and social sciences, Currier believed that the Internet could be used to help people learn more about themselves. People could visit www.tickle.com to take several different kinds of personality and self-assessment tests, most backed by scientific research, to understand areas of human behavior (and also to find out what breed of dog they most closely resembled).

Tickle was acquired by Monster in 2004 for about $100 million. Shortly after this interview, Currier founded Ooga Labs, a digital media studio that develops consumer Internet applications.

Livingston: How did you come up with the idea for an online testing company?

Currier: After college, I got an early introduction to digital media before there was Internet: I worked in Hollywood for a venture group that invested in companies involved in digital media for the movie industry. A lot of digital content was getting pushed over AT&T's broadband network, which was proprietary at the time. I worked at Star TV in Hong Kong and did more digital media, and got back to venture capital in Boston where the company was investing in the early-stage Internet companies like Infoseek.

When I was at business school, I would think about the media companies that were popular at the time—like Broadcast.com, Women.com, and iVillage—and they didn't make any sense to me. They were basically trying to put old media experiences online. For example, Spinner.com was putting radio online, and they got sold for $340 million. I thought that was crazy.

I knew the Internet was going to bubble up its own unique media form. It was probably going to be user-generated, and it wasn't going to be like anything that we see on the other mediums. So I was looking and looking for what that was going to be at the same time I was getting my degree at business school.

At class one night, they gave us a few pieces of paper and a number 2 pencil, and we filled out circles for a Myers-Briggs corporate personality test, which is something they administer to Harvard Business School students. Eleven days later, we got our results in manila envelopes—all in black-and-white text with a little graph—and soon we exploded into conversation. People in that community talked about the test for about 2 weeks—at dinner conversations, on the basketball court. I watched this and thought, "I've never seen anyone talk about a movie for this long. That's powerful media. Why?"

So I discussed this with my family, who were involved in psychology, and asked, "Are we our own favorite subjects?" We're very concerned about ourselves and the people we know. I realized that no other technology allowed us to get media about ourselves. All the other media technologies allow us to learn only about people we will never know. Tom Cruise, Tom Brokaw—we know a ton about those people and yet we'll never know them.

I believed that the Internet would allow you to have a media experience about you and the people you know—though it wasn't going to be the best video, audio, or magazine—and that was going to take a lot of different forms. And I thought this testing could be incredibly powerful because people love talking about themselves, love talking about the people they know, and it could be viral.

At the venture firm, I saw how most online media companies were getting killed by acquisition costs, and I realized that to build a successful company, you had to have very low—if not zero—expenses for acquiring users. So I thought that these tests could be a very promising area to start a digital media company through.

A lot of these tests were trapped in the ivory tower. Why couldn't we just release them online, make them inexpensive, and just benefit humanity? It could be a good foundation for a media business, and even if it failed it would be doing something good for the world.

Livingston: How did you get started once you had this idea?

Currier: I had to come up with what the product would actually do. And then I had to start talking to people about it and getting their ideas. There's a balance between thinking that you have this fantastic idea that you don't want anyone else to know about and the need to talk about it and get broad-ranging opinions so that you make as few mistakes as possible.

I was really paranoid because I thought this idea was incredibly obvious. It seemed like this was the best thing to do online—it would be incredibly viral and it would be deep because you'd get so much data on people. You could help them find the right job, get a great date, decide whether to get an SUV or a minivan, help facilitate conversations within the family. And people would answer honestly, because the test was about them and they'd want accurate results. It was just obvious to me that you could build a huge media company on the back of this thing. So I was relatively paranoid about that and only talked to people that I trusted.

But what I got back was, "I don't understand what the heck you're talking about." All the people that I had been talking with about digital media, self-help, and psychology with, they still didn't understand what the hell I was trying to do. I couldn't find the words to describe the vision.

Livingston: Why did they not get it? What did they misunderstand?

Currier: I think there are very few people who have a capacity to see the future. So it can be difficult when you are talking about something where nothing about it exists yet.

At the time, everyone was caught up in the success of Broadcast.com, iVillage, and Women.com, so they believed in their value. Instead of saying, "The people who are buying those companies are stupid," they were saying, "Those guys must know something I don't know."

Since most humans have a much easier time understanding what is, if you suggest that what they see is wrong, it's very disconcerting and they hate it. Because they are trying to understand their world and predict their future—that's the main function of the cerebrum, to find the patterns and predict what is going to happen next—and insofar as they realize that the future to them is somewhat gray, or even black, it's scary. So then they go and have another conversation and everyone says, "Broadcast.com, oh that's so cool." Everyone nods and smiles and that's the type of pack animal collective creating reality. And when you go against that, it's painful.

Livingston: What else was challenging?

Currier: Where you are is never enough for the people around you. Because starting a company is the act of collecting and organizing the human energy that is in the ether. You are trying to take all this matter that's around you and shape it into something that fits with what's in your head. And all these people who are being shaped want to know where you are now and want you to take another step along the path so that they can feel more confident. They are always searching for more confidence points.

For example:

"What are you calling it? Give it a name so we can talk about it."

So you decide on a name—Emode.

"Do you have a business plan?"

So I would give them a one-page business summary.

"No, I want a real business plan."

So I wrote a business plan.

"Do you have any employees?"

"No, I don't have any employees. I need to go get some."

"Do you have any money?"

And you go talk to some angels.

"Do you have an office?"

And you go sign a lease somewhere.

"Do you have business cards?"

"No, let me go get business cards."

"Do you have a website?"

"We just launched it."

"Well, is anyone coming?"

"No one's coming yet, but I'll get back to you when people are coming."

"When you hit this level, then I'll be interested."

Everyone is looking for the next step. And so as you go along with each of these confidence steps, you can pick up more and more people into what's going on.

So then you go talk to a venture capitalist, and they ask if any other venture capitalist is interested. And then once you get other VCs interested, you say, "Yes, they're interested and maybe you guys could syndicate them and do the round." They say, "Well, have you received a term sheet from them?" Then once you've received a term sheet, then the VCs get interested, and then acquirers get interested. Women.com offered to buy us out for $32 million once we got our term sheets.

You have to get to these levels to attract more people, and then you hit these spark points, and in my process the spark point was getting the term sheets from the VC. People suddenly want to work with you, loan you money; PR firms want to spend your money, investment bankers want to meet you.

Livingston: Which spark point would you consider most significant for Tickle?

Currier: The launching of the dog test. When we started the company, we wanted to change the world, and we had all these tests on the site to help people in their lives. We had the anxiety test; the parenting, relationship, and communication tests. And no one came.

I remembered that advertising agencies say if you want people to remember an ad, include babies and puppies. So I thought, "We should make a fun test. Let's do a test for what kind of breed of dog are you." So they came up with a 15-question test that wasn't scientific at all. We put it online, and 8 days later we had a million people trying to enter our site. Our server was going down every 10 minutes. We had to emergency unplug it from the wall, throw it in the back of the car, and plug it into a T3 at an ISP in Lynn, Mass.

Once we got crazy traffic, we were able to then show the graphs to the venture guys, and we were on our way. They said, "Anyone with traffic can make a lot of money on the Internet, so I'm in."

Livingston: Were there other hair-raising moments in the early years?

Currier: Most of them had to do with people. We had a VP of engineering who wasn't working out, and we had to let him go. But because he seemed unstable, we arranged for a marshal to be ready to create peace once we let this guy go if he really blew up and went crazy.

Livingston: Could you have recognized that this employee was bad news from the beginning?

Currier: You might have, but I wasn't experienced enough at the time, since I had never done one of these before. I was 30 and I knew a lot about the industry and the technology, but I was very green on people. And that is a painful way to start a company.

I also hired a head of HR, and she was pregnant at the time but didn't tell us. When I asked her to create the maternity leave policy, she suggested 5 months with full pay. Since I was so busy, I said, "I want to trust you and empower you to do everything we need on this side, so if you think that's right, great."

So a few weeks later she told me she would be leaving soon for maternity leave. By that time, several of us were off salary because we were running out of money, and here she was going home to spend 5 months at full pay, and we were practically out of money. Never having built a company, I didn't know where I wanted the lines drawn. It was like a big, white piece of paper. And I got taken on that.

Livingston: Was there ever a time when a competitor did something that made you fearful?

Currier: iVillage started copying us, and I was very worried about it for probably a year, and then it all just faded away. Probably because it's hard to get the engineers, the psychologists, and the writers to talk to one another. You've got to build a culture and communication amongst a small group of people so that they can get things done.

Livingston: What was different about the way you motivated them?

Currier: My willingness to communicate with people and my understanding of their need to form their brains and their language around their relationships with each other and the product we needed to create. I genuinely cared about my people, and I built a culture where you communicate—you don't blame— and you learn what the heck the other person's talking about. You, psychologist, you need to learn a little about engineering. You, engineer, you need to learn a little about what the user actually experiences. You have to understand why they like the question this way so that the writers can do their job. So it was really just a matter of empathy that I had for the team, and communication style.

You have to figure out how to hire people who are nice, communicative, smart, and capable. If you're missing one of those four things, you can't stay. And so you have to churn people out and be willing to let them go. It was painful, but I knew from the beginning we were going to have to do that.

Livingston: What was most surprising to you about starting a startup?

Currier: How painful it was. I woke up on October 3, 1999, at around 4 a.m. with my chest burning from fear and pain about not knowing what to do, and worrying that I had taken my friends' and mentors' money. I had realized that what I was trying to do was not working, and that I didn't know how to fix it and I was in way over my head.

Livingston: How did you keep going?

Currier: I put one foot in front of the other. I was sleeping 4 hours a night with the help of NyQuil, and then I'd just keep thinking, keep trying to find the language and find new employees, trying to meet the VC who would understand my vision and back me. I met with 43 VCs.

Livingston: Since you were a VC, could you speak their language better than most technology founders?

Currier: I remember saying to them, "Look, in 4 years, we'll be doing $18 million in revenue with $4.5 million of profit. After that the sky's the limit. I'm an ex-venture guy; I'm telling you the truth. We can get to $18 million in year 4, and 30 times $4 million is a $120 million valuation for the company at that time. You'll get 20 times your money."

They all told me $18 million wasn't interesting. And I'd say, "But most people will tell you $50 million, and you know they're lying. I'm already discounting it because I'm a venture guy just like you are." And they'd say, "Yeah, but $18 million just isn't interesting."

So I changed my spreadsheet to say $50 million. And they said, "OK, that's pretty interesting."

Livingston: Can you think of another example where you had to pull off a trick to advance?

Currier: Well, of course you sometimes have to exaggerate. If you think there are three places where you can get a lease, then you just say you have a lease so you can move to the next step. You've got to say you are a step ahead of where you actually are to move to the step that you want to be at.

To move to step two, people have to believe that you're already at step two so there's no risk for them. Because they don't want to take on your risk—you have to take it all on. And then you have to take on the risk of fibbing.

Livingston: What would you tell someone who was considering starting a startup?

Currier: That it is incredibly painful and it will take over your life. If you care about it and if you have any chance of succeeding, you will stop being present for the softer things in life like your family, friends, or dating life. And when you are there with them, you're not really there with them; you're thinking about this thing because you're creating it, and it takes that amount of passion to make it work.

Livingston: Did this ever hurt any of your relationships?

Currier: I almost didn't marry my wife. She and I started dating about 2 months before I came up with the idea, so she hasn't really known me without it. I couldn't figure out if we should get married, but then I hired a new VP of engineering and he transformed my life. Because I could trust him to do a lot of important work, he gave me breathing room to actually feel something. Four months after I hired him, I proposed and we got married. We now have four great kids. I almost really blew it; the whole haze of the thing made it unclear.

At an HBS reunion, we had a roundtable for all of us who had been entrepreneurs, and one of our professors asked, "What didn't HBS teach you about this?" And I said, "Pain."

I only remember one class that came close: the professor walked out of the class with tears in his eyes, having recounted the story of his friend who had started a cable company, and it destroyed his life, destroyed his family, and moved him to a place where his life was a waste of time. That was the only indication I had at HBS about how painful this is.

Having gone through this already, my ability to start another startup is now much higher. If you could give a student a tenth of that understanding at business school, it would be worth hundreds of thousands of dollars, and years of effort to understand that you will sleep for 4 hours a night for 18 straight months if things are not going well.

Livingston: Would you do it again?

Currier: Oh yeah. But it won't be nearly as hard this time because I have money in the bank now, and I know what I'm doing. And I know what the probabilities of different things working are, and I would know how to do it, so it would be a lot less painful. You'd still have to be obsessed with it; you'd still not be present with anything else; but if I thought it could do something important, then I would do it again.

Livingston: Your company was acquired by Monster. How do you preserve the startuppyness of Tickle within this big company?

Currier: You try like hell to preserve the startup feel because you are the personality that likes to start things and you don't like an environment that's not starting. We've kept our doors as desks; we refuse to move from our office; and Monster has been fantastic about leaving us alone. We're just out here doing our thing. We are very lucky, and I still enjoy and want to build a great legacy for Monster. But I won't be here forever. I can't. I'm a starter.

If Yahoo had acquired us, they would have made us move to Mountain View, and would have made us a widget on a feature on a division of a department, and everyone would have left, and the whole thing would have died. And Wall Street would have applauded roundly.

Whereas Wall Street has been perplexed by Monster's acquisition of Tickle. Yet it's so obvious: we're the largest career testing site in the world, we've got matchmaking capabilities between people for romance, and we can use the same matchmaking capabilities by measuring different dimensions for jobs. We can take job matching to the next level—the next stage for high-end job finding. And Monster gets the value of every person and every product we have here because there was no overlap.

Blake Ross
Creator, Firefox

Blake Ross and Dave Hyatt started Firefox as a side project while working at the Mozilla Foundation. They were working to revive the struggling Netscape browser, but became frustrated by the constraints imposed on them. So Ross and Hyatt decided to build a browser that they would actually want to use.

Working in their spare time, they began developing a new browser that was fast, simple, and reliable. In 2002, they launched the initial version, called Phoenix, and in 2004 they released Firefox 1.0, which was an instant hit.

Like a lot of things described in this book, Firefox was something new. It was an open source project run like a startup, both in the concern for the end user and in the attention paid to marketing. The results were impressive: Firefox has cut into the formerly overwhelming market share of Internet Explorer, and dominates among technical users.

In 2005, Ross took a leave from Stanford University to start a startup with fellow Firefox developer Joe Hewitt.

Livingston: Tell me about how Firefox got started.

Ross: Firefox grew out of Mozilla, which itself has a very long history that I won't go into now. I personally started working on the Mozilla project in 2000. It was open source; anyone could work on it. I started working closely with the Netscape team, because they were basing their product on Mozilla. I was helping them fix bugs, and they invited me out for an internship one summer, so I went out to Netscape, which was a pretty cool first job.

Livingston: You were only 14, right?

Ross: Right. I worked out in California, and it was great the first summer. Then I started working from home, and when I came back the next summer, things had gotten much worse. Netscape kept sliding further and further in the market. At this point, they had something like 5 percent market share. This is post-AOL, post–browser war and all that. Things got a lot more desperate when AOL tanked and started to demand more revenue from the browser. They wanted a return on investment, and they'd bought Netscape for about $4 billion.

So the browser started to turn into nothing more than a vehicle to drive people to Netscape.com. There were search buttons everywhere, advertisements everywhere. It was a mess. The culture didn't focus on users. It was painful to be working there.

Firefox was more a response to our experience at Netscape than to the dominant browser, Internet Explorer. Explorer had basically been abandoned at that point; in 2001, Microsoft disbanded the IE team. So we started Firefox as a way to work on the browser that we knew we could make if we weren't being controlled by marketing, sales, and all these other influences inside Netscape. It started off with just three or four of us—the people who had always been fighting these battles within Netscape to make the right decisions for users.

For example, we wanted to include pop-up blocking in Netscape 7. It would have been the first mainstream browser to include pop-up blocking. The Mozilla folks had all the code ready, but Netscape wouldn't include it because Netscape.com had a pop-up ad. Those kinds of decisions were painful, and it was frustrating to have our names on the product that was getting released. So we started a project called Phoenix, which was supposed to be an allusion to the mythical bird that is reborn from its own ashes. It was like the project was being reborn from the ashes of Netscape.

Livingston: Who was involved?

Ross: David Hyatt, Joe Hewitt—who is now my partner on a new startup, Parakey—and I were on the development side, with Brian Ryner and Asa Dotzler providing build and QA support. The project was like an afterthought for the first 6 months to a year, something we worked on at Denny's after work. I went back home to Miami, and we worked on it online for a while.

Phoenix was basically a fork of the Mozilla code base that we controlled. We closed off access to the code, because we felt it was impossible to create anything consumer-oriented when you had a thousand Netscape people in search of revenue and a thousand open source geeks who shunned big business trying to reach consensus. We just wanted to close it off and do what we thought was the right thing. We went through a couple name changes, Mozilla offered us more support, and that's kind of how it all got started.

Livingston: What were some of the other names?

Ross: It started off as Phoenix, and we quickly encountered trademark issues. It was just the three of us, we weren't lawyers, and we were broke, so at that point we probably would have done anything someone asked of us. In this case, Phoenix Technologies complained because they had some kind of web browser, too. We renamed it Firebird, because it's the same imagery, but there was an open source database already called Firebird. So we renamed it again. At that point, it was fairly popular—though not nearly as popular as it is now—so we wanted to keep the "Fire" part of the name. We just went through Fire-anything names for a couple of months, and somebody came up with Firefox, which is actually the Chinese name for a red panda.

Livingston: Were the Firefox developers all in different places?

Ross: When we first started doing it, we were all at Netscape. Then Dave left to go to Apple to work on Safari, and we had some other folks like Ben Goodger from New Zealand, Pierre Chanial from France, and Jan Varga from Slovakia come on board. I went back to Miami, and we continued to work together online.

Joe and I still collaborate through IM on Parakey, even though we're about 20 minutes apart, because we're so used to that environment from Firefox. It's just so much faster to collaborate online than it is for him to drive down to me or me to drive up to him.

Livingston: Were there any conflicts with Dave working at Apple?

Ross: Yes. They were also making a simple end-user browser, and he was not really supposed to be working on a competitor to that. It wasn't on our end that we had a problem.

Livingston: Did he leave Apple?

Ross: No. He still works on Safari right now. He did Firefox and then went off to Apple.

Livingston: So then it was just a few of you.

Ross: The Firefox team is always changing. It's not fair to say there are just a few of us, because we're based on Mozilla, which obviously has dozens of developers, and there are a lot of developers working on Gecko, the core layout engine. The Firefox team itself—the people worrying about everything wrapped around the engine and working on the separate fork of the code base—was always about four or five different people for the first year.

Now there are a lot more, obviously, because it's the main source tree. All those people that were working on Mozilla now work on Firefox.

Livingston: What was the first turning point when you knew you were really onto something?

Ross: I think it was when we put out our first milestone, which wasn't even . . . We put it on an FTP site and had an article on mozillaZine, which is a community news site. It was already getting as many downloads as a Mozilla milestone.

On the one side, you had a lot of Mozilla people—the hardcore developer types—who didn't like what we were doing, because focusing on "mom and dad" is heretical in much of the open source world. Then there were a lot of people who were saying, "Finally, Mozilla is stepping away from its geek roots and doing something more mainstream." We got a lot of coverage early on from bloggers and *PC World* and stuff like that. It got out of control pretty quickly.

Livingston: Did you have problems getting users at the beginning?

Ross: No, but the users we were getting weren't really the target audience; these were people that downloaded beta builds from Mozilla. So it was still a geek audience. We had to transform the culture at Mozilla because it was all based around open source ethos, which says programmers are kings, marketers are sleaze, and everyone else can read the manual. All the branding for Mozilla looked very Communist—the logo was a dinosaur and the banners ads were . . . I can't even describe it, but very odd, technical kind of imagery that didn't appeal to most people. We had to move a lot of that into a more mainstream world.

Livingston: How did you do that?

Ross: The first thing that happened was that Netscape split off Mozilla into an independent entity. Mozilla was once just the open source technology arm of Netscape—they made technology and Netscape distributed it. When Netscape said goodbye, Mozilla didn't really have any kind of major distributor anymore.

As Firefox matured, Mozilla decided that they could try to distribute it directly to the user without having to go through a middleman like Netscape. At that point, the culture started to shift out of necessity; the organization had to cater to more users or potentially collapse.

Livingston: As you were working on this, did you worry about competitive threats?

Ross: No, Firefox was very different from traditional startups. Companies usually worry about competition for financial reasons, but when we did Firefox, money was just always sort of there. There were donations, seed money from AOL; we eventually got this Google deal, but it wasn't a source of fear for us, because we knew if it didn't make money . . . It wasn't even supposed to make money—it was a hobby, right, so we didn't really care. I was in school. It didn't have to succeed.

It sounds bad, but the project was kind of just for us at the beginning—to make something that we knew we could make, but not inside Netscape. It was an outlet for those frustrations. We wanted people to use it, but we weren't going to kill ourselves if it failed. We defined success in terms of users, not competitors.

In any case, the IE team had been disbanded, and Netscape had bowed out, so the market was wide open. We didn't crunch numbers or conduct market analysis; we relaxed and followed our gut. There's a lot more pressure now with Parakey. People expect another Firefox or something like that.

Livingston: People must have high expectations for you, which is not a bad thing, I suppose.

Ross: Not a bad thing, but you have to deliver. It's hard to under-promise and over-deliver when everyone's promising things for you. We're trying not to hype up what we're doing until we've got something people can use. People expect the world, so if you hype up what you are doing, you have to deliver, and it's not easy.

Livingston: Did any competitors ever do anything to anger you?

Ross: Not directly. The only thing that bothers me is that Microsoft seems completely driven by competition. We tried to be driven entirely by users. There was a need, so we tried to cater to it. We didn't say, "We're going to try to crush Microsoft" just to crush Microsoft. That wasn't the intent, even though that's kind of the stated goal of some misguided open source projects.

Whereas Microsoft, they win a browser war, so in 2001, they bow out. Which is completely irresponsible, because this is the most used software application in the world, and they just stopped developing it. Now they are back in the game, because they have competition, so that pulls them back in. I will say that Internet Explorer 7 is shaping up to be a good browser; I just wish it came a few years earlier.

We also see them trying to emulate a lot of the more genuine community spirit that we've built up. People like Mozilla because we're open source; we try to be transparent and honest with the community. We're a free product. We work with people. And we're starting to see that kind of thing emanate from Microsoft. They have a team blog now and they are trying to be very buddy-buddy, but it feels like a PR pitch, as if they looked at our situation and now they are trying to bring that sense of goodwill over there. If it were genuine, it would be great, but it feels like a sales pitch. It's getting better though.

I respect companies like Opera, which also produces a browser. They aren't doing that well right now, but at least they're in it for the right reasons. They've been around for a decade now, and they are passionate about the Web. Microsoft just kind of comes and goes with the money and the competition, and that doesn't seem like the right motivation to make a good product.

Livingston: Looking back, what did people misunderstand about Firefox?

Ross: Many die-hard open source fans misunderstood our goal. Usually, in an open source project, if you're not a developer, it's kind of like, "What are you doing here?"

A lot of people misunderstood the real audience we were going after. It's hard to explain exactly what that means, but you can imagine, here's this Mozilla project, it's very open, everyone gets a say. If you are a developer, you get to vote on whether or not a feature gets implemented. Then we come along and say, "We're making a product for mom and dad. You still have a voice here, but some of the features that you think we should add may not be the ones that they want to use. So you have to take our word for it that, even though 500 of you want something right now, you may actually be in the minority of a much larger group that we're pursuing that's going to be silent during this phase of development."

It's hard to convince 500 flesh-and-blood developers that their pet feature may not be desirable to 500 million imaginary users, especially when you have no hard evidence to back it up. In some ways, I'm glad it's just the two of us again on Parakey. We can work very fast and there are no politics.

Livingston: So in open source projects, you have to listen to the opinions of other developers.

Ross: Sure, they're the ones building the product. We just have to be wary of our inner geek voices and make sure we're considering the needs of the world at large. I don't think Mozilla did that, and the project stagnated at a few million users.

Livingston: Do you think Firefox has reached the mainstream because it is better?

Ross: There are a million different reasons. Many people think it's easier. Others were just sort of weaned onto it when their children put it on their computers.

Of course, we've also done plenty of legwork to reach the mainstream. It's all word-of-mouth marketing. We have a site called Spread Firefox that Asa Dotzler and I started in 2004 when we launched Firefox. It's basically a way to leverage the talents of people who are not coders. We said, "Instead of just being developer-only, like most open source projects, how do we leverage college students and Toastmasters and people who knit—just every kind of talent you have and every organization you're a part of. How do we match you up with other people in your region and give you tools to spread Firefox?" That was a huge success. We've had over 250,000 people sign up.

We also did an ad in the *New York Times*. Ten thousand people donated between $10 and $30 each to buy two full-page facing ads in the *New York Times* when Firefox launched. Of course, that's a couple hundred thousand dollars, but we didn't have a marketing budget. That was all community-funded, which is pretty unusual for any software project, let alone an open source project.

Livingston: So Firefox spread because the browser is better and through word of mouth?

Ross: Yes. We don't have people shaping a message or working the press. It's all been grassroots, word of mouth, done through Spread Firefox. It's been interesting because we've seen about a dozen companies adopt the same model since then. There's GoTrillian.com, SpreadOpenOffice.org—there are all these different copycat sites.

Livingston: Was there ever a point when you were really worried?

Ross: Not really. But I'm making it seem like startups are so stress-free, and of course that's just not true. It's just really freeing not to be . . . We weren't trying to strike it rich with Firefox. It's open source and it's free. We weren't trying to take over the world; we had kind of modest goals, and it was OK if it failed. We were a lot freer to make risky decisions.

If you can afford to do things that way, it's just so much better. You're not thinking about venture capitalists or marketing or sales. Just product and users, all day every day.

Livingston: You were pretty young when you worked on Firefox. Was there anything you found you were better at than you thought?

Ross: I thought marketing was something that required a degree and formal experience. It turns out that marketing is just making the product good enough that people spread it on their own, and giving them ways to do that. It's a lot easier and more natural than I thought it would be. Now I can't stand meeting with professional marketers who try to "craft" the "message" and all that junk.

Livingston: What surprised you most?

Ross: How easy it was to get Firefox to take off, at least in light of the death knell people had been sounding for years. We'd been hearing forever that nobody downloads a client anymore, and browsers are dead, and Mozilla can't make it. It's never going to go anywhere; the market has been monopolized. We just ignored all that and did it anyway, and it worked.

It's a bit harder to take analysts and other "industry insiders" seriously now, because Firefox proved them wrong. There are a lot of people in the industry who aren't actually the ones writing the code or contributing to the project, but they want to feel like they are relevant somehow, so they make sweeping predictions that draw attention. I think you have to be in the project and be the one moving it forward to truly understand whether you have a shot at success. One analyst has already announced he's "skeptical" about Parakey and he barely even knows what it is, let alone tried it out. Smells like Firefox all over again. Those kinds of comments are so motivating. I love the challenge.

We talked to plenty of people at the very beginning of Firefox. It was obvious that people were not happy with their browser, and it was very clear that, if we could do something better, we might be able to get them to use it.

Livingston: Do you remember people's reactions when you gave an early demo of it?

Ross: People loved the simplicity and went crazy over tabbed browsing. What's weird is that I didn't really talk to anyone I knew personally throughout the course of Firefox development. My parents and my friends—most of them didn't really know I was working on Firefox until it came out and there was the *Business 2.0* article. That's when everyone was like, "Wait, you work on Firefox?" They knew I "did something" with computers, but . . .

Livingston: Your parents didn't know?

Ross: Kind of. I think they knew I worked on Mozilla. They knew I worked at Netscape, so they knew I worked in browsers, but they didn't really know my involvement in Firefox until they read about it in a magazine. Which is kind of how I prefer it, because it's much easier to spend a couple months on something, fail silently, and just go back to school, than it is to tell everyone that everyone is going to use our product. It's easier if people aren't bugging you until you have something to put in their hands, and then they can tell you if it's good or not.

Livingston: So the stakes were lower. Did you ever want to quit?

Ross: Well, I did in a way. I went back to school for 6 months, and I wasn't working on the project much during that time. It wasn't that I walked away—we knew there were people working on it—but it was leisurely because we knew that Microsoft wasn't coming back any time soon.

Livingston: Now you are in a "real" startup. How did you get started?

Ross: In some ways, the media and the venture capital industry made it happen. From our earliest days at Netscape, Joe and I were always shooting the breeze about how terrible software was and what we would change if we could. After some Firefox press hit, we started getting emails from investors saying, "We want to meet." And we'd think, "Meet about what? It's an open source hobby project." Then we realized, "They want to meet about funding us, so we should probably get some kind of company together." We figured this was the perfect opportunity to act after years of talk.

Livingston: You wanted to take advantage of the rising tide?

Ross: Right. We already had ideas around software, and we said, "This is the time to do it if we are going to do anything. People are going to listen to us right now, so we might as well go for it."

Livingston: Do you have a name?

Ross: We're calling it Parakey for now, but who knows if it will stick. Firefox was our fourth name.

Livingston: Can you tell me about any of the challenges you've faced?

Ross: One thing is just time. Whenever I'm doing something now, I feel like I should be doing something else instead. If I got married tomorrow, I'd probably be worrying about a code issue during the ceremony and deliver my vows in Python. It's a nonstop state of stress. The first couple months we did the startup and all these venture capitalists were emailing us, we felt like we had to meet with all of them. We thought, "Oh my God, we have to say yes; we can't say no to these people." Now we realize that time is our most valuable resource, and every minute we spend in one of these meetings just sitting there is time wasted.

Things are getting better. We're starting to push people away to give us space to work, but in some respects it would be so much easier if the Firefox thing hadn't happened. We should be setting our own timeline, but people are already waiting for what we're going to do next, so it's hard to relax under these kinds of circumstances. It's a lot of pressure.

Livingston: Who are your mentors? Is this Joe's first startup, too?

Ross: Yes. That's kind of the problem. We don't have that one person who has done this a thousand times who can advise us. We have a good lawyer. We're looking for a mentor who doesn't have ulterior motives and who is aligned with our interests.

Livingston: Which also must be a problem since you are so well known. Some people must think, "This is my ticket!"

Ross: I can't tell you how many times I get an email from someone who just wants to have dinner. So we'll have dinner, and we'll chat about politics, the weather, whatever. Then we'll have dinner again, and slowly it comes out that they want something. Eventually you find out that they want to come work for you, or they want to . . . sometimes they don't even know what they want, but they know they want something. It's hard to see what people's intentions are at the beginning.

We're also overly paranoid because the first thing we did when we started the company was talk to a bunch of entrepreneurs who told us, "Don't tell anyone what you are doing. VCs are sharks." Meanwhile, you hear from the VCs, "You're too paranoid." So it's hard to find the right balance and be human, because you don't know who's genuine and who's not.

Livingston: It must be frustrating not to be able to share your idea.

Ross: Incredibly. If you ever want to stop a conversation dead in its tracks, just use my magic words: "stealth mode." I've also found "programmer" to work well in many situations. But we'll have our day.

Livingston: Are there any lessons that you learned in the Firefox days that you are applying to this new startup?

Ross: One is to make sure you are always in communication with the people who are eventually going to use your product. It's very easy to just lock yourself in a room and code all day, and you forget what the real problems are that people are having. So you have to keep talking to people and keep refining what you are doing.

I also learned how you build up the right kind of buzz about your product in an honest way. With Firefox, we catered to the bloggers first, even though they weren't our primary target audience. Once you get the prominent bloggers to pick up the scent, you attract the intermediate press, the *PC Worlds* and the CNETs. You still don't have any moms or dads yet, you don't have any non-techies, but once the mainstream press sees *PC* magazine talking about it, then *they* start to cover the story, and they actually make it kind of a self-fulfilling prophecy. They write that "everyone is talking about Firefox" when, of course, mainstream users haven't even heard of it yet. But they are going to, now that the *New York Times* wrote about it.

Livingston: What are your biggest challenges starting a startup?

Ross: One is, in general, not knowing what's "normal." Investors hand us "normal" term sheets, consultants ask for "normal" fees. I'm 21—I haven't seen enough of the extremes to know what's normal. Our approach has been to make decisions slowly and methodically, do our research, and figure out who's on the level and who's selling us lines before signing anything.

The other problem is just finding the time to finish the project and still see my family, my friends, my girlfriend. It's very hard as two people. It's a very big project.

Livingston: Is your time horizon several years?

Ross: No. It's short term for launch.

Livingston: Because there will be a race?

Ross: We don't know of anyone doing specifically what we are doing, but you can just feel in the air that everyone's moving toward this kind of model. Who knows, someone could announce it tomorrow.

Livingston: Are you able to say who you are most nervous about as a competitor?

Ross: I'd say Google or Microsoft. It's a big enough project that I'm not sure a startup would be trying to do it, except us because we're nuts, but it's possible. Of the known companies, it would be Google or Microsoft.

Livingston: So right now you are operating on a small amount of seed funding? Is that to pay your rent, etc.?

Ross: We're going to take more before we launch, but we're trying to take as little as possible. We don't want $12 million. I don't know what we'd do with that. We don't even have an office. We're just working out of our apartments.

Livingston: Do you plan to get one?

Ross: Eventually. I need to see how many engineers I can fit in my bathroom and closet first.

Livingston: Are you nervous that this idea is too big for two people?

Ross: Yes. But we're also nervous about finding someone else, so it's hard. Just finding and interviewing candidates is stressful, because it's not like there's a team back home coding. If Joe and I are at a meeting, no one is pushing the product forward, and that's scary. There's a question of, "Is it better for us to spend all of our time iterating very quickly, or potentially ruin that dynamic by bringing on someone that we don't know well?"

In short, I'm nervous about everything. If you're doing a startup and you're relaxed, you should be very worried.

Livingston: So far, what has surprised you most about starting your own startup?

Ross: One thing I didn't know was how tightly connected everyone is in the Valley. We'll meet someone, and then we'll meet someone who I would never expect to even know that person, and they'll say, "I heard you met Tony last week." It's such a small industry, and so much business is done through the network circuit, which is kind of upsetting, because I'd rather the good companies get the good deals and the bad ones don't get deals at all. Instead, it's more like, "Who do you know?"

I can definitely see where the Google guys came from when they refused to play by these rules. They didn't know anyone, and they didn't schmooze their way in.

Mena Trott
Cofounder, Six Apart

Husband-and-wife cofounders Mena and Ben Trott started Six Apart (named for the number of days between their birthdays) in their apartment in 2001. Trott's personal blog, Dollarshort, was growing in popularity, and she was dissatisfied with the blogging software available at the time. So she and Ben decided to develop their own and share it with some friends. Movable Type became popular almost immediately on its launch in October 2001.

In April 2003, Six Apart received funding from Joi Ito's Neoteny. They launched their hosted service, TypePad, later that fall. In January 2005, the company announced the acquisition of Danga Interactive, the makers of LiveJournal. Six Apart launched Vox (formerly known as Comet), a hosted blogging platform with a social networking component, in 2006.

Livingston: Take me back to how things got started.

Trott: I started with a blog called Dollarshort in about April of 2001. I did it because I felt that I needed a creative outlet. I just started writing a blog, writing stories. I was still at my job, but I didn't feel incredibly fulfilled. My blog was getting more and more popular, and we were getting more involved in seeing what people were doing.

When the company closed and we got laid off, we said, "Let's start working on a blogging tool—just release it as donationware and see where that goes." We didn't expect anything from it. We thought we'd get donations and maybe some stuff off our Amazon Wish List, but we never imagined anything more than that.

As we got more and more involved, we became more ambitious, but I don't think we ever would have woken up and said, "Let's start a company." It just never occurred to us that it was even possible. When Ben and I were in college (we've been together since we were in high school), we started to think about a web design company, but it always seemed overwhelming. We had no idea where to start. When I look back, it seemed like the hardest thing in the world.

Luckily, it was all kind of accidental. When we released Movable Type, it became popular pretty quickly, and it became a full-time job. I think having customers from day one was the thing that really forced us to be a company. If we had been just talking about a product and we had to build up a customer base and figure out how to market it, that would have been incredibly hard. So what we did was just jump in with no desire to do anything more than create something that we love.

Later on when we were talking to VCs, they would say, "What problem does this solve?" We weren't giving pitches, it was just conversational, but that's the thing that never occurred to us. We were never trying to solve anyone's problem other than mine or a few bloggers'.

But there was a big demand for what we were creating, and Movable Type became really popular. Around July 2002, we were at a fork in the road and we asked ourselves, "Do we want to become consultants and focus on building out customizations of Movable Type and doing implementations?" We went that way for a little bit and then said, "This is not fun." (I still have an invoice that we were never paid and we ended up paying out of pocket.) So we said, "Let's do something even harder. Let's go straight to the consumer." And we started working on TypePad.

We formed the LLC in July of 2002, right before we decided to start doing TypePad. We still didn't have funding—it was Ben and I still in the apartment in Richmond. We used the spare bedroom and our desks were literally back to back. We spent a lot of time there, 18 months in total. It's funny when I tell these stories. It seemed like a different world. It's kind of like when people have babies and they say they can't remember how painful it was and they say, "Let's have another baby." I think there's a chemical in my brain that forces me to forget how painful the time was.

Livingston: Tell me about some of the painful times, when it was just the two of you sitting in a room.

Trott: I think that was painful enough!

One of the reasons that I started my blog was that I felt like I didn't really have any friends. When Ben and I were together at college, we never forced ourselves to make friends with other people because we had each other. It was a new thing for us because we had started going out when we were seniors in high school, and then we spent the rest of the time joined at the hip. We always had each other. Plus we got so involved with the Web and doing work that it never occurred to us to make friends.

So I wanted my blog to have a connection with people online, all these people that I wanted to be friends with. My blog helped facilitate that. One of the things that was really painful about those times in the apartment was that Ben and I really didn't have any friends, and we really didn't do anything extracurricular. We went to parties occasionally, but it was never fun. So one of the hard things was that we shut ourselves in for so long working on this. It was such a different experience because Ben and I became such a team, everything we did was together. There was probably a 2-year period where we didn't spend more than 6 hours apart. The first time I went on a business trip for the company was the first overnight trip where we were apart longer than 6 hours.

It's really good that we now have other people, because you can get really caught up in living with someone and being so part of it. But I think we didn't know any better. We could definitely form a company again, but we couldn't do it that way, because you get drained.

Even after we became more of a company and we had employees, it wasn't until about a year ago that we've been able to say, "No, I don't want to talk about work at home." Having an office made a difference. Working out of the home is the hardest thing to do, because you can never leave work.

Livingston: You were working on Movable Type. Were you just planning to launch it and see what happened?

Trott: We had a lot of excitement before the launch because I announced it on my blog. About 2000 people signed up to be notified when we launched. All these people were like, "Movable Type's coming this week, we're really excited." And we thought, "Oh my God, there's so much pressure." We were looking at each other saying, "Should we do this or not? It could be tethering us to this product forever."

We made the decision to do it. Of course, if I knew then all the stuff that would happen to us, certainly I would do it. But the first couple months were pretty hairy.

Ben and I sort of have this perfectionism about what we do. We can't do it halfway. So we said that we were going to figure out how to make this something that could sustain itself. But at the same time we knew that we were going to have to get jobs. At least that's what we thought, because it was free—it was just donations. You can't make money off of shareware. But luckily people started donating very quickly, and we were at break-even just about after the second month. And it was break-even pretty much until we got funding.

Livingston: How did you get people to donate?

Trott: We never actively asked for money because we thought that was obnoxious. We had one page up that said, "We take donations and this is why you should donate." There were two factors why people would donate. One was that they liked the product. The other was that we'd give recently updated keys.

When you posted your blog, it would appear on our main site, and if you paid around $20 you'd get a key to do that. So people would say in the email, "Can I have my key? Here's my money." Well, you could kind of think that you are paying for the software, but here's your key. I actually sent those emails out with their keys up until probably January of 2004. It was a really long time. I felt that they were giving money, so I wanted to honor that and thank them.

Livingston: So you're taking donations, it's paying the rent and keeping things moving. Did you then try to seek out VC money?

Trott: No. We never sought out money. Joi Ito contacted us because he was using the product, and he was interested. He was actually probably more interested in just talking to us about what we were doing. And then he said, "If you're ever interested . . ." We kind of ignored him because we didn't know what to do. We didn't have any desire to take money. We had heard all these horror stories about people receiving venture money (this is 2001/2002), and even though we didn't think we could have the aspirations to be something huge, we certainly didn't want to crash and burn because we took money when we shouldn't have.

And we didn't know anything about it. Are you supposed to pay them back? We didn't understand that investors put money in and they own a part of your company. All we had heard were bad things that happened, and we didn't know why.

So Joi contacted us and he was smart because he was also a user of the product. He knew that we wouldn't ignore user questions. He was asking technical questions and he donated, so then we felt really obliged. Then in December of 2002 we finally met him at the Supernova conference. We met him with Barak [Berkowitz], who is now our CEO, and they talked about what we were interested in doing, and we said, "We're working on this hosted service"—it didn't have a name yet—"It's easy and it's this thing that we think we can get a lot of people using." But to us, a lot of people meant that if we had 130 people using it, we'd break even. If we had 3,000 users, we'd be set for life. And we would maintain a service where it was 3,000.

Barak said, "That's great for a niche or personal lifestyle business, but we're not interested in investing in that." At that time we thought, "Who is this asshole? Why is he saying that to us?" First, we didn't care—we didn't seek him out. And also we didn't want someone else telling us that our goals weren't ambitious enough.

After that lunch, they invited us to go to Japan to talk. We were like, "OK, we get a free vacation." We didn't think that we would take any money. The fact that Barak was challenging whether we could do it made us want to do it more. We also knew that, if they didn't invest in us, they'd invest in somebody else. At the time, Blogger hadn't been bought by Google yet, and we thought, "OK, Blogger will get the money if we don't." (Which was probably true if they hadn't been bought.) And we didn't want that—we wanted a stake in it and didn't want to be a footnote.

We always had an ambitious, "we want to win" attitude, but we never had the stakes so high, because it never occurred to us that we could do it. I think that's one of the good things, too: since it never occurred to us that we could do it, it didn't occur to us that we couldn't do it. We just had to put our minds on it. And that has been really key to what we've done. The lack of experience made us think, "Why can't this just be done?"

So time flies and we grow the company, and we acquired a couple companies in between.

Livingston: How much funding did you take?

Trott: Initially it was less than a million dollars—so angel money, really.

Livingston: So you now had the money to hire some people and get an office. What were some of the first things you did?

Trott: Nothing, that's the funny thing. We treated the money like it was our own. We were so concerned about it. Suddenly we had this money and we couldn't spend it all because, if we spent it all, we'd need more, and then we'd need more and then we'd have zero ownership of our company. That terrified us.

As a result, we didn't hire fast enough and we weren't in an office. We had closed in April, but we didn't move into an office until August. We had one employee who was working out of his house in San Jose, one in New York, and our support person was in Minnesota. It was like a remote office and nothing was really changing because we thought, "We can't spend this money."

We bought operations stuff for TypePad—servers, etc.—and we had payroll for the first time. Five people on payroll. Five people is a lot more than zero. And Ben and I were never really taking a salary other than what we earned from consulting, which was just kind of recycling itself.

We were the complete opposite of the things that typified the Bubble. We saw the Bubble, and we saw people spending too much money on things that didn't matter. Then you have us, who didn't even want to buy a refrigerator for the office because it cost $150. I think that there's a middle road that's a lot better.

Livingston: Why did you set yourself up as an LLC instead of a C corporation?

Trott: Because we read that LLCs can't take investments. So we figured, if we formed an LLC, we couldn't have stockholders. But then, you can always change from an LLC to a C corp. It's a funny kind of stupid thing that we did, like, "Let's form a company that can't take investors," not realizing that you can just change the structure of your company. We were looking at the California incorporation book, and we said, "We have to figure out if we're going to be a partnership, a sole proprietary, a C corp., or an LLC." And we were looking at the checklist and we saw "can't take money," so we said, "Let's do that one." It's amazing. For anyone who is starting a company, it's so hard.

Ben and I were 24, and where are you supposed to learn this stuff? We got the Nolo book on incorporating and we looked online, but it's so hard.

We owe a lot to Barak. He became a board member (for Neoteny) after the investment, and he was the best board member because not only did he help us figure out the business strategy, but he also helped us figure out how to get an office, how to get insurance, how to wire our office and do the business stuff. That's one of the reasons we made him CEO—because he was so willing to do everything that we needed and he wasn't an investor who would just give us money and check on us every quarter.

He did allow us to make mistakes, however. For example, he let us not ramp up as fast as we could because we had to learn for ourselves that that was not the best idea. Another example was when we went to look at offices. Barak went, because Ben was at home working. We'd look at offices that had like 10 or

20 offices, and I said, "If we need an office that big in a year from now, then I don't know what we're doing, because we don't need that many people." He said, "OK. You can make that decision." So we got like a 1,500-square-foot office that we outgrew in 8 months. People asked why we got such a small office, and it was because I thought everything else was too big. I realized that on my own. It was really important; he did it in a good way.

Livingston: This is surprising, based on the stories I've heard about investors.

Trott: The Neoteny investment was such an anomaly. We were this incredibly early-stage company that had no structure, no employees, no really good accounting, nothing but the LLC. But we had a huge customer base, which I don't think most startups have. We had hundreds of thousands of people using our products, and it had been operated with so few resources. So we had to really start from scratch.

If it wasn't for Barak, I don't know where we would be now. We knew what we knew, which was the product. But there were all these little things that you just have no clue about. It was incredibly overwhelming. But if you think about it too much, then you don't do it. You almost have to not know what you're getting into to actually do it.

Livingston: Tell me about other things that went wrong.

Trott: Ben and I were still trying to do everything ourselves, and that was incredibly stupid because we just wore ourselves to death. Ben and I pretty much were the only people that built the first version of TypePad. We said, "Let's not hire anybody. We did Movable Type on our own. We can do TypePad on our own." And it killed us.

The slow pace at which we hired was good for the budget because we were able to operate on that $600,000 for a really long time. But at the same time, it wasn't good that it was at the expense of our health.

I made the decision to put Barak in at CEO in November of 2002, but he didn't become CEO until July of 2003. He was kind of acting like CEO in January 2003. He worked without a salary. He got paid eventually, but he worked under just a promise that he'd be made CEO, which was amazing. To work 6 months with just an understanding—he had a lot of faith in us.

Livingston: Why did it take so long?

Trott: Because we were just so focused on operating the business. He had his employment letter that I had to write and we had to consult a lawyer—it's kind of a big thing to put a CEO in. Because of all the negotiations (that were really minor, actually), it just always got put on the back burner.

Livingston: What else went wrong?

Trott: Skimping on hardware sometimes. I wouldn't recommend that. We often had to replace the stuff we bought because we had been so worried about costs.

But that's not always a bad thing. With LiveJournal, Brad [Fitzpatrick] wrote everything instead of buying things. That worked for him. He did his thing for 6 years. So I think it works, but we had a different scale than LiveJournal, which took a long time to get a large base.

Livingston: Why did you build new software for TypePad instead of reusing the code you had for Movable Type?

Trott: Movable Type is download software that you install on your own server. It was meant for people who knew their way around installing server software. We realized that more and more people were coming to blogging with less and less experience. That's relative to the people who are coming in now, who probably have only installed one web application.

So we wanted to have a service that anybody could use. That's why we started developing TypePad. It's a lot more like WYSIWYG, and you can drag and drop items into your templates, and you don't have to know any coding. It's a very different product than Movable Type.

Livingston: You have distinct audiences?

Trott: Movable Type and TypePad are kind of the same audience, and then there's LiveJournal. Movable Type and TypePad are both about 50/50 gender split and it skews toward people in their 30s. With LiveJournal, 70 percent are under-21 females.

Livingston: I heard that you planned to transfer the code behind TypePad to Movable Type. Is that true?

Trott: No. We always thought that the features of TypePad would go into Movable Type. But as time went by, more people who want to use TypePad have just gone to TypePad, and Movable Type tends to be more of a professional business tool. Even though there are still "prosumers" that are using Movable Type, it's easier to deploy the features that people want on TypePad.

It's funny, because Movable Type is a tricky install, but it would be almost impossible for someone to install TypePad because there are so many things that are required with the server setup. It's kind of trying to decide what the best of all the worlds are. That's what we're doing with the Comet stuff that we announced at DEMO. It's kind of the next-generation platform. It's all the features of LiveJournal that are really good—privacy per post, friends aggregation, to be able to read people's posts—with the publishing options of Movable Type and TypePad. So the reason why TypePad didn't become Movable Type is because the audience is differentiated and it didn't make sense to have that on an installable.

Livingston: What did people misunderstand about what you were doing?

Trott: There was licensing. From October 2001 to May 2004, Movable Type was always free and you had paid options. Commercial was the one level that was never completely free. So if you were using it in a commercial way, you'd have to pay $150. The thing was that we had these huge companies using Movable Type, paying $150 and putting 150 to 200 people on it. We never felt that was right. That's why we had a strict license that basically said that you don't make money off the stuff that we're not making money off of. It wasn't that we didn't want people to make a living off of Movable Type; it's just that, if we weren't making a living, we didn't think that other people should be making money.

Some people say that's not a good attitude, but it was the attitude that kept us functioning as a business. That's some advice for people: don't apologize for wanting to be a company. You see so many people who say, "Oh, we won't charge; things should be free." It's like you don't think you're worth being paid for your time. I feel even more strongly about this when it's an entire company rather than just me and Ben. We can be kind of the fools that will work for free, but I'm not going to make other people suffer for that.

With Movable Type, we said, "Why should businesses get this for free? Why should we get taken advantage of?" There were so many people that were setting up hosted services using Movable Type, and they would charge users money. So we set up these limitations with the licensing saying that you can only have x number of blogs and x number of authors. We just wanted to target the people who were making money off the software that way. But we applied it to personal users too much; we said personal users couldn't have this and people freaked out. They went crazy. Our biggest mistake was that it shouldn't have been across the board.

When we changed the licensing, people flipped out. They were like, "These are the people that screwed you. We supported you for all these years." It was really hard for us because we had always been the darlings in the industry. We never tried to be that, but people just thought we did no wrong. And we didn't do any wrong. I don't think we did wrong with that, but, as soon as you charge for something, it changes people's impression. So we suddenly became evil because we wanted to make some money from our product. It's unfortunate because it's kind of the mindset that people have on the Internet—that things shouldn't cost money. But you have to pay people and pay the rent.

It's really complicated, and I think that most people who aren't in our situation can't really pass accurate judgment. I remember when Ev [Williams] sold Blogger to Google, and people were like, "Ev sold out!" We thought, "OK, he started a business and he sold his business." You shouldn't be ashamed of wanting to be a successful business. Of course, you shouldn't do things that are unethical, and we have never done anything unethical.

Livingston: What competitors did you worry about most?

Trott: We never really obsessed about it. We were always worried about Blogger. I think we always knew that Yahoo or Microsoft would enter the space, and they did. When AOL Journals came out, I thought, "There were these big companies that have entered the market and still haven't done anything really to innovate."

At Six Apart, we're a little bit behind what our vision is because we've been talking about this stuff that we're finally getting to start to trickle out and shipping just now, even though we've been working on it for a year or two—like the Comet stuff we've been working on since day one of the founding of the company. Other than that, there's the open source software, the free software that competes with us.

What we want to do is get tons of people blogging—hundreds of millions of people blogging—and there's room to have more than one software doing that. I don't think people realize that. They see it as an all-or-none game. I think it's really important to realize that you are building a market, and you have to build for the most number of people and not be so worried about counting. It's not as much a numbers game as much as innovation.

Livingston: Was there ever a time when you wanted to quit?

Trott: Yeah, it was really the pre-launch of TypePad. That was the hardest time because Ben was doing more of the operations stuff. I remember I was in the shower, and I just lost it. I was crying and I was like, "This is never going to end. I can't do this anymore."

I don't know why I broke down in the shower, but I remember it because we were at our old apartment. I remember looking at the tiles, and I just could not imagine how we could get out of it. It's really hard to think about it because it was a really hard time. I've never blogged about it. Maybe I should, because people don't understand how hard it was.

Livingston: Was it the pressure?

Trott: It was the pressure. Paying customers. I think it was actually after TypePad had launched because we had paying customers. It just didn't seem like there was any light at the end of the tunnel.

But it's like when you look back at your teenage years and you think about how horrible they were, but then you realize that they weren't that bad. What, you didn't go to a dance? That's the worst thing in your life? It's like, "Well, it wasn't that bad," but it always seems worse when you're in the midst of it.

When we went to Japan for that trip, we said that if nothing ever came out of this company other than this trip to Japan, we've accomplished a lot. We never thought we'd go to Japan, let alone on somebody else's dime. What we have to realize is that we've had so many good opportunities and we've learned so much that, if everything failed tomorrow, we would still have gotten so much out of it.

I think it's really important that you have a realization of what's important. You can't stress over things that you can't necessarily control. Even though we can control the success of the company to a certain extent, you have to be grateful for what you've got. We were able to buy a house. We never thought we'd be able to buy a house. That's a huge thing.

Four years ago, I never thought we'd have the stuff we have now—not material, but a company and a house and have friends and be respected. Would I have quit? No, I wouldn't have, because I didn't. But we came pretty close.

I think it was even harder because of the marriage. It's hard to be so stressed out and not have any outlet that's not work. But at the same time, Ben knew what I was going through more than anybody else could in the world, and so I didn't have to tell him how I was feeling because he knew what was bothering me.

Livingston: Did you ever argue at work?

Trott: It's not like that anymore, but when we fought, we fought out in the open. That's one thing that people told me I had to stop. If I'm freaking out about something, I freak out on the one person I think I can. I mean, I can't yell at Barak necessarily, so I'll yell at the person that I'm married to because it's easier to do that.

Whenever we got into really big fights, it was always about something not working right. And it was me. If something breaks, usually it's going to be engineering. It's not going to be design, because design is something that doesn't break. It may not work the way people want it to, but it's not going to be noticeable. So I would freak out and say to Ben, "This is down! Don't you know it's down? Don't you care about the company?" But yelling at Ben isn't going to fix it. That's something I realized. But it's back to that pregnancy thing; I've blocked out the really bad fights.

Livingston: Why do you think there aren't more female startup founders?

Trott: This is the part that I always end up regretting because I set the gender back. I think one of the reasons happens to be that women aren't always necessarily that motivated to prove themselves in the way that men are. It's not saying that they don't have ambition; it's saying that there's something in our makeup that makes us be confident more in what we are and what we've accomplished independently without having to say, "I'm a founder, I'm an entrepreneur."

When I was in school, I was always a class clown. And if I think about the other people in my class who were class clowns, they weren't girls. It was me and a bunch of boys. I think there's that same sort of personality that makes you want to do something like start a company, and you can't do something like that without wanting to be exposed.

I've kind of retreated a bit. I want to be exposed less now. But I'm more confident in what I've done. I've always identified more with guys at school and I've always been competitive with them. If you try to figure out the single thing that made us get to where we are now, it's my competitiveness with Ben.

When we were in high school, I was practically failing out of my classes. I hated school. It wasn't that I wasn't smart, but I just didn't care about math and science. My English and history grades were great, but everything else was horrible. And then I started going out with Ben and he was valedictorian. I went from a D average to hanging out with the valedictorian, and I thought, "I don't want to be considered the stupid one of us," so I brought my grade point average up in the quarter from a D to a B+.

In college, we were always competitive in every class we took. I'd get pissed off because he was a math major and I was an English major and he decided to minor in English and then he'd come into my classes and there were a few where he'd do better than me. I'd say, "Stay in your own field!" But the thing was with the business, too, I wanted to be successful and he wanted to be successful at the same time, and so we've been competing because we have to be better than each other.

Livingston: Any other reasons why there aren't more female founders?

Trott: People do ask me that all the time, and I have to step back and try to fig-ure out why it is. I'm at a weird age group where I haven't been in the industry for a long time and I haven't seen it first hand, but then it's like, "It can't be a problem because I'm here."

If I'm forced to think about women who are in this field, I can't usually. But I know there are. Many women are in marketing or design. I think marketing and design are a lot harder to learn than engineering. That's my opinion. People put value judgments on engineering like, "There are more men; therefore, it must be a smarter field that women should get into." I don't think that's the case at all. I say, look at women, they're strong designers and strong at marketing and communication. That's a harder skill to acquire in life. Being able to write and being able to figure out what people want in their product, how to sell it to them.

There aren't that many women in technology and maybe it doesn't really matter. I mean, why aren't there more men in design?

Livingston: Looking back in your whole experience, what would you say is the most surprising thing?

Trott: There's the whole, "I can't believe we have a company that has 100 people." The surprising thing is that there's going to be someone here now that I don't know personally. It's not just to a point where I'm not good friends with them, like other employees; it's like, "I don't know this person's name." I feel badly, and I should know everyone's name, but it's hard.

The good part of it is that I don't have to interview everybody. It's not like a small company where, if I don't interview this person, then they can't get a job. So I'm very happy. We still have our staff meetings every Friday where every-body comes in, and we talk and introduce people. So we're still a small com-pany in that sense.

It's surprising that we're still doing it after 4 years and that I actually like this job. I never liked any of the jobs that I had (even though I only had two). This is something that I enjoy doing. I love work. Last night I thought about it because we just sat around all weekend watching TV, and for a little while I was like, "I don't want to go to work tomorrow because I want to finish watching *Lost*" but then I thought, "I like work and I like coming in and talking to people."

I'll be sad the day that the company doesn't exist in some form, but maybe that will be longer. With Amazon, it's been 10 years.

Livingston: Is there anything that your colleagues would describe as a Mena-ism?

Trott: There's the whole joke about me being self-absorbed. I believe I am, but in a way that I'm very self-aware about, and it's one of the ways that I make fun of myself. So I say, "I can't be that self-absorbed because I'm most critical of myself." The running joke at the company is that I'm self-indulgent, but that's me. I'd say that the worst part of me is all out there, so if you see me and I'm being snappish or egotistical, that's the worst it gets. It doesn't get much deeper in terms of my bad things. I think less people know my good parts than my bad.

Livingston: What's your best quality?

Trott: Can you even say what your best quality is without sounding . . . I guess I'm not humble. I really care about people. I think that's one of the reasons I tend to be flippant at work or critical of people and make fun of them in a joking way. It's that I care about everybody. And I don't want to be that sensitive person, so if I have a choice of complimenting a person or making a joke, I'll make a joke. I'm like that dad that won't hug. It's really pathetic.

Livingston: How did it feel to get famous so quickly?

Trott: It's weird because—and I'm not comparing myself to a celebrity—when people want to be celebrities or actors and they say that "this is the thing I want most," then they get to that point and they realize, "I feel the same way." I feel the same way that I really did 4 years ago. I have more confidence now, which is a really important thing, and I'm happier. I can actually say I'm happier, which I think the people who get famous can't say.

I'm not famous in the sense that anybody outside of weblogging will know who I am, but I'm still famous to the point where I don't feel comfortable just writing about anything online anymore, because people will dissect it. That's hard. But it's been good, too, because I think we've gotten closer to what people really want. You can't have someone leading a company who is so concerned about the whole world knowing what they're doing and caring about being famous, because that's not how most people are.

It's been better that I've become more inward, because I think that that's how people function. If I cared most about getting the most number of readers for my blog, that's not going to scale, because most people aren't that way. I went from that in 2002—that was probably the height of the popularity of my blog—to where I am now, and it's just like, "I like my LiveJournal because 20 people read it." And figuring out how to make that experience better is really important.

Livingston: How do you handle people who criticize you?

Trott: There are a lot of people, especially competition, who really criticize the company for no reason. They personally attack us. They say we're stupid. It's really mean. That stuff bothers me. Not as much anymore, because you have to realize that people don't do this sort of stuff unless they're really . . . It's like when your mom tells you that the reason a girl is picking on you in school is probably because she's depressed. You have to understand they're coming from a place where they feel like they have to do it. We've never done things like that. Sometimes I wish these people would get told off. But we're successful and that's one of the reasons why we get picked on. You don't pick on the underdog.

But it's hard, and that's why I'd recommend doing something like the LiveJournal for some friends that know you in real life, because it's not fun to be torn apart or written about. I got a lot of that and that's kind of why I stopped blogging—because people were critical of me.

There was one post where I made a joke about wanting a banjo, and it was like, "Ben, he's such a tyrant, he won't let me have a banjo." I don't have any instruments, and why should I buy a $300 banjo?

He was right, but I was trying to make him seem like this villain. The point of the joke was, "Boy, she's really stupid about wanting something and he's being reasonable." And I got all these emails saying, "You should leave your husband," and "How much does he spend on beer in a year?" All these things that were such judgments. And it's like, (1) you didn't get my joke (it's really hard to translate humor on the Web), and (2) shut up, don't talk about my husband that way.

That was the peak of my wanting to talk about everything. Or wanting to talk to a lot of people.

Bob Davis
Founder, Lycos

Lycos was started in 1995 when CMGI's investment group, @Ventures, bought a search engine developed by Michael Mauldin at Carnegie Mellon University and Bob Davis signed on as CEO. The company grew rapidly over the next several years as Internet usage exploded.

By the peak of the Internet Bubble, it was the fourth most popular site on the Web. In 2000, Lycos was acquired for $5.4 billion by Terra Networks, a subsidiary of the Spanish telephone company, Telefonica.

Davis is currently a managing general partner at venture capital firm Highland Capital.

Livingston: Lycos's original technology came out of CMU. How was the company started?

Davis: The technology was invented back in 1994 by a brilliant computer scientist at Carnegie Mellon University named Michael Mauldin, whose nickname was Fuzzy. It was a research project, the result of a federal research grant. So it was Fuzzy by himself in a closeted office at the research lab at CMU.

He knew he had something, but wasn't really sure what to do with it and didn't want to be a businessperson in a commercial entity. So he worked with CMU's Tech Transfer Office to try to sell the technology. They came across Dan Nova of CMGI, which at the time was a small, early-stage, $35 million venture capital fund, and grew into one of the most successful Internet investment firms of its era. CMGI's venture firm was founded by Dave Wetherell, who understood the magnitude of what this medium would become while most others were still learning how to spell *Internet*. Making a long story short, he acquired 80 percent of the company, and 20 percent of it continued to be owned by a combination of Fuzzy and Carnegie Mellon—10 percent apiece.

Livingston: How did you get involved in the founding of Lycos?

Davis: I was VP of sales for an old-line technology company that sold memory for big IBM mainframes, which wasn't a very exciting job, and I was unhappy. One day my friend Dan Nova called me just to check in socially. He told me about how he was trying to put a deal together with Carnegie Mellon for a technology and that, if he got it done, he wouldn't have a CEO. At that point he was in the early stages of thinking about the deal. I said, "What about me?" He laughed. I said, "I'm serious."

So we talked more about it and I worked with him as he went through the process of wrapping up the deal with Carnegie Mellon. I then joined as the CEO of a company that didn't exist yet because Carnegie Mellon still had the technology and hadn't closed the deal with CMGI. So for about a week in June of '95, I was the CEO of Lycos, but Lycos didn't exist. We had no other employees, no customers, no products.

Livingston: But you had the technology.

Davis: We had the technology. But Lycos was little about the technology and all about consumer brand.

Livingston: What were you focused on doing in the first month?

Davis: Job number one for the first month was about building a team, getting some core people in place. And trying to understand what we were doing for a living and how we were going to go about doing it. Were we a technology company? A media company? Or some hybrid thereof?

We were a little late to the game because, by the time we incorporated, other search engines like Infoseek and Yahoo were in the marketplace. So we showed up trying to figure out what we wanted to do. We were somewhat indecisive in the sense that I couldn't make the call between technology and media. They're different, so we coined the phrase "Technomedia," which meant that we were licensing our technology at the same time we were building our own branded site, selling advertising. It wasn't a good term. We eventually abandoned the technology piece of it and became a pure-play media company.

Livingston: Wasn't the technology group located in Pittsburgh?

Davis: Fuzzy was very committed to being a research scientist and didn't want to join the company or be involved with the business side of it. But our agreement with Carnegie Mellon required us to keep a presence in Pittsburgh. So despite the fact that Lycos was headquartered in Boston, we were obligated to have a meaningful presence in Pittsburgh.

We were fortunate in the sense that Carnegie Mellon gave us a good draw of students, postgraduates, and alumni in the area, since it's a premier computer science institution. We hired our first few technical engineers out of Carnegie Mellon—one that was Fuzzy's student assistant and another that was working in their data labs. I think we probably peaked with 300 employees in Pittsburgh, and certainly substantial pieces of our engineering operation were there.

Livingston: Was this difficult to manage, especially in a startup environment?

Davis: Yes, it was very hard to manage. It's only a short plane ride from Boston to Pittsburgh, but it was almost the equivalent of oceans between us, because you're not able to walk down the corridor and say, "Hello. What can we do next?" This added a substantial burden for the company.

Livingston: So what were some of the other big problems that you faced early on?

Davis: What weren't they? Hiring people, firing people, understanding our business model, getting customers, servicing the customers, finding office space, scaling the company, staring down competitors, going public, raising money, satisfying shareholders. That's all in the first 9 months.

Livingston: Did you know from the beginning that your goal was to go public?

Davis: No. When we started, I felt we could make a big business, but I didn't think it would be quite to the extent that it became. The week after we had started the company, Dan Nova said to me, "This will never be a people-intensive business." But when I finally left the company, we had 3,500 employees. We also joke about the fact that we once said, "At some point, if we're lucky, maybe we'll get up to a million users of Lycos." I think at the time, we had maybe 50,000 or 100,000. When I left the company, we had about 110 to 120 million, monthly.

Livingston: What were the big turning points?

Davis: There was no turning point per se. It was a complete evolution and there was a new opportunity and a new challenge every day. As you mow down one obstacle, there's always another one waiting. We'd be fighting six or seven fires at any given point in time on any given day, and you're fighting all these fires at the same time you're trying to construct the blueprint of the house. So you're dealing with emergencies du jour while you're trying to build a business.

But that's the nature of the entrepreneur and that's the nature of a young business. We'd be hard-pressed to find a company in the history of business that has laid out a blueprint and been able to follow that blueprint chapter and verse throughout its life. It just doesn't happen. It's a changing environment out there.

So there were many issues we faced. Staffing was a huge challenge. Lycos became sexy after a few years, but early on, no one had heard of Lycos, and those that had thought it was this crazy idea that wasn't destined to continue. Never mind the company—people didn't believe in the medium then, so recruiting employees was a challenge. Getting good people on board was tricky because we had no proof points for employees in the sense that there was no demonstrable success.

Livingston: This was before joining a startup was a popular thing to do?

Davis: Well, startups have been around forever, but working for a startup didn't have the euphoria that it had a few months later. But there have always been entrepreneurs and people willing to take risks. The Internet wasn't cool, for sure, and Lycos was unheard of when we started the business.

Livingston: What did you find people misunderstood?

Davis: I think it was more of a lack of a clear vision as to what the Internet would become. There was very little appreciation that it would ever become a household tool. But bear in mind, at this point in '95, even computers in the home were somewhat unusual. We had them on our office desktop, not at home with our kids using them. We look back retrospectively at the Internet and say it's the greatest medium that's ever existed. But in '95 email was unheard of other than in the office.

Livingston: How did Lycos get its first traffic?

Davis: We were fortunate in the sense we had a good product at that point in time, despite the fact that there were others ahead of us. We promoted, we advertised, we aggressively sought PR. Over the years we got a lot of press. We evangelized in a big way. We encouraged our employees to tell their friends, families, and neighbors about Lycos and how they could utilize it. Eventually over a period of about 18 months, we had this snowball that had become a giant snowball rolling down the hill with a lot of momentum that was very difficult to stop.

Livingston: So who were your first customers?

Davis: We talked all the time at Lycos about the three customers we had: employees, our advertisers (the paying customers), and our users. From my standpoint, users were on the top of the list because without the users, we'd have no company. So it's interesting that those who were most removed, in the sense that we had no formal interaction with them—the viewers of our product—were the most important to our success.

And we didn't know who was watching, especially early on. We didn't know when they were watching, but we knew they were watching. We knew from the logs the audience was growing rapidly.

AT&T was our first paying customer—an advertiser. It was tiny: a $5,000 insertion order. But it was euphoria—our investors were excited, employees were excited. And then we took the order and quickly realized that we didn't have any technology to place an ad on our server! We had the technology guys going crazy for about a week and a half, but they figured out a way and we got that first banner ad for AT&T running on Lycos.

Livingston: What was Lycos doing that was different from its competitors?

Davis: We did an awful lot that was similar to one another in terms of the products we sold. If you went to Lycos, Yahoo, Infoseek, or Excite, the products had more in common than they had apart. But where we differentiated ourselves was less so with technology and more so with the consumer, and that's brand.

And we worked very hard on our positioning and our branding of the company in terms of what we wanted it to be. We tried to be this safe, comfortable environment for folks that were just trying to figure out the Internet. We thought of ourselves as the Internet on training wheels. A good way to find your way around was using Lycos, and we worked really hard to position ourselves that way. So we weren't trying to be the souped-up Maserati (as a VP of marketing used to say) that could go 120 miles an hour. And we weren't trying to be a cramped little Beetle. We liked to think of ourselves in that analogy as the family sedan, the Ford Taurus. Not the sexiest out there, but very purposeful in what we did.

We also were different because we focused on earnings from the day we incorporated, and many others did not do that. We were a profitable company very early on, maybe a year and a half or so into our life, and we really were the exception.

Livingston: Which competitor did you worry about most?

Davis: It depends what day of the week it was. Probably Yahoo. Early on, Google didn't exist; they didn't show up until around '98. We worried about Microsoft's intentions for getting into the online world. Its pocketbook was boundless. They could show up with a strong offering and advertise the heck out of it.

Then we also worried about Yahoo because back then it was the 800-pound gorilla. Yahoo had a larger audience than we did. We were playing catch-up with them.

Livingston: Do you remember if you ever had to somehow make yourselves seem bigger than you actually were?

Davis: All the time. We became the most popular destination on the Web in April '99—I remember it well. At that point we were the busiest spot on the Internet—we overtook Yahoo. But for the previous four years we were playing catch-up to Yahoo. So we were always trumpeting ourselves and talking about the Lycos advantage. And over time, the parts became a little bit different, but to the consumer not all that different.

We in the industry saw it differently. Lycos became more search and Yahoo became a directory. If you remember Yahoo back in '95/'96, there really wasn't the search feature. You'd click your way down into things. So you would say literature, books, founders, books about founders—and you would click your way down rather than just doing a simple search.

Livingston: You went public in what was the fastest IPO in the NASDAQ ever.

Davis: It still is.

Livingston: How did you manage that? How did you manage creating a business plan and vision for the company, growing the company, doing all the PR, and preparing?

Davis: We developed a business plan, but I'd be lying to say that we referred to it every day. We spent a lot of time on the plan trying to identify what business we were in and where we'd go, but so much of our life was reactionary. But we focused on increasing users. We focused on expanding the advertising base. We focused on partnerships; getting others to promote Lycos was very effective for us. We had a wide number of customers, like AT&T, CompuServe, and Prodigy, that licensed Lycos technology and put their own search engine online with

"Powered by Lycos" underneath it. Interestingly enough, all three of those companies are gone today.

They were our early licensees. We also did some joint ventures overseas. Probably less than a year into it, we struck a joint venture with Bertelsmann, which was the largest media company in Europe. We put in our technology and they put in about $10 million, and we created Lycos Europe, which was Lycos in native languages for a dozen countries in Europe, initially.

Livingston: So these partnerships and licensing helped drive a lot of new users?

Davis: They were incredibly important for us early on. We had a number of license agreements with companies that would pay us several hundred thousand to millions of dollars to use our technology. So we got a lot of cash from that and then we had a lot more visibility as well.

Livingston: So Lycos was focused on building visibility in many different ways.

Davis: Yes. We were PR evangelists of the highest order and were constantly self-promoting. PR is the cheapest form of advertising and it was always pretty powerful for us. It was the most effective way we had to get the word out to customers.

We eventually became a large national advertiser: there were Lycos commercials, a Lycos race car, Lycos parachutes jumping out of the sky.

I think the life of an entrepreneur is a life of setbacks, challenges, disappointments, and failures. It's not how you celebrate the successes, it's how you overcome the adversity and the hardship that determines how the business succeeds. And I think that's what we were able to do well.

We had a saying at Lycos called, "Let up, you lose." It was all about perseverance and hunkering down and overcoming the tough times and saying, "How can I succeed?" Certainly every day something had to be done, and we needed to have a focus on a lot of priorities at the same time.

We always needed to focus on hiring good people. People are the foundation of any company. Machiavelli said you judge a leader by the strength of his generals, and it's so true. The team that we put in place would determine how successful Lycos would become over time, so we tried to hire very well. And there hadn't been the Internet industry, which made it harder to assess people's skills.

So we focused on hiring. We focused on building customers, going out and developing customer relationships, and of course that meant hiring a sales team to go out and find advertisers for us. We focused on putting infrastructure in place. Bear in mind we had none. We needed computers to operate the equipment, and that was difficult. Early on we had no money to pay for computers, or very little, so we worked on arrangements with companies like Sun Microsystems and others where they'd give us hardware at a hugely discounted rate and in return we would put on our site "Powered by Sun." And eventually it became "Powered by Digital Equipment." We didn't call it that at the time, but in reality, that was a form of advertising. People were trading us product in return for impressions.

Livingston: Did you ever get any other money except from the original deal?

Davis: No. We had, I think, in total, a couple of million dollars of venture capital money.

As part of the purchase agreement, we were also obligated to pay Carnegie Mellon 50 percent of our first $1.5 million in revenues. So from cash flow, another $750,000 went to Carnegie Mellon. For real working capital, we had a million and a quarter, and that was all we ever had.

So we focused on building our infrastructure, which was difficult. We were always nomads in the sense that we were outgrowing our facility and moving from space to space, trying to stay one step ahead in the urgent need to move.

We were also constantly working at integrating the product. Keeping up with the Joneses, or staying ahead of the Joneses, was always a tricky thing to do. There was massive copying in the industry. Not in the legal sense of taking someone's intellectual property, but in the sense that when we would put a new service online, it generally wouldn't take more than a week for a competitor to do the same thing. For example, when we added the ability to search images online (which is now common, but we were the first to do it), two months later it was everywhere.

Many services that are so commonplace today were all brand new back then. We were a day at a time. There was massive innovation, and this innovation has changed the way the world will communicate for decades.

Livingston: Was the innovation technological innovation?

Davis: There was very little technology. We would have engineers in Pittsburgh come up with an idea and roll it through. We would have product marketing specialists, management or individual contributing employees come up with ideas, and the Pittsburgh guys would develop them. We would outsource a lot. We would license products ourselves.

After a year or so, our audience became substantial. Soon the industry had what was then called the four horsemen: Lycos, Yahoo, Infoseek, and Excite. And then all others were looking for business online to leverage our audience. Among the four of us, we had it all. Search is the ultimate killer app.

Picture the Internet as this giant card catalog in the Library of Congress, and all of a sudden the card catalog tips over and all the papers are on the floor and you can't find anything. You don't know where the books are. Search is your order to that chaos, and so people came to us in big, big numbers.

Livingston: You accomplished so much so quickly as a first-time CEO. What did you find you were better at than you thought?

Davis: I think how much we grew so fast surprised me, and I think the most satisfying thing for me was being able to scale the company through all of that growth. We were growing 200 percent to 300 percent a year, every year. People don't realize that a rapidly growing company is crumbling within and feels pain every hour of every day because nothing works the way it was designed as little as a year before.

In a growth business—which is where you always want to be as an entrepreneur, because it's a lot more fun than the alternative—things are breaking every day. The accounting system that I used in '95 was useless in '98. The systems and the computers that I used weren't powerful enough 12 months later. The facilities that we would lease weren't big enough. The data center wasn't powerful enough to manage the computers we needed. Everything would crumble, and you needed to be one step ahead of that all the time. So amazing growth was a challenge, but it was an awful lot of fun. And it's important that you do it with perseverance. You do it with a sense of determination and doggedness that says, "I can overcome."

Livingston: I usually ask people when did they most want to quit, but I have a feeling you never did.

Davis: That's not true. There were times where you're overwhelmed. Though I am not sure I actually wanted to quit, I was probably close. The time I was feeling most overwhelmed was when we had an attempted merger with Lycos and Barry Diller's USA Networks in 1999. That became a very controversial transaction, as it was the first attempt to merge offline and online assets. We announced the merger, and then in the face of shareholder dissent, I failed to complete it.

Livingston: Was it hard to be in the limelight like that?

Davis: If there was any good thing that came out of it, I'd say it was the enormous publicity we had. In a perverse sense it was valuable to us because, throughout all this, the Lycos audience was soaring. Lycos was in the news every day in a way we never could have bought. At the same time we killed the deal with USA, we overtook Yahoo for the number one destination online. And then back to the importance of perseverance, we stayed with it, and a year later, Terra came knocking at the door and offered us a very attractive price. We sold Lycos for $5.4 billion, which represented a return on venture capital investment of about 300,000 percent.

Ron Gruner
Cofounder, Alliant Computer Systems; Founder, Shareholder.com

In 1982, Ron Gruner, Craig Mundie, and Rich McAndrew founded Alliant Computer Systems to build parallel supercomputers. Their goal was to build a machine that used multiprocessing to achieve better performance than the fastest single-CPU machines, but in a way that was transparent to developers.

In 1985, after 3 years of work, they'd done it, and for the next several years Alliant was one of the leading players in the turbulent parallel computer industry. But the company lost its way; Gruner left in 1991 after disagreement about the company's direction; and a year later Alliant filed for bankruptcy.

Looking for something to do next, Gruner started a new company at the opposite end of the spectrum: a web-based service business. His experience as CEO of Alliant had taught him the importance of investor relations. In 1992, he founded Shareholder.com with the goal of using technology to automate the process. Shareholder.com pioneered a new, broader approach toward investor relations. Shareholder.com grew steadily, and in February 2006 was acquired by NASDAQ.

Livingston: Give me a little background on your career and how you got started with Alliant.

Gruner: I've really had three jobs in my life, starting with Data General in 1969. I moved up from Oklahoma to Massachusetts to work for Data General, which got a lot of visibility in the late '60s, even though it was a very small company. I started as their 43rd employee and saw them grow to over 15,000 when I left in 1982.

My background was in computer design. My first half at Data General, I was an engineer doing most of the work myself, and then in the second half I was managing most of the time.

Data General was a very entrepreneurial—almost Darwinian—kind of environment. Ed de Castro and the other founders would try hard to hire the best, most aggressive people they could find, and then let those people go off and oftentimes compete on their own.

The book *The Soul of a New Machine* characterizes that environment fairly well. It talks about two competing teams—the Eagle Team and the Fountainhead Team—how they competed internally, and how the Eagle Team eventually won out because they got to market sooner. I was the head of the Fountainhead project. Spending 13 years there was a really good background for me to understand a truly entrepreneurial kind of environment.

I left Data General in the spring of '82 and, with two other cofounders, Craig Mundie and Rich McAndrew, I started Alliant Computer Systems. Our mission was to build very high-performance computer systems that provided a growth path from Digital's Vax line of machines, which were topping out at half a million dollars.

Our machines provided anywhere from four to ten times the performance of Digital's largest Vax, for maybe 50 percent more, using parallel processing technology. But because this was a very complex technology—obviously all hardware-based; back in those days everything was proprietary hardware—we had to raise a lot of money. We took the traditional approach of going out and raising venture capital.

We knew, even then, having watched how Data General financed itself, that you wanted to generate two things when you're looking for money. One is a sense of exclusivity, saying, "This is a very special kind of deal and not everybody is going to get into it." And secondly, a sense of urgency, so you can get people to make a decision.

A former boss of mine, Carl Carmen at Data General, knew the VC community pretty well. We brought him in, and another partner of his, Jesse Aweida, who was the founder of Storage Technology Corporation. We didn't call them this at the time, but they were angel investors. Together they put in a couple of hundred thousand to help us get launched and spend 6 months writing a business plan on how to commercialize parallel processing technology.

We then contacted Kleiner Perkins, who even then were viewed as one of the premier venture capital firms. We told them that we thought we had a really interesting idea. We weren't prepared to talk about it, but we would talk about it in about 6 months. We thought, having been at Data General and knowing the computer business very well, it could be something even approaching a revolutionary idea.

One of the big wins Kleiner Perkins had in the '70s was Tandem Computer. Tandem's gone now, but it was a big hit in the '70s and early '80s. They rethought computer architecture to build what they called Non-Stop Computing. They used redundant computers, so if one computer failed, the system kept running. For transaction processing, it was very reliable.

It was really elegant, sexy technology. We thought that we were doing the same thing on the performance side through parallel processing. We didn't want to talk about it until we felt we had it really fleshed out well. So we let Kleiner Perkins know that we weren't ready to talk, but we'd contact them when we were.

Livingston: How did they respond?

Gruner: They said "Fine." What they thought, I don't know. But we did go back to them about 4 months later, when we had a first draft of the business plan done. We worked very hard on that plan and then went out to San Francisco and pitched the idea to them. This was John Doerr. He had been there a few years at the time, but he was just really getting started in his career. Frank Caufield, Brook Byers, and Tom Perkins—that whole crew.

They liked the idea because they could draw analogies with Tandem Computer. They looked at our backgrounds, having been in the business, etc. So we were able to raise money from Kleiner Perkins. The first round, as I recall, was about $4.7 million, and back in those days, that was a lot of money for a first round of financing.

They then introduced us to Hambrecht & Quist—Bill Hambrecht—and Venrock, which was the venture management arm of the Rockefeller family—Peter Crisp in New York City. We were able to put together that consortium of three VCs in about 3 months.

We closed in early October of 1982 and set up the board. Tom Perkins came on the board. Bill Hambrecht did not, but he liked to be able to observe. It all worked pretty well. We raised three additional rounds with those investors for a total of about $30 million.

We kept it to those three investors, or some subset of those. As the game moved on, Hambrecht & Quist, being an investment banking house and, frankly, hoping to take us public someday, stepped up and took a larger share than Kleiner Perkins did, but they were all substantial investors.

We announced the initial product in the summer of 1985.

Livingston: Three years later?

Gruner: Yes. It took 3 years. We got financing in the fall of '82. It took 2 1/2 years to hire a development staff, design the computer, develop the software, and announce it. We shipped initial systems, which were not beta systems but were really production systems, in September of '85. So it was approaching 3 years. It was a complex task. And that consumed the better part of $30 million.

The first year we did approaching $5 million dollars in revenue. Then the next year, in '86, we did about $30 million in revenue.

Livingston: That's impressive.

Gruner: Because it was hardware. We went public in December of '86. Morgan Stanley and Hambrecht & Quist took us public.

That was a very positive experience. We found a lot of plain, simple wisdom from some of the venture capitalists we had—particularly Tom Perkins. Tom was on our board. Even at that point he was quite wealthy, very successful. And he made almost every single board meeting. He had to make them in Boston by taking a red-eye from San Francisco to Boston, coming into a meeting at, say, 9:30 in the morning, going to a 4- to 5-hour typically boring board meeting, then flying back that night. And he was in his early 50s at that time. He always had great insights, and always tinged with a nice touch of humor, too.

We had other great members of the board. We felt that most of the venture capital community added a lot of value—also in terms of contacts, we were very positive about that.

We grew very quickly, and at one point we had a market valuation of approaching half a billion dollars, about $450 to $475 million.

Livingston: Wow.

Gruner: That was back in the '80s. But then we absolutely hit the wall.

Livingston: Why?

Gruner: A couple of things happened. We were significantly late on one of the next generations of our computers. You would think that high-performance computers designed out of the most advanced parallel processing technology, with a number of patents behind it, would be a highly differentiated product. In reality, it was just the opposite of that.

High-performance computers are the ultimate commodity. The reason is that the customer comes in and says, "Here's my benchmark; here's my program. Run this on your computer and tell me how long it takes to run." So they wind up buying a computer based on performance divided by dollars, megaflops per dollar. It's just like buying a tank of gas.

When you miss a generation—when you miss a major product cycle or you're late significantly, and the competition has caught up with you and they're providing performance that's better or the same as yours—you're at a very significant loss because that's really all that matters. We were selling engineering or scientific computers. Ease of use, reliability, and all those things were small factors. The major factor was, "How fast is your machine and what's it cost?"

The other thing that affected us, that we just simply weren't smart enough to turn on a dime, was the workstation. It's a market that's disappeared now completely, but workstations were personal computers that sat on a desk of an engineer or scientist that they could use for computing rather than having to send their job to a centralized computer facility, run it, and then get the results back the next morning. Workstations began to really take off in the mid '80s. Sun Microsystems and Apollo Computer pioneered that.

As that was coming, the personal computer was getting faster and faster all the time. So many of our large customers—Bell Labs for example—stopped buying the large computers like Vaxes and our kinds of machines and started buying workstations and personal computers.

At the same time that was going on, the Cold War was coming to an end. Many of our customers were defense-related. Major customers were large intelligence agencies in the United States, for example, or other defense-related applications. So that market dried up. Revenues turned down very steeply in the late '80s.

Livingston: How did your investors react?

Gruner: We had a situation where a lot could be learned about the pros and cons of using venture capital. Things were going south quickly and badly. We at the board level had to make a decision as to what we should do. One part of the board was saying, "Let's take our time; work this thing through; live with this for 2 or 3 years; get things fixed; transition into another segment, and move in that direction." Another segment of the board was saying—and I don't mean this in a derogatory way—"Let's take more risk, roll the dice. If it works, it will work out big, and, if it doesn't, it disappears and let's move on to the next deal."

One of the things that I think is dogma within venture capital is that you don't want to manage what they call the "living dead." I don't know what the numbers are now, but back when I was working with venture capitalists, their rules of thumb were: typically one out of ten companies is a really big hit; roughly three out of ten go belly up pretty quickly, and you get rid of them. The other five to six are what they call the "living dead." They grow nicely, organically, but don't generate spectacular returns, and they take management time and energy. Those are the kinds of companies they prefer not to deal with, because it simply doesn't make sense. They have a fiduciary responsibility to their limited partners to generate a significant return, so they want to deal with firms that will tend to do that.

The lesson I learned at Alliant in dealing with venture capitalists was that they're quite impatient with a difficult situation. They have to be. They have no choice.

So it came down to making a decision. What were we going to do with the company and how were we going to transition it? I was in disagreement. I was saying, "Let's take the slower, more methodical approach over time, and we can work it out." The other approach was, "No. Let's change the architecture of the computer, move into the newer technologies quickly, etc." You can argue either one.

So I left the company. I left the board of directors. I was chief executive for 10 years. I basically got fired when it came down to saying, "I can't live with this strategy because I think it's wrong." They said, "We understand that; we respect you; but you can't stay." So I left.

And, unfortunately, it didn't work out. A year later, the company was bankrupt. Certainly, at the point that I'd left, I'd left a lot of problems for them to clean up. The company was not healthy; it was headed in the wrong direction. So I share a good deal of that responsibility.

But then I was at the stage of, "What am I going to do next?" Here I was, in my early 40s, and clearly the computer designer in hardware development was a dying breed. Back in the '60s and '70s, there were lots of people designing computers, mainframes and minicomputers, and all kinds of things—because they were all built out of parts. But with microprocessors, there's only one Intel and a few other smaller firms like AMD. You only need a few dozen designers. So that went away.

I said, "I've got to change careers." I had to think about what I wanted to do. I had some offers to join venture capital firms, which I thought about. There's always the role of corporate consultant. But I decided I really enjoyed being an entrepreneur, and I wanted to go off and do it again.

Livingston: How did you decide what to do?

Gruner: I had a couple of very clear criteria in my mind. I wanted to build a business that had a recurring revenue stream. At Data General—and Alliant even more so, because it sold computers that were in the half million to one million dollar range to large defense companies, universities, and the government, who had very sophisticated purchasing agents—we typically generated 80 percent of our revenue the last 2 weeks of the quarter. People don't believe this today, but it's true.

And we were a public company. So if we had to make $15 million in revenue in a quarter, we'd be 2 weeks from the end of the quarter and we might have $3 million on the books. We were fairly confident we'd close the other $12 million, but it was horrible.

I remember one time we got a call on a Friday, the last day of the quarter. The call was from a very large defense contractor located in Sunnyvale, California. It was a purchasing agent saying, "Well, it's 5 o'clock in Boston right now, isn't it?" I said, "Yes, sir, it sure is." He says, "It's the last day of the quarter, isn't it?" I said, "Yes, sir, it is." He said, "Well, let's negotiate."

So we went into extended negotiations with this guy for a couple of hours, until 7 p.m. our time, until he signed the contract and faxed it to us. Having been through that, I said, "I really want to build a strategy that has a recurring revenue stream."

The second thing was, having been chief executive at Alliant for 10 years, about halfway through that process I realized, "As the boss, I'm spending 40 percent of my time on things that don't directly contribute to getting computers out to customers." In other words, raising money, dealing with investors, dealing with lawyers, those kinds of issues. So I said, "In the next company I do, I want to be able to spend 98 percent of my time focused on the customer and only 2 percent on secondary factors that lead to that."

I said, "I want to start a company that I can bootstrap up from a small amount of capital that gives us an opportunity of being a big fish in a small pond. Because I can't be in a big pond if I'm going to take just a small amount of money. I can only do so much. And then just let the thing grow organically, just take our time."

I actually made the conscious decision to, rather than put together a 5-year business plan, put together my basic thoughts on strategy and manage the company quarter to quarter. Turn quickly if things have to change, but manage it that way.

The third requirement, having been through Alliant with all people working in good faith but losing control of the company, I said, "I ain't going to lose control. I want to be the sole owner. I'm going to be the majority owner of the company. I want to be the sole founder. It may be harder that way because I have to do most of it myself, but I've got control."

My notion for the new company was something I would not have expected when I was at Alliant. It was to go into shareholder communications, which was a micro-niche. The way I got that idea was two things kind of segued in my mind. First, when I was at Alliant, we actually had an investor relations person; we were leading in that in the '80s. She and I spent a great deal of time talking to investors. We had a policy that we would try extremely hard to be open and transparent and get back to every single investor.

There were times when the stock took a bad hit and we would get a couple of hundred phone calls. This was before email, so you did everything by phone. Conference calls were just getting started. So we literally would return every phone call. I remember making phone calls at 9 o'clock, 10 o'clock at night to some mom and pop in Topeka, Kansas. I'd call and say, "My name's Ron Gruner from Alliant Computer Systems. I'm returning your call about our company." And the man would call out and say, "Honey, Gruner's on the phone from Alliant, get on the other telephone." And I'd explain to them what was going on.

Incidentally, that was the decade of class action suits. We never got sued, and I attribute that partly to the fact that we worked really hard to be open and transparent with investors. I don't think we gave anybody any room to say they were misled. But maybe we were just lucky.

Livingston: Did most CEOs call back individual retail investors?

Gruner: I can't say, but we did. So when I thought about what I was going to do next, I said, "This whole area of shareholder communications, it seems to me the individual shareholder is an under-served constituency." Institutional investors got a lot of attention by every company, which makes sense because they're major shareholders. I felt the middle tier and the small tier were being ignored, so I thought, "Let me think about starting a company that uses technology to reach out and communicate with shareholders." That's how we got started.

I really knew nothing about the industry itself, had no contacts. I was starting from scratch. I hired several consultants who knew the industry well, who had been in trade organizations or otherwise had credibility. I had them educate me about the industry and also take me around to opinion leaders in the industry. We talked about what they'd like to have and the opportunities they saw, as well as me talking about my more abstract ideas.

Fairly quickly I hit on the idea that, "OK, here's a specific business opportunity. We can turn this abstraction into revenues." Back in the early '90s, most companies were still sending out printed quarterly reports. These were glossies, typically a trifold piece of paper in an envelope, that were sent out a month to 6 weeks after the release of financial results.

Even back before the Web, back in the early '90s, most investors viewed that as junk mail, because they could have looked in the newspaper the day after the earnings were announced and seen what they were. By the time this thing showed up, it was kind of like yesterday's oatmeal. It was old news.

So I had a concept and I'll tell you how I got it. I had a friend who was a really good programmer, and he told me in the summer of '92 about a project he had recently done for the *Boston Phoenix*, the underground newspaper. That project was writing a program to do personal ads over the telephone—personal voicemail ads. People could leave a message saying, "Hi, my name's Ron Gruner, I'm single, I enjoy this and that, etc." This is before the Web.

The *Boston Phoenix* had personal ads in back, but then they moved in this thing called voicemail ads. When I heard that, I said, "That's kind of an incredible idea." It generates revenues—people call these numbers and you pay per minute—but you can also hear the person, you get a feel for what they're like. I said, "You know, that concept could be applied to companies. Chief financial officers and executives could communicate to the shareholders using telephone technology."

Telephone technology in the early '90s was really hot. It seems like ancient history now, but 800 numbers were coming in—interactive voice response systems, voicemail was all fairly new technology. The concept was to put together an 800 line for each company, which was a customized information service, a hotline for shareholders.

A typical pitch was one we made to IBM, who became a client. We had done some research. We said, "You guys are spending about a million and a half dollars on printing quarterly reports. Every survey that's been done, including your own, shows that most shareholders think of those as junk mail. We propose to stop sending quarterly reports out. Replace the service with what we call our Shareholder Direct service, so all your interested shareholders only have to make a toll-free call to your 800 number and they can then hear the latest quarterly results, answers to frequently asked questions; and they can hear an overview of the company. If you choose to, they can hear Lou Gerstner or the chief financial officer commenting about the quarter.

"Based on our analysis of your shareholder base and the demographics, we think that will cost you about a quarter million dollars a year. So you're spending $1.5 million now. You can take $1.25 million and drop that to bottom line in savings. Spend a quarter million for our service, and the shareholders that are interested in getting the information can get it much faster and in a more personal form than they get it now."

That's how we got started. It generated cash immediately, because we charged what we called a "subscription fee." We didn't want to call it this, but it was really a retainer fee. We called it a subscription fee, billed in advance every quarter: $4,000 in advance plus a per-minute charge.

And rather than going off and buying all the telephone systems ourselves, which would have been my natural inclination as a technology guy, I outsourced that to a large firm in Omaha called West Interactive. So I had no capital costs.

We turned profitable in the summer of 1994.

Livingston: That's less than 2 years.

Gruner: Yes. We had a seed financing in July of '92.

Livingston: Who were your investors?

Gruner: It was just a small group of about 8 to 10 of my friends and business associates, who put in about $25,000 each. We raised $276,000. I nursed that money very carefully, worked without a salary for quite a while. It turned profitable in the summer of '94, and I just grew the company organically until I sold it to NASDAQ in January of 2006.

Of course, we had some really good breaks. The Web was a huge one. When that developed, starting in '95, we jumped right on that. People were saying, "What are you going to do? You're all telephone-based technology, and here's this thing called the Internet." So we thought, "It's just another technology." Having learned from Alliant about not moving quickly enough, we were on it right away.

Campbell's Soup, for example, was one of our earliest clients, and the first time they had a corporate website was through us. If you look back at their annual report in, I think, '95, they said, "If you would like shareholder information, please call 1-800-XXX-SOUP"—that was their Shareholder Direct line—"or visit our website at www.shareholder.com/campbell."

So we started the web service and took it a day at a time, built the business up. We focused very strongly on client satisfaction. We'd do everything it took to keep a client happy. And we focused on the bigger clients.

Livingston: The Internet was just making a splash in corporate America. Was it hard to convince big companies to embrace the Internet?

Gruner: It really wasn't too hard. The initial costs were very low. We would go in and say, "Look, we are investor relations specialists. We know this area very well and we know you have a web development team. But this is a very specialized area. If you want to do this well, you need real-time SEC feeds and stock quotes. When you put up a news release, it needs to be done"—even back then—"in a few hours. You can't wait a few days to put a news release up." So that wasn't too hard to sell.

Livingston: They could outsource all these things to Shareholder.com?

Gruner: That's right. In the '80s and early '90s, the investor relations officer was really an underappreciated asset. They were understaffed and underbudgeted. So we would go in and say, "Our job is to make your life easier. You send us the information; we'll take care of it." And we told them discreetly, "If anything gets screwed up, we take the bullet. We're here to help you."

Then we just kept adding functionality and functionality. And the government helped us too. We had three big breaks with the SEC.

The first was in the early '90s when the SEC put out a comfort letter saying alternatives to the printed quarterly report should be considered, including 800-based telephone numbers. That's essentially like the SEC jumping up and saying, "Go, go, go!" That's about as aggressive as they get. We had asked for a comfort letter because some of the clients were saying, "We don't even know what the SEC says about this." And the SEC said, "We won't say 'yes' or 'no,' but we think it's an interesting idea."

Regulation FD came along in 2000. It had pros and cons, but, for us, it opened things up tremendously. And then, of course, Sarbanes-Oxley came out a few years ago. All of those things basically said that it's much more important to communicate with shareholders uniformly and democratically. Because, believe me, even when I was at Alliant, and in the early '90s, it was very exclusionary—who could attend conference calls, for example.

Mark Coker, the founder of BestCalls, played a very important part in breaking that whole thing open. Back before Regulation FD, conference calls were by invitation only, for institutional investors. Unless you had a significant share in a company or were a recognized security analyst, you did not get an invitation to participate in a conference call.

Regulation FD changed all that. Basically it said, if you've got material information as a public company, you've got to get that out to everybody, including the individual investor that might have a hundred shares. So that opened up the conference calls. And because it wasn't possible to have a conference call with 10,000 people on it, webcasting (fortunately that technology was becoming available) made that possible. At the same time that some people may be talking on the telephone, that conversation was being webcast live to anybody that wanted to listen to it. So that was a major market that opened up to us.

Livingston: Did you know any of this was going to happen?

Gruner: No, of course not. In the early '90s, I just felt that there was an opportunity to somehow use technology to find a way to better reach out to shareholders and save money for companies. That was the basic concept. Just like 10 years before that, when I started Alliant, I said, "There's this whole new technology, what was called parallel processing. There's been a lot of research on it. If we can commercialize that, it may be a really good business opportunity." That was the core concept of Alliant. That's how we left Data General, how we got started. That's all we knew.

So that's how we got started with Shareholder.com, the notion of commercializing technology around shareholder communications.

Livingston: Back to when you started Alliant, when the three of you who worked at Data General decided, "We're going to start our own company . . ."

Gruner: Two of us left Data General at the same time. The third founder had left Data General a few years before that, but we had stayed in contact.

Livingston: You said you spent about 4 months putting together a business plan. What kind of things were you doing in that 4 months? Were you doing any programming to test any ideas?

Gruner: No.

Livingston: It seems like a long time, by today's standards, I guess.

Gruner: Well, it may be by today's standards, but we worked 7 days a week, 10 hours a day. We spent a huge amount of time at the MIT library doing research on parallel processing. What we wanted to do was to find a technology that would allow us to use parallel processing to run existing programs. That was critical. Let's say, an existing Fortran program from 5 years before: take that, recompile it, and then have it run faster.

There were a lot of people doing development in that area academically. We felt the University of Illinois had the best approach. So we then contacted Dr. David Kuck, the lead professor—called him up out of the blue, explained who we were, and invited ourselves up to visit him. Then we began to get a feel for how concrete this technology was. So part of that 4 months was building high-level models to test whether or not this could take existing programs and run them in parallel.

Another part of the time was doing all the competitive analysis in terms of who the companies were in the marketplace and where they might be going. We had pretty good contacts with the industry, as well as startups. And then, being engineers, we probably overengineered the business plan to give it extremely detailed financials.

At that time, it was just at the point when the personal computer and the spreadsheet had come out. The first time I saw a spreadsheet, I thought it was like a miracle. People take it for granted now, but you type a few numbers in the top left of the spreadsheet, and everything else changes automatically. This is incredible! This is like giving us a microscope we can study a company with. So we said, "We can educate ourselves about the financial aspects of a company by building a P&L, a cash flow, and a balance sheet, and making sure they all tie together correctly—changing things and see how that affects the company."

At the same time, over those 4 or 5 months, we were networking with people that we could bring on board as our initial core development team.

Livingston: What were some of the first things you did once you got the $5 million?

Gruner: The first thing we did was hire the first four key people: two very strong software people and two very strong hardware people. They were the architects, along with the founders ourselves, of the computer system.

We wanted to keep expenses as low as possible, so we were initially in a small office in a shopping center in Acton, Massachusetts. And we began hiring people to design and build the product. We spent 2 years doing that. We wanted to be very selective in how we hired people. We had a process we called "chemistry, mechanics, and religion."

Once again, we wanted to build a sense of exclusivity, but also filter people very carefully. It typically consisted of at least three interviews. Chemistry was first. We would bring the person in; we would interview the person on a personal level, and it had to go both ways. Is he or she the right kind of person for us? Does he or she have the right kind of work ethic, background, all those kinds of things. The next step was mechanics. There, we would talk about the specifics of the job. "Here's the job we have in mind for you. We cannot, by the way, tell you what we're doing. We can't tell you what our strategy is or what the project is, but your piece of it is going to be roughly this." At the conclusion, we would give them a written offer, including compensation, and say, "Here's your high-level job description, and, if you feel, after having spent this much time with us, that you would like to join us, you sign the offer letter; and then we will then tell you what the project is." That was religion.

After they had accepted, we brought them in and told them what the project was about: it's basically taking parallel processing, which nobody was doing at the time, and commercializing it. Everybody got really excited about that.

Livingston: Why were you so secretive? Were you nervous about competitors?

Gruner: We were nervous about competitors; we thought we had a very specific edge. And we also thought it was a good recruiting technique in terms of having people focus on three things we thought were important. First of all, "Let's focus in both directions on the people, on the culture, on the environment, see if that makes sense to you." Because we asked them some extraordinary things. We said, "This project is going to take about 2 years, and it's going to be a lot of work. Furthermore, we are going to institutionalize it by saying, 'We need you to work every other Saturday.'"

Livingston: Really?

Gruner: Yeah. "You gotta be here. It's a regular work day. And the other Saturdays and Sundays you might have to be here too, but every other Saturday is a regular work day, gotta be here on time, full day, no monkey business. And that's for 2 years." We told them that early on. We wanted to get people to focus on that first, and then get psyched up about the project. We didn't want to reverse it, where people got really psyched up, "Oh, I want to work on this sexy technology." We held that to the very end.

During that 2-year period, where we were working very hard, we had virtually no attrition. At the time we announced, we had, I think, 40 people in the company, and I think over the 2 years, the attrition was one or two people. It as very small, because we did a careful job of filtering people. And they didn't come in saying, "I feel like there was misrepresentation here," or "I didn't understand what was going on."

Livingston: Do you remember any big turning points as you were building these parallel processing systems?

Gruner: We were using a technology called gate arrays. These were custom integrated circuits. In our case, we were using technology by Fujitsu in Japan. They were very expensive to design, very expensive to tool. They had a very long development cycle. So in building the design, the computer that would use the first revision of gate arrays was really critical. If we had to go through revisions, we had budgeted that, but that would make things a lot more expensive and more complicated. So when our first gate arrays came back, representing a total investment at that point of probably $3 million, and essentially worked almost completely, that was a huge milestone in the project. That was a year before we announced.

So we had hardware that began to work, and then the next step was the Fortran compiler. Fortran is a computer programming language, and the compiler is what took a Fortran program, say, written for a Digital Vax computer, which at the time was a very successful high-end machine, and converted it to run on our machine. The key question was, "Can we take these off-the-shelf Vax programs, recompile them for ours, and actually have them (1) run correctly and (2) significantly speed up as you add more computers?" When we demonstrated that to ourselves, that was a huge milestone. At that point we knew. By early '85, we knew we've got technology that works and is viable. And if we can execute from that, we've got a viable company.

Livingston: Did you have any competitors at that point?

Gruner: We had one competitor that wasn't using quite the same technology, but had moved into our same market, had identified the same opportunity, and that was Convex Computer in Dallas, Texas. They took a completely different strategy. The leading supercomputer at the time was Cray Research, and they said, "We're going to build a computer that's compatible with the Cray." It's ironic in that the lead architect on that project was Steve Wallach, who was the architect of the Eagle computer at Data General.

The Eagle computer was absolutely compatible with the Eclipse computer, which I had designed at Data General. He built the Eagle to be compatible with Eclipse and was very successful. He took that same strategy and did it at Convex. We took a strategy of saying, "Let's pioneer parallel processing technology." They were somewhat different strategies in different approaches, but we were in a horse race with them and they with us.

We announced the product in the summer of 1985, and it was very successful for about 5 years after that.

Livingston: Do you remember any stories about the things that went wrong? Times you thought you were dead?

Gruner: At Alliant, we had dozens of people working and we had lots of money, so once we got past where we could take a program from a Vax and run it on our computer, we weren't too concerned that there was some bullet that could put us out of business.

We had done enough work with the marketplace. We had a number of key customers lined up: Bell Labs is an example. The University of Illinois was going to use our computers in their future research projects. So we could see, even in early '85, $10 million of business lined up, and, if we could deliver the computers, we'd be in good shape. The scares that I had in my career came at Shareholder.com.

Livingston: OK. Let's jump ahead to Shareholder.com.

Gruner: Shareholder.com was a whole different kind of thing, because the first few years there were only three or four people, including myself. We were delivering news for public companies that was very visible, under scrutiny. If you screwed up, either by being late or by getting the wrong information, you were in big trouble. We had a couple of things that scared me to death.

I think the one that was probably scariest, that definitely could have put us out of business, happened in '94 or '95. A very large pharmaceutical company had decided to go with us. We had everything underway, and they were going to announce this new service on their annual report. Everything is fine except that I get a call one afternoon saying, "Ron, we've got a really serious problem. The annual report has come out and it's got the wrong 800 number on it!"

They were frantic. There were two issues: one, they had printed over a million annual reports loaded on pallets at the facility, and two, they had a legal requirement to distribute the reports 30 days before the annual meeting. The reports and the proxies had to be in the shareholders' hands at least 30 days before the annual meeting, so they were really under the gun. As I recall, they had 5 or 6 days to get those reports in the mail; otherwise they had to reset the annual meeting, and it would have been a huge disaster. It would have clearly put us out of business instantly—even though we had told them the right number and we could prove it by showing them the fax we sent them.

So I called the 800 number and it was going to somebody's pager. Back in those days, you couldn't leave a voicemail. It just said, "Please leave a number to call." So we did that. Nobody ever called back. Because we had a good relationship with AT&T, we identified who owned the 800 number. It was a paging company down in Dallas, Texas.

We called the paging company and without revealing what the situation was specifically, we said, "We have a situation here where we got a number mixed up and your customer will be getting a lot of phone calls he doesn't want to get. We'd like to make it right by him and by you." The company wouldn't give us the time of day. They said, "No. Because of privacy issues, we won't contact him and you certainly cannot contact him. All you can do is leave a message." So we tried and tried, and worked it up the ladder. They wouldn't budge. They were just intractable. This consumed about 2 days. Then Josiah Cushing, one of the college grads I had hired, during our staff meeting said, "Ron, why don't you try hiring a private detective?"

I said, "Well, let's try this. It's an interesting idea." So I went to the Boston Yellow Pages, looked under "private investigators," and found an ad that appealed to me. I called the private investigator and I said, "Here's an 800 number. It belongs to somebody that has a pager. All I need from you is to know the name and the personal phone number of this person." He said, "No problem. It'll cost you $100." And I said, "That's fine. How long will it take?" He said, "It will probably take about 4 hours." I thought that was pretty impressive.

He calls back 3 or 4 hours later and said, "Ron, I've got good news and bad news." I said, "Give me the good news first." "The good news is I've got who it is." "Well, what's the bad news?" "It's going to cost you $200, because when we got the name of the person, he had an unlisted number, so we had to do two searches." I said, "Fine. We'll send you a check for $200. It will be in tonight's mail."

I then call the person up. He is in Dallas, Texas. The whole company was hinging on this, plus the situation with the pharmaceutical company, and I was scared to death about how to make this call. So I just thought, "Be as honest as possible," and I said, "Look, I represent a company that's printed your number in a document that's going to be very widespread shortly. Otherwise, they have to republish the whole thing, and it's a real mess. What I'd like to ask you is: we'd like to acquire your 800 number. Give us the right to that and we'll do whatever we can do to make it right for you. All you have to do is tell us what you'd like to have us do." And he said, "I understand. I'll be happy to help you out. If you could buy me a years' worth of pager subscriptions, that will be fine." That was like $400. He could have said $100,000, and they would have done it. He actually said a year, but I said, "No, we'll give you 2 years. We'll be happy to do that."

So we did that and everything was fine, and then he calls back about an hour later. I thought to myself, "Oh my God! He has talked to an attorney. This whole thing is going to get blown off the tracks." And he said, "You know, I was talking to my wife and she would really like a pager. Could you do the same thing for her?" I said, "Sure." The long and short of it is, we met a very decent person. He dealt with us fairly. We bought him $500 or $600 worth of subscriptions for his pager. We got the number literally within hours because AT&T expedited it for us, and everything worked out. But that was probably the scariest incident we had in these 15 years.

Livingston: Were you a hero with the client?

Gruner: Yes, we were, but we didn't fall on the sword too much on that. We basically told them that we got it worked out. I don't think I even told them we used a private investigator. We absorbed all the costs. Turns out, there were two people involved: a client plus a very large stock transfer agent that was working with the client. Of course, the transfer agent really felt good about that, so they threw a lot more business in our direction at that point.

One of our take-aways from that was that you can almost always take a negative situation and turn it to your advantage if you work hard at it. We took something that was a very negative potential situation and made some real friends. Anytime we had a client situation that blew up—and those happen in the business, things go wrong—we would always say, "How do we take this and turn this into a big opportunity, where the client comes back even more loyal than they were before?"

Livingston: Shareholder.com was doing a lot of new stuff for the industry at the time. Do you remember any things that your clients wanted or asked for that surprised you?

Gruner: Having been in the computer business, particularly the high-performance, engineering and scientific aspect of it, that's populated by a lot of early adopters that want the very latest technology, even if it doesn't quite work. Financial people and investor relations people, and legal people in general, are very conservative. So we had to do a lot of missionary work to have them feel comfortable with the technology.

The kinds of things that clients would ask us for were, "How can you make this easier to use? How can you simplify it? How can you make this such that my administrative assistant can manage the system?" One of the things we did early on was to try to make as much of the system self-administrative as possible. They could go into a private, password-protected site and manage aspects of their telephone system as well as their website.

As Regulation FD and Sarbanes-Oxley came in and became real factors, the thing they would come to us for was direction on interpretation. At the time, we had 500 to 700 clients, and they'd want to know, "What are other companies doing?"

They weren't saying, "We're looking for this new feature." That wasn't so common, whereas that would be very common in the computer business. This was more interpretation of the regulations, and how to take stress out of their lives.

Livingston: So you became a source of advice for these companies as well as a source of new technology?

Gruner: Yes, I would say Shareholder.com played a significant role in the late '90s and up until now, interpreting both the technology and the regulatory environment. And from 1995 to 2000, the company and I personally spent a lot of time going to trade conferences, luncheons that NIRI (National Investor Relations Institute) would host, talking about "What's the Internet?" and giving demonstrations, trying to make that less intimidating, explaining it. And then, starting in 2000, we did a similar thing with Regulation FD and Sarbanes-Oxley. Not explaining it so much, but showing examples of what other companies were doing.

Livingston: Did you worry about any competitors?

Gruner: At Shareholder.com we had several competitors. By far our most serious competitor was also a Boston-based company, called CCBN. CCBN was a very smart company. They were funded by Thomson Financial, a major company in a lot of aspects of corporate services, financial services. They were our arch-competitor.

But at the same time, with the dot-com boom, about a dozen companies popped up in investor and shareholder communications, funded by venture capitalists. At one point, by late 1999, I calculated that over $85 million of venture capital had flowed into this little niche of shareholder communications.

And we were still living on our quarter-million-dollar capitalization and doing fine. We were offered investments many times by VCs and turned them down. We just felt growing organically was how we wanted to proceed.

Livingston: You didn't want to give up control.

Gruner: I did not want to give up control. At the time, I owned about two-thirds of the company, and I felt that just makes life so much simpler, particularly for me. But I think for everybody else, too, because we would sit in a conference room, talk about something, make a decision, and be going. We could make important strategic decisions in an afternoon if we chose to.

For example, we had been pricing our Shareholder Direct service at a fixed cost of $4,000 a quarter, plus telephone fees and other variable charges of the Internet. That $16,000 was highly, highly profitable. That was one of the things that allowed us to grow organically all through the '90s. But as these new competitors are coming in—like I said, about a dozen competitors offering websites, webcasting, conference calls, and all kinds of services, financed by $85 million of venture capital—they were going in and just bombing prices and even giving stuff away for free.

We realized that we would have to adjust prices. So we sat down and talked about it and, literally in a day, made the decision to completely restructure our product line and roll that out pretty quickly. That's the kind of thing that would have been difficult to do in a more complex, let's say, structure.

Livingston: You could be more flexible and move faster.

Gruner: Yes. So we were able to compete with all these startups—almost all of which went out of business or were acquired. We acquired two, for literally a penny on the dollar. We acquired one firm that had well over $20 million of venture capital invested for a few hundred thousand dollars. They just blew up.

Many of these guys got in the business not understanding shareholder communications. Most importantly, not understanding it's very much a "people" kind of business and that investor relations officers are typically "people" kind of people. Their job is to communicate. So coming in and selling technology—particularly technology as an unknown—was a very hard sell. They had a hard time breaking into the market, whereas we had worked a company at a time. We had had consultants early on that educated us, brought us in to companies, gave us credibility—kind of put their name on the line after they got to know us well.

CCBN did well because they were backed by Thomson Financial. Their key founder, Jeff Parker, had great visibility in that community, and credibility. But everybody else disappeared.

Livingston: Did you get acquisition offers?

Gruner: We had a number. At one point we had an acquisition offer by a dotcom whose stock price had gone up by a factor of seven in the prior 3 months. They gave us an offer at the time that was valued in the tens of millions of dollars. This was a point where we had revenues of about $3 million. It was denominated in stock. We thought very seriously about it, but basically got cold feet—because at that point we had been doing it for 7 years. We just felt, if the stock collapses, we've lost it all.

Nine months later, that stock was worth $205 million! So if we had done the deal, had I been smart enough to negotiate the deal where we could have gotten out of the stock, it would have been a $200,000,000 kind of deal.

We had other deals that were a lot less, but we never saw anything that was the right fit, the right kind of liquidity, and the right kind of chemistry. We didn't want to sell the company to somebody that was going to disembowel it.

So that's why, when we had an offer from NASDAQ—and we had a couple of offers from them; I can't talk too specifically about it—we felt that it was the right strategy. We've known the people for a long time; we've had marketing relationships with them; they're going into corporate services and they're very sincere about that. They want to use Shareholder.com as the foundation for building their corporate services. They're keeping the name. The valuation was right. It all happened very quickly.

Livingston: The stars were aligned.

Gruner: Yeah, they were all aligned. Somebody told me a long time ago that generally companies are bought, not sold. And that's what we did. We didn't hire an investment bank or anything like that to go off and sell us. We just waited for the right opportunity.

Livingston: Is there anything you might have done differently with Shareholder.com?

Gruner: Well, I think that bootstrapping the company on a quarter of a million dollars made us a little myopic. We became so proud of that fact that we didn't find the middle ground. I think that in '98, '99, or 2000, we could have taken a million, $2 million of capital, at a very attractive valuation, and retained control and grown the company twice or three times as fast as we did. Perhaps that was a mistake, not doing that. I don't know, because everything worked out fine. And when you only have so much money, it makes decisions much easier.

Here's an example: back when the whole Internet thing was getting started, I hired a computer consultant to come in and advise us about what our Internet infrastructure should be. He was a well-credentialed, Microsoft-accredited engineer, etc. He came in and said, "You need to buy x number of servers and this kind of software and all that, and it's a quarter of a million dollars to do it right."

We said we couldn't even come close to doing that. So I went down to Barnes & Noble, bought several books, including some of the Dummy series. And we built our first Internet servers, which lasted us several years, on Gateway desktop computers, using Microsoft Access as our database system and using basically off-the-shelf server software. We did that for $3 [thousand] or 4,000, and it worked great.

Livingston: Did having a background in technology give you an edge? I would think a lot of financial services companies at the time didn't.

Gruner: Well, in financial services, that may be. But we were kind of a different breed of cat in financial services. We were a technology company providing great service to public companies. So we were always viewed as a technologist kind of company, and many companies liked that. Some didn't like that so much. But that was our niche. That was our differentiation. We understood technology better.

Livingston: Who did you learn from? Did you have any mentors?

Gruner: I had several. I tried to learn and listen to them. The whole founding group at Data General were really smart people. There were four founders there: Ed de Castro, who was the president, who was an investor in Shareholder.com, and who remains a friend after 35 years; Henry Burkhardt, who was the VP of software; Dick Sogge, the VP of engineering; Herb Richman in marketing. They're all really smart guys, and I learned a lot from watching and listening to them.

Because de Castro was a hardware engineer like I was, I would view him as my primary mentor during those years. During the '80s, like I said, we had a good board of directors. Tom Perkins played a very key role. I think I absorbed a lot of the wisdom from him by osmosis—just in board meetings, and how he conducted himself. How he did a good job, I thought, of managing conflict and disagreements. I have to say I'm surprised, though, by how public he's let the internal HP board battle become. Seems to me that it's been very costly to HP.

Livingston: Was there ever a time at Shareholder.com when you wanted to quit?

Gruner: No, not really. I really enjoyed most every day. I enjoyed driving into work, looked forward to it. Every company has its pros and cons. The nice aspect of Shareholder.com was that it was indeed a recurring revenue stream. So we had almost no financial worries. We could predict our quarterly revenues within a couple of percent the first day of the quarter.

The worries that we had came from the fact that we were basically in the news business. When earnings season came out, we might be doing 50 earnings calls and webcasts and news releases on the same day. Every one had to be done on time and perfectly, because an earnings release, for all intents and purposes, is a legal document. So where we sweated was just managing that process. It's like running 50 television stations at the same time.

If you screwed up, it was very visible. On rare occasions we did. We might get one webcast mixed up with another company. We'd fix it within 3 or 4 minutes, but it's extremely embarrassing. And, believe me, chief executives don't like that at all.

I'd be the one to call up and apologize, and that was just part of the job. Most people were very reasonable, and they would understand—things go wrong. I would use the analogy of a cell phone (that was when cell phones were really getting hot). I'd say, "Look, we've all got cell phones or car phones. Sometimes they just screw up and they go wrong. And this is the same kind of stuff; this is pretty advanced technology and sometimes things go wrong."

But we did occasionally lose a client that was just irrational, saying, "My boss told me to fire you because you made this mistake." We'd typically give them a credit for the whole thing, and we'd say, "If you ever want to come back, we'd love to have you back." And many did.

Livingston: What advice would you give to someone who had never started a startup but was thinking about it?

Gruner: I went to an executive conference several years ago in New York. One of the most interesting sessions had about six chief executives, all of whom were very successful, and the moderator asked, "If you could describe in one word the key to success for your company, what would that word be?" Very few answered in one word. Some of them said integrity, or communications, and things like that. The last person to talk was Michael Dell, and he said one simple word: persistence.

I can relate to that. Things never work out right the first time. You've always got to do it two or three times to get it right. And things always go wrong. So persistence is the key to success.

I had seen that in my career. I had seen that in computer design projects. I had seen that through my whole life. And so that word is the best single advice I can give to entrepreneurs. The key to success, if you had to sum it up in one word, is persistence.

The Alliant management team in 1985: (from left to right) Rich McAndrew, Craig Mundie, Ronald Gruner, John Clary, and David Micciche

Index

X

Y